Moreton Morrell Site

Purchasing and Supply Chain Management

. is t⌐
st⌐

PEARSON
Education

We work with leading authors to develop the strongest educational materials in purchasing, bringing cutting-edge thinking and best learning practice to a global market.

Under a range of well-known imprints, including Financial Times Prentice Hall, we craft high-quality print and electronic publications that help readers to understand and apply their content, whether studying or at work.

To find out more about the complete range of our publishing, please visit us on the World Wide Web at: www.pearsoned.co.uk

Purchasing and Supply Chain Management

KENNETH LYSONS

MA, MEd, PhD, Dipl.PA, Ac.Dip.Ed.,
DMS, FCIS, FCIPS, FInst M, MILT

BRIAN FARRINGTON

BSc(Econ), MSc, PhD, FCIPS

Prentice Hall
FINANCIAL TIMES

An imprint of **Pearson Education**
Harlow, England • London • New York • Boston • San Francisco • Toronto • Sydney • Singapore • Hong Kong
Tokyo • Seoul • Taipei • New Delhi • Cape Town • Madrid • Mexico City • Amsterdam • Munich • Paris • Milan

Pearson Education Limited

Edinburgh Gate
Harlow
Essex CM20 2JE
England

and Associated Companies throughout the world

Visit us on the World Wide Web at:
www.pearsoned.co.uk

First published 1981 Macdonald & Evans Limited
Second edition 1989 Longman Group UK Limited
Third edition 1993 Longman Group UK Limited
Fourth edition 1996 Pitman Publishing, a division of Pearson Professional Limited
Fifth edition 2000 Pearson Education Limited
Sixth edition 2003 Pearson Education Limited
Seventh edition 2006 Pearson Education Limited

© Macdonald & Evans Limited 1981
© Longman Group Limited 1989, 1993
© Pearson Professional Limited 1996
© Pearson Education Limited 2000, 2006

ISBN 0 273 69438 3

British Library Cataloguing-in-Publication Data
A catalogue record for this book is available from the British Library

Library of Congress Cataloging-in-Publication Data
A catalog record for this book is available from the Library of Congress

10 9 8 7 6 5 4 3 2 1
10 09 08 07 06 05

Typeset in 10/12pt Sabon by 35
Printed and bound in Great Britain by Ashford Colour Press, Hants

The publisher's policy is to use paper manufactured from sustainable forests.

Contents

Part 4   Strategy, tactics and operations 3: negotiation, support tools and performance   545

Preface to seventh edition

The first edition of this book appeared in 1981 as a short revision aid for purchasing students. In the intervening years the book has increased in size and content. The present seventh edition may fairly claim to be the most comprehensive textbook on purchasing and supply chain management published in the UK. In particular it offers the following features provided by no other competing UK text:

- An Instructor's Manual and PowerPoint slides online at www.pearsoned.co.uk/lysons.
- Every chapter has a case study, discussion questions and sample past examination questions taken (by permission) from the examinations of the Chartered Institute of Purchasing and Supply.
- A glossary of purchasing and supply definitions, acronyms and foreign words and phrases.
- An index of names and organisations referred to in the text.

There are three important changes in this seventh edition that require special mention.

1. There is a change in authorship; Dr Brian Farrington is now co-author with Dr Kenneth Lysons. Dr Lysons and Dr Farrington have been friends and colleagues over many years. Together they bring to the writing of this book both sound academic knowledge and a wide practical experience of purchasing and supply chain management both as practitioners and consultants.

2. There is a change of content. To allow for more in-depth discussion of purchasing and supply chain issues the chapters on storing supplies, transporting goods and human resources in the supply chain included in the sixth edition have been omitted. New chapters relate to supplier relationships and product innovation, supplier involvement and development. Every one of the remaining chapters has been extensively revised. Redundant material has been ruthlessly pruned and a substantial amount of new material added. While a separate chapter on public sector purchasing has not been included there are a number of references at appropriate places throughout the book.

3. The sixth edition stated that the book aimed to be both a textbook for students and a guidebook for practitioners.

   As a textbook, coverage is provided of the syllabus of the Chartered Institute of Purchasing and Supply at both the Foundation and Professional stages.

   Candidates for all the papers comprising the Foundation Stage examination will find the book helpful and complete coverage is provided of the *Introduction to Supply and Materials Management* syllabus.

   At the professional stage, complete coverage is provided for the compulsory syllabuses in *Strategy and Strategic Procurement* and *Tactics and Operations*. Candidates for the optional examinations in *Commercial Relationships* and *Operations Management* will also find their needs substantially met. The book should also be useful to students taking the examinations of the Institute of Logistics and Transport and first and higher degrees in Business Studies and Management which contain Purchasing and Supply Management Elements.

As a guidebook, the text should provide a quick source of reference for practitioners on may aspects of purchasing and supply.

As stated in the preface to the first edition, the modern emphasis is on integrated study, and in writing the book the authors have draw on may disciplines that contribute to a sound knowledge of purchasing and supply chain management. These include financial and management accountancy, economics, ethics, law, operations management, marketing, negotiation, psychology, sociology and strategy. Career progress in the purchasing and supply field increasingly requires the critical thinking that derives from wide perspectives. The range of disciplines referred to above indicates that any person aspiring to become a 'purchasing professional' must be well acquainted with the many areas of knowledge that contribute to efficient purchasing and also dedicated to continuing self-development.

Acknowledgements

The writers are indebted to many organisations and people. Although research is greatly facilitated by the Internet, authors are still indebted to libraries and we would put on record the courteous assistance from the staffs of the British Library, UK Department of Trade and Industry Library, Institute of Management Foundation, Institute of Logistics and Transport, Picton Library of the City of Liverpool, Prescot Branch of the Metropolitan Borough of Knowsley Library Service, St Helens College, Cranfield University, University of Liverpool and John Rylands and Business School Libraries of the University of Manchester.

The Chartered Institute of Purchasing and Supply kindly gave permission to use questions and a case study from papers set at the Foundation and Diploma Stage examinations and quote from publications written for the Institute by Kenneth Lysons.

It is impossible to mention by name everyone who has contributed to this book, but the authors would specifically thank Roy Ayliffe, Director of Professional Practice at CIPS, Rob Atkins of Bracknell Forest Borough Council, Professor Andrew Cox, David Eakin, Nicolas Graham, Professor Peter Hines, Peter Huggett and Lynn Mayhew, Howard Jones, Gerry Johnson and Kevan Scholes, Dr David Jones, Professor Richard Lamming, Jonathan Lyles and Robert Payne, Gerald Morris, Drs S. New and S. Young, Dr P. Niruwenhuis, Elizabeth Stanton Jones, Professor John Smith and Steven Young.

Kenneth Lysons would again place on record the help given by Jeanne Ashton, a loyal friend and assistant over many years. The authors would also thank their respective wives, Audrey Lysons and Joyce Farrington, for their patience during a lengthy period of writing.

Most of the book has again been expertly word-processed by Judith Ray who has patiently coped with idiosyncrasies of handwriting and changes in the text. Judith has received some help from Jeanne Ashton and Julie Ellison. Our thanks to Karen Mclaren who project edited the book on behalf of the publishers and Barbara Massam for her careful proofreading.

Publisher's acknowledgements

We are grateful for permission to reproduce the following copyright material. Dr David Jones for Table 1.5 and Figure 1.3, Russell Syson for Figures 1.6 and 1.7. The NHS Purchasing and Supply Agency for the statement of aims and objectives in Figure 2.8 and statement of 2003–4 objectives. The Harvard Business School Corporation for permission to use Figure 2.13 from the *Harvard Business Review*. The Bracknell Forest (UK) Borough Council for the use of Figure 2.17. The Chartered Institute of Purchasing and Supply for Figure 2.19 and other material specified in relevant chapters of this book. Professor Peter Hines for permission to use Figures 3.14 and 3.15 and the aims and objectives of *Kyoryoku Kai* on page 259, and Professor Hines and Nick Rich for Table 4.9. The Bourton Group for Figures 3.16 and 3.17. The Volvo Corporation for Figure 5.2. Market Research Focus Ltd for Figure 5.3. Addison-Wesley for Table 6.1. The ACTIVE Secretariat for Figure 6.6. The Buy IT e-Procurement Best Practice Network for Figure 6.8. Professor Andrew Cox and the Reed Elsevier Group for Figure 7.2. M. Bensaou and the *Sloan Management Review* for Figures 7.3 and 7.4. The Industrial Marketing and Purchasing Group (IMP) for Figure 7.5. F. Wynstra for Figure 8.4 and F. Wynstra, A. van Weele and B. Axelsson and the *European Journal of Purchasing and Supply* for Table 8.3. The British Standards Institution for Figure 9.1. The Ford Motor Co. for Tables 9.3 and 9.4. The Society of British Aerospace Companies for Figure 11.4. P. Batram and Policy Publications for Figure 11.7. Gerald Morris and the British Electrotechnical and Allied Manufacturers Association for providing Example 12.6. The Institute of Supply Management (USA) and Blackwell Publishing for Tables 14.1, 14.2 and 14.8.

The UK Ministry of Defence for the list of key principles in e-tendering on page 579 and the UK Office of Government Commerce for the list of debriefing topics on page 580. HM Treasury and HMSO for Example 16.2. The International Council for Local Environment Initiatives for Figure 17.8. Peter Kileen for Figure 17.9. The examination questions are taken, by permission, from recent CIPS Graduate Papers.

In a very few instances no replies have been received from applications to use material or we have been unable to trace the owners of copyright material. We would appreciate any information that would enable us to do so. Any infringement of copyright is unintentional.

Plan of the book

Part 1 Introduction and strategy					
Chapter 1 What is purchasing?	Chapter 2 Strategy and strategic procurement	Chapter 3 Logistics and supply chains	Chapter 4 Structure and supply chains	Chapter 5 Purchasing structure and design	Chapter 6 Purchasing procedures

Part 2 Strategy, tactics and operations 1: purchasing factors					
Chapter 7 Supplier relationships	Chapter 8 Purchasing: product innovation, supplier involvement and development	Chapter 9 Specifying and managing product quality	Chapter 10 Matching supply with demand	Chapter 11 Sourcing and the management of suppliers	Chapter 12 Buying at the right price

Part 3 Strategy, tactics and operations 2: buying situations	
Chapter 13 Contrasting approaches to supply	Chapter 14 Buying from overseas

Part 4 Strategy, tactics and operations 3: negotiation, support tools and performance		
Chapter 15 Negotiation	Chapter 16 Support tools	Chapter 17 Purchasing research, performance and ethics

Part 1

Introduction and strategy

Chapter 1

What is purchasing?

Learning outcomes

This chapter aims to provide an understanding of:

- perspectives on purchasing
- the stages of purchasing development and future trends in purchasing development
- factors influencing the internal and external status of purchasing.

Key ideas

- Purchasing as a function, process, supply or value chain link, a relationship, discipline and profession.
- Definitions of purchasing.
- The evolution of purchasing and supply management (PSM) from a reactive transactional to a proactive strategic activity.
- Globalisation, information technology, changing production and management philosophies as factors in the evolution of purchasing.
- Characteristics of purchasing in the future and world class purchasing.
- Leverage, focus and professionalism as factors contributing to the status of purchasing within a particular organisation.

1.1 Perspectives on purchasing

The study of purchasing can be approached from several perspectives. Such perspectives include those of function, process, link in the supply or value chain, relationship, discipline and profession.

1.1.1 Purchasing as a function

In management studies, a 'function' is often defined as a unit or department in which people use specialised knowledge skills and resources to perform specialised tasks. A

3

function is also what a resource is designed to do, so, for example, the function of a pen is to make a mark. A distinction can therefore be made between the purchasing *function* and the *purchasing department*. The former in a business context involves acquiring raw materials, components, goods and services for conversion, consumption or resale. The latter is the organisational unit responsible for carrying out this function. In many organisations, purchasing is still part of a segmented, departmentalised structure in which the procurement of supplies is a discrete activity in the sequence of activities from the acquisition of supplies to the delivery of a finished product to the ultimate user. The challenge of global competition is, however, increasingly leading many organisations to replace segmented structures with integrated structures in which purchasing is part of a larger grouping, such as materials, logistics or supply chain management. Such structures emphasise the importance of cross-functional decision making.

1.1.2 Purchasing as a process

A *process* is a set of subprocesses or stages directed at achieving an output. The various tasks or stages can be depicted as a process chain. Thus, as with Figure 1.1, purchasing can be depicted as a sequential chain of events leading to the acquisition of supplies.

The link in the purchasing process chain is information. Thus, each subprocess in the chain is responsible for capturing or otherwise processing information that enables us to answer the questions 'What are we required to purchase?' and 'Where and how can the required supplies be obtained?' A process chain relationship can therefore also be considered a message chain relationship. Previously messages, both internal (such as requisitions) and external (such as orders and payments), were transmitted on paper documents via the mail. As shown later, electronic transmission has revolutionised the cost and speed of purchasing processes.

Figure 1.1 The purchasing process chain

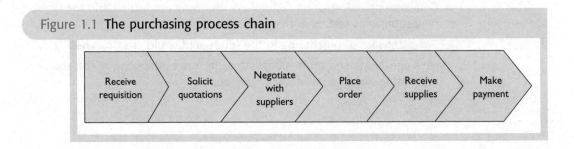

1.1.3 Purchasing as a link in the supply or value chain

Purchasing, along with such activities as production, warehousing and transportation, is one of the links in the supply chain or sequence of processes by which supplies are converted into finished products and delivered to the purchasers. Supply and value chains are discussed in Chapter 3, where it is shown that, in his value chain model, Porter[1] regards procurement as one of four support activities that contribute to the competitive advantage of a business.

1.1.4 Purchasing as a relationship

Purchasing relationships may be both internal and external, short- or long-term.

Internal relationships are with other links in the supply chain, such as initiator(s) of a purchase and the users of the goods procured. Increasingly, internal relationships are cross-functional and based on teamwork.

Externally, relationships with suppliers, as shown later, may represent a continuum from arm's length to supplier alliances. Many organisations now rely on suppliers to design, develop and manufacture items that they would previously have produced themselves. As Ford et al.[2] observe:

> The main issue facing managers is no longer about 'buying the right products at the right time at the right price' but of handling and developing relationships with key suppliers over long periods.

1.1.5 Purchasing as problem-solving

The following is the view of the IMP (Industrial Marketing and Purchasing Group):[3]

> Customers are not looking for a product from a manufacturer. Instead they seek a solution to a problem from a supplier. Business purchases are problem driven. A problem may relate to the customer's need to carry out its basic activities efficiently and economically. Examples include the problems of wastage of material, poor utilisation of staff or an unacceptable failure rate in components. We refer to these as problems of 'rationalisation'. A problem can also arise for positive reasons such as when a company is trying to develop relationships with new customers or enhance the performance of a product. We refer to these as problems of 'development'.

1.1.6 Purchasing as a discipline

A discipline is a branch of knowledge, an area of study. The academic content of purchasing lacks the clearly defined focus associated with other fields of study, such as mathematics, economics and law, and draws heavily on other subjects to build its knowledge base. Such subjects include accounting, economics, ethics, information technology, law, management accounting, operational research, marketing, management and psychology. Purchasing as a subarea of study is often included in wider-ranging courses, including logistics management, operations management and marketing. The discussion of purchasing as a field of study in its own right is continued in 1.7.3, later in this chapter.

1.1.7 Purchasing as a profession

Purchasing professionalism and professionalisation are also discussed in 1.7.3.

1.2 Definitions

Day[4] has rightly pointed out that 'no definition can wholly incorporate the demands placed on a purchasing team's set of skills'. Situational diversities, such as strategic importance, amount of spend, contribution to profitability, supplier relationships and the recognition given to purchasing in a particular organisation, mean that any definition of purchasing is open to criticism. Apart from integrated definitions, such as materials, logistics and supply management, some definitions are considered below.

1.2.1 The classic definition of purchasing

This defines the objectives of purchasing as:

> To buy materials of the right quality, in the right quantity from the right source delivered to the right place at the right time at the right price.

Some criticisms of this definition centre on the difficulties associated with the word 'right'.

- What is 'right' is contingent on a particular organisation or situation.
- In practice, some of the above 'rights' are irreconcilable and a particular 'right' can only be obtained by trading off another. Thus, it may be possible to obtain the right quality but not at the right price. In practice, the right suppliers are often, but not necessarily, the busiest and also the most expensive.

The above definition is outmoded as it implies that purchasing is:

- *reactive rather than proactive* – that is, purchasing is a service activity buying what it is instructed to buy rather than one that takes the initiative in helping to determine purchasing policies
- *transactional rather than relational* – that is, purchasing is primarily concerned with the mechanics of order placing on a one-off basis rather than the establishment, where appropriate, of long-term, collaborative supplier relationships
- *tactical rather than strategic* – that is, purchasing is focused on short-term buying rather than on contributing to the achievement of long-term corporate goals.

1.2.2 Purchasing as procurement

Procurement is a wider term than purchasing, which implies the acquisition of goods or services in return for a monetary or equivalent payment. Procurement, however, is the process of obtaining goods or services in any way, including borrowing, leasing and even force or pillage. As procurement is, strictly, a more accurate term, it is unsurprising that the word procurement is often supplanting 'purchasing' in job titles, such as 'procurement manager', 'procurement agents' and 'head of procurement'.

1.2.3 Purchasing as organisational buying

Organisational buyers have been defined by Marrian[5] as:

> Those buyers of goods and services for the specific purpose of industrial or agricultural production or for use in the operation or conduct of a plant, business, institution, profession or service.

Organisational buyers are, therefore, those who buy on behalf of an organisation rather than for individual or family use or consumption. Organisational buyers can, as shown in Table 1.1, be considered to belong to one of four buying groups, each of which can be further subdivided.

Table 1.1 **A typology of organisational buyers**

Types of organisation	Characteristics	Examples
Industrial/producer organisations	Purchase of goods and services for some tangible production and commercially significant purpose	Manufacturers: primary (extractive) producers – agriculture, forestry, fishing, horticulture, mining
Intermediate organisations	Purchase of goods and services for resale or for facilitating the resale of other goods in the industrial or ultimate consumer markets	Distributors, dealers, wholesalers, retailers, banks, hotels and service traders
Government and public-sector organisations	Purchase of goods and services for resale or use by organisations providing a service, often tangible, and not always commercially significant at national, regional and local levels	Central and local government, public utilities
Institutions	Purchase of goods and services for institutions that buy independently on their own behalf	Schools, colleges, hospitals, voluntary organisations.

Some of the categories in Table 1.1 may overlap. Thus, in the National Health Service, some supplies may be bought centrally by government agencies, regionally by health authorities and locally by hospitals themselves.

1.2.4 Purchasing as supplier management

Supplier management may be defined as:

> That aspect of purchasing or procurement concerned with rationalising the supplier base and selecting, coordinating, appraising the performance of and developing the potential of suppliers and, where appropriate, building long-term collaborative relationships.

Supplier management is a more strategic and cross-functional activity than 'purchasing', which is transactionally and commercially biased. The relationship between procurement purchasing and supplier management is shown in Figure 1.2.

1.2.5 Purchasing as external resource management

The following is the view of Lamming:[6]

> The new strategic function will probably not be called purchasing – that is much too limited a word. The connotations of purse strings and spending money have no relevance to the setting up and management of strategic interfirm relationships. This task is concerned with ensuring the correct external resources are in place to complement the internal resources. Perhaps 'external resource managers' is a term that future purchasing managers will adopt.

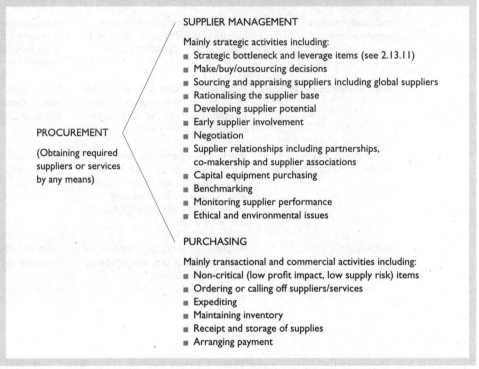

Figure 1.2 **The relationship between procurement, supplier management and purchasing**

PROCUREMENT

(Obtaining required suppliers or services by any means)

SUPPLIER MANAGEMENT

Mainly strategic activities including:
- Strategic bottleneck and leverage items (see 2.13.11)
- Make/buy/outsourcing decisions
- Sourcing and appraising suppliers including global suppliers
- Rationalising the supplier base
- Developing supplier potential
- Early supplier involvement
- Negotiation
- Supplier relationships including partnerships, co-makership and supplier associations
- Capital equipment purchasing
- Benchmarking
- Monitoring supplier performance
- Ethical and environmental issues

PURCHASING

Mainly transactional and commercial activities including:
- Non-critical (low profit impact, low supply risk) items
- Ordering or calling off suppliers/services
- Expediting
- Maintaining inventory
- Receipt and storage of supplies
- Arranging payment

The perspective of external resource management is also adopted by van Weele,[7] who defines purchasing as:

> Obtaining from external sources all goods and services which are necessary for running, maintaining and managing the company's primary and support activities at the most favourable conditions.

Against these definitions, it may be held that 'external resources' includes people, the recruitment and management of whom, as individuals, is primarily a human resource management responsibility. Services provided by people collectively, as in outsourcing or the procurement of facilities, may, of course, fall within the purchasing remit. As a staff manager, the purchasing executive will also be responsible for the management of internal resources.

1.2.6 A composite definition

In spite of its inadequacies, the term 'purchasing' is used in the title of this book as it is still retained in the names of both the British Chartered Institute of Purchasing and Supply (CIPS) and the journals such as *The European Journal of Purchasing Management*. The following definition of purchasing is offered as including aspects discussed above:

> The process undertaken by the organisational unit that, either as a function or as part of an integrated supply chain, is responsible for procuring or assisting users to procure, in the most

efficient manner, required supplies at the right time, quality, quantity and price and the management of suppliers, thereby contributing to the competitive advantage of the enterprise and the achievement of its corporate strategy.

The significant words or terms in the above definition are the following.

- *Processes* – the chain or sequence of activities involved in procuring supplies.
- *Organisational unit* – this may be a department, team, cost or profit centre responsible for all purchasing activities under the control of a designated manager. An alternative term might be 'responsibility centre'.
- *Function* – a discrete organisational unit.
- *Integrated supply chain* – refers to the absorption of formerly discrete organisational units, such as purchasing, production and sales, into a continuous flow of interaction.
- *Procurement* – as stated above, is the process of obtaining goods or services by any means.
- *Assisting users to procure* – refers to the increasing practice of negotiating contracts with one supplier for a range of items, such as office supplies. Users can then order their requirements directly online, using a procurement card. It also refers to advice given by purchasing as part of a purchasing team.
- *The most efficient manner* – the elimination, so far as possible, of all non-value-adding activities in the purchasing process.
- *Quality, quantity, time and price* – these concepts are discussed in appropriate chapters of this book.
- *The management of suppliers* – this is defined above and, as stated, is sometimes regarded as a support activity distinct from the actual procurement of supplies.
- *Competitive advantage* – is a special edge that enables an organisation to deal with market and environmental forces better than its competitors do. Purchasing power and well-developed supplier relationships are two ways in which an organisation may obtain competitive advantage over its competitors.
- *Corporate strategy* – the aims and objectives of an enterprise together with the means by which these are to be achieved. Functional strategies such as a purchasing strategy should be related to corporate strategy.

1.3 The evolution of purchasing

Purchasing represents a stage in the evolution of civilised human relationships as it enables a desired object to be obtained by trading rather than conquest, plunder or confiscation. It is a very ancient activity. A cuneiform clay tablet excavated at El-Rash Shamra, northern Syria, dated about 2800 BC carries an inscription that, roughly translated, reads: 'HST to deliver 50 jars of fragrant smooth oil each 15 days after [a starting date] and during the reign of AS. In return he will be paid 600 small weight in grain. This order will continue indefinitely until the purchaser or his son removes his consent.'

Despite its long history, it was only in the latter half of the twentieth century that the importance of efficient purchasing was widely recognised and even later when its strategic aim – as opposed to operational significance – was acknowledged with an

Table 1.2 **The evolution of purchasing**

Stage	Characteristics
Stage 1 Product-centred purchasing	Product-focused – concerned with the five 'rights', which concentrate exclusively on the purchasing of tangible products and outcome dimensions by means of which this product can be described and mentioned
Stage 2 Process-centred purchasing	Product-focused – moves beyond a concern with outcomes and begins to measure the process via which the outcome is delivered
Stage 3 Relational purchasing	Process- and relationally-focused – expanded to include purchaser–supplier relationships and how these might be used to manage the quality and nature of the supplier
Stage 4 Performance-centred purchasing	Focused on best product management methods. Employs an integrated methodology to manage relationships, processes and outcomes. Jointly resources this methodology with suppliers

emphasis on purchasing processes, relationships and performance rather than on products. Stannack and Jones[8] have identified four stages of purchasing evolution, as shown in Table 1.2.

An alternative model of purchasing evolution is provided by Reck and Long[9] who identify four stages of development that purchasing must pass through to become a competitive weapon in the battle for markets (see Table 1.3).

Reck and Long also identify the effect at each of the four stages of 12 non-operational development variables, as shown in Table 1.4.

Other attempts to trace the evolution of purchasing are those of Syson[10] and Morris and Calantone[11] who each identify three stages. Syson refers to 'the changing focus of purchasing as it evolves from a purely clerical routine activity to a commercial stage in which the emphasis is on cost savings and finally a proactive strategic function concerned with materials or logistics management'. Morris and Calantone differentiate between (i) clerical, (ii) 'asset management' and profitability and (iii) 'core-strategic' function stages.

Jones,[12] however, criticises the above approaches on two grounds. First, they are non-operational and merely indicate the stage of development of purchasing activity, the criteria for which may differ from one procurement organisation to another. Second, the models have a restricted number of development measurement variables. In an attempt to remedy those deficiencies Jones suggests a 5-stage development model using 18 measurement criteria. The five stages of purchasing development measured on a scale of 1–5 are shown in Table 1.5.

The purchasing profile shown in Figure 1.3 enables the stage of development reached by a particular organisation to be identified and assessed on a scale of 1–5. The profile also indicates areas where further development is required, as measured in the 18 criteria shown in Figure 1.3. Appropriate strategies to meet identified shortcomings can then be devised.

Table 1.3 Strategic stages of the development of a purchasing function

Stage	Definition and characteristics	
Stage 1 Passive	Definition	Purchasing function has no strategic direction and primarily reacts to the requests of other functions
	Characteristics	■ High proportion of time on quick-fix routine operations ■ Functional and individual communications due to purchasing's low visibility ■ Supplier selection based on price and availability
Stage 2 Independent	Definition	Purchasing function adopts the latest purchasing techniques and processes, but its strategic direction is independent of the firm's competitive strategy
	Characteristics	■ Performance based primarily on cost reduction and efficiency disciplines ■ Coordination links are established between purchasing and technical disciplines ■ Top management recognises the importance of professional development ■ Top management recognises the opportunities in purchasing for contribution to profitability
Stage 3 Supportive	Definition	The purchasing function supports the firm's competitive strategy by adopting purchasing techniques and products, which strengthen the firm's competitive position
	Characteristics	■ Purchasers are included in sales proposal teams ■ Suppliers are considered a resource, with emphasis on experience, motivation and attitude ■ Markets, products and suppliers are continuously monitored and analysed
Stage 4 Integrative	Definition	Purchasing's strategy is fully integrated into the firm's competitive strategy and constitutes part of an integrated effort among functional peers to formulate and implement a strategic plan
	Characteristics	■ Cross-functional training of purchasing professionals and executives is made available ■ Permanent lines of communication are established with other functional areas ■ Professional development focuses on strategic elements of the competitive strategy ■ Purchasing performance is measured in terms of contribution to the firm's success

Source: adapted from Reck, R. F., and Long, B., 'Purchasing: a competitive weapon', *Journal of Purchasing and Materials Management*, Vol. 24, No. 3, 1998, pp. 2–8

Table 1.4 Stage characteristics – Reck and Long's development model

Characteristics (variable)	Passive	Independent	Supportive	Integrative
Nature of long-range planning	None	Commodity or procedural	Supportive of strategy	Integral part of strategy
Impetus for change	Management demands	Competitive parity	Competitive strategy	Integrative management
Career advancement	Limited	Possible	Probable	Unlimited
Evaluation based on	Complaints	Cost reduction and supplier performance	Competitive objectives	Strategic contribution
Organisational visibility	Low	Limited	Variable	High
Computer systems focus	Repetitive	Techniques	Specific to concern	Needs of concern
Sources of new ideas	Trial and error	Current purchasing practices	Competitive strategy	Interfunctional information exchange
Basis of resource availability	Limited	Arbitrary/affordable	Objectives	Strategic requirements
Basis of supplier evaluation	Price and easy availability	Least total cost	Competitive objectives	Strategic contributions
Attitude towards suppliers	Adversarial	Variable	Company resource	Mutual interdependence
Professional development focus	Deemed unnecessary	Current new practices	Elements of strategy	Cross-functional understanding
Overall characteristics	Clerical function	Functional efficiency	Strategic facilitator	Strategic contributor

Table 1.5 Purchasing development stages and performance capabilities

Stage of development	Capabilities	Estimated organisational contribution
Stage 1 Infant	Fragmented purchasing	None or low
Stage 2 Awakening	Realisation of savings potential	Clerical efficiency. Small savings via consolidation 2–5 per cent
Stage 3 Developing	Control and development of purchasing price/negotiation capabilities	Cost reduction 5–10 per cent
Stage 4 Mature	80/20 recognised Specialist buyers Cost reductions Commencement of supplier base management	Cost reduction 10–20 per cent Acquisition costs 1–10 per cent
Stage 5 Advanced	Devolution of purchasing Strong central control Supply chain management	Cost reduction 25 per cent Cost of ownership Acquisition cost and supply chain management 30 per cent + Leverage buying Global sourcing Understanding and practice of acquisition cost and cost of ownership

Figure 1.3 Purchasing profile analysis

Measurement area	Stage of development				
	1 Infant	2 Awakening	3 Developing	4 Mature	5 Advanced
Activity breakdown analysis					
Purchasing organisational structure					
Purchasing services					
Function position in the business					
Extent of training/ development of buyer					
Relative remuneration levels					
Measurement of purchasing performance					
Standard of information systems					
Computer technology					
Standard of operating procedures					
Interface development (buying centre)					
Buying process involvement					
Buyer characteristics/ development					
Degree of purchasing specialism					
Supplier interface development					
Policy on ethics					
Hospitality					
Quality of buyer/supplier relationship					

1.4 Purchasing and change

At least three drivers have influenced and are influencing changes in purchasing philosophies, processes and procedures, globalisation, information technology and changing approaches to production and management and the emphasis on core competencies.

1.4.1 Globalisation

There are numerous definitions of globalisation and considerable controversy regarding its real significance and the extent to which it is really a new concept.

A useful definition of globalisation is:[13]

> The increasing interdependence across national and geographical boundaries of people, trade and commerce driven in large part by information technology and technology generally.

An even more concise definition is:[13]

> The integration of the world's economies.

From the standpoint of this book an important aspect of globalisation is global sourcing, which may be defined as:[14]

> A process of manufacturing and/or purchasing of components in various parts of the world and then assembling them into a final product: an international division of labour in which activities are performed in countries where they can be done well at the lowest level.

Christopher[15] provides a 'classic' example of global sourcing by referring to the Singer Sewing Machine Company:

> It buys sewing machine shells from a subcontractor in the United States, the motors from Brazil, the drive shafts from Italy and assembles the finished machine in Taiwan. It then markets the finished machines in most countries of the world.

Global sourcing is a wider term than 'import purchasing' or 'international procurement' as it involves strategic product lifecycle decisions relating to long-term supplier relationships based on such factors as purchase price and lead time reliability, supplier flexibility and political stability. Global purchasing will be considered further in Chapter 14.

1.4.2 Information technology

As stated in the above definition, globalisation is driven in large part by information technology, or IT. IT – comprised of computers and telecommunications, especially the Internet – has already had a significant effect on purchasing processes and procedures. By sharing information and processing electronic transactions over the Internet suppliers are being converted into e-suppliers. Large undertakings, such as Ford, have indicated that eventually all their suppliers will be e-suppliers. IT and its applications to purchasing and supply management (PSM) are dealt with in Chapter 6.

1.4.3 Changing production and management philosophies

Global competition has intensified the search for strategies that will yield competitive advantage. Such competitive advantage may be sought via reduced inventories, lower costs, Just-in-Time, Total Quality Management (TQM), supplier collaboration, time-based competition, lean and agile production and supply chain management. Such models and approaches should not be viewed as discrete concepts but as part of purchasing evolution. Gadde[16] considers that the two main trends in purchasing since the 1990s have been outsourcing and supply chain management. Outsourcing in some instances will result in virtual management – a management core that excels at production while seamlessly integrating external organisations, such as suppliers. Some of the ways in which purchasing has changed over the last three decades are shown in Table 1.6.

Table 1.6 Changing aspects of PSM

Aspect	Traditional	Changing
Structure	Vertical, hierarchical, functionally orientated	Horizontal, flatter, involving self-managed teams and cross-functional relationships
	Purchasing regarded as a separate function	Purchasing regarded as part of an integrated supply chain
Procedures	Paper-based Slow, high cost All procurement routed through purchasing	Based on IT applications Rapid, low cost Increased emphasis on centre-led, user procurement
Purchase considerations	Price only	Total cost of acquisition and use
	Buy what we can't make	Subcontract or outsource non-core business
Sourcing	Multisourcing Local or national Little use of purchasing consortia	Reducing supplier base Global Increasing use of purchasing consortia
Supplier relationships	Short-term Adversarial and confrontational Win–lose negotiations Retention of information	Long-term Partnerships and collaborative Win–win negotiations Sharing of information
Quality and specification	Purchaser specifications of design and quality Inspection of goods on receipt	Supplier specifications of design and quality Supplier certification
Inventory and lead times	High to provide security	Low due to JIT requirements, thus obviating waste by such causes as holding costs, obsolescence, etc.
Purchasing performance	Assessed mainly on price differences and savings	Assessed mainly on its value-added activities as part of the supply chain

1.5 Purchasing in the future

Research in the USA[17] indicates that, within the decade commencing 2000, future trends relating to PSM will include:

- an increase in the strategic importance of PSM – key activities will include supplier evaluation, selection and management
- tactical purchasing activities, such as ordering and expediting, will increasingly be automated and selected low-value, non-critical, standard commodity purchases are likely to be outsourced to full-service providers
- most non-tactical items will be bought under master contracts enabling transactions such as releasing, receiving and accounting to be undertaken by users who will select their requirements from online databases maintained by suppliers and consortia
- the Internet/World Wide Web will be the main vehicle for electronic purchasing, which increasingly will be used for purchase transactions and also be the key to globalisation
- while the core procurement organisation will remain, leading organisations will establish strategic purchasing competency centres with highly trained, cross-functional personnel responsible for achieving competitive advantage via their choice of supply chain partners, influencing design, sourcing, production and integrating the innovations and contributions of suppliers
- strategic alliances with suppliers will increase
- organisations in the supply chain will increasingly share resources, including intellectual properties information, people and other assets
- increased coordination of suppliers via supplier associations modelled on the *Kyoryoku Kai* pattern, discussed in Chapter 8
- global supplier development will be critical to global penetration
- there will be an increasing emphasis on win–win negotiation
- dominant companies in the supply chain will influence the sourcing decision of first-, second- and third-tier suppliers
- while the price paid will be an important measure of purchasing performance, this will be considered as part of the overall contribution of PSM to profit
- environmental factors will become increasingly important to purchasing considerations
- the absolute number of purchasing jobs will decrease, especially of staff employed in tactical purchasing
- personnel employed in PSM will require a higher level of training, including that in leadership and influence skills.

1.6 World class purchasing

The term 'world class' was popularised by the book *World Class Manufacturing* by Schonberger[18] published in 1986. Schonberger defined world class manufacturing as analogous to the Olympic motto 'citius, altius, fortius' (translated as faster, higher, stronger). The world class manufacturing equivalent is continual and rapid improvement.

Twelve characteristics of world class supplier management were identified by the USA Center for Advanced Purchasing Studies,[19] namely the following.

■ *Commitment to total quality management (TQM).*

■ *Commitment to just-in-time (JIT).*

■ *Commitment to total cycle time reduction.*

■ *Long-range strategic plans* that are multidimensional and fully integrated with the overall corporate plan, including the organisation's supply strategy, and related to customers' needs.

■ *Supplier relationships*, including networks, partnerships and alliances. Relationships include such matters as supply base rationalisation and the segmentation of suppliers as 'strategic', 'preferred' and 'arm's length'. Relationships with strategic suppliers include a high level of trust, shared risks and rewards, sharing of data and supplier involvement in product improvement.

■ *Strategic cost management* – this involves a total life acquisition approach to evaluating bids and the use of IT to support a paperless and seamless purchasing process across the whole supply chain.

■ *Performance measurements*, including regular benchmarking with and across industries. Performance measures are developed in consultation with customers, other organisational units and suppliers.

■ *Training and professional development*, including identification of required skills for higher-level purchasing posts and the maintenance of employee skills inventories.

■ *Service excellence* – purchasing is proactive, anticipates customers' needs and demonstrates flexibility.

■ *Corporate social responsibility*, especially regarding ethical, environmental and safety issues and support of local suppliers.

■ *Learning* – world class purchasing recognises that learning and education are critical factors in continuous improvement.

■ *Management and leadership* – although listed last, this is probably the key factor. Purchasing executives earn and enjoy top management support and recognise the importance of transformational change. Such leaders have vision, foster open communications, treat others with respect and develop the potential of both their staff and suppliers.

Ultimately, world class purchasing depends on obtaining world class suppliers. World class suppliers will tend to mirror the characteristics of world class purchasing listed above. Research reported by Minahan[20] indicates that, while to be considered 'world class' suppliers must excel in such areas as competitive price, quality and lead times, these attributes are 'just the price of entry to get into the game'. The research identified the following three characteristics of world class suppliers:

■ *continuous improvement* world class suppliers have a formal and proven commitment to achieve year-on-year products and process improvements

■ *technology and innovation* world class suppliers are technology leaders in their respective industries, providing customers with next-generation technologies and a 'leg-up' on their competition

■ *adaptability* world class suppliers are willing to invest in new equipment, develop new technologies and rework their businesses to better support the strategies of their customers.

World class supplier management is therefore concerned with:

■ searching for suppliers with the above characteristics or the potential to achieve them

■ providing such suppliers with specifications of the purchaser's expectations relating to products and services and agreeing how supplier performance will be measured against expectations

■ recognising outstanding supplier performance by such means as the award of long-term contracts and sharing the benefits of collaborative innovation or performance that enhance the purchaser's competitiveness.

Strategic purchasing partnerships are partnerships of equals in which suppliers are regarded as a source of the competitive edge responsible for a major share of product costs. As Saunders[21] rightly observes:

> For a firm to reach world class standards in serving its own customers, it is vital to achieve world class standards in controlling its network of suppliers.

1.7 The status of purchasing and supply management (PSM)

Within a particular organisation the status of PSM is influenced by leverage, focus and professionalism.

1.7.1 Leverage

Leverage in the present context is the power of purchasing to enhance profitability.

The greatest scope for making savings lies in the areas of greatest expenditure. For most organisations the areas of greatest expenditure are purchasing and payments to personnel. As a result of technology, labour costs in manufacturing enterprises are tending to reduce substantially. Conversely, manufacturing organisations may find it cheaper to outsource assemblies and components from specialist suppliers that were formerly made in-house. These tendencies are shown by Figures 1.4 and 1.5, which relate to the expenditure of a manufacturing company for the years 1979 and 2004 respectively.

The greatest scope for savings lies in the area of bought-out items, which in 2004 had superseded labour as the area of greatest expenditure. It follows therefore that:

■ assuming other variables remain constant, every pound saved on purchasing is a pound of profit

■ for many reasons, such as increased defects or poorer deliveries, a pound off the purchase price does not necessarily represent a pound of profit

■ when purchases form a high proportion of total costs, a modest saving on bought-out items will result in a similar contribution to profits as would a substantial increase in sales, so, as shown below, a 4 per cent reduction in purchase costs makes the same contribution to profits as a 20 per cent expansion in turnover.

SALES			
Then	Now	Increase	Extra profit
£	£	%	£
100,000	120,000	20	2000 (assuming 10 per cent on turnover)
PURCHASING			
50,000	48,000	−4 (i.e. a saving)	2000

This argument must, however, be used carefully.

■ Cost reduction can be counter-profitable if the result is lower quality or higher expenditure on production.

■ The total cost of ownership (TCO) approach emphasises that not just the purchase price but also all costs associated with the acquisition, use and maintenance of an item should be considered.

■ As the proportion of expenditure on supplies and the complexity of bought-out items varies widely from organisation to organisation, it follows that there will be a corresponding variance in the contribution of purchasing to profitability.

The profit contribution may be low, for example, in the pharmaceutical industry where the ingredients of a patent medicine can be insignificant compared with the costs of marketing the product. Conversely, it will be significant in the motor vehicle industry where the proportion of material costs to total factory costs will be high.

Figure 1.4 **Costs of a manufacturing company in 1979**

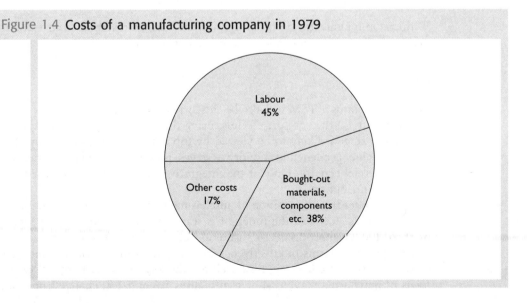

Figure 1.5 **Costs of the same manufacturing company in 2004**

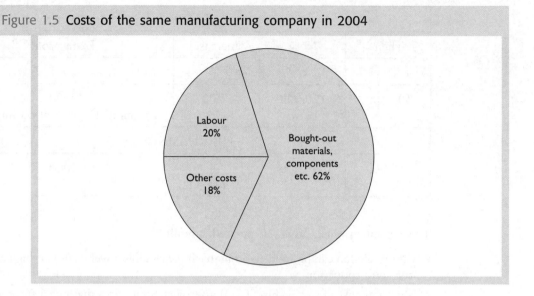

Purchasing as a factor in profitability is likely to be critical where:

■ bought-out items form a high proportion of total expenditure
■ short-run prices fluctuate
■ judgements relating to innovation and fashion are involved
■ markets for the finished product are highly competitive.

Purchasing will be less critical, though still important, where:

■ bought-out items form a small proportion of total expenditure
■ prices are relatively stable
■ there is an absence of innovation in operations.

Within non-manufacturing organisations the savings resulting from value-for-money efficiency purchasing may allow increased expenditure in other areas.

1.7.2 Focus

The internal status of PSM will also be closely related to the stage of development reached by the activity in the enterprise. Thus, using the Reck and Long model, purchasing at the passive stage is likely to be viewed by top management as a mainly clerical function. At the independent and supportive stages, purchasing will be regarded as a significant commercial activity. Only at the integrative stage is PSM recognised as making a strategic contribution.

Syson[22] states that the position of purchasing within a particular organisation depends on whether the focus of the function is transactional, commercial or strategic. Each of these foci is appropriate to sustaining commercial advantage for different types of enterprise: 'in terms of effectiveness, the key question is whether the correct focus exists. In terms of efficiency, how well are the key tasks discharged?' Over time, the focus of purchasing may, as shown in Figures 1.6 and 1.7, change from transactional

Figure 1.6 **Positioning graph: strategies/policies**

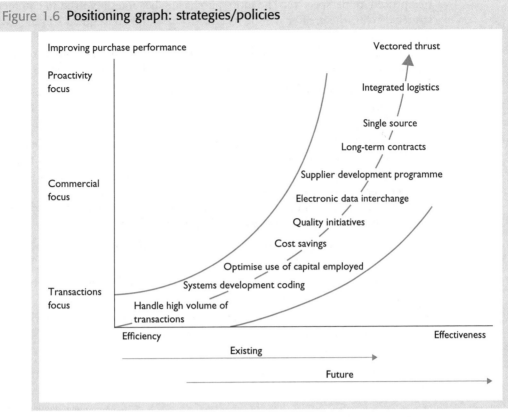

Figure 1.7 **Positioning graph: measures of performance**

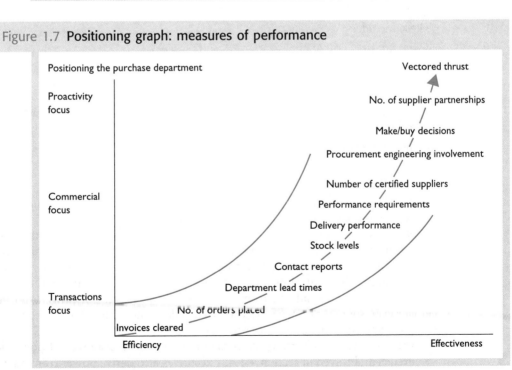

to a procedure perspective. The more purchasing becomes involved in commercial and strategic areas, the greater will be its effectiveness and consequent standing within the organisation.

In Figures 1.6 and 1.7 it will be noticed that as PSM moves from a transactional to a proactivity focus, performance measures also change from efficiency to effectiveness.

> *Efficiency* is a measure of how well or productively resources are used to achieve a goal. *Effectiveness* is a measure of the appropriateness of the goals the organisation is pursuing and of the degree to which those goals are achieved.

Syson[23] refers to the level of the purchasing department, implying that the level at which purchasing is placed in a hierarchical structure reveals its status within that company. From a different perspective, broadly similar considerations will apply in determining the recognition given to purchasing by other supply chain members.

A somewhat different approach to determining the internal status of purchasing is provided by the three laws propounded by Farmer:[24]

1 purchasing increases in perceived importance in direct relationship with the reduction in length of the product lifecycle times

2 purchasing is perceived to be important when the business concerned interfaces significantly with (a) volatile market(s)

3 purchasing is important whenever the organisation concerned spends a significant proportion of its income on purchasing goods and services in order to allow it to do business.

Empirically, the importance of purchasing both organisationally and within the supply chain is indicated by structural and influential factors.

Structural factors

These include:

- the job title of the executive responsible for PSM
- to whom and at what level the executive in charge of PSM reports
- the total spend for which PSM is responsible
- the financial limits placed on PSM staff to commit the undertaking without recourse to higher authority
- the committees on which PSM staff are represented.

Influential factors

Ibarra[25] has identified network centrality, power and innovative involvement as important influential factors in the determination of status.

Network centrality, like format authority, implies a high position in a status hierarchy and also varying degrees of access to and control over valued resources. As stated in section 3.2.1, purchasing is frequently a key activity in materials management. Purchasing is also central in supply chains, as indicated in section 3.11.

Power may be considered from two aspects: the sources of power and the use of power. The sources of power are briefly considered in section 4.1.4. The use of power may be defined as the ability to affect outcomes.

The executives in charge of PSM may have all the five sources of power identified by French and Raven in section 4.1.4. Executives also derive power from having access to information or occupying a boundary-spanning position that links organisations' internal networks to external suppliers and information sources.

Innovative involvement, as Ibarra shows, may be either administrative or technical and may itself be an indicator of power as any change in the status quo requires an individual to use power and mobilise support, information and material resources to overcome resistance to change. Persons with a high position in the organisation are more likely to be successful innovators than those further down with less or little power.

Technical innovators are directly related to the primary work activity of an organisation and include the introduction of new products, services and production technologies.

Administrative innovations involve changes in structure and administrative processes and are more directly related to internal management than the other types of innovation. Kanter's[26] observation that 'corporate entrepreneurs have often to pull in what they need for their innovation from other departments or areas, from peers over whom they have no authority and who have the choice about whether or not to ante up their knowledge, support or resources to invest in or help the innovator' is of relevance to both supply chain management and the centrality of purchasing within it.

The status of PSM in any organisation depends on two key factors. First, the ability to impact positively on the bottom line of corporate strategic planning and, second, recognition by PSM of the value of its contribution to profitability and competitive advantage and being able to market that contribution to top management and other supply chain members.

1.7.3 Professionalism

As long ago as 1928, Carr-Saunders[27] made a distinction between professionalism and professionalisation. *Professionalism* is traditionally associated with certain attributes, including:

- skill based on theoretical knowledge
- prolonged training and education
- demonstration of competence by means of tests and examinations
- adherence to a code of professional ethics.

Professionalisation is associated with the development of associations that seek to establish minimum qualifications for entrance to a professional practice or activity, enforce appropriate rules and norms of conduct among the members of the professional group and raise the status of the professional group in the wider society. Thus, attempts to raise the external perception of purchasing have included:

- the establishment of institutions concerned with promoting the concept of 'professional' purchasing, such as the Chartered Institute of Purchasing and Supply (CIPS) in the UK and the Institute of Supply Management (ISM) in the USA (in 2004, over 42 national purchasing associations were affiliated to the International Federation of Purchasing and Materials Management)
- the development of undergraduate and postgraduate courses with a purchasing content
- the establishment of 'chairs' in purchasing or logistics at some universities

- research into PSM and related fields
- the publication of textbooks and specialist journals relating to purchasing, such as *Supply Management (UK)*, *European Purchasing Management* and the *International Journal of Purchasing and Supply Management*, as well as, in the logistics field, *Logistics Focus* and the *International Journal of Logistics*.
- published codes of ethics (see Appendices 1 and 2).

Notwithstanding the enhanced status of purchasing in the UK by the granting in 1992 of a Royal Charter to the Institute of Purchasing and Supply, the occupation has to surmount difficulties in its quest for professional status.

Such difficulties include:

- no regulation of entry – it is not necessary to have a professional qualification in purchasing to enter the occupation
- purchasing practitioners are at all levels of evolution, so those with only an operational or transactional knowledge of purchasing might experience difficulty in moving to strategic purchasing
- limited powers to enforce ethical standards.

The general problem, however, is what constitutes the academic content. Purchasing is a hybrid subject that draws heavily on other disciplines to build its knowledge base. Such disciplines include accounting, economics, ethics, information technology, marketing, management and psychology.

Even the study of subjects such as negotiation can be enhanced by a knowledge of the approaches to negotiation in such fields as politics and industrial relations.

Cox[28] regards much contemporary academic work relating to procurement as 'unscientific', characterised by uncritical accounts of what purchasing practitioners do, untheoretical research and the development of 'fads and short-term fixes'. Such academic work is often regarded as irrelevant by purchasing practitioners. Cox therefore calls for a proactive, scientific approach to the academic study of purchasing. He believes that such an approach will involve the use of systematic theory to provide general laws and the application of deductive and inductive reasoning to respectively 'construct optional procurement strategies based on "fit for purpose" awareness of business and market processes and indicate the optional role for procurement in business'.

The change in emphasis from purchasing as a reactive administrative activity to one that is proactive and strategic has resulted in numerous lists of the skills and attributes that purchasing staff should possess in order to maximise their contribution to the achievement of organisational goals. Two typical surveys in the USA are those by Kolchin[29] and Giunipero and Pearcy.[30]

The first of these studies, based on the responses of a large sample of American purchasing executives, identified the following ten subjects as the most important to purchasers in the year 2000:

1 total cost analysis
2 negotiation strategies and techniques
3 supplier/partner management
4 ethical conduct
5 supplier evaluation

6 quality techniques

7 purchasing strategy and planning

8 price/cost analysis

9 electronic data interchange

10 interpersonal communication.

The second study, based on a review of relevant literature and a rating by 136 purchasing/supply management professionals identified 32 skills required of a world class purchaser. These skills were categorised under seven headings:

1 strategic

2 process management

3 team

4 decision making

5 behavioural

6 negotiation

7 quantitative

Examples of strategic, behavioural and quantitative skills are:

Strategic skills	Behavioural skills	Quantitative skills
Strategic thinking	Interpersonal/communication	Computational
Supply base research	Risk-taking/entrepreneurship	Technical
Structuring supplier relationships	Creativity	Blueprint reading
Technology planning	Inquisitiveness	Specification development
Supplier cost targeting		

One further writer, Whittington,[31] has stated that 'the buying task as we know it will disappear . . . Organisationally purchasing will often find itself in a place called "distribution functionality" or "strategic supply" located where the customer is'. She also believes that the purchasing professional of the future will be concerned with three types of tasks:

- *facilitating* that is, team leadership and providing the 'proper blending and use of all necessary skills'

- *contract negotiating and developing* that is, purchasing people – this will still be required – to write and negotiate advantageous contracts for the organisation

- *technical expertise (computer skills)* that is, the challenges of purchasing on the Net and funding products in the world of cyberspace as well as other EDI tasks.

This view is supported by Lamming (see 1.2.5) and others. In the Kolchin study referred to above, almost two-thirds of the respondents believed that the designation of purchasing would change. The three most cited new names were 'supply management', 'sourcing management' and 'logistics'.

Case study

The GHTB Group is engaged in financial services and has banking, insurance and building society interests. There is a new Chief Executive of the group who has moved into the position from an international manufacturing organisation. She has engaged the services of a strategic consultancy group to study the way in which purchasing operates in GHTB Group. Having received its report she is appalled at the findings. In summary, they include the following points:

- each part of the organisation is empowered to create contracts with suppliers – there is no strategy or coordination
- the banking and insurance arms of the business have purchasing managers whereas the building society employs a chief buyer
- there are over 15,000 suppliers to the organisation, but no expenditure analysis is available
- in the past year there were 50,000 purchase orders placed with suppliers, 40 per cent after receipt of an invoice
- in each part of the organisation, many departments and individuals have authority to place contracts without the involvement of purchasing, including marketing, information and communications technology (ICT), travel, printing, warehousing and legal affairs
- the group training director has no budget for training the purchasing staff and has never conducted a training needs analysis
- there are, currently, four major disputes with suppliers relating to infringement of intellectual property rights, breach of contract for not taking agreed quantities of printing, the late installation of an IT system and theft of goods from a third-party leased warehouse
- there is no cost reduction target, supplier rationalisation or relationship management strategy in any part of the organisation
- the banking group is about to engage in a corporate identity package involving £5 million of expenditure and the whole deal has been handled by the facilities management sections, together with external architects and quantity surveyors, who have handled the purchasing process and their fees are based on 6 per cent of expenditure
- there are no model contracts in any part of the group.

The Chief Executive realises that this style of purchasing operation is unacceptable and intends to change it materially. If you were asked to give advice on the way forward, what would be your thoughts?

Tasks

1 Would you create a group purchasing activity?
2 How would you persuade the marketing directors that purchasing can add value to their expenditure?
3 What would you recommend regarding the disputes with suppliers?
4 Would you take any action regarding the corporate identity package?

Discussion questions

1.1 In certain organisations the functional approach to purchasing has decided advantages. Consider the extent to which this statement is true.

1.2 Prepare a flow chart showing the processes involved in procuring supplies in your organisation. Compare your flow chart with those prepared by other students and consider where and how improvements might be made.

1.3 Supply chain management was initially developed by wholesaling and retailing organisations. Why do you think organisations in the distributive sector led the way?

1.4 In the text, an example was given of how it might not be possible to reconcile the 'right quality' with the 'right price'. Discuss some other problems of reconciling the six 'rights'.

1.5 List five ways in which buying for industrial/producer organisations may differ from buying from (i) intermediate organisations and (ii) institutions.

1.6 Why do some organisations pay insufficient attention to supplier management?

1.7 Consider the four stages of the development of the purchasing function identified by Reck and Long. State, with reasons, the stage reached by purchasing in your organisation.

1.8 Use the purchasing profile developed by Jones to identify the stage reached by your organisation regarding each of the 18 criteria listed under 'measurement area'.

1.9 Why is 'globalisation' a wider term than 'import purchasing' or 'international procurement'?

1.10 Using the format of Table 1.2, compare reactive and proactive approaches to purchasing.

1.11 The absolute number of purchasing jobs will decrease, especially staff members employed in tactical purchasing. Prepare a self-development plan to ensure that you will be prepared to take advantage of the career opportunities presented by the move to strategic procurement.

1.12 Rate your organisation (1) low, (2) average or (3) high for each of the following criteria relating to world class purchasing.

Characteristic	High (3)	Average (2)	Low (1)
1 Commitment to TQM			
2 Commitment to JIT			
3 Commitment to total cycle time reduction			
4 Long-range strategic plans			
5 Supplier relationships			
6 Strategic cost management			
7 Performance management			
8 Training and professional development			
9 Service excellence			
10 Learning			
11 Management and leadership			

Consider what action you could take to improve the rating on any of the criteria to which you have given a low rating.

1.13 Consider the following figures relating to a company (all figures are in thousands of pounds).

	£	£
Sales		100,000
Purchases	20,000	
Pay, etc.	20,000	
Cost of sales		40,000
Gross profit		60,000
Operating costs		55,000
Net profit		5000

(a) Assume that there are savings of 5 per cent on purchases and that turnover and operating costs remain constant. What, in percentage terms, will be the effect on net profit?

(b) What increase in sales will have to be achieved to obtain a similar percentage increase in profit, assuming no purchasing savings and the same proportionate cost of sales and operating expenses?

1.14 Discuss the following statement:

> Theoretical study alone cannot make managers. Their success will depend on their innate qualities, acquired knowledge, experience under competent guidance and, above all, on the degree to which they combine these elements into a balanced personality.
>
> (Urwick Report, 1947, adapted)

Why then study purchasing?
What are the characteristics of 'balanced personality'?

1.15 Consider the examples of strategic behavioural and quantitative skills given in section 1.7.3. What skills would you include under the headings of (a) process management, (b) team skills and (c) decision making?

Past examination questions

1 How is the buyer's role likely to change as the buyer becomes more involved with proactive strategic purchasing?

CIPS, *Purchasing and Supply Chain Management Strategy*, May 1997

2 Using a purchasing development model or framework with which you are familiar, explain how such a model could be usefully employed in assisting the development of the purchasing activity.

CIPS, *Purchasing*, November 1998

References

[1] Porter, M. E., *Competitive Advantage*, Free Press, 1985

[2] Ford, D., Gadde, L-E., Hakansson, H., and Snehota, I., *Managing Business Relationships*, 2nd edn, John Wiley, 2003, p. 92

[3] As 2 above, p. 3

 4 Day, M. (ed.) in Farmer D., and Day, M. (eds), *Handbook of Purchasing Management*, 3rd edn, Gower, 2002, Introduction, p. 2

 5 Marrian, J., 'Market characteristics of industrial goals and buyers', in Wilson, A. (ed.), *The Marketing of Industrial Products*, Hutchinson, 1965, p. 11

 6 Lamming, R., 'The future of purchasing: developing lean supply', in Lamming, R., and Cox, A., *Strategic Procurement Management in the 1990s*, Earlsgate Press, 1985, p. 40

 7 Van Weele, A. J., *Purchasing Management*, Chapman & Hall, 1994, p. 9

 8 Stannack, P., and Jones, M., *The Death of Purchasing Procedures*, PSERA, 1996

 9 Reck, R. F. and Long, B., 'Purchasing a competitive weapon', *Journal of Purchasing and Materials Management*, Vol. 24, No. 3, 1998, p. 4

10 Syson, R., *Improving Purchasing Performance*, Pitman, 1992, pp. 254–5

11 Morris, N., and Calantone, R. J., 'Redefining the purchasing function', *International Journal of Purchasing and Materials Management*, Fall, 1992

12 Jones, D. M., 'Development models', *Supply Management*, 18 March, 1999. The authors are particularly grateful to Dr Jones for the use of Figures 1.6 and 1.7

13 These two definitions are taken from 'Globalisation and the Triple Bottom Line', Australian Public Service and Merit Protection Commission 1999

14 Schermerborn, J. R., *Management for Productivity*, 4th edn, John Wiley, 1993, glossary p. G6

15 Christopher, M., *Logistics and Supply Chain Management*, 2nd edn, Prentice Hall, 1998, p. 129

16 Gadde, L. E., and Hakansson, H., *Supply Network Strategies*, John Wiley, 2001, pp. 23–4

17 See, for example, Carter, J. R., 'Purchasing and supply management: future directions and trends' and especially *The Future of Purchasing and Supply Management – a Five and Ten Year Forecast*, Joint Research Initiative of Center for Advanced Purchasing Studies, NAPM and AT Kearnly, 1998

18 Schonberger, R. J., *World Class Manufacturing: The Next Decade: Building Power, Strength and Value*, Free Press, 1986

19 Carter, P. L., and Ogden, J. A., *The World Class Purchasing and Supply Organisation: Identifying the Characteristics*, Center for Advanced Purchasing Studies, University of Arizona

20 Minahan, T., 'What Makes a Supplier World Class?', *Purchasing On Line*, 13 August, 1988

21 Saunders, M., *Strategic Purchasing and Supply Chain Management*, Pitman, 1994, p. 11

22 Syson, R., as 10 above

23 Syson, R., as 10 above

24 Farmer, D., 'Organisation for purchasing', *Purchasing and Supply Management*, February, 1990, pp. 23–7

25 Ibarra, H., 'Network centrality, power and innovation involvement, determinants of technical and administrative power', *Academy of Management Journal*, Vol. 36 (3), June, 1993, pp. 471–502

26 Kanter, R. M., 'When a thousand flowers bloom' in Staw, B. M., and Cummings, L. L. (eds), *Research in Organisational Behaviour*, Vol. 10, 1988, p. 189

27 Carr-Saunders, A. M., and Wilson, P. A., *The Professions*, Oxford University Press, 1928

28 Cox, A., 'Relational competence and strategic procurement management', *European Journal of Purchasing and Supply Management*, 1996, Vol. 2 (1), pp. 57–70

29 Kolchin, C., 'Study reveals future educational and training trends', *NAPM Insights*, July, 1993

30 Giunipero, L. C., and Pearcy, D. H., 'World class purchasing skills: an empirical investigation', *Journal of Supply Chain Management*, 2000, Vol. 36 (4), pp. 4–13

31 Whittington, E., 'Will the Last Buyer Please Stand Up!', Proceedings NAPM 84 Annual Conference, May 1999

Chapter 2

Strategy and strategic procurement

Learning outcomes

With reference, where applicable, to purchasing and supply, this chapter aims to provide an understanding of:

- the origins and development of strategic theory
- corporate, business and functional/operating strategies
- strategic management
- strategic analysis
- strategy formulation
- the evaluation of alternative strategies
- strategy implementation
- the post implementation, evaluation, control and review of strategies.

Key ideas

- Mintzberg, Johnson and Scholes and the definitions of strategy.
- Mintzberg's ten schools of strategic development.
- Rational planning, incremental and emergent views of strategy.
- Growth, stability, combination and retrenchment strategies.
- Strategic purchasing and purchasing strategy.
- Environmental and internal scanning.
- Critical success factors.
- Vision and mission statements and business, purchasing and supply objectives.
- Lifecycles, scenario planning, cost–benefit, profitability and risk analysis as approaches to the evaluation of strategies.
- Portfolio planning with special reference to Kraljic and Kamann.
- Policies and strategy implementation plans.
- The CIPS procurement and supply chain model.

Introduction

Two presidents of rival United States companies went walking in a forest to discuss a possible merger. They were confronted by a grizzly bear that rose on its hind legs and snarled menacingly. One president took off his knapsack and put on a pair of running shoes. The other president shouted 'Hi you can't outrun that bear!' 'No' was the reply 'I can't outrun the bear but I'm making darned sure that I can outrun you!'[1]

Faced by an environmental threat, he thought strategically.

Strategic thinking is an important factor in both the long-term success of an organisation and effective procurement within the organisation. If purchasing is of strategic importance, then purchasing professionals must learn to think strategically. What, though, is strategic thinking?

2.1 Strategic thinking

Five elements that make up strategic thinking – as identified by Liedtka[2] – are shown in Figure 2.1.

The characteristics of each of the five elements are discussed in a fine paper by Lawrence,[3] as follows.

1 *Systems perspective* A 'system' is a set of independent and interrelated parts that is dependent for survival on its environment. Strategic thinking, from a systems perspective, requires an understanding of:

■ the external, internal and business ecosystem in which the organisation operates (an ecosystem in a business context is a network of interrelated enterprises that may cross a variety of industries) and managing within such an ecosystem requires the ability to think strategically about the position of the enterprise within it and the relationships and alliances with the enterprises that it is comprised of

■ how corporate, business and functional strategies relate vertically to the external environment and horizontally across departments, functions, suppliers and buyers

■ interrelationships between the individual parts of the system

Figure 2.1 **The elements of strategic thinking**

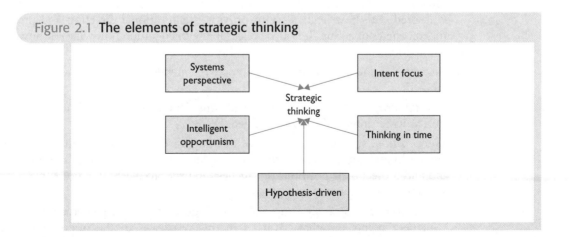

■ individual roles within the larger system and how individual behaviour impacts on other parts of the system and the final outcome.

2 *Intent focus* Strategic thinking is concerned with the identification of goals and devising strategies for their achievement.

3 *Intelligent opportunism* Strategic thinking is 'openness to new experiences which allows one to take advantage of alternative strategies that may emerge as more relevant to a rapidly changing business environment'.

4 *Thinking in time* Strategic thinking is concerned with 'bridging the gap' between current reality and future intent. Thus, when current resources and capabilities are insufficient, the organisation must bridge the gap by making the best of what is available. 'By connecting the past with the present and linking this to the future, strategic thinking is always "thinking in time".'

5 *Hypothesis driven* Strategic thinking accommodates both creative and analytical thinking. Hypothesis *generation* poses the creative question 'What if . . . ?' Hypothesis *testing* follows up with the critical question 'If . . . , then' and evaluates the data relevant to the analysis. Taken together and repeated, this process allows an organisation to pose a variety of hypotheses without sacrificing the ability to explore novel ideas and approaches.

2.2 What is strategy?

Strategy, derived from the Greek word *strategia*, means 'generalship' and is primarily a military concept that, since the end of World War II, has been used in a business context.

2.2.1 Definitions – Mintzberg

Mintzberg[4] observes that the word strategy 'has long been used implicitly in different ways even if it has been traditionally used in only one'. He therefore provides five different definitions of strategy as plan, ploy, pattern, position and perspective.

1 As a *plan*, strategy is some sort of consciously intended course of action, a guideline (or set of guidelines) to deal with a situation. From this perspective, strategy is concerned with how leaders try to provide organisational direction and predetermined courses of action. It is also concerned with cognition (knowing) or how plans or intentions are initially conceived in the human brain.

2 As a *ploy*, strategy is a specific manoeuvre intended to outwit an opponent or competitor.

3 As a *pattern*, strategy is a stream of actions demonstrating consistency in behaviour, whether intended or not intended.

4 As a *position*, strategy is a means of locating an organisation in an environment. The positional approach sees strategy as 'a mediating force by which organisations find and protect their positions or "niches" in order to meet, avoid or subvert competition in the external environment'.

5 As a *perspective*, strategy is a concept or ingrained way of perceiving the world. Mintzberg points out that 'strategy in this respect is to the organisation what

personality is to the individual' – that is, distinct ways of working deriving from the culture or ideology of the undertaking that become the shared norms, values and determinants of the behaviour of the people who collectively form the organisation.

Mintzberg's five definitions help us to avoid attaching simplistic meanings to strategy. As he observes:[5]

> Strategy is not just a notion of how to deal with an enemy or set of competitors in a market . . .

> A good deal of confusion . . . stems from contradictory and ill-defined uses of the term strategy. By explicating and using various definitions we may thereby enrich our ability to understand and manage the processes by which strategies form.

2.2.2 Definitions – Johnson and Scholes

Johnson and Scholes[6] identify eight characteristics of strategy that include most of those described above:

1 strategy is likely to be concerned with the *long-term* direction of an organisation
2 strategic decisions are normally about trying to achieve some *advantage* for the organisation over its competitors
3 strategic decisions are likely to be concerned with the *scope* of an organisation's activities
4 strategy can be seen as the *matching* of the resources and activities of an organisation to the environment in which it operates – sometimes known as the strategic *fit*
5 strategy can also be seen as *building on* or 'stretching' an organisation's resources and competences to create opportunities to capitalise on them
6 strategies may require major *resource changes* for an organisation
7 strategic decisions are likely to affect *operational decisions*
8 the strategy of an organisation is affected not only by environmental forces and resources availability but also the *values and expectations* of those who have *power* in and around the organisation.

By combining the above characteristics, Johnson and Scholes provide the following definition:

> Strategy is the *direction* and *scope* of an organisation over the *long term* which achieves *advantage* for the organisation through its configuration of resources within a changing *environment* and to fulfil *stakeholder* expectations.

2.2.3 Strategy and tactics

Tactics – sometimes termed 'operational planning' – are short-term decisions made in response to changing circumstances so as to make the best use of currently available resources to achieve limited goals.

Tactical plans relate to functional areas, such as finance, purchasing, production and marketing and have shorter timeframes than strategic plans.

Quinn[7] points out that 'what appears to be a tactic to the Chief Executive may be a strategy to the marketing head'.

2.3 Strategy development

2.3.1 Mintzberg's ten schools

Mintzberg et al.[8] have identified ten 'schools' that have appeared at different stages in the development of strategic development, which they classify under three headings: prescriptive, descriptive and configuration.

Prescriptive schools are concerned with how strategies *should* be formulated, rather than how they actually are. Mintzberg's three prescriptive schools are shown in Table 2.1.

Table 2.1 **Mintzberg's prescriptive schools of strategy formation**

Designation	Strategy formation process
The design school	Strategy making as a process of *conception* – that is, abstract thinking or reflective activity. Strategy making is an acquired, not a natural or intuitive, skill and must be learned formally
The planning school	Strategy formation as a *formal* process – that is, a course of action or procedures
The positioning school	Strategy formation as an *analytical* process – that is, strategy formation is the selection of generic, specifically common, identifiable positions in the marketplace based on analytical calculations

Descriptive schools are concerned with representing how, in reality, strategies are formulated rather than how they 'ought' to be made. Mintzberg's six descriptive schools are shown in Table 2.2.

The *configuration school* emphasises two aspects of strategy. The first describes 'organisational states' and their surroundings as *configurations*. An organisation 'state' implies entrenched behaviour. Configurations are therefore relatively stable clusters of characteristics relating to a particular school. Thus, 'planning' is predominant in mechanistic conditions of relative stability and 'entrepreneurship' in more dynamic configurations of start-up and turnaround. The configuration school, therefore, can integrate the preceding nine schools as it recognises that each school represents a particular configuration contingent on its time and context.

The second aspect is concerned with *transformation*. The configuration school sees strategy formation as a process of transformation or 'shaking loose' entrenched behaviour so that the organisation can make the transformation or development to a new state or configuration. The key to strategic management, therefore, is to sustain stability but periodically recognise the need for change to a new configuration.

2.3.2 Rational planning and incremental and emergent views

Rational planning encompasses all Mintzberg's prescriptive schools and is the traditional view of strategy formation based on the economist's concept of a rational economical person. The rational economical person is assumed to:

Table 2.2 Mintzberg's descriptive schools of strategy formation

Designation	Strategy formation process
The entrepeneurial school	Strategy formation as a *visionary* process – that is, strategy exists in the mind of the leader as a vision of the organisation's long-term future
The cognitive school	Strategy formation as a *mental* process – that is, strategy formation takes place in the mind of the strategist as a process of perceiving, knowing and conceiving the environment in an objective way, distinct from emotion or volition
The learning school	Strategy formation as an *emergent* process of learning over time, in which, at the limit, formulation and implementation become indistinguishable
The power school	Strategy formation as a process of *negotiation* – that is, strategy is shaped by political games involving transient interests and coalitions of those holding internal or external power who seek to arrive at a consensus on strategy by means of persuasion, bargaining and sometimes direct confrontation
The cultural school	Strategy formation as a *collective* process – that is, strategy formation is a process of social interaction based on beliefs and understandings shared by organisational members
The environmental school	Strategy formation as a *reactive* process – that is, adapting to the environment rather than by initiating changes in the environment.

- make decisions to maximise returns
- consider all the alternatives
- know the costs and consequences of all the alternatives
- allow decisions to be made by a single person
- order consequences according to a fixed preference.

Such planning normally involves two stages:

1 summarising external and internal strengths and weaknesses, opportunities and threats (SWOT analysis) and identifying goals or objectives that can be translated into measurable targets

2 identifying the means by which such goals can be achieved and specifying appropriate plans.

Lawrence[9] states that traditional notions of strategic planning have been attacked on the ground that such planning 'often takes an already agreed upon strategic direction and helps strategists decide how the organisation is to be configured and resources allocated to realise that direction'. Fahey and Prusak[10] regard this predisposition to focus on the past and the present rather than on the future as one of the 11 deadly sins of knowledge management. Other criticisms are that:

- planning is overly focused on analysis and extrapolation rather than creativity and invention

- planners rarely know all the available alternatives and, therefore, have a limited ability to process information

- rational planning assumes a stable environment, yet, when the environment changes, strategic priorities also change.

Incremental and emergent views encompass Mintzberg's descriptive and configuration schools and emphasise that strategies may be formulated over time and implemented step by step.

Logical incrementalism is primarily associated with Charles Lindblom[11] who also referred to this approach as 'muddling through'.

In this view, managers make incremental changes as they learn from experience. Intelligent or strategic opportunism or the managerial ability to stay focused on long-term objectives while retaining the flexibility to cope with short-term problems and opportunities has already been identified in section 2.1 above as an essential element of strategic thinking. Waterman[12] states that, in leading organisations, managers 'sense opportunity where others can't, act while others hesitate and demur when others plunge'.

Such considerations led Mintzberg to develop the concept of *emergent strategies*. Such strategies evolve in an organisation without being consciously intended or formulated as managers learn from and respond to work situations.

As Mintzberg observes:[13]

Managers who craft strategy do not spend much time in reading reports or industry analyses. They are involved, responsive to their materials, learning about their organisation and industries through personal touch. They are also sensitive to experience, recognising that while individual vision may be important, other factors may determine strategy as well.

An example of emergent strategy is provided by the Japanese Honda Company.

Honda attempted to enter the United States' motorcycle market in 1959. It had four machines: a 50cc Supercub and larger 125cc, 250cc and 305 models. The initial annual target was 6000 machines, with each model representing approximately 25 per cent of the total number. The sales value was, of course, heavily weighted towards the larger bikes.

Little effort was made to sell the 50cc machines, which were regarded as unsuitable for the US market where everything was big and luxurious. The larger machines, however, developed oil leaks and clutch failures as they were being driven harder and longer than they were in Japan.

The 50cc model attracted attention when used by Honda staff to ride around Los Angeles on errands. Due to the faults in the larger models, Honda had to sell more of the smaller 50cc machines to raise funds. Supported by the slogan 'You meet the nicest people on a Honda', the 50cc model proved popular with people who had not previously bought motorcycles. By 1965, Honda had captured 63 per cent of the US motorcycle market.

The Honda story illustrates the general principle that successful strategies need not be clearly formulated in advance. Such strategies can just *emerge*. An emergent strategy may therefore be defined as:

A strategy developed out of a pattern of behaviour not consciously imposed by senior management.

2.3.3 Intended, realised, unrealised and emergent strategies

Intended strategies are the strategic directions deliberately formulated by managers. Such strategies are sometimes referred to as *deliberate strategies*.

Realised strategies are those that are actually being followed. *Unrealised strategies* are those that, due to such failures as interference by market, technological or political forces, are not realised or not realised as intended. As Robert Burns[14] observed:

> The best laid schemes o' mice and men
> Gang aft agley (often go wrong)
> An' lea'e us nought but grief and pain
> For promised joy

Emergent strategies, as we have seen, develop incrementally over time via a process of learning by doing.

Most strategies lie on a continuum between intended and emergent strategies, as shown in Figure 2.2.

Figure 2.2 Strategy development routes

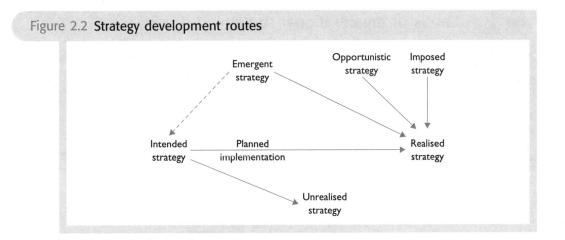

Realised strategy, therefore, is a variable combination of intended and emergent strategies.

2.3.4 Strategic drift

This refers to situations in which organisational strategies fail to develop in line with gradual changes in the environment. Ultimately, if left unchecked, the long-term consequence of strategic drift is business failure.

> Gradually, incrementally, perhaps imperceptibly, the organisation drifts away from its established strategies, perhaps to everyone's eventual regret. The well-known story of the boiled frog applies here. Put a frog into boiling water and it jumps out. Put it in cold water that is slowly brought to the boil and it apparently remains to die. The frog does not want to die; it just does not notice until too late.[15]

Perseverance with strategies that are no longer relevant to the environment may be due to the fact that, when faced with pressures to change, managers tend to minimise uncertainty by turning to that which is known and familiar. This often results in slow, incremental changes building on existing knowledge skills and routines when what is required is rapid, transformational change.

The main symptoms of strategic drift are:

- a homogeneous culture – established routines, little questioning, resistance to new ideas
- major political barriers to change, such as resistant, dominant leaders, stakeholder conflicts, 'concrete ceilings'
- introspection – lack of sensitivity to environmental and competitive factors
- deteriorating relative performance, market share or profits.

The prevention of strategic drift requires strategies to question their taken-for-granted assumptions and beliefs with a view to fostering critical debate on the relevance of current strategies.

2.4 Levels of organisational strategy

As shown in Figure 2.3, in a typical large, diversified business, strategies are formulated, evaluated and implemented at three levels.

For non-diversified undertakings and those with only one line of business, corporate and business strategies are normally synonymous.

Figure 2.3 Levels of organisational strategy

2.5 Corporate strategy

Generally, corporate strategies are concerned with:

- determining what business(es) the enterprise should be in to maximise profitability
- deciding 'grand' strategies (see below)
- determining the 'values' of the enterprise and how it is to be managed

- coordinating and managing major resources and relationships between the enterprise, its markets, competitors, allies and other environmental factors
- deciding on business locations and structures.

Because corporate strategies provide long-term direction, they change infrequently. Corporate strategies are usually less specific than those at lower levels and, consequently, are more difficult to evaluate.

'Grand' or 'master' strategies referred to above fall into four categories: growth, stability, combination and retrenchment.

2.6 Growth strategies

These are adopted when an organisation seeks to expand its relative market share by increasing its level of operations. Growth strategies can be classified as shown in Figure 2.4.

2.6.1 Integration strategies

Vertical integration strategies reflect the extent to which an organisation expands *upstream* into industries that provide inputs (*backward integration*), such as a car manufacturer acquiring a steel rolling mill, or *downstream (forward integration)* into industries that distribute the organisation's products, such as a car manufacturer acquiring a car distribution chain.

Backward integration

Backward integration seeks to ensure continuity of supplies by owning or controlling suppliers. David[16] has identified the following conditions that might cause an organisation to adopt a backward integration strategy, all of which have purchasing and supply applications:

- when an organisation's present suppliers are especially expensive, unreliable or incapable of meeting the firm's needs for parts, components, assemblies or raw materials
- when the number of suppliers is few and the number of competitors is many
- when an organisation competes in an industry that is growing rapidly (in a declining industry, vertical and horizontal strategies reduce an organisation's ability to diversify)

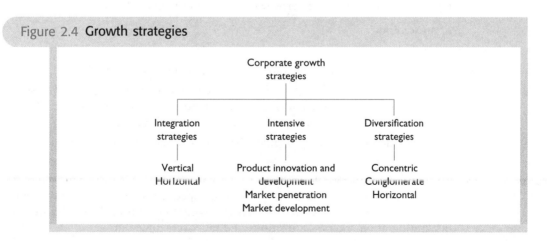

Figure 2.4 **Growth strategies**

- when an organisation has both the capital and human resources needed to manage the new business of supplying its own raw materials
- when the advantages of stable prices are particularly important (this is a factor because an organisation can stabilise the cost of its raw materials and the associated price of its product via backward integration)
- when present suppliers have high profit margins, which suggest that the business of supplying products or services in the given industry is a worthwhile venture
- when an organisation needs to acquire a needed resource quickly.

A further important factor may be:

- to reduce dependence on suppliers of critical components.

Forward integration

Forward integration can:

- avoid dependence on distributors who have no particular allegiance to a particular brand or product and tend to 'push' items that yield the highest profits
- provide production with stable, continuous and predictable demand requirements
- provide cost savings by eliminating intermediaries or distributors.

Some disadvantages of vertical integration include:

- difficulties in balancing capacity at each stage of the supply chain as the efficient scale of operation of each link in the supply chain can vary, so, when internal capacity is inadequate to supply the next stage it will be necessary to supply the deficiency by buying out and, conversely, excessive capacity gives rise to the need to dispose of the surplus
- high investment in technology and development may inhibit innovation and change due to the need to redesign, retool and retrain.

Backward or forward integration often call for highly diversified skills and abilities, such as manufacturing, transport and distribution, which require different business capabilities.

For the above reasons, many manufacturers – particularly in car and food manufacture – have abandoned vertical integration in favour of:

- outsourcing
- tiering
- long-term partnerships or joint-venture agreements with suppliers
- *Keiretsu* strategies (*Keiretsu* is the Japanese word for 'affiliated chain' and such chains are comprised of mutual alliances that extend across the entire supply chain of suppliers, manufacturers, assemblers, transporters and distributors)
- the creation of virtual companies that use suppliers on an 'as needed' basis.

Horizontal integration

Horizontal integration focuses on expanding operations by acquiring other enterprises operating in the same industry or merging with competitors. Examples of horizontal integration are mergers, acquisitions and takeovers aimed at:

- reducing competition
- increasing economics of scale
- transferring and integrating resources and competences.

2.6.2 Intensive strategies

These are termed 'intensive' because they are 'vigorous' efforts to improve an organisation's competitive position in relation to its competitors.

- *Product innovation and development* seeks to increase sales by improving present products or services or developing new ones. Purchasing can contribute to this strategy in such ways as advising on specifications, value management and suggesting alternative materials, components and production methods.
- *Market penetration* seeks to enhance the market share for existing products or services by greater marketing efforts.
- *Market development* seeks to increase the demand for a product by discovering new uses for it or introducing it into new geographical areas.

2.6.3 Diversification strategies

These seek to reduce dependence on a single industry or product. Such strategies may be:

- *concentric* – that is, adding new, but related, products to the existing range
- *conglomerate* – that is, adding new, unrelated products or services
- *horizontal* – that is, adding new, unrelated products or services for existing customers, such as a car distributor offering insurance.

The current trend is away from diversification and in favour of 'sticking to the knitting', or concentrating on the core business.

2.6.4 Stability, combination and retrenchment strategies

Stability focuses on maintaining the present course of action and avoiding, so far as possible, major changes. It is not necessarily a 'do nothing' approach but a considered decision that the present way of working is the most appropriate in a given situation.

Combination is the simultaneous adoption of several strategies according to the needs of a particular aspect of a business. Thus, in a divisionalised organisation, a strategic decision may be to pursue a growth strategy in some divisions and one of stability in others.

Retrenchment, or defensive, strategies are clearly the opposite of those focusing on growth. Typical retrenchment strategies include:

- *harvesting* maximising short-term profits and cash flow while maintaining investment in a product flow
- *turnaround* attempting to restructure operations to restore earlier performance levels
- *divestiture* selling off one or more units of an enterprise to raise cash or concentrate on core activities
- *liquidation* the decision to cease business and dispose of all assets.

2.7 Business-level strategy

A strategic business unit (SBU) has been defined[17] as:

> An operating unit or planning focus that groups a distinct set of products or services that are sold to a uniform set of customers facing a well-defined set of competitors.

Generally business strategies are concerned with:

- coordinating and integrating unit strategies so that they are consonant with corporate strategies
- developing the distinctive competences and competitive advantages of each unit
- identifying product market niches and developing strategies for competing in each
- monitoring products and markets so that strategies conform to the needs of product markets at their current state of development.

The selection of a business strategy involves answering the strategic question 'How are we going to compete in this particular business area?'

Two approaches to business-level strategy are the competitive strategy of Michael Porter[18] and the adaptive strategy of Miles and Snow.[19]

2.7.1 Porter's competitive strategy

Competitive strategies are based on some combination of quality, service, cost and time. Porter's typology identifies three strategies that can be used to give SBUs a competitive advantage.

- *Cost leadership* – operating efficiencies so that an organisation is the low-cost producer in its industry. This is effective when:
  - the market is comprised of many price-sensitive buyers
  - there are few ways to achieve product differentiation
  - buyers are indifferent regarding brands (Coke v Pepsi)

  Some potential threats to this strategy are that:
  - competitors may imitate this strategy, thus driving profits down
  - competitors may discover technological breakthroughs
  - buyer preferences may be influenced by differentiating factors other than price (see also 3.9.1).
- *Differentiation* – attempting to develop products that are regarded industry-wide as unique (see also 3.9.2).
- *Focus* – concentration on a specific market segment and within that segment attempts to achieve either a cost advantage or differentiation. Because of their narrow market focus, firms adopting a focus strategy have lower volumes and therefore less bargaining power with their suppliers.

2.7.2 Miles and Snow's adaptive strategy

Adaptive strategies are based on the premise that an organisation should formulate strategies that will allow each of its SBUs to adapt to its unique environmental challenges. Four major strategies are identified:

- *defender* – this emphasises output of reliable products for steady customers and is appropriate for very stable environments
- *prospector* – this emphasises a continuous search for new market opportunities and innovation and is appropriate for dynamic environments with untapped customers
- *analyser* – this emphasises stability while responding selectively to opportunities for innovation and is appropriate for moderately stable environments
- *reactor* – this is really no strategy as reactors respond to competitive pressures by crisis management.

2.7.3 Functional strategies

These are concerned with the formulation of strategies relating to the main areas or activities that constitute a business – finance, research and development, marketing, purchasing, production/manufacturing, human resources and logistics/distribution.

Functional strategies are expected to derive from and be consistent with corporate and business strategies and are primarily concerned with:

- ensuring that the skills and competencies of functional specialists are utilised effectively
- integrating activities within the functional/operating area, such as purchasing, marketing
- providing information and expertise that can be utilised in the formulation of corporate and business strategies.

The selection of functional strategies involves answering the strategic question 'How can we best apply functional expertise to serve the business needs of the SBU or organisation?'

Strategic purchasing and purchasing strategy

Strategic purchasing is the linking of purchasing to corporate or business strategies.[20] Some comparisons between purchasing at the corporate and functional levels are shown in Table 2.3.

Table 2.3 **Purchasing strategy at corporate and functional levels**

Corporate/business level	Functional/operational level
Formulated at higher levels in the hierarchy	Taken at lower levels in the hierarchy
Emphasise purchasing effectiveness	Emphasise purchasing efficiency
Based on widespread environmental scanning. Some of this information will be communicated upwards from functional level	Based on information from a more limited environmental scanning. Some information obtained from suppliers etc. may be communicated upwards
Corporate strategy must be communicated downwards	Integrated with corporate strategies so far as these are communicated and understood
Focused on issues impacting future long-term procurement requirements and problems	Focused on issues impacting current tactical procurement requirements and problems

Some purchasing decisions, such as those relating to the acquisition of capital equipment, outsourcing and entering into long-term partnership alliances, are generally made at the corporate/business level, often on the basis of information or recommendations from purchasing at functional or operational levels. As stated in Chapter 1 the extent to which purchasing is involved in the formation of organisational strategies is largely dependent on the extent to which procurement is perceived by top management as contributing to competitive advantage. The purchasing executive who reports directly to the chief executive is clearly in a stronger position to influence organisational strategy than one lower in the hierarchy who reports to a materials or logistics manager. Irrespective of their level of reporting, purchasing staff should seek to contribute to corporate strategy by the provision of intelligence on the basis of which decisions can be made and to competitive advantage by improving the effectiveness of the function.

Kraljic[21] states that a company's need for a supply strategy depends on:

- the strategic importance of purchasing in terms of the value added by the product line and the percentage of materials in total costs
- the complexity of the supply market, gauged by supply scarcity, pace of technology and/or materials substitution, entry barriers, logistics cost or complexity and monopoly or oligopoly condition.

Kraljic claims that:

> By assessing the company's situation in terms of these two variables, top management and senior purchasing executives can determine the type of supply strategy the company needs both to exploit its purchasing power vis-à-vis important suppliers and reduce its risk to an acceptable minimum.

2.7.4 Purchasing strategy

Purchasing strategy relates to the specific actions that purchasing may take to achieve its objectives.

2.7.5 Global purchasing strategy

This is discussed in Chapter 14.

2.8 Strategic management

Strategic management, as shown in Figure 2.5, refers to the processes of strategic analysis, formulation, evaluation, implementation, control and review.

2.9 Strategic analysis

A useful definition is:[22]

> developing a theoretically informed understanding of the environment in which the organisation is operating together with an understanding of the organisation's interaction with its environment in order to improve organisational efficiency and effectiveness by increasing the organisation's capacity to deploy and redeploy its resources intelligently.

Figure 2.5 **The cycle of strategic management**

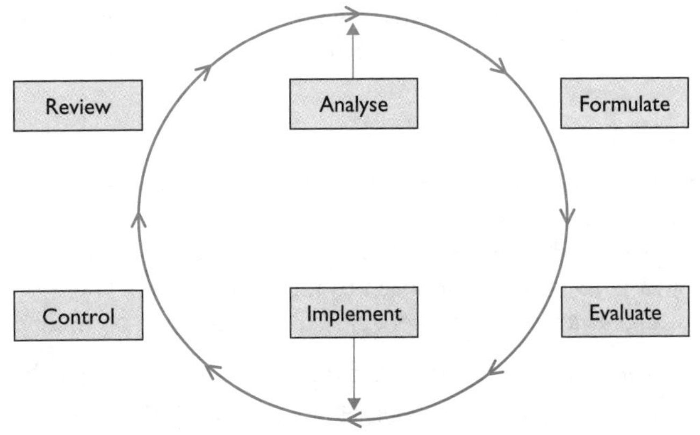

The tools of strategic analysis include environmental scanning, Porter analysis, scenario analysis, organisational appraisal, critical success analysis, gap and SWOT analysis.

2.9.1 Environmental scanning

Some writers regard 'the environment' as relating to all factors relevant to strategic management that are outside the boundaries of a particular organisation. Others think of the environment as encompassing both external and internal environments.

Environmental scanning has been described as 'a kind of radar to scan the world systematically and signal the new, or unexpected, the major and minor'.[23] Choo[24] states that organisations monitor their environments to:

> Understand the external forces of change so that they may develop effective responses which secure or improve their position in the future. They scan to avoid surprises, identify threats and opportunities, gain competitive advantage and improve short- and long-term planning.

2.9.2 Scanning methods

Scanning can be:

- *passive* – for example, reading a quality newspaper or professional journal
- *active* – such as desk or field research in which attention is focused on information relating to a specific industry or task
- *electronic* – this uses a field intelligence agent (FIA), which is comprised of a database, knowledge base, reasoning engine and datamining unit. FIAs provide environmental information from multiple sources, comment on environmental trends and changes and enable users to ascertain whether or not current assumptions are valid or new patterns have emerged.

2.10   Important environmental factors

Important external environmental factors relating to the strategy of an organisation are sector, industry and macro-environmental.

2.10.1 Sector

Sector relates to whether the enterprise is located in the private, public or voluntary sectors of the economy.

The *private sector* includes single traders, partnerships and companies owned by private investors as opposed to the government. There is a wide variety of such undertakings that can be loosely classified according to their primary function into:

- *primary*, or extractive, organisations, such as agriculture, mining, fishing
- *secondary*, or manufacturing and assembly, organisations, such as food or car manufacturers
- *tertiary*, or distributive, organisations, concerned with the physical distribution of goods from producers to consumers, such as transport, wholesalers, retailers or providers of services, such as schools, hospitals.

The *public sector* is comprised of the national government, local government, government-owned and controlled agencies and corporations and monetary institutions, such as the armed forces and the National Health Service.

The *voluntary sector* describes bodies that are independent of government and business and are non-profit making, such as charities and churches.

Because of the wide variety of enterprises, some writers prefer to use the term 'organisational' in preference to 'corporate' strategy. Sector factors influence strategic management both at the organisational and functional levels.

At both levels, strategy is influenced by the underlying philosophy of the sector. Thus, what is known as the public–private paradox emphasises that, while business and government have much in common, ultimately they are different. Public- and private-sector purchasing members of staff, for example, do many of the same things and are both increasingly focused on competitiveness. There are, however, substantial differences that, as shown in Table 2.4, help to determine their respective purchasing strategies.

2.10.2 Industry

An industry can be defined as a group of companies within a sector offering products or services that are close substitutes for each other.

Rivalry among competitors is central to the forces contributing to industrial competitiveness. It is important to understand, therefore, the environmental factors that contribute to the attractiveness and competitiveness of an enterprise within the industry.

The five forces model devised by Michael Porter is by far the most widely used model to evaluate industry attractiveness.

Porter's five forces model

Reference has already been made to Porter's competitive strategy (2.7.1). Porter's five forces model is shown in Figure 2.6.

Table 2.4 Comparison of some public- and private-sector factors relating to procurement strategies

Factor	Public sector	Private sector
Aims	To provide the end users, members of the general public, with what they need when they need it and at the best value for money	To provide the enterprise with supplies that will enable it to achieve competitive advantage via positioning, cost and differentiation
Profit	Value for money spent irrespective of profit	Value for money spent commensurate with and as a contribution to profitability
Accountability	Purchasing officers in central and local government are accountable and subject to audits for the spending of public money	Private purchasing is accountable to the shareholders or owners of the undertaking for the spending of private money
Transparency	In the context of public purchasing, transparency refers to the ability of all interested parties to know and understand how public procurement is managed	In the context of private purchasing, the requirement for transparency is confined to those directly concerned, such as customers, suppliers and similar stakeholders
Procedures	In the interests of transparency, public procedures are characterised by: ■ well-defined regulations and procedures open to public scrutiny, such as standing orders, EU directives ■ clear standardised tender documents and information ■ equal opportunity for all in the bidding process	Fewer standardised procedures and greater flexibility on the part of purchasing staff to make unilateral strategic decisions than in the public sector

Figure 2.6 illustrates Porter's main principles.

■ In any industry, five competitive forces dictate rivalry between competitors and the generic industry structure. These forces are the main players (competitors, buyers, suppliers, substitutes and new entrants), their interrelationships (the five forces) and the factors behind those forces that help to account for industry attractiveness.

■ In aggregate, the five forces determine industry profitability because they directly influence the prices an enterprise can charge, its cost structure and investment requirements.

■ No enterprise can successfully perform at above average level by endeavouring to be all things to all people. Management must therefore select a strategy that will give the business a competitive advantage. As stated earlier, Porter argues that there are only three generic strategies that can be used singly or in combination to create a defensible position or outperform competitors: cost leadership, differentiation and focus on a particular market niche.

Figure 2.6 Porter's analysis of industry structure in his five forces model

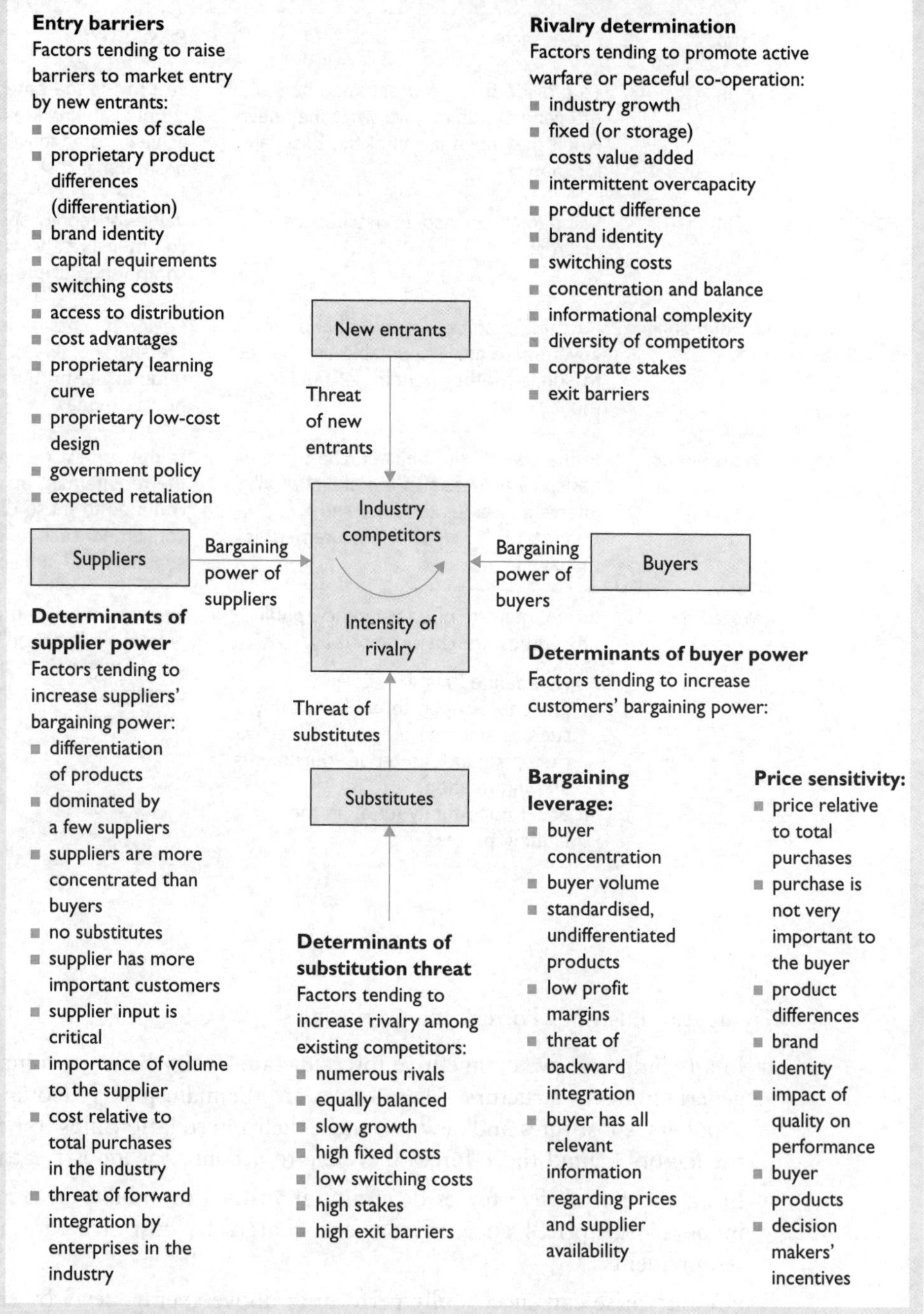

Entry barriers
Factors tending to raise barriers to market entry by new entrants:
- economies of scale
- proprietary product differences (differentiation)
- brand identity
- capital requirements
- switching costs
- access to distribution
- cost advantages
- proprietary learning curve
- proprietary low-cost design
- government policy
- expected retaliation

Rivalry determination
Factors tending to promote active warfare or peaceful co-operation:
- industry growth
- fixed (or storage) costs value added
- intermittent overcapacity
- product difference
- brand identity
- switching costs
- concentration and balance
- informational complexity
- diversity of competitors
- corporate stakes
- exit barriers

New entrants

Threat of new entrants

Industry competitors

Intensity of rivalry

Suppliers

Bargaining power of suppliers

Bargaining power of buyers

Buyers

Determinants of supplier power
Factors tending to increase suppliers' bargaining power:
- differentiation of products
- dominated by a few suppliers
- suppliers are more concentrated than buyers
- no substitutes
- supplier has more important customers
- supplier input is critical
- importance of volume to the supplier
- cost relative to total purchases in the industry
- threat of forward integration by enterprises in the industry

Threat of substitutes

Substitutes

Determinants of substitution threat
Factors tending to increase rivalry among existing competitors:
- numerous rivals
- equally balanced
- slow growth
- high fixed costs
- low switching costs
- high stakes
- high exit barriers

Determinants of buyer power
Factors tending to increase customers' bargaining power:

Bargaining leverage:
- buyer concentration
- buyer volume
- standardised, undifferentiated products
- low profit margins
- threat of backward integration
- buyer has all relevant information regarding prices and supplier availability

Price sensitivity:
- price relative to total purchases
- purchase is not very important to the buyer
- product differences
- brand identity
- impact of quality on performance
- buyer products
- decision makers' incentives

Source: Competitive Strategy: Techniques for Analysing Industries and Competitors (Free Press, 1980), p. 4 (adapted)

A critique of Porter's five forces model

Porter's model has been criticised on several grounds including the following.

- *Changed economic conditions* Porter's theories relate to the economic situation of the 1980s, characterised by strong competition, interenterprise rivalry and relatively stable structures. They are less relevant in today's dynamic environment in which the Internet and e-business applications have the power to transform entire industries.

- *Identification of new forces* Downes[25] has identified digitalisation, globalisation and deregulation as three new forces that influence strategy.
  - *Digitalisation* – putting data into digital form for use in a digital computer – has provided all players in any given market with access to more information, thus enabling even external players to change the basis of competition.
  - *Globalisation* enables businesses to buy, sell and compare prices globally. Competitive advantage can be derived from cooperation, ability to develop strategic alliances and manage extensive global networks for the mutual advantage of buyers and sellers.
  - *Deregulation* – that is, a much reduced involvement of central government in the control of such industries as airlines, banking and public utilities.

  Downes states that the foremost differences between what he terms the 'Porter world' and 'the world of new forces' is information technology (IT). The old economy used IT as a tool for implementing change. Today, technology has become the most important driver of change.

  The three forces of digitalisation, globalisation and deregulation have effectively removed the barriers to industrial entry and enabled new competitors and new ways of competing to develop at an accelerated speed.

- *Relationships* Porter's wording 'bargaining power of suppliers and buyers' suggests adversarial relationships. Current thinking regards suppliers as partners, the relationships with them needing to be nutured and strengthened so that they become resources based on lasting friendly relationships derived from performance and integrity. Outsourcing relationships may enhance both the efficiency and effectiveness of purchasing.

Nevertheless, Porter's work should still be closely studied by purchasing professionals as it provides perspectives on how suppliers may regard their customers and, conversely, how customers may regard their suppliers.

2.10.3 Macro-environmental factors

These are the changes in the political, economic, social, technological, environmental and legal environments that directly or indirectly affect the organisation, both sector and industry-wise, as well as nationally and globally. The list of each of these factors, which can be recalled by the mnemonic PESTEL, is long. Typical examples are:

- Political – the role of government, that is, regulator or participator, political ideology
- Economic – gross domestic product (GDP), labour rates, monetary and fiscal policies
- Social – social trends, socio-economic groupings, value systems, ethics

- _T_echnological – changes, rates of technological change, costs and savings, patents
- _E_nvironmental – 'Green' considerations, disposal of products, atmospheric factors
- _L_egal – laws relating to competition, employment, the environment, consumer protection.

2.11 Internal scrutiny

This, in effect, is the internal scanning of resources, culture, value chains, structure and critical success factors.

2.11.1 Resources

Resources commonly identified are money, physical facilities and human and IT resources.

- _Money_ enables an organisation to have the maximum choice between alternatives. An important aspect of money is liquidity or ready availability. Too much money tied up in plant or stocks may limit the ability of an enterprise to take advantage of opportunities.
- _Physical facilities_ include plant and machinery. Important strategic factors are location, life, flexibility or alternative uses and the dangers of obsolescence. Such factors influence decisions regarding whether to buy or hire facilities or outsource certain operations.
- _Human resources_ include the specialised competences of the workforce and how easily specific attributes can be acquired or replaced. A further factor is the extent to which human resources can be replaced by technology. Non-availability of resources may limit the achievement of corporate goals and lead to the search for alternative means of acquiring them, such as via partnership agreements or outsourcing. Other resources, including patents and reputation, may provide an organisation with a competitive advantage over rivals in the same industry.
- _IT resources_ facilitate rapid communication between the organisation and its external contacts, including suppliers and customers, in addition to being a source of intelligence.

2.11.2 Culture

Culture is 'the way things are done round here'. More formally, culture is the system of shared values, beliefs and habits within an organisation that interacts with the formal structure to produce behavioural norms. A very simple structure of culture at the operational level is that purchasing staff should never keep sales representatives waiting. Representatives who cannot be seen with the minimum of delay should be informed so that their time is not unduly wasted. Culture is an important aspect of strategy because, if a supportive culture does not exist or cannot be cultivated, strategy changes can be difficult to implement. A model of the elements that comprise the culture web of an organisation is shown in Figure 2.7.

Figure 2.7 **Culture web of an organisation**

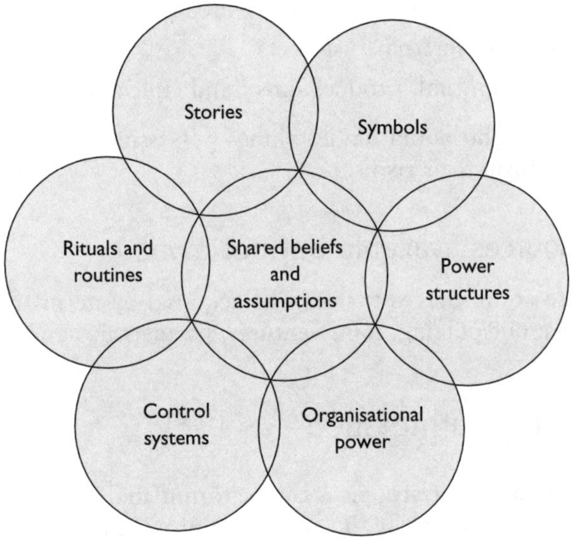

2.11.3 Value chains and structure

These are dealt with in Chapters 3 and 4 respectively.

2.11.4 Critical success factors (CSFs)

A CSF has been defined as:[26]

> An element of organisational activity which is central to its future success. Critical success factors may change over time and may include such items as product quality, employee attitudes, manufacturing flexibility and brand awareness.

In the design of new products, the early involvement of suppliers may be a critical success factor.

CSFs are linked to key tasks and priorities. *Key tasks* are what must be done to ensure that each critical success factor is achieved. *Priorities* indicate the order in which key tasks are performed.

Some critical success factors relating to purchasing strategies include:

- total quality management
- smaller supply bases
- just-in-time deliveries
- total cycle time reduction
- supplier relationships
- total cost management

- e-purchasing
- performance management
- training and development of purchasing staff
- service to internal customers
- environmental, product safety and ethical standards.

Research shows that undertakings possessing strengths in their critical success factors outperform their rivals.

2.11.5 Resources available but not owned

These are resources that can be acquired by means of lease, hire, consultancy agreements, outsourcing, joint ventures, partnerships and shared use arrangements.

2.12 Strategy formulation

As we have seen, strategies can be formulated by a process of rational planning or may emerge incrementally. These two approaches are sometimes presented as conflicting, based on the concept that strategic planning is inimical to creative thinking. Instead, however, the two approaches should be seen as complementary. A great enterprise such as the World War II Normandy landings in 1944 could not have been accomplished without creative thinking involving vision, creativity and incremental learning based on constantly changing intelligence. Such thinking, however, had to become operationalised by means of strategic thinking. As Lawrence[27] observes:

> The essential point . . . is that strategic thinking and strategic planning are both necessary and none is adequate without the other, in an effective strategy making regime. The real challenge is how to transform today's planning process in a way that incorporates, rather than undermines strategic thinking.

Strategy formulation at corporate, business and functional levels relates to the:

- formulation of a vision statement
- preparation of a mission statement
- derivation of objectives
- application of SWOT analysis.

2.12.1 Vision statements

Vision, from a strategic aspect, has been defined as:[28]

> A mental representation of strategy, created or at least expressed in the head of the leader. That vision serves both as an inspiration and a sense of what needs to be done.

Such a vision is often the starting point for strategy formulation. The vision must, however, be communicated to others in a mission statement.

A vision statement articulates a realistic, credible and positive projection of the future state of an organisation or functions or operations within that operation.

A typical vision statement for the purchasing activity might be:

To develop, as part of an integrated supply chain, world class purchasing strategies, policies, procedures and personnel to ensure that, by means of effective sourcing, competitive advantage is achieved by, for example, lowered supplies costs, commensurate with quality, shortened supply cycles and good supplier relationships.

The vision statement of Rolls-Royce PLC reads:

It is our vision to make Rolls-Royce the first choice for power systems, products and services. Our mission is to be trusted to deliver excellence to our customers and investors with the support of employees, partners and suppliers.

A rider to the above states:

It is the responsibility of each supplier/partner to become part of the vision and to orchestrate its own business practices to deliver the excellence required.

2.12.2 Vision and mission statements

Vision and mission statements are sometimes considered to be synonymous, but Campbell and Yeung[29] point out some differences.

- Vision refers to a future state, 'a condition that is better than now'. Thus, British Airways aspires to become 'The world's favourite airline' and Microsoft to have a PC in every home. Mission statements refer to the 'here and now'.
- When a vision is achieved, a new vision needs to be developed, but a mission can remain the same.
- A vision is associated with a goal, whereas a mission is associated with a way of behaving.

The mission statement answers the question 'What is our business?' It is the sense of purpose provided by a mission statement that helps in both strategy formulation and maintaining the focus of strategic plans.

At the operating level, a mission statement should indicate the following.

- The aims of the function or operation. These should be carefully considered and reflect the needs and expectations of both internal and external customers. Aims, especially at the organisational level, may be narrowly or broadly defined. A building society may define its mission narrowly as to provide mortgages to prospective house purchasers. More broadly, this purpose is to provide financial services. Similarly, for a film company, 'to provide entertainment' is a broader aim than 'to make films'.
- How the aims will be achieved.
- The basis of internal and external relationships.
- The link with organisational strategies.

These four points are exemplified in Figure 2.8.

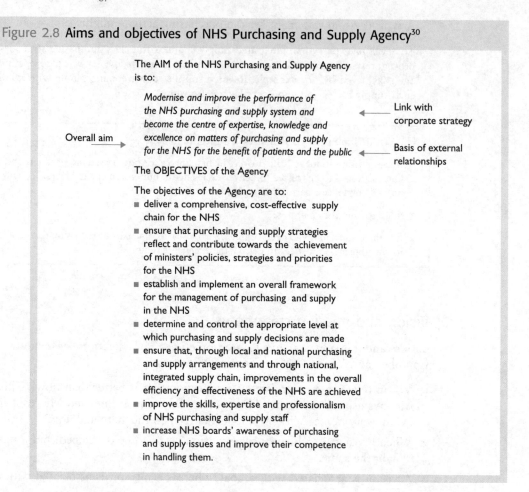

Figure 2.8 **Aims and objectives of NHS Purchasing and Supply Agency**[30]

2.12.3 Objectives

Objectives are explicit statements of the results the organisation wishes to achieve. Corporate and business objectives are medium- to long-term, strategic and general and usually cover growth, profitability, technology, products and markets. Functional or operational objectives are short-term, tactical and specific. Thus, 'Elements of strategy at a higher management level become objectives at a lower one.'[31]

As we saw earlier, the classic definition of the overall purchasing task is:

To obtain materials of the right *quality* in the right *quantity* from the right *source* delivering to the right *place* at the right *time* at the right *price*.

As you will also recall, this definition is somewhat simplistic for the following reasons:

■ the term 'right' is situational – each company will define 'right' differently

■ what is 'right' will change as the overall purchasing context and environment change

■ the above rights must be consistent with corporate goals and objectives from which functional/operating goals and objectives are derived

■ in practice, some rights are irreconcilable – for example, it may be possible to obtain the right quality, but not the right price as 'the best suppliers are often the busiest but also the dearest'.

Purchasing objectives have therefore to be balanced according to overall corporate strategy and requirements at a given time.

An alternative definition of the key purpose for the purchasing and supply chain, derived for the UK Purchasing and Supply Lead Body for National Vocational Qualifications by the University of Ulster, is:

> To provide the interface between customer and supplier in order to plan, obtain, store and distribute as necessary, supplies of materials, goods and services [m, g, s] to enable the organisation to satisfy its external and internal customers.

As shown in Table 2.5, purchasing objectives derive from corporate objectives.

Short-term objectives are those set for a short period – one year, say – so that actual achievement can be measured against the original objectives, distinguishing between factors relating to attainment or non-attainment for which the purchasing activity and its staff can be held accountable. The technique of management by objectives is discussed in Section 17.7.

Table 2.5 Purchasing and corporate objectives

Business objectives	Purchasing and supply objectives
A statement of the position the organisation is aiming for in its markets, including market share	The objective of providing the quantity and quality of supplies required by the market share and market positioning objectives
A key objective of, say, moving out of speciality markets and entering volume markets	A key objective of developing new, larger suppliers and materials flow systems more geared to larger numbers of fewer parts while keeping the total inventory volume low
A key objective to build new businesses that will generate positive cash flow as well as reasonable profits	Contribute to cash flow improvement by means of lower average inventory and by negotiating smaller delivery lots and/or longer payment terms
A plan to develop some specific new products or services	A plan to develop appropriate suppliers
An overall production/capacity plan, including an overall policy on make or buy	A plan to develop systems that integrate capacity planning and/or purchase planning, together with the policy on make or buy and partnering relationships
A plan to introduce a cost reduction programme	A plan to introduce supplies standardisation, supplier reduction programmes and e-procurement
A financial plan, setting out in broad terms how the proposed capital expenditure is to be financed, together with an outline timescale and an order in which the objectives need to be achieved	A financial plan, setting out broadly the profit contribution expected from purchasing and supply, together with the time in which it should be achieved and the priorities of the objectives

The NHS Purchasing and Supply Agency, for example, is required to produce an annual business plan that details its planned activities for the coming year and how they relate to its overall objectives. For the year 2003–4, the Agency set the following targets:[32]

■ Target 1: We will work jointly with selected supply confederations to collect data and determine the most appropriate sourcing and supply strategy using recognised analytical techniques and the considerable expertise in the Agency of managing markets and suppliers.

To do this we will:

– determine by 30 September 2003 an effective decision-making toolkit to establish the most appropriate level of purchasing and supply activity

– roll out the findings and assist supply confederations and key trusts with implementation by 31 March 2003.

■ Target 2: Increase the value of NHS expenditure, influenced by professional purchasing and supply management. To do this the Agency will need to:

– increase the value of Agency-influenced expenditure from £5.4 billion to £6 billion

– establish with supply confederations a consistent and scientific approach to identify total NHS-influenced expenditure, as opposed to contractual spend, and publish this approach, reporting quarterly, and monitor and revise where necessary.

■ Target 3: The Agency will consistently manage the performance of its contracts and agree criteria for measuring supplier performance. All new contracts with effect from June 2003 will have specific measurement criteria. This will enable us to:

– identify best practice and performance with a view to achieving even greater value for money and continuity of supply for the NHS

– identify in a timely and effective manner those suppliers failing to meet contractual requirements and deal with them.

■ Target 4: To achieve purchasing savings of at least 5 per cent of the value of the Agency's contracts by 31 March 2004. To do this we will:

– implement purchasing strategies and contracts in order to optimise value for money

– report on these in accordance with the Operational Purchasing Procedures Manual and to the Ministerial Advisory Board and trusts on a quarterly basis.

2.12.4 SWOT analysis

Environmental scanning and internal scrutiny described earlier in this chapter provide the intelligence for a SWOT (strengths, weaknesses, opportunities and threats) analysis. Figure 2.9 indicates that some form of SWOT analysis or matrix is an essential preliminary step in the formulation of strategies designed to convert the inspirations expressed in vision and mission statements into realities and ensure that the objectives are achieved.

Figure 2.9 **SWOT matrix**

		Internal scrutiny	
		What are our *strengths?*	What are our *weaknesses?*
Scanning the internal environment	What are the *opportunities* we can exploit?	S → O strategies	W → O strategies
	What are the *threats* affecting our business?	S → T strategies	W → T strategies

In Figure 2.9:

- *S → O strategies* are those that seek to utilise organisational strengths to exploit external opportunities
- *W → O strategies* are those that seek to rectify organisational weaknesses so that external opportunities can be exploited
- *S → T strategies* are those that utilise organisational strengths to reduce vulnerability to external threats
- *W → T strategies* establish defensive plans to prevent organisational weaknesses from being highly vulnerable to external threats.

SWOT analysis can be undertaken at all three organisational levels – corporate, business and functional. An example of a SWOT analysis leading to some possible W → T strategies is where the organisation is under some threat as the manufacture of a major product requires the purchase of a highly sensitive material for which there is a high demand and few suppliers. In such a case, the SWOT/TOWS matrix may be used, as shown in Figure 2.10.

Figure 2.10 **SWOT analysis applied to a supplies situation**

STRENGTHS	WEAKNESSES
▪ Purchasing power ▪ Regular demand ▪ Purchasing probity and goodwill	▪ Highly sensitive imported material
THREATS	**OPPORTUNITIES**
▪ Competition for the material from competitors ▪ Few suppliers ▪ Exchange rates	▪ Alternative materials ▪ Possibility of vertical integration with a supplier ▪ Outsourcing ▪ Partnerships ▪ Virtual company formation

SWOT analysis has been criticised on the grounds that, in practice, such exercises are often poorly structured, hastily conducted and result in vague and inconsistent lists of subjective factors reflecting the interests and prejudices of the proposers. Such criticisms can be countered by:

- *making the analysis a group process* in which the free flow of ideas is encouraged
- *the use of qualifiers* this requires the movers of statements for inclusion in the analysis to give reasons, so, instead of just saying 'too much reliance on one supplier', the proposer would be required to add 'because the supplier takes our business for granted and we are possibly paying more than necessary'.

2.13 The evaluation of alternative strategies

In a given situation, there are normally several alternative strategies that are available. The aim is to evaluate several strategic options – including a 'do nothing' or 'do the minimum' option, which, where appropriate, may be included, even if it is unacceptable in operational terms.

Rumelt[33] identifies four principles that can be applied to strategic evaluation:

- *consistency* the strategy must not present mutually inconsistent policies
- *consonance* the strategy must represent an adaptive response to the external environment and the critical changes occurring within it
- *advantage* the strategy must provide for the creation and/or maintenance of a competitive advantage in the selected area of authority
- *feasibility* the strategy must neither overtax available resources nor create insoluble problems.

An alternative set of criteria is that a given strategy should, first, meet the requirements of a given situation, second, provide sustainable competitive advantage and, third, improve company performance.

2.13.1 Methods of strategy evaluation

There are several possible approaches to choosing a strategy that meets the above criteria. Porter's positional approach to strategy formation is simply the selection of one of three generic positions based on an analysis of the organisation's position in the environment.

Other important approaches include lifecycle analysis, scenario planning, return analysis, profitability analysis, risk analysis, resource deployment analysis, non-financial factor appraisal and portfolio planning and analysis.

2.13.2 Lifecycle analysis

This is based on the concept that all products in their original, unmodified form have a finite lifespan, as shown in Figure 2.11.

The product lifecycle or Gopertz curve plots the actual or potential sales of a new product over time and shows the stages of development – growth, maturity, decline and eventual withdrawal. Important aspects of product lifecycles are:

Figure 2.11 **Product lifecycle**

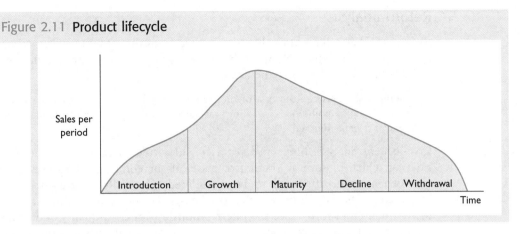

- *their length* from development to withdrawal, which may be short with products subject to rapid technological advances
- *their shape* not all products have the same shape to their curve – so-called high learning, low learning, fashion and fad products have different curves reflecting different marketing strategies
- *the product* this can vary depending on whether the product lifecycle applies to a *class* – that is, the entire product category or industry – a *form* – that is, variations within the class – or a *brand*.

From the strategic aspect, the lifecycle approach has become increasingly important for the following reasons:

- *environmental factors*, such as the relative environmental performance of a product, as in the case of purchasing packaging, paper and the subsequent management of waste
- *durability factors*, such as competition between substitute commodity products – aluminium and steel in the car industry, for example
- *obsolescence* with regard to capital equipment, which may be a factor in deciding to adopt an outsourcing strategy
- *changing demand* this concept of the product lifecycle helps marketing managers to recognise both that products may need to be continually changed to prevent sales decline and that there is a need to formulate marketing strategies to stimulate demand – this strategy may impact purchasing strategies, such as how far in advance to place orders for materials or components that are likely to change.

2.13.3 Scenario planning

Scenario planning consists of developing a conceptual forecast of the future based on given assumptions. Thus, by starting with different assumptions, different future scenarios can be presented. The assumptions can be based on the examination of trends relating to economic, political and social factors that may affect corporate objectives and supply and demand forecasts. Planning therefore involves deciding which scenario is most likely to occur and devising appropriate strategies for it. An example is examining how the prices of sensitive commodities change in the scenarios of glut and shortage.

2.13.4 Return analysis

Return analysis – the returns likely to accrue from the adoption of a particular strategy – may be done by such means as cost–benefit analysis or profitability analysis. Cost–benefit analysis may be defined as:

> A comparison between the cost of the resources used, plus any other costs imposed by an activity (such as pollution, environmental damage) and the value of the financial and non-financial benefits derived.

Cost–benefit analysis often involves a consideration of trade-offs. Thus, when considering which of several alternative materials or components to use, a number of cost–benefit trade-offs need to be considered. Generally, increased quality means increased prices and, ultimately, increased costs. The decision on which to specify must therefore attempt to balance the interrelationships of cost, quality and projected selling prices with company objectives relating to sales quantities and profitability.

2.13.5 Profitability analysis

This uses a number of ratios to measure the ability of the business to make a profit, including:

- *sales growth* indicates the percentage increase (or decrease) in sales between two time periods – that is:

$$\frac{\text{Current year's (or other period) sales} - \text{Last year's sales}}{\text{Last year's sales}}$$

and if overall costs and inflation are on the rise, then a related increase in sales should be expected; if not, this is an indication that prices are not keeping up with costs

- *costs of goods sold to sales* an indication of the percentage of sales used to pay for expenses that vary directly with sales – that is:

$$\frac{\text{Cost of goods sold}}{\text{Sales}}$$

- *gross profit margin* indicates profit earning on products without consideration of selling and administrative overheads – that is:

$$\frac{\text{Gross profit}}{\text{Total sales}}$$

- *net profit margins* indicates how much profit comes from every £1 of sales – that is:

$$\frac{\text{Net profit}}{\text{Total sales}}$$

- *return on assets* indicates how effectively assets are used to provide a return – that is:

$$\frac{\text{Net profit}}{\text{Total assets}}$$

Profitability analysis can also include such measures as return on capital employed (ROCE), payback and discounted cash flow, referred to in Chapter 13.

2.13.6 Risk analysis

From a strategic perspective, a risk is something that may have an impact on the achievement of objectives.

Risks can be assessed from three standpoints.

- *The likelihood of the risk being realised* A realised risk is known as an issue and, as such, must be dealt with.
- *The impact of risk* Thus the breakdown of a JIT contract may have quantitative and qualitative consequences. *Quantitative* consequences include the costs of a breakdown in production, obtaining substitute supplies and, possibly, funding a new supplier. *Qualitatively*, the reputation of the purchasing activity may be adversely affected by sourcing from an unreliable supplier.
- *The costs and benefits of taking steps to reduce either the risk or its impact* should the risk become an issue. Risks from a strategic viewpoint do not always have a negative connotation. Risks present opportunities to be embraced, such as global sourcing, as well as dangers to be avoided.

Some approaches to the reduction and control of strategic risks include the following.

- *Decision support modelling and information systems* These software programs use information from both internal and external sources to support decision making.
- *Probability analysis* This determines the probability of a risk occurring on a scale of 0 to 1. The probability of an event can be computed by the formula:

$$\frac{\text{Number of ways an outcome could occur}}{\text{Total number of outcomes}}$$

Thus the probability of obtaining the number 3 when rolling a six-sided dice is:

$$\frac{1}{6} \text{ or } 0.167$$

In the real world, the calculation of probability is often impossible due to insufficient data. Even when it can be done, statistical conclusions should be supported by some form of qualitative assessment. From experience we know that a dice can be rolled six times without a 3 occurring once.

- *Sensitivity analysis* This is used to determine how 'sensitive' a strategy is to changes in the assumptions on which it is based. Such analysis questions or challenges each of the assumptions underlying the strategy and determines how sensitive the desired or predicted outcome is to each assumption. Essentially sensitivity looks at the question of 'What if . . . ?' when a variable is different from that originally expected. Thus, except for the initial purchase price, all data relating to the purchase of a capital asset such as life, return on investment and cost of maintenance are estimates. Any estimate, however, is subject to error. Sensitivity analysis identifies an error range for the various estimated values over which the purchase will be acceptable. While sensitivity analysis of each variable, such as the estimated life of the asset, will be reduced by obsolescence resulting from improved technology, it does provide a tolerance factor for estimation errors by providing upper and lower ranges for selected variables.

■ *Hedging* is a method of minimising investment risk, particularly in the contexts of investment management and commodity dealing. The financial tools most frequently used for hedging are forward buying, futures and options. Collectively, these tools are known as *derivatives*. Hedging is discussed further in Section 13.13.4.

■ *Satisficing* This is a concept introduced by Cyert and March[34] who argue that managers do not attempt to discover every alternative. When managers satisfice, they choose acceptable solutions based on the information available to them rather than trying to make the optimum decision.

2.13.7 Resource deployment analysis

Resource deployment analysis is the assessment of the likely effect on key resources of adopting a particular strategy. Thus, a decision whether or not to adopt an outsourcing strategy with regard to a support service will be preceded by an analysis of the effects on tangible and intangible resources, including finance, human resources, competitive advantage and growth.

2.13.8 Non-financial factor appraisal

When making strategic decisions, it is important to consider such non-financial aspects as:

■ enhancement (or otherwise) of the organisational image
■ effects on suppliers, customers, competitors and the general public
■ environmental and ethical factors
■ the likelihood of change, development, obsolescence
■ staff and union reaction to the strategy
■ ethical implications of the proposed strategy.

2.13.9 Portfolio planning and analysis

Portfolio planning and analysis aim to assist with strategic decisions as to where to invest scarce organisational resources among a number of competing business opportunities. This approach is analogous to an investment manager deciding which shares to buy with the aim of creating a portfolio designed to meet a given investment strategy, such as achieving growth or providing income.

2.13.10 The BCG portfolio

One of the most popular portfolio approaches is the Boston Consulting Group (BCG) matrix. This approach to strategy formulation analyses business opportunities according to market growth rate and market share. As shown in Figure 2.12, based on these criteria, businesses can be categorised as:

■ *stars* businesses with high market share and high growth
■ *cash cows* businesses with high market share and low growth

Figure 2.12 Corporate strategies within the BCG matrix

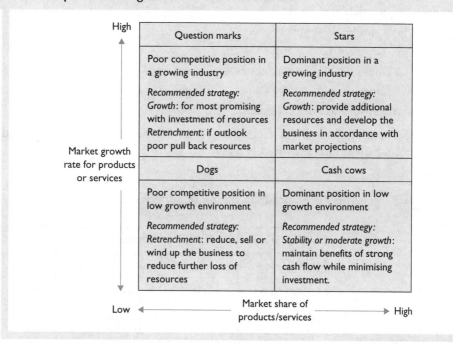

- *question marks* businesses with low market share and high growth
- *dogs* businesses with low market share and low growth.

The BCG matrix can be used to decide what strategy(ies) to adopt at all three strategic organisational levels: corporate, business and functional/operational.

2.13.11 Purchasing portfolio management

In 1983, Kraljic[35] introduced the first portfolio approach for use in purchasing and supply management, although a similar 'matrix' was described by Fisher[36] in 1970. Kraljic's starting premise is that:

> Threats of resource depletion and raw materials scarcity, political turbulence and government intervention in supply markets, intensified competition and accelerating technological changes have ended the days of no surprises. As dozens of companies have learned, supply and demand patterns can be upset virtually overnight.

The Kraljic portfolio aims to guide managers so that they can recognise the weakness of their organisation and formulate strategies for guarding against supplies disruption.

Kraljic states that the *profit impact* of a given supply item can be defined in terms of:

- volume purchased
- percentage of total cost
- impact on product quality or business growth.

Supply risk for that item is assessed in terms of availability:

- availability
- number of suppliers
- competitive demand
- make-or-buy opportunities
- storage risks
- substitution opportunities.

These profits and risk factors enable all purchased items to be assigned to one of the four quadrants shown in Figure 2.13.

Figure 2.13 The Kraljic portfolio matrix (adapted)

	Leverage products (Examples: steel plate and sections)	Strategic products (Examples: assemblies, gear boxes, engines, optics)	Balance of power in purchaser/ supplier relationship
High ↑ Purchasing importance and profit impact of a given supply item measured against criteria such as cost of materials, total costs, volume purchased ↓	■ Relatively large share of product price ■ Small change in price has large impact on profit Risk small as: ■ many alternative suppliers ■ substitution possible Buyer-dominated segment Competitive bidding	■ Together with leverage products can account for 80% of turnover ■ Small changes in price will have an immediate and significant impact on costs Risk significant due to high dependence on supplier Balance of power may differ between purchasers and suppliers. Performance-based partnership	
	Non-critical (routine) products (Examples: standard office supplies, MRO items, fasteners, consumables)	Bottleneck products (Examples: natural flavours, vitamins, pigments)	
	■ Can require up to 80% of purchasing activity for 20% of purchasing turnover ■ Low product/high administrative cost No risk due to: ■ many alternative suppliers ■ large product variety Reduce number of suppliers Use systems contracting and e-procurement solutions	■ Relatively limited in value but danger of sudden price rises High risk due to: ■ few, if any, alternative suppliers ■ suppliers may be technology leaders Supplier-dominated segment Secure long- and short-term supply Seek alternative suppliers	

Low (many suppliers) ←——— Supply risk measured against such criteria as short- and long-term availability, number of potential suppliers, structure of supply markets. ———→ High (one or few suppliers)

Nellove and Söderquist[37] state that all portfolio approaches to procurement involve three common steps:

1 analysis of the products and their classification
2 analysis of the supplier relationships required to deliver the products
3 action plans to match product requirements to supplier relationships.

Thus, the steps for the use of the matrix in Figure 2.13 are:

■ list all purchases in descending value order

■ analyse the risk and market complexity of each purchase

■ position each item on the matrix accordingly

■ periodically, decide whether or not to move a particular purchase to an alternative quadrant.

The aims and possible tasks associated with each quadrant are shown in Table 2.6.

Gelderman and van Weele[38] point out that 'in general little is known about *the actual use* of purchasing portfolio models or how purchasing professionals position commodities and suppliers into the portfolio and develop strategies from its use'. To gain insights into such issues, we interviewed a limited number of executives and purchasing professionals employed by a large Dutch chemical company. The interviewees were selected for their experience in the use of portfolio models in actual purchasing situations. Their findings in relation to the company DSM may be summarised as follows.

Basic

■ Generally matrix movements follow a clockwise pattern from bottleneck to non-critical; non-critical to leverage; leverage to strategic.

■ DSM works on the principle that the non-critical and bottleneck quadrants should be as empty as possible.

Bottleneck items

For processed materials, a key question is whether standardisation is possible, permitting movement to the leverage quadrant.

Where standardisation is not possible, approaches reported are:

■ capacity deals concentrating purchases with one supplier

■ obtaining a better bottleneck position by reducing supply risk on the one hand and obtaining a better negotiating position on the other

■ 'staying in the corner and making the best of it' by keeping stocks, hedging, broadening the specification, searching for alternative suppliers and so on.

Many non-critical (MRO) and equipment items are 'bottleneck' due to overspecification. Less complicated and more generic specifications allow 'pooling' of purchases across units/groups and consequent movement from the bottleneck quadrant to the non-critical one and/or non-critical to the leverage quadrant.

Table 2.6 **Aims, tasks and information associated with each procurement focus**

Procurement focus	Aims	Main tasks	Required information
Leverage aims (high profit impact, low supply risk)	■ Obtain best short-term deal ■ Maximise cost savings	■ Ensure suppliers are aware that they are in a competitive situation ■ Group similar items together to increase value and quality for quantity discounts ■ Utilise blanket orders but keep contract terms relatively short (1–2 years) ■ Search for alternative products/suppliers ■ Negotiate value-added arrangements – VMI, JIT, storage ■ Consider moving into strategic quadrant	■ Good market data ■ Short- to medium-term demand planning ■ Accurate vendor data ■ Price/transport rate forecasts
Strategic items (high profit impact, high supply risk)	■ Maximise cost reductions ■ Minimise risk ■ Create competitive advantage ■ Create mutual commitment to long-term relationships	■ Prepare accurate forecasts of future requirements ■ Carefully analyse supply risk ■ Seek long-term supplier/partnering agreements (3–5 years) with built-in arrangements for continuous improvement and performance measurement ■ Consider joint ventures with selected suppliers and customers to gain competitive advantage ■ Take prompt action to rectify slipping performance ■ Possibly move purchasing back into leverage quadrant until confidence restored	■ Highly detailed market data ■ Long-term supply and demand trend information ■ Good competitive intelligence ■ Industry cost curves
Non-critical (routine) items (low profit impact, low supply risk)	■ Reduce administrative procedures and costs ■ Eliminate complexity ■ Improve operational efficiency	■ Simplify requisitioning, buying and payment ■ Standardise where possible ■ Consolidate and buy from consortia ■ Encourage direct ordering by users/internal customers against call-off contracts ■ Use e-procurement ■ Consider clustering into leverage quadrant	■ Good market overview ■ Short-term demand forecast ■ Economic order quantity ■ Inventory levels
Bottleneck items (low profit items, high supply risk)	■ Reduce costs ■ Secure short- and long-term supply	■ Forecast future requirements as accurately as possible ■ Consolidate purchases to secure leverage ■ Determine importance attached to purchases by supplier ■ See if specification measures – buffer stocks, consigned stocks, transportation ■ Search for alternative products/supplies ■ Contract to reduce risk	■ Medium-term demand/supply forecasts ■ Very good market data ■ Inventory costs ■ Maintenance plans

Non-critical items

At DSM, the main products are office supplies and services. As stated above, the main considerations influencing movement to the leverage quadrant are standardisation and pooling. Where pooling is not an option, purchase cards are useful for individual non-strategic commodities.

Leverage items

DSM distinguishes between 'strategic partnerships' and 'partnerships of convenience'.

Only a limited number of supplies qualify for movement from the leverage to the strategic quadrant, which is feasible when:

- the supplier has proper capabilities for co-design
- the purchaser (DSM) is prepared to spend time on supplier development
- the purchaser has sufficient levels of trust in the supplier at all organisational levels.

When a supplier does not qualify as a strategic supplier, the focus is on efficiency and cost reduction rather than design optimisation.

Partnerships can be either technology (joint venture, codevelopment, concurrent engineering) or logistics-driven (JIT). The latter are regarded as 'partnerships of convenience' or tactical solutions to tactical problems and reside in the leverage quadrant.

Strategic items

Successful strategic partnerships are rare and DSM policy is to reduce or restrict dependence on the supplier involved. Partnerships, over time, may become unsatisfactory or the supplier does not wish to be involved in joint development.

With underachieving partners, DSM may adopt such approaches as supplier development, making the product less complicated and developing new suppliers.

Conclusions

While recognising the limitation of their investigation, Geldermann and van Weele concluded that:

- the portfolio approach is helpful in positioning commodities/supplies in different matrix quadrants
- the pre-eminent value of the approach is in helping purchasing practitioners to move commodities/suppliers around specific quadrants to reduce dependence on specific suppliers
- the Kraljic portfolio is 'an effective tool for discussing visualising and illustrating the possibilities of differentiated purchasing strategies . . . it is a powerful tool for coordinating purchasing strategies among various, fairly autonomous business units'.

In addition, the Kraljic categories provide a useful way of classifying purchases by total spend under each heading.

There are various modifications or variants to the Kraljic matrix, of which possibly the best-known one is that of Bensaou.[39] One objection to purchasing portfolio models is that they do not take account of the supplier's perspective. Using the complexity of the supply market (ask yourself, 'In practice are there many or few suppliers?') and

Figure 2.14 The buyer's market from the supplier's perspective

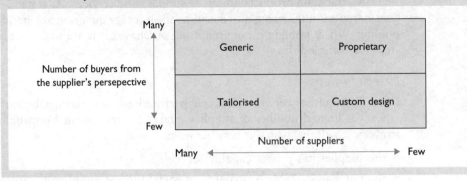

the complexity of the buyer markets ('Many or few buyers?'), Kamann[40] has developed the alternative matrix shown in Figure 2.14.

Figure 2.14 identifies four classifications of products:

- *generic items* standardised commodities
- *tailorised items* items produced using flexible technology – mass customisation
- *proprietary products* brand names, such as Microsoft
- *custom design* the real one-to-one relationships.

By combining the Kamann and Kraljic matrices, we obtain a cube, as shown in Figure 2.15. This cube reflects both the complexity of the supplier's market (from the purchasing perspective) and the buyer's market (from the supplier's perspective).

Figure 2.15 The Kamann cube

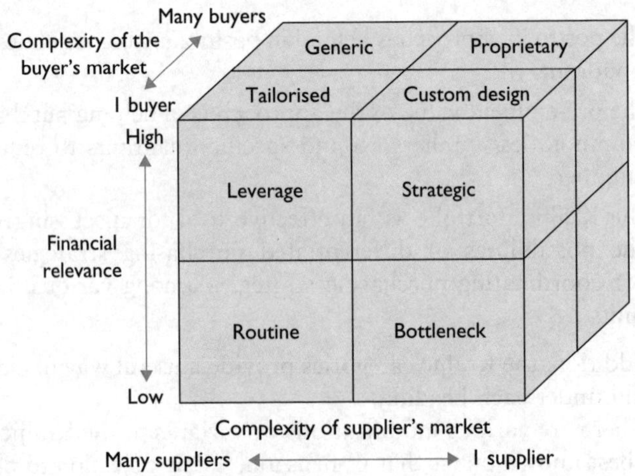

Kamann observes, inter alia, the following.

- *Part of the strategic and bottleneck items belong to the proprietary column (one monopolistic or very few oligopolistic suppliers and many buyers)* The chances of getting adapted product specifications for such items is therefore small. This is especially true for smaller buyers, who may deal with agents rather than directly with producers.

- *Many companies differentiate between various types of leverage items in their supplier strategy* A food multinational, for example, differentiates between simple products (such as potatoes) and more complicated products (such as a complete meal). For complicated products, joint value analysis, involving customers and suppliers, is used to standardise products across markets and producers.

- *Purchasing procedures* Generic, tailored and proprietary items can be well integrated. Custom design requires many face-to-face contacts. Suppliers can be categorised as:

  - brokers – potentially virtual organisations that just redistribute orders, organise and collect leveraged buying power, combined with spot buying on the Internet

  - capacity suppliers – actually produce goods and services

  - codevelopers – concerned with product development and design requiring much face-to face contact and long-term relationships. Logistics is 'the glue that blends the business processes of brokers, capacity suppliers and codevelopers'. These relationships are depicted in Figure 2.16.

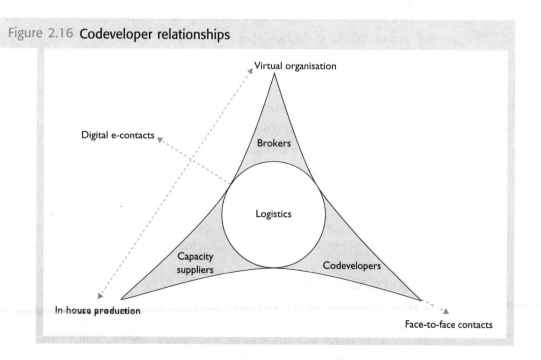

Figure 2.16 **Codeveloper relationships**

Table 2.7 **Contrasts between strategy formulation and implementation**

Strategy formulation	*Strategy implementation*
The positioning of forces before the action	Management of forces during the action
Focuses on effectiveness	Focuses on efficiency
Is primarily an intellectual process	Is primarily an operational process
Requires good initiative and analytical skills	Requires special motivation and leadership skills
Requires coordination of a few individuals	Requires coordination of many people

2.14 Strategy implementation

Strategy implementation is concerned with converting a strategic plan into action and doing what needs to be done to achieve the targeted strategic goals and objectives. The principal differences between strategy formulation and strategy implementation are shown in Table 2.7.

Strategy implementation should be seen as a learning process from which all organisational levels can benefit.

2.14.1 The main stages of strategy implementation

1 Communicate strategic plans to all who have not been involved in their formulation. Good communication helps to avoid negative reactions, particularly where strategies involve significant change.

2 Obtain commitment from those concerned. This involves disclosure and discussion in consultative processes, such as meetings and team briefings.

3 Framing policies and procedures.

4 Setting operational targets and objectives and ensuring that these are related to corporate objectives.

5 Assigning responsibilities and commensurate authority to individuals and teams for the achievement of objectives.

6 Changing organisational structures, where necessary.

7 Allocation of resources and agreeing budgets.

8 Providing employees with required training.

9 Constantly monitoring the success or otherwise of strategies and making required revisions.

Resource allocation and policies are important aspects of the above activities. Organisational structures are considered in Chapter 4 and procedures in Chapter 6.

2.14.2 Resource allocation

In most organisations the financial, physical, human and technological resources allocated to a function/activity will be reduced to quantitative terms and expressed in budgets or financial statements of the resources needed to achieve specific objectives or implement a formulated strategy.

2.14.3 Policies

Policies are instruments for strategy implementation. A policy is:

> a body of principles, expressed or implied, laid down to direct an enterprise towards its objectives and guide executives in decision making.

Policies are mandatory and must be adhered to by all people and activities throughout the organisation.

It is useful to consider the advantages of policy generally and policies for purchasing specifically.

The advantages of policies

At corporate, functional and operational levels, policies have the following advantages:

- corporate policies provide guidelines to executives when formulating functional and operating strategies
- policies provide authority based on principle and/or precedent for a given course of action
- they provide a basis for management control, allow coordination across organisational units and reduce the time managers spend making decisions
- they provide management by exception, providing guidelines for routine actions, so a new decision is required only in exceptional circumstances
- policies lead to uniformity of procedures and consistency in thought and action.

Purchasing policies

Typical examples include the following.

- Policies relating to supply relationships

  > Our policy is to be selective about the types of relationships we establish with suppliers, but in all cases to treat them with professional respect and hold our dealings with them as confidential to the parties concerned.

  > We should aim to actively promote an image rather than let one form by default. We wish to be seen as fair, tough, totally professional and demonstrably operating according to the highest standards of business practice.

- Internal policies

  > Our policy is to support internal suppliers to the fullest extent and develop product and service quality to the same high standards as those available in the external market. Employees may not use the company's name or purchase leverage to obtain materials or services at preferential rates for their personal use or for use by other parties in whom the 'buyer' has an interest.

- Sourcing policies

  > Only those suppliers who satisfy the requirements of the company's supplier appraisal process and are able to meet their contractual obligations to the company in full should be used. Buyers should actively source from the world market where practical, taking into account corporate guidelines and statutory regulations.

Policy statements can be written in relation to virtually every aspect of purchasing activity. Other important areas for which policy statements may be prepared include:

- purchasing authority – who may purchase and limitations on authority
- use of purchasing cards
- purchase of capital equipment
- environmental policies
- disposal of waste and surplus
- purchasing from SMEs and local purchasing
- e-procurement
- ethical policies.

In general, the procurement policies of individual organisations should conform to three basic principles:

- procurement policies should aim to select and procure, in an economically rational manner, the best possible goods and services available
- suppliers worldwide should be eligible to participate in procurement transactions on open, fair and transparent principles and easy-to-understand, simple procedures
- procurement transactions have an important contribution to make to society worldwide – for example, corporate purchasing practices should consider the effective preservation of natural resources and protection of the environment.

Purchasing policies are usually specified in a purchasing manual that is regularly revised. The policies may be varied to meet an exceptional situation, such as a breakdown in supplies, but this should only be done on the authority of the executive who has ultimate responsibility for purchasing.

2.14.4 An example of a strategy implementation plan

An example of a public-sector organisation plan is shown in Figure 2.17.[41] The 11 headings of the plan can easily be adapted to the requirements of a private-sector enterprise.

2.15 Post-implementation evaluation, control and review

This is concerned with verifying the degree to which implemented strategies are fulfilling the mission and objectives of the organisation. Evaluation differs from control. Post-implementation evaluation can apply the principles listed in section 2.12 above. Spekman[42] states that the objective of evaluation is to enable procurement managers to understand both the process and result of strategic planning and offers the following list of evaluation criteria.

- *Internal consistency*
  - Are the procurement strategies mutually achievable?
  - Do they address corporate/division objectives?
  - Do they reinforce each other? Is there synergy?
  - Do the strategies focus on crucial procurement issues?

Figure 2.17 **An example of a strategy implementation plan**

Aims
To support the achievement of the Council's key objectives and allow concentration of more resources, both financial and staff time, on delivering core tasks. This will be done by securing best value for money, reducing or managing risk and modernising related business processes by adopting best practice procurement techniques for all bought-in external goods and services.

Objectives

1 Take a *strategic overview* of corporate procurement.
- Undertake portfolio analysis to identify key spend areas and suppliers.
- Identify scope for aggregation of demand into large/corporate contracts.
- Identify scope for collaborative arrangements.
- Identify the procurement community within BFBC.
- Create procurement performance measures against agreed baseline.
- Prepare an annual report to the executive board.

2 Establish procurement as specific element in *corporate and departmental planning process*.
- Incorporate council's procurement strategy and this implementation plan into the council's annual policy and performance plan.
- Establish procurement strategy/plan for each individual department as part of annual service plans.
- Review plans annually in normal planning process.

3 Adopt a commercial approach, in line with *best value principles*, to all procurement decisions.
- Evaluate all bids on quality as well as whole life cost whenever appropriate.
- Review procurement processes and contract regulations (and keep them under review).
- Prepare process guide in the form of a procurement manual and best practice toolkit with standard documentation and procedures to help department staff.
- Ensure, in addition, that departments have access to professional advice/involvement wherever needed.

4 Develop scope for *e-procurement*.
- Forge links with neighbouring authorities to identify scope for collaborative procurement and establishment of local e-marketplace.
- Ensure new contracts incorporate requirements for e-trading wherever possible.
- Identify scope for e-tendering and e-auctions.

5 Commit to principles of *sustainability and ethical procurement* where these can be achieved within the terms of best value principles.
- Develop appropriate best practice guidance with staff.

6 Simplify *business processes*.
- Establish framework agreements for high-volume/low-value goods and services.
- Prepare process guide in the form of a procurement manual and best practice toolkit with standard documentation and procedures to help departmental staff.
- Ensure effective interfaces with other council systems and processes.

7 Improve *communications* with markets.
- Publish annual procurement plan/programme of forthcoming contracts.
- Identify markets that do not deliver optimum performance and seek to develop/manage them to better effect.
- Identify opportunities for greater partnerships working/collaboration with suppliers/markets.
- Initiate development programme with major suppliers and partners.

8 Ensure availability of appropriate *training and guidance* for all staff involved in procurement (including schools).
- Undertake procurement skills gap analysis.
- Develop training programme, buying in expertise as required.
- Prepare procurement guidance reference manual covering principles and processes and summarised mini guide.
- Prepare detailed best practice toolkit with standardised documentation.

9 The *organisation of procurement* will remain unchanged but:
- improve communications with staff and schools
- develop feedback system for identifying lessons learnt from individual procurement exercises and sharing best practice
- ensure clarity in all guidance issued (use plain English).

10 Ensure all suppliers are treated fairly and openly in the awarding of council contracts.
- Prepare ethical code as part of procurement manual and integrate with council's code of conduct.

11 Commit to *continuous improvement* of all procurement practices and procedures.
- Regularly review contracts regulations, procurement manual and toolkit.
- Initiate benchmarking review of procurement and refresh biannually.
- Establish and monitor key performance indicators for procurement.

- *Environmental fit*
  - Do the purchasing strategies exploit environmental opportunities?
  - Do they deal with external threats?
- *Resource fit*
  - Can the strategies be carried out in the light of resource constraints?
  - Is the timing consistent with the department's and/or business's ability to adapt to the change?
- *Communication and implementation*
  - Are the strategies understood by key implementers?
  - Is there organisational commitment?
  - Is there sufficient managerial capability to support effective procurement planning?

The control process involves four stages, as shown in Figure 2.18. Setting standards is not easy, owing to the multitude of possibilities.

Normally, specific performance standards can be grouped under four headings:

- service to internal and external customers
- contributors to the competitive advantage of other elements in the supply chain
- staff effectiveness and efficiency
- financial measures – that is, cost reductions, conformity to budgets.

Performance measurement, as applied to the purchasing function, is considered in Chapter 17.

Johnson and Scholes[43] state that, in reviewing strategic options, it is important to distinguish between three interrelated aspects of any strategy. The typical purchasing strategies/tactics or contributions for each of the three aspects of strategic development are shown in Table 2.8.

Figure 2.18 **Steps in the control process**

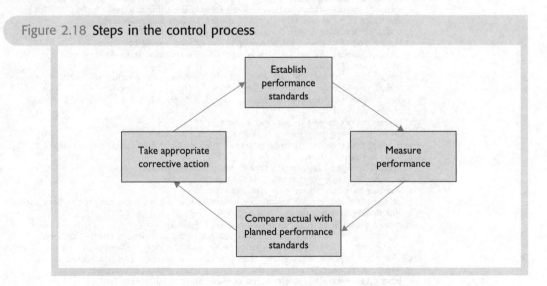

Table 2.8 Typical aspects of purchasing strategies, tactics or contributions to corporate development strategies

Aspects of strategic development	Typical purchasing strategies/tactics contributions
Generic strategy (the basis on which the organisation will compete or sustain excellence)	
Cost leadership	Lower purchase costs achieved by consolidation of purchases, single sourcing, global procurement. Reduction in costs of purchasing system and administration. Value for money spent. Logistical contributions to competitive advantage. Buying subassemblies in lieu of components, etc.
Differentiation	Involvement of suppliers in product design and development, value analysis, total quality management, alternative materials. Stimulation of technological developments in one supplier market, etc.
Focus	Location of specialist suppliers, make-or-buy decision for specialist components, subcontracting, outsourcing, etc.
Alternative strategy directions in which the organisation may choose to develop	
Do nothing	
Withdrawal	Running down/disposal of inventory. Negotiating contract cancellations, etc.
Consolidation	Moving to standard/generic materials/components to increase potential use. Negotiation of limited period contracts, etc.
Market penetration	Provision of information regarding competitors, price volatility, unused capacity in the supplier market. Negotiation of contracts with options for increased supply or stocking of inventory at suppliers, etc.
Product development	Liaison with design and production. Partnership sourcing; supplier appraisal. Negotiation regarding ownership of jigs and tools for bought-out items. Timing of supply deliveries. MRP II. Value engineering, etc.
Market development	Liaison with marketing. Partnership sourcing, specifying packaging and shipping instructions. Identification of vital points in the supply/value chain.
Diversification	Supply considerations, such as effect on set-up costs and productions runs. Purchasing quantity considerations. Promotion of interchangeability of materials and components, etc.
Alternative methods by which any direction of development may be advanced	
Internal development	Organisational aspects of purchasing. Recruitment or development of purchasing staff. Integration of purchasing into materials management or logistics
Acquisition	Corporate level issues relating to: ■ backward integration – activities concerned with securing inputs, such as raw materials by acquisition of supplies ■ forward integration – activities concerned with securing outputs, such as acquisition of distribution channels, transport undertakings, etc. ■ horizontal integration – activities complementary to those currently undertaken, such as consortia, franchising, licensing or agency and outsourcing agreements.

2.16 Strategic purchasing and supply chain process models

2.16.1 What are models?

Models are representations of real objects or situations. A model aeroplane, for example, is a representation of the real thing. Physical replicas are referred to as *iconic models*. Alternatively, we can have models that are physical in form but do not have the same appearance as the things that they purport to represent. These are known as *analogue models*. A thermometer, which represents temperature, is an analogue model. Today, computers are used to simulate situations and provide answers to 'What if . . . ?' questions. In general, models can be classified as:

■ *mathematical* – these represent a problem by a system of symbols and mathematical relationships or expression (the formulae used in Chapter 9 are of this type)

■ *non-mathematical* – these can take the form of charts, diagrams and similar visual representations that communicate information.

2.16.2 The CIPS procurement and supply management model

Much of what has been discussed in this chapter is admirably summarised in the CIPS procurement and supply management model.[44] This is a generic representation of an organisation and shows where purchasing and supply management fit into it at both strategic and operational levels. The model shows where the organisation's purchasing and supply management strategy fits in, too, what it covers and how it can be implemented. The model shows the high-level stages of purchasing and supply management activity and the key steps at each stage. The model can also be used by purchasing and supply management practitioners to explain to colleagues where their role fits into their organisation and what it covers.

The overall CIPS model is shown in Figure 2.19.

The model shows how organisational vision, mission, values and corporate strategy are derived from environmental factors, such as the government, customers, competitors, stakeholders and other external influences, and an evaluation of organisational competences.

The model also shows how purchasing strategies interface with and are related to other organisational functions/activities such as R&D, finance, marketing and technical ICT strategies.

The aspects of procurement indicated under the headings of strategic sourcing analysis, proactive demand management and acquisition pre- and post contract are dealt with in appropriate chapters of this book.

2.16.3 Other procurement models

Other purchasing models include the Ministry of Defence's acquisition management system (AMS), the supply chain operations reference (SCOR) and the European Federation of Quality Management (EFQM) model. All these can be accessed on the Internet.

Figure 2.19 The CIPS procurement and supply management model

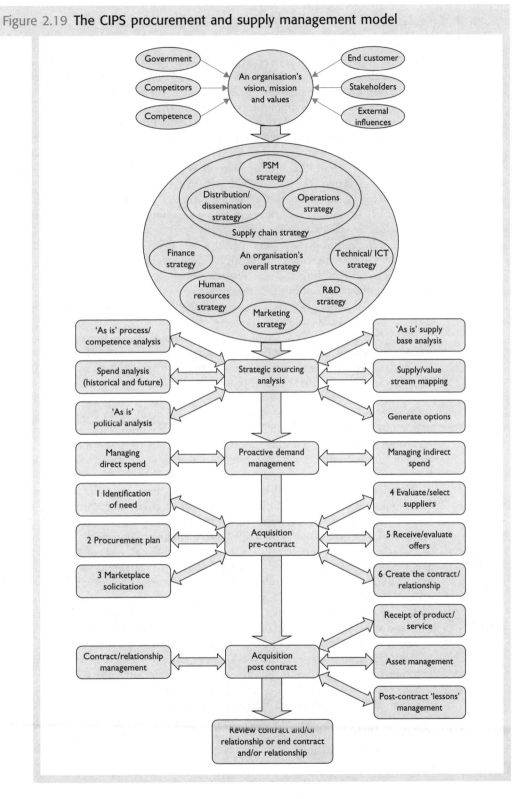

Case study[45]

The Government Waste Services Agency (GWSA) is a government body with its head-quarters situated within the Midlands of England but has offices throughout the country that are responsible for matters concerning waste for all government bodies.

The main aims for the organisation are to improve services for the citizens of England by investing in a greener, cleaner and safer community environment and operate in an efficient manner with taxpayers' monies. Funds for the agency are derived from the budgets of all other government bodies, which essentially contribute to the running of this agency on their behalf. Procurement activity is fully devolved throughout the GWSA and is managed on a regional basis. Its chief executive recognises that there are European Union (EU) regulations that apply to the GWSA, although the organisation has generally operated a policy of obtaining keen prices by approaching local suppliers and buying on the basis of largely spot purchases.

Little information on suppliers is held at the GWSA's headquarters and central contracts have not been created. While all office managers have the ethos of 'green buying' and a focus on recycling and waste management, it is generally up to each of them to execute a policy and put in place practices that satisfy that ethos. The chief executive is aware that this strategy often leaves the agency in difficulties in terms of a lack of prediction of future needs and that it allows variations in practice and price.

Research has recently come to him from a university that, in five years' time, the demand for waste disposal facilities will outstrip supply. Costs for recycling and waste removal for England as a whole are also a concern over the next five years. The GWSA is aware that a strategy is required for each public-sector body to determine how they are going to face environmental issues. Each public-sector organisation can be perceived to have a high or low environmental risk depending on a range of factors, including energy consumption. While each public-sector body is responsible for its own organisational behaviour, it is also responsible for all the inhabitants of the country as it connects with them in various activities while carrying out its responsibilities. No policy or strategy has been developed for this.

Waste Service Management Ltd (WSML), a supplier, began life as a family concern in 1960 and considers itself to be at the forefront of environmentally friendly approaches to waste removal and recycling. WSML has been a small, but important, supplier to a regional office of the GWSA and looked into the requirements of the citizens of the region. It has assessed that there are 300,000 people in the region from 160,000 families. The average family in this region throws out, yearly, over 2 tonnes of rubbish and waste – mostly domestic and garden refuse. WSML has a forward-thinking approach. It has set up facilities for recycling garden waste, paper, glass, engine oil, tins, cloth, scrap metal and fridges and freezers. Some 32 such facilities exist throughout its region at amenity sites and supermarket car parks. Many are merely skip-like containers from which the company collects 'rubbish' deposited by the population living in the area.

WSML is keen to expand and work more closely with the GWSA as a whole, not just with one regional office as is the case now. It wants to offer the GWSA more options to promote recycling and provide a full package for the citizens of England in order to spread the success achieved thus far. WSML is planning, over the next five years, to diversify into litter collection from the 844 kilometres of streets it serves currently, the home collection of waste newspapers and to address the increasing problem of removal of chewing gum from pavements.

Tasks

1 Identify the approach to procurement strategy that has been adopted by the GWSA.

2 Discuss the linkage between the GWSA's procurement strategy and the achievement of its corporate objectives.

3 Identify strategic choices open to WSML and how these choices may be implemented.

Discussion questions

2.1 Figure 2.1 identifies five elements of strategic thinking. Complete the following table by providing one example of each of the five elements that you have encountered in your own experience or reflection.

Element	Example
Systems perspective	
Intent focus	
Intelligent opportunism	
Thinking in time	
Hypothesis driven	

2.2 From a purchasing perspective, provide an example of strategy as:
(a) a plan
(b) a ploy
(c) a pattern
(d) a position.

2.3 (a) What, from the standpoint of strategic 'fit', is the relationship between (1) opportunities in the business environment and (2) resources and competences?
(b) What strategy(ies) might you adopt if you have recognised a good opportunity in the environment that you can't exploit because of lack of resources?

2.4 Think of an example relevant to purchasing to illustrate the statement 'What appears to be a tactic to the chief executive may be a strategy to the purchasing head.'

2.5 What approaches other than rational planning may influence strategy formation?

2.6 According to Mintzberg, there are five activities involved in strategic management:
(a) managing stability – knowing when and when not to change
(b) declining discontinuity – recognising changes of significance to their work and the organisation
(c) knowing the business – having an awareness and understanding of the operations of the organisation
(d) managing patterns – having the ability to detect emerging positions and helping them to take shape
(e) reconciling change and combining or bringing together of the future, present and past and recognising that an obsession with either change or continuity can be counterproductive.

Give examples of each of the above five activities in a purchasing context.

79

2.7 Prepare simple diagrams of vertical and horizontal integration for:
   (a) food production
   (b) book production.

2.8 Give examples of the following retrenchment strategies.

Strategy	Example
Harvesting	
Turnaround	
Divestiture	
Liquidation	

2.9 Thinking about the organisation in which you are employed, list up to three examples under each of the following headings:
   ■ key strengths
   ■ key weaknesses
   ■ key opportunities
   ■ key threats.

2.10 Using the guidelines given in this chapter, write a mission statement for the purchasing function/activity in which you are employed.

2.11 From the mission statement prepared in answer to question 2.10, derive some relevant objectives.

2.12 Identify some operational strategies for achieving the objectives stated in answer to question 2.11.

2.13 Peters and Waterman state (*In Search of Excellence*, Harper, 1982) that members of staff are capable of exceptional loyalty and effort if the organisational culture is attuned to this. How, as Chief Purchasing Executive, would you seek to create a culture of loyalty and effort?

2.14 In Kraljic's purchasing portfolio, under which of the headings 'leverage', 'routine' and 'bottleneck' would you place the following items?
   (a) Office supplies.
   (b) Bottling equipment for a brewery.
   (c) Steel plate.
   (d) Natural flavourings for a food manufacture.
   (e) Cleaning materials.
   (f) Pigments for the paint industry.
   (g) Nuts and bolts.

2.15 Prepare a policy statement relating to one of the following:
   (a) quality required from suppliers
   (b) training of purchasing staff
   (c) payment of suppliers
   (d) purchases from local suppliers.

2.16 Taking the scenario in question 2.13, prepare a purchasing strategy implementation plan for your organisation.

2.17 A smaller competitor has developed a product that has twice the performance of that manufactured by your organisation at half the cost.

(a) What generic and alternative strategies might you adopt to counter the threat?

(b) By what alternative methods might you endeavour to develop your own competitive product?

Past examination questions

All the questions below are taken from the CIPS Professional Stage papers, Purchasing and Supply Chain Management 1: Strategy.

1 (a) Explain the term 'strategic drift'.

(b) Using examples, identify five symptoms of strategic drift.

(May 2003)

2 Explain and evaluate the approaches to strategy development identified below.

(a) A rational approach.

(b) An emergent approach.

(May 2003)

3 (a) Explain one model used to analyse organisational culture.

(b) Evaluate the role of this model in the implementation of strategic change.

(May 2003)

4 (a) Explain the purpose of strategic analysis.

(b) Distinguish four examples of models that can help to develop strategic analysis.

(November 2003)

5 Describe the processes that a business can undertake with regard to the evaluation and selection of a corporate strategy.

(November 2003)

6 Identify and discuss activities that add value that are to be undertaken by a purchasing and supply function.

References

[1] We are indebted for this anecdote to David, F. R., *Concepts of Strategic Management*, Macmillan, 1991, p. 4

[2] Liedtka, J. M., 'Strategic thinking; can it be taught?', *Long Range Planning*, Vol 31 (1), 1998, pp. 120–9

[3] Lawrence, E., 'Strategic thinking', paper prepared for the Research Directorate Public Service Commission of Canada, April 27, 1999

[4] Mintzberg, H., 'Five Ps for strategy' in Mintzberg, H., Lampel, J., Quinn, J. G., and Ghoshal, S. *The Strategy Process*, Prentice Hall, 2003, pp. 3–10

[5] As 4 above, p. 9

[6] Johnson, G., and Scholes, K., *Exploring Corporate Strategy*, 6th edn, Prentice Hall, 2002, pp. 4–10

[7] Quinn, J. B., 'Strategies for change' in Mintzberg, H. et al. as 4 above, p. 11

[8] Mintzberg, H., Ahlstrand, B., and Lampel, J., *Strategy Safari*, Prentice Hall, 1998, pp. 1–21

[9] As 3 above

[10] Fahey, L., and Prusak, L., 'The eleven deadliest sins of knowledge management', *California Management Review*, Vol. 40, spring, 1998

[11] Lindblom, C., *The Intelligence of Democracy: Decision Making Through Mutual Adjustment*, Free Press, 1965

[12] Waterman, R. H., *The Renewal Factor*, Bantam Books, 1987

[13] Mintzberg, H., 'Crafting Strategy' in Mintzberg et al., as 4 above, p. 147

[14] Burns, R., *Collected Poems, To a Mouse*

[15] As 8 above, p. 226

[16] As 1 above, p. 65

[17] Hax, A. C., and Majluf, N. S., *The Strategy Concept and Process*, Prentice Hall, 1999, p. 416

[18] Porter, M., *Competitive Strategy: Techniques for Analysing, Industries and Competitors*, Macmillan, 1980

[19] Miles, R. E., and Snow, C. C., *Organisational Strategy, Structure and Process*, McGraw-Hill, 1978

[20] Carr, A. S., and Smeltzer, L. R., 'An empirically based definition of strategic purchasing', *European Journal of Purchasing and Supply Management*, Vol. 3, 1997, pp. 199–207

[21] Kraljic, P., 'Purchasing must become supply management', *Harvard Business Review* Sept/Oct, 1983, p. 110

[22] Worral, L., 'Strategic analysis: a scientific art', Occasional paper No. OP001/98, University of Wolverhampton, 27 May, 1998

[23] Brown, A., and Weiner, E., *Supermanaging: How to Harness Change for Personal and Organisational Success*, Mentor Books, 1985, p. ix

[24] Choo, C. W., 'Environmental scanning as information seeking and organisational learning', *Information Research*, Vol. 7, No. 1, Oct, 2001

[25] Downes, L. 'Beyond Porter' in *Context Magazine*, available at: www.contextmag.com/archives/199712/technosynthesis.asp

[26] ICMA, *Management Accounting 2000: Official Terminology*

[27] As 3 above

[28] As 8 above, p. 124

[29] Campbell, A., and Yeung, S., 'Creating a sense of mission' in De-luit, B., and Meyer, R., *Strategy: Process, Content, Context*, West Publishing, 1994, pp. 153–4

[30] NHS Purchasing and Supply Agency, Framework Document, 2003/4

[31] As 20 above

[32] As 30 above

[33] Rumelt, R. P., 'Evaluating business strategy' in Mintzberg et al., as 4 above, p. 81

[34] Cyert, K., and March, J., *Behavioural Theory of the Firm*, Prentice Hall, 1963

[35] As 21 above, pp. 109–17

[36] Fisher, L., *Industrial Marketing: An Analytical Approach to Planning and Execution*, Brandon Systems Press, 1970

[37] Nellove, R., and Söderquist, K., 'Portfolio approaches to procurement', *Long Range Planning*, Vol. 33, 2000, pp. 245–67

[38] Gelderman, C. J., and van Weele, A. J., 'Strategic direction through purchasing portfolio management: a case study', *International Journal of Supply Chain Management*, Vol. 38, spring, 2002, pp. 30–8

39 Bensaou, M., 'Portfolio of buyer–supplier relationships', *Sloan Management Review*, summer, 1999, pp. 35–44

40 Kamann, D., and Jan, F., 'Extra dimensions to portfolio analysis', paper presented at the IPSERA meeting London, Ontario, Canada, 1999

41 This figure is reproduced by kind permission of Rob Atkins and the Bracknell Forest (UK) Borough Council

42 Spekman, R. E., 'A strategic approach to procurement planning', *Journal of Purchasing and Supply Management*, spring, 1989, pp. 3–9

43 Johnson, G., and Scholes, K., *Exploring Corporate Strategy Text and Cases*, 3rd edn, Prentice Hall, 1993, pp. 203–43

44 CIPS, procurement and supply management model. Full details of this model are shown on the CIPS website

45 This is taken by permission of CIPS from the November 2003 Professional Stage Examination in Strategy and Strategic Procurement

Chapter 3

Logistics and supply chains

Learning outcomes

This chapter aims to provide an understanding of:

- the origin and scope of logistics
- materials logistics and distribution managements
- reverse logistics
- supply chains and supply chain management (SCM)
- supply chain vulnerability
- value chains
- value chain analysis
- supply chain optimisation
- supply chains and purchasing.

Key ideas

- Military and non-military logistics.
- The scope of materials and physical distribution management (MM and PDM).
- Total systems management, trade-offs, cooperative planning and manufacturing techniques as important logistics concepts.
- Reverse logistics as the opposite of forward logistics.
- Networks, linkages, processes, value and the ultimate 'customer' as key supply chain characteristics.
- Supply chain classifications.
- Infrastructure, technology, strategic alliances, software and human resource management (HRM) as key supply chain enablers.
- External and internal supply chain risks.
- Porter's value chain model.
- Hines's value chain model.
- Cost and differentiation as means to competitive advantage.
- Objectives and factors in supply chain optimisation.
- The influence of the supply chain concept on traditional purchasing.

Introduction

Purchasing is increasingly considered within the wider context of supply chains. Logistics, however, is a much older term. It is therefore appropriate that the present chapter should begin with a consideration of logistics.

We next define the terms 'supply chain' and 'supply chain management' (SCM) and identify some types of supply chains, the processes that comprise supply chain management and the enablers via which SCM is implemented. An aspect of SCM that has only recently received serious attention is supply chain vulnerability.

The chapter ends with a consideration of supply chain optimisation, the impact of SCM on traditional purchasing and some contributions of purchasing to the supply chain management field.

3.1 What is logistics?

3.1.1 Military logistics

The supply chain approach developed from logistics. Logistics, initially a military term dating from the Napoleonic Wars, refers to the technique of moving and quartering armies – that is, quartermasters' work. The scope of logistics in a military sense is reflected in the definition adopted by NATO:[1]

> The science of planning and carrying out the movement and maintenance of forces. In its most comprehensive sense the aspects of military operations which deal with:
>
> (a) design and development, acquisition, storage, transport, distribution, maintenance, evacuation and disposition of material;
>
> (b) transport of personnel;
>
> (c) acquisition of construction, maintenance, operation and disposition of facilities;
>
> (d) acquisition or furnishing of services; and
>
> (e) medical and health support.

NATO also distinguishes between two important aspects of logistics: acquisition logistics and operational logistics (Figure 3.1).

The importance of military logistics is apparent from a consideration of the enormous problems relating to the supply of the Allied forces involved in the D-Day invasion of Europe in World War II, the Falklands War of 1982 or the invasion of Iraq.

3.1.2 Non-military applications of logistics

Non-military applications of logistics, although generally less complicated, still cover the same ground, as indicated by the following definitions:

> Logistics is the total management of the key operational functions in the supply chain – procurement, production and distribution. Procurement includes purchasing and product development. The production function includes manufacturing and assembling, while the distribution function involves warehousing, inventory, transport and delivery.[2]

> Logistics is the process of managing both the movement and storage of goods and materials from the source to the point of ultimate consumption and the associated information flow.[3]

Figure 3.1 **The scope of military logistics**

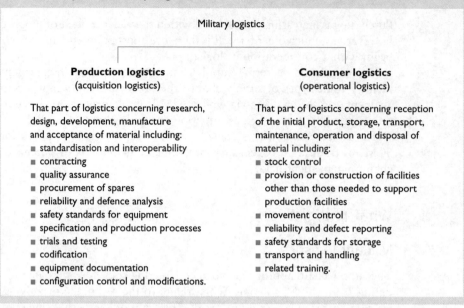

Source: NATO, *Logistics Handbook*, 1997, paragraphs 103–4

Logistics is that part of the supply chain process that plans, implements and controls the efficient, effective flow and storage of goods, services and related information from the point of origin to the point of consumption in order to meet the customers' requirements.[4]

3.2 Materials, logistics and distribution management

As shown in Figure 3.2, logistics is comprised of both materials management and physical distribution management.

3.2.1 Materials management

Materials management (MM) is concerned with the flow of materials to and from production or manufacturing and has been defined as:[5]

> The planning, organisation and control of all aspects of inventory embracing procurement, warehousing, work-in-progress and distribution of finished goods.

Some aspects of MM that may be included under the heading 'Materials flow' are listed in Table 3.1.

The factors influencing the activities assigned to MM include the following:

- purchasing is frequently the 'key' activity
- production planning and control may be assigned to MM or the manufacturing function where this is separate – the former tends to apply when production is materials orientated, such as in an assembly factory; the latter when production is machine/process orientated.

Figure 3.2 **Scope of logistics management**

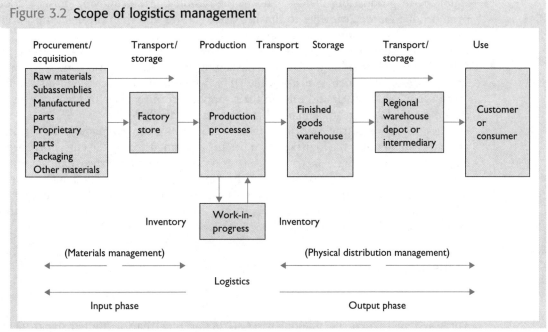

Source: adapted from Gattorna, J., 'Strategic issues in Logistics', *Focus on Physical Distribution and Logistics Management*, Oct./Nov., 1986

Table 3.1 **Materials flow activities**

Materials flow	Typical activities
Planning	Preparation of materials budgets, product research and development, value engineering and analysis, standardisation of specifications
Procurement	Determining order quantities, processing works and stores requisitions, issuing enquiries, evaluating quotations, supplier appraisal, negotiation, placing contracts, progressing deliveries, certifying payments, vendor rating
Storage	Stores location, layout and equipment, mechanical handling, stores classification, coding and cataloguing, receipt of purchased items, inspection, storage or return, protection of stores, issuing to production, providing cost data, stock records, disposal of obsolete, surplus or scrap material
Production control	Forward ordering arrangements for materials, preparing production schedules and sequences, issuing orders to production, emergency action to meet material shortages, make-or-buy decisions, quality and reliability feedback and adjustment of supplies flow to production line or sales trend

3.2.2 Physical distribution management

Physical distribution management (PDM) is often considered to be concerned with the flow of goods from the receipt of an order until the goods are delivered to the customer. An alternative view, adopted in this text, is that, whereas MM is concerned with the *input* phase of moving bought-out items, such as raw materials and components from suppliers, to production, PDM relates to the *output* phase of moving finished goods from production departments to finished goods stores and then through appropriate channels of distribution to the ultimate consumer.

The main activities associated with PDM are inventory control, warehousing and storage, materials handling, protective packaging and containerisation and transportation. Developments such as just-in-time (JIT), where both producers and distributors carry a few hours' stock and rely on their suppliers to meet their production or sales requirements, have greatly enhanced the importance of PDM.

The perspective of the logistician is that 'what flows can be made to flow faster'. From this standpoint, the logistician studies the costs incurred by the enterprise, beginning with the initial input factor, time spent on the production process and terminating when the customer pays for the product or service received. The longer the time spent at each stage of the process, the higher the costs incurred. A reduction in the time taken at any stage will provide an opportunity for cost reduction, which can, in turn, lead to a reduction in price.

3.2.3 Some important logistics concepts

Total systems management

Total systems management emphasises a total rather than a limited departmental viewpoint. Total systems management has been facilitated by the availability of IT. Functions or groups of processes or activities with a total system may be regarded as subsystems.

Trade-offs

A trade-off is where an increased cost in one area is more than offset by a cost reduction in another, so that the whole system benefits. This may give rise to interdepartmental conflicts owing to different objectives. Thus, purchasing may advocate bulk purchases of materials to secure larger supplier discounts. This policy might be opposed by finance because of money tied up in working capital and in inventory because of the increased cost of warehousing. Conflicts should be settled on the basis of which policy yields the greatest trade-off. Similarly, purchasing may have to consider whether or not the security of supply consequent on having a number of suppliers is offset by the economies resulting from single-source buying. Thus, the effects of trade-offs may be assessed according to their impact on total systems costs and sales revenue. Higher inventory costs, for example, may result from increased stocks, yet quicker delivery may increase total sales revenue. Obtaining information for computerised exchange requires the breaking down of functional barriers that protect departmental 'territory' and discourage information sharing.

Cooperative planning

This can work forwards to customers and backwards to suppliers. The change from product- to customer-orientated supply chains and, thus, faster supply resources, can provide customers with alternatives such as make to stock, make to order and finish to order. Conversely, from the inward supply side, effective, cooperative planning may relate to zero defects, on-time delivery, shared products and information exchanges relating to such matters as shared specifications, design support, multiyear commitments and technology exchange. Overall, both suppliers and customers can benefit from reduced costs of inventory, capacity, order handling and administration. Cooperative planning utilises, as appropriate, manufacturing and scheduling techniques including the following.

■ *Manufacturing techniques*
  – computer-aided design (CAD)
  – computer integrated manufacture (CIM)
  – flexible manufacturing systems (FMS)
  – materials requirement planning (MRP)
  – manufacturing resources planning (MRP II)
  – optimised production technology (OPT)
  – strategic lead time management (STM)
■ *Scheduling techniques*
  – just-in-time (JIT)
  – materials requirement planning (MRP)
  – manufacturing resources planning (MRP II)
  – enterprise resource planning (ERP).

This can be explained by the cost–value curve shown in Figure 3.3.

1 The lowest cost value is at the procurement stage when supplies are purchased.
2 During transportation of supplies, value remains low because little capital is invested until raw materials and components enter production – the only costs incurred relate to acquisition and holding.
3 The curve becomes steeper as raw materials and components are gradually incorporated into the final product. This is because of accumulated manufacturing costs and increasing interest costs that reflect the value of capital invested.
4 The curve becomes flatter at the end of the production process because no more manufacturing costs apply. At this stage the invested capital is at its highest value and the cost of stocking finished goods instead of selling them involves higher opportunity costs than holding the initial supplies. This shows why the logistician is, if anything, more concerned with PDM than MM as the potential for cost reduction

Figure 3.3 The added value aspect of logistics

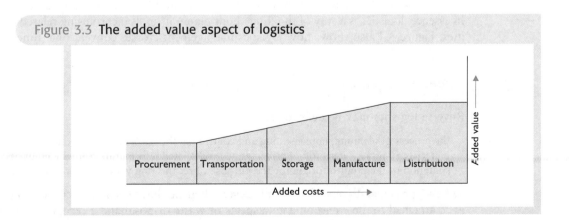

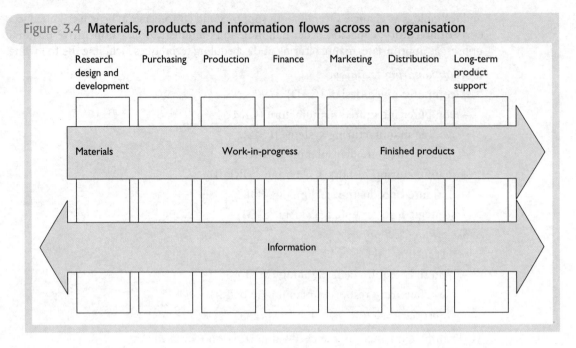

Figure 3.4 **Materials, products and information flows across an organisation**

is the highest at this point of the total supply chain. Cost reduction by speeding flows of materials, work-in-progress and finished products is not the only concern of the logistician. Logistics management involves two flows. The first, as stated above, is the flow of materials and work-in-progress across the organisation to the ultimate customer. The second, as shown in Figure 3.4, is a reverse flow of information, in the form of orders or other indicators on which future demand forecasts can be based. Such forecasts, as Gattorna stated, can in turn 'trigger replenishment orders which produce inventories at distribution centres. These orders influence production schedules which, in turn, help to determine the timing and quantities with which raw materials are procured.'

Logistics management may be regarded as a subsystem of the larger enterprise or a system of which purchasing, manufacturing, storage and transportation are subsystems. In essence, logistics is a way of thinking about planning and synchronising related activities. Figure 3.4 also shows how logistics management crosses conventional functions.

3.3   Reverse logistics

Reverse logistics may be defined as:[6]

> the process of planning, implementing and controlling the efficient, cost-effective flow of raw materials, in process inventory, finished goods and related information from the point of consumption to the point of origin for the purpose of recapturing value or proper disposal.

The two principal drivers of interest in reverse logistics have been the increased importance attached to the environmental aspects of waste disposal and a recognition of the

Figure 3.5 **Reverse logistics network**

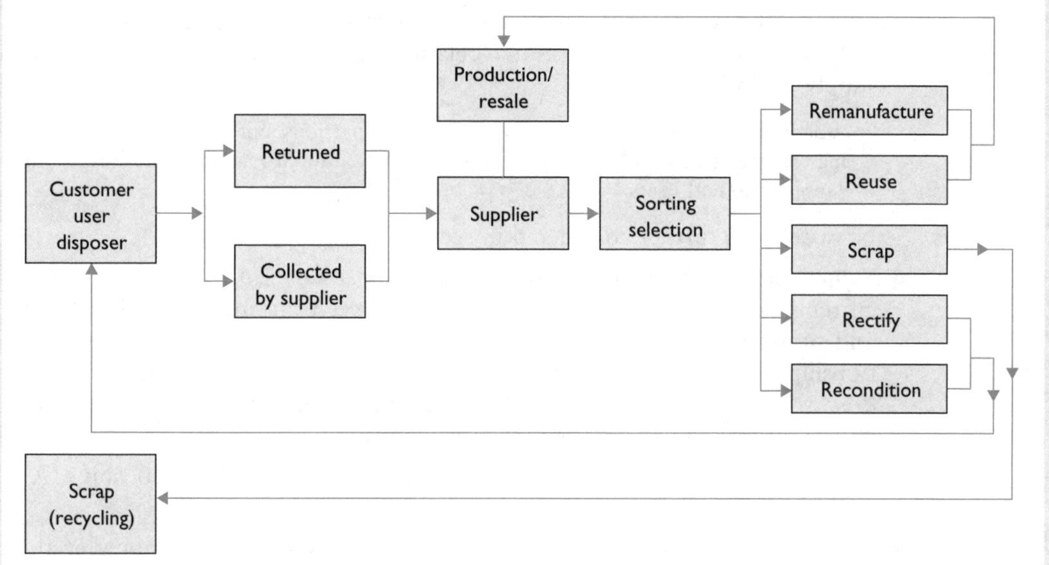

potential returns that can be obtained from the reuse of products or parts or the recycling of materials. Reverse logistics may also apply to goods sent to distributors on a sale-or-return basis, unused materials to be returned to stores from contracts or project sites or from subcontractors. The main activities involved with reverse logistics are therefore as shown in Figure 3.5.

Figure 3.5 shows that the main reverse logistics activities include collection of returnable items, their inspection and separation and the application of a range of disposition options, including repair, reconditioning, upgrading, remanufacture, demanufacture (parts reclamation) and recycling. Disposition logic also includes channel or routing logic – that is, the returned items and components can be sent back to the customer, routed to a warehouse or production or sold in secondary markets.

In the computer industry, for example, companies such as IBM are seeking ways of enabling customers to refurbish existing computers or buy used parts. A number of software providers have devised programs to provide logistics solutions along the entire lifecycle of a product, including the options available at the end of its working life.

3.4 Supply chains

3.4.1 Definitions

There are many definitions of the term 'supply chain', of which the following is typical:[7]

> A supply chain is that network of organisations that are involved, through upstream and down-stream linkages, in the different processes and activities that produce value in the form of products and services in the hands of the ultimate customer or consumer.

The above definition emphasises the following key characteristics of supply chains:

■ *Supply chains are 'networks'* Traditionally, supply chains were loosely linked associations of discrete businesses. The network concept implies some coordination of 'cow to customer' processes and relationships. An alternative definition is that a supply chain is:

> A network of connected and interdependent organisations mutually and cooperatively working together to control, manage and improve the flow of materials and information from suppliers to end users.[8]

Networks are further considered in section 4.3.

■ *Supply chain linkages are upstream and downstream Upstream* means 'against the current' and relates to the relationships between an enterprise and its suppliers and suppliers' suppliers. *Downstream* is 'with the current' and relates to the relationship between an enterprise and its customers. There can also be *upstream–downstream*, as is the case with organisations that have returnable containers, pallets, drums and so on or trade-in products.

■ *Linkages* The coordination of supply chain processes and relationships. A supply chain is only as strong as its weakest link.

■ *Processes* In the context of a business, a process is defined by Cooper et al.[9] as:

> A specific ordering of work activities across a time and place with a beginning and an end and clearly identified inputs and outputs, a structure of action.

From a purchasing standpoint, the processes that comprise the supply chain are shown in Figure 3.6.

Figure 3.6 Supplier chain processes from a purchasing perspective

Search	Acquire	Use	Maintain	Dispose

From a supplier's standpoint the processes are shown in Figure 3.7.

■ *Value* is defined by Porter[10] as 'what buyers are willing to pay'. Superior value stems from offering lower prices for equivalent benefits or providing unique benefits that more than offset a higher price.

■ *The ultimate customer* A customer is simply the recipient of the goods or services that result from all the processes and activities of the supply chain. A function or subsystem can be the customer of the preceding or succeeding link in a supply chain.

Figure 3.7 Supply chain processes from a supplier's perspective

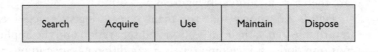

Research	Design	Manufacture or Provide	Sell	Service

Customers may be either internal or external. The definition refers to the 'ultimate customer or consumer' so that the supply chain may extend beyond the customer from whom the direct order for goods or services emanates.

3.4.2 Types of supply chains

Supply chains can be classified in numerous ways. An organisation such as a food retailer will have many types of supply chains reflecting differences in products, services, production and distribution methods, customer–supplier relationships and information flows. Supply chains may be roughly classified according to four customer–supplier characteristics and also in relation to virtuality, scope, service, complexity, products, purpose and value.

Customer–supplier characteristics

These may give rise to:

- *concentrated chains* found in businesses such as the automotive industry that have:
  - few customers but many suppliers
  - customers with demanding requirements
  - EDI systems or a requirement for JIT deliveries
- *batch manufacture chains* that have:
  - many customers and many suppliers
  - complicated relationship webs – an undertaking with which an enterprise is in contact may, at different times, be a customer, supplier, competitor or ally
- *retail and distribution chains* that have:
  - many customers but relatively few suppliers
  - customised methods, such as vendor-managed inventory (VMI) of facilitating dealings with suppliers
- *service chains* that implement the mission statements of organisations such as hospitals, libraries and banks concerned with the delivery of services, books, information and financial services or restaurants and cinemas delivering food and entertainment, for example – essentially service chains are not different from manufacturing chains as every service involves people, something physical (an asset or part of something performed), an action and a time element.

Other characteristics

- *Virtuality* Virtual is the opposite of real. Thus, a 'virtual' enterprise is the counterpart of a real, tangible business. As Christopher[11] states, 'a virtual supply chain is, in effect, a series of relationships between partners that is based upon the value-added exchanges of information'. In a virtual supply chain, information replaces the need for inventories. A mail-order business may have no inventory and simply call for supplies from the manufacturer when orders are received from customers.
- *Scope* Supply chains may be local, regional and international in scope. Some suppliers of gas, such as BP, for example, have the ability to put together delivery chains to bring gas supplies from Trinidad to Spain, from Siberia to China and from North Africa to Southern Europe.

■ *Complexity* Mentzer et al.[12] identify three degrees of supply chain complexity: 'direct', 'extended' and 'ultimate'. A *direct* supply chain, as shown in Figure 3.8, is comprised of a company or supplier and a customer involved in the upstream and/or downstream flow of products, services, finances and information.

Figure 3.8 **Direct supply chain**

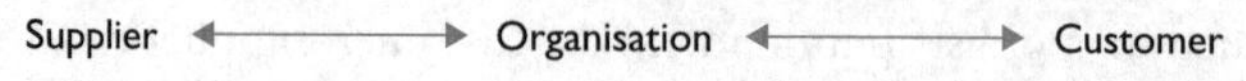

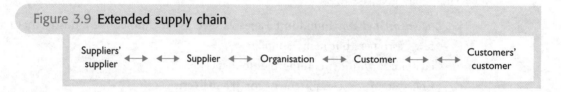

An *extended* supply chain, as shown in Figure 3.9, includes suppliers of the immediate supplier and customers of the immediate customer.

Figure 3.9 **Extended supply chain**

An *ultimate* supply chain, as shown in Figure 3.10, includes all the organisations involved in all the upstream and downstream flows of products, services, finances and information from the ultimate supplier to the ultimate customer.

Figure 3.10 **Ultimate supply chain**

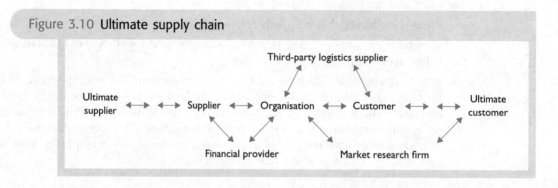

■ *Purpose* A distinction can be made between *efficient* and *responsive* supply chains. *Efficient* supply chains are primarily concerned with reducing the cost of operations, as in lean supply chains. These work best when forecast accuracy is high and product variety low. *Responsive* supply chains are primarily concerned with minimising the delivery cycle time, as in agile supply chains. These work best when forecast accuracy is low and product variety high.

■ *Products* Supply chains vary widely according to the end product. Examples are build-to-forecast and build-to-order supply chains and ones for innovative and functional products (see section 4.3.2).

■ *Value chains* These are dealt with later in the present chapter.

3.5 Supply chain management (SCM)

There is no universally agreed definition of SCM but one is given in section 3.7 below. Mentzer et al.[13] state that the many published definitions can be classified into three categories – a management philosophy, implementation of a management philosophy and a set of management processes.

SCM as a management philosophy

Mentzer et al. suggest that, as a management philosophy, SCM has the following three characteristics:

- a systems approach to viewing the supply chain as a whole and managing the total flow of goods inventory from the supplier to the ultimate consumers
- a strategic orientation towards cooperative efforts to synchronise and converge intra-firm and interfirm operational and strategic capabilities into a unified whole
- a customer focus to create unique and individualised sources of customer value, leading to customer satisfaction.

SCM as a set of activities to implement a management philosophy

The seven activities listed below as essential to the implementation of a management philosophy are:

- integrated behaviour
- mutually shared information
- mutually shared risks and rewards
- cooperation
- the same goal and same focus on serving customers
- integration of processes
- partners to build and maintain long-term relationships.

These activities are implied in the following list of SCM objectives:

- the integration of both internal and external competencies
- the building of alliances, relationships and trust throughout the supply system
- the reduction of costs and improvement of profit margins
- the maximisation of return on assets (net income after expenses/interests)
- the facilitation of innovation and the synchronisation of supply chain processes
- the optimisation of the delivery of products, services, information and finance both upstream and downstream and across internal and external boundaries.

SCM as a set of management processes

As shown by Figure 3.11, Lambert et al.[14] list eight SCM processes originally postulated by the International Centre for Competitive Excellence.

Figure 3.11 Supply chain management: integrating and managing business processes across the supply chain

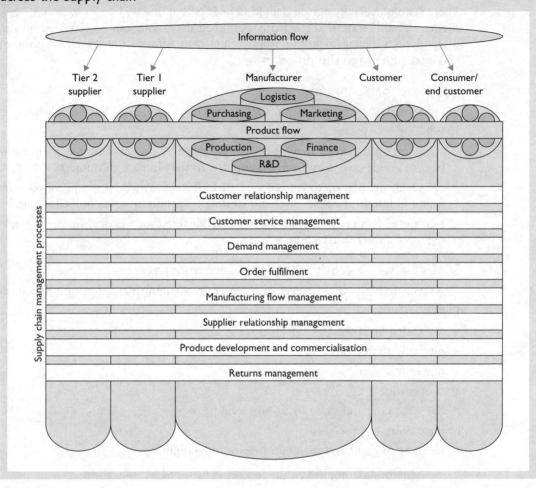

Each of the above eight processes is briefly described below.

- *Customer relationship management (CRM)* is concerned with learning about customers' needs and behaviour and the integration of sales, marketing and service strategies. CRM software, as Kalakota[15] states, 'helps organisations to manage their customer relationships better by tracking down customer interactions of all types'.

- *Customer service management (CSM)* is concerned with providing internal and external customers with high-quality goods and services, at the lowest cost, with the shortest waiting times and maximum responsiveness and flexibility to their needs. This is clearly aligned with efficient customer response (ECR).

- *Demand management* is concerned with balancing the requirements of internal and external with supply chain capabilities. It includes forecasting demand, synchronising supply and demand, increasing flexibility, reducing the variability of demand by means of standardisation and the control of inventory, for example. This is closely aligned with materials requirements planning (MRP) and JIT.

- *Order fulfilment* is concerned with the fulfilment of customers' orders efficiently, effectively and at the minimum total cost.

- *Manufacturing flow management* is concerned with all the processes and activities required to transform inputs and a variety of resources into finished goods and services. Order fulfilment is therefore closely aligned with operations management (OM) and such approaches as manufacturing resources planning (MRP II), manufacturing execution systems (MES) and quick response manufacturing (QRM). These approaches are described in most texts on OM.

- *Supplier relationship management (SRM)* is concerned with how an enterprise interacts with its suppliers and, therefore, is the mirror image of CRM. Relationships may be either short- or long-term and vary in intensity from 'arm's length' to high involvement. SRM is becoming increasingly critical as organisations concentrate on core competencies and rely on suppliers to maintain critical advantage or a superior position over competitors.

- *Product development and commercialisation* is concerned with all the processes and activities involved in the development and marketing of new or existing products. In general, product development involves four main phases. First, idea generation, second, concept development, third, product and process design and, fourth, production and delivery. Marketing can contribute to product development (PD) in such ways as trial tests in limited markets or with customer panels to ascertain likely customer reactions to specific product features. SCM is involved because PD extends across internal and external boundaries. Internally, PD involves teamwork between marketing, design, purchasing, production, quality engineering and transportation. Externally, the uncertainties of supply and demand, shorter lifecycles, faster rates of technological change and the increased use of manufacturing, distribution and logistics partners has resulted in increasingly complicated supply chain networks. Some advanced companies have begun to transfer design responsibility upstream to the supplier base. Thus, Exostar, founded by BAE Systems, Lockhead Martin, Raytheon and Boeing, is designed to improve collaboration across the aerospace industry. Exostar, covering more than 37,000 suppliers worldwide, offers services that will allow trading partners and suppliers to collaborate on design, products and programmes that aim to provide customers with better products in a shorter timeframe.

- *Returns management* is concerned with the activities indicated in section 3.3 relating to reverse logistics. Alternative terms such as 'green logistics', 'end of chain management' and 'post-consumer logistics' emphasise the importance of environmental factors, both in product design and SCM. Returns management has extended the supply chain to beyond the end consumer. It also extends relationships beyond customers and suppliers to include cooperation with agencies such as local authority and private waste collection, recycling and disposal.

3.5.1 SCM enablers

Research by Marien[16] identified four key enablers, all of which must be fully leveraged if SCM is to be successful. Marien also observed that these four enablers become barriers to effective SCM if they are not in place. Each of the four enablers also has its own set of attributes. The four enablers and their relative rankings by Marien's respondents are:

- organisational infrastrucuture   3.44 (4 = highest importance)
- technology   2.14
- strategic alliances   2.07
- human resource management   2.05

Organisational infrastructure

How business units and functional areas are organised, how change management programmes are led and coordinated with the existing organisational structure – these constitute organisational infrastructure. Important attributes of organisational infrastructure include:

- having a coherent business strategy that aligns business units towards the same goal
- having a formal process – flow methodologies to enable SCM improvements
- having the right process metrics to guide the performance of operating units towards the strategic organisational SCM objectives.

It is of interest that respondents ranked organisational infrastructure considerably ahead of technology.

Technology

The word 'technology' (not just IT but also the 'physical' materials management technologies for material design operations and materials handling) here also is a factor in the selection of business allies and how intercompany relationships are built and managed. Important attributes of technology include:

- having operations, marketing and logistics data coordinated within the company
- having data readily available to managers and the coordination of operations, marketing and logistics data between supply chain members.

Strategic alliances

This factor covers how external companies (customers, suppliers and logistics-service providers) are selected as business allies and how intercompany relationships are built and managed. Important attributes of strategic alliances include:

- having expectations clearly stated, understood and agreed to upfront
- collaboration on supply chain design and product and service strategies
- having top management of partnering companies interface on a regular basis
- having compatible IT systems.

Human resource management

This area involves managing how job descriptions are designed, positions filled, people are recognised and compensated and career paths directed. Important aspects of human resource management include:

- sourcing, hiring and selecting skilled people at all management levels
- finding change agents to manage SCM implementation
- having compensation and incentive programmes in place for SCM performance
- finding internal process facilitators knowledgeable about SCM.

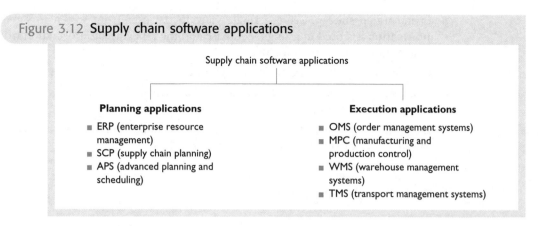

Figure 3.12 **Supply chain software applications**

3.5.2 Software as an SCM enabler

Four essential supply chain requirements are connectivity, integration, visibility and responsiveness.

Connectivity is the ability to exchange information with external supply chain partners in a timely, responsible and usable format that facilitates interorganisational collaboration.

Integration is the process of combining or coordinating separate functions, processors or producers and enabling them to interact in a seamless manner.

Visibility is the ability to access or view pertinent data or information as it relates to logistics and the supply chain.

Responsiveness is the ability to react quickly to customers' needs or specifications by delivering a product of the right quality, at the right time, in the right place, at the lowest possible cost. System availability is 24/7.

Initially, software providers specialised in either management planning or execution applications, as shown in Figure 3.12.

The current emphasis is on the creation of software that integrates each of the software types shown in Figure 3.12 and deals with the supply chain as a continuous process rather than as individual stages. Thus, enterprise resource management (ERP) may be defined as:

> a software solution that addresses the enterprise's needs, taking the process view of an organisation to meet the organisational goals by tightly integrating all functions of an enterprise.

The core ERP subsystems are sales and marketing master scheduling, materials requirements planning (MRP), capacity requirements planning (CRP), bills of materials, purchasing, shop floor control, accounts payable and receivable and logistics.

Leading ERP vendors have either purchased or partnered with advanced planning and scheduling (APS) vendors and have developed Internet versions of their supply chain offerings. Internet supply chains cause the walls between internal and external supply chains to break down. Enterprise application integration (EAI) enables providers to convert their entire suites of enterprise applications into e business applications and provide a framework that ties businesses electronically to their customers, suppliers, electronic trading communities and business partners. Such suites offer several advantages, including that:

- an integrated suite presents a single view to the user from screen to screen and information is stored in a single database and the rekeying of information from one system into another is eliminated

- a single database provides a tighter integration of business processes

- maintenance is cheaper and upgrades easier when there is only one system to upgrade and one supplier to deal with

- for the above reasons, connectivity, integration, visibility and responsiveness are essential attributes of supply chain software.

3.6 Supply chain vulnerability

Supply chains are vulnerable due to both external and internal risks.

External risks are those attributed to environmental, economic, political and social causes, such as storms, earthquakes, terrorism, strikes, wars, embargoes and computer viruses.

Internal risks are those attributable to interactions between organisations in the supply chain. A Cranfield University report[17] identifies five categories of supply chain risk.

- *Lack of ownership* due to the blurring of boundaries between buying and supplying organisations arising from factors such as outsourcing and the creation of complicated networks of business relationships with confused lines of responsibilities.

- *Chaos risks* due to mistrust and distorted information throughout the supply chain. An example is the so-called 'bullwhip' effect, in which fluctuations in orders increase as they move upstream from retailers to manufacturers to suppliers.

- *Decision risks* due to chaos that makes it impossible to make the right decision for every player in the supply chain.

- *JIT relationship risks* due to the fact that an enterprise has little capacity or stock in reserve to cater for disruptions in the supply chain due to late deliveries, such as transport breakdowns.

- *Inertia risks* due to a general lack of responsiveness by customers or suppliers to changing environmental conditions and market signals with consequential inability to react to competition moves or market opportunities.

To the above may be added:

- *supplier base reduction*, especially single sourcing in which an enterprise is dependent on one supplier

- *globalisation* in which advantages of sourcing abroad may be offset by extended lead times, transport difficulties and political events

- *acquisitions, mergers and similar alliances* that may reduce supply chain availability.

The Cranfield report observes that 'supply chain risk management starts with the identification and assessment of likely risks and their possible impact on operations'. To assess risk exposure, the company must identify not only direct risks to its operations, such as the loss of critical raw materials or process capability, but also the potential causes of those risks at every significant link along the supply chain.

The report also lists ten ways in which to manage supply chain risk. The first three of these measures run counter to current supply chain trends:

- *diversification* – multiple sourcing
- *stockpiling* – use of inventory as a buffer against all eventualities
- *redundancy* – maintaining excess production, storage, handling and transport capacity
- *insurance* – against losses caused by supply chain disruption
- *supplier selection* – more careful assessment of supplier capability and risks of dealing with particular suppliers
- *supplier development* – working closely with suppliers, sharing information and collaboration initiatives
- *contractual obligation* – imposing legal obligations with stiff penalties for non-delivery
- *collaborative initiatives* – spreading risk among grouped companies on an ad hoc basis or as part of a trade association
- *rationalisation of the product range* – companies, particularly distributors, may wish to exclude products with supply problems from their product ranges
- *localised sourcing* – reduction of risks arising from congested transport networks or intermodal transport transfer by shortening transport distances.

3.7 SCM and logistics

Some writers regard SCM and logistics as practically synonymous. Others, however, distinguish between them. Cooper[18] regards logistics as concerned with material and material flows and SCM as the integration of all business processes across the supply chain.

The relationship between SCM and logistics is well summarised by the UK Institute of Logistics and Transport:[19]

> The management of logistics makes possible the optimised flow and positioning of goods, materials, information and all resources of an enterprise.
>
> The supply chain is the flow of materials through procurement, manufacture, distribution, sales and disposal, together with the associated transport and storage.

The application of logistics is essential to the efficient management of the supply chain.

3.8 Value chains

Supply chains and value chains are synonymous. A value chain is:

> a linear map of the way in which value is added by means of a process from raw materials to finished delivered product (including service after delivery).

Important value chain models have been developed by Porter and Hines.

Figure 3.13 **Porter's supply chain**

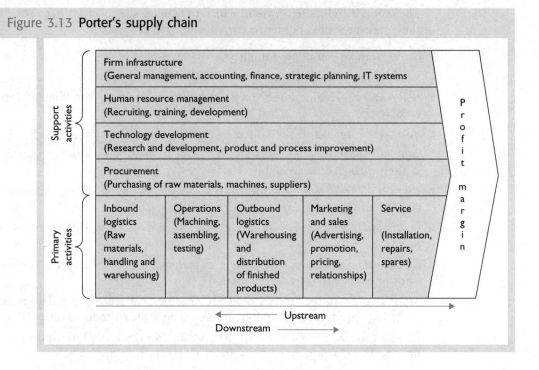

3.8.1 Porter's value chain model

Porter states that the activities of a business can be classified into five primary and four support activities, each of which will potentially contribute to competitive advantage. The activities, shown in Figure 3.13, comprise the value chain.

The five *primary* activities are as follows.

- *Inbound logistics* all activities linked to receiving, handling and storing inputs into the production system, including warehousing, transport and stock control.

- *Operations* all activities involved in the transformation of inputs to outputs as the final product(s). In a manufacturing enterprise, these would include production, assembly, quality control and packaging. In a service industry, these include all activities involved in providing the service, such as advice, correspondence and preparation of documents by a legal firm.

- *Outbound logistics* activities involved in moving the output from operations to the end user, including finished goods warehousing, order processing, order picking and packing, shipping, transport, maintenance of a dealer or distribution network.

- *Marketing and sales* activities involved in informing potential customers about the product, persuading them to buy and enabling them to do so, including advertising, promotion, market research and dealer/distributor support.

- *Service* activities involved in the provision of services to buyers offered as part of the purchase agreement, including installation, spare parts delivery, maintenance and repair, technical assistance, buyers' enquiries and complaints.

The four *support* activities for the above primary activities are the following.

- *Firm infrastructure* or general administration, including activities, costs and assets relating to general management safety and security, management information systems and the formation of strategic alliances.

- *Human resource management* all the activities involved in recruiting, hiring, training, developing and compensating the people in an organisation.

- *Technology development* activities relating to product design and improvement of production processes and resource utilisation, including research and development, process design improvement, computer software, computer-aided design and engineering and development of computerised support systems.

- *Procurement* all activities involved in acquiring resource inputs to the primary activities, including the purchase of fuel, energy, raw materials, components, sub-assemblies, merchandise and consumable items from external vendors.

The word 'margin' on the right side of the Figure 3.13 indicates that the enterprise obtains a profit margin that is more than the cost of each of the individual activities or subsystems that comprise the value chain. Viewed differently, the end customer is readier to pay more for a product or service than the total cost of all the value chain activities or subsystems.

Linkages are the means by which the interdependent parts of the value chain – both internal and external – are joined together. Such linkages take place when one element affects the costs or effectiveness of another element in the value chain. Thus, intranets and the Internet are useful linkages as they may reduce the cost of supply chain administration. Linkages require coordination. Ensuring that products are delivered on time, for example, requires the coordination of operations (production), outbound logistics and service activities. Linkages are considered further in section 4.3, on networks.

3.8.2 Hines's value chain model

Writing in 1993, Peter Hines[20] recognised that Porter made two valuable contributions to our understanding of value chain systems.

First, Porter places a major emphasis on the materials management value-adding mechanism, raising the subject to a strategic level in the minds of senior executives. Second, he places the customer in an important position in the supply chain.

3.8.3 A critique of Porter

Hines also identified three major problems with Porter's model.

- Neither Porter nor the firms discussed concede that consumer satisfaction – not company profit – should be their primary objective. The focus of Porter's model is on the profit margin of each enterprise, not the consumer's satisfaction.

- Although Porter acknowledges the importance of integration, his model shows a rather divided network, both within the company and between the different organisations in the supply chain.

- Hines believes that the wrong functions are highlighted as being important in Porter's primary and support activities.

Hines suggests that the above three criticisms result from the fact that Porter's model is based solely on American cases 'without reference to more innovative Japanese enterprises'. Porter's conclusions may therefore 'prove inappropriate for companies facing the challenges of the 21st Century with the prospect of an array of more developed competitors. Indeed in some cases close adherence to Porter's methodology may prevent firms from further continual development'.

3.8.4 Alternative models

To correct the above problems, Hines offers two models:

- a *micro* integrated materials value pipeline
- a *macro* ten forces partnership model.

The micro integrated materials value pipeline is shown in Figure 3.14.

The main contrasts between the Porter and Hines models are summarised in Table 3.2.

The following are the important features of Hines's model.

- The value chain points in the opposite direction to that in Porter's model, emphasising differences in both objectives and processes.
- Demand is determined by collective customer-defined price levels.
- Primary functions in each of the separate firms in the value chain must be integrated and 'traditional arm's length external barriers and internal divisions broken down'. The emphasis is on collaboration rather than competition.
- Key primary functions and secondary activities differ, as shown in Table 3.2. The significance of each of the secondary activities identified by Hines is, briefly, as follows.

Figure 3.14 Hines's micro integrated materials value pipeline

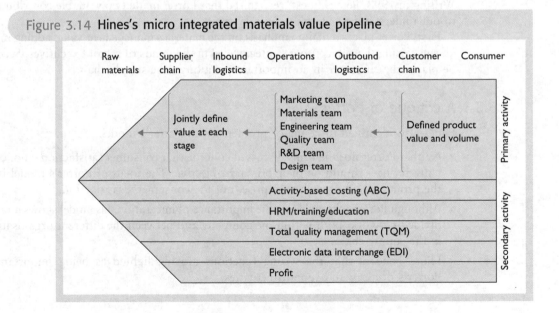

Table 3.2 **Porter's and Hines's models contrasted**

	Porter	*Hines*
Principal objective	Profitability	Consumer satisfaction
Processes	Push system	Pull system
Structure and direction	Series of chains linking firms pointing from raw materials source to customer	One large flow pointing from consumer to raw material source
Primary activities	Inbound logistics, operations, outbound logistics, marketing and sales service	Teams concerned with marketing, materials, engineering, quality, R&D and design
Secondary (support) activities	Firm infrastructure, HRM, technology development, procurement	Activity-based costing (ABC), HRM/training/education, TQM, EDI, profit

- Activity-based costing (ABC) enables the exact cost of products and the benefits of activities such as *kaizen* and value analysis to be ascertained. By allocating costs to activities rather than functions, we can identify the true costs involved in delivering the product. A simpler method of value chain analysis is to call the price charged to the customer at the end of the supply chain 100 per cent and, by working backwards, ascertain the cost of each supply activity. ABC is considered further in section 16.8. It enables the most serious non-value-adding problems to be identified first and addressed promptly.

- Human resources management (HRM) – especially employee training and education – facilitates effectiveness, efficiency and proactive thinking.

- Total quality management (TQM) provides a culture for all network members.

- Electronic data interchange (EDI) together with intranets, extranets and so on facilitate quick response to customers' requirements and draw network members closer together.

- Profit should be roughly equalised between network members and result from reducing total production and consumption costs to below what consumers are willing to pay for products meeting their specifications.

The macro ten forces partnership model shown in Figure 3.15 widens the analysis from that of a company with a single source to the whole range of supply pipelines and identifies the forces that encourage rapid and sustained development. The whole network includes several tiers or layers of supplying companies.

Hines states that the ten forces identified in Figure 3.15 describe a variety of forces that encourage rapid and sustained continual development. It should be noted that the model as shown by Hines in Figure 3.15 relates to assembly-type production. Thus, the first of the ten forces is the creative tension developed between competing final assemblers or original equipment manufacturers (OEMs). This creative tension results from both cooperation and competition between them. The cooperation derives from OEMs developing common suppliers. The competition is rivalry in attempting to meet

Figure 3.15 Hines's macro ten force partnership model

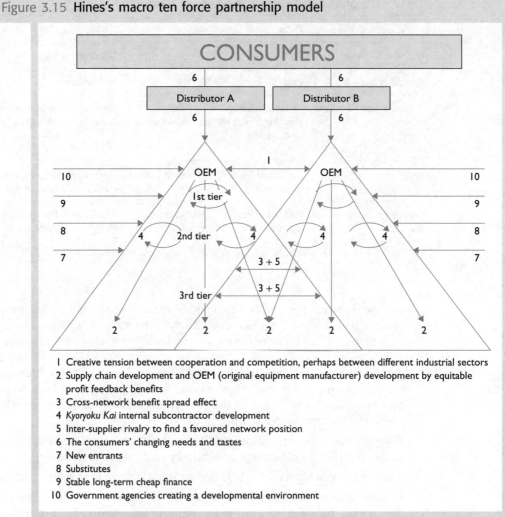

1 Creative tension between cooperation and competition, perhaps between different industrial sectors
2 Supply chain development and OEM (original equipment manufacturer) development by equitable profit feedback benefits
3 Cross-network benefit spread effect
4 *Kyoryoku Kai* internal subcontractor development
5 Inter-supplier rivalry to find a favoured network position
6 The consumers' changing needs and tastes
7 New entrants
8 Substitutes
9 Stable long-term cheap finance
10 Government agencies creating a developmental environment

consumers' requirements. Cooperation is fostered by supplier associations, referred to in section 8.8.

3.9   Value chain analysis

Value chain analysis is concerned with a detailed examination of each subsystem in a supply chain and every activity within these subsystems with a view to delivering maximum value at the least possible total cost, thereby enhancing value and synergy throughout the entire chain.

Porter[21] states that there are two ways in which an enterprise can obtain a sustained competitive advantage: first, cost and, second, differentiation.

3.9.1 Cost

Cost analysis with regard to value chains is performed by assigning costs to the value chain activities. The approach of activity-based costing (ABC) is, as stated above, of particular relevance in this context.

Porter identifies ten major cost drivers that determine the value or cost of activities.

- *Economies or diseconomies of scale* Fixed costs spread over a large volume of production are more cost-effective than producing small quantities of an item. Diseconomies of scale in procurement can occur if large requirements meet an inelastic supply, forcing up input prices.

- *Learning and spillovers* Learning can reduce costs and can spill over from one industry to another via suppliers, ex-employees and reports of representatives.

- *Capacity utilisation* Changes in the level of capacity utilisation will involve costs of expanding or contracting.

- *Linkages between activities* The cost or value of an activity is frequently affected by how other activities are performed. Linkages with suppliers centre on the suppliers' product design characteristics, such as service and quality. The way in which a supplier performs activities within the value chain can raise or lower the purchasers' costs.

- *Interrelationships* Sharing a value activity with another business unit can reduce costs. Certain raw materials can be procured more cheaply by combining units' requirements.

- *Degree of vertical integration* Every value activity employs or can employ purchased inputs and thus poses integration choices. The cost of an outbound logistics activity may vary depending on whether or not the enterprise owns its own vehicles.

- *Timing of market entry* An enterprise may gain an advantage from being the first to take a particular action.

- *Firm's policy of cost or differentiation* 'The cost of a value activity is always affected by policy choices a firm makes independently of other cost drivers. Policy choices reflect a firm's strategy and often deliberate trade-offs between cost and differentiation.

- *Geographic location* Location relative to suppliers is an important factor in inbound logistical cost.

- *Institutional factors* Government regulations, taxation, unionisation, tariffs and levies constitute major cost drivers.

An enterprise that controls the above drivers better than its rivals will secure a competitive advantage over them.

A cost advantage can also be gained by reconfiguring the value chain so that it is significantly different from those of competitors. Such reconfigured chains can derive from differing production processes, automation, direct instead of indirect sales, new raw materials or distribution channels and shifting the location of facilities relative to suppliers and customers.

3.9.2 Differentiation

Porter[22] states that a firm differentiates itself from its competitors when it provides something unique that is valuable to buyers beyond simply offering a new price. A differentiation advantage can be obtained either by enhancing the sources of uniqueness or reconfiguring the value chain.

The drivers of uniqueness are often similar to the cost drivers listed above and include:

- *policy choices* about what activities to perform and how to perform them, such as what product features to include, services to provide, technology to employ or quality of outputs
- *linkages between activities* such as delivery time, which is often influenced not only by outbound logistics but also by the speed of order processing
- *timing* being the first to adopt a product image may pre-empt others doing so
- *location* convenience of use for customers and other such factors
- *interrelationships* sharing technologies or sales effort, for example
- *learning and spillovers* learning how to perform an activity better – Porter observes that only proprietary learning leads to sustainable differentiation
- *integration* providing a service in-house instead of leaving it to suppliers may mean that the organisation is the only one to offer the service or provide the service in a unique way
- *scale* large-scale operations can allow an activity to be performed in a unique way not possible at a smaller volume
- *institutional factors* good union relationships may avoid losses in production time due to strikes and so on.

Reconfiguring a value chain to create uniqueness can involve devising a new distribution chain or selling approach, forward integration to eliminate channels of distribution, backward integration to enhance quality and the adoption of new production technologies.

3.9.3 The main steps in value chain analysis

Porter[23] provides lists of the main steps in strategic cost analysis and differentiation analysis.

For *strategic cost analysis* these steps are:

1 identify the appropriate value chain and assign costs and assets to it
2 diagnose the cost drivers of each value activity and how they interact
3 identify competitors' value chains and determine the relative costs to competitors and the sources of cost difference
4 develop a strategy to lower your relative cost position by controlling cost drivers or reconfiguring the value chain and/or downstream value
5 ensure that cost reduction efforts do not erode differentiation or make a conscious choice to do so
6 test the cost reduction strategy for sustainability.

Poirier[24] reports the following range of expenditures as percentags of the sales dollar for a large sample of USA manufacturing organisations.

- purchasing   55–65 per cent
- transport   3.5–7 per cent
- labour   2.5–6 per cent
- inventory   3–9 per cent
- system and administration   1.5–3 per cent
- facilities   0.7–2 per cent

Poirier observes that, although costs could be reduced in almost every category, most paled in comparison to purchasing. Dramatic results were recorded as organisations focused some of their best talent on this, the most costly segment.

3.10 Supply chain optimisation

Supply chain optimisation is different from SCM. The latter concentrates on controlling the various elements in the supply chain. Optimisation is about removing the non-value-added steps that have infiltrated or been designed into the link of processes that constitutes a particular supply chain. Optimisation is concerned with the removal of supply chain inefficiencies and has been defined as:

> the management of complicated supply chains in their entirety with the objectives of synchronising all value-adding production and distribution activities and the elimination of such activities that do not add value.

3.10.1 The objectives of supply chain optimisation

The above definition emphasises the importance of:

- synchronising all value-adding production and distributing activities
- eliminating activities that do not add value.

Other objectives include the following.

- *Providing the highest possible levels of customer service* Research shows a strong relationship between customer satisfaction and customer loyalty. Customer service levels should aim to create delighted customers by exceeding customers' expectations. Such expectations include responsiveness and value.
- *Achieving cost-effectiveness* Cost-effectiveness is also referred to as value for money and may be expressed as a ratio:

$$\frac{\text{Value of benefit received}}{\text{Cost of the benefit}}$$

- *Achieving maximum productivity from resources expended or assets employed* Productivity is also a ratio, relating outputs to one or more inputs. An increase in output per unit of input is an increase in productivity. Thus, the total productivity of a supply chain is:

$$\frac{\text{Total output}}{\text{Total input}}$$

The challenge is to increase the value of output relative to the cost of input. Productivity also increases when the same output is achieved with less input.

■ *Optimising enterprise profits* Cudahy[25] points out that 'the logic and aim of enterprise profit optimisation (EPO) is the simultaneous optimisation of the supply and demand sides of a business both within an enterprise and throughout its trading network. Thus by simultaneously improving operational efficiency and achieving profitable growth, EPO can enhance revenue and thereby complement cost reduction and asset productivity as a means of enhancing profitability.'

Cudahy states that the introduction of a pricing and revenue optimisation (PRO) system involves the following four basic steps.

– *Step 1: Segmenting the market* Identifying from historical transaction data the selection of groups of people who will be most receptive to a product. Frequent segmentation methods include demographic variables, such as age, sex, race, income and occupation, and psychographic variables, such as lifestyle, activities, interests and opinions.

– *Step 2: Calculating customer demand* Use of pricing software to predict how a customer or micro segment will respond to products and prices based on current market and other conditions.

– *Step 3: Optimising prices* This is concerned with deciding what prices to offer to a particular customer to maximise a particular profit objective, market share or other strategic goals. Based on an analysis of cost, demand, market position, price elasticity and competitive pressures, it recommends optimum – not lowest – prices to achieve these goals.

– *Step 4: Recalibrating prices* This is the fine-tuning of prices to customer buying behaviour.

Cudahy observes that pricing and revenue optimisation are not about competing on price but extracting the maximum value from a company's products and capacity.

■ *Achieving maximum time compression* Time compression is an important aspect in achieving customer satisfaction, cost-effectiveness and productivity. Wilding[26] rightly observes that while cost and transfer price comparisons are open to a variety of interpretations, time is a common measure across all supply chain partners. Speeding up the flow of materials downstream and the flow of information upstream increases productivity, provides competitive advantage by virtue of rapidly responding to customers' requirements and eliminates non-value-adding process time. Beesley[27] claims that at least 95 per cent of process time is accounted for by non-value-adding activities. Time compression has applications for all aspects of the supply chain but is of particular importance as, unlike material, time wasted cannot be replaced. In general, non-value-adding activities relating to time can be categorised as:

– queueing time – materials waiting to be processed

– rework time – rectifying errors

– time wasted due to managerial decisions (or indecisions)

– cost of inventory in the supply chain.

Regarding inventory, Beesley claims 'as a general rule the volume of inventory held in a supply chain is proportional to the length of time expressed as the total time to customer'. If the supply chain is compressed work-in-progress, cycle and buffer stocks are reduced, with consequent lower overhead, capital and operating costs.

3.10.2 Factors in supply chain optimisation

The important factors in supply chain optimisation are described below.

Reduction of uncertainty

Davis[28] refers to 'three distinct sources of uncertainty that plague supply chains':

- *suppliers* failure to fulfil delivery promises
- *manufacturing* machine breakdowns, computer foul-ups that route materials to the wrong place and so on
- *customers* uncertainty regarding order quantities and the 'bullwhip' effect or increase in demand variability further up the supply chain, e-orders from distributors fluctuating more than retail rates, which are fairly uniform.

All the above increase inventory. Inventory exists as a simple insurance against uncertainty of supply. Reduction of uncertainty – by means of reliable, accurate and valid forecasts, the study of demand trends and use of statistical methods – can optimise the supply chain by avoiding holding excess stock and, conversely, delay in responding to customers' demands due to stockouts.

Collaboration

Optimisation is normally most likely to be achieved by collaboration between cross-functional teams within the organisation and customers and suppliers external to it. Such collaboration may optimise product and process design and customers' and suppliers' satisfaction.

Benchmarking

Before we can optimise, we must know what performance is possible. Benchmarking has been defined by Naylor[29] as:

> the practice of recognising and examining the best industrial and commercial practices in industry or in the world and using this knowledge as the basis for improvement in all aspects of business.

Benchmarking is more than imitation. As Naylor states, 'it is through analysis of success and a spreading of learning throughout the organisation'.

Key performance indicators (KPIs)

KPIs express abstract supply chain objectives in financial or physical units for the purpose of comparison. Data relating to various functions, processes or activities is assembled, quantified and transformed into physical or financial information that can be used to compare results – often against benchmarks – and then measure relative performance. Thus, the performance of both suppliers and customer with regard to delivery of orders on time can be expressed as a percentage of the orders placed. KPIs, considered in detail in section 11.10.2, can provide not only objectives to achieve but also the motivation to achieve or better the required performance.

Leadership

The impetus for supply chain optimisation and world class SCM must either derive from or have the support of top management. This requires two-way communication between top management and the senior managers responsible either for the integrated supply chain or functions and processes within it. Important leadership characteristics are the ability to articulate the vision of an optimised supply chain to other team members, set and motivate the team to achieve goals, innovate and introduce change, nurture the competences of team members, foster a culture of continuous learning and improvement and display high levels of personal integrity.

Actions to improve supply chain performance

Davis[30] suggests a number of actions that can be used to improve supply chain performance and reduce vulnerability to demand uncertainty in both products and processes.

For products, these actions include the use of standard components and sub-assemblies, lower tolerances, fewer product offerings and the production of a generic product.

For processes, typical actions may be to reward suppliers' performance, subcontract, inbound freight handling, remove bottlenecks, introduce self-managed work teams and devise improved forecasting techniques.

The strategic, tactical and operational level decision-making processes should all be influenced by the search for supply chain optimisation. Strategies also lead to structures, as described in Chapter 4.

3.11 Supply chains and purchasing

Most of this book is concerned with purchasing as a major supply chain subsystem. Purchasing has been well described as the glue that holds the expanded supply chain together.

The supply chain concept has profoundly influenced traditional purchasing philosophies, practices and procedures in such ways as the following.

- Purchasing is increasingly ceasing to be a discrete function and becoming a group of activities within an integrated supply chain.

- Research by the USA *Purchasing* magazine showed that, in 2002:[31]
  - one in four purchasing professional respondents identified SCM as their principal job responsibility
  - virtually all the other respondents viewed SCM as an important component of their job
  - SCM is generally regarded as expanding purchasing's role.

- The head of purchasing may report to a materials, logistics or supply chain manager rather than to someone at a higher level. Figures 3.16 and 3.17 are based on a 1997 survey by the Bourton Group.[32] Figure 3.16 shows that responsibility for supply chain issues is headed by a dedicated director in about 15 per cent of responding companies and by a specific manager in another 45 per cent. In a further 20 per cent, responsibility lies with an operations or production director. Figure 3.17 indicates that the person running the supply chain reports to the managing director and chief executive officer in just under half of the responding companies. In the other half, ultimate responsibility is mainly with directors and general managers or with operations or production mangers or directors. Reporting

Figure 3.16 **The people who run the supply chain in a sample of 344 companies**

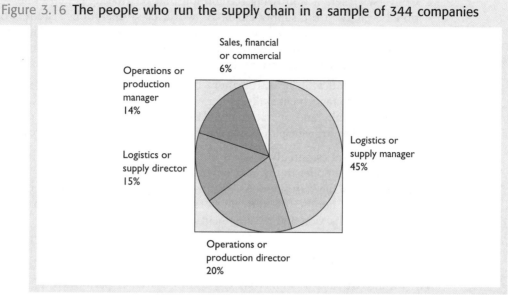

Figure 3.17 **The reporting levels of people with supply chain responsibility in a sample of 344 companies**

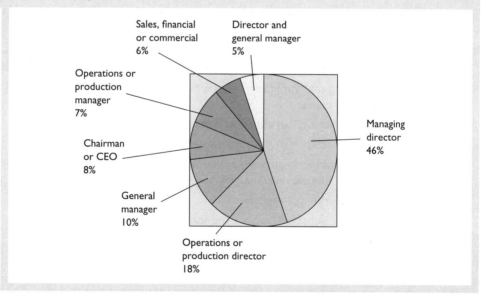

responsibility for the supply chain appears to be below director level in about 16 per cent of cases.

■ The number of purchasing staff is likely to be reduced, owing to some former purchasing activities being made redundant by IT or taken over by other teams, such as supplier selection or inventory control.

- Conversely there is a growing recognition that purchasing is more than a transactional activity in the supply chain. As world class operations require world class suppliers, the emphasis of purchasing will be less on price and more on supplier relationships and alliances and on contributing to the achievement of enterprise objectives along the entire supply chain.

- Purchasing staff will have to acquire competence in other supply chain activities and general management skills, along with the capacity to think strategically rather than functionally and operationally. This gives further force to the observation of Lamming, that strategic purchasing requires a broad rather than a narrow knowledge.

Supply chains are essentially a series of suppliers and customers. Every customer in turn becomes a supplier to the next downstream activity or function until the finished product reaches the customer. As an upstream supplier-facing member, purchasing can undertake a number of strategic roles. Gadde-Lars and Hakansson[33] distinguish between rationalisation and development roles.

3.11.1 Rationalisation roles

These roles are 'all the numerous day-to-day activities performed to decrease costs successively' and are of three types.

- *Discovering what needs to purchased and where*:
  - determining specifications for purchased goods and services in association with design, production, transportation and other supply chain functions
  - providing critical information to strategic managers on materials, prices, availability and supplier issues
  - selecting and rationalising the number of first-tier suppliers
  - advising on make-or-buy decisions, outsourcing, leasing and similar strategies
  - ensuring that suppliers meet performance expectations with regard to price, quality and delivery
  - evaluating the benefits and dangers of global sourcing
  - forging relationships and long-term partnerships with key suppliers
  - endeavouring to obtain maximum possible value from all suppliers by implementing value management, analysis and engineering.

- *Rationalisation of logistics*:
  - locating suppliers so that the least possible interruption is likely to occur to JIT and similar delivery arrangements
  - negotiating the best possible contracts and arrangements for transportation and distribution
  - undertaking responsibility for reverse logistics and the disposal of scrap and surplus by environmentally acceptable means
  - providing suppliers with accurate forecasts of requirements and facilitating such approaches as JIT and MRP.

- *Rationalisation of procurement routines, procedures and policies*:
  - involvement in the selection of appropriate supply chain packages and the reduction of purchasing costs via e-procurement

- involvement in the design of all purchasing and supply chain structures
- ensuring that staff receive appropriate training in general management, SCM and special aspects of purchasing
- monitoring the ethical aspects of procurement
- measuring all aspects of supply chain and purchasing performance.

3.11.2 Development roles

These involve coordinating the internal R&D activities of the purchaser with those of suppliers. Research by McGinnis and Vallopra[34] has shown that early supplier involvement in new product development contributes to competitive advantage in the areas of new products, time-to-market, achieving high quality, cost advantages, sales and profits. Supplier involvement is more likely in the design of manufactured than non-manufactured products, though it can apply to both. In general, enterprises that focus on upstream product specification and design activities where they can best use their resources will want to outsource downstream activities where they are not cost-effective or less competent than specialised suppliers, such as component manufacture, so that suppliers will have a greater roles to play in these areas. Important purchasing roles in supplier involvement in product development include participation in cross-functional product development teams, the identification of suppliers capable of contributing and supplier development and monitoring.

Case study

Household Appliances PLC buys a wide range of components that are assembled into washing machines, cookers, dishwashers and similar 'white goods' on a continuous assembly line basis. Such products are sold mainly in large retail outlets stocking domestic appliances but also directly to some major users, such as hospital and local and central government authorities. There is also rapidly growing overseas demand.

The retail outlets operate a form of computer-assisted ordering so that, as soon as an item is sold, a replacement is ordered automatically from Household Appliances. Delays in the replacement of showroom stock can result in lost sales as, if a Household Appliances model is not on view, customers buy competitors' products.

A major cause of delays is transport problems. Household Appliances has no transport fleet of its own and has negotiated an outsourcing agreement with a large logistics company. This company combines drops of Household Appliances' products with deliveries to other customers. Because of this policy, delays of several days can occur in replenishing the retailers' stock.

Originally, Household Appliances had several suppliers of critical components. Following a consultancy exercise, it decided to adopt a policy of single sourcing for some items. This policy has led to several problems. The manufacture of two critical die-cast items involves the use of expensive moulds. The present supplier of these two items agreed to supply the moulds free of charge on the conditions that the moulds would remain the supplier's property and that Household Appliances would not source elsewhere for a minimum of two years. This supplier is located some 150 miles from Household Appliances' factory.

▶

Household Appliances' production line also experienced a serious hold-up during an industrial dispute affecting deliveries of a third component. Subsequent enquiries elicited the facts that the supplier of the component manufactured the same item for three of Household Appliances' competitors, all of whom placed substantially larger orders. It also emerged that a preferred alternative supplier for this component has entered into a collaborative arrangement with one of Household Appliances' competitors for the joint development of an alternative item offering substantial cost and performance advantages over that currently in use.

To obviate losses, which, due to the above factors have been significant, Household Appliances has adopted a policy of keeping significant stocks of critical components.

Tasks

1 Identify the sources of vulnerability in Household Appliances' supply chain.

2 As purchasing manager of Household Appliances PLC, what steps would you recommend taking to improve the situation?

Discussion questions

3.1 Consider the activities listed under production and consumer logistics in Figure 3.1. In what ways will the execution of such activities differ in civilian as distinct from military situations?

3.2 In the nineteenth century, the standard grain and hay ration for horses was about 11.4 kilograms (25 pounds) and the daily forage of a corps of 10,000 cavalry weighed as much (allowing for remounts) as the food for 60,000 men. Forage requirements also tended to be self-generating as the animals needed to transport forage also had to be fed.

In World War II, without counting transoceanic shipments, fuel made up half the resupply and replacement needs of US troops in Europe, and the average ammunition requirements of Western forces in combat zones was 12 per cent of total needs.

Consider some of the logistical implications of the above facts.

3.3 Under what conditions would you recommend a materials management approach as appropriate to the needs of an enterprise? What are some possible disadvantages of materials management?

3.4 In what ways, if any, can reverse logistics add value?

3.5 A frequent observation is that the traditional supply chain is on its way out, to be superseded by new models reliant on information flow and cooperation for supply chain success.

How may modern supply chains differ from older models in terms of the four characteristics of:

■ connectivity
■ execution
■ creativity and innovation
■ speed?

3.6 Sovereign is a producer of chair lifts for use in homes, hospitals and hotels. The main elements of the chair lift are the electronics, including the motor, track and seat mechanism. The electronics and seat mechanisms are fairly standard and are purchased from outside suppliers. The track varies in length and shape according to the individual application and is ordered for a specific application. The chair lifts are distributed via hospitals and local authority social service departments, as well as being sold directly to customers responding to advertising. It is necessary for either Sovereign or distributors to install and maintain the chair lifts and sometimes remove them from the premises of users when they are no longer required.

Draw a supply chain showing the acquisition of bought-out parts for the installation of the chair lift. What are the main logistical problems to be considered?

3.7 Flint[35] suggests five supply cost areas where specific ideas for cost savings can be made. These are shown in the figure below. Under each heading, insert examples of possible cost savings.

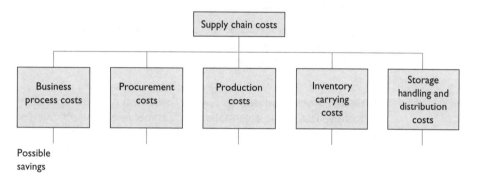

3.8 From your experience, provide examples to support the following statement by Peter Drucker: 'The economy is changing structure. From being organised around a flow of things and the flow of money, it is becoming organised around the flow of information.'

3.9 Writing in the 1950s, W. H. Bower in *Some Ethical Problems of Management*, declared: 'The object of industry or commerce is not to make a profit and incidentally thereby to render a product or a service to the community but rather the object of industry is to provide a needed product or service and thereby make a profit.'

Has this statement any relevance to the differing views of value chains of Porter and Hines?

3.10 What, if any, are the differences between a supply chain and a 'pipeline'. If there are differences, are there problems that could occur with pipelines and not supply chains and vice versa?

3.11 A speaker addressing an aerospace conference observed: 'The common snail travels at 0.007 miles per hour. This is more than ten times the average velocity of a part flowing through a typical fighter aircraft production system.'

What is the relevance of this statement to time compression? If you were a logistics manager in the aircraft factory, what steps would you take to compress time?

3.12 In supply chains, there is a danger that purchasing will be seen as an unimportant activity that can be outsourced. How can purchasing staff show that they are important contributors to supply chain effectiveness?

3.13 Take a typical product of the organisation in which you are employed and
   (a) draw a supply chain from the acquisition of the materials or supplies through operations to the final consumer
   (b) list the main activities or processes involved in operations
   (c) starting with the selling price of the product, work backwards and estimate the amount of value added by each supply chain activity. (You may need to consult with your management accountant.)

3.14 How may efforts to obtain a competitive advantage by means of cost reduction erode the competitive advantages obtained by differentiation?

Past examination questions

The following questions are taken from the CIPS Professional Stage examination: *Strategy and Strategic Procurement*

1 (a) Define what is meant by the concept of strategic management of the supply chains.
  (b) Discuss what impact such a strategic approach to supply chain management might have on its participants.

(November 2003)

2 Customer-driven organisations operate three main approaches: understanding the customer, responsiveness by the organisation to customer need, and provision of real value for money by the organisation.
  Discuss these approaches from a strategic management perspective.

(November 2002)

3 There are inefficiencies along the supply chain in respect of delays, inventory, decisions and rules, and uncertainties. Identify what might cause these and suggest some strategic supply chain solutions to address these inefficiencies.

(November 2002)

4 (a) Identify and discuss activities that add value that are to be undertaken by a purchasing and supply function.
  (b) Define and appraise different approaches that might be taken to organising a purchasing and supply function.

(November 2003)

5 Evaluate the role, objectives and contribution of supply chain strategies to corporate strategy and the strategic planning process.

(November 2003)

References

[1] NATO, *Logistics Handbook*, 1997, paras 103–4

[2] Knight Wendling, 'Logistics Report', 1988 (published for private consultation)

[3] Crompton, H. K., and Jessop, D. A., *Dictionary of Purchasing and Supply*, Liverpool Business Publishing, 2001, p. 88

[4] Council of Logistics Management Professionals USA, 12 February, 1998

[5] Institute of Logistics and Transport, *Glossary of Inventory and Materials Management Definitions*, 1998, p. 10

[6] Rogers, D. S., and Tibben-Lembke, R., *Going Backwards: Reverse Logistics Trends and Practices*, Reverse Logistics Executive Council, Pittsburgh, USA

[7] As 6 above

[8] Atken, J., quoted in Christopher, M., *Logistics and Supply Chain Management*, 2nd edn, 1998, Pearson Education, p. 19

[9] Cooper, M. C., Lambert, D. M., and Pugh, J. D., 'Supply Chain Management – more than a new name for logistics', *International Journal of Logistics Management*, Vol. 8, No. 1, 1997, pp. 1–4

[10] Porter, M. E., *Competitive Advantage*, Free Press, 1985, p. 3

[11] Christopher, M., as 8 above, p. 266

[12] Mentzer, J. T., De-Witt, W., Keebler, J. S., Soonhong, M., Nix, N. W., Smith, C. D., and Zacharia, Z. G., 'Defining supply chain management', *Journal of Business Logistics*, Vol. 22, No. 2, 2001

[13] As 12 above

[14] Adapted from Lambert, Douglas M., Cooper Martha C., and Pagh, Janus D., 'Supply chain management: implementation, issues and research opportunities', *The International Journal of Logistics Management*, Vol. 9, No. 2, 1998, p. 2

[15] Kalakota, R., and Robinson, M., *E-business 2.0 Roadmap for success*, 2nd edn, Addison-Wesley, 2001, p. 172

[16] Marien, E. J., 'The four supply chain enablers', *Supply Chain Management Review*, Vol. 4, No. 1, March/April 2000

[17] Cranfield University School of Management, 'Supply chain vulnerability', Final Report, 2002, pp. 35–7

[18] As 9 above

[19] Institute of Logistics and Transport Publicity Leaflet, *What is Logistics and what does a Career in Logistics Involve?* Undated

[20] Hines, P., 'Integrated materials management: the value chain redefined', *International Journal of Logistics Management*, Vol. 4, No. 1, 1993, pp. 13–22

[21] As 10 above, pp. 62–118

[22] As 10 above, pp. 119–63

[23] As 10 above, pp. 118 and 162–3

[24] Poirier, C. C., *Advanced Supply Chain Management*, Berrett-Koehler Publishers, 1999, p. 15

[25] Cudahy, G., 'The impact of pricing on supply chains' in Gattorna, J. L. (ed.) *Gower Handbook of Supply Chain Management*, 5th edn, 2003, Gower, pp. 62–75

[26] Wilding, R., 'Supply chain optimisation: using the three "Ts" to enhance value and reduce costs', *IFAMM Global Briefing*, 2004, pp. 18–19

[27] Beesley, A. T., 'Time compression: new source of competitiveness in the supply chain', *Logistics Focus*, June, 1995, pp. 24–5

[28] Davis, T., 'Effective supply chain management', *Sloan Management Review*, summer, 1993, pp. 35–45

[29] Naylor, J., *Introduction to Operations Management*, 2nd edn, Prentice Hall, 2002, p. 535

[30] As 28 above

[31] 'Supply chain management – what is it?', *Purchasing*, Sept. 4, 2003, pp. 45–9

[32] Bourton Group, 'Half delivered: a survey of strategies and tactics in managing the supply chain in manufacturing businesses', 1997, pp. 26–7

[33] Gadde-Lars, Erik, and Hakansson, H., *Supply Network Strategies*, John Wiley, 2001, pp. 8–10

[34] McGinnis, M. A., and Vallopra, R. H., 'Purchasing and supplier involvement' in *New Product Development and Production/Operations Process Development and Improvement Center for Advanced Purchasing Studies*, University of Alabama, 1998

[35] Flint, C., 'Buzzword logistics', *Logistics Focus*, Nov., 1997, p. 27

Chapter 4

Structure and supply chains

Learning outcomes

With reference, where applicable, to supply and value chains, this chapter aims to provide an understanding of:

- specialisation, coordination and control as aspects of organisational structure
- some determinants of organisational structure
- why and how traditional bureaucratic structures have been replaced with new approaches, including networks, lean and agile organisations
- supply chain mapping.

Key ideas

- Specialisation and outsourcing, coordination as integration and the essentials of 'control'.
- Age, technical systems, power and the environment as determinants of structure.
- The reasons for and characteristics of new type structures.
- Network structures: basic concepts, classifications, configurations and optimisation.
- Tiering: levels, reasons for tiering, responsibilities of first-tier suppliers and the consequences of tiering.
- Lean organisations and lean thinking, production, structures and the advantages and disadvantages of lean production.
- Agile organisations: the drivers, characteristics and enablers of agile manufacturing and the concepts of postponement and agility.
- Supply chain mapping: forms, purposes, methodology of supply chain mapping and value stream mapping tools.

Introduction

This chapter falls into two broad sections. The first provides a general introduction to organisational structures. The second is concerned with 'new type' structures, such as networks, lean and agile organisations and the implications for supply chains. Purchasing organisations are dealt with in Chapter 5.

4.1 Organisational structures

Mintzberg[1] has defined organisational structure as:

> The sum total of the ways in which the enterprise divides its labour into distinct tasks and achieves coordination among them.

4.1.1 Specialisation

Traditionally, specialisation was the division of organisational activities into functions, occupations, jobs and tasks. By means of vertical integration, enterprises also aimed at self-sufficiency – both in the supply of materials and the in-house manufacture of products.

Stemming from the work of Prahalad and Hamel,[2] however, the present emphasis of specialisation relates to *core competences*, or competitive advantage, that satisfy three criteria:

- potential access to a wide variety of markets
- significant contribution to the perceived benefit of the end product(s)
- ideally, a core competence should be difficult for a competitor to imitate.

Core competences arise from the integration of specialist technologies and the co-ordination of diverse production skills. They result in core products. Examples of enterprises and their core products are:

- Pilkingtons and glass products
- Black and Decker and small electric motors
- Honda and petrol engines.

Such core products can be used to launch a variety of end products. Honda engines have applications ranging from cars, motorcycles and lawnmowers to portable generators.

Concentration on core competences has led to the outsourcing of non-core activities. Six consequences of outsourcing include the:

- transfer of non-core manufacturing activities to specialist contract manufacturers that, by leveraging their fixed costs over multiple customers, can produce more for less
- transfer of non-core service activities, such as catering or training, to specialist providers
- removal from corporate balance sheets of manufacturing assets, such as tools and equipment
- reduced payroll by eliminating non-core employees
- ability to combine the power of several highly specialised contributions into a single, flexible, value-adding entity
- opportunity for purchasing to create better leverage of procured parts, products and services.

4.1.2 Coordination

Traditionally, coordination as an aspect of organisational theory related to ensuring that people and resources grouped into discrete functions worked together to accomplish organisational goals. The hierarchy of authority was itself a powerful coordinating influence.

Today, coordination is synonymous with *integration*. Essentially, integration is conflict resolution. On the assumption that separate organisational elements and interests will inevitably conflict over scarce resources, objectives, status and similar factors, there must be integrating mechanisms to ensure unity of effort. Where such integration is not achieved, the result will be waste, conflict and low productivity, or *suboptimisation*. Integration can be both intra- and interorganisational.

Intra-organisational integration

Figure 4.1 indicates a continuum of intra-organisational mechanisms to enhance communication and integration between the parts of an organisation, or, in the present context, supply chain elements.

Figure 4.1 A continuum of intra-organisational mechanisms

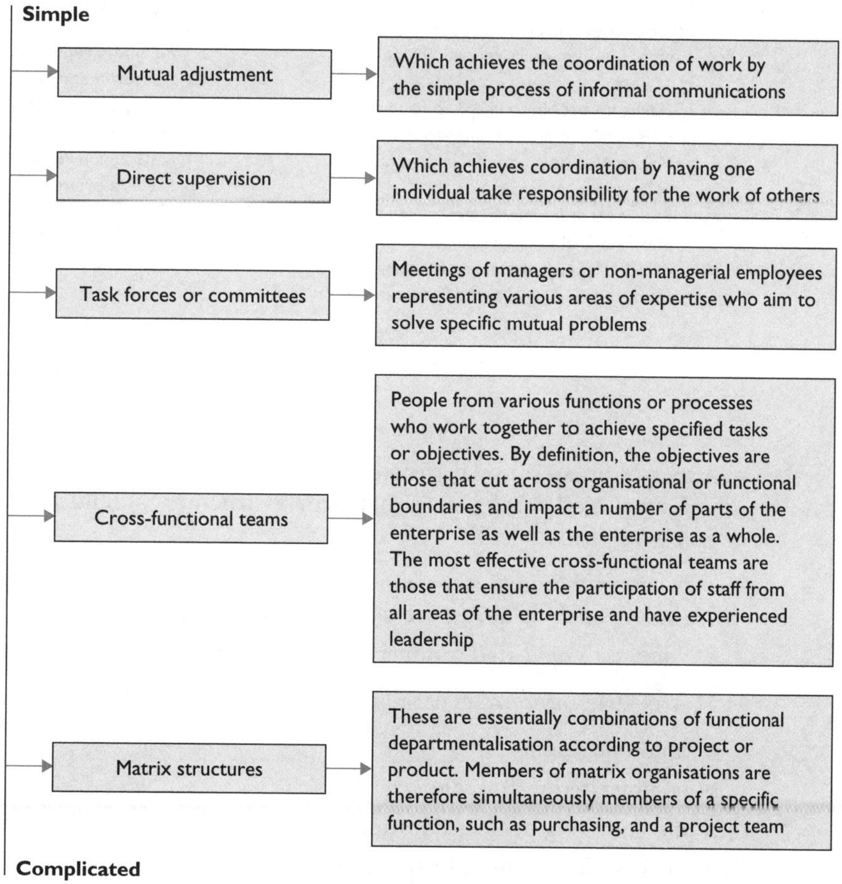

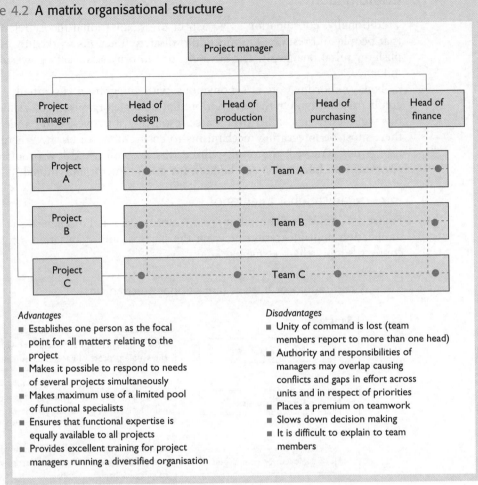

Figure 4.2 **A matrix organisational structure**

Advantages

- Establishes one person as the focal point for all matters relating to the project
- Makes it possible to respond to needs of several projects simultaneously
- Makes maximum use of a limited pool of functional specialists
- Ensures that functional expertise is equally available to all projects
- Provides excellent training for project managers running a diversified organisation

Disadvantages

- Unity of command is lost (team members report to more than one head)
- Authority and responsibilities of managers may overlap causing conflicts and gaps in effort across units and in respect of priorities
- Places a premium on teamwork
- Slows down decision making
- It is difficult to explain to team members

A matrix organisational structure is shown in Figure 4.2.

Grinnel and Apple[3] state that matrix structures should be considered only for the following situations:

- when complicated, low-volume production runs are the principal outputs of an organisation, such as aerospace construction products
- when a complicated product design calls for both innovation and timely completion.

Matrix structures are generally applicable when the following factors obtain:

- high uncertainty
- complicated technology
- medium/long project duration
- medium/long internal dependence
- high differentiation.

Most of the disadvantages of matrix structures derive from the dual or multiple relationships that may lead to conflicts between resources and business managers and confusion about where authority lies. More positively, the horizontal communication linkages of matrix organisations encourage integration and teamwork. Horizontal structures and cross-functional management structures are referred to in Chapter 5.

Integration also involves *formalisation*, or the extent to which work behaviour is constrained by rules, regulations, policies and procedures. Formalisation is greatest when the individual discretion given to employees is low. The extent to which an organisation is formalised indicates how top decision makers view their subordinates. Douglas McGregor[4] proposed two contrasting sets of managerial assumptions about the work attitudes and behaviour of their subordinates, which he termed Theory X and Theory Y.

Theory X assumes that the average worker is lazy, dislikes work, will do as little as possible, lacks ambition and seeks to avoid responsibility. Managers therefore maximise their control over worker behaviour.

Theory Y assumes that the work setting determines whether workers consider work to be a source of satisfaction or a chore. Where work is a source of satisfaction, close control of worker behaviour is unnecessary as employees will exercise self-control and be committed to organisational goals.

Interorganisational structures

No business is an island. Every organisation has relationships as customers, suppliers or as collaborators in innovation with many other organisations. Mechanisms, must therefore be developed to resolve possible interorganisational conflicts arising from factors such as loss of control and influence, increased uncertainty, consensus problems and standardisation issues.

By far the most important influence in both intra- and interorganisational integration is IT. Prior to IT, it was important that organisational structures should, for reasons of coordination or integration, be in physical proximity. With IT, grouping tasks, functions or people in close physical proximity is unnecessary. With electronic mail, video conferencing and fax machines, it is possible to establish and integrate links within and across all organisational boundaries. Software applications such as MRP, MRPII, ERP, ECR and VMI are all approaches to the integration of resources and relationships.

4.1.3 Control

Control is a third aspect of organisational structure. A control system requires two essential elements:

- a power base
- a control mechanism, which may be of one of the following generic types.
  - *Centralisation* – decision making is either carried out by a centralised authority or requires the approval of the centralised authority before it is implemented.
  - *Formalisation* – as stated under the heading 'Intra-organisational integration' in section 4.1.2 above, this relates to regulations, policies, rules and procedures that provide guidelines, objectives or goals.

- *Output control* – determining objectives or goals that provide the criteria for decision making.

- *Cultural control* – the shared values and norms that guide decision making. It is often suggested that where culture is strong, strong structures are unnecessary. Cultural control is often exercised via informal structures. Informal organisation covers not only the friendships and animosities of people who work together but also their shared traditions and values that guide their behaviour sometimes to achieve and sometimes to block organisational goals. In practice, the relationship of the informal to the formal organisation determines how effectively the latter will function. No manager can succeed without understanding the informal structures that operate within a particular work setting.

4.1.4 The determinants of structure

What is known as the contingent approach emphasises that there is no one ideal structure. Mintzberg[5] has identified four contingency or 'situational' factors, which are age and size, technical systems, power and the environment.

Age and size

Mintzberg states that the older and larger an organisation, the more standardised will be its behaviour, policies and procedures. Because of these factors, changes are more difficult to implement in older, larger organisations.

Technical systems

Mintzberg suggests that the more a technical system controls the workforce, the more standardised will be the operating system and bureaucratic the organisational structure. Conversely, information and computer technologies may transform a bureaucratic to a flexible structure and lead to changes in the nature of managerial work, job design and working practices.

Power

Power may be defined as the capacity of an individual or group to influence decisions or effect organisational outcomes. Five sources of power are identified by French and Raven[6] under the classifications shown in Figure 4.3.

- *Reward power* is based on individual or group perceptions that another individual or group has the ability to provide varying amounts and types of rewards.

- *Legitimate power* is based on the values held by an individual or the formation of particular values as a result of socialisation. It exists when an individual or group accepts that it is legitimate for another individual or group to influence their actions.

- *Coercive power* is based on individual or group perceptions that another individual or group has the ability to administer penalties.

- *Expert power* is based on individual or group perceptions that another person or group has greater knowledge or expertise than them and is thus worth following.

- *Referent power* is based on the desire of an individual or group to identify with or be like another person or group.

Figure 4.3 **The sources of power**

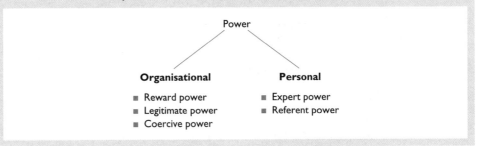

There are significant differences between organisational and personal power. Organisational power is conferred and dependent on the position of the individual or group in the organisational hierarchy. Personal power is inherent and dependent on the personal characteristics of the holder. Personal power is therefore less removable from the holder than organisational power.

Often the importance of purchasing in an organisation derives from the reputation of the head of purchasing or team leader for competence and the attractiveness of his or her personality to others. Political power, for example, has been described as a combination of respect and liking.

Other research[7] has shown that, in relation to departments or operations, those who are most powerful in an organisation control important resources, have to cope effectively with uncertainty and have scarce expertise. This research implies that the most powerful departments or operations are those concerned with uncertainty, such as marketing in highly competitive industries and purchasing where materials form a high proportion of the total cost, particularly where the prices of the materials are unstable. The factors determining buyer and supplier power in the marketplace as identified by Porter are set out in Figure 2.6 in Chapter 2.

The environment

The importance of environmental scanning to the formulation of strategies was discussed in Chapter 2. The environment may be defined as 'all factors external to an organisation'. Environments are both general and specific. Both these aspects must be considered in relation to organisational structures and decision making.

The general environment is comprised of the political, economic, legal, social and technological conditions within which all organisations operate at a given time. The specific environment consists of the people, groups and organisations with whom a particular enterprise must interact. These include clients, customers, regulators, resource suppliers, trade unions and numerous others.

Both general and specific environments have specific significance for organisations that operate internationally.

Mintzberg[8] states that environments can range from:

- *stable to dynamic* in stable environments, more mechanistic structures will apply; the more dynamic the environment, the more organic will be the structure
- *simple to complicated* the more complicated the environment, the more decentralised the organisational structure, and vice versa

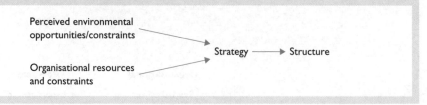

Figure 4.4 **The environment–strategy–structure link**

- *integrated to diverse* the more diversified the organisation's markets, the greater the propensity for it to split into market-based units (these give favourable economies of scale)
- *munificent (liberal and friendly) to hostile* an extremely hostile environment will drive an organisation to centralise its structure, at least temporarily.

Strategy and structure

Mintzberg's analysis emphasises that different environments lead to different strategies. Different strategies require different structures. Thus, as Chandler[9] concluded after a study of almost 100 large American companies, changes in corporate strategy precede and lead to changes in organisational structure – that is, structure follows strategy. This environment–strategy–structure link is shown in Figure 4.4.

Later writers,[10] however, suggest that Chandler's strategy–structure relationship is too simplistic, that structure may constrain strategy and, once an organisation has been locked into a particular environment–strategy–structure relationship, it may have difficulty pursuing activities outside its normal scope of operations. Often an organisation cannot change strategy until it implements changes in structure.

4.1.5 McKinsey's 7S model

McKinsey, as quoted by Waterman,[11] also regarded Chandler's strategy–structure model as inadequate and identified seven interrelated factors that organisations wishing to become more customer-orientated need to address. These factors are shown in Figure 4.5.

Figure 4.5 shows that shared values are at the core of the organisation. While formal structure is important, the critical issue is not how activities are divided up but, rather, the ability to focus on those dimensions that are important to organisational development. From a purchasing standpoint, these seven dimensions are the following.

- *Shared values* The importance of purchasing sharing in the corporate culture or 'ways in which things are done around here'. The recognition by the organisation and purchasing that procurement is a contributor to the achievement of organisational objectives. Relating all purchasing activities to the ethical and environmental policies of the organisation.
- *Structure* The breaking down of functional barriers based on specialisation and the integration of purchasing into logistics and supply chain processes in a seamless manner.
- *Skills* The development of staff knowledge and competences relative to purchasing and the sharing of such knowledge and competence with both internal and external suppliers

Figure 4.5 McKinsey's 7S model

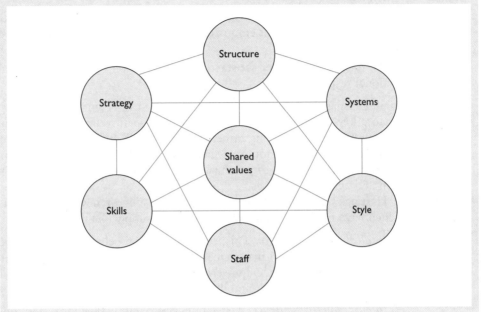

- *Strategy* In what ways can purchasing contribute to the achievement of marketing, alliance, growth, diversification, outsourcing and similar strategies?
- *Style* The building of supplier goodwill and cooperation by creating good supplier relationships based on trust, courtesy, information sharing and adherence to ethical principles.
- *Staff* Securing the right mix of purchasing and support staff to ensure that procurement contributes to competitive advantages, training and rewarding staff.
- *Systems* The development of procedures, information flows and the facilitation of e-procurement.

4.2 New type organisations

Traditional bureaucratic structures characterised by vertical 'silos', departmentalisation of functions, rigid hierarchies and 'red tape' are becoming dysfunctional because they are widely regarded as too rigid, slow and insufficiently innovative to meet the requirements of flexible, fast-moving and rapidly changing enterprises and their customers.

Quinn[12] lists five factors that have influenced the reform of traditional hierarchical organisations.

- the pursuit of 'right-sizing' and 'horizontal' organisations, resulting in the reduction of management layers and flat structures
- concurrent actions, including the re-engineering of business processes, followed by organisational redesign and the greater use of multifunctional teams

- the need for precision, speed and flexibility in the execution of programmes and strategies
- the development of powerful information systems and automated knowledge capture, with the resultant empowerment of employees in the management of business processes
- the focus on customer satisfaction and retention by means of enhanced organisational responsiveness.

In purchasing, a further factor is the transition from being a purely transactional activity to a key contributor to organisational competitiveness and performance in which the emphasis is on sourcing rather than buying. While many organisations still organise purchasing along traditional hierarchical lines, the above factors are increasingly leading to the adoption of purchasing and supply chain networks and the adoption of lean and agile philosophies.

Hastings[13] has identified seven characteristics of new type organisations, all of which have implications for purchasing and supply chain management.

- *Radical decentralisation* This, combined with a belief that 'small is beautiful', splits the organisation into many small, autonomous units, the smallest of which is the individual who, when 'empowered', is given considerable autonomy with consequent responsibility and accountability.

- *Intense interdependence* This emphasises interdependence and multidisciplinary approaches and is implemented by assembling teams and coalitions to pursue common objectives. Both individuals and the organisation itself realise that in order to compete they have to cooperate.

- *Demanding expectations* Organisations and the individuals in them have a clear sense of the goals that they are expected to achieve. Individuals are demanding of others and expect their cooperation as a right.

- *Transparent performance standards* Demanding performance standards and performance measures are set and communicated in a transparent fashion so that all are aware of how they are doing in relation to others. The emphasis is on improvement, not winners and losers.

- *Distributed leadership* Leadership is not confined to senior management but is distributed among people in the company generally, who are required to display maturity and responsibility.

- *Boundary busting* To achieve adaptability and flexibility, physical, personal, hierarchical, functional, cultural, psychological and practical barriers to cooperation and communication are identified and systematically eliminated.

- *Networking and reciprocity* Direct relationships and communication between individuals – irrespective of their roles, status, functions, culture or location – are encouraged and facilitated by the abandonment of conventional rigid organisation structures so that a pervasive culture of reciprocity and exchange mediates all relationships.

The movement from traditional bureaucratic/mechanistic to modern adaptive/organic structures is described in Table 4.5.

Examples of new type organic structures – emphasising empowerment, functional redundancy and the facilitation of communication between employee 'teams' and external 'parties' – are networks, which are lean and agile.

4.3 Networks

4.3.1 Network structures

A network structure is a series of strategic alliances that an organisation forms with suppliers, manufacturers and distributors to produce and market a product. Such structures enable an enterprise to bring resources together on a long-term basis, reduce costs and enhance quality without the high expenditure involved in investing in specialised resources, including research and design, and dedicated technology or the employment of an army of managers and operatives. It follows that:

- a network, as Ford et al.[14] point out is 'not a world of individual and isolated transactions. It is the result of complex interactions within and between companies in relationships over time', so, as Ford et al.[15] state elsewhere, 'the time dimension of a relationship requires managers to shift their emphasis away from each discrete purchase or sale towards tracking how things unfold in the relationship over time and changing these when appropriate'

- network structures allow organisations to bring resources (especially expertise), together on a long-term basis to reduce costs, which is why enterprises in Europe and the USA are increasingly turning to global networking as a means of gaining access to low-cost overseas inputs

- networks relate to all aspects of the supply chain, including marketing and distribution, but this book is primarily concerned with networking with suppliers.

4.3.2 Network basics

The typical supply chain network is shown in Figure 4.6.

Figure 4.6 Typical supply chain network

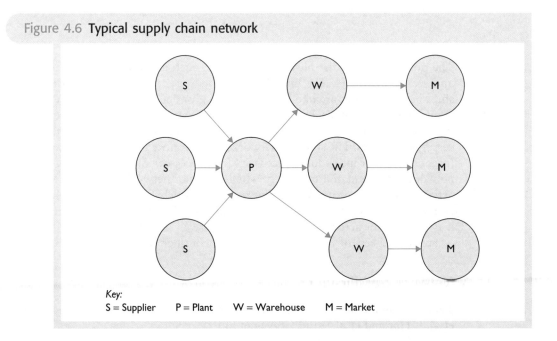

Key:
S = Supplier   P = Plant   W = Warehouse   M = Market

Figure 4.7 Network model

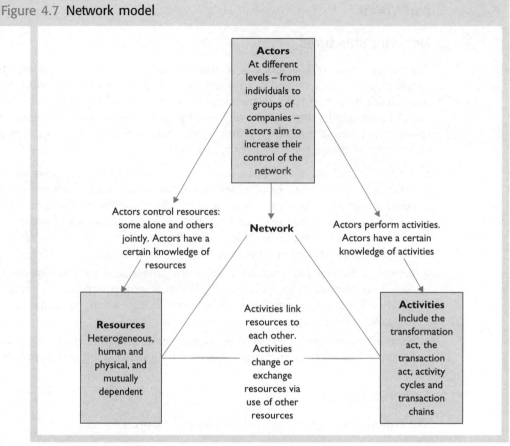

Source: Hakansson, H., *Industrial Technological Development*, Croom Helm, 1987

The nodes represent the business or 'actors', such as suppliers, producers, customers and service providers. The links between the nodes represent relationships. Relationships between actors are like bridges as they give one actor access to the resources and competences of another. Harland[16] points out that some researchers use the term 'network' to describe a network of actors, while others use it to discuss a network of processes or activities. The study of networks can therefore be related to networks of actors (organisations or individuals), activities (or processes) and resources. When discussing networks, it is essential to specify whether or not networks of actors or networks of activities are being considered. The network model shown in Figure 4.7[17] shows the connections between actors, resources and activities and how, via their relationships, it is possible for actors to mobilise resources.

Further aspects of network structure are considered in section 4.4 below.

4.3.3 Network classifications

Typical of numerous classifications of networks are those of Snow et al.,[18] Lamming et al.,[19] Harland et al.[20] and Craven et al.[21]

Figure 4.8 **Common network types**

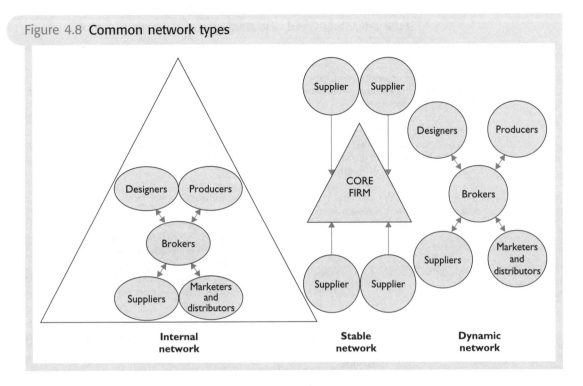

Snow et al.[18] distinguish between internal, stable and dynamic structures – shown in Figure 4.8.

Internal network firms own most or all of the assets associated with the business and endeavour to capture entrepreneurial and market benefits without engaging in much outsourcing.

In *stable networks*, assets are owned by several firms but dedicated to a particular business. As shown, the suppliers nestle round a large core enterprise, either providing supplies or distributing its products.

With *dynamic networks*, there is extensive outsourcing. The lead firm identifies and assembles assets owned wholly or largely by other enterprises on whose core skills it relies. Examples of such core skills cited by Snow et al. are manufacturing, such as Motorola, research and development, such as Reebok, or design and assembly, such as Dell Computing. In dynamic organisations, key managers create and assemble resources controlled by outside resources and can therefore be thought of as brokers. Some enterprises rely purely on brokering and are therefore virtual organisations. In virtual organisations an enterprise designs and markets a product but outsources manufacturing to specialist providers and possibly distributors. Some advantages and disadvantages of dynamic networks are shown in Table 4.1.

Lamming et al.,[19] building on earlier work by Fisher,[22] suggest two distinctive types of supply networks relating, respectively, to products that are 'innovative-unique' (such as drugs, communications technology and electronics) and 'functional' (such as canned soft drinks, brake cylinders and car window wipers). In each case, a distinction is made, as shown in Table 4.2, between products of higher or lower complexity, competitive priorities and sharing of resources and information.

Table 4.1 Some advantages and disadvantages of dynamic networks

Advantages	Disadvantages
Networks allow organisations to specialise in what they do best and, thus, develop distinctive competences	Network structures have less control over operations. Even slight misunderstandings can result in product misspecifications
Networks can display the technical specialisation of functional structures, the market responsiveness of divisions and the balanced orientation of matrix structures	Network organisations are vulnerable to competition from their manufacturing contractors
Synergy – that is, the whole is greater than the sum of its parts – results from the cooperation of the network partners	If a network partner fails or goes out of business, the entire network can break down. It is difficult to guard innovations developed, designed and manufactured by network partners. Dynamic organisations lose their organic advantage when they become legalistic, secretive and too binding on the other partners

Table 4.2 Characteristics of supply networks for products (Lamming et al., 2000)

Characteristics	Products	
	Innovative and unique	Functional
Higher complexity	*Competitive priority*: speed, flexibility, quality, supremacy. *Sharing of resources and information*: large amounts of non-strategic information enabled by IT – problematic when involving sensitive information and knowledge	*Competitive priority*: cost reduction, quality, sustainability, service. *Sharing of resources and information*: large amounts of non-strategic information enabled by IT – generally unproblematic, but may include cost breakdowns and strategic knowledge
Low complexity	*Competitive priority*: speed and flexibility, innovation, quality, supremacy. *Sharing of resources and information*: problematic, exchange of sensitive information and knowledge – IT less critical	*Competitive priority*: cost (by high-volume production), service. *Sharing of resources and information*: generally unproblematic – may include cost and strategic knowledge – IT less critical

Harland et al.[20] provides a taxonomy of supplier networks based on two dimensions, which are, first, whether the supply network operates under dynamic or stabilised (routinised) conditions and, second, whether the influence of the focal firm over other supply chain actors, such as customers and suppliers, is high or low.

The contributions of the above dimensions provide four types of supply networks, as shown in Table 4.3. The taxonomy outlined in the table aims to provide insight into ways of networking for managers to employ in dealing with different types of networks.

Table 4.3 **A taxonomy of supply networks (Harland et al., 2001)**

Network designation	Dynamic/stability factors	Factors in focal firm influence	Applicable networking activities
Type 1 dynamic/low degree of focal firm influence	Internal process characteristics: ■ high process variety, including large numbers of network configurations, low volumes or both ■ sometimes high levels of promotional activity External market conditions: ■ uncertain demand ■ many competitors ■ high frequency of new product launches	Low influence due to: ■ direct network value added by focal firm producing low volumes relative to other network players ■ focal firm has low profile in the network relating to its lack of drive to innovate	■ Human resources integration and knowledge capture within the network ■ Encouraging other network players to invest in innovation by motivating (incentives) and risk and benefit sharing ■ Demand management problems – buffer stocks ■ Coping with the network
Type 2 dynamic/high degree of focal firm influence	As above	High influence due to: ■ direct value added by focal firm producing large volumes relative to other network players ■ reputation for innovative capability ■ focal firm provides access to rest of the network, either as a bottleneck or a conduit, which will influence the network	■ Human resources integration and knowledge capture to advance innovation ■ Motivation and risk and benefit sharing less critical to focal firm but still important for successful partnerships ■ Focal firm in a position to choose partners ■ Focal firm's decisions have implications for other actors ■ Demand management problems – buffer stocks managing the network
Type 3 routinised/ low degree of focal firm influence	Internal process characteristics: ■ low variety ■ high volumes ■ promotional/activities not frequent enough to make network dynamic External market conditions: ■ stable demand ■ few competitors ■ difficulty of switching ■ low frequency of product launches	Low influence due to Type 1 factors	■ Process rather than product innovation critical to improving operational processes. Enhance quality and minimise costs ■ Critical activities are: – equipment resource integration and information processing – motivation and risk and benefit sharing ■ Stock minimisation ■ Coping with network
Type 4 routinised/ high degree of focal firm influence	As Type 3	High influence due to Type 2 factors Focal firm often in a position to gain control of the network	■ Focal firm in a position to choose with whom to work and make decisions on behalf of the supply network ■ Equipment resource integration and information processing ■ Stock minimisation ■ Managing network

Figure 4.9 **Classification of network organisations**

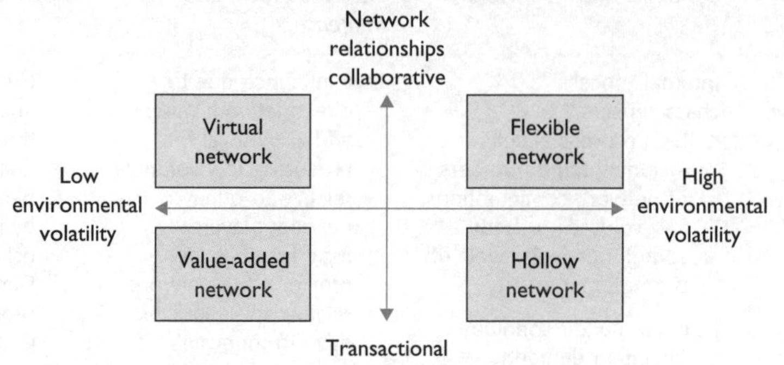

Source: based on Archol (1991), Powell (1990), Quinn (1992) and Webster (1992), from Craven et al. (1996) 'New organisational forms for competing in highly dynamic environments', *British Journal of Management*, Vol. 7, pp. 203–18

Craven et al.[21] proposed two dimensions for the classification of network organisations: the volatility of environmental changes and the type of relationship between network members, whether it is collaborative or transactional.

Highly volatile situations require that enterprises should have:

■ flexible internal structures capable of rapid adjustment to new environmental conditions

■ flexible external relationships that allow for alteration or termination in a relatively short time period.

Network relationships may range from highly collaborative to largely transactional links. *Transactional linkages* imply discrete exchanges of values where a major issue is price, typified in the economics model of buyer–seller relationships. Transactional links are most likely to occur between parties that do not require collaboration.

Collaborative links may:

■ involve various forms of interorganisational cooperation and partnering, including the development of formal alliances and joint ventures

■ considerate interactions between organisations to achieve common objectives

■ continuing relationships between the parties that, when they are long-term ones, are likely to involve strategic alliances as a networking method.

Based on the two dimensions of volatility and relationships, Craven classifies networks as hollow, flexible, value-added and virtual, as shown in Figure 4.9.

As shown by Figure 4.9, virtual and value-added networks are appropriate to conditions of low environmental volatility. When environmental volatility is high, flexible and hollow networks are applicable. Conversely, value-added and hollow networks are appropriate to transactional relationships. When relationships are collaborative, virtual and flexible networks are applicable. The conditions under which a core organisation is most likely to employ each of the four networks are set out in Table 4.4.

Table 4.4 **Characteristics of alternative network forms, from Craven et al., 1996**

Characteristics	Flexible network	Hollow network	Virtual network	Value-added network
Environmental fluctuations	Short-term	Short-term	Long-term	Long-term
Network coordinator/ member relationships	Collaborative but flexible	Transactional	Collaborative (vertical and horizontal)	Transactional
End-user relationships	Transactional	Collaborative	Collaborative/ transactional	Transactional
Market structure	Diverse end-users' needs/wants	Highly segmented end-user focus	Complicated, segmented and dynamic	Diffused preferences difficult to segment
Technological complexity	Production/ distribution processes are complicated	Technology is centred on network's members	High level of technology involving an array of capabilities	Product innovation
Core competency of coordinating organisation	Market knowledge and process design leveraging with specialists	Marketing function/focus	Product innovation and production skills	Product design, production and marketing coordination
Network members' core competency	Specialists	Network members' capabilities matched to end-users' needs	Market access and specialised technological capabilities	Specialists in narrowly defined functions with major cost advantages

4.3.4 Network configuration and optimisation

Configuration

Deciding the configuration of the network – the number, location, capacity and technology of suppliers, manufacturing plants, warehouses and distribution channels – is important for the following reasons:

- the strategic configuration of the supply chain influences tactical decisions relating to the aggregate quantities and material flows relating to the purchasing, processing and distribution of products
- the supply chain configuration involves the commitment of substantial capital resources, such as plant and machinery, for long time periods
- factors such as changes in consumer demand and technology and global sourcing lead to changes in network configurations. There is, however, evidence that configurations, once determined, are difficult to change.

Arbulu and Tommelein[23] studied supply chain practices for pipe supports used in the construction of power plants. A pipe support is an assembly of components including springs, bearings and pipe shoes (pieces of pipe that transfer gravity loads to a structure underneath the pipe). Although relatively inexpensive, problems relating to the design and supply of pipe supports can compromise the success of the overall power plant project.

Arbulu and Tommelein identify the following five supply chain configurations for the supply of pipe supports.

- *Configuration 1*: Engineering firm designs the pipe supports. Supplier details, fabricates and supplies the supports. Contractor installs. (This is the common practice.)
- *Configuration 2*: Engineering firm routes pipes and performs pipe stress analysis. Supplier designs, details, fabricates and supplies the supports. Contractor installs.
- *Configuration 3*: Supplier fully designs pipe supports. Contractor installs.
- *Configuration 4*: Contractor takes responsibility for pipe support design and fabrication, though, usually, subcontracts the work and then installs.
- *Configuration 5*: Fabricator takes responsibility for pipe support design and fabrication. Contractor installs.

Optimisation

The optimisation of supply chain networks is concerned with decisions relating to what constitutes the ideal number of operating facilities and their locations, as well as the amount of supplies to purchase, the quantity of outputs to manufacturing and the flow of such outputs through the network to minimise total costs.

Network optimisation models (NOM) aim to facilitate optimal materials sourcing, processing, activity and material and product flows throughout the supply chain, taking into account forecasts of future demand. They are a measure of the performance of all the key supply chain operating characteristics and provide indications of risks and returns under a variety of operating environments. A large number of commercial off-the-shelf (COTS) supply chain optimisation software packages are available that focus on both strategic and tactical issues.

4.4 Factors in configurations

Network configurations are contingent and will vary widely among organisations. Lambert et al.[24] state that an explicit knowledge and understanding of how the network structure is configured is a key element of supply chain management and identify three primary elements: identification of the supply chain members, structural dimensions and the horizontal position of the focal enterprise.

- *Identification of the supply chain members* – that is, all the organisations with which the focal company interacts directly or indirectly via its suppliers or customers from the point of origin to the point of consumption. These may be divided into primary and supporting network members. The former are those who actually perform operational or managerial activities in the processes leading to the production of a final product. The latter are organisations that provide resources, knowledge, utilities or assets for the primary members of the network, such as those that lease machinery to a contractor or banks that lend money to a retailer.

- *The structural dimensions of the network* These dimensions are the horizontal and vertical structures and the horizontal position of the focal company within the parameters of the supply chain. The *horizontal structure* is the number of tiers across the supply chain. Supply chains may be short with few tiers or long with many tiers. The *vertical structure* is the number of suppliers or customers represented within each tier. Thus, an enterprise can have a narrow or wide vertical structure with few or many suppliers or customers respectively.

- *Horizontal positioning* This refers to the positioning of the focal organisation in the supply chain. An enterprise may be located at or near the initial source of the supply, at or near to the ultimate customer or at some intermediate supply chain position.

4.4.1 Tiering

Tiering levels

Lamming[25] points out that the terms 'first' and 'second' tiers are 'used to indicate the degree of influence the supplier exerts in the supply chain, rather than some fixed position in the hierarchy', and offers the following definitions:

> First-tier suppliers are those that integrate for direct supply to the assembler or who have a significant technical influence on the assembly while supplying indirectly.

> Second-tier suppliers are those that supply components to first-tier firms for integration into systems or provide some support service, such as metal finishing, etc.

Tiering may extend further. Exceptionally, an enterprise may have six or more tiers.

Reasons for tiering

Lamming shows that tiers may form for three reasons:

- because the assembler may require first-tier suppliers to integrate diverse technologies not possessed by one organisation
- components required for systems will be very specialised and, thus, made by a small number of (large) firms, in large quantities (such as electronic parts), so it is sensible for first-tier suppliers to buy these from specialist makers
- the third level of subcontracted work covers simple, low value-added items required by first- and second-tier suppliers, such as presswork, fasteners.

Responsibilities for tiering

First-tier suppliers are direct suppliers, usually making high-cost, complicated assemblies. They are empowered to relay the assembler's standards to second-tier or indirect suppliers and are responsible for large numbers of second-tier suppliers.

The responsibilities of first-tier suppliers as identified by Lamming include:

- research and development, especially relating to technologies that are being applied to the assembler's product for the first time
- management of second-tier and lower-tier suppliers, including integration previously undertaken by the assembly

- true JIT supply
- customer-dedicated staff who work in association with the design and production departments of the assembler
- warranties and customer claims.

Some consequences of tiering

The key word at all levels of tiering levels is *collaboration* as much of the competitive advantage required for lean production (described below) derives from the ability to deal with subcontractors as collaborators or partners.

Where tiering is carried out for either the first or second reasons stated above, the relationship between the two suppliers becomes more akin to a strategic joint venture than a purchasing link. The product technology resides in both firms, so the first-tier supplier would find it just as difficult to replace the specialist second-tier supplier as vice versa. In this situation, the suppliers may even set up special companies to conduct business as joint ventures.

Tiering and linking

Tiering is closely related to linking.

Lambert et al.[26] identified four 'fundamentally different' process links that can be identified between supply chain members. These links provide indications of how closely focal firm executives integrate and manage links further away from the first tier.

- *Managed process links* The focal company integrates and manages process links with first-tier customers and suppliers, although it may be actively involved in the management of other process links beyond the first tier. These are critical processes in the supply chain shown in Figure 4.10 (the managed process links are shown by the thickest solid lines).
- *Monitored process links* The focal company monitors or audits as frequently as necessary how the process links are integrated and managed between other member companies. These will be less critical but still important processes (in Figure 4.10, the monitored process links are indicated by the thick dashed lines).
- *Not-managed process links* The focal company fully trusts other supply chain members to manage the process links appropriately or, because of limited resources, leaves it to them. These will be links that the focal company is not actively involved in or critical enough to use resources for monitoring. Thus, a manufacturer may have one or more suppliers of wooden pallets. Normally, the focal company will not choose to integrate and manage the links beyond the pallet manufacturer all the way back to the growing of the trees (in Figure 4.10, the not-managed process tasks are shown by the thin solid lines).
- *Non-member process links* Non-member process tasks are links between members of the focal company's supply chain and non-members of the supply chain. Such non-members links are not considered to be links of the company's supply chain structure, but they can, and often will, affect the performance of the focal company and its supply chain – a supplier to the focal company may also be a supplier to a competitor, for example. Such a supply chain structure may have implications for the supplier's allocation of manpower to the focal company's development process,

Figure 4.10 **Types of intercompany business process links**

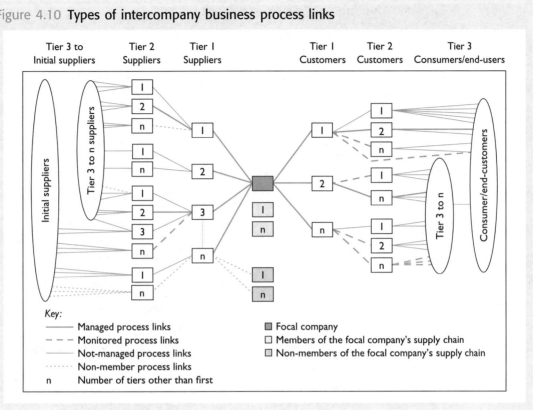

Key:
——— Managed process links
– – – Monitored process links
——— Not-managed process links
········· Non-member process links
n   Number of tiers other than first

■ Focal company
□ Members of the focal company's supply chain
□ Non-members of the focal company's supply chain

availability of supplies in times of shortage or con-fidentially of information (in Figure 4.10 non-member process links are shown by the thin dashed lines).

Lean organisations

4.5.1 Lean thinking

The core concept of lean thinking is the Japanese term *muda*, exemplified by the practices of Japanese motor manufacturers described by Womack et al.[27] in their book *Machines That Changed the World*. *Muda* means 'waste' or any human activity that absorbs resources but creates no value. Examples of *muda* are spoiled production, unnecessary processing steps, the purposeless movement or movements of employees and goods, time wasted in waiting for materials, uneconomic or unnecessary inventories and goods and services that fail to meet customers' requirements. Lean thinking is mean because it does more with less.

A report by research teams from the Universities of Bath and Warwick[28] on the 'people' implications of lean organisations identified three phases of lean development and their associated production and human resources approaches. These are shown in Table 4.5.

Table 4.5 **The three phases of lean development**

Phase	Concerned with	Approaches
1 Leanness as transition	Efforts made by the organisation to become lean	Delayering – flattening the organisation Downsizing – a reduction in the workforce Outsourcing – focusing on core activities and subcontracting non-core activities to outside providers
2 Leanness as an outcome	Assumed structural flexibility following a period of delayering, downsizing and outsourcing	Business process re-engineering (BPR) The fundamental rethinking and radical redesign of business processes to achieve dramatic improvements in critical contemporary measures of performance, such as cost, quality, service, speed Lean production characterised by: ■ elimination of waste in terms of both material and human resources ■ low inventories ■ zero defects – prevention rather than rectification of faults ■ integrated production chains ■ teamworking ■ involvement of all employees and suppliers in a continuous process to improve products and job design
3 Leanness as a process	Focuses attention on the attributes of those organisations that can respond to environmentally produced change	Total quality management (TQM). Management philosophy and company practices that aim to harness the human and material resources of the organisation in the most effective way to achieve the objectives of the organisation just-in-time (JIT). An inventory control philosophy whose goal is to maintain just enough material in just the right place at just the right time to make just the right amount of product

4.5.2 Lean production

Some aspects of lean production, such as the attempt to eliminate waste, the purchase of whole assemblies and tiering, have been referred to above. Other aspects of lean production, as identified by Womack et al., include the following.

■ Target costing – for example, a car assembler establishes a target price for the vehicle, then the assembler and suppliers work backwards to ascertain how the car can be made for the price, while allowing a reasonable profit for both the assembler and suppliers. This differs from the traditional approach in which:

$$\text{Sales price} = \text{Cost} + \text{Profit}$$

The lean production approach is:

$$\text{Profit} = \text{Sales price} - \text{Cost}$$

■ The use of value engineering, value analysis and learning curves to reduce initial and subsequent cost of suppliers.

■ The use of cross-functional teams of highly skilled workers and highly flexible automated machines.

■ A just-in-time (JIT) pull system in which nothing is moved or produced until the previous process is completed.

■ Zero defective parts. When a supplier fails to meet quality or reliability requirements, a cooperative effort is made to ascertain the cause. In the interim, part of the business is transferred to another supplier.

■ Cooperation between the assembler and first-tier suppliers effected by supplier associations. They meet to share new findings on better ways to make parts. Some companies also have associations with their second-tier suppliers.

■ After negotiations, the assembler and supplier agree on a cost-reduction curve over the four-year life of the product. Any supplier-derived cost savings beyond those agreed go to the supplier.

■ Relationships between the assembler and suppliers are based on a 'basic contract' that expresses a long-term commitment to working together for mutual benefit. The contract also lays down rules relating to prices, quality assurance, ordering, delivery, proprietary rights and materials supply.

4.5.3 Lean production structures

Lean production, as Toni and Tonchia[29] point out, leads to a management by process organisation designed to link all the activities in order to achieve the unified objective of customer satisfaction in all its aspects.

The primary justification of management by process is to overcome functional rigidity (functional silos) where single functions of units often have different and contradictory performance objectives (such as manufacturing versus delivery punctuality).

In a manufacturing organisation, three processes can be considered fundamental:

■ product development
■ manufacturing or assembly (materials processing)
■ logistics (material handling).

Features of process-orientated organisations are:

■ they are end product-orientated and determined by the aggregation of competences and activities
■ responsibility is linked to roles rather than levels
■ they become horizontal, as with materials management and supply chains
■ their aim is the integration of subtasks, with functional responsibilities coordinated by the process logic.

4.5.4 Advantages and disadvantages of lean production

Advantages include greater flexibility, reduced waste, quicker response to customers' demands, shorter throughput time, lower supervision costs, lower stock levels and improved quality as feedback is quicker.

Trade union objections to lean production include:

- increases in workers' responsibilities can lead to pressure and anxiety not present in traditional systems
- expansion of job requirements without comparable increases in pay
- the company is the main beneficiary of employee-generated improvements.

The two principal limitations of lean production, however, are its inability to deal with turbulence and change and that the pursuit of perfection may eliminate the scope for flexibility. Lean production depends on a stable business environment as then it can maximise its efficiencies of scale.

4.6 Agile organisations and production

Agile production is the latest stage of a development away from the mass production of the 1970s, through the decentralised production of the 1980s and on to the supply chain management and lean production of the 1990s.

4.6.1 Drivers of agility

The main drivers of agility include rapidly changing and unpredictable markets, the rapid rates of technological innovation, customers' requirements for customisation and choice, competitive priorities of responsiveness, shorter lifecycles, concern for the environment and international competitiveness. Goldman et al.[30] state that the four underlying components of agility are:

- delivering value to the customer
- being ready for change
- valuing human knowledge
- forming virtual partnerships.

4.6.2 Agile characteristics

Based on Goldman, Aitken et al.[31] have identified the core characteristics of agile manufacture shown in Table 4.6.

4.6.3 Postponement

Postponement and decoupling are important concepts of agility. By making customised product changes as close as possible to the time of purchase by the end-customer it is possible to provide a wide variety of customised products without incurring high inventory, processing and transportation costs. Suppose the manufacture and assembly of a product requires 40 steps. By proceeding as far as step 30 and then putting the partly completed product into inventory, the final 10 steps have been postponed.

Table 4.6 **Comparison of lean and agile production systems**

Factor	Lean production	Agile production
Primary purposes	Meeting predictable demand efficiently at the lowest possible cost Elimination of waste from the supply chain	Rapid response to unpredictable demand to minimise stockouts, forced markdowns and obsolete inventory
Manufacturing focus	Maintenance of a high average utilisation unit	Deployment of excess buffer capability
Inventory strategy	High stock turnover and minimum inventory	Deployment of significant buffer stocks of parts to respond to demand
Lead time focus	Shortened lead time, providing it does not increase cost	Investing aggressively in resources that will reduce lead times
Approach to supplier selection	Selecting for cost and quality	Selecting primarily for speed, flexibility and quality
Supply linkages	Emphasis on long-term supply chain partnerships that are consolidated over time	Emphasis on virtual supply chains where partnerships are reconfigured according to new market opportunities
Performance measurement	Emphasis on world class measures based on such criteria as quality and productivity	Emphasis on customer-facing metrics, such as orders met on time, in full
Work organisation	Emphasis on work standardisation – doing it the same way every time	Emphasis on self-management and ability to respond immediately to new opportunities from all involved in work processes
Work planning and control	Emphasis on the protection of operation's core by a fixed period in the planning cycle to help balance resources, synchronise material movements and reduce waste	Emphasis on the need for immediate interpretation of customer demand and instantaneous response

The above is an example of *manufacturing postponement*, the object of which is to maintain flexibility by keeping products in a neutral or uncommitted state for as long as possible. Examples of manufacturing postponement are found in vehicle manufacturers when colours and non-standard components or additions are deferred until the receipt of specific instructions from the customer. In housebuilding, the basic shell may be constructed, but kitchen and bathroom fitting and decorating will not proceed until the requirements of the individual customer have been ascertained.

There is also *geographic*, or *logistics*, *postponement*, which is the exact opposite. The basic notion of geographic postponement according to Bowersox et al [32] is 'to build and stock a full line inventory at one or two strategic locations'. Forward deployment of inventory is postponed until customers' orders are received. An example is the keeping of critical spares at a service centre to ensure their rapid availability to customers. Once an order for spares is received, it is transmitted electronically to the central service centre, from where the required items are rapidly transported to the customer and replacements manufactured. The outcome is highly reliable customer service with low inventory.

Van Hoek[33] has identified the following advantages of postponement:

- inventory can be held at a generic level so that there will be fewer stock variants and, therefore, less total inventory
- because inventory is generic, its flexibility is greater – that is, the same components or modules can be embodied on a variety of end products
- forecasting is easier at the generic level than for finished products
- the ability to customise products locally means that a higher level of variety may be offered at a lower cost.

4.6.4 Decoupling

The decoupling point is defined by Christopher[34] as 'the point to which real demand penetrates upstream in a supply chain'. Decoupling is closely associated with postponement and the type of customer demand. Figure 4.11 shows how the positioning of the decoupling point changes with different supply chain structures.

The organisations downstream from the decoupling point are organised for agility and the ability to cope with variability in demand volume and high levels of product variety. Upstream organisations work to a stable demand with relatively low variety and can therefore focus on lean, low-cost manufacture.

Christopher and Towill[36] point out that, in real-world supply chains, there are actually two decoupling points. The first relates to 'material' and is where strategic inventory is held in as generic a form as possible. Inventory should therefore lie as far downstream in the supply chain and as near to the final marketplace as possible. The second is the 'information' decoupling point. Ideally this should lie as far as possible

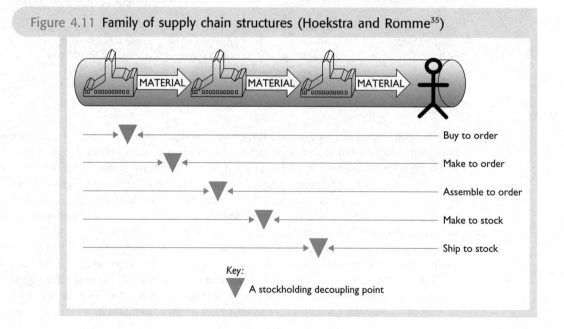

Figure 4.11 **Family of supply chain structures (Hoekstra and Romme[35])**

upstream as, in effect, it is the furthest point to which information on real final demand penetrates. Reference to the concept of 'leagility' is made in section 4.6.6 below.

4.6.5 Enablers of agile manufacturing

Gunasekaran[37] identified seven enablers of agile manufacturing:

- *virtual enterprise* each functional aspect of the manufacturing design, production and marketing of a product may be performed by many different organisations using an Internet-assisted manufacturing system
- *physically distributed teams and manufacturing* 'the physically distributed enterprise is a temporary alliance of partner enterprises located all over the world, each contributing their core competences to take advantage of a specific business opportunity or fend off a market threat'
- *rapid partnership formation tools/metrics* achievable by means of such tools as IT, including the Internet, EDI, quality function development (QFD) techniques and financial and non-financial metrics
- *concurrent engineering* provides a quick response to the need for shorter product development cycles and appropriate tools for this include functional analysis, computer-aided manufacturing (CAM), solid modelling, value engineering, failure mode and effect analysis (FEMA) and robust engineering
- *integrated product/production/business information systems* the diverse systems of participating organisations must be integrated, either by redesign or the adoption of strategies aimed at the sharing of information by means of advanced technologies, such as the Internet and EDI
- *rapid prototyping tools* 'prototyping refers to the design and generation of an early version of a product. Advanced computer technologies such as computer-aided design (CAD), computer-aided estimates (CAE) and computer engineering (CE) help to improve responsiveness to customer requirements by reducing product development times and non-value added activities at the design stage'
- *e-commerce* this can improve responsiveness to customers' demands by directly collecting their requirements via an online communication system, such as the Internet, and reducing cycle and order fulfilment times.

4.6.6 Lean and agile production

Lean and agile production are sometimes regarded as synonymous, but there are significant differences. Aitken et al.[38] note that 'Webster's Dictionary makes the distinction clearly when it defines lean as "containing little fat" whereas agile is defined as "nimble"'. Some comparisons between lean and agile production systems are shown in Table 4.6.

Naylor et al.[39] distinguish between the two terms as follows:

Leanness means developing a value stream to eliminate all waste, including time, and to enable a level schedule.

Agility means using market knowledge and a virtual corporation to exploit profitable opportunities in a volatile marketplace.

An alternative comparison of lean and agile supply is shown in Table 4.7.[40]

Table 4.7 **Comparison of lean and agile supply: the distinguishing attributes**

Distinguishing attributes	Lean supply	Agile supply
Typical products	Commodities	Fashion goods
Marketplace demand	Predictable	Volatile
Product variety	Low	High
Product lifecycle	Long	Short
Customer drivers	Cost	Availability
Profit margin	Low	High
Dominant costs	Physical costs	Marketability costs
Stockout penalties	Long-term, contractual	Immediate and volatile
Purchasing policy	Buy goods	Assign capacity
Information enrichment	Highly desirable	Obligatory
Forecasting mechanism	Algorithm	Consultative

In general, lean production is best in situations where volumes are high, variety low and demand predictable. Conversely, agile production is suited to volatile demand and where products are customised. Thus, as Mason-Jones et al.[41] observe, 'fashion products, such as trendy clothing, have a short lifecycle and high demand uncertainty and therefore expose the supply chain to both stockouts and obsolescence risks. Commodities e.g. tinned soups have relatively long lifecycles and low demand uncertainty due to the fact that they tend to be well-established products with a predictable consumption pattern.'

Leanness and agility are complementary rather than competing terms and leanness should often be regarded as an enabler of agility. As indicated in section 4.6.4, the strategic use of a decoupling point may combine leanness and agility and thereby exploit the benefits of both approaches. Naylor et al.[42] have termed this combined approach 'leagility', which they define as:

> The combination of the lean and agile paradigms within a total supply chain strategy by positioning the decoupling point so as to best suit the need for responding to a volatile demand yet providing level scheduling upstream from the marketplace.

4.7 Supply and value chain mapping

A map is a visual representation of some actuality. Maps also enable us to comprehend and communicate information. Maps assist comprehension as a picture is 'worth a thousand words'. Maps also communicate specific and general information. Architects' plans and road maps communicate specific and general information respectively. A supply network diagram is a form of supply chain mapping.

4.7.1 Forms of mapping

As supply and value chain mapping is undertaken for a specific purpose – normally for supply chain redesign or modification or the elimination or reduction of waste – the number of options for mapping to meet the needs of users is large. Gardner and Cooper[43] distinguish between strategic supply chain mapping and process mapping

Table 4.8 **Distinguishing strategic supply chain and process mapping**

Characteristics	Supply chain mapping	Process mapping
Orientation	*External*: focuses on how goods, information and money flow upstream and downstream and through a firm	*Internal* (typically): focuses on a single operation or system with an enterprise
Level of detail	*Low to moderate*: emphasises high-level measures, such as volume, cost or lead time. Gives an overall perspective on how processes work together between enterprises. May exclude non-critical entities	*High*: breaks down a process into activities and steps. Every step includes information to characterise the system being mapped
Purpose	*Strategic*: mapping aims to create a supply chain conforming to a strategy or ensure that the current chain fulfils that strategy adequately	*Tactical*: process map originates from the recognition of a problem area and the need to improve operating efficiency. Goal is to make changes in current operations. Efforts normally limited to one process or function at a time

regarding three characteristics: orientation, level of detail and purpose. These distinctions are set out in Table 4.8.

4.7.2 The purpose of supply chain mapping

Gardner and Cooper[44] state that a well-executed strategic supply chain map can:

> . . . enhance the strategic planning process, case distribution of key information, facilitate supply chain redesign or modification, clarify channel dynamics, provide a common perspective, enhance communications, enable monitoring of supply chain strategy and provide a basis for supply chain analysis . . . Thus a map can be quite helpful in understanding a firm's supply chain, for evaluating the current supply chain and for contemplating realignment of a supply chain.

4.7.3 The methodology of mapping

A supply chain map may be linked to or built directly from a database or built by hand. Gardner and Cooper state that 'the complexity of mapping is influenced by three supply chain map attributes: geometry, perspective and implementation issues'.

Geometry is concerned with such aspects as:

- the number of sequential business units performing transactions leading to the final consumer
- direction – whether it is supplier- or customer-orientated or both
- length – the number of tiers up and down
- aggregation (width) – the degree of specificity within a tier, which may be high (one box per tier), medium (types of firms at each level identified) or low (some firms are named at each level)
- spatial – is the map geographically representative?

Perspective is concerned with issues relating to:

■ the focal point – whether the maps takes a firm- or industry-centred view

■ scope – whether the breadth of product coverage included in the map is SBU-wide or by product category, product or component

■ whether or not the map includes key processes beyond logistics

■ whether or not the map includes a complete set of key business processes

■ whether or not the map includes reverse logistics and other feedback loops.

Implementation issues:

■ whether the density of information integrated into the visual map is high or low

■ whether or not the map is linked to an existing corporate or supply chain database

■ how the completed map shall be made available – paper, electronically or on the Web?

4.7.4 Value stream mapping tools

Hines and Rich[45] distinguish between traditional supply or value chains and value streams. The former include the complete activities of all the companies involved, while the latter refers only to the specific parts of the firms that actually add value to the product or service under consideration.

Hines and Rich identify seven mapping tools designed to reduce or eliminate seven forms of waste in a manufacturing organisation – overproduction, waiting, transportation, inappropriate processing, unnecessary inventory, unnecessary motion and defects. These take three forms, which are product (not identified by inspection and passed on to customers), service (not directly relating to products but to service, such as late delivery or incorrect documentation) and internal scrap (defects identified during inspection). The seven mapping tools are described in Table 4.9.

It is impractical in this book to give a detailed explanation of the implementation of the above tools[46] so we will confine ourselves to the following observations.

The process activity mapping tool provides an example of a typical mapping exercise directed at eliminating or reducing waste.

The first step is the preparation of a *process map* – a detailed flow chart that indicates every activity involved in making or doing something. It is critical to include all activities – not only those that are obvious.

Once the process map has been developed, a value chart can be constructed that attaches a cost or value to every activity. This cost is obtained after considering factors such as the machine or area used for the activity, distance moved, time taken and number of people employed.

Activities fall into four categories:

■ production or service time (value-added activity)

■ inspection time – performing quality control (non-value-added activity)

■ transfer time – movement of products or components (non-value-added activity)

■ idle time – storage time or timewasting during the production process (non-value-added activity).

Table 4.9 **Hines and Rich's seven value stream mapping tools**

Mapping tools	Purpose and application
Process activity mapping	Reducing waste by eliminating unnecessary activities, simplifying other activities or changing process sequences
Supply chain response matrix	Reducing lead times and inventory amounts
Production variety funnel	Targeting inventory reduction and changes in the processing of products in companies with varying activity patterns
Quality filter mapping	Identifying, for the purpose of improvement, the location of product and service defects, internal scrap, and other problems, inefficiencies and wasted effort
Demand amplification mapping	Identifying demand changes along the supply chain within varying time buckets to manage or reduce fluctuations in regular, exceptional and promotional demand
Decision point analysis	Particularly applicable for regular, unvarying production of multiple identical items, as in a chemical plant. Involves identifying the point at which products stop being made in accordance with actual demand and start to be made against forecasts alone. Identifying this point indicates whether processes are aligned with push or pull philosophies
Physical structure	Overviewing a particular supply chain from an industry perspective. This information may result in a redesign along the lines indicated for process activity mapping

The lead time for the process is therefore:

Production time + Non-value-added time

While in theory inspection and transfer time are regarded as non-value-added activities, they cannot, in practice, be completely eliminated.

The final stage involves using the process map and value chart to identify where savings can be made or value added.

Case study

Petersons is a manufacturer of mechanical handling equipment used by airlines, food, mining and sea port organisations. The company, a private limited company, was founded in 1960 by the present Managing Director, Joe Peterson. He has three sons, all of whom have worked their way through the business and are now directors. Other senior managers have all served a long time in the business. The business reached its peak of 300 employees 15 years ago. Since then, there has been a steady decline to the existing workforce of 180. Petersons has a small foundry and a well-equipped machine shop, mainly employed making small gears and turned parts. The company assembles its own gearboxes. A large percentage, by value, of gears and other components are bought ▶

because of their complexity or size. There are other purchases, including steel sections, plate and tubing, ball and roller bearings, conveyor belting, electric motors and an increasing amount of electronic control equipment.

The company keeps large stocks of spares and is proud of the fact that it can normally provide spares on demand for conveyor installations of up to 20 years ago. The current stock turn is 1.2 times per annum. There has been no analysis of the range of spares and the equipment it was designed for. It is probable that many of the spares will never be ordered by customers because they have disposed of the installation without telling Petersons.

The sales force amounts to five people, employed on an agency basis. They have large territories, including overseas, South Africa, USA and Scandinavia. There is no effective marketing or sales plan and the sales force makes its own plans for sales activities. Joe Peterson is an engineer by training and has little empathy with marketing and selling. In the past a lot of reputational selling has taken place. There remains a core of committed customers and the equipment has a reputation for quality. Of course, many of the original contacts were those of Joe Peterson.

There has been a continual loss of business. This has been caused by three main factors. First, the airlines and sea ports have not been investing in capital plant and equipment. Second, competitors have incorporated sophisticated electronic and computerised remote control technology into their products. Third, Petersons have not invested in CAD design systems, new manufacturing technology and not looked at outsourcing.

The Purchasing Manager has just retired and been replaced by Lucy Ashcroft, who has come from the automotive sector. She has produced a report that says there have to be radical changes to the relationships with suppliers, who are at arm's length, and the transactional way in which buying is undertaken. She is horrified at the extent of the spares inventory and the fact that customers do not have solus contracts for the supply of spares (meaning that they can go anywhere for spares). There is also too much working capital tied up in the business.

Joe Peterson has acknowledged the points with considerable grace and recognises that the skills needed to make significant business and purchasing changes are not present in the existing team. He is, of course, faced with other decisions, such as redundancy possibilities, capital investment in design capability, unless this is outsourced, a marketing campaign aimed at sectors not traditionally supplied by Petersons and investment in training and development.

Task

Prepare a report for the Board of Directors setting out your recommendations for change, including the impact on purchasing and supply chain management.

Discussion questions

4.1 Specialisation had its origins in the concept of the division of labour described by Adam Smith in *The Wealth of Nations* (1776). Smith showed that if a man set out to make pins by his unaided labour, he could scarcely produce one pin a day. When, however, even a few people divide up the work of pin making into tasks, such as measuring and cutting the wire, putting on the points and pinheads and so on, it is possible to produce thousands of pins daily. The concept of the division of labour led to mass production and assembly lines. Can you identify at least four advantages and disadvantages of specialisation?

4.2 What are the core competences of the organisation that is your present employer?

4.3 Why is communication the basis of all coordination?

4.4 Committees are another important coordination mechanism. Why, then, has a camel been described as 'a horse designed by a committee'?

4.5 Why are Theory Y managers sometimes unsuccessful?

4.6 Can you think of any examples of cultural control applied to working practices?

4.7 Give one example of each of the five types of power identified by French and Raven.

4.8 Attempt to draw a simple supply chain network for the supply of materials/components for a product with which you are familiar.

4.9 Why are so many new type structures described as 'boundary busting'?

4.10 Why is it important for a purchasing or supply chain professional to know whether they are employed by organisations concerned with innovative-unique or functional-type products?

4.11 What is the usefulness of Craven's classification of network organisations to the practical purchasing officer or supply chain manager?

4.12 How many tiers are involved in the supply of a product or assembly used by your organisation?

4.13 The three key characteristics of networks have been identified as:
   (a) transactional – what is exchanged between network members
   (b) the nature of links – the strengths and qualitative nature of the network relationships, such as the degree to which members honour their network obligations or agree about the appropriate behaviour in their relationships
   (c) cultural characteristics – how members are linked and the roles played by individuals within the network

   With reference to suppliers with whom you network, identify examples to illustrate each of the above characteristics.

4.14 Lamming has stated (in *Beyond Partnerships*, Prentice Hall, 1998, p. 32) that the comparison of the term 'lean' with 'the concept of removing bodily fat to reach fighting weight is appropriate'. Give examples of ways which, by adopting a lean philosophy, organisations can become more competitive.

4.15 Explain the following sentence: 'When it comes to agility, a supply network must be able to turn on a shilling, navigating the competitive waters like a canoe, not an ocean liner.' Why are many enterprises liners rather than canoes?

Past examination questions

1 Explain the concept of the supply chain and discuss the role of flow within it.
   CIPS, *Purchasing and Supply Chain Management 1: Strategy*, May 2003

2 Explain the underlying principles, features and application of the Boston Consulting Group (BG + CG) box used in portfolio analysis
   CIPS, *Purchasing and Supply Chain Management 1: Strategy*, May 2002

3 (a) Modern society is a 'now' society in that people want things instantly. List and explain the pressures this has placed on the supply chain.

   (b) How can the pressures you have identified in (a) be reduced, alleviated or eliminated.

Chartered Institute of Logistics and Transport,
Level 4: Supply Chain Elective Unit, mock examination

4 (a) What is meant by the term 'lean supply chain' and what are the principles of lean thinking?

   (b) What benefits or disbenefits does a lean supply chain provide for:

     (i) customers

     (ii) companies in the supply chain?

   (c) Explain the seven wastes associated with lean thinking and give examples of each for a food supply chain to supermarkets.

CILT (UK), Level 4 Professional Diploma in Logistics and Transport:
Supply Chain Elective Unit, mock examination

References

1 Mintzberg, H., *The Structure of Organisations*, Prentice Hall, 1979, p. 2

2 The main ideas about core competences were developed by Prahalad, C. K., and Hamel, G., in a series of articles in the *Harvard Business Review*, Vol. 88, 1990, and in their book *The Core Competence of the Corporation*, Harvard Business Press, 1990

3 Grinnel, S., and Apple, H. P., 'When two bosses are better than one', *Machine Design*, 9 January 1975, p. 86

4 McGregor, D. M., *The Human Side of Enterprise*, McGraw-Hill, 1960

5 As 1 above, Ch. 15

6 French, P., Jr., and Raven, B., 'The basis of social power' in Cartwright, D. (ed.), *Studies in Social Power*, Michigan Institute for Social Research, 1959

7 Hickson, D., et al., 'A strategic contingencies theory of organisational power', *Administrative Science Quarterley*, No. 16, 1971, pp. 216–19

8 As 1 above

9 Chandler, A. D., *Strategy and Structure: Chapters in the History of the Industrial Enterprise*, MIT Press, 1962

10 For a discussion of this point, see Banter, D. K., and Gogne, T. E., *Designing Effective Organisations*, Sage, 1995, Ch. 16

11 Waterman, R., 'The seven elements of strategic fit', *Journal of Business Strategy*, No. 3, 1982, pp. 68–72

12 Quinn, J. B., *Intelligent Enterprise*, Free Press, 1992

13 Hastings, C., *The New Organisation*, McGraw-Hill, 1993, pp. 7–8

14 Ford, D., Gadde, L-E., Hakansson, H., and Snehota, I., *Managing Business Relationships*, 2nd edn, John Wiley, 2003, p. 18

15 As 14 above, p. 38

16 Harland, C. M., 'Supply chain management: relationships, chains and networks', *British Journal of Management*, Vol. 7, March, 1996, Special Issue, pp. 63–80

17 This diagram, attributed to Hakansson, H., *Industrial Technological Development: A Network Approach*, 1987, Croom Helm, is used by Harland in 16 above.

18 Snow, C. C., Miles, R. E., and Coleman, H. J., 'Managing 21ˢᵗ century network organisations', *Organisational Dynamics*, 20:3, winter, 1992, pp. 5, 20

19 Lamming, R., Johnsen, T., Zheng, J., and Harland, C., 'An initial classification of supply networks', *International Journal of Operations and Production Management*, Vol. 20, No. 6, 2000

20 Harland, C., Lamming, R. C., Zheng, J., and Johnsen, T. E., 'A taxonomy of supply networks', *Journal of Supply Management*, Vol. 37, No. 4, fall, 2001, pp. 21–7

21 Craven, D. W., Piercy, N. F., and Shipp, S. H., 'New organisational forms for competing in highly dynamic environments', *British Journal of Management*, Vol. 7, 1996, pp. 203–18

22 Fisher, M. L., 'What is the right supply chain for your product?', *Harvard Business Review*, March/April, 1997, pp. 105–16

23 Arbulu, R. J., and Tommelein, I. D., 'Alternative supply chain configurations for engineered or catalogued made-to-order components: case study on pipe supports used in power plants', *Proceedings IGLC*, 10 Aug, 2002, Granada, Brazil

24 Lambert, D. H., Cooper, M. C., and Pagh, J. D., 'Supply chain management implementation issues and research opportunities', *International Journal of Logistics Management*, Vol. 9, No. 2, 1998, pp. 1–9

25 Lamming, R., *Beyond Partnerships: Strategies for Innovation and Supply*, Prentice Hall, 1998, p. 17, and 1993 edn, pp. 186–90

26 As 24 above

27 Womack, J. P., Jones, D. T., and Roos, D., *The Machine that Changed the World*, Maxwell Macmillan, 1990

28 See 'People management: applications of leaner ways of working', Chartered Institute of Personnel and Development, Working Party Paper No. 13. The authors are indebted to the CIPD for permission to use this table

29 Toni, A. D., and Tonchia, S., 'Lean organisation, management by process and performance measurement', *International Journal of Operations and Production Management*, Vol. 16, No. 2, 1996, pp. 221–36

30 Goldman, S. L., Nagel, R. N., and Preiss, K., *Agile Competitors and Virtual Organisations: Strategies for Enriching the Customer*, Van Nostrand Reinhold, 1995

31 Aitken, J., Christopher, M., and Towill, D., 'Understanding, implementing and exploiting applications', *Supply Chain Management*, Vol. 5, No. 1, 2002, pp. 206–13

32 Bowersox, D. J., Class, D. J., and Cooper, M. B., *Supply Chain Logistics Management*, International edition, 2002, McGraw-Hill, pp. 16–19

33 Van Hoek, R., 'Reconfiguring the supply chain to implement postponed manufacturing', *International Journal of Logistics Management*, Vol. 9, No. 1, 1998, pp. 1223–47

34 Christopher, M., 'Managing the global supply chain in an uncertain world', India Infoline Business School at: www.Indiainfoline.com/bisc/gscm.html, pp. 1–5

35 Hoekstra, S., and Romme, J., *Integral Logistics Structures: Developing Customer-orientated Goods Flow*, McGraw-Hill, 1992, quoted in Naim, M., Naylor, J., and Barlow, J., 'Developing lean and agile supply chains in the UK housebuilding industry', Proceedings IGLC-7, 26–28 July 1999, University of California, pp. 159–68

36 Christopher, M., and Towill, D. R., 'Supply chain migration from lean and functional to agile and customised', *Supply Chain Management*, Vol. 5, No. 4, 2000, pp. 206–13

37 Gunasekaran, A., 'Agile manufacturing: enablers and implementation framework', *International Journal of Production Research*, Vol. 36, No. 5, 2000, pp. 1223–47

38 As 31 above

39 Naylor, J. B., Naim, M. M., and Berry, D., 'Leagility: interfacing the lean and agile manufacturing paradigm in the total supply chain', *International Journal of Production Economics*, Vol. 62, 1999, pp. 107–18

40 Taken from Mason-Jones, R., Naylor, J. B., and Towill, D. R., 'Engineering the leagile supply chain', *International Journal of Agile Management Systems*, 2000

41 Mason-Jones, R., Naylor, J. B., and Towill, D. R., 'Lean, agile or leagile? Matching your supply chain to the marketplace', *International Journal of Production Research*, Vol. 38, No. 17, 2000, pp. 4061–70

42 Naylor, J. B., Naim, M. M., and Berry, D., 'Leagility: integrating the lean and agile manufacturing paradigm in the total supply chain', *International Journal of Production Economics*, Vol. 62, 1999, pp. 107–18

43 Gardner, J. T., and Cooper, M. C., 'Strategic supply chain mapping approaches', *Journal of Business Logistics*, Vol. 24, No. 2, 2003, pp. 37–64

44 As 43 above

45 Hines, P., and Rich, N., 'The seven value stream mapping tools', *International Journal of Operations and Production Management*, Vol. 17, No. 1, 1997, pp. 37–64

46 Interested readers are referred to Hines, P., Lamming, R., Jones, D., Cousins, P., and Rich, N., *Value Stream Mapping*, Part One, Pearson, 2000, pp. 13–92

Chapter 5

Purchasing structure and design

Learning outcomes

This chapter aims to provide an understanding of:

- the influence of environmental factors on purchasing structures
- purchasing as a functional department
- horizontal organisations, processes and teams
- teams in purchasing and supply
- cross-functional teams and their problems
- cross-organisational teams
- divisional purchasing structures
- centralised purchasing
- decentralised purchasing
- purchasing in multiplant organisations
- evolving purchasing structures
- organisational change.

Key ideas

- Mechanistic and organic structures.
- Downsizing, e-commerce, global sourcing, partnering and outsourcing as factors influencing purchasing organisation.
- The advantages and disadvantages of functional purchasing.
- Silo mindsets.
- The principles of horizontal organisation.
- The concept of core processes.
- The nature, purpose, structure, advantages and disadvantages of cross-functional teams.
- The basis of divisionalisation.
- Economies of scale and control as aspects of centralised purchasing.
- The advantages and disadvantages of decentralised purchasing.
- Purchasing structure in multiplant organisations.
- Some new type purchasing structures.
- The driving forces for organisational change.
- Structural, cultural and individual perspectives on organisational change.
- Approaches to the implementation of change.

Introduction

Contingency theory states that there is no best way to organise. The organisational structures and control systems adopted for a particular enterprise and for functions or groups of activities within the enterprise depend on or are contingent on the external environment in which the enterprise operates. Burns and Stalker[1] identified two basic structures derived from the ways in which the activities of an enterprise can respond to the environment. In a *mechanistic structure*, authority is centralised at the summit of the managerial hierarchy and vertical authority is used to control human and material resources. Mechanistic structures operate most effectively in stable environments. In an *organic structure*, authority is decentralised, employees are empowered to respond effectively to the unexpected and departments are encouraged to share information and other resources and take a cross-functional perspective. Organic structures operate most effectively in conditions of uncertainty and turbulence.

Major changes in purchasing structure are therefore beyond the control of the purchasing function. How purchasing is organised must be congruent with the overall organisation of the enterprise of which purchasing is part, which, as stated above, will be determined by the external environment.

After a brief discussion of some business environmental factors that influence both organisation and purchasing structures, this chapter will consider functional, centralised, decentralised and hybrid purchasing structures, some alternative structures, purchasing in multiplant enterprises and, finally, some aspects of purchasing interfaces with other functions and the implementation of structural change.

5.1 Business environmental factors and purchasing structures

Five such factors are downsizing, e-commerce, global sourcing, partnering and outsourcing.

5.1.1 Downsizing

The aim of downsizing is to create leaner and more responsive organisations as a result of the planned elimination of positions and jobs. During the 1980s and early 1990s, between one third and one half of all medium- and large-size UK firms downsized. Two thirds of the companies that downsized did so more than once.[2] Being smaller and leaner, concentrating on core competences and eliminating functions, hierarchies and organisational units are now regarded as successful strategies. Along with other factors, downsizing affects purchasing structures in such ways as fewer staff, flatter structures, redesigning jobs, merging activities, empowering lower-level employees, forming self-managed work teams and changing performance criteria. The drivers of downsizing include the elimination of non-value-adding activities, reduction in overhead costs, the introduction of labour-saving technology, global competition and recession.

5.1.2 E-commerce

This facilitates communication between suppliers and customers and makes possible the streamlining of purchasing (and other) operational and management processes. By means of e-commerce and e-procurement, paper-based systems, bureaucratic authorisation processes and multilayered decision structures are superseded by source data capture, integrated transaction processing, electronic data interchange (EDI), real-time systems, online decision support and document management and expert systems. E-commerce also supports networking and reduces non-value-adding activities. E-commerce also impacts payment processes and requires fewer accounting staff.

5.1.3 Globing sourcing

Global sourcing has several structural aspects. Because of its complexity, responsibility for global sourcing will be vested in a special section or team reporting at a high organisational level. When contract values are high or relationships long-term, sourcing may be decentralised by employing an agent or having an office in the supplier's country. Many large clothing retailers, for example, have buying offices in the Far East, such as Hong Kong. Global sourcing often involves the coordination of a complicated network of actors and relationships relating to the exchange of products, expertise, technology and finance across national boundaries. Such coordination is facilitated by IT.

5.1.4 Partnering

With partnership arrangements, there may be a great deal of interfirm interaction between many functional areas. Coordination arrangements are therefore required to keep the relationship operating with a minimum of friction. Teams may also be formed to select and appraise potential partners and monitor the working of the relationship. The roles of coordinator and team leader are often a purchasing responsibility.

5.1.5 Outsourcing

This is often used to effect downsizing. A major consequence of outsourcing has been the replacement of vertical, self-sufficient enterprises with horizontal organisations. This strategy results in fewer employees and the elimination of departments or functions providing support services. In an extreme form, outsourcing may result in virtual companies that rely on a network of suppliers to produce goods and services.

5.2 Purchasing as a functional department

Although the supply chain approach regards purchasing as a process, many organisational structures show purchasing as a separate rather than an integrated activity. Functional departmentalism is associated with vertical organisations, which have the following characteristics:

- work is divided into functions, then departments, then tasks
- the primary building block of performance is the individual and his or her job
- the chain of command goes up the functional ladder
- the manager's job is to match the right people to the right tasks and then measure, evaluate and reward their performance (vertical or mechanistic organisations, as stated earlier, are associated with environmental stability)

- the guiding principle of functional departmentalisation is that all people contributing to the same functional area need to be physically located together in departments.

5.2.1 The advantages of functional departments

These include:

- availability of specialist personnel to the whole organisation
- high morale among departmental staff arising from the fact that people appear to enjoy working with 'their own kind'
- ease of supervision and control
- simplification of training
- operational efficiency.

5.2.2 The disadvantages of functional departments

Ofstroff and Smith[3] point out that, while the crucial advantage of vertical organisations is functional excellence, their central defect is coordination across functions, departments and tasks. This lack of integration results in 'silo mindsets'. Spanyi[4] has identified the following characteristics of a traditional functional thinker:

- more concerned about reporting relationships and authority than on the flow of work to create value for customers
- closely guards his or her 'big picture' view and is sometimes called 'Attila' behind his or her back
- takes pride in his or her grasp of department-specific issues and solutions and pleads ignorance of other areas of knowledge
- sends subordinates to cross-group meetings with orders to 'protect our interests'
- clearly prefers one-on-one problem-solving sessions
- focuses mainly on actual-to-budget metrics to assess progress
- insists that even minor cross-departmental issues be elevated for his or her review
- when confronted with problems not directly within his or her control, the reply is, 'not my problem'
- perceives goal-setting to be a top-down, unidirectional activity
- is visibly uncomfortable in meetings with a broad cross-departmental representation.

Functional silos have two characteristics:

- each silo has a discrete core competence, such as purchasing, production and marketing
- functions complete their part of the total process and then 'throw it over the wall' to the next link in the supply chain.

The disadvantages of silo mindsets associated with departmentalisation include:

- coordination among related functional areas is more difficult, hence the move to supply chain and cross-functional approaches
- departmentalisation can foster a parochial emphasis on functional objectives with a minimum appreciation of or concern for overall organisational goals

- employees' identification with a specialist group or function can make it difficult to implement change
- training of managers with broad perspectives and wide understanding of business may be inhibited
- interdepartmental rivalry and conflict may be encouraged
- where purchasing staff lack technical knowledge, time is often saved if design or user departments deal directly with suppliers
- user departments will resort to informal procedures if formal purchasing procedures are too slow, unreliable or otherwise unsatisfactory
- departmentalisation tends to look inwards whereas, in today's competitive environment, the emphasis is on the customers and how the enterprise can respond quickly to their requirements
- departmentalisation can result in many activities that involve expenditure and time without adding value.

Silo mindsets are incompatible with turbulent environments, lean and agile philosophies, complicated, highly interdependent technologies and the communication and information-sharing possibilities of IT, all of which require organic structures and horizontal-type organisations.

5.3 Horizontal organisations and processes

Horizontal organisations are not completely flat, but they have fewer layers than their vertical counterparts. Neither is necessarily incompatible with vertical structures.[5] Ostroff and Smith[6] point out that each company must seek its own unique balance between the vertical and horizontal features needed to deliver performance. These writers also provide the following working list of ten principles 'at the heart of' horizontal organisations.

5.3.1 Horizontal organisations' principles and characteristics

- Organise around the process not the task.
- Flatten hierarchy by minimising the subdivision of work flows and non-value-adding activities.
- Assign ownership of processes and process performance.
- Link performance objectives and evaluation to customer satisfaction.
- Make teams, not individuals, the principal building blocks of the organisations' performance and design.
- Combine managerial and non-managerial activities as often as possible.
- Treat multiple competences as the rule, not the exception.
- Inform and train people on a 'just-in-time to perform' basis, not on a 'need to know' basis.
- Maximise supplier and customer contact.
- Reward individual skill development and team performance, not just skilled performance.

Table 5.1 **Differences between vertical and horizontal organisations**

Aspect	Vertical/functional organisation	Horizontal/process organisation
Performance objective	Profitability, shareholder value, financial results	Customer satisfaction
Focus of effort	Functional specific improvement	Company-wide processes linked to customer satisfaction
Business structure	Linking together business units, functions, departments and tasks	Linking together work flows
Basis of organisation	Individuals, positions and tasks	Teams
Management and non-managerial activities	Separate	Combined so far as possible – emphasis on empowerment
Expertise	Emphasise task specialisation in the service of functional excellence	Emphasise the importance of multiple competences
Information	Used for decision making and managerial control	Provided directly to users on a just-in-time basis
Supplier/customer contact	Often at arm's length	Encouraged as a means of ascertaining customers' needs, encouraging improvement and participation
Rewards	Individual performance, promotion	Wider roles within the team and core processes

In essence, the main differences between vertical and horizontal organisations can be summarised as in Table 5.1.

Essentially, horizontal organisations are concerned with core processes and teams, both of which have implications for purchasing structures.

5.3.2 Core processes

Kaplan and Murdoch[7] define a core process as: 'A set of interrelated activities, decisions and informational material flows which together determine the competitive success of the company.'

Core processes have the following important characteristics.

- An enterprise will generally have no more than three or four core processes that are critical to the achievement of its strategic objectives, core competences and core products. Such processes are not unrelated to Porter's primary activities, shown in Figure 3.13.

- Each core process is comprised of a number of key activities.

- Kaplan and Murdoch state that, as shown in Figure 5.1, with core processes 'work flows, decision-making organisation and information systems are redesigned in a parallel, integrated fashion rather than sequentially or independently. Core processes therefore cut across the functional, geographic and even company boundaries

Figure 5.1 The characteristics of core processes

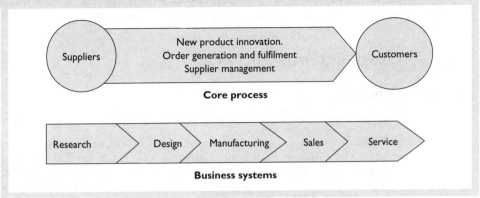

that apply in a typical value chain or business framework which views a company as a sequence of functional activities each pursuing its own frequently conflicting objectives.'

■ Core processes may extend beyond organisational boundaries. This is clearly the case when new product innovation involves suppliers and, possibly, suppliers' suppliers.

In most organisations, purchasing is a support rather than a primary activity, such as supply management, logistics or materials management. A possible exception is retailing where 'buying' is a critical factor and satisfies the criteria for a core competence set out in 4.1.1. Whether purchasing is a core process or an activity within such a process determines reporting levels, the content of the purchasing task and the positioning of purchasing in an organisational structure.

5.4   Teams

Teams are groups of people working together to achieve a common objective, such as customer satisfaction. The growing consensus is that teams are the best way to:

■ integrate tasks
■ integrate information
■ maximise competence
■ manage performance
■ manage resources
■ promote employee satisfaction and reduce stress
■ implement quality management and improvement.

The team concept also has implications for purchasing structures. If the person in control of purchasing or an area of purchasing is regarded as a team *leader*, it is arguable that the job content is different from that of a team *manager*. Although leadership – in the sense of directing the work of others – is one of the four functions frequently ascribed to management (the other three being planning, organising and controlling), it is widely agreed that the important qualities that distinguish leaders from managers are vision, innovation and adaptability. It is the possession of these qualities that transforms purchasing managers into purchasing strategists.

5.5 Cross-functional purchasing

5.5.1 Definition

The Institute of Supply Management (USA)[8] states that cross-functional teams are:

> Groups of individuals from various organisational functions who are brought together to achieve clear, worthwhile, and compelling goals that could not be reached without a team. Teaming leverages organisational resources while utilising the expertise of team members. Purchasers typically participate in teams dealing with sourcing, commodities, quality, and new product/service development.

5.5.2 Reasons for the formation of cross-functional teams

The involvement of purchasing in multiskilled teams drawn from several functions is attributable to at least six factors:

- the involvement of purchasing in strategic procurement decisions
- the concept of the 'supply chain', which emphasises the need to deal with work flow in an integrated way by means of materials management and logistics approaches
- teams may make better use of the vastly increased information availability and ability to communicate effectively provided by IT and ICT
- the development of such approaches as ERP, MRP and JIT, together with single and partnership sourcing and outsourcing
- the recognition that, because of such developments as global purchasing, more complicated price and cost analyses, the need to integrate purchasing processes with those of manufacturing and the enhanced importance of quality, purchasing often needs expert advice and support in decision making
- the recognition, based on research findings, that 'Teams out-perform individuals acting alone or in large organisation groupings, especially when performance requires multiskills judgements and experience.'[9]

5.5.3 The purpose and structure of cross-functional teams

Cross-functional teams may be formed for a wide variety of purposes covering the whole supply chain spectrum. Aspects of purchasing for which cross-functional teams have special relevance include sourcing, global sourcing, outsourcing, new product development, value management and analysis, quality management, capital equipment buying and staff development and training.

Cross-functional teams may be either short- or long-term in duration. Short-term cross-functional teams are essentially task forces formed for a particular purpose and are disbanded when that purpose has been accomplished. Long-term teams are permanent or semi-permanent. With a project such as nuclear submarine design, development, build and commission, for example, the total cycle to decommissioning could exceed 20 years.

Short-term cross-functional teams will probably adopt a matrix-type structure, as shown in Figure 4.2. In such a team, staff will be seconded from various functions, either on a part- or full-time basis, for the duration of the team's existence.

Long-term cross-functional teams will serve full time in a project team as members of a self-contained unit headed by a project manager.

5.5.4 The advantages of cross-functional teams

Parker[10] has listed six important competitive advantages that accrue to organisations that successfully implement cross-functional teams:

- *speed* reduction in the time it takes to get things done, especially the product development process
- *complexity* improvement in the organisation's ability to solve complicated problems
- *customer focus* focusing the organisation's resources on satisfying the customers' needs
- *creativity* by bringing together people with a variety of experiences and backgrounds, cross-functional teams increase the creative capacity of the organisation
- *organisational learning* members of cross-functional teams are more easily able to develop new technical/job skills, learn more about other disciplines and how to work with people who have different team player styles and cultural backgrounds
- *single point of contact* the promotion of more effective cross-functional teamwork by identifying one place to go for information and decisions about a project or customer.

Another advantage is an increased understanding between functions of each other's problems. Production and quality assurance may develop an enhanced appreciation of the difficulties of dealing with suppliers and purchasing an awareness of the problems faced by production and design.

The quality of the contributions made by procurement staff to cross-functional teams can also do much to enhance the reputation and recognition given to purchasing by other team members.

5.6 Some problems of cross-functional teams

A number of problems have been reported in relation to cross-functional teams. Sobek et al.[11] point out that:

> Cross-functional coordination has improved, but at the cost of depth of knowledge within functions, because people are spending less time within their own functions. Organisational learning across products has also dropped as people rapidly rotate through positions. Standardisation across products has suffered because product teams have become autonomous. In organisations that combine functional and project-based structures, engineers are often torn between the orders of their functional bosses on the one hand and the demands of project leaders on the other.

Other problems of cross-functional teams include:

- the need for a substantial investment in the training and retraining of team leaders in interpersonal skills and of team members in adopting a cross-functional, rather than a silo, orientation
- cross-functional teams require members to attend numerous meetings

■ because of their expertise, some members are required to participate in several teams concurrently with a resultant competition for priorities.

Finally, it should not be forgotten that the basic reason for cross-functional teams is to break down functional silos. This does not mean the abdication of functional responsibilities, however. Those responsible for product design must retain that responsibility even when working in a product team. While cross-functional sourcing may share responsibility for decision making, purchasing is not absolved from the duty of ensuring that the team has full information on potential suppliers and products and services that provide maximum value for money spent.

5.7 Cross-organisational teams

These are a development on cross-functional teams, involving the inclusion of suppliers or customers in teams. As with functions, such involvement can give organisations a greater understanding of common problems. Trent and Monczka[12] state that, on average, teams that include qualified suppliers as members demonstrate greater overall performance. They also list four further benefits that can result from supplier participation:

■ greater satisfaction concerning the quality of information exchange between the team and its key suppliers

■ a greater reliance on suppliers to support directly the teams' goals and objectives

■ greater supply base management effectiveness and

■ greater supplier contribution in a number of critical areas; one significant development is that of the 'Guest Engineer', in which a member of the supplier's staff is permanently located in the works of the purchaser.

Such interfirm cooperation is of special importance in relation to product innovation and development (see Chapter 8).

5.8 Divisional purchasing structures

As shown in Table 5.2, the focus of divisionalisation can be on the product or service, geography or customer.

Divisionalisation is usually the pattern for large, highly diversified organisations that, often, operate in several countries or continents, as with Volvo's 3P purchasing organisation, shown in Figure 5.2. The 3P organisation covers Mack, Renault and Volvo brands, involving 5 billion euros in spend across multiple categories of purchase.

Table 5.2 **The basis of divisional structures**

Type	Focus	Examples
Product or service	Product or service provided	ICI Paints Division; Rentokil Pest Control
Geographical	Location of activity	UK Division; European Division
Customer	Customer or client	UK government contracts

Figure 5.2 Volvo's 3P purchasing organisation

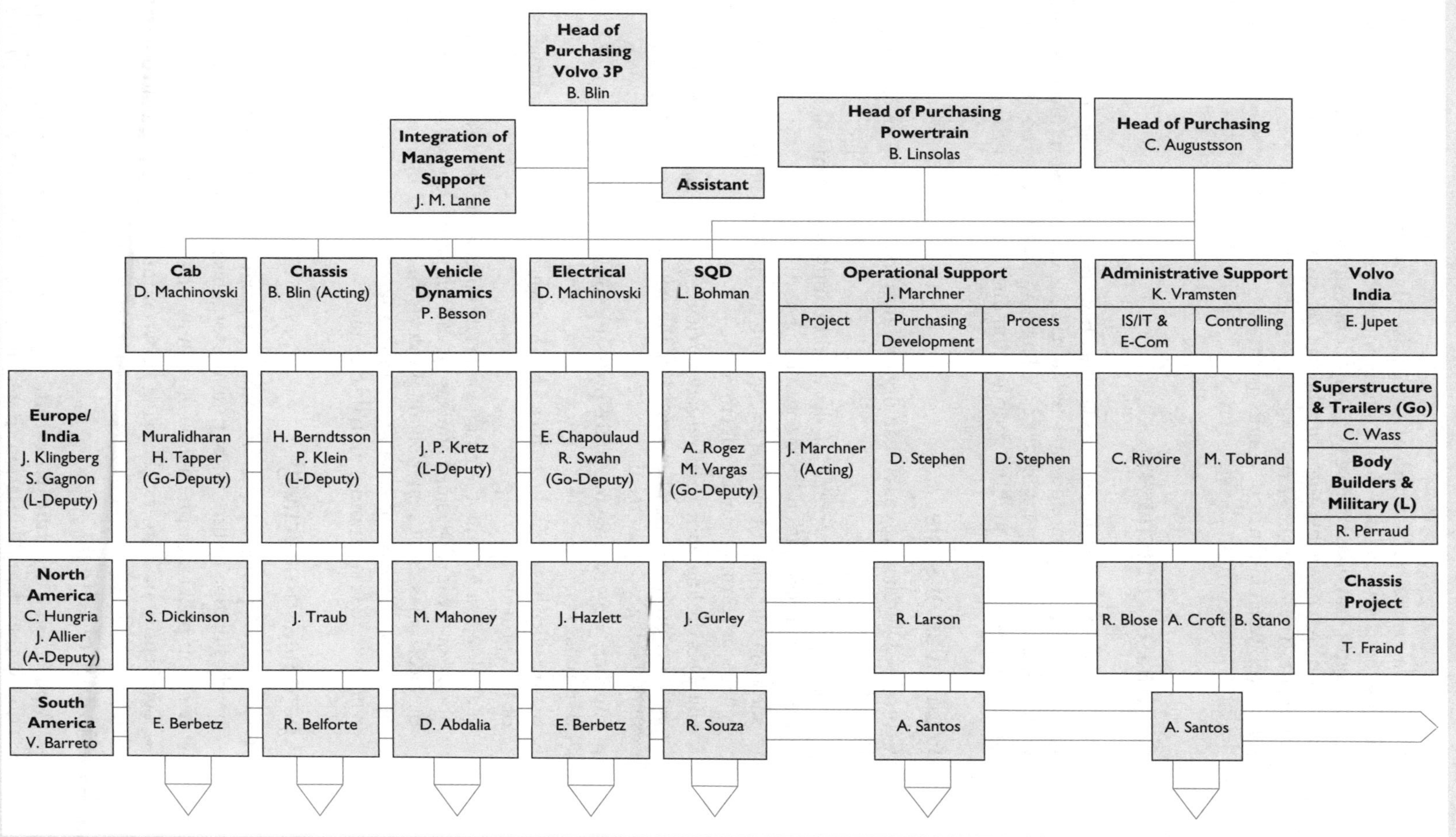

Head of Purchasing Volvo 3P
B. Blin

Integration of Management Support
J. M. Lanne

Assistant

Head of Purchasing Powertrain
B. Linsolas

Head of Purchasing
C. Augustsson

Volvo India
E. Jupet

	Cab	Chassis	Vehicle Dynamics	Electrical	SQD	Operational Support			Administrative Support		Superstructure & Trailers (Go)
	D. Machinovski	B. Blin (Acting)	P. Besson	D. Machinovski	L. Bohman	J. Marchner			K. Vramsten		C. Wass
						Project	Purchasing Development	Process	IS/IT & E-Com	Controlling	**Body Builders & Military (L)** R. Perraud

Operational Support sub-cells: J. Marchner (Acting); D. Stephen; D. Stephen; C. Rivoire; M. Tobrand

Europe/India	Muralidharan	H. Berndtsson	J. P. Kretz	E. Chapoulaud	A. Rogez				R. Blose	A. Croft	B. Stano
J. Klingberg S. Gagnon (L-Deputy)	H. Tapper (Go-Deputy)	P. Klein (L-Deputy)	(L-Deputy)	R. Swahn (Go-Deputy)	M. Vargas (Go-Deputy)						
North America C. Hungria J. Allier (A-Deputy)	S. Dickinson	J. Traub	M. Mahoney	J. Hazlett	J. Gurley	R. Larson					
South America V. Barreto	E. Berbetz	R. Belforte	D. Abdalia	E. Berbetz	R. Souza	A. Santos		A. Santos	A. Santos		

Chassis Project
T. Fraind

Once established, each division is organised in a functional form with its own hierarchies and is self-contained and autonomous in terms of day-to-day operations. Most writers agree that divisionalised organisations exhibit superior profitability to centralised ones as it makes visible the contribution of each division to the profitability of the enterprise. The mere act of creating a division will not, however, of itself increase performance. What ultimately counts is the way in which resources are allocated and decisions made within the structure.

5.9 Centralised purchasing

This implies that purchases are made either from company headquarters or some regional or divisional level. The advantages claimed for concentrating purchasing in a strong central department responsible for coordinating purchasing across the organisation relate to economies of scale and the coordination and control of procurement activities.

5.9.1 Economies of scale

Centralised purchasing enables an organisation to leverage its purchasing power to the best effect as:

- forecasts can be prepared of the total quantities of items likely to be required by the whole organisation for a specified period
- such consolidation of quantities can form the basis for negotiating quantity discounts, rebates or learning curve reductions
- suppliers dealing with a centralised purchasing department have an incentive to compete for 'preferred supplier status' or the whole or a substantial proportion of the undertaking's requirements
- suppliers may be able to reduce prices by spreading overheads over longer production runs
- the supplier base may be reduced by the award of 'preferred supplier status' to one or two providers
- centralisation permits the employment of purchasing professionals in a way that is not possible with diversified purchasing and who can become expert in the procurement of special classes of materials or products following market trends and the development of reliable and economic supply sources or of import and export procedures where there is substantial global sourcing.

5.9.2 Coordination of activity

- Centralised purchasing tends to have a greater strategic focus than divisionalised purchasing due to proximity to major organisational decision makers.
- Uniform policies can be adopted, such as single sourcing.
- Competitive or 'maverick' buying between functions is eliminated.

5.9.3 Control of activity

- A purchasing department or team may become either a separate *cost centre* (a location within the organisation to which costs may be assigned), an *activity cost pool* (with activity costing) or a *profit centre* (a unit in the organisation responsible for revenue and profits as well as expenditure).

■ Budgetary control may be applied to both the purchasing function as an operating unit and the total expenditure on supplies.

■ Uniformity of prices obtained by centralised purchasing assists in standardising costing.

■ Inventories can be controlled reducing obsolescence and loss of working capital tied up in excessive stock.

■ The performance of a centralised purchasing function can be monitored by setting objectives and comparing actual results with predetermined standards.

Many of the above advantages are not restricted to a functional approach and apply equally when purchasing is a group or team within an integrated supply chain structure.

5.10 Decentralisation

Traditionally, decentralisation referred to purchasing done by plants or divisions. As stated later, however, increasingly purchasing is delegated to actual users. Some of the advantages and disadvantages of decentralised purchasing are shown in Table 5.3.

Table 5.3 **Advantages and disadvantages of decentralised purchasing**

Advantages	Disadvantages
Closer to users and better understanding of local needs	Reduced leverage that exists with consolidation of purchases
Response time to divisional or plant needs may be rapid and of higher quality	Focus on local rather than corporate and operational rather than strategic considerations
Possibly closer relationships with suppliers	Purchasing will tend to report to a lower organisational level
Local suppliers and consequent lower transportation costs	Limited expertise in requirements and few opportunities for cross-functional collaboration
Where plants are profit centres the view is expressed that if purchasing costs are a high percentage of total costs then each profit centre should make its own decisions regarding purchasing and suppliers	Possibly lack of standardisation Restricted career opportunities for local purchasing staff Cost of purchasing relatively high
Geographical, cultural, political, environmental, social, language and currency appropriateness	

5.11 Purchasing in multiplant organisations

Decentralisation implies that an organisation's activities are spread over a number of plants or locations. The issue of centralisation or decentralisation, therefore, arises:

An investigation by Lyles and Payne[13] of 74 UK companies indicated 3 'models' of procurement:

- coordinated devolved procurement
- centralised procurement
- consultative centralised procurement.

These models are shown in Figure 5.3.

Figure 5.3 Models of procurement for multiplant organisations

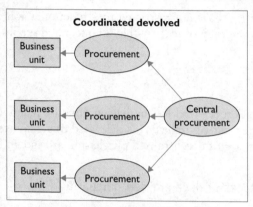

Coordinated devolved

- Most procurement activities are carried out within the business units or operating divisions of the organisation, but they are coordinated by a centralised procurement function
- Procurement of products and services common to more than one area of the business is usually centralised
- Procurement strategy, policy, systems and standards are controlled centrally

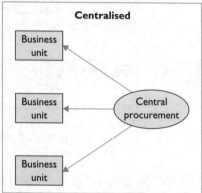

Centralised

- No independent procurement departments or staff exist within the business units of operating divisions of the organisation
- Procurement strategy, policy, systems and standards are controlled centrally and all procurement activities are carried out centrally

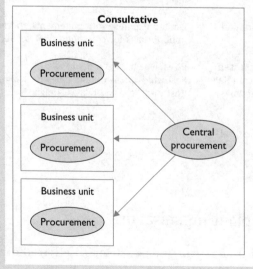

Consultative

- Procurement activities of both a strategic and operational nature are carried out within the business units or operating divisions, but taking guidance and advice from a centralised procurement function
- The overall control of procurement strategy, policy, systems and standards rests with the central procurement function

In the above investigation, Lyles and Payne report the following findings.

■ Most organisations that now have a centralised or consultative structure have evolved from a devolved model, such as that shown in Figure 5.3.

■ In 2000, the most common procurement model in the companies researched was one of centralised control and devolved authorisation. Of the respondents, 93 per cent considered that the control over the purchasing of products and services in their organisation was centralised – only 5 per cent describing such control as devolved. Conversely, 84 per cent of respondents stated that the authorisation of expenditure was devolved, 14 per cent that it was centralised. It can be deduced that about 9 per cent of the sample had both centralised control and authorisation of expenditure.

Purchasing will tend to be completely centralised where the items required at each plant are largely homogeneous. An example would be a confectionery company with a large number of plants each using large quantities of flour, sugar and other common ingredients. In this case, orders would be placed centrally and deliveries made against contract as required by the local plants.

Purchasing may be coordinated and devolved where the group is a conglomerate consisting of a number of plants, each producing dissimilar products. In this case, purchasing is done at plant level as the materials and components used are specific to that location. Reasons for organising purchasing in this way include that:

■ as the efficiency of purchasing influences profitability, the manager of each plant should have control over the expenditure incurred for materials for that plant

■ centralised purchasing proliferates paperwork and leads to delays

■ some plants are so large that the economies of scale referred to earlier are already present and there is an optimum after which *diseconomies* of scale set in.

One relevant objection to complete decentralisation is that the competition between plants may lead to a loss of group purpose.

As Lyles and Payne show, in most group undertakings there is a compromise – some purchasing activities being undertaken centrally and others at plant level. It is, therefore, necessary to determine:

■ what activities shall be undertaken centrally

■ what activities shall be centralised

■ how coordination between central and plant-level purchasing shall be achieved.

In each case, the options chosen will depend on the undertaking, but the following arrangements are typical.

5.11.1 Centralised activities

■ Determination of major purchasing strategies and policies, such as vertical integration, outsourcing, single and partnership sourcing, countertrade, reciprocal sourcing.

■ Purchase of leverage, strategic and bottleneck products (see Figure 2.13).

■ Purchase of capital equipment and systems.

■ Negotiation of bulk contracts for homogeneous supplies used by a number of plants.

■ Purchasing research into market conditions, vulnerability and similar matters.

- Rationalisation of the share of orders to be received by specific suppliers. This will apply particularly when the purchasing organisation controls a large proportion of the available orders or, for social reasons, needs to spread its purchasing power fairly among a number of dependent suppliers.
- Control of group inventory.
- Staff training and development.

5.11.2 Decentralised activities

- Small-value orders and maintenance, repair and operating (MRO) items.
- Items used only by that plant.
- Emergency purchases – where local initiative may avoid an interruption of production, for example.
- Local buying to save transport costs.
- Local purchasing undertaken for social reasons – that is, a plant is part of the community in which it is situated and can, by exercising its purchasing power, contribute to the prosperity of the locality.
- Staff purchases.

5.11.3 Procurement councils

Procurement councils as Cavinato[14] points out are a variant of decentralisation. The councils are comprised of purchasing staff who, although located at different plants, have similar requirements for products and services. The council members meet and coordinate a single source or quantity as though they were one group, thus removing the disadvantages of reduced leverage resulting from the non-consolidation of purchases, adversity of suppliers and lack of standardisation. In practice, procurement councils may disband due to the absence of leadership or top management support.

5.12 Evolving purchasing structures

Cavinato[15] suggests that, increasingly, organisations are moving away from defined departments and issues such as centralisation and decentralisation, to whom purchasing should report, and the title of the most senior purchasing officer are of less consequence now than in the past: 'Suppliers are accessing the firm through links other than just the purchasing department. The firm is increasingly gaining entry into customer operations through channels other than sales and marketing.'

Apart from traditional centralised and decentralised purchasing, Cavinato identifies five other models of purchasing organisation that have evolved and have significant implications both for purchasing and logistics.

5.12.1 The centralised coordinator model

This is when decentralised purchasing reports to a plant or divisional general managers with a centralised coordinating purchasing group at corporate headquarters. The central group takes a macro view of purchasing and logistics issues concerning the entire organisation and provides services and information to the individual plants or divisions.

Cavinato claims that this model has the advantage of scope and authority in dealing with suppliers without the full overhead cost often associated with fully centralised groups.

5.12.2 The area planner concept model

In this model, a central procurement group handles issues of vendor sourcing, selection and performance monitoring while users handle the processing of requisitions and day-to-day orders for inbound supplies.

The area planner approach thus removes procurement from the transaction cycle.

5.12.3 The supply manager concept model

Here, one person has responsibility for the flow of a product or a few products from the supplier input, through production to delivery to the ultimate customer. Performance is based on a contribution margin computed from selling price less costs accumulated up to the packing end of the production line.

A major problem with this arrangement is the difficulty of recruiting people with the wide range of skills required for each product.

5.12.4 Commodity teams

Like the supply manager concept model, this is a supply chain rather than primarily purchasing model. Logistics pipelines seek to enhance collaboration between purchasers and suppliers. An example is the collaborative forecasting and replenishment (CFAR) initiative developed between Wal-Mart and Proctor & Gamble. Teams from both companies forecast sales of Proctor & Gamble products at Wal-Mart stores and jointly plan replenishments. Continuous replenishment programs (CRP) are driven by withdrawals of products from retailers' warehouses rather than by point-of-sale (POS) data at retail stores and vendor-managed inventory (VMI), where inventories at the wholesaler or retailer are monitored and replenished by the manufacturer or wholesaler, are variations on the pipeline model. With pipeline models, the supplier is undertaking many of the processes traditionally performed by purchasers.

5.12.5 The market segmentation model

This model is associated with Cannon.[16] The 'market' in this model comprises all the orders/contracts that the organisation wishes to place. Each item purchased can be categorised according to four variables:

- rapidity of technological change associated with the item
- total volume of spend
- number of orders placed annually
- number of suppliers.

Cannon suggests that, on the basis of such segmentation, interaction between purchasing and its internal customers can be related to the following three scenarios.

- Where the total value of spend is low, the internal customer should do the buying and the purchasing function should provide training in areas such as vendor appraisal, the legal significance of contract terms and conditions, tender/quotation evaluation, negotiation, contracts administration and dispute resolution. This arrangement has the advantages of eliminating requisitions, enhanced speed and reduced costs.

- Where the total value of spend is high and there is also a high rate of technological change, internal customers/users should collaborate when procuring the organisation's requirements. In this scenario, purchasing will again provide training in the areas listed above. Service agreements will, additionally, demarcate areas of buying responsibility and the possibility of using targeted added-value approaches should be investigated by both parties.

- When the total value of spend is high but the rate of technological change is low, procurement should be the responsibility of purchasing, which offers its internal customers added value, service and expertise.

All the above five models have important structural and organisational implications for purchasing. Often they will change the responsibilities and reduce the size of the purchasing function and expedite the change from vertical to horizontal structures. In extreme cases, purchasing may become a virtual activity.

5.13 Organisational change

5.13.1 Types of change

Daft[17] has identified four basic types of change that affect organisations and apply to purchasing and other functions:

- *technology* such as IT and e-procurement
- *product or service* purchasing, for example, was traditionally mainly a transactional process, concerned with obtaining items for production or other internal use, but is increasingly involved with strategic issues
- *administrative* the movement from discrete purchasing 'departments' to cross-functional procedures, such as the scanning, screening and selection of suppliers by cross-functional teams, for example
- *people* such as the need for trained purchasing professionals
- *business relationships* which arise from acquisitions, mergers, joint ventures and partnership alliances.

5.13.2 Forces for change

Forces for change may be both external and internal.

External forces are those outside the organisation that create pressure to devise and implement new strategies to meet the challenges of competition or technology.

Internal forces are those within the organisation that may be the result of changing environmental conditions, such as declining competitive advantage, rising production costs or outdated facilities. Such factors may create internal pressure for new corporate strategies.

5.13.3 Perspectives on organisational change

Changes due to the above causes can be considered from three perspectives – structural, cultural and individual.

Structural change

If structure follows strategy, then changes in strategy arising from any of the above five drivers will be followed by structural changes. This can be exemplified by technological drivers, such as IT, and administrative or business drivers resulting in the decision to outsource.

IT, with its capability to communicate and share information, has caused traditional hierarchies to be replaced with horizontal structures. The need to physically locate people and units together to ensure coordination and supervision or to choose between centralised or decentralised structures is also increasingly invalidated by IT, with a consequent focus on projects and processes rather than standard procedures and tasks. IT can be substituted for layers of management and a number of managerial tasks. Lucas and Baroudi[18] give examples of how IT can create virtual organisations that do not exist in physical form. Mail-order companies, for example, employ individuals working from home using a special phone connected to an 0800 number to take orders from customers who have their catalogues. Manufacturers can use parts suppliers to substitute for their inventory. The supplier, linked electronically with the manufacturer, can use overnight delivery to ensure that the parts are delivered just-in-time for production. The manufacturer, thus, has a virtual parts inventory that is owned by the supplier until it arrives for production.

Outsourcing may lead to the complete disappearance of a function from an organisational structure.

Cultural change

Organisational culture is a 'pattern of belief and expectations shared by organisational members'[19] or 'the way things are done around here'.[20]

Culture is an important aspect of change as culture might either block or facilitate it and also because changes in organisational strategies usually require changes in organisational structure. Thus, a change from transactional to partnership purchasing will require a cultural reorientation on the part of the staff involved so that its suppliers are no longer regarded as adversaries to be kept at arm's length, but, instead, as allies. Developments such as total quality management (TQM) require the acceptance by all employees of a culture of continuous improvement in which people at all organisational levels accept responsibility for identifying quality problems early on. TQM also requires a culture of 'learning together', with guidance and support for the learning process being provided by management. With TQM it is also a management responsibility to develop a culture in which every employee is encouraged and empowered to take ownership of outputs, customer problems and improvement actions. Such changes in cultural outlook will usually require a significant investment in education and training and the use of an internal or external change agent responsible for ensuring that the planned change is properly implemented.

Individual change

People usually respond to change with hostility and apprehension due to numerous factors, including insecurity, lack of information regarding proposed changes, the break-up of work groups, perceived threats to expertise, status or earnings, inconvenience of new working conditions and changes in management and supervisory personnel.

Preparing for change

An evaluation by management of structural, cultural and individual issues is the essential first step in the implementation of change at both organisational and functional levels.

5.13.4 The implementation of change

Kurt Lewin,[21] a behavioural scientist, argues that the process of implementing change involves three basic steps:

1 *unfreezing* enabling people or organisations to be willing to change
2 *changing* selection of techniques to implement change
3 *refreezing* reinforcing and supporting the change so that it becomes a relatively permanent part of organisational processes.

Lewin's view of the change process is shown in Figure 5.4.

Numerous writers have produced step-by-step guides for the implementation of change and the following extension of Lewin's approach by Kotter and Schlesinger[22] is typical. This model suggests an eight-step process for the successful implementation of change – the first four steps being directed at the defrosting of a hardened status quo (or culture), steps five and seven introduce new practices and the last step corresponds to Lewin's 'refreezing', which helps to make them stick. The eight steps are:

1 *establishing a sense of urgency* recognising the need for the enterprise or a function within the enterprise to change if it is to achieve and retain competitive advantage or cope with crises and opportunities
2 *creating the guiding coalition* creating and empowering a group to lead change and encouraging the group to work as a team
3 *developing a vision and a strategy* 'vision' in this context means having a clear sense of what the future requires and the strategies required to turn the vision into reality
4 *communicating the change vision* using every available communication media to create an awareness of the visions and strategies to employees and others affected and secure their cooperation and involvement

Figure 5.4 Lewin's view of the change process

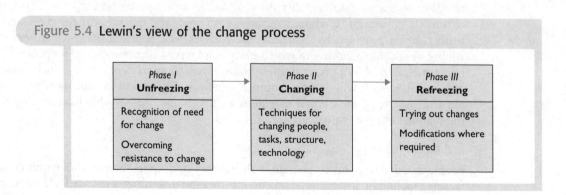

Phase I **Unfreezing**	Phase II **Changing**	Phase III **Refreezing**
Recognition of need for change Overcoming resistance to change	Techniques for changing people, tasks, structure, technology	Trying out changes Modifications where required

5 *empowering broad-based action* removing obstacles, changing structures or systems and encouraging new approaches

6 *generating short-term wins* strategies usually involve some shorter-term goals as the achievement of these goals provides encouragement to sustain people in their efforts to attain longer-term objectives

7 *consolidating gains and producing more change* reinvigorating the process with new projects, themes and change agents

8 *anchoring new approaches in the culture* stabilising change at the new level and reinforcing it by means of such supporting mechanisms as policies, structure or norms.

Collins[23] criticises what he terms 'n-step' models of change implementation on three grounds:

■ they assume that organisations act in a rational predictable way, while the reality is that they consist of a diverse range of people with diverse ideas and opinions about the right course of action

■ n-step models assume that change management can be reduced to a number of discrete, sequential steps and that change has an identifiable beginning and end, while the reality is that it is uncertain, unpredictable and contingent and 'we cannot expect the processes and final outcomes of change to map out clearly before us'

■ n-step models fail to recognise that the creative and critical skills required by managers to successfully engender change cannot be captured in 'a few rules or simple recipes for success'.

Collins, therefore, concludes that, rather than offer simplistic n-step accounts, writers should recognise that their models need to incorporate some of the complexities of real life. N-step models are dishonest and paint an inaccurate and oversimplified picture of the change process.

Probably the best approach is to recognise the importance in all change situations of communicating the need for change, consultation with all affected by the change and commitment to the successful implementation of change by all involved. In any event, learning organisations do not suddenly adopt strategic change but, rather, are perpetually seeking it.

Case study

Background of the Devillier Group

The Devillier Group has its headquarters in the United Kingdom and is engaged in four specific areas of work, each trading as an operating division. These divisions are Building and Civil Engineering, Rail and Transportation Services, Specialist Engineering and Facilities Management. Divisional managing directors are accountable for the business performance of each division and agree a five-year rolling business plan with the Group Chief Executive. The total turnover of the Devillier Group is £980 million, of which 88 per cent is generated within the United Kingdom. The remaining 12 per cent is largely generated in France and Germany. A new Group Operations Director has been appointed to review the existing structures, including purchasing.

Group turnover by division and purchasing expenditure profile

	Division turnover (£m)	Purchasing expenditure (£m)	Companies in the division
Building and Civil Engineering	400	210	6
Rail and Transportation services	275	180	2
Specialist Engineering	125	80	3
Facilities Management	180	130	6

The Existing Purchasing Structure

Group

There is a Group Purchasing Executive who is acknowledged to lack teeth. The appointment was made two years ago and no group purchasing strategy has ever been agreed. There has been resistance to the concept of group purchasing, particularly from the divisional managing directors, who have argued that if they are profit centres, they must be allowed to control expenditure as they think fit.

Only two group deals have been put in place. The first is for travel, but only 15 per cent of all travel expenditure is currently put through the group contract. The second is for vehicles. Last year, 1500 new vehicles, cars and vans were purchased using a reverse auction process. This saved 30 per cent on the previous costs and put £2.5 million into the group's bottom line.

Building and Civil Engineering

This division is engaged in major projects, including new buildings, highways, bridges and pipe laying.

Each company within the division has a chief buyer and support staff. In truth, most of the buying is done by estimators and quantity surveyors. Buying is transactional and orders placed with a multitude of suppliers who are selected on a project-by-project basis.

The Divisional Managing Director has publicly stated that he will not support group purchasing because it will not be responsive to his needs.

Rail and Transportation Services

There are only two companies in this division and each has a purchasing manager. It is the most advanced in the group and the Divisional Managing Director is very supportive of purchasing. The expenditure is quite different from that of other divisions in the group, except for IT, vehicles and office supplies.

Specialist Engineering

This division came into existence three years ago with the acquisition of a highly specialised engineering group serving Formula 1 racing and advanced engineering research projects for the nuclear industry. There is no formal buying structure in any of the companies, but the division is very profitable, achieving a 40 per cent return on capital employed.

The view of the Divisional Managing Director is that technical and financial competence matter more than 'shaving a few per cent off a purchase price'.

Facilities Management

This division is growing the fastest in the group. It anticipates growth of 20 per cent in each of the next five years. It is growing on the outsourcing actions of central and local government and the private sector. The expenditure is on an array of services procurement, including security, building maintenance, call centres and, interestingly, procurement.

There is currently a vacancy for its Divisional Purchasing Director. This would be a huge step forward for both the group and the division. This decision was made without the involvement of the Group Purchasing Executive.

Tasks

1   If you had the task of advising the Devillier Group on the most appropriate purchasing structure, what factors would you take into account?

2   What information would you require to inform your decision?

3   How would you approach the divisional managing directors?

4   List the options for structures and list the advantages and disadvantages of each option.

Discussion questions

5.1   From your own experience, give one example of how downsizing, e-commerce, global sourcing, partnering and outsourcing can affect the design of purchasing structures.

5.2   Many organisations, such as the armed forces, work on a functional basis because a commanding officer can give directions to and receive advice from line and staff officers who can then translate these orders into the language and contexts of the different areas for which they are responsible. This allows for tight control at the top and accountability upwards. Why might a system that works well in, say, the Army, be less successful in a civilian context?

5.3   What steps would you take to change the outlook of a purchasing manager who has a 'silo mindset'?

5.4   In which type of structure would you prefer to work: (i) vertical or (ii) horizontal? What does your choice probably reveal about you?

5.5   Does the concept of purchasing as a support rather than a primary activity tend to lower or enhance the importance of procurement?

5.6   'Project teams are a waste of resources when a task can be handled effectively through the existing structure' (Charles Handy, *Understanding Organisations*, 4th edn, Penguin, 1993, p. 269). Discuss this statement with special reference to cross-functional teams.

5.7   You are the Purchasing Manager reporting to the Managing Director of a company organised on a functional basis. Write a one-page memo to the Managing Director outlining the benefit of having regular meetings between the heads of design, marketing production and yourself.

5.8   Write another memo setting out the possible advantages of involving suppliers in the preparation of specifications for bought-out items.

5.9   What are the implications for supply chain management of centralised and decentralised purchasing?

5.10 A centralised purchasing system is often regarded as outdated. Give reasons for many organisations believing that devolved purchasing is the most effective approach.

5.11 Consider the applicability of each of the five evolving purchasing structures described in section 5.12 to your organisation.

5.12 Resistance to change may come from individuals, groups or be organisational. What steps would you take to overcome such resistance?

Past examination questions

All the following questions are taken from CIPS Graduate Diploma papers in *Purchasing and Supply Chain Management 1: Strategy*.

1 Centralisation refers to an organisational approach in which decisions about staffing, investments, budgets, etc., are primarily taken by a central head office function. In a decentralised organisational approach, the authority to take such decisions is delegated down the line to local management.

Discuss these types of organisational approach in the context of the factors involved in a decision to totally centralise or decentralise the purchasing function in an organisation.

(November 1999)

2 (a) Discuss why strategic change is challenging.
 (b) Analyse the causes for strategic change in organisations. (November 2001)

3 (a) Explain one model used to analyse organisational culture.
 (b) Evaluate the role of this model in the implementation of strategic change.

(May 2003)

4 (a) Identify and discuss activities that add value that are to be undertaken by a purchasing and supply function.
 (b) Define and appraise the different approaches which might be taken to organise a purchasing and supply function. (November 2003)

References

[1] Burns, T., and Stalker, G. H., *The Management of Innovation*, Tavistock, 1968

[2] Cameron, K. S., 'Downsizing (historical)' in Cooper, C. L., and Argyris, C. *The Concise Blackwell Encyclopedia of Management*, Blackwell, 1998, p. 176

[3] Ofstroff, F., and Smith, D., 'Redesigning the corporation: the horizontal organisation', *McKinsey Quarterly*, No. 1, 1992, pp. 148–67

[4] Spanyi, A., 'Transforming the traditional functional mindset' at: www.anclote.com/spanyi.html

[5] Stewart, T. A., and Jacoby, R., 'The search for the organisation of tomorrow', *Fortune*, Vol. 125, Issue 10, May 18, 1992, pp. 148–67

[6] As 3 above

[7] Kaplan, R. B., and Murdoch, L., 'Rethinking the corporation: core process redesign', *McKinsey Quarterly*, No. 2, 1991, pp. 27–43

[8] Institute of Supply Management, *Glossary of Key Purchasing and Supply Terms*

[9] Torrington, D., and Hall, L., *Personnel Management*, Prentice Hall, 1991, p. 208

[10] Parker, G. M., 'How to succeed as a cross-functional team', Proceedings of 79th Annual International Purchasing Conference of the National Association of Purchasing Managers, 1 May, 1994

[11] Sobek, I. I., Durward, K., Liker, J. K., and Ward, A. C., 'Another look at how Toyota integrates product development', *Harvard Business Review*, Vol. 76.4, July/Aug., 1998, p. 36

[12] Trent, R. J., and Monczka, R. M., 'Effective cross-functional sourcing teams: critical success factors', *International Journal of Purchasing and Materials Management*, fall, 1994, pp. 3–13

[13] Lyles, J., and Payne, R., 'Strategic purchasing review report', prepared for *Market Research Focus 2000*, p. 7. The authors are grateful to Market Research Focus Ltd for permission to quote from the report

[14] Cavinato, J. L., 'Evolving procurement organisations: logistics implications', *Journal of Business Logistics*, Vol. 1, No. 1, 1992, pp. 27–44

[15] As 14 above

[16] Cannon, S., 'Purchasing's segmented market', *Purchasing and Supply Chain Management*, Nov. 1994, pp. 35–9

[17] Daft, R. L., *Organisation Theory and Design*, West Publishing, 1983, quoted in Thomason, J. L., *Strategic Management*, Chapman & Hall, 1990, p. 590

[18] Lucas, H. C., and Baroudi, J., 'The role of information technology in organisation design', *Journal of Management Information Systems*, Vol. 10, No. 4, spring, 1994, pp. 9–23

[19] Hellriegel, D., Slocum, J. W., and Woodman, R. W., *Organisational Behaviour*, West Publishing, 1986, p. 340

[20] Handy, C., *Understanding Organisations*, 4th edn, Penguin, 1993

[21] Lewin, K., *Field Theory in Social Science*, Harper & Row, 1951

[22] Kotter, J. P., and Schlesinger, L. A., 'Choosing strategies for change', *Harvard Business Review*, March–April, 1979, pp. 107–9

[23] Collins, D., *Organisational Change*, Routledge, 1998. The authors are indebted to Harty, C., 'Do n-step guides for change work?', CIPS Knowledge in Action series, for the information contained in this section

Purchasing procedures

With reference to purchasing and supply management, this chapter aims to provide an understanding of:

- traditional purchasing procedures and their inefficiencies
- e-commerce, e-business, e-SCM and e-procurement
- e-procurement tools
- purchasing and supply manuals
- legal aspects of purchasing.

- Phases of traditional purchasing.
- E-commerce, e-business, e-SCM and e-procurement.
- Electronic data interchange (EDI).
- E-hubs, exchanges and marketplaces.
- E-catalogues and reverse auctions.
- E-payment.
- Processing of small-value orders.
- Purchasing and supplier manuals.
- Contract essentials, 'the battle of the forms' and the general structure of contracts.

Introduction

A *procedure* is a system of sequential steps or techniques for getting a task or job done. Procedures are also the formal arrangements by means of which policies linking strategies are implemented. A cluster of reliable procedures, each comprised of a number of operations that, together, provide information enabling staff to execute and managers to control those operations, is called a system.

6.1 Traditional purchasing procedures

Apart from prepurchase activities, such as participation in the preparation of specifications and budget decisions, purchasing has traditionally involved three main phases, each requiring specific documents and considerable transactional activity.

6.1.1 The identification phase

Notification of the need to purchase by either:

- a requisition issued by the stores, stock control or a potential user.
- a bill of materials issued by the drawing office, production control or equivalent department.

6.1.2 Ordering phase

On receipt, the requisition or bill of materials will be checked by the buyer for accuracy, conformity to specifications and purchase records to ensure whether the purchase is a 'rebuy' or a 'new buy' request. If the item is a standard rebuy request for an item that has been previously purchased from a satisfactory supplier at an acceptable price, a repeat order may be issued. If, however, the item is a new buy, the following steps will be involved.

1 *Enquiries or requests for quotation (RFQs)* will be sent to possible suppliers, accompanied by additional documents, such as drawings, specifications and so on that will enable them to submit a quotation.

2 *Quotations* will be received in response to the enquiries and details of price, quality, delivery, tool costs and so on and terms of business compared.

3 When quantities are substantial and quality and/or delivery of great importance, further negotiation with suppliers – including an evaluation of their capacity to undertake the order – may be required.

4 A *purchase order* will be issued to the vendor that gave the quotation, amended where necessary by subsequent negotiation, that was most acceptable. A copy of the order will be retained in the purchasing department. (sometimes two copies are retained for filing both alphabetically and numerically). Further copies of the order may be provided for:

- the department originating the requisition
- expediting section
- production control
- computer section
- accounts
- inspection.

5 An *order acknowledgement* should be required from the vendor. On receipt, the acknowledgement should be examined to ensure that the order has been accepted on the terms and conditions defined by the buyer or as subsequently agreed between the parties and then filed.

6.1.3 Post-ordering phase

1 It may be necessary to expedite the order to ensure that delivery dates are met or to expedite delivery of overdue orders.

2 An advice note, notifying that the goods have been dispatched or are ready for collection, will be issued by the supplier. Copies of the advice note may be sent to relevant departments, such as expediting and stores.

3 On receipt, the goods will be checked for quantity by the stores. Where matters of quality or specification are involved, they will be examined by the inspection department. If satisfactory, a goods received note will be completed and copies sent to the purchasing department. If they are not satisfactory, the purchasing department will be notified so that the complaint can be taken up with the supplier.

4 An invoice for the value of the goods will be received from the supplier. This will be compared with the purchase order and goods received note. Usually, prices will be checked by the purchasing department, paying special attention to the legitimacy of any variations from the quoted price. If satisfactory, the invoice will be passed to the accounts department for payment.

5 On completion, the order will be transferred to a completed orders file.

6.2　Inefficiencies of traditional procedures

The inefficiencies of traditional procedures include:

- A sequence of non-value-adding clerical activities.
- Excessive documentation – for a new buy purchase, a minimum of seven different documents (requisition, enquiry, quotation, order acknowledgement, advice note, goods received note and invoice) will be involved, with expensive copying for purchase department records and information to other departments.
- Excessive time in processing orders, both internally and externally.
- Excessive cost of purely transactional activities. Clearly the act of placing a traditional purchase order will differ from one organisation to another, but the average cost of the labour and services for requesting, locating suppliers, order placement, postage, receiving and payment has been variously estimated in the range £100 to £150. Assuming a figure of £125, this means that the true cost of a £1000 order is £1125 or $12\frac{1}{2}$ per cent just to transact the business. This amount can represent a substantial burden per £1 spent to the purchaser, especially, as mentioned later, on low-value purchases. Moreover, suppliers report comparable costs for the reciprocal operations of processing orders received.

It is because of such inefficiencies that many organisations are increasingly recognising that:[1]

Administrative paperwork often serves merely to document a chain of events or to provide a logistical trail. Leading-edge purchasing organisations need to transform this administrative function into value-added processes by reducing, eliminating or combining steps whenever possible.

All organisations are therefore being forced to embrace the strategic implications of IT and e-procurement. Some writers use the generic 'e-supply strategy' to refer to any initiative by which an organisation adopts an Internet software application to assist with the management of procurement, logistics or supply chain activities, whether it is for many or single applications.

6.3 E-commerce, e-business, e-SCM and e-procurement

6.3.1 E-commerce

The UK Department of Trade and Industry (DTI) definition of electronic commerce is:

> Any forms of business transaction carried out electronically over public telephone systems.

While this definition encompasses the whole scope of business activities, e-commerce is usually concerned with buying and selling via the Internet and World Wide Web.

6.3.2 E-business

The DTI's definition relates to what IBM refers to as electronic business (e-business) and the two terms are often used synonymously. The consensus, however, is that e-commerce is a subset of e-business.

E-commerce relates primarily to *transactions*, or the buying and selling of products or services on the Internet. It usually refers to a website that has an online storefront or catalogue and the facility for electronic order processing. It should be noted that e-commerce may also be conducted via more limited forms of electronic communication, including e-mail, fax and the emerging use of telephone calls over the Internet.

E-business, however, incorporates a wide range of production, customer and internal processes that are only indirectly related to commercial transactions.

- *Production-focused processes* include electronic links with suppliers, especially manufacturing resource planning (MRP II), enterprise resource planning (ERP) and advanced planning and scheduling (APS).
- *Customer-focused processes* include online customer support and customer relationship management (CRM).
- *Internal* or *management-focused processes* include automated employee services, training, information sharing, video conferencing and recruiting.

There are also many general benefits of e-business, such as:

- provision of 24 hours a day, 7 days a week information access
- aggregation of information from several sources
- accurate audit trails of transactions, enabling businesses to identify areas offering the greatest potential for efficiency, improvements and cost reduction
- personalisation and customisation of information.

6.3.3 E-SCM

E-supply chain management (e-SCM) is concerned with streamlining and optimising the whole supply chain by means of internal applications, with the aim of ensuring maximum sales growth at the lowest possible cost. This includes setting up an internal online purchasing system, joining an industrywide electronic marketplace and implementing e-SCM across the entire value chain.

The concepts of supply chain management and supply chain optimisation were discussed in sections 3.5 and 3.10 above. Unsurprisingly, the Internet provides present and future benefits to both the management and optimisation of supply chains. Purchasers and suppliers can derive the following benefits from e-SCM.

Purchase benefits include:

- the ability to purchase, both directly and indirectly, materials at a lower cost, primarily due to price transparency and competition, so, while large purchasers can exert powerful leverage to obtain more substantial price reductions and discounts, small purchasers using such systems can obtain more favourable prices as many suppliers are competing for the business of purchasers via the medium of e-marketplace and trading exchanges
- achievements of greater efficiency when purchasing goods and services and ultimately lowering the overall cost of transactions, as business-to-business marketplaces often offer smaller purchasers opportunities to discover lower prices for things that would be prohibitively expensive to discover by human effort alone
- purchasers being able to form strong ties with suppliers, in forecasting, scheduling and planning production data and sharing product data designs to develop supplier collaboration.

Supplier benefits

Supplier benefits tend to fall into two classes, depending on whether the e-SCM program emphasises collaboration or commercial opportunities. The latter includes the enhancement etc. Supplier benefits include the enhancement of forecasting ability, resulting in the capacity to meet and exceed customers' demands, achieve the right combination of products and services at the right time and align their production schedules, manufacturing capacity and inventory to customers' buying patterns.

When the emphasis is on collaboration, suppliers can benefit from participating in large, active online marketplaces. If frequented by a critical mass of buyers, such marketplaces can provide a cost-effective way to reach new customers and increase sales.

6.3.4 E-procurement

The CIPS definition of e-procurement is:

> E-procurement is using the Internet to operate the transactional aspects of requisitioning, authorising ordering, receiving and payment processes for the required services or products.

The CIPS statement also points out that e-procurement is typically the focus of local business administrators (one of the key goals of e-procurement is to devolve buying to local users) and covers the following areas of the buying process:

- requisition against agreed contract
- authorisation
- order
- receipt
- payment.

The key enabler of all the above is the ability of systems to communicate across organisational boundaries. While the technology for e-commerce provides the basic means, the main benefits derive from the resultant changes in business procedures, processes and perspectives. E-commerce is made possible by the open standard of extensible markup language (XML) – a structured computer programming language that allows for the easy identification of data types in multiple formats and can be understood across all standard Internet technologies. Adoption of XML will help organisations to integrate applications seamlessly and exchange information with trading partners.

6.4 The evolution of e-procurement models

Kalakota and Robinson[2] have identified seven basic types of e-procurement trading models. These, together with their key differences, are shown in Table 6.1.

Table 6.1 **Comparison of various e-procurement models (Kalakota and Robinson[2])**

Trading model	Characteristics
EDI networks	■ Handful of trading partners and customers ■ Simple transactional capabilities ■ Batch processing ■ Reactive and costly value-added network (VAN) charges
Business-to-employees (B2E) requisition applications	■ Make buying fast and hassle-free for a company's employees ■ Automated approvals routing and standardisation of requisition procedures ■ Provide supplier management tools for the professional buyer
Corporate procurement portals	■ Provide improved control over the procurement process and let a company's business rules be implemented with more consistency ■ Custom, negotiated prices posted in a multisupplier catalogue ■ Spending analysis and multisupplier catalogue management
First-generation trading exchanges: community, catalogue and storefronts	■ Industry content, job postings, and news ■ Storefronts: new sales channel for distributors and manufacturers ■ Product content and catalogue aggregation services
Second-generation trading exchanges: transaction-orientated trading exchanges	■ Automated requisition process and purchase order transactions ■ Supplier, price and product/service availability discovery ■ Catalogue and credit management
Third-generation trading exchanges: collaborative supply chains	■ Enable partners to closely synchronise operations and enable real-time fulfilment ■ Process transparency, resulting in restructuring of demand and the supply chain ■ Substitute information for inventory
Industry consortia: buyer and supplier led	■ The next step in the evolution of corporate procurement portals

6.5   Electronic data interchange (EDI)

6.5.1 Definition

Electronic data interchange (EDI) may be defined as follows:

> The technique based on agreed standards, which facilitates business transactions in standardised electronic form in an automated manner directly from a computer application in one organisation to an application in another.

A *transaction* in EDI-speak is a term used to describe the electronic transmission of a single document. Each transaction set is usually referred to by a name and number, which are defined by the ASCx12 or EDIFACT standards referred to below. Thus, a purchase order in x12 is number 850. Each line of a transaction is termed a *segment* and piece of information in the line an *element*. In a purchase order, for example, the segment is the name and address of the purchaser or supplier. The segment is broken down into such data elements as organisation name, address line 1, address line 2, address line 3, postcode and country.

6.5.2 Standards

Data elements and codes are described in a directory relating to the message standard used. By the use of trade, national and international standards, organisations can trade electronically. Early message standards were developed by communities of organisations relating to an industry, such as automotive, construction and electronic enterprises, that had an interest in trading together. Thus, automotive manufacturers, including Ford, General Motors, Saab, Renault, Fiat, Austin Rover and Citroën and suppliers Lucas, Perkins, Bosch, GKN, SKF and BCS, set up ODETTE (Organisation for Data Exchange by Tele-Transmission in Europe). ODETTE sets the standards for e-business, engineering data exchange and logistics management that link the 4000 plus businesses in the European motor industry and their global partners.

Although there are still many EDI standards, only two – namely ASCx12 and EDIFACT – are widely used and recognised. ASCx12 standards were created in 1979 by the Accredited Standards Committee of the American National Standards Institute. These standards define the data formats and encoding rules for business transactions, including order placement and transportation. EDIFACT (EDI for Administration, Commerce and Transport) was developed by the United Nations in 1985 for the purpose of providing EDI standards that would support world trade. This international standard has been ratified as ISO 9735. UN/EDIFACT directories are published twice yearly by the United Nations.

6.5.3 How EDI works

How EDI is implemented is shown by Figure 6.1. The sequence is as follows:

1 company A creates a purchase order using its internal business software
2 EDI software translates the order
3 company A sends the 850 purchase order to company B over a third-party value-added network (VAN) or encrypted in EDIFACT format over the Internet

Figure 6.1 **EDI implementation**

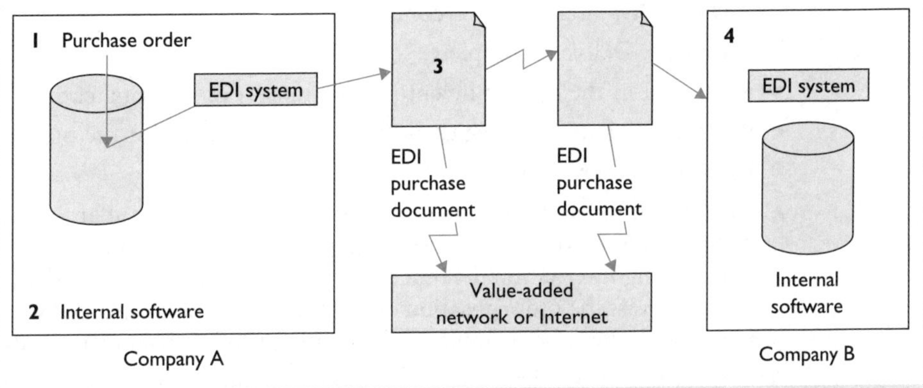

4 company B receives the 850 purchase order document and will translate it from EDI to its proprietary format and, typically, company B will send an acknowledgement to company A.

6.5.4 The advantages of EDI

- Replacing the paper documents – purchase orders, acknowledgements, invoices and so on – used by buyers and sellers in commercial transactions with standard electronic messages conveyed between computers, often without the need for human intervention.

EDI at the supermarket

One of the best examples of EDI is EPOS (electronic point-of-sale) at the supermarket. When a product is purchased, the checkout operator scans a barcode on its label, which automatically registers the price on the cash till.

That same signal also triggers a computer process that reorders the item from the manufacturer, sets off a production cycle, and arranges invoicing, payment and transportation of the new order. EDI effectively puts the product back on the shelf with no paperwork and a minimum of human involvement.

- Reduction in lead times as buyers and suppliers work together in a real-time environment. Armstrong and Jackson[3] provide a real-life example of pre- and post-EDI lead times. The latter shows a reduction of eight days for acknowledging the order and five days to deliver it. The total time was therefore reduced from 19 to 11 days.
  - Day 1: Order prepared and authorised electronically, then posted to EDI service.
  - Day 2: Order taken from EDI service by recipient and put straight into order processing system. An acknowledgement is created automatically and sent to the EDI service.

189

- Day 3: Manufacturing process begins (seven days). The acknowledgement is received by the originator and processed automatically.
- Day 9: Manufacturing is completed.
- Day 11: Delivery complete.

- Reduction in the cost of inventory and release of working capital.

- Promotion of such strategies as JIT as a consequence of the previous two points.

- Better customer service.

- Facilitation of global purchasing using international standards, such as EDIFACT, which is compatible with most equipment in most countries. In 1970, SITPRO (Simplifying International Trade Procedures Board) was established 'to guide, stimulate and assist the rationalisation of international flows associated with them'. SITPRO works with the British Standards Institution (BSI) in connection with EDI standards.

- Facilitation of invoice payments by the computer–to–computer transfer of money, which eliminates the need for the preparation and posting of cheques.

- The integration of functions, particularly marketing, purchasing, production and finance.

- EDI tends to promote long-term buyer–supplier relationships and increase mutual trust.

6.5.5 Some potential problems in implementing EDI

Killen and Kamauff[4] point out that before adopting EDI an organisation should:

- ensure that exchanging information electronically supports the overall organisational strategy

- consider the cost and ramifications of EDI's standard tools and techniques, including implementation, software maintenance, manpower and participant training and how to promote systems and applications integration

- consider the organisational and process changes involved.

In relation to the second point, Norman[5] states that the more the data is processed and reprocessed, the more room there is to save time and money. Potential EDI users should therefore calculate the cost per transaction. If it is cheaper to fax or manually perform the task, the buyer probably lacks the volume to invest in EDI. Monczka and Carter[6] propose the following indicators of a reasonable opportunity for the application of EDI in the purchasing environment:

- a high volume of paperwork transaction documents
- numerous suppliers
- a long internal administration lead time associated with the purchasing cycle
- a desire for personnel reductions, new hire avoidance or both
- a need to increase the professionalism of purchasing personnel.

6.5.6 EDI limitations

Historically, the two principal limitations of EDI relate to cost and flexibility.

Table 6.2 **Comparison of EDI and extranets**

Characteristics	EDI	Extranets
Infrastructure	Customised software	Packaged solutions that leverage and extend existing Internet technology and intranet investment
Transmission costs	Extensive VANS or leased lines, slow dial-up connections	Inexpensive and fast Internet connections
Access	Proprietary software	Web browsers support EDI protocols as well as many other open standards
Scale	Restricted to only the largest vendors who can support EDI infrastructure	Support real-time buying and selling, allowing for tighter and more proactive planning

Cost

EDI was, and still is, an expensive option, given that, until recently, organisations sent all EDI transactions over a VAN (value-added network) that had set-up and running costs often on a per thousand characters transmitted basis. The scope of EDI was also intentionally limited to ensure controlled activity within a closed door environment. The heavy overheads associated with EDI infrastructure were prohibitive for many small- to medium-sized enterprises.

Internet and extranet approaches can, however, enable a small business to link into secure EDI networks at minimal cost. The Internet pricing model of flat monthly rates has forced most of the VAN networks to lower their pricing structures. A new market shift is also underway in which organisations are moving from proprietary technology to extranet solutions. A comparison of EDI and extranet technologies is shown in Table 6.2.

Small businesses using the Internet can compete on a level playing field with large competitors, expand globally and improve their trading partner relationships.

Inflexibility

EDI is a cumbersome, static and inflexible method of transmitting data, most suited to straightforward business transactions, such as the placement of purchase orders for known requirements. It is not suitable for transactions requiring tight coupling and coordination, such as the consideration of several possible purchase alternatives or supply chain optimisation. Unlike human beings, computers are poor at interpreting unstructured data and cannot derive useful information from Web documents that are not predefined and permanent. The standard document language used to create web pages is hypertext mark-up language (HTML). While HTML is able to display data and focuses on how data look, it cannot describe data. While HTML can state what items a supplier can offer, it cannot describe them. Traditional EDI approaches do not, therefore, provide the flexibility required in a dynamic Internet environment.

6.5.7 EDI and XML

XML (referred to in 6.3.4 above) is an attempt to meet the problems of cost and inflexibility and the provision of a whole new way of communicating across the Internet and beyond.

The major difference between EDI and XML is that the former is designed to meet business needs and is a *process*. XML is a *language* and its success in any business will always depend on how it is being used by a given application.

As a language, XML provides a basic syntax that can be used to share information between many kinds of computer, different applications and different organisations. XML can also describe – as distinct from display – data. It can, for example, enable a purchaser to understand in detail what a supplier has to offer. It also ensures that a purchase order accurately describes what the purchaser requires. It therefore provides a direct route between purchaser and supplier, irrespective of the size of either, that was unavailable with EDI.

XML/EDI is an attempt to provide a standard framework for the exchange of different types of data, such as a purchase order, invoice or healthcare claim, so that the information, whether in a transaction, exchanged in an application program interface (API) database portal catalogue or a work flow document or message, can be searched, decoded, processed and displayed consistently and correctly by first implementing EDI questionnaires and extending our vocabulary via online repositories to include our business language, rules and objectives. Thus, by combining XML and EDI, we create a new, powerful approach that is different from XML and EDI.

In addition to EDI and the Internet, there are other ways of transmitting data electronically between two or more organisations. For small businesses, encrypted e-mails are very cost-effective. Orders can be collected securely online and put into existing in-house systems that automatically e-mail suppliers when stock values reach lower limits. Technology is also changing. Although until recently PCs were the Internet access device of choice, preferred substitutes, such as mobile phones and personal digital assistants (PDAs), are outselling PCs several times over. As an IBM[7] publication states:

> By 2003 the number of cellular phones around the world is expected to exceed one billion, with about 80 per cent of them having some form of access to the Internet. This rapid proliferation of new network access devices is referred to as persuasive computing-migration of the Web beyond PCs to a new generation of devices that can access any service utilising both wireless and wired connections.

The National Computing Centre[8] points out that, 'The latest business buzz word is Business Process Integration' (BPI), which is all about the processes that cross the buying and selling organisations – that is, there is greater benefit from automating the interactions than in the transactional aspects of ordering and invoicing.

The principle of BPI, which is based on XML standards, is similar to EDI. The main difference is that BPI can handle business rules – that is, it can recognise that an enquiry is from known client X and can therefore reply with stock/price availability specific to client X. EDI can only provide data in such a situation.

6.6 E-hubs, exchanges, portals and marketplaces

Some writers believe that a distinction can be made between these terms.

Figure 6.2 **A star network**

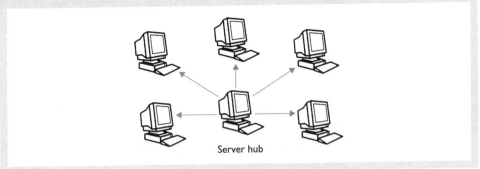

Server hub

6.6.1 Hubs

In the context of internal technologies, a hub is a device that connects several networks together. As used in e-businesses, a hub generally means a central repository or private exchange, such as the star network shown in Figure 6.2.

In the network shown in Figure 6.2, the *server* is a control computer that holds databases and programs for many PC workstations or terminals, which are called *clients*. The clients of the information hub may be internal customers or external organisations, such as suppliers.

6.6.2 Exchange

An exchange is a business-to-business (B2B) website where purchasers and suppliers meet to transact business. A distinction may be made between private and public exchanges.

Private exchanges can be either one-to-one (1T1) or one-to-many connections (1TM). The former are direct connections, while the latter connect all the actors through the central Internet hub. Private exchanges are normally specified by a single operation and available by invitation only to the organisation's suppliers and trading partners. Such private exchanges are frequently used for collaborative business procedures, such as real-time supply chain management and logistics.

Public exchanges – often referred to as *portals* – extend outside the boundaries of the company and involve many-to-many (MTM) interactions. Public exchanges may be run either by a consortium of big players within a specific industry (consortium portals) or by an independent entity starting up its business as an intermediary (independent portals). An example of the former is Covisent, founded in 2000 by General Motors, Ford, DaimlerChrysler, Nissan, Renault, Commerce One and Oracle to improve the effectiveness of critical processes, such as collaborative product development, procurement and supply chain management. By 2004, Covisent had over 29,000 registered customers and was connected to more than 146,000 active users in 96 countries.

Independent portals, such as ChemConnect and Verticainet, have some advantages relative to consortia and private e-markets. They can act more rapidly as they do not

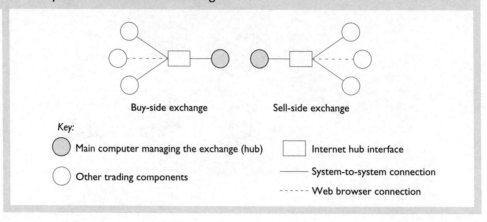

Figure 6.3 **Buy-side and sell-side exchanges**

Buy-side exchange   Sell-side exchange

Key:

⬤ Main computer managing the exchange (hub)   ▭ Internet hub interface

◯ Other trading components   —— System-to-system connection

---- Web browser connection

need to mediate among multiple owners as consortium portals do. Because they have comparatively few proprietary interests, they are also seen to be neutral, unlike the consortia and private e-markets. With all public exchanges, organisations pay a fee to become a member and possibly an additional transaction fee.

Both private and public exchanges can be either buy-side or sell-side, although this distinction is more usual with private exchanges. A *buy-side exchange* is built to interact with suppliers. Conversely a *sell-side exchange* is built to interact with customers. These are shown in Figure 6.3.[9]

6.6.3 Marketplace

Like an exchange, a marketplace is a website that enables purchasers to select from many suppliers. With e-marketplaces, the buyer is in control as open marketplaces enable purchasers to evaluate all potential suppliers for a particular product or service and make informed decisions regarding what and where to buy.

E-marketplaces are particularly applicable where:

■ markets are large and the search costs to find suppliers are high because of the large number of potential suppliers

■ product specifications and information are subject to rapid change

■ buyers have difficulty in comparing similar products from different vendors because of an excess of features and characteristics that may not be clearly indicated

■ internal costs of such processes as locating, appraising and evaluating the performance of suppliers are high.

In summary, it may be said that e-marketplaces offer greater functionality than exchanges, which, in turn, offer more functionality than hubs.

Figure 6.4 shows how hubs, exchanges and marketplaces interrelate in context with existing electronic communications, such as EDI, e-mail and fax.

Figure 6.4 **Hubs, exchanges and marketplaces in context**

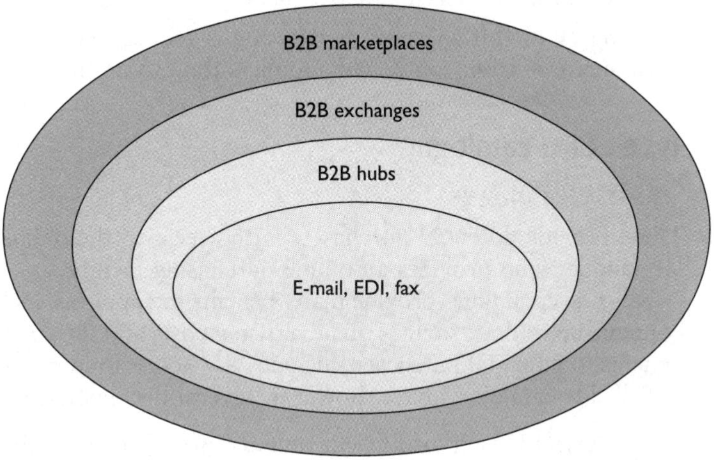

6.7 E-catalogues

Printed catalogues or products lists provide specifications, prices and, frequently, illustrations of the items that suppliers can provide. The disadvantages of hard copy catalogues are that they may be obsolete even before they are published and are too slow to provide information in a dynamic marketplace.

6.7.1 Definition

At their simplest, B2B marketplaces are just online catalogues. An e-catalogue may be defined as:

> A web page that provides information on products and services offered and sold by a vendor and supports online ordering and payment capabilities.

6.7.2 Advantages of e-catalogues

E-catalogues benefit both purchasers and suppliers in that they:

■ facilitate real-time two-way communication between buyers and sellers
■ allow for the development of closer purchaser–supplier relationships due to improved vendor services and by informing purchasers about products of which they might otherwise be unaware
■ enable suppliers to respond quickly to market conditions and requirements by adjusting prices and repackaging
■ virtually eliminate the time lag between the generation of a requisition by a catalogue user and the issue of the purchase order as:
  – authorisation, where required, can be done online and notified and confirmed by e-mail

195

- where users are authorised to generate their own purchases (subject to value and item constraints), the order can be automatically generated without the intervention of the purchasing department

■ maverick or 'off-contract' purchasing is reduced because it is simpler and quicker to purchase from contracted suppliers than to go outside the official system.

6.7.3 Types of e-catalogue

Sell-side catalogues

These provide potential purchasers with access to the online catalogues of a particular supplier who provides an online purchasing facility.

Sell-side catalogues provide many benefits to suppliers, including ease of keeping the contents up to date, savings on advertising costs and the costs of processing a sale. The benefits to potential purchasers include 24/7 access to information and ease of ordering.

Sell-side catalogues have, however, several disadvantages, including:

■ purchasers having insufficient time to surf all the available supplier websites

■ buyers perhaps becoming overly dependent on particular suppliers as training in the use of new software may be required if suppliers are changed

■ where the price of a product differs from one purchaser to another, the use of personalised, restricted, prenegotiated catalogues or encrypted catalogues may be necessary.

Buy-side catalogues

These are catalogues created by purchasing organisations. Normally, such catalogues are confined to goods covered by prenegotiated prices, specifications and terms and run by a program that is integrated into the purchasing organisation's intranet. An example of the operation of buy-side catalogues is shown in Figure 6.5.

The benefits to purchasers include:

■ reduced communication costs

■ increased security

■ many catalogues can be accessed via the same intranet application.

The compilation and updating of buy-side catalogues does, however, require a large investment in clerical resources that will be uneconomical for all but the largest organisations. Suppliers wishing to be included in the catalogue will also be required to provide their content in a standard format. For suppliers dealing with a large number of purchasers, the workload in terms of providing information in the form required by each online catalogue will be unsustainable.

Third-party catalogues

The disadvantages of sell- and buy-side catalogues can be minimised by outsourcing the process to an electronic marketplace or buying consortium. This can be done by linking the in-house e-procurement catalogue to a master catalogue administered by the marketplace, as shown in Figure 6.6.[10]

■ Standard information for inclusion in the 'market site' or 'master catalogue' is provided by the suppliers. This information is then made available to the in-house catalogues of individual purchasing organisations.

Figure 6.5 **Buy-side catalogue operation**

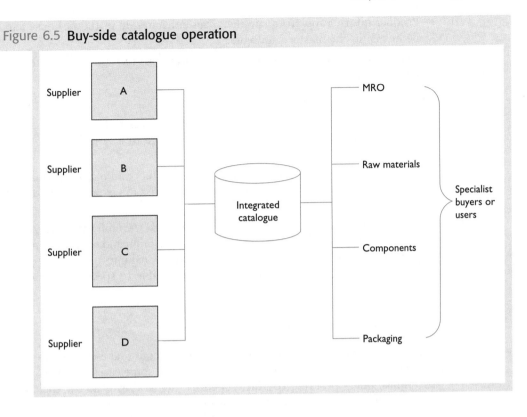

Figure 6.6 **Third-party catalogues**

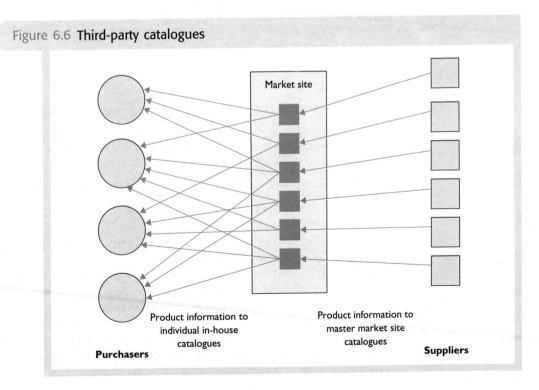

- Product information from suppliers can either reside in the in-house catalogue or be hosted in the master catalogue.
- The responsibility of managing and updating product and other information rests with the suppliers.

Advantages of this system include that:

- suppliers have a good incentive to provide information in the specified standard format as the master catalogue will be available to a large number of purchasing organisations
- the in-house procurement catalogues draw product and other information from the master catalogue and purchasers or users can pass electronic orders to suppliers via the market site
- product information can be divided into two parts – public and encrypted and public information will include a basic product description and specification, often accompanied by an illustration or diagram, while encrypted information will provide details of prices, discounts and similar matters applicable to specific purchasers that cannot be accessed by unauthorised users.

6.7.4 The future of e-catalogues

The UK National Computing Centre[11] has pointed out that e-catalogues used for indirect spend are expensive to create and maintain. In some cases they may not be needed as requisitioners ordering routine, repetitive items already know their requirements and organisations may simply need pick lists of MRO items based on a spreadsheet accessed on an intranet site. Where a supplier knows the purchaser's requirements, ordering history, required lead time and similar information, catalogues may be obsolete. Even so, catalogues offer so many advantages that they are here to stay.

6.8 E-auctions

One step up from e-catalogue is e-auctions. An e-auction may be defined as:[12]

> An electronic market, which can exist in both business-to-business and business-to-consumer contexts. Sellers offer goods or services to buyers through a website with a structured process for price setting and fulfilment.

Web auctions may follow English, Dutch, sealed-bid and reverse-bid processes.

- *English bid process* In this process, bids are successively replaced by higher bids to obtain the highest price for a given item.
- *Dutch bid process* The English process is unsuitable for selling thousands of items to a number of different buyers. This can, however, be easily and quickly done in a 'Dutch auction', developed in the seventeenth century in Amsterdam for the sale of flowers. In a Dutch auction, the auctioneer starts at a high price and then descends by steps until a bid is received. The successful bidder then decides whether to buy the whole or a portion of the items on offer at that price. The auctioneer increases the offer price for any items remaining in the current lot and then again descends by steps and continues in this manner until either all the items comprising the lot are sold or a reserve price is reached.

- *Sealed-bid process* This is broadly similar to tendering. A potential purchaser issues a request for bids to be submitted by a prescribed date and time according to a sealed format. At the specified date and time, the purchaser's representatives will evaluate and compare the bids according to a rating grid. The winning bid is the one that achieves the maximum score. Should several bids obtain the same score, the bid offering the best price is the winner.
- *Reverse-bid processes* See section 6.9.

6.9 Reverse auctions

6.9.1 What is a reverse auction?

In a reverse auction, buying organisations post the item(s) they wish to buy and price they are willing to pay while suppliers compete to offer the best price for the item(s) over a prescribed time period.

For example, a buying organisation is interested in purchasing 1000 castings to a published specification at the lowest possible price. It therefore creates a reverse auction, stating the dimensions, quality, performance and delivery requirements and, often, bid decrements. Suppliers enter the marketplace and bid on the auction. Winners are declared according to the agreed auction rules. Thus, e-auctions may be structured using the lowest price or most economically advantageous tender (MEAT) options.

At the conclusion of the auction, both purchaser and supplier are bound by the sale. If a reserve price is set but not met, the buying organisation decides the winning bid. Suppliers can bid more than once in the prescribed time. Apart from the names of the suppliers and reverse sealed bid auctions, all the bids are available for everyone to see. Most online auction sites use automatic bidding against agents or a 'proxy bidder' that automatically place bids on the suppliers' behalf.

Example 6.1

Reverse auction 1

Bids are solicited for 100 product Xs. The opening bid is £25 per product, with bid decrements of £5:

- supplier A bids £25 each for 100 items
- supplier B bids £20 each for 50 items
- supplier C bids £15 each for 50 items.

The result of the auction is that:

- supplier A is unsuccessful
- supplier B sells 50 items for £20
- supplier C sells 50 items for £15.

There are several variations on the bidding process. In what is known as the reverse English manual system, the buying organisation specifies the opening bid and the supplier bids higher. At the conclusion of the auction, the purchaser selects the winners manually. Each winning bidder sells at the bid price made. The criteria for the winning bid may not be disclosed.

Example 6.2

Reverse auction 2

Bids are solicited for 100 product Xs. The opening bid is £25:

- supplier A bids £18 per item for 100 items
- supplier B bids £20 per item for 100 items
- supplier C bids £20 per item for 100 items.

The result of the auction is that:

- supplier A is unsuccessful
- supplier C sells 100 items for £20, because of closer geographical proximity to the purchaser than supplier B.

6.9.2 When to use reverse auctions

Most reverse auctions are used for spot buying and eliminate the time-consuming offline process of selecting suppliers, requesting quotations and comparing quotes received. Marketplaces with many suppliers can offer purchasers a compiled list of suppliers. Purchasing organisations conducting reverse auctions on their own sites must invite prospective suppliers in advance if they wish such suppliers to participate. Reverse auctions are particularly useful in the following circumstances:

- when there is uncertainty as to the size of the market and the willingness of sellers to supply a product
- when purchasing large quantities of an item for which clear specifications are possible
- when selling surplus assets
- for some services, such as car rentals, freight services, travel.

The consensus used to be that the lowest-price reverse auction process should be used only when there is little concern about production specifications or the selected suppliers. Reverse auctions were not considered appropriate for complicated products or projects requiring collaboration or considerable negotiation. Buy IT,[13] however, states that software providers are now expanding their offerings to ensure that online auction tools become an integral part of the broader procurement strategy process, including the creation and management of optimal long-term value partnerships. As the goods or services became more difficult to specify and the relationships between purchasers and suppliers became more integrated, online auctions became less about driving cost out of the supply chain and more of a tool for collaboration.

6.9.3 The reverse auction process

Figure 6.7 indicates the principal steps involved.

Figure 6.7 **The reverse auction process**

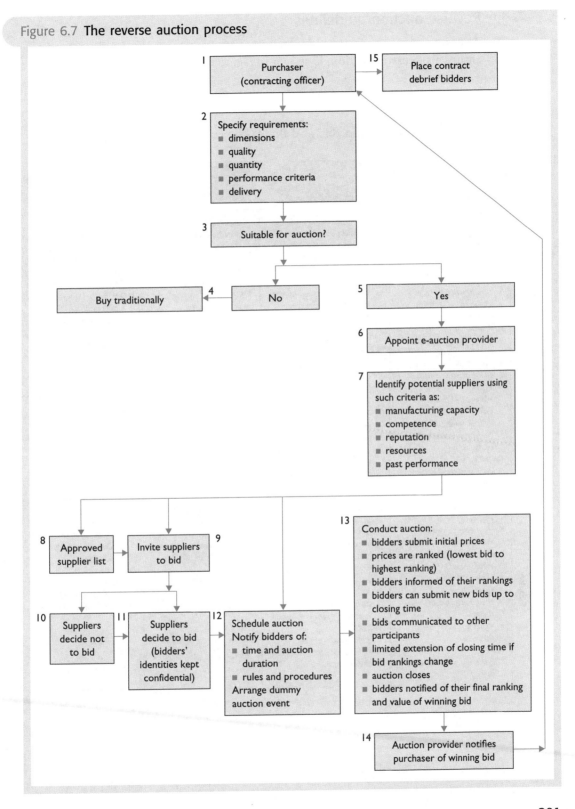

6.9.4 Reverse auction guidelines

A useful summary of online auction 'dos and don'ts', which, if followed, all help to ensure a successful auction, is shown in Figure 6.8.[14]

Figure 6.8 Online reverse auction dos and don'ts

	Strategy	Preparation	Event	Follow-up
Buyer	■ Is this a core competence for my business? ■ How does this fit with other e-procurement activities? ■ How will this fit with other e-procurement activities? ■ What approach to take: full service, supported or self-service? ■ What percentage of my spend is e-auctionable? ■ What do I want to achieve by running e-auctions? ■ What impact will this have on key supplier relationships? **DON'T** ■ Plan to reverse auction everything	■ Decide on number of suppliers to invite ■ Provide clear specification ■ Ensure there is sufficient market competition – or review approach ■ Gain internal commitment to implement the result ■ Develop robust lot strategy ■ Agree evaluation criteria ■ Set bid decrements ■ Train suppliers ■ Agree bid format and timing of events ■ Set clear rules for the event ■ Set opening price **DON'T** ■ Underinform participating suppliers ■ Plan the event at the wrong time, such as public holiday in the home country of participating suppliers	■ Ensure proxy bidding process in place ■ Monitor supplier bidding ■ Monitor technology reliability ■ Monitor bidding tactics **DON'T** ■ Act unethically ■ Get carried away with the hype, the lowest bid isn't always the best answer	■ Finalise sourcing decision ■ Obtain internal approval to decision if required ■ Give feedback to all suppliers, successful or not ■ Capture knowledge gained **DON'T** ■ Underestimate the importance of follow-up
Supplier	■ How much will this impact my sales pipeline? ■ How best to respond? ■ How will this impact my customer's relationships? ■ How will I tailor my approach by customer/product/ timing? ■ What do I want to achieve? **DON'T** ■ Refuse to participate on pricing	■ Respond promptly to all buyer's requests ■ Undertake all training offered ■ Preprepare initial bid ■ Consider event-specific strategies ■ Agree who will be on the bid team ■ Research your competition **DON'T** ■ Ignore offers of help and coaching from the customer or provider	■ Have your first bid ready before the start of the event ■ Submit bids – you have to be in it to win it **DON'T** ■ Bid below a sustainable cost ■ Act unethically	■ Provide cost breakdown, if requested ■ If unsuccessful, use benchmark to analyse market price gap **DON'T** ■ Ignore lessons learnt – there will almost certainly be a next time

6.9.5 Advantages of reverse auctions

Reverse auctions provide benefits for both buyers and sellers. The benefits for buyers include:

■ savings over and above those obtained from normal negotiations as a result of competition – on average, the auction process drives down supplier process by 11 per cent, with savings ranging from 4 to 40 per cent.[15]

■ reductions in acquisition lead times

■ access to a wider range of suppliers

■ a global supply base can be achieved relatively quickly

■ sources of market information are enhanced

■ more efficient administration of requests for quotations (RFQs) and proposals

■ auctions conducted on the Internet generally provide total anonymity so time is not wasted on seeing suppliers' representatives.

The benefits for suppliers include:

■ an opportunity to enter previously closed markets, which is particularly important for smaller companies

■ reduced negotiation timescales

■ provision of a good source of market pricing information

■ clear indications of what must be done to win the business.

6.9.6 Disadvantages of reverse auctions

Some objections to reverse auction include that they:

■ are based on a win–lose approach – the seller is trying to get the most money while the buyer is after the best deal and the goal is to screw your opponent to win either a good deal or a profitable deal at the other person's expense, so the logical progression is always towards cheating and, therefore, such a system cannot be sustained without burdensome watchdogs and regulators

■ can cause an adverse shift in buyer–seller relationships as the supplier may feel exploited and become less trustful of buyers

■ can have long-term adverse effects on the economic performance of both suppliers and purchasers as:

 – some suppliers may not be able to sustain sharp price reductions in the long term

 – suppliers that cannot compete at the lower price levels may be removed, or ask to be removed, from the purchaser's approved supplier list so those purchasers eventually have reduced supplier bases

 – in order to ensure that the exact goods and services required are obtained, considerable time may be needed to complete detailed specification sheets.

Figure 6.9 **Solutions landscape for electronic invoicing and payments**[16]

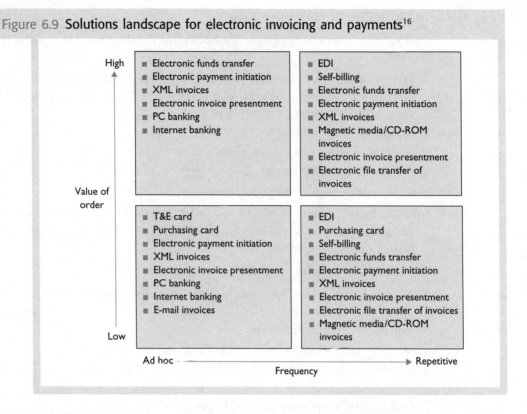

6.10   E-payment

E-payment may be by a standalone method, as with a purchasing card, or incorporated into software, as with the UK Ministry of Defence's purchaser to payment (P2P) system. This last system enables:

- an electronic order for goods and services to be sent to a trading partner
- an electronic receipt to be held and linked to the order for goods and services
- an electronic invoice to be sent to the MOD
- the order, receipt and invoice to be matched online, generating an electronic message authorising the processing of payment that is sent to the trading partner.

Figure 6.9 provides a useful map of e-payment and invoicing applications and the vendors that provide them, placing the different options according to whether the value of the purchase to which the payment relates is high or low and also the frequency of payments.

Security and auditing are important aspects of e-payments. Security risks include unauthorised access by hackers, illegal acquisition of PINs and data theft. Approaches to security concerns include:

- *encrypted technologies* the art of encoding information in such a way that only the holder of a secret password can decode and read it
- *certification authorisations* organisations that clarify and provide proof that a signature is valid.

In any e-payments system, it is vital that each invoice and payment is traceable throughout the system. The audit trail should track every line of data right back to the file where it originated.

6.11 The advantages of e-procurement

Buy IT[17] states that the benefits of an investment in e-procurement can be both hard – that is, directly measurable – and soft – indirectly measurable.

6.11.1 Hard measures

Hard measures include:

- automated purchase to buy process (order processing time and cost of auction)
- automation of P-card purchasing
- electronic payment of invoices
- lower prices by means of strategic sourcing
- average inventory reduction
- reduced head count
- supply base rationalisation.

6.11.2 Soft measures

Soft measures include:

- freeing up of purchasing staff time, enabling them to focus on more strategic procurement issues
- reduction in maverick buying (which is when staff buy from suppliers other than those with whom a purchasing agreement has been negotiated)
- improved monitoring of supplier performance
- improved order tracking and tracing
- improved availability of management information and accounting.

6.11.3 Intangible benefits

Intangible benefits include such things as cultural changes consequent on the implementation of e-procurement. These benefits cannot be measured within the business case but may support it.

Buy IT[18] states that, in order to identify e-procurement cost savings as distinct from those achieved by means of other procurement best practice, the measurement system needs to discriminate between 'business as usual' type savings and those directly attributed to the implementation of the e-procurement system.

6.12 Small-value purchases

A 1997 enquiry by the National Audit Office into low-value purchases by the Ministry of Defence found that procurement costs for such items were high. For example, obtaining quotes and issuing a purchase order for a padlock costing 80p amounted to £90. Low-value orders increase costs and hamper purchasing and accounting productivity. Low-cost procedures for the efficient handling of low-value purchases include the following.

6.12.1 Delegated order placement to users

Placement of own orders by users within specified limits and with approved suppliers over the Internet.

6.12.2 Purchasing cards

These are similar to credit cards and involve a provider such as American Express and usually an issuing bank. When used for low-value purchases, they enable any user, such as a foreman on a building site, to make purchases and provide payments to suppliers. Richardson[19] has listed the following benefits of using purchasing cards:

- compliance levels can improve where more orders are going through preferred suppliers, which can lead to better volume discounts
- average transaction and order processing costs can drop dramatically
- implementation costs are 10 to 100 times less than for an ERP or e-procurement system
- suppliers are paid faster, enabling then to invest in their business and improve their services to clients
- greater and improved documentation of data on accounts, suppliers and taxes
- less purchasing employee time spent on order paperwork and chasing, allowing more time for strategic and tactical work.

Clearly the issue and use of purchasing cards has to be carefully controlled. The cardholder should be held responsible for protecting the purchasing card and for all purchases made using a particular purchasing card number.

Neither the physical purchasing card nor its account number should be shared with or transferred to any other person to use. A purchasing card internal review should be held periodically to ensure compliance with controls, appropriateness of purchases, that cards are actually in the possession of the authorised holders and that there is general adherence to specific purchase procedures.

6.12.3 Other methods of dealing with low-value purchases

Other methods of dealing with low-value purchases are listed below.

- *Telephone orders* Requirements are telephoned to the supplier who is provided with an order number. The agreed price is recorded on the order form, but this is not sent to the supplier. The goods are invoiced by the supplier against the order form.
- *Petty cash purchases* Items are obtained directly from local suppliers on presentation of an authorised requisition form and paid for at once from petty cash. The main problem is that of controlling the numbers and sizes of such purchases. This can be done by providing potential users with a petty cash imprest, out of which such payments are made.

- *Standing orders* All orders for a range of items, such as electrical fittings, fasteners, are placed with one supplier for a period of, say, 12 months. A special discount is often negotiated and quantities may or may not be specified. Required items are called off by users who transmit releases directly from the supplier via a fax, telephone or computer interface. The amount due is summarised by the supplier, either electronically or tabulated as a single invoice, and segregated by users' cost centres for easier coding by the accounts function.
- *Self-billing* This uses EDI. When the former Rover Group, which traded electronically, received goods from a supplier, it checked that the goods were ordered and then simply paid. The supplier did not need to raise an invoice. Self-billing enables both customer and supplier to make saving.
- *Blank cheque orders* A system devised in the USA. A cheque form with a specified liability is attached to the order form. On forwarding the goods, the supplier fills in the cheque, which he or she deposits in his or her own bank. The cheque can only be deposited, not cashed, until authorised by the purchaser. The need for invoicing and forwarding of payment is thus avoided.
- *Stockless buying* This is virtually the same as blanket ordering, but the supplier agrees to maintain stocks of specified items.

6.13 Purchasing manuals

6.13.1 What is a purchasing manual?

Essentially, a purchasing manual is a medium for communicating information regarding purchasing policies, procedures, instructions and regulations.

- *Policies* may be general or consequential. *General policies* state, in broad terms, the objectives and responsibilities of the purchasing function. *Consequential policies* state, in expanded form, how general polices are applied in specific activities and situations, such as the selection of suppliers.
- *Procedures* prescribe the sequence of activities by which policies are implemented, such as the receipt of bought-out goods.
- *Instructions* give detailed knowledge or guidance to those responsible for carrying out the policies or procedures, such as suppliers with whom call-off contracts have been negotiated.
- *Regulations* detailed rules regarding the conduct of purchasing and ancillary staff in the various situations arising in the course of their duties, such as concerning the receipt of gifts from suppliers.

When drafting a purchasing manual, it is useful to keep these distinctions clearly in mind.

6.13.2 Advantages of purchasing manuals

Advantages claimed for purchasing manuals include the following:

- writing it down helps with precision and clarity
- the preparation of the manual provides an opportunity for consultation between purchasing and other departments to look critically at existing policies and procedures and, where necessary, change them

- procedures are prescribed in terms of activities undertaken or controlled by purchasing, thus promoting consistency and reducing the need for detailed supervision of routine tasks
- a manual is a useful aid in training and guiding staff
- a manual can help the annual audit
- a manual coordinates policies and procedures and helps to ensure uniformity and continuity of purchasing principles and practice, as well as providing a point of reference against which such principles and practice can be evaluated
- a manual may help to enhance the status of purchasing by showing that top management attaches importance to the procurement function
- computerisation, which needs detailed and well-documented systems, has given further impetus to the preparation of purchasing manuals.

6.13.3 Disadvantages of purchasing manuals

Some disadvantages of manuals are that they:

- are costly to prepare
- tend to foster red tape and bureaucracy and stifle initiative
- must be continually updated to show changes in procedures and policy.

6.13.4 Format

Although hard copy manuals are still produced, the most suitable format is that of an operational database used to process the information needed to perform operational tasks. This can be available internally via an intranet or externally on the Internet. As the manual is freely accessible, it encourages transparency and can easily be updated.

Contents

A purchasing manual may consist of three main sections, dealing respectively with organisation, policy and procedures.

- *Organisation*
  - Charts showing the place of purchasing within the undertaking and how it is organised, both centrally and locally.
  - Possibly job descriptions for all posts within the purchasing function, including, where applicable, limitations of remits.
  - Teams relating to purchasing and supply chain activities.
  - Administrative information for staff, such as absences, hours of work, travelling expenses and similar matters.
- *Policy*
  - Statements of policy, setting out the objectives, responsibilities and authority of the purchasing function.

- Statements, which can be expanded, of general principles relating to price, quality and delivery.
- Terms and conditions of purchase.
- Ethical relationships with suppliers, especially regarding gifts, and entertainment.
- Environmental policies.
- Supplier appraisal and selection.
- Employee purchases.
- Reports to management.

■ *Procedures*
- Descriptions, accompanied by flow charts, of procedures relating to requisitioning, ordering, expediting, receiving, inspecting, storing and payment of goods with special reference to procurement.
- Procedures relating to the rejection and return of goods.
- Procedures regarding the disposal of scrap and obsolete or surplus items.

6.14 Supplier manuals

Purchasing manuals are primarily for internal use, whereas supplier manuals provide information for the providers of goods and services. Such manuals may relate to a specific aspect of supplier relationships, such as quality or delivery requirements and ethical or environmental issues, or be a comprehensive publication covering all aspects of supply.

6.14.1 The purpose of supplier manuals

Supplier manuals may achieve the following.

■ Set out the parameters within which the purchaser is prepared to trade with the supplier. Most supplier manuals contain a statement that:

variation from the requirements/standards prescribed in this manual will only be permitted with the specific written agreement of the supply manager.

■ Provide the legal basis for trading, such as:

compliance with the requirements of this manual is a requirement of the conditions of purchase that form part of the XYZ trading terms and conditions and that suppliers accept when agreeing to supply goods or services to XYZ. Failure to comply is a breach of contract.

■ Provide essential information required by the supplier relating to the purchaser's requirements regarding such issues as packaging, transportation, deliveries, delivery locations, environmental and ethical polices and e-procurement.

6.14.2 The content of supplier manuals

The following are typical headings for a supplier manual.

- *Introduction*
  - The purpose of the manual.
  - Non-variation statement, similar to that in 6.14.1 above.
  - Compliance with the manual as a condition of purchase.
- *Conditions of purchase*
  - Definitions, such as the meanings attached to such terms as the 'purchaser', 'the supplier' and 'goods'.
  - Supply of goods.
  - Quality of goods.
  - Remedies for supplier non-compliance.
  - Payment.
  - Intellectual property rights.
  - Termination.
  - General provisions relating to subcontracting, privacy of information, law governing contracts.
- *Preorder requirements*
  - Procedures that the supplier must observe before the dispatch of goods.
- *Predelivery requirements*
  - First production samples.
  - Pallet requirements.
  - Configuration of palletised stock.
  - Split deliveries.
- *Transportation and delivery requirements*
  - Carriers.
  - Timeliness and time of deliveries.
  - Documentation.
- *Post delivery requirements*
  - Post delivery procedures.
  - Pallet redemption.
  - Misdeliveries.
  - Goods for return.
- *Policies and quality*
  - Purchaser's environmental policies.
  - Health and safety policies.
  - Code of conduct for ethical trading.
  - Quality assurance terms and conditions.
- *Appendices*
  - Glossary of terms.
  - Warehouse addresses, telephone and fax numbers.

- *Agreements (to be signed and returned)*
  - Purchaser's trading terms and conditions.
  - New supplier account agreement.
- *Questionnaire (to be completed and returned)*
  - Supplier EDI questionnaire.

6.14.3 Format

This will be similar to that for a purchasing manual, as described in 6.13.4.

6.15 Legal aspects of purchasing

Although purchasing procedures may have changed from manual to electronic methods, all commercial transactions must conform to the requirements of a valid contract.

6.15.1 The essentials of a contract

A valid contract is a promise or agreement that the law will enforce. To be legally enforceable, a contract must satisfy the following essentials.

- *Intention* Both parties must intend to enter into a legal relationship.
- *Agreement* In a dispute, the court must be satisfied that the contracting parties had reached a firm agreement and were not still negotiating. Agreement will usually be shown by the unconditional acceptance of an offer. It is important to determine by whom the offer is made, whether the offer is valid and if it has been accepted.
- *Consideration* English law of contract is concerned with *bargains*, not mere promises. Thus, if A promises to give something to B, B will have no remedy if A breaks his promise. If, however, B has undertaken to do something in return so that A's promise is dependent on B's, the mutual exchange of promises turns the arrangement into a contract. The consideration must also exist and have some ascertainable value, however slight, otherwise there is no contract.
- *Form* Certain exceptional types of agreement are only valid if made in a particular way, such as in writing. Thus, conveyances of lands and leases for over three years must be by deed. The absence of written evidence, while not affecting the validity of a contract, may make it unenforceable in the courts. This evidence may be from correspondence or any other documentation made at the time the contract was made or subsequently. Such written evidence must clearly identify the parties against whom the evidence is to be used or by authorised agent.
- *Definite terms* There will be no contract if it is not possible to determine what has been agreed between the parties. Where essential terms have yet to be decided, the parties are still in the stage of negotiation. An agreement to agree in future is not a contract.
- *Legality* Some agreements, such as contracts to defraud the Inland Revenue, or immoral contracts, such as agreements to fix prices or regulate supplies, while not illegal are void under the Competition Acts, unless the parties can prove to the Restrictive Practices Court that their agreement is beneficial and in the public interest.

211

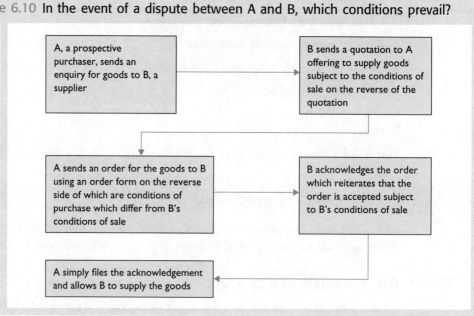

Figure 6.10 In the event of a dispute between A and B, which conditions prevail?

6.15.2 The 'battle of the forms'

One of the essential elements of a valid contract (that is, a contract that can be enforced) is an unconditional acceptance by the offeror (that is, the party to whom the offer is made) of an offer made by the other party, known as the offeree. If the acceptance seeks to vary the terms of the offer in any way, there is a counter-offer and the original offer lapses.

Thus, in the case of *Hyde* v *Wrench* (1840), Wrench (W) offered to sell his farm to Hyde (H) for £1000. H replied, offering £950, which W refused and, without informing H of his intention, sold the farm elsewhere. H later wrote, accepting the original price of £1000 and, on finding the farm sold, sued W for breach of contract. The contract held that the counter-offer of £950 rejected the original offer, which could only be revived by W.

Quotations, order forms and acknowledgements often contain, on their reverse side, or make reference to standard conditions of sale or purchase. The situation that can arise is shown in Figure 6.10.

The term 'battle of the forms' was coined by Lord Denning in the case of *Butler Machine Tool Co. Ltd* v *Ex-Cell-O Corporation (England) Ltd* (1979), which arose from differing sets of standard conditions. Butler, the sellers, made a quotation offering to sell a machine tool to Ex-Cell-O, the buyers, for £75,000. The offer was stated to be subject to terms and conditions that 'shall prevail over any terms and conditions in the Buyer's order'. These included a price variation clause for the goods to be charged at the price ruling on the date of delivery. The buyers ordered the machine, their order being subject to terms and conditions materially different from those of the sellers' and containing no price variation clause. At the foot of the buyers' order was a tear-off acknowledgement of receipt of the order stating, 'We accept your order on the Terms and Conditions stated hereon'. The acknowledgement was completed by the sellers and returned to the buyers with a letter stating that the buyers' order was being entered in accordance with the sellers' quotation.

On delivery, the sellers claimed a price increase of £2892, which the buyers refused to pay. The sellers brought an action, claiming that the variation clause entitled them to increase their price. Although the buyers contended that the contract had been concluded on their terms and was therefore a fixed-price contract, the judge found for the sellers on the grounds that the contract had been concluded on the basis that the sellers' terms were to prevail as variation was stipulated in the opening offer and this applied to subsequent negotiations.

This verdict was, however, reversed on appeal on the grounds that the sellers, by completing and returning the buyers' terms, could not therefore claim to increase the price under the price variation clause contained in their offer. The sellers' letter referring to the quotation was irrelevant as it referred only to the price and identity of the machine and did not incorporate the sellers' terms into the contract.

This case is important as it emphasises that whether or not the buyers' or sellers' terms and conditions apply depends on the facts of the case. As Lord Denning stated:

> In most cases when there is a battle of forms there is a contract as soon as the last of the forms is sent and received without any objections being taken to it . . . The difficulty is to decide which form or part of which form is a term or condition of the contract. In some cases the battle is won by the man who fires the last shot. He is the man who puts forward the latest terms and conditions and, if they are not objected to by the other party, he may be taken to have agreed to them. In some cases the battle is won by the man who gets his blow in first . . . There are yet other cases where the battle depends on the shots fired by both sides . . . The terms and conditions of both parties are to be construed together.

Thus, in the situation shown in Figure 6.10, it would be the sellers' terms and conditions that would prevail.

It is advisable for buyers to include a clause in their conditions of purchase stating that liability will only be accepted for orders placed subject to the terms and conditions stated on their order forms, which the sellers accept by signing and returning an acknowledgment form referring to those conditions within a stipulated time – say 14 days.

6.15.3 Law and the buyer

Commercial or mercantile law includes agency agreements, contracts for the sale of goods and services, insurance, negotiable instruments and carriage by land, sea and air. Clearly all such legislation, together with that relating to electronic trading and European procurement, is applicable to purchasing. There are at least three good reasons for all purchasing professionals to have a working knowledge of commercial law. First, the principle of *ignorantia juris non excusat* (ignorance of the law does not excuse) means that a company (which, in law, is a legal person) and its servants, such as purchasing specialists, are presumed to know the law. Second, all purchasing staff should have an awareness of the possible legal consequences of their actions. Third, 'a little knowledge is a dangerous thing' and a knowledge of the law should indicate when it is advisable for buyers to seek professional advice.

6.15.4 The general structure of a contract

■ *The agreement* This names the parties to the contract. In a standard contract, it is only necessary to change the names and any other relevant details. If the parties sign on the front page, this saves leafing through the whole, but there should be a statement that the parties have read and understood all the terms and conditions appertaining to the contract.

■ *The terms and conditions* These are comprised of the following points.

– *Definitions* These are inserted to avoid ambiguity and avoid the repetition of long sentences. When, in the text, a capital letter is used for a word, it indicates that the word has been defined in the 'definitions' section.

– *General terms* These are the general agreements clause, changes, alterations and variations clause, 'notice' clause – stating how and by what method any notice relating to the contract is to be sent – and a clause stating that the headings and definitions are for information only.

– *The commercial provisions* These set out the rights and obligations of the supplier and, in a separate clause, the rights and obligations of the purchaser. Another separate clause will specify payment terms.

– *Secondary commercial provisions* These deal with such matters as conditions, warranties, confidentiality, intellectual property, indemnity and termination.

– *Boilerplate clauses* These are standard clauses that appear in almost all contracts, such as the following.

  ■ *severability* the right of a court to remove a term or condition that is invalid, void or unenforceable without prejudice to the rest of the contract

  ■ *waiver* a statement that failure to enforce a 'right' at a given time will not prevent the exercise of that right later

  ■ *force majeure* applicable where a 'major force', such as an act of God, war, riots, floods, tempests and so on, prevents or delays the performance of the contract

  ■ *law and jurisdiction* the law that governs the contract – *The Principles of International Contracts*, produced by the International Institute for the Unifications of Private Law (UNIDROIT) in 1994 aim to:

  > . . . establish a balanced set of rules designed for use throughout the world, irrespective of the legal traditions and the economic and political conditions of the countries in which they are to be applied.

These principles have no legal force and depend for their acceptance on their perceived authority. When, however, the parties agree, they can become legally binding.

6.15.5 The interpretation of contracts

It is usual for purchasing staff to know something of the general principles of interpretation and the rules of evidence, including how the courts will construe the words used, resolve ambiguities, take account of trade usages, vary written terms and 'fill in the gaps' with regard to issues not covered in the contract.

Case study

Introducing e-procurement

Background

The Grant Group supplies a wide range of packaged food products to the large supermarket chains and other selected, independent food retailers. The group has always recognised the importance of buying in a retail context and employs a team of 20 buying specialists. It has commodity responsibility, including buying, own-brand tinned products, such as salmon, branded tinned soups and meats, packaging, including outers and inners (cardboard, cans, tins, bottles, capital equipment and engineering and office consumables), and short shelf-life products. The group's margins are not very good because of concentrated buying power in the hands of a few supermarkets. The Buying Director has recognised that savings can be made by getting smarter and using e-procurement.

The data transfer relating to buying actions, including market enquiries, quotations, purchase orders, shipping and dispatch details and invoicing, are done by using mailed hard copies, e-mails and fax. The data is sent in various formats, including Word, Excel, Text and so on.

The Grant Group purchases from a range of suppliers, some of which are extremely sophisticated but others have legacy systems. Traditionally, the IT focus has been on customer-facing systems, receiving EPOS data and interfacing warehouse and dispatch/transportation systems. It is worth noting that some of the Grant Group's customers have made it a mandatory condition of being a supplier to invest in IT technology.

What next?

The Buying Director has asked you to join a working party to review the introduction of e-procurement into the Grant Group. The working party will have representatives from buying, marketing, IT and finance.

Your first formal meeting is due next week and you have been asked to present a paper on the required functionality of any proposed system. The Buying Director suggests that you consider:

- online connectivity with key suppliers
- provision for paperless buying
- electronic generation of requests for quotations and subsequent receipt and analysis of quotations
- linkage between receipt of customer demand and repeat buying actions
- purchase order generation
- shipping and dispatch data
- payment
- use of reverse auctions.

Obviously, you will formulate your ideas and seek to present a structured response that will include your views on success factors, barriers to change and the expected business benefits from the introduction of e-procurement.

Task

Prepare your presentation for the working party, ensuring that there are sufficient points of substance to obtain the support of your colleagues.

Discussion questions

6.1　(a) Prepare a flow chart of a traditional, paper-based purchasing system from the receipt of a requisition to the payment of the supplier.

(b) Estimate the time taken and the cost of each stage in the above process.

(c) Prepare a flow chart showing how the same activities would be done under e-procurement.

(d) Estimate the savings in time and cost using e-procurement.

6.2　Why, in many organisations, is e-procurement limited to MRO (maintenance, repair and operating) items?

6.3　Does your organisation:

(a) currently use e-procurement?

(b) plan to use e-procurement?

(c) not plan to use e-procurement?

If the answer is (c) state why.

6.4　A consultancy undertook research into the most significant benefits that a sample of 200 major UK companies derived from e-procurement and those aspects that the companies regarded as 'not at all significant'. Arrange the following into two lists: (1) those that *you* would consider 'very significant' and (2) those that you would consider 'not at all significant':

- savings from enterprisewide contracts
- improved supplier relationships
- increase in purchases under approved contracts
- improved management information
- reduced requisition to payment time
- reduced cost per transaction.

Give reasons for your rankings.

6.5

Type of purchase	High frequency, low value	Low frequency, low value	High frequency, high value	Low frequency, low planning
Example of product Possible e-commerce method				

Complete the above chart by:

(a) allocating the following products to the appropriate headings:

- incidental items
- raw materials
- capital equipment
- MRO (maintenance, repair and operating items)
- urgently required low-cost items
- insurance and legal services
- product components
- commodities.

(b) allocating the following e-commerce methods to the appropriate headings (some may be suitable for more than one heading):
- Internet for sourcing
- online catalogue
- EDI
- e-mail
- ERP systems
- fax.

6.6 XML offers its users many advantages, including:
- simplicity
- extensibility
- interoperability
- openness.

Give one example of how XML provides each of the above advantages.

6.7 You have several items of production plant that are now surplus to requirements. What benefits might be obtained from offering them for sale in a reverse auction?

6.8 Is it possible to use reverse auctions and also build long-term supplier relationships?

6.9 Draft rules and guidelines for the information of staff to whom purchasing cards have been issued.

6.10 The following legal terms are not referred to in the text. From your knowledge of the law, how many can you define or explain?
- Accord and satisfaction
- Anticipatory breach
- Agent
- Assumpsit
- *Caveat emptor*
- Condition
- Disclosure
- Duress
- Estoppel
- Express terms
- Frustration
- Fundamental breach
- Implied conditions
- Impossibility of performance
- Liquidated damages
- Misrepresentation
- Mistake
- *Quantum meruit*
- Rescission
- Restraint of trade
- Specific performance
- *Uberrima fides*
- Vicarious performance
- Warranty

Past examination questions

All the following are taken, with permission, from the CIPS Professional Stage Examinations *Purchasing and Supply Chain Management* II: Tactics and Observations.

1   The application of information technology (IT) can have a significant impact upon the management of the supply chain in general and a profound effect upon the purchasing function in particular.

Discuss the extent to which you agree with this statement with reference to the impact of IT on both the management of the supply chain and the purchasing function.

(November 2001)

2   E-commerce impacts upon the supply chain by offering a number of important advantages to the buyer and it will shift the balance of power to buyers. What do you consider to be these advantages and how will they impact upon the supply chain?

(May 2002)

3   Identify ways in which information technology can be applied to the purchasing and supply function and evaluate the possible benefits.

(November 2003)

4   Identify and discuss the ways in which e-commerce and information technology in general have affected the management and operations of the purchasing function and how they may continue to do so in the future.

(May 2003)

References

1   Killen, K. H., and Kamauff, J. W., *Managing Purchasing*, Irwin, 1995, pp. 17–18

2   Kalakota, R., and Robinson, M., *E-business* 2.0, 2nd edn, Addison Wesley, 2001, p. 310

3   Armstrong, V., and Jackson, D., 'Electronic data interchange: a guide to purchasing and supply', CIPS, 1991, pp. 15–16

4   As 1 above, p. 60

5   Norman, G., 'Is it time for EDI?', Logistics Supplement, *Journal of Purchasing and Supply Management*, June, 1994, p. 20

6   Monczka, R. M., and Carter, J. R., 'Implementation of electronic data interchange', *Journal of Purchasing and Supply Management*, Summer, 1998, pp. 2–9

7   *IBM Computing in an E-business World*, IBM, 2000, p. 16

8   National Computing Centre, 'The impact of e-purchasing on supply chain management', *My IT Adviser*, 17 Sept., 2002

9   Adapted from Ronchi, Stefano, *The Internet and the Customer Supplier Relationship*, Ashgate, 2003, p. 48

10 We are indebted to the ACTIVE Secretariat, 20 Eastbourne Terrace, London W2 6LE, for permission to use this figure, taken from 'The e-Business Study', 2000, p. 20

11 As 8 above

12 Epicor 2000, *The Strategy*, p. 91

13 Buy IT, 'Online auctioning: e-procurement guidelines', issued by Buy IT Best Practice Network, Oct., 2001, pp. 13–14

14 The authors are grateful to David Eaton and the Buy IT e-procurement Best Practice Network for permission to use this figure, taken from 'Buy IT Online Auctions', 2001, p. 5

15 Lascelles, D., *Managing the Supply Chain*, Business Intelligence, 2001, p. 44

16 We are grateful to CIPS for permission to reproduce this figure, taken from 'The CIPS E-procurement guidelines: e-invoicing and e-payment'

17 Buy IT, 'E-procurement guidelines: measuring the benefits', Sept., 2002

18 As 17 above

19 Richardson, T., 'Guide to purchasing cards', Supplement, *Purchasing and Supply Management*, 2003, p. 7

Part 2

Strategy, tactics and operations 1: purchasing factors

Chapter 7

Supplier relationships

Learning outcomes

This chapter aims to provide an understanding of:

- relationship purchasing and purchasing relationships
- models of supplier relationships
- the termination of supplier relationships.

Key ideas

- Transactional and relationship purchasing.
- Relationship formation.
- Classification and analysis of supplier relationships.
- The practical usefulness of supplier relationship models.
- Factors to consider when terminating supplier relationships.

Introduction

This chapter is concerned with providing an understanding of purchasing–supplier relationships from the perspectives of both theory and practice.

7.1 Relationship purchasing and purchasing relationships

A relationship is defined, inter alia, as a 'connection or association'.[1] Relationships apply when individuals, organisations and groups within and external to an enterprise interact. Apart from the field of industrial sociology, concerned with the study of group interaction within a workplace environment, the application of the study of business relationships began with the concept of relationship marketing.

As currently used, relationship marketing describes a long-term marketing strategy in which the emphasis is on building and maintaining long-term relationships with customers, rather than on 'one sale at a time' approaches. On a business-to-business level, relationship marketing applies to the management of a range of purchasing–supplier relationships in the context of a broader network of interconnected purchasing, supplier and competitor organisations.

As purchasing is the mirror image of marketing, relationship purchasing aims to achieve strong, lasting relationships with suppliers with a view to securing mutual benefits and the added value of competitive advantages for both parties. There is, however, a difference between relationship purchasing and purchasing relationships. Not all purchasing relationships are concerned with long-term purchasing–supplier associations. Purchasing relationships may be considered as having two aspects: relationship formation and relationship forms.

The most successful relationships are those where customers and suppliers develop trust and an understanding of their respective requirements and interests, accompanied by a concern for both learning from and providing assistance to each other. Where such conditions exist, the ultimate outcome should be the creation of established and dependable purchasing–supplier relationships. Such relationships are the basis of networks and provide competitive advantages for both parties.

7.2 The differences between transactional and relationship purchasing[2]

These are shown in Table 7.1.

Table 7.1 **The main differences between transactional and relationship purchasing**

Transactional	Relationship
Focus on short, discrete purchasing	Focus on supplier retention
Short-term orientation	Long-term orientation
Arm's length	Closeness
Simple buyer–seller relationship	Complicated, including internal relationships
Emphasis on price, quality and delivery in the offered product No innovation	Emphasis on improving price, quality, delivery and other factors, such as innovative design as a collaborative exercise between purchaser and supplier
Moderate supplier contact	High level of supplier contact, with each contact being used to gain information and strengthen the relationship
Little sharing of information; opaqueness	Significant sharing of information, including cost information; transparency
Reverse auctions may be applicable	Reverse auctions generally not applicable

Figure 7.1 **Processes and outcomes on different interaction levels**

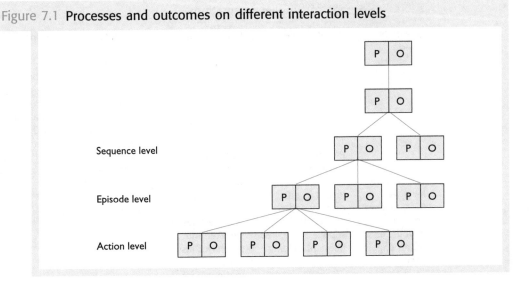

7.3 Relationship formation

As shown in Figure 7.1, Holmlund and Strandvik[3] classify interactions between two or more enterprises as taking place on five different aggregation levels – actions, episodes, sequences, relationships and partner base. These are hierarchical levels, ranging from a single exchange to the portfolio of relationships of one particular enterprise.

- *Actions* 'individual initiatives by the focal enterprise', such as a telephone call or plant visit, that may relate to products, information, money or social contacts.

- *Episodes* groups of interrelated actions, such as a negotiation encompassing a number of actions.

- *Sequences* larger and more extensive entities of interactions. This level may be defined in terms of a contract, product, campaign or project. Holmlund and Strandvik[4] also point out that:

  > a sequence, in enterprises, can also be related to the presence of a significant human action in either of the organisations. A sequence may then end when a particular person is replaced by another in either firm. Even if the relationship continues, the quality of the relationship may change due to the influence of one single person . . . The completion of a sequence constitutes a vulnerable period of time during which the parties make important evaluations. The evaluation may cause a potential termination of the relationship, since a sequence represents a time-framed commitment, which is defined by the particular sequence.

- *Relationships* comprised of all the sequences, which, in turn, are comprised of all related episodes and actions in one particular relationship between two firms.

- *Partner base* the relationship portfolio of a particular enterprise – that is all the relationships that a particular enterprise has at a particular point of time.

The formation of long-term personal relationships usually develops by going through the same stages. Thus, a meeting (action level) may develop into a friendship (episode

Table 7.2 **Stages of supplier integrations**

One-night stand	Regular date	Going steady	Living together	Marriage
				Cobusiness integration
				Core competences totally aligned, such that rationalisation will release added value
			Strategic alliances	
		Performance partnerships	Single sourcing and joint investment strategies; interdependence becomes the driving force	
	Preferred suppliers	Benchmarking still applied to assess value but now joint definition of improvement plans and priorities, joint supplier and purchaser fusion teams with specific improvement objectives, some job rotation		
Competitive leverage Bids, tenders and tactical negotiation on an ongoing basis	Proven track record in quality, delivery and cost, hence smaller supplier base, less frequent bidding			

Low ◄——————————————————————————————————► High

Degree of strategic alignment and integration of core competences

Source: Johnson, S., Tinsley Bridge Ltd, 'Managing change through teamwork', ISCAN, Sheffield, 1997, pp. 7–17

level), courtship (sequential level) and marriage (relationship level). Each level is normally of a longer and more permanent duration than the preceding one. The model of supplier integration shown in Table 7.2 follows this pattern.

Jarvelin,[5] however, argues that, for practical purposes, the quality of relationships can be studied at two levels: episodes and relationships.

7.4   Models of supplier relationships

There are several classifications, of which the following, by Cox, Bensaou, and the IMP Group, are typical.

7.5   The Cox model

Cox[6] presents a stepladder of external and internal relationships, as shown in Figure 7.2.

Cox gives two reasons for the omission from the ladder of 'partnership sourcing', referred to later in this book.

■ the concept of partnership sourcing is generic and refers to a complicated range of collaborative relationships, such as from preferred supplier to strategic alliance

■ the term partnership sourcing is used to refer to all forms of non-adversarial collaborative relationships.

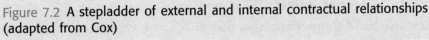

Figure 7.2 **A stepladder of external and internal contractual relationships (adapted from Cox)**

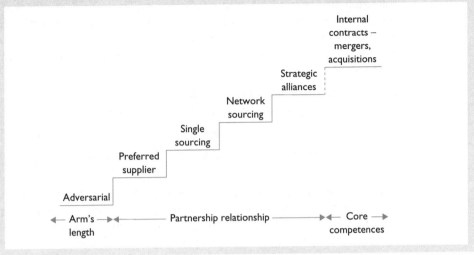

The Cox model draws heavily on concepts associated with transaction cost and resource-based theories of the firm.

7.5.1 Transaction cost theory (TCT)

Transaction cost theory (TCT), associated with Coase[7] and Williamson,[8] refers to the idea of the cost of providing for some good or service if it was purchased in the marketplace rather than from within the firm. Three key concepts are those of transaction costs, asset specificity and asymmetrical information distribution.

Transaction costs are comprised of:

- search and bargain costs
- bargaining and decision costs
- policing and enforcement costs.

Asset specificity is the relative lack of transferability of assets intended for use in a given transaction to other uses. Williamson identifies six main types of asset specificity:

- site
- physical asset
- human asset
- brand names
- dedicated assets
- temporal.

Asymmetrical information distribution means that the parties to a transaction have uneven access to relevant information. One consequence is that, within contractual relationships, either party may engage in post-contractual opportunism if the chance of switching to more advantageous partnerships arises.

7.5.2 Resource-based theory (RBT)

Resource-based theory emphasises that each firm is characterised by its own unique collection of resources of core competences. Thus, Kay[9] argues that the source of competitive advantage is the creation and exploitation of distinctive capabilities that are difficult to build and maintain, codify and make into recipes, copy and emulate and can't simply be bought off the shelf. Kay identifies three basic types of distinctive capability.

- *Corporate architecture* the capacity of the organisation to:
  - create and store organisational knowledge and routines
  - promote more effective cooperation between network members
  - achieve a transparent and easy flow of information
  - adapt rapidly and flexibly.
- *Innovation* the capacity to lower costs, improve products or introduce new products ahead of competitors. The successful exploitation of new ideas incorporating new technologies, designs and best practice is difficult and uncertain. Often, innovation can only be achieved by cooperating and collaborating with partners.
- *Reputation* the capacity to instil confidence in an organisation's credibility, reliability, responsibility, trustworthiness and, possibly, accountability. Organisations can only achieve a positive reputation over time, but, once achieved, their ability to provide quality assurance may enable them to obtain a premium price for products.

From the insights provided by TCT and RBT, Cox derives the following propositions.

- *Arm's length relationships* are associated with low asset specificity and low supplier competences that can easily be bought off the shelf as there are many potential suppliers.
- *Internal contracts* – in-house provision – are associated with high asset specificity and core competences:

  The more competences approximate to core competences of high asset specificity, then the greater the likelihood that external relationships may lead to merger or acquisition or, failing that, result in very close, single-sourced negotiated contracts in which both parties have some clear ownership rights in the goods and services produced.[10]

- *Partnership relationships* (as shown in Figure 7.2) apply to assets of medium specificity and ascend in steps according to the distance of the complementary competences provided by external suppliers from the core competences of a particular firm:

  The nearer they [complementary competences] are to the core competences of the firm, the more the firm will have to consider vertical integration through merger and acquisition. The further away from the core competences of the firm the less there is a need for medium asset-specific skills to be vertically integrated.[11]

7.5.3 Cox's classification of contractual relationships

The five steps in the ladder of contractual relationships shown in Figure 7.2 each represent a higher level of asset specificity and strategic importance to the firm of the specific goods and services. Each step also represents relative degrees of power between the relationship's participants and in the relative ownership of the goods and services emanating from the relationships. Strategic supplier alliances are the final stage before a firm considers a complementary supplier to be so important that vertical integration through merger and acquisition is undertaken.

■ *Adversarial leverage* Up to the mid 1980s, approaching the marketplace on an adversarial basis was the norm. Thus, Porter,[12] writing in 1980, advocates that purchasers should multisource, negotiate short-term contracts, maintain secrecy regarding costs, sales and product design and make (or receive) no improvement suggestions to (or from) suppliers.

■ *Preferred suppliers* Providers of complementary goods and services of medium asset specificity or strategic importance who have been placed by the purchaser on a restricted list of potential suppliers after a process of vendor rating and accreditation.

■ *Single sourcing* Purchasing from a single supplier of medium asset specificity complementary goods or services of relatively high strategic importance. As Cox observes, the aim of single sourcing is to reduce transaction costs and economise, but without the costs associated with vertical integration.

■ *Network sourcing and partnerships* Networks have been considered earlier in section 4.3. According to Cox, network sourcing 'is the idea that it is possible to create a virtual company at all levels of the supply chain by engineering multiple tiered partnerships at each stage, but without moving to vertical integration'. With network sourcing:

　– the prime contracting firm acts as the driver for the reduction of transaction costs within the whole supply and value chain

　– cost reduction is achieved by a partnership between the prime contractor and a first-tier supplier who controls an important medium asset for the prime contractor and also forms similar partnerships with second-tier suppliers (see 4.4.1 above)

　– each tiering level of the supply chain is effectively a joint venture in which firms at each stage will inform and educate their respective partners by sharing best practice and 'fit for purpose' techniques

　– such network sourcing relationships will only be possible in mature industries 'where asset specificity has constantly been reduced and multiple and serial subcontracting thereby facilitated. In such supply chain relationships issues of ownership, control and power become increasingly difficult to allocate.'

■ *Strategic supplier alliances* Classically referred to as joint ventures, these are defined by Cox as 'negotiated single-sourced relationships with the supplier of a complementary product or service'. Such relationships form a completely new and independent legal entity, distinct from the firms comprising the alliance. As both parties have some degree of proprietorship (not necessarily 50/50) in the outcome of the relationship, the basis of such relationships is power equivalence and a high degree of complimentarity.

7.6　The Bensaou model

The Bensaou model is based on a study of 11 Japanese and 3 US automobile manufacturers. Bensaou[13] suggests a framework for managing a portfolio of investments for the purpose of enabling senior managers to answer two questions.

- Which governance structure or relational design should a firm choose under different external contingencies?

This is a strategic decision because it affects how a firm defines its boundaries and core activities.

- What is the appropriate way to manage each different type of relationship?

This is an organisational question.

Bensaou suggests four buyer relationship profiles:

- market exchange
- captive buyer
- captive supplier
- strategic partnerships.

For each profile, Bensaou identifies distinguishing product, market and supplier characteristics.

Finally, he suggests that the four profiles can be arranged in a matrix to indicate whether the buyer's and supplier's tangible or intangible investments in the relationship are high or low. Tangible investments, in this context, are buildings, tooling and equipment. Intangible investments are people, time and effort spent in learning supplier–purchaser business practices and procedures and information sharing.

The Bensaou matrix, as adapted, is shown in Figure 7.3.

Bensaou also identified three management variables for each profile, which are:

- information-sharing practices
- characteristics of 'boundary-spanner' jobs
- the social climate within the relationship.

The management practices that high performers in each cell use to match the coordination, information and knowledge exchange requirements presented by the external context shown in Figure 7.3 are shown in Figure 7.4.

Bensaou concluded the following.

- Many large firms in manufacturing are moving away from traditional vertical integration and towards the external contracting of key activities.
- As interfirm relationships increase, firms cannot manage with one design for all relationships and so need to manage a portfolio of relationships.
- There are two kinds of successful relationship: high requirement–low capabilities and low requirements–high capabilities. There are also two paths to failure: underdesigned and overdesigned relationships. *Overdesign* takes place when firms invest in building trust as a result of frequent visits and cross-company teams when the market and product context call for simple, impersonal control and information exchange. Such overdesign is both costly and risky, especially in terms of the intangible investments in people, information or knowledge.
- Building or redesigning relationships according to the Bensaou model therefore involves the following three analytical steps:

Figure 7.3 Supplier's specific investment

High	**Captive buyer** Product characteristics: ■ technically complicated ■ based on mature, well-understood technology ■ little innovation and improvement to the product Market characteristics: ■ stable demand with limited market growth ■ concentrated market with few established players ■ buyers maintain an internal manufacturing capability Supplier characteristics: ■ large supply houses ■ supplier proprietary technology ■ few strongly established suppliers ■ strong bargaining power ■ car manufacturers heavily depend on these suppliers, their technology and skills	**Strategic partnership** Product characteristics: ■ high level of customisation required ■ close to buyer's core competency ■ tight mutual adjustments needed in key processes ■ technically complicated part or integrated subsystem ■ based on new technology ■ innovation leaps on technology, product or service ■ frequent design changes ■ strong engineering expertise required ■ large capital investment required Market characteristics: ■ strong demand and high growth market ■ very competitive and concentrated market ■ frequent changes in competitors due to instability or lack of dominant design ■ buyer maintains in-house design and testing capability Partner characteristics: ■ large multiproduct supply houses ■ strong supplier proprietary technology ■ active in research and innovation (R&D costs) ■ strong recognised skills and capabilities in design, engineering and manufacturing
Low	**Market exchange** Product characteristics: ■ highly standardised products ■ mature technology ■ little innovation and rare design changes ■ technically simple product or well-structured complicated manufacturing process ■ little or no customisation to buyer's final product ■ low engineering effort and expertise required ■ small capital investments required Market characteristics: ■ stable or declining demand ■ highly competitive market ■ many capable suppliers ■ same players over time Supplier characteristics: ■ small 'mom and pop' shops ■ no proprietary technology ■ low switching costs ■ low bargaining power ■ strong economic reliance on automotive business	**Captive supplier** Product characteristics: ■ technically complicated products ■ based on new technology (developed by suppliers) ■ important and frequent innovations and new functionalities in the product category ■ significant engineering effort and expertise required ■ heavy capital investments required Market characteristics: ■ high growth market segment ■ fierce competition ■ few qualified players ■ unstable market with shifts between suppliers Supplier characteristics: ■ strong supplier proprietary technology ■ suppliers with strong financial capabilities and good R&D skills ■ low supplier bargaining power ■ heavy supplier dependency on the buyer and economic reliance on the automotive sector in general

Relationship investment   Low   High

231

Figure 7.4 Management profile for each contextual profile

Captive buyer	Strategic partnerships
Captive buyer	**Strategic partnerships**
Information-sharing mechanisms:	Information-sharing mechanisms:
■ 'broadband' and important exchange of detailed information on a continuous basis ■ frequent and regular mutual visits	■ 'broadband' frequent and 'rich media' exchange ■ regular mutual visits and practice of guest engineers
Boundary-spanner tasks' characteristics: ■ structured tasks, highly predictable ■ large amount of time spent by buyer's purchasing agents and engineers with supplier	Boundary-spanner tasks' characteristics: ■ highly ill defined, ill structured ■ non-routine, frequent, unexpected events ■ large amount of time spent with supplier's staff, mostly on coordinating issues
Climate and process characteristics: ■ tense climate, lack of mutual trust ■ no early supplier involvement in design ■ strong effort by buyer towards cooperation ■ supplier does not necessarily have a good reputation	Climate and process characteristics: ■ high mutual trust and commitment to relationship ■ strong sense of buyer fairness ■ early supplier involvement in design ■ extensive joint action and cooperation ■ supplier has excellent reputation
Market exchange	**Captive supplier**
Exchange-sharing mechanisms: ■ 'narrowband' and limited information exchange, heavy at time of contract negotiation ■ operational coordination and monitoring along structured routines	Information-sharing mechanisms: ■ little exchange of information ■ few mutual visits, mostly from supplier to buyer
Boundary-spanner tasks' characteristics: ■ limited time spent directly with suppliers' staff ■ highly routine and structured tasks with little interdependence with supplier's staff	Boundary-spanner tasks' characteristics: ■ limited time allocated by buyer's staff to the supplier ■ mostly complicated, coordinating tasks
Climate and process characteristics: ■ positive social climate ■ no systematic joint effort and cooperation ■ no early supplier involvement in design ■ supplier fairly treated by the buyer ■ supplier has a good reputation and track record	Climate and process characteristics: ■ high mutual trust, but limited direct joint action and cooperation ■ greater burden put on the supplier

1 the strategic selection of relational types to match the external conditions relating to the product, the technology and the market (see Figure 7.3)

2 the identification of an appropriate management profile for each type of relational design

3 matching the design of the relationship, which could be over- or underdesigned, to the desired management profile.

7.7 The IMP model

This model, as indicated by its title, was developed by Hakansson[14] and the Industrial Marketing and Purchasing Group (IMP), formed in 1976 by researchers from five European countries.

In the IMP model, the marketing and purchasing of industrial goods is seen as an interaction process between two parties within a specific environment. The model analyses industrial marketing and purchasing in terms of four basic elements, each of which is subdivided.

First is the *interaction process*. This involves the analysis of two factors: episodes and relationships. An *episode*, as stated earlier, is a group of interrelated actions involved in a process, such as placing an order. In an industrial market, relationship episodes involve the exchange of products or services, information, money and social attitudes or values, such as mutual trust between suppliers and purchasers. Episodes, especially social exchange episodes, are critical to the establishment of long-term supplier–purchaser *relationships*. The building of relationships may involve *adaptations* to products, financial arrangements, information routines or social relations on the part of either party. The exchange of information or communication may also involve *contact patterns* between people filling different roles or functions. Over a period of time, the exchange of products or services, money, information and social relationships lead to clear expectations by both parties of the roles and relationships of their opposite numbers, which eventually become *institutionalised* so that they go unquestioned by either party.

The second element is the *interacting parties*. In addition to episodes and relationships, the process of interorganisational interaction will be influenced by the *characteristics* of both the organisations themselves and the people who represent them. *Organisational factors* include the position of an undertaking in the market as manufacturer, wholesaler or distributor, the products of the selling company, the production and application of the two parties and their respective relative expertise. *Individual factors* are the people, such as the salesperson and buyer or groups of individuals (representatives of design, selling, transport and so on) involved in interorganisational interactions. The exchange of information and relationships lead to the creation of social bonds between the individuals concerned, which, in turn, influence the decisions of each enterprise involved in the business relationship. The varied personalities, experience, expertise and motivations of the individuals representing each enterprise will result in various ways of dealing with episodes that will, in turn, affect the development of long-term interorganisational relationships. Individual experiences may also result in preconceptions concerning customers or suppliers that affect attitudes on the part of those involved and others who know about them. The experience gained in individual episodes aggregates to create a total experience. The experience of a single episode – such as incivility or delayed delivery on the part of the supplier or slow payment by a buyer – can radically change attitudes that may then persist over a long period.

The third element is the *interaction environment*. Interorganisational interaction takes place in an environmental context that includes the market structure, the degree of dynamics within the market and relationship, internationalism, the position of the relationship in the supply chain and the wider social system.

The fourth element, the *atmosphere*, is the power dependence that exists between suppliers and purchasers and such relationship variables as conflict, cooperation, closeness or distance as well as the mutual expectations of the respective parties. This closer interaction between suppliers and purchasers will result in reduced costs or higher profits for one or both organisations. Another aspect of atmosphere is the ability of either party to control the other, which derives from the perception of the power exercised by the other party in the relationship.

The IMP interaction model can be conceptualised as shown in Figure 7.5.

Figure 7.5 An illustration of the IMP interaction model[15]

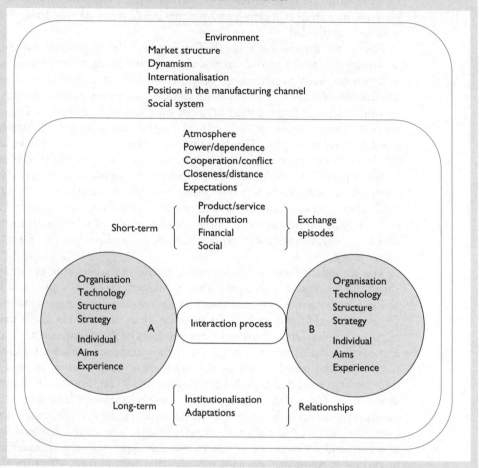

7.8 The practical usefulness of supplier relationship models

There are various other models of supplier relationships in addition to the three described above, including those by Helper[16] and Tang.[17]

Helper suggests that a useful way in which to classify a supplier relationship is by the methods used to resolve problems that arise between the parties and distinguishes between 'exit' and 'voice' relationships. In an *exit* relationship a customer who has a problem with a supplier finds a new supplier. In a *voice* relationship, the customer works with the existing supplier to resolve the problem.

Tang classifies supplier relationships into four types: vendor, preferred supplier, exclusive supplier and partner. For each category he provides a useful analysis of nine relevant operational characteristics:

- type of contract
- length of contract
- product/service type
- information exchange
- pricing scheme
- delivery schedule
- senior management involvement
- supplier development programmes offered by the buyer
- number of suppliers.

To practising purchasing staff, models of supplier relationships often appear academic and remote from the realities of day-to-day purchasing. There are, however, several reasons for purchasing students and practitioners to study such models:

- they increase awareness of the large number of variables that impact supplier relationships
- reflecting on them provides us with a deeper understanding of relationships in general and of an individual relationship in particular – as Sutton-Brady[18] indicates:
  - relationships are the results of interactions
  - interactions do not take place within an emotional vacuum – they must have some 'emotional setting' that sets the scene for relationship development, generally referred to as the relationship atmosphere or climate
  - atmosphere is derived from the perceptions of the parties to the interaction: 'This leads to the belief that there is a "good" or "bad" relationship atmosphere conducive to the positive or negative development of the relationship and subsequently to the nature and quality of future exchange episodes between the actors'

  so the study of such variables and concepts as power/dependence, cooperation/competition, trust/opportunism and expectations may lead to a better understanding of the causes of purchaser–supplier antagonism or conflict and the need for adaptations in the perceptions of both sides
- reflecting on such models provides an understanding of the importance of a supplier to a particular purchaser and vice versa and the risks, benefits and opportunity costs of such relationships
- the use of such models assists in developing appropriate strategies, such as single or multiple sourcing, making or buying and the reasons for such strategies
- they enable purchasers to find a balance between the internal resources of their firm and the external resources possessed by the supplier
- they enable purchasers to clarify what they want from a given supplier – in some cases, the purchaser wishes to use the supplier's ability to design or assist in the design of a special product, in others, the purchaser wishes to utilise the supplier's ability to provide a standardised product at a competitive price
- as Bensaou states, models can indicate the factors contributing to both successful and unsuccessful purchasing and supply relationships.

7.9   The termination of relationships

No relationship can or should be expected to last forever as organisations operate in a dynamic environment. The ending of a relationship does not necessarily mean failure and there may be positive as well as negative outcomes for one or both of the parties involved.

7.9.1 Reasons for termination

Mitchell[19] describes how it is possible to detect that a relationship is changing:

> A primary tip-off that the nature of the relationship is changing can be seen in requests that are made by you or by the supplier. Are multiple requests necessary before action is taken? Are requests necessary for items or service that used to be offered without asking? Perhaps the request is granted, but the requester feels like he or she is cashing in on his or her last favour with each request . . . When you start to work out issues and compromises and you get the impression that your partner is nickel and dimeing you all the way you know that your alliance is coming to an end.

Mitchell also points out that, although partnering principles and objectives can be well outlined at an organisational level, success is often dependent on individuals:

> All individuals for both organisations must be committed and resistance can begin on either side of the fence. If the problems have roots in the purchasing and supply organisation, at least the purchasing supply manager will be able to take an active part in determining the cause and correcting it . . . If the problem seems to stem from the supplier organisation, the outcome is a bit more unpredictable.

In practice, most partnership break-ups derive from:

- inadequate understanding of what 'partnership' means
- rapidly changing circumstances that cause one or both parties to revise their priorities and concentrate on achieving their own organisational objectives at the expense of the partnership.

Such circumstances, as identified by Southey[20] in the UK and Campbell and Pollard[21] in the USA, include:

- *changes in business direction(s)* an existing partnership may no longer have value if either the purchasing or supplier organisation has shifted its strategic direction
- *product obsolescence* the product or service provided by the supplier is becoming obsolete without any replacement options
- *the supplier is unable to meet service levels* certain objectives basic to the partnership can no longer be met
- *short-term attitude* either partner may consider that the long-term benefits of the partnership have not been realised sufficiently quickly or have been insufficient to warrant a continued commitment to a particular supplier/purchaser
- *economic factors* a supplier has become 'at risk' financially, with the danger of potential liquidation
- *external economics* a recession may force suppliers to cut back on product development, training and other resources, such as product engineers, and, consequently, they will be unable to meet the 'continuous improvement' objectives of the partnership

- *mergers and acquisitions* such ventures can create new business models for either the purchaser or supplier
- *corporate divestiture* may create a situation where, because parts of the business have been sold, the organisation can no longer provide a product or service
- *instability and inconsistency* acquisitions or disposals of companies or rapid changes in key personnel or organisational philosophy often adversely affect years of previous relationship-building based on trust and stability.

In the last analysis, however, successful partnerships can only be built if trust and co-operation exist between purchaser and supplier.

7.9.2 The process of termination

It is a truism that good contract management is not reactive but aims to anticipate and respond to future contingencies. Every well-written contract should anticipate the possibility of terminating the relationship.

Some writers, however, criticise the inadequacies of legal contracts for governing partnerships, especially in the face of uncertainty and dependence. Sitkin and Roth,[22] for example, describe legalistic remedies as weak, impersonal substitutes for trust. Contractual provisions may also lack flexibility, that might enable terminations to be made more amicably and easily than following the 'letter of the law'. Ouchi,[23] however, points out that formal control mechanisms are more effective in obtaining compliance with specifiable objectives than in obtaining commitment to a general value orientation.

Timing, relationship aspects, legal considerations and succession issues are important aspects of termination.

7.9.3 Timing

Mitchell[24] states that, whenever possible, the timing of the termination should be synchronised with the expiration of the agreement currently in force. Giving too much advance warning to a supplier can lead to a deterioration in service. Conversely, termination may not come as a surprise to a supplier that has received regular negative feedback on performance. Decisions may also have to be made on whether the termination should be immediate or gradual. Such decisions may be governed by terms and conditions relating to termination in the current agreement.

7.9.4 Relationship aspects

Terminations may be amicable or hostile. Campbell and Pollard[25] refer to the three Ps that can aid in minimising possible hostility encountered in the termination process:

- positive attitude
- pleasant tone
- professional treatment.

A positive attitude recognises that both organisations will survive apart and that recriminations will help neither. Further, both organisations may need each other in the future. A pleasant tone can be more effective than harsh words. Professional justification for the termination is essential. Termination is not a personal issue. The purchasing executive's job is to obtain the best possible value in order that his or her organisation can remain ahead of the competition.

7.9.5 Legal considerations

Among such factors are:

- *the financial consequences of terminating the agreement* in some cases, it may be possible to negotiate a settlement, in others the contract will be specific
- *confidentiality agreements* where such agreements are part of the contract terms, they must be honoured for the prescribed time
- *intellectual property issues* drawings, designs prepared during the agreement, computer software and so on
- *capital property issues* especially in relation to materials or capital equipment located at the supplier's site
- *security issues* it is necessary to change passwords or security codes shared with the other party to the agreement
- *obtaining clear signed records of any settlement*
- *employee rights* if they were transferred under the Transfer of Undertakings (Protection of Employment) (TUPE) Regulations.

7.9.6 Succession issues

Before deciding to terminate, it will be necessary to ensure that steps have been taken to ensure a continuity of supplies. This will entail:

- discussion with internal customers regarding groups, systems and projects that will be affected by the change of supplier
- reflecting on the lessons learned from the terminated relationship
- conducting market analysis to determine other supplier options
- preparing specifications (possibly revised)
- selection of a new supplier – an important factor will be the potential supplier's reputation for trustworthiness
- negotiation of a relationship agreement.

Finally as Campbell and Pollard[26] observe:

> As a result of thinking through the options and creating a professional plan for separation, supply managers can disprove the old maxim that 'marriages are made in heaven, but the divorce is the very devil'.

7.10 Further aspects of relationships

These include collaboration in innovation and design, the supply base, supplier appraisal, outsourcing, make-or-buy decisions, partnerships and supplier performance and they are dealt with in appropriate sections elsewhere in this book.

Case study

Telespecialists Ltd (TL) is engaged in the manufacture and supply of fixed and mobile communications networks. It is based in the UK and has two manufacturing plants in Birmingham and Milton Keynes. Over the past two years, there have been financial pressures due to weaker markets, leading to a limited inflow of capital. The Chief Executive Officer has addressed this with a strategy to deal with improving the profitability and performance of the company.

You are the Purchasing Manager and have been asked to submit a paper to the next Board meeting in four weeks' time. You are asked to reply to three specific questions.

1 How can supplier relationships be improved?

2 What financial benefits will accrue?

3 How long will it take to produce an appropriate supplier relationship strategy?

You begin to reflect on how suppliers are currently managed and decide to put your thoughts into bullet points. These are:

■ No formal partnership is in place.

■ All key items are dual sourced for supply security.

■ All key items are tendered at least twice a year.

■ Reverse auctions have been introduced.

■ Generally there are adversarial relationships.

■ Benchmarking shows purchase prices are competitive.

■ When a supplier delivers late three times, it is dropped.

■ Supplier meetings only take place when there is a problem.

■ Technical staff do not trust suppliers enough to be open with them about technological ideas.

■ No contracts commit to quantities.

■ Payments to suppliers have been moved from 30 days to 90 days without consultation.

■ Some products have been brought in-house to ensure that the company's production staff members are gainfully employed.

■ The company has threatened to move more purchases to China and India.

■ The general business stance is to keep suppliers 'on their toes' using a variety of tactics, including threats to force prices to drop by 6 per cent in the next 6 months.

You decide to meet your four chief buyers and share your thoughts. At the same time, you will produce a response for the CEO. There is an obvious opportunity to change many practices, but how?

Task

Produce a draft outline response to the three questions raised by the CEO.

Discussion questions

7.1 'The most successful relationships are those where customers and suppliers develop trust and an understanding of their requirements and interests, accompanied by a concern for both learning from and providing assistance to each other.'
   (a) Define the words 'trust' and 'understanding'.
   (b) Can there be trust without understanding?
   (c) What are the characteristics of a 'learning organisation'?

7.2 Why are organisations increasingly moving from transactional to relationship purchasing?

7.3 Try to provide an example from your own experience of the progression of a supplier relationship from episodes to relationships.

7.4 Give two examples each of:
   (a) transaction costs
   (b) asset specificity
   (c) asymmetrical information distribution.

7.5 To what extent do you consider 'adversarial leverage' to be still prevalent? Can you provide an example of adversarial leverage from your own experience?

7.6 Compare the Bensaou matrix with the Kraljic portfolio in Chapter 2. To which of Bensaou's 'profiles' would you assign:
   (a) leverage products
   (b) strategic products
   (c) non-critical products
   (d) bottleneck products?

7.7 One of the factors associated with 'the environment' in the IMP model is the 'social system'. By this is meant the interactions between purchasers and suppliers that take place in the context of the values (aims on broad guides to action) and norms (rules governing performance) that govern relationships in a particular environment. Why is a knowledge of values and norms (which may be influenced by economics, political, ethical, legal and religious factors) important in the context of global purchasing?

7.8 Try to complete the matrix below using the nine characteristics identified by Tang in 7.8 above. (The first line has been completed as an example.)

Characteristic	Vendor relationship	Partnership relationship
Type of contact	Purchase order	Detailed contract
Length of contract		
Product/service type		
Information exchange		
Pricing scheme		
Delivery schedule		
Senior management involvement		
Supplier development programme offered by the supplier		
Number of suppliers		

7.9 What argument would you use to either support or rebut the view that 'legal agreements are weak, impersonal substitutes for trust'?

Past examination question

1 As the purchasing manager for a manufacturer of domestic appliances, you are to source the door seal for a new model of microwave oven. This component has caused problems in the past, but the design problems have now been overcome. The market has become increasingly competitive and any problems with the new model would be disastrous. Preliminary sourcing indicates that Permaseal Ltd has a substantially lower price than other competitors including your current supplier Thermalbond Ltd. However, the last time you did business with Permaseal was six years previously and at that time you had some quality and delivery problems.

Explain in detail how you would undertake this sourcing exercise in order to ensure that you select the best possible supplier for the long term.

CIPS, *Purchasing and Supply Management II: Tactics and Operations*, November 2001

References

1 *The Concise Oxford Dictionary*, Oxford University Press

2 The authors gratefully acknowledge permission to quote from the CIPS booklet 'How to manage supplier relationships', written by Dr Kenneth Lysons

3 Holmlund, M., and Strandvik, T., 'Perception configuration in business relationships', *Management Decision*, Vol. 37 (9), 1999, pp. 686–96

4 As 3 above

5 Jarvelin, Anne Marie, 'Evaluation of relationship quality in business relationships', academic disseration, University of Tampare, Finland, 2001, p. 38

6 Cox, A., 'Regional competence and strategic procurement management', *European Journal of Purchasing and Supply Management*, Vol. 2, No. 1, 1996, pp. 57–70

7 Coase, R. H., 'The nature of the firm', *Economica*, No. 4, 1937, pp. 386–405

8 Williamson, O. E., 'Transaction cost economics: the governing of contractual relations', *Journal of Law and Economics*, Vol. 22, 1979, pp. 232–61

9 Kay, J., *Foundations of Corporate Success: How Business Strategies Add Value*, Oxford University Press, 1995

10 As 6 above, p. 64

11 As 6 above, p. 63

12 Porter, M., *Competitive Strategy*, Free Press, 1980, pp. 106–7

13 Bensaou, M., 'Portfolio of buyer–supplier relationships', *Sloan Management Review*, summer, 1999, pp. 35–44

14 Hakansson, H., *International Marketing and Purchasing of Industrial Goods*, John Wiley, 1982

15 IMP Group, 'An interaction approach', *International Marketing and Purchasing of Industrial Goods*, winter, 1982, pp. 10–27

16 Helper, S., 'How much has really changed between US automakers and their suppliers?', *Sloan Management Review*, summer, 1991, pp. 15–28

17 Tang, C. S., 'Supplier relationships map', *International Journal of Logistics: Research and Applications*, Vol. 2, No. 1, 1999

18 Sutton-Brady, C., *Towards Developing a Construct of Relationship Atmosphere*

19 Mitchell, L. K., 'Breaking up is hard to do – how to end a supplier relationship', ISM resource article at: www.ism.ws/ResourceArticles/2000/cpoomitchell.cfm

20 Southey, P., 'Pitfalls to partnering in the UK', PSERG Second International Annual Conference 1993, in Burnett, K. (ed.) *Readings in Partnership Sourcing*, CIPS, 1995

21 Campbell, P. and Pollard, W. M., 'Ending a supplier relationship', *Inside Supply Management*, Sept. 2002, pp. 33–8

22 Sitkin, S. B. and Roth, N. L., 'Explaining the limited effectiveness of legalistic "remedies" for trust/distrust', *Organisation Science*, Vol. 4 (3), 1993, pp. 367–92

23 Ouchi, W. G., 'A conceptual framework for the design of organisational control mechanisms', *Management Science*, Vol. 25 (9), 1979, pp. 833–48

24 As 19 above

25 As 21 above

26 As 21 above

Chapter 8

Purchasing: product innovation, supplier involvement and development

Learning outcomes

With reference, where applicable, to purchasing and supply management, this chapter aims to provide an understanding of:

- product and process innovation
- new product development
- supplier development
- supplier associations.

Key ideas

- Innovation and *kaizen*.
- Drivers of innovation.
- The stages of new product development.
- Environmental factors in design.
- Purchasing contributions to new product development.
- Early buyer involvement (EBI).
- Early supplier involvement (ESI).
- Results and process-orientated supplier development.
- The steps involved in supplier development.
- The aims and objectives of *Kyoryoku Kai*.
- Perceived benefits and disadvantages of supplier associations.

8.1 Innovation and *kaizen*

8.1.1 Innovation

Innovation is the process of turning ideas and knowledge into products and services that create a consumer demand within the marketplace.[1]

- *Product innovation* is the process of transforming technical ideas or market needs and opportunities into a new product (or service) that is launched on to the market.

- *Process innovation* is the introduction or development of new methods or technology by means of which products or services can be manufactured or delivered more effectively or efficiently. An example of process innovation is the introduction of robots and other forms of automated equipment.

- *Breakthrough innovation* is completely new or revolutionary products, such as new scientific discoveries in pharmaceuticals. Commonplace products, such as the radio, television and aircraft were once breakthrough innovations.

- *Incremental innovations* are gradual improvements in a product or service.

Treasy[2] points out that every innovation carries two risks: a technology risk – 'Will it work'? – and a marketplace risk – 'Will people buy it?' The technology risk arises when we seek to achieve breakthrough innovations. The marketplace risk can arise because the cost of the resultant product to potential customers is too high or because the market is not ready for the innovation.

8.1.2 *Kaizen*

Kaizen is a Japanese term and means continuous improvement. The concept of *kaizen* is the basis of total quality management (TQM) and is strongly associated with Japanese lean production.

Although analogous to incremental innovation, *kaizen* is, as shown by Table 8.1, generally different from innovation.

Both innovation and *kaizen*, however, share the common objective of enabling an organisation to achieve a sustainable advantage.

Table 8.1 **Differences between innovation and *kaizen***

Characteristics	Innovation	Kaizen
Focus	Large, short-term, radical changes in products	Small, frequent, gradual improvements over a long time
Expertise	Leading-edge breakthrough	Conventional know-how
Sources	Scientific or technological discovery or invention	Design, production and marketing
Capital requirements	Substantial investment in equipment and technology	Relatively modest investment
Progress	Dramatic breakthroughs	Small incremental steps
Results	Spontaneous	Continuous
Risks	High	Low
Involvement	Corporate activity	Individual or small team
Recognition	Results	Effort

8.1.3 Drivers of innovation

In addition to achieving sustainable advantage, these drivers include:

- the need to meet the challenges of global and domestic competition
- the challenges of rapid and complicated technological advances
- the enhancement of the value of the enterprise derived from a reputation for innovation and new product development.

8.1.4 Important aspects of innovation

- Recognition of an unmet need in the market.
- Time or the need to bring an innovatory product or service to the market ahead of competitors. There is strong evidence that speed to market creates enhanced market share and a reputation for market leadership:

> By introducing 6 all new vehicles within a 14-month period, Toyota captured a 43 per cent share of the auto sales in Japan . . .

A 1987 study showed that the Japanese could then, on average, create a new car about 18 months faster than either their US or Western-European competitors, at a cost of about half a billion dollars in lost profits to the lagging firms.[3] Time-based strategies embody the value-added dimensions of time-responsiveness and customisation. For engineered products, time-to-market can be reduced by advanced computer-aided engineering and concurrent engineering.

Computer-aided engineering (CAE) eliminates entirely some of the traditional steps in the new product development process and allows others to be performed simultaneously. Mikeham et al.[4] state that, where used properly, appropriate software can reduce cycle times, costs and risks by 90 per cent.

Concurrent or simultaneous engineering is the concept that all major functions or activities that contribute to getting a product to market have a continuing product development involvement and responsibility for it from the initial idea through to sales. Concurrent engineering recognises that the traditional sequential or 'pipeline' approach to product development, in which individuals are only responsible for a specific function, is no longer adequate. In concurrent engineering, multifunctional teams of 4 to 20 members are involved. The two most significant features of concurrent engineering are:

- customer focus, based on an understanding of what the ultimate user requires
- reduced cycle time, the reduction being based on doing the right thing right, first time.

Concurrent engineering is a key factor in improving quality, reducing production costs and delivery times and enabling design problems to be identified and rectified at an early stage. Carlson[5] reports that the application of concurrent engineering at McDonnell Douglas reduced scrap by 58 per cent and rework by 29 per cent, while Boeing gained a parts lead time reduction of 30 per cent.

The concurrent approach is not limited to engineering, but can also be applied in industries such as food, pharmaceuticals and furniture manufacture where biologists, nutritionists, chemists, physicists and other disciplines perform the technical roles in cross-functional development teams.

8.1.5 The stages of new product development

The process of new product development normally involves seven stages, as shown in Figure 8.1.

1 *Initial concept*

Ideas for new products can derive from:

- consumer research into what customers want by means of buying pattern analysis, focus groups and consumer surveys
- research and development (R&D) departments concerned with both pure and applied research
- reverse engineering or stripping down competitors' products to discover design improvements that can be applied to your own products
- suggestions from customers
- government regulations that create a demand for new products.

Figure 8.1 **The seven stages of new product development**

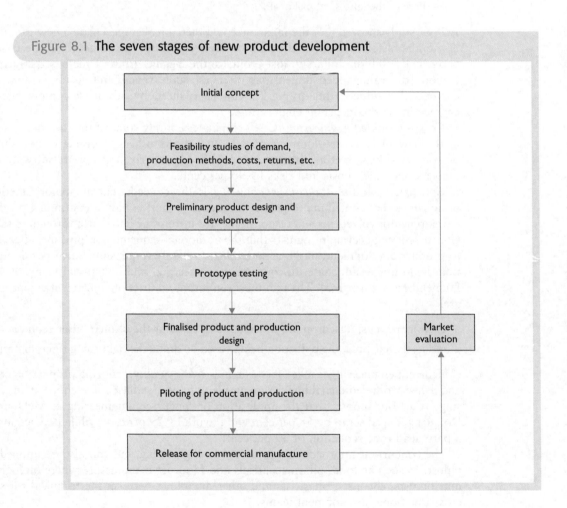

2 *Feasibility studies*

At this stage, many innovative ideas will be discarded on such grounds as:

■ insufficient customer demand

■ difficulty or complexity of manufacture

■ proposed product does not fit into current operations

■ high risk

■ high cost of manufacture

■ likely profit margin too low

■ need to outsource

■ required high investment in plant, equipment and human resources.

3 *Preliminary product design*

■ Usually undertaken by a design team comprised of representatives from design, R&D, production, marketing, purchasing and human resource management (HRM). The design team will use such approaches as brainstorming, value analysis and engineering.

4 *Prototype testing*

■ Prototypes may include life-size models or computer visualisation such as computer animation and virtual reality.

5 *Finalised product and production design*

This is concerned with ensuring that the product meets customers' requirements. The final design is not just a series of drawings of the product. This stage involves decisions relating to how the product is to be made, including details of processes, quality specifications, materials to be used, the supply chain and everything else that appertains to the final product.

6 *Piloting product and production*

This involves both marketing and production. Marketing will try out the product on a sample of customers. Production will ensure that the product moves smoothly through the various stages of manufacture. At this point, feedback will be obtained in the form of answers to such questions as the following.

■ What features do customers like/dislike most?

■ Do customers consider that the product is worth the purchase price?

■ Are there opportunities to customise the product to meet the unique needs of customers?

■ How does the product compare with those of competitors?

■ What production snags need to be ironed out?

■ Is the product safe to use?

■ How might the product and its manufacture be further improved?

7 *Release for commercial manufacture*

Waters[6] points out that many new products are not successful and are quickly withdrawn and instances IBM's PC, Junior, which lost £100 million by 1985, and the

1994 launch by Lever Brothers of Persil Power, taken off the market when it was discovered to weaken fabrics and fade colours. As Waters states:

> Very few of the initial ideas reach the point where they are launched on the market and even fewer become commercial successes. One rule of thumb suggests that 250 ideas lead to one product, and 25 products lead to one success. A pharmaceutical industry study showed that it took 10,000 chemicals to find one that they could market – which partly explains the cost of one billion dollars to develop a new drug.

It has been estimated that approximately 80 per cent of the manufacturing costs of a product are determined by its design. Further opportunities for savings lie in the integration of product design and the supply chain. An integrated supply chain brings suppliers and customers closer to the manufacturer so increased value can be created.[7]

8.2   Environmentally sensitive design

8.2.1 Factors in environmentally sensitive design

Pressures exerted by environmental groups and relevant legislation, such as the UK Clean Air Act 1956, the Radioactive Substances Act 1993 and the Environmental Protection Act 1990, require designers to devise socially responsible products. In the design of such products, special consideration must be given to:

- increasing their efficiency and economy in the use of materials, energy and other resources
- minimising pollution from chosen materials
- reducing any long-term harm to the environment caused by using the product
- ensuring that the planned life of the product is the most appropriate in environmental terms and that the product functions efficiently for its full life
- ensuring that full account is taken of the end-disposal of the product
- specifying packaging that can be recycled easily
- minimising nuisances, such as noise or odour
- analysing and minimising safety hazards.

Attention given to the above factors at the design stage can simplify production, enhance the manufacturer's reputation and prevent investment in products and processes that environmental legislation may make obsolete.

8.2.2 Approaches to environmentally sensitive design

Four important approaches are lifecycle analysis (LCA), design for disassembly (DFD), the use of environmentally preferred materials and guidance by the International Standards Organisation (ISO).

8.2.3 Lifecycle analysis

This is based on the concept that all products have a lifecycle. The product lifecycle, or Gopertz curve, is shown in Figure 8.2.

Figure 8.2 **Product lifecycle**

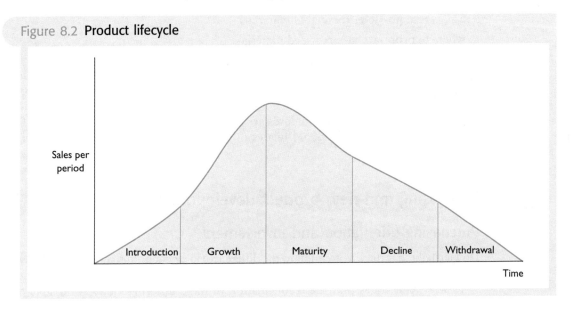

8.2.4 Design for disassembly (DFD)

This has two aspects:

- *Recyclability* This saves both energy and resources. Recycling aluminium, for example, requires 95 per cent less energy than producing aluminium from bauxite ore. Making paper from recycled stock requires 64 per cent less energy than using wood pulp. About 70 per cent of all metal discarded is used only once before it is discarded.

- *Repairability* The aim is to prolong the life of products by ensuring that they can be repaired easily at low cost.

8.2.5 Use of environmentally preferred materials

Industrial ecology aims to manage human activity on a sustainable basis by:

- minimising energy and materials usage
- ensuring acceptable quality of life for human beings
- conserving energy and natural resources, such as minerals and forests.

Industrial ecology advocates the application of the following principles when selecting materials for product design:

- choose abundant, non-toxic materials whenever possible
- choose materials familiar to nature – for example, cellulose, rather than synthetic materials, such as chlorinated aromatics
- minimise the number of materials used in a production process

- use, where possible, recyclable materials
- where appropriate, use recycled materials.

8.2.6 Guidance from the International Standards Organisation for Standardisation (ISO)

The main ISO environmental standards are BS EN 14001, 14004, 14010, 14011, 14012, 14040 and 14050. ISO Guide 64 relates to the inclusion of environmental aspects in production standards.

8.3 Purchasing and new product development

8.3.1 Purchasing orientation and involvement

Dowlatshahi[8] has drawn attention to the differences in orientation that may arise between purchasing and design and these are set out in Table 8.2.

Dowlatshahi states that the reconciliation of these differing views is possible only in a concurrent engineering environment, which he defines as:

> The consideration and inclusion of product design attributes such as manufacturability, procurability, reliability, maintainability, schedularability, marketability and the like in the early stages of product design.

Wynstra et al.[9] state that purchasing participation in product development can range from ad hoc limited involvement to formal and extensive participation in the development team. A typology of six possible configurations of purchasing participation in product development is presented by Lakemond et al.[10]

A Engineers contact purchasing specialists external to the project team on an ad hoc basis.

B Purchasing specialists are integrated into the project team on a part-time basis and work closely with an engineer regarding specific parts/materials/technologies.

Table 8.2 **Differences in orientation between purchasing and design**

Purchasing orientation	Design orientation
- Minimum acceptable margin of quality, safety and performance	- Wide margins of quality, safety and performance
- Use of adequate materials	- Use of ideal materials
- Lowest ultimate cost	- Limited concern for cost
- High regard for availability	- Limited regard for availability
- Practical and economical parameters, specification, features and tolerances	- Close or near-perfect parameters, specifications, features and tolerances
- General view of product	- Conceptual abstraction of product quality
- Cost elimination of materials	- Selection of materials
- Concern for JIT delivery and supplier relationship	- Concern for overall product design

Figure 8.3 Lakemond et al.'s typology of possible configurations of purchasing's participation in product development

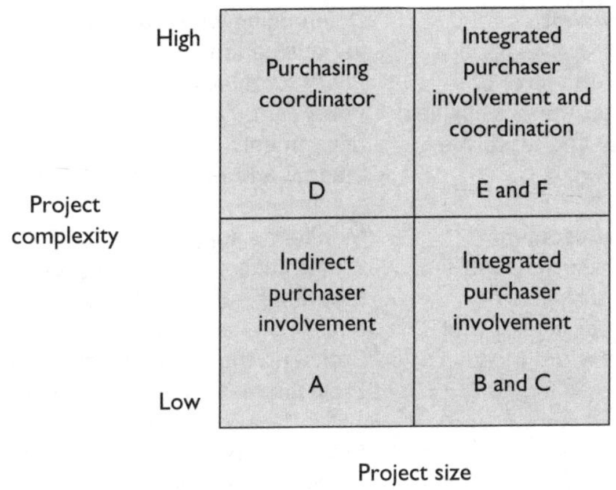

C Purchasing specialists are integrated into the project team on a full-time basis (dedicated) and work closely with engineers regarding specific parts/materials/technologies.

D A purchasing coordinator is added to the project team and takes care of coordinating purchasers external to the project team.

E A purchasing coordinator is added to the project team in combination with purchasing specialists integrated into the project team on a part-time basis.

F A purchasing coordinator is added to the project team in combination with purchasing specialists integrated into the project team on a full-time basis.

The above writers suggest that some configurations are more appropriate for certain projects than others, depending on the variables of project complexity and project size, as shown in Figure 8.3.

8.3.2 Early buyer involvement (EBI)

With EBI, purchasing specialists are involved in a new development project from its inception. As shown in Figure 8.3, this is more likely to be the case in projects of high complexity and large size.

8.3.3 Some areas of purchasing involvement in product development

Wynstra et al.[11] have identified four areas of purchasing involvement in product development, each of which has a different time horizon and each involves different activities. These are shown in Table 8.3.

Table 8.3 Areas of purchasing involvement in product development

Area of involvement	Associated activities
Development management The higher the level of availability and stability and the lower the level of dependence, the greater the possibilities to 'buy' the technology and leave the development to suppliers	Determining which technologies to keep/develop in-house and which to outsource Policy formulation for supplier involvement Policy formulation for purchasing-related activities of internal departments Internal and external communication of policies
Supplier interface management Proactive, continuous research with the aim of identifying suppliers or technologies that may be relevant for the development of new products	Monitoring supplier markets for technological developments Preselecting suppliers for product development collaboration Motivating suppliers to build up/maintain specific knowledge or develop certain products Exploiting the technological capabilities of suppliers Evaluating suppliers' development performance
Project management Involves two subareas – product planning and project execution	Product planning activities are primarily carried out during or before initial development and include: ■ determining specific develop-or-buy solutions ■ selecting suppliers for involvement in the development project ■ determining the extent of supplier involvement Project execution involves activities during the project and includes: ■ coordinating development activities between suppliers and manufacturers ■ coordinating development activities between different first-tier suppliers ■ coordinating development activities between first- and second-tier suppliers ■ ordering and chasing prototypes

Product management
Directly contributing to the specifications of the new product
	Activities can be divided into two categories:
	■ extending activities – those aimed at increasing the number of alternatives, including:
	  – providing information on new products and technologies already available or in course of development
	  – suggesting alternative suppliers, products and technologies that can yield higher-quality results
	■ restrictive activities – those aimed at limiting the number of alternative specifications:
	  – evaluating product designs in terms of part availability, manufacturability, lead time, quality and costs
	  – promoting standardisation and simplification

8.4 Relationships between purchasers and suppliers in new product development

Such relationships can take a number of forms:

- *codevelopment* the ability of a customer to design competitive products in collaboration with their first-tier suppliers
- *comakership* close cooperation between buyer and seller organisations on product development, manufacture or supply

■ *codestiny* where the future of all the participating organisations depends, to a greater or lesser extent, on the success of a partnership relationship in which each organisation has made an investment.

8.5 Early supplier involvement (ESI)

ESI has been defined as:[12]

> A practice that brings together one or more selected suppliers with a buyer's product design team early in the product development process. The objective is to utilise the supplier's expertise and experience in developing a product specification that is designed for effective and efficient product roll-out.

ESI aims to secure access to the competences and technologies of selected suppliers in situations that preclude the option of vertical integration due to resource limitations and managerial constraints.

8.5.1 Development responsibility and risk

Wynstra and Ten Pierick[13] identified two important variables relating to the management of supplier involvement: the degree of responsibility for product development contracted out to the supplier and development risk.

Development responsibility

This is the level of responsibility delegated to the supplier in the development of a building block or component. Calvi et al.[14] state that this responsibility or 'supplier autonomy' is a function of the supplier's know-how and the importance of intellectual property rights owned.

The degree of supplier responsibility to be contracted out is determined by the manufacturer after answering such questions as the following.

■ Considering the organisation's core technological competences, into how much detail should it go when developing specifications?

■ Are there suppliers that have relevant product or production knowledge in relation to the component that is greater than that of the manufacturer?

■ Are there suppliers that can do the development work more efficiently than the manufacturer?

■ To what extent does the manufacturer need the development capacity (person hours) of suppliers to meet the project targets?

Development risk

Calvi et al. identify six combinative categories of risk that can be ascertained by asking the following questions.

■ What is the link between the building block or component and the performance of the final product?

■ What is the level of newness and differentiation brought by the building block or component?

Figure 8.4 Wynstra and Ten Pierick's supplier involvement portfolio

	Low	High
High	Arm's length development	Strategic development
Low	Routine development	Critical development

- What is the position of the building block or component on the critical path – that is, what is the reliability of the supplier's capacity in meeting delivery schedules?
- How new are the production technologies involved?
- What is the weight of the building blocks' cost in the final product?
- How many different technologies are used in this building block? The presence of different technologies may produce difficulties in co-ordination among different suppliers.

Deciding the level of responsibility to assign to suppliers is a strategic decision because it involves an evaluation of the purchaser's and supplier's competences. It also involves an outsourcing or make-or-buy decision by a cross-functional team.

On the basis of the two variables of degree of assigned responsibility and development risk, Wynstra and Ten Pierick developed the supplier involvement portfolio shown in Figure 8.4.

The normal approach to 'filling' the portfolio is to:

1 ■ decide the degree of supplier responsibility for the development
  ■ decide the degree of development risk
2 position the supplier component in the portfolio
3 reflect on the distribution of the various supplier/component combinations across the portfolio and, if necessary, reposition.

8.6 Advantages and problems of ESI

8.6.1 The advantages of ESI

The advantages of ESI in product development may be briefly summarised as:

- reduced concept-to-customer development time
- improved product specifications
- enhanced quality
- lower development costs
- access to new technologies ahead of competitors
- joint problem-solving
- interchange of knowledge and information
- improved manufacturability of products.

8.6.2 The disadvantages and problems of ESI

The disadvantages and problems of ESI have been summarised by Mikkola et al.[15] and Handfield et al.[16]

The major risks of collaborative product development listed by Mikkola et al. include 'leakage of information, loss of control or ownership, longer development lead time, conflicts due to different aims and objectives and collaborators becoming competitors'.

Handfield et al. point out that ESI raises such considerations as 'tier structure, degree of responsibility for design, specific responsibilities on the requirements selling process, when to involve suppliers in the process, intercompany communication, intellectual property agreements, supplier membership on the project team and alignment of objectives with regard to outcomes'.

Petersen et al.[17] highlight four factors as being of particular importance to the integration of suppliers into new product development.

- *Customer knowledge of the supplier* Such knowledge facilitates the integration of the supplier's staff into new product development teams and helps to achieve an alignment between the buying company's needs and the supplier's capabilities, from both technical and cultural standpoints.

- *Technology and cost information sharing* Technology sharing can often lead to better supplier solutions, which may also result in lower costs. Petersen and his colleagues report that several organisations in their sample employed 'target pricing methods', which involved joint buyer–seller teams exploring alternative solutions to meeting a target cost. Such efforts might require suppliers to 'open their books' and reveal their methods of cost allocation. Such transparency is only likely to take place when a high level of trust exists between the purchasers and suppliers.

- *Supplier involvement in decision making* Suppliers are often asked to colocate a design engineer on the purchasing company's design team. This colocation may be on a full- or part-time basis. In Petersen's research, the extent of the supplier's participation was the factor most strongly associated with the achievement of project goals.

- *Technology uncertainty* Such uncertainty can derive from new-to-the-world technologies, new applications of existing technologies and technologies outside the company's field of expertise. In general, the greater the technological uncertainty or the complexity of the product, the greater the need for ESI in new product development. The degree of collaboration will also be higher for customised products and where the rate of technological change is fast.

Dowlatshahi[18] makes the point that the investment in research and development required by purchasers and suppliers respectively should be clearly delineated. A supplier's specific suggestions with regard to a new product should be viewed as equivalent to the R&D invested by the purchaser. Realistically, only suppliers with long-term contracts can be expected to make a significant investment in R&D.

8.7 Supplier development

8.7.1 Definition

Supplier development has been defined as:

> Any activity that a buyer undertakes to improve a supplier's performance and/or capabilities to meet the buyer's short- or long-term supply needs.[19]

Supplier development programmes can be either results- or process-orientated.

■ *Results-orientated programmes* focus on solving specific problems for suppliers and normally involve step-by-step changes relating to supplier's costs, quality and delivery. Hartley and Jones[20] identify three characteristics of results-orientated supplier development:

  – the process is standardised and buyer-driven

  – the changes made are primarily technical

  – the process is of short duration and requires limited follow-up.

  With this approach, the supplier improves while the buyer's supplier development team is on site and the achieved level of performance can be maintained after the team has left. The results approach is basically an attempt to transfer an organisation's in-house capabilities across boundaries.

■ *Process-orientated programmes* focus on increasing the supplier's ability to make production improvements without hands-on assistance from the buyer. This requires the supplier to learn the problem-solving techniques required for continuous improvements. Such learning is complicated, may require the 'unlearning' of old practices and the encoding of new knowledge in organisational routines.

Kaizen, referred to in 8.1.2, is an important aspect of supplier development.

8.7.2 The steps of supplier development

The actual process may differ according to the organisation and, as stated above, whether the development is primarily results- or process-orientated. The generalised model shown in Figure 8.5 involves nine steps.

The nine steps may be briefly explained as follows:

1 *Identify critical products* This is done using a portfolio approach, such as that of Kraljic (see 2.13.11). These will be mainly strategic and bottleneck products.

2 *Identify critical suppliers* This involves consideration of such questions as the following.

  ■ What is the capability of the suppliers? Sako[21] identifies three levels of capability:

    – *maintenance capability* – the ability to maintain a particular level of performance consistently

    – *improvement capability* – that which affects the pace of performance improvements

    – *evolutionary capability* – the capacity for capability building, which is different from dynamic capabilities in that the emphasis is less on 'adapting, integrating and reconfiguring internal resources in response to changing environments and more on the sustained accumulation of the other two capabilities'.

  ■ Are the present suppliers capable of meeting future needs?

  ■ Are the present suppliers worth developing or is it time to source new ones?

3 *Appraise supplier performance* Supplier performance appraisal is considered in Chapter 11.

4 *Determine the gap between present and desired supplier performance* Gap analysis involves identifying the differences between the current and a desired business

Figure 8.5 General steps in a supplier development programme

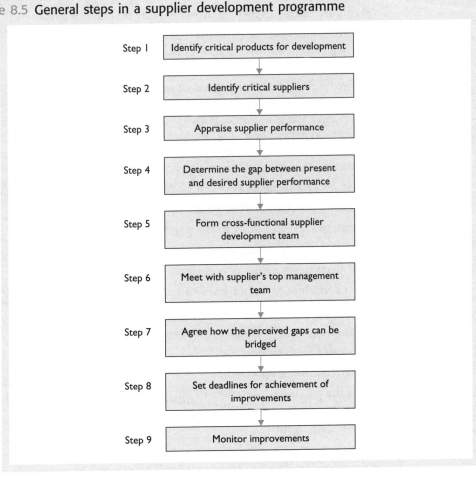

Step 1 — Identify critical products for development

Step 2 — Identify critical suppliers

Step 3 — Appraise supplier performance

Step 4 — Determine the gap between present and desired supplier performance

Step 5 — Form cross-functional supplier development team

Step 6 — Meet with supplier's top management team

Step 7 — Agree how the perceived gaps can be bridged

Step 8 — Set deadlines for achievement of improvements

Step 9 — Monitor improvements

situation. It is important to recognise that gaps may be considered from a supply-side as well as a demand-side perspective.

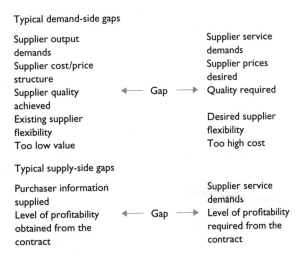

Typical demand-side gaps

Supplier output demands		Supplier service demands
Supplier cost/price structure		Supplier prices desired
Supplier quality achieved	← Gap →	Quality required
Existing supplier flexibility		Desired supplier flexibility
Too low value		Too high cost

Typical supply-side gaps

| Purchaser information supplied | | Supplier service demands |
| Level of profitability obtained from the contract | ← Gap → | Level of profitability required from the contract |

There may also be combined gaps, such as the level of collaboration or where the level of purchaser–supplier relationships satisfies neither party.

5 *Form cross-functional supplier development team* This team will be responsible for appraising present and potential suppliers, identifying gaps and negotiating with suppliers to try to devise mutually acceptable resolution of problems.

6 *Meet with supplier's top management team* Meeting with the top management team of the supplier provides an insight into the extent to which a collaborative relationship with the purchaser is required. It also provides an opportunity for both sides to know each other as individuals, discuss areas of cooperation not previously identified, exchange views frankly and build trust. Negotiated improvements can also be minuted and thereby provide an agreed record of decisions made.

7 *Agree how the perceived gaps can be bridged* Approaches may include:

- seconding purchaser's staff to the supplier
- seconding supplier's staff to the purchaser
- purchaser on site audits at the supplier's premises
- third-party assessment, as is required for ISO 9000 registration
- loan of machinery and IT hardware
- granting access to IT systems, such as CAD
- negotiating improved transportation contracts
- joint value analysis exercises
- improved costing approaches
- using the purchaser's leverage to obtain materials and other items for the supplier at cheaper cost
- the offer of incentives
- the formation of a supplier association (see section 8.8).

8 *Set deadlines for achieving improvements* These should be reasonable, agreed by both parties and strictly enforced. The supplier should understand that failure to effect improvements by the agreed date may lead to loss of business. The emphasis, however, should be on constructive help rather than punitive measures.

9 *Monitor improvements* Even after achievement of the required standards, the performance of suppliers should be carefully monitored. Handfield et al.[22] state that the pitfalls of supplier development fall into three categories: supplier-specific, buyer-specific and buyer–supplier interface. Supplier-specific pitfalls stem chiefly from the supplier's lack of commitment or lack of technical or human resources. Buyer-specific factors derive from a reluctance to commit to supplier development fully when the purchaser sees no obvious potential benefits in so doing, such as a supplier being considered of insufficient importance to justify the investment. The principal buyer–supplier interface pitfalls are due to lack of mutual trust, poor alignment of organisational cultures and insufficient inducements to the supplier. As Handfield and his coauthors state:

> Initiating supplier performance improvement is not an easy task . . . Our findings suggest that such an accomplishment takes time and is only achieved by patient relationship managers who are tenacious enough to pay follow-up visits to suppliers and continually enforce a strong programme of supplier evaluation and performance feedback.

8.8 Supplier associations (SA)

8.8.1 What is a supplier association?

The supplier association (SA), or *Kyoryoku Kai*, has been a feature of Japanese manufacturing since the 1950s. Assisted by *Kyoryoku Kai*, large Japanese manufacturers such as Toyota have been able to both coordinate and develop their subcontractors in such ways as the dissemination of best practice, provision of technical assistance and, in some instances, training. Supplier associations also help to develop a climate of trust between the parties involved.

Hines and Rich[23] define a supplier association (SA) as:

> A mutually benefiting group of a company's most important suppliers brought together on a regular basis in order to achieve strategic and operational alignment through the development of awareness, education and implementation programmes designed to achieve both radical and incremental improvements.

The above writers report that, in 1998, about 50 customer companies in the UK and Europe were using the SA approach with a total of approximately 600 suppliers. Originally associated with the automotive sector, SA has now been adopted by a range of industries, including office equipment, distribution, telecommunications, steel, general engineering, aerospace and medical equipment.

8.8.2 The aims and objectives of *Kyoryoku Kai*

These have been summarised by Hines[24] as being to:

- improve the abilities and skills of suppliers, particularly in terms of JIT, TQM, statistical process control (SPC), value analysis, value engineering (VA/VE), management flexibility and cost reduction
- produce a uniform supply system using the same types of techniques
- facilitate the flow of information and strategy formulation to and from and within supplier networks
- increase trust between buyer and supplier, allowing for closer business relationships
- keep suppliers and customers in touch with market developments and, hence, aid the translation of 'the voice of customers'
- enhance the reputation of the customer as something suppliers should try to do (and increase) business with
- help smaller suppliers lacking specialist trainers
- increase length of business relationships
- allow development benefits to be shared
- provide an example to subcontractors of how to coordinate and develop their own suppliers.

Gullander[25] refers to two kinds of SAs that he designates steering groups and working groups.

A *steering group* is comprised of one or two representatives from each supplier and the customer. Representatives – normally the CEO or director of quality production or purchasing – are normally empowered to make important decisions on SA joint advisers.

259

The steering group meets two to three times a year with some ten to fifteen members present and, most often, all member firms represented.

A *working group* focuses on a specific task, such as the introduction of a quality technique, and continues until the task has been completed. The group is comprised of representatives of member firms, but only those firms that believe in competence improvement in the selected area participate. Normally, there is one representative per firm. Gullander states that being excellent in a particular field is not a reason for non-participation. Such a firm might take the role of teacher or facilitator of the work in the working group. Several working groups with different foci may operate simultaneously.

8.8.3 Perceived benefits and disadvantages of SAs

In a study of eight Welsh SAs, Izushi and Morgan[26] reported that:

- a majority of the firms surveyed thought that their SA helped them to form good relationships with other suppliers and build mutual trust between the participants
- the majority also considered that their SA gave them a better understanding of the customer firm and built mutual trust, the understanding deriving from improved communication and 'stable orders' for goods from the customer, early announcement of the customer's development plans and a less than arm's length approach on the customer's part to problem-solving in scheduling and delivery
- a majority of the firms found their SA useful in assessing the competitive positions and learning general principles of best practice.

There were, however, a number of reservations. There was significant, if minority, support for the following statements:

- 'A supplier association is no more than a gesture to show loyalty to a customer firm'
- 'A customer firm uses a supplier association to gain more control of its suppliers'.

In addition, SAs were criticised on the following grounds:

- they may become 'talking shops' about general techniques that the customer leaves to suppliers to implement themselves
- generalised presentations of techniques often pose difficulties in implementation because of suppliers' idiosyncrasies and problems
- the 'implement it yourself' approach may inhibit the development of mutual trust between customers and suppliers so that, for example, a customer asks suppliers to introduce techniques but refuses to disclose the results of implementation in its own organisation
- there may be difficulty in keeping momentum going between meetings.

Izushi and Morgan suggest that such shortcomings might be overcome by:

- customer leadership in putting techniques into action and disclosing to customers how it implements them at its site
- making the best use of expertise possessed by member suppliers
- use of measurable goals and regular checking of achievements
- selection of member suppliers who are conducive to collaboration and focus on particular products or processes
- provision of training for the staff of supplier development teams to enable them to communicate with suppliers as partners.

8.8.4 Further aspects of design, including 'robust design'

QFD and FMEA are discussed in 9.9.6 and 9.9.7, respectively, value management, engineering and analysis in 9.11.

Case study

The Veroxide Group (VG) manufactures a range of pharmaceutical products, namely prescription drugs and human vaccines. VG has its headquarters in Berne, Switzerland, a research and development unit in Stockholm, Sweden, and manufacturing sites in Leeds, UK, Pretoria, South Africa, and Berne. In the past year, R&D spending rose 3.9 per cent, equivalent to 17.3 per cent of core business sales. There are several potential new products in the pipeline but 'Zentonex' is widely anticipated to receive regulatory approval in six months' time.

VG has located its production buying operation in Leeds, but it may be noted that the R&D unit has its own buying function. There is little contact between the two buying functions, largely because the R&D Director insists that he is the custodian of his budget. When a drug goes into mass production, much larger quantities of feedstock are required.

When 'Zentonex' enters production, one of the stock items needed is 'Onolun' – a special chemical. To meet the forecasted production scheme, 2 tonnes of it will be required every three months. This chemical has been supplied to VG by Gardners Ltd, which produces it in its Birmingham, UK, manufacturing plant. Gardners has been a regular supplier to the R&D unit for five years and has impeccable delivery and quality performance. Gardners has three competitors located in Brazil, Canada and France. VG plans to make 'Zentonex' in its Pretoria location.

Anne Fortescue, the VG Buying Director, commissioned a report on Gardners' ability to manufacture and supply 'Onolun'. The salient extracts from the report are:

Buying is done by an untrained buyer who takes instructions from the plant director. Buying is an unsophisticated operation and would require three key suppliers to provide stock for 'Onolun'. These suppliers can manufacture in the quantities required and to the quality standards. The quality management is excellent and we have complete confidence in this aspect.

It became evident that Gardners will need to invest £500k in new plant and equipment. The company has not planned this expenditure and would need to extend its bank overdraft to fund the purchase. The lead time for purchasing, installing and commissioning the new facility would be 18 weeks. The Chief Engineer would be accountable for the project, including procurement.

The feedback is that shelf-life is restricted (seven weeks) and so the supply chain and inventory management will be critical. The person accountable for this is the Stores Manager. This causes us serious concern and is identified as a major risk.

If VG signs a contract with Gardners it will have to make a commitment to supplier development. This is our key recommendation.

Task

If you were Anne Fortescue, what would you identify as being the key features of a supplier development programme in the above circumstances?

Discussion questions

8.1 Give two examples each of:
   (a) product innovation
   (b) process innovation
   (c) incremental innovation.

8.2 Figure 8.6 shows the main stages of research and development

Figure 8.6 **The main stages of research and development**

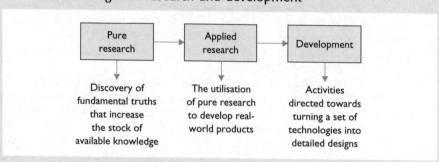

Explain this diagram with reference to:
   (a) the discovery of a new drug for the treatment of a specific disease or medical condition
   (b) the innovation of float glass by Pilkington
   (c) the evolution of integrated circuits through transistors and valves.

8.3 How can a knowledge of production methods for a particular product help purchasing staff to make recommendations for the use of specific materials or components?

8.4 To what extent do you consider environmental issues when buying:
   (a) a car
   (b) furniture?

8.5 What is your response to the following statement?

   It has seemed to me that we have been treating the world's resources and its delicate ecological system with the recklessness of a Pools winner whose motto is 'spend, spend, spend' and who gives little thought if any to the longer term.

8.6 Long-standing barriers between design, production and purchasing can be difficult to overcome. Suggest how such barriers might be broken down and what benefits might accrue from replacing conflict with collaboration.

8.7 Consider Wynstra's six possible configurations of purchasing participation described in 8.3.1. Which of the configurations most nearly describes purchasing participation in your own organisation?

8.8 Supplier integration into new product/process/service development suggests that suppliers are providing information and directly participating in decision making for purchases used in the new product/process/service. This integration can occur at any point in the five-stage product/process/service development model.[27]

The 'five stages of development' are:

1 idea generation: the voice of the customer
2 business technical assessment (preliminary)
3 product/process/service concept development
4 product/process/service engineering and design
5 prototype, build, test and pilot for operations leading to full-scale production.

Try to think of at least two contributions that purchasing can make to each of the five stages in relation to a product.

8.9 How should purchasing and/or other managers weigh the relative strengths and weaknesses of potential suppliers in areas such as technological knowledge, manufacturing capabilities, length of relationship with the supplier, degree of trust and alignment of technology?

8.10 Discuss the viewpoints that, in supplier involvement or development
(a) 'the customer receives most of the benefits and the supplier receives few'
(b) 'cooperative relationships are often cooperative in name and suppliers do more than their fair share of cooperating.'

How might you seek to deal constructively with these objections?

Past examination questions

1 The design process necessitates many participants from various functions providing the right information at the right time to pursue new product development. Explain how the procurement function might participate in providing information for this process.

CIPS, Purchasing and Supply Chain Management: Strategy, May 2001

2 Involving the supplier at the outset of the product development cycle is referred to as early supplier involvement (ESI). Explain why ESI may be desirable and identify the possible benefits of such involvement. Suggest some of the possible disadvantages of embarking on ESI.

CIPS, Purchasing and Supply Chain Management II: Tactics and Operations, May 1999.

References

[1] London Development Agency, Why Innovate?

[2] Treasy, M., 'Innovation as a last resort', *Harvard Business Review*, July–Aug., 2004, pp. 29–30

[3] Mendez, E. G., and Pearson, J. N., 'Purchasing's role in product development', *International Journal of Purchasing and Materials Management*, Jan., 1, 1994, pp. 3–12

[4] Mikehams, A. R., Morgan, E. J., and Chatting, J., 'An attribute approach to concurrent engineering', Proceedings of the Institute of Mechanical Engineers, Vol. 218, Part B, 2004, pp. 995–1005

[5] Carlson, S. E., 'Planning for concurrent engineering', *Medical Device and Diagnostic Industry Magazine*, May, 1996

[6] Waters, D., *Operations Management*, 2nd edn, Pearson Education, 2002, p. 95

[7] Mikkola, J. H., and Joetti-Larsen, S. K., 'Early supplier involvement: implications for new product development outsourcing and supplier–buyer interdependence', *Global Journal of Flexible Systems Management*, Vol. 4, No. 4, 2003, pp. 31–41

[8] Dowlatshahi, S., 'Purchasing's role in a concurrent engineering environment', *International Journal of Purchasing and Materials Management*, winter, 1992, pp. 21–5

[9] Wynstra, F., Axelsson, B., and van Weele, A. J., 'Driving and enabling purchasing involvement in product development', *European Journal of Supply Management*, Vol. 6, No. 2, 2000, pp. 129–41

[10] Lakemond, N., van Echtelt, F., and Wynstra, F., 'A configuration typology for involving purchasing specialists in product development', *Journal of Supply Management*, Vol. 37, No. 4, Nov., 2001, pp. 11–20

[11] Wynstra, F., van Weele, A., and Axelsson, B., 'Purchasing involvement in product development', *European Journal of Purchasing*, Vol. 5, 1999, pp. 129–41

[12] Institute of Supply Management, 'Glossary of key purchasing and supply terms', ISM

[13] Wynstra, F., and Ten Pierick, E., 'Management of supplier involvement in new product development', *European Journal of Purchasing and Supply Management*, Vol. 6, 2000, pp. 49–57

[14] Calvi, R., Le-Dain, M. A., Harbis, A., and Bonotta, H. V., 'How to manage early supplier involvement (ESI) into the new product development process (NPDP)', Proceedings of the 10th International Annual IPSERA Conference, 2001, pp. 158–62

[15] As 7 above

[16] Handfield, R. B., Raqatz, K., Petersen, K. J., and Monczka, R. M., 'Involving suppliers in new product development', *California Management Review*, Vol. 42, No. 1, fall, 1999, pp. 59–82

[17] Petersen, K. J., Handfield, R. B., and Ragatz, G. L., 'A model of supplier integration into new product development', *Journal of Production and Innovation Management*, Vol. 20, 2003, pp. 284–99

[18] Dowlatshahi, S., 'Early supplier involvement: theory versus practice', *International Journal of Production Research*, Vol. 37, No. 18, 1999, pp. 4119–39

[19] Handfield, R. B., Krause, D. R., Scannell, T. V., and Monczka, P. M., 'Avoid the pitfalls in supplier development', *Sloan Management Review*, winter, 2000, pp. 37–48

[20] Hartley, J., and Jones, G., 'Process oriented supplier development', *International Journal of Purchasing and Materials Management*, Summer, 1997

[21] Sako, M., 'Supplier development at Honda, Nissan and Toyota', *Comparative Case Studies of Organisational Capability Enhancement*, Nov., 2003

[22] As 19 above

[23] Hines, P., and Rich, N., 'Outsourcing competitive advantage', Proceedings of the Second Worldwide Research Symposium on Purchasing and Supply Chain Management, IPSERA, London, 1–3 April, 1998, pp. 268–94

[24] Hines, P., *Creating World Class Suppliers*, Pitman, 1994, p. 143

[25] Gullander, S., 'Supplier associations: a tool for regional development', paper presented at the conference SMES and Districts, Castellanza, Italy, 5–7 Nov., 1998

[26] Izushi, H., and Morgan, K., 'Management of supplier associations: observations from Wales', *International Journal of Logistics Research and Application*, Vol. 1., 1998, pp. 75–91

[27] Quoted in Handfield, as 16 above

Chapter 9

Specifying and managing product quality

Learning outcomes

With reference to purchasing and supply management this chapter aims to provide an understanding of:

- concepts of quality and reliability
- total quality management (TQM)
- specifications
- standardisation
- quality assurance and controls
- tools for quality control and reliability
- the costs of quality
- value management, engineering and analysis.

Key ideas

- Definitions and dimensions of the right quality.
- The principles of total quality management (TQM).
- Specifications and specification writing from a purchasing perspective.
- Alternatives to individual specifications.
- Standardisation with special reference to BS EN ISO specifications.
- Standardisation from a purchasing perspective.
- Inspection, statistical quality control, quality loss function, robust design, quality function deployment (QFD) and failure mode and effects analysis (FMEA) as tools for quality control and reliability.
- Costs of quality conformance and non-conformance.

9.1   What is quality?

9.1.1 Definitions

There are numerous definitions of quality. ISO 8402, which defines the fundamental terms relating to quality concepts, states that quality is:

> The totality of features and characteristics of a product that bears on the ability to satisfy stated or implied needs.

In this definition, 'features and characteristics of product' implies the ability to identify what quality aspects can be measured or controlled or constitute an acceptable quality level (AQL), while 'ability to satisfy given needs' relates to the value of the product or service to the customer, including economic value as well as safety, reliability, maintainability and other relevant features.

Crosby[1] defines quality as 'conformity to requirements not goodness'. He also stresses that the definition of quality can never make any sense unless it is based on what the customer wants – that is, a product is a quality product only when it conforms to the customer's requirements.

Juran[2] defines quality as 'fitness for use'. This definition implies quality of design, quality of conformance, availability and adequate field services. There is, however, no universal definition of quality. Garvin, for example, has identified five approaches to defining quality[3] and eight dimensions of quality.[4] The five approaches are as follows.

- The *transcendent approach* quality is absolute and universally recognisable. The concept is loosely related to a comparison of product attributes and characteristics.
- The *product-based approach* quality is a precise and measurable variable. In this approach, differences in quality reflect differences in the quantity of some product characteristics.
- The *use-based approach* quality is defined in terms of fitness for use or how well the product fulfils its intended functions.
- The *manufacturing-based approach* quality is 'conformance to specifications' – that is, targets and tolerances determined by product designers.
- The *value-based approach* quality is defined in terms of costs and prices. Here, a quality product is one that provides performance at an acceptable price or conformance at an acceptable cost.

These alternative definitions of quality often overlap and may conflict. Perspectives of quality may also change as a product moves from the design to the marketing stage. For these reasons, it is essential to consider each of the above perspectives when framing an overall quality philosophy.

Garvin's eight dimensions of quality are:

- *performance* the product's operating characteristics
- *reliability* the probability of a product surviving for a specified period of time under stated conditions of use
- *serviceability* the speed, accessibility and ease of repairing the item or having it repaired

- *conformance* measures the projected use available from the product over its intended operating cycle before it deteriorates
- *durability* measures the projected use available from the product over its intended operating cycle before it deteriorates
- *features* 'the bells and whistles' or secondary characteristics that supplement the product's basic functioning
- *aesthetics* personal judgements about how a product looks, feels, sounds, tastes or smells
- *perceived quality* closely identified with the reputation of the producer and, like aesthetics, it is a personal evaluation.

While the relative importance attached to any of the above characteristics will depend on the particular item, the most important factors in commercial or industrial purchasing decisions will probably be performance, reliability, conformance, availability and serviceability.

Other factors that determine 'the right quality' for a particular application include:

- *price* as the competitive selling price of the product in which the item is to be incorporated will determine the prices paid for bought-out items
- *customer specifications* or those laid down by statutory or similar organisations
- *durability* this influences the quality specifications for components as, if the expected life of the final product is only three years, for example, there is little point in incorporating a component with a life of five years where cheaper alternatives are available, though the reputation of the product must, however, be of paramount consideration.

Quality is therefore determined by balancing technical considerations, such as fitness for use, performance, safety and reliability, with economic factors, including price and availability. It is therefore the *optimum* quality for the application that should be sought, rather than the *highest* quality.

In drafting quality specifications, the aim should always be the minimum statement of optimum (not the highest) quality so as not to increase the cost unnecessarily, restrict processes of manufacture nor limit the use of possible alternatives.

9.1.2 Reliability

As shown above, reliability is an attribute of quality. It is, however, so important that the terms 'quality and reliability' are often used together. Reliability has been defined as:[5]

> A measure of the ability of a product to function successfully when required, for the period required, under specified conditions.

Reliability is usually expressed in terms of mathematical probability, ranging from 0 per cent (complete unreliability) to 100 per cent (or complete reliability).

Failure mode and effect analysis (FMEA), performed to evaluate the effect on the overall design of a failure in any one of the identifiable failure modes of the design components and to evaluate how critically the failure will affect the design of performance, is referred to in section 9.9.7 below.

9.2 Quality systems

9.2.1 What is a quality system?

A *quality system* is defined as:[6]

> The organisational structure, responsibilities, procedures, processes and resources for implementing quality management.

A quality system typically applies to, and interacts with, all activities pertinent to the quality of a product or service. As shown in Figure 9.1 it involves all phases, from the initial identification to final satisfaction of requirements and customer expectations.

All organisations have a quality management system. This may, however, be informal and insufficiently documented. The advantages of a properly documented system, such as that required by BS EN 9001:2000, are that it:

- ensures all aspects of quality are controlled
- ensures consistent, efficient work practices
- indicates best practice
- provides objective evidence for determining and correcting the causes of poor quality
- increases customer confidence
- gives competitive advantage.

Figure 9.1 **The quality loop**

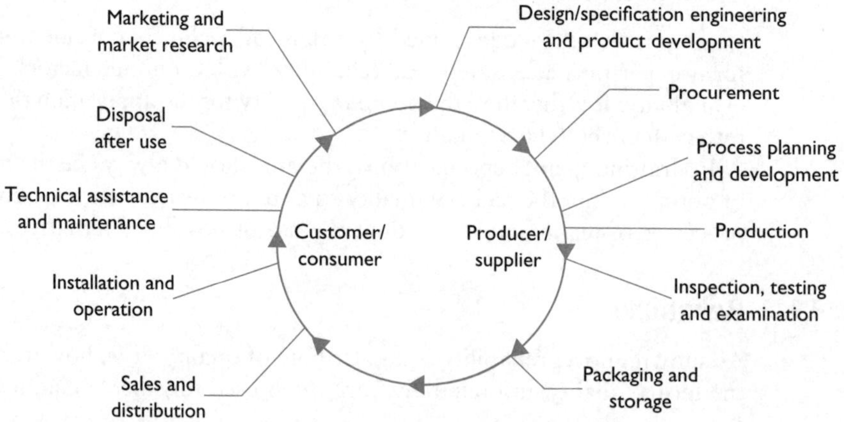

Source: British Standards Institution, reproduced with permission

9.3 The importance of TQM

9.3.1 Definitions

Total quality management (TQM) has been defined as:[7]

> A way of managing an organisation so that every job, every process, is carried out right, first time and every time.

This means that each stage of manufacture or service is 'total' – that is, 100 per cent correct before it proceeds. An alternative definition is:[8]

> An integrative management concept of continually improving the quality of delivered goods and services through the participation of all levels and functions of the organisation.

9.3.2 TQM principles

TQM is based on three important principles.

■ *A focus on product improvement from the customer's viewpoint* The key ideas in this principle are product improvement and customer product improvement. Juran[9] emphasised the importance of achieving annual improvements in quality and reductions in quality-related costs. Any improvements that take an organisation to levels of quality performance that they have previously not achieved is termed a 'breakthrough'. Breakthroughs are focused on improving or eliminating chronic losses or, in Deming's[10] terminology, 'common causes of variation'. All breakthroughs follow a common sequence of discovery, organisation, diagnosis, corrective action and control. The term 'customer' in this context is associated with the concept of 'quality chains', which emphasises the linkages between suppliers and customers. Quality chains are both internal and external. Thus, internally, purchasing is a customer of design and supplier production. Staff within a function or activity are also suppliers and customers. Like all chains, the quality chain is no stronger than its weakest link. Without strong supplier–customer links, both internally and externally, TQM is doomed to failure. Quality chains are one way in which to outmode the functional conflict and power tactics referred to elsewhere in this book. The first step in implementing an internal quality chain approach is for each activity to determine answers to the following questions relating to customers and suppliers.[11]

– Customers
  ■ Who are my internal customers?
  ■ What are their true requirements?
  ■ How do, or can, I find out what their requirements are?
  ■ How can I measure my ability to meet their requirements?
  ■ Do I have the necessary capability to meet their requirements? (If not, then what must change to improve the capability?)
  ■ Do I continually meet their requirements? (If not, then what prevents this from happening when the capability exists?)
  ■ How do I monitor changes in their requirements?
– Suppliers
  ■ Who are my internal suppliers?
  ■ What are my true requirements?
  ■ How do I communicate my requirements?
  ■ Do my suppliers have the capability to measure and meet the requirements?
  ■ How do I inform them of changes in the requirements?

The second step, based on answers to questions such as the above, is to determine the level of service that a function such as purchasing will provide. Cannon[12] has identified four factors affecting decisions about service types and levels:

– what the customer wants
– what the function can provide

– close collaboration to solve disagreements

– redefining both type and level of service at regular intervals.

It is also important to determine the technical expertise of purchasing as 'it is this expertise which enables the function to add value to the procurement activity beyond that which the internal customer can perform without the function's assistance'. The questions posed earlier in this section can also be reframed by substituting the word 'external' for 'internal' so that external quality chains can be considered from both supplier and customer angles, too. In the capacity of customers, purchasing organisations expect suppliers to compete in terms of quality, delivery and price. Zaire[13] states that the best approach to managing suppliers is based on JIT, which, from its inception, has the objective of obtaining and sustaining superior performance. The other important aspect of external customer supplier value chains refers to the management of customer processes as the purpose of TQM is customer enlightenment and long-term partnerships.

■ *A recognition that personnel at all levels share responsibility for product quality* The Japanese concept of *kaizen*, or ongoing improvement, affects everyone in an organisation, at all levels. It is therefore based on team rather than individual performance. Thus, while top management provides leadership, continuous improvement is also understood and implemented at shop floor level. Some consequences of this principle include:

– provision of leadership from the top

– creation of a 'quality culture' dedicated to continuous improvement

– teamwork – that is, quality improvement teams and quality circles

– adequate resource allocation

– quality training of employees

– measurement and use of statistical concepts

– quality feedback

– employee recognition.

Zaire[14] states:

> Once a culture of common beliefs, principles, objectives and concerns has been established, people will manage their own tasks and will take voluntary responsibility to improve processes they own.

■ *Recognition of the importance of implementing a system to provide information to managers about quality processes that enable them to plan, control and evaluate performance.*

Most of this chapter is concerned with various aspects of quality implementation.

9.3.3 Factors that have contributed to the development of TQM

■ *Global competition* for sales, profits, jobs and funds in both the private and public sectors, leading to the concept of 'world class manufacturing', with the emphasis on using manufacturing to gain a competitive edge by improving customer service.

■ *JIT* and other similar strategies based on the philosophy of zero defects – that is, it is cheaper to design and build quality into a product than attempt to ensure quality by means of inspection alone.

■ *Japanese quality procedures* such as *kaizen* (unending improvement) and *Poka-Yoke* (foolproofing), and a quality culture implemented in European manufacturing units, such as at Toyota and Nissan.

■ *Quality philosophies* associated with internationally respected experts.

9.3.4 The development of TQM

TQM originated in Japan as a result of a group of American management consultants and statisticians helping to rebuild Japanese industry after World War II. TQM transformed cheap and unreliable products labelled 'Made in Japan' into goods with an international reputation for high quality, innovation and reliability. These consultants were principally W. Edwards Deming, Joseph Juran and A. V. Feigenbaum. The DTI publication *The Quality Gurus* identifies 'three clear groups of quality gurus' (a 'guru' is an influential teacher) covering the period since World War II. Brief details of these gurus are set out in Table 9.1.

Table 9.1 **The quality gurus**

Name	Principal book	Important principles
The early Americans		
W. Edwards Deming (1900–1993)	*Quality, Productivity and Competitive Position*, MIT Press, 1982	Deming's 14 points. Points 3, 4 and 9 are especially relevant to purchasing: 3 cease dependence on inspection to achieve quality, eliminate the need for inspection on a mass basis by building quality into the product in the first place 4 end the practice of awarding business on the basis of price tag and, instead, minimise the total cost by moving towards a single supplier for any one item for a long-term relationship of loyalty and trust 9 break down barriers between departments – people in research, design, sales and production must work as a team to foresee problems of production and use that may be encountered with the product or service
Joseph M. Juran (1904–)	*Quality Control Handbook 1988*, McGraw-Hill, 1988	■ Quality is 'fitness for use', which can be broken down into quality of design, quality of conformance, availability and field service ■ Companies must reduce the cost of quality ■ Quality should be aimed at controlling sporadic problems or avoidable costs and unavoidable costs. The latter requires the introduction of a new culture intended to change attributes and increase companywide knowledge
Armand V. Feigenbaum (1920–)	*Total Quality Control*, McGraw-Hill, 1983	■ 'The underlying principle of the total quality view ... is that ... control must start with identification of customer quality requirements and end only when the product has been placed in the hands of a customer who remains satisfied. Total quality control guides the coordinated actions of people, machines and information to achieve this goal. The first principle is to recognise that quality is everybody's job'

Table 9.1 **(cont'd)**

Name	Principal book	Important principles
The Japanese		
Kaoru Ishikawa (1915–1989)	*What is Total Quality Control? The Japanese Way*, Prentice Hall, 1985	■ The first to introduce the concept of quality control circles ■ Originator of fishbone or Ishikawa diagrams, now used worldwide in continuous improvements to represent cause–effect analysis ■ Argues that 90–95% of quality problems can be solved by simple statistical techniques
Genichi Taguchi (1924–)	*Introduction to Quality Engineering*, Asian Productivity Association, 1986	■ Defines the quality of a product as the loss imparted by the product to society from the time the product is shipped. The loss may include customers' complaints, added warranty costs, damage to company reputation, loss of market lead, etc. ■ Uses statistical techniques additional to statistical process control (SPC) to enable engineers/designers to identify those variables that, if controlled, can affect product manufacture and performance
Shigeo Shingo (1909–1990)	*Zero Quality Control: Source Inspection and the Poka-Yoke System*, Productivity Press, 1986	■ Development of just-in-time and, consequently, the Toyota production system ■ *Poka-Yoke*, or fool proofing, also known as the zero defects concept
The new Western wave		
Philip B. Crosby (1926–)	*Quality is Free*, McGraw-Hill, 1983	Five absolutes of quality management: 1 'Quality conformity to requirements – not elegance' 2 'There is no such thing as a quality problem although there may be an engineering machine problem' 3 'It is always cheaper to do the job right first time' 4 'The only performance indicator is the cost of quality' 5 'The only performance standard is zero defects'. The 14-step quality improvement programme traits
Tom Peters (1942–)	*A Passion for Excellence*, Profile Books, 1964	Twelve traits of quality revolution based on a study of the quality improvement programmes of successful American companies
Claus Moller (1968–)	*A Complaint is a Gift* (with Janelle Barlow), Time Management International	■ Administrative rather than production processes offer more opportunity for productivity gain ■ Personal development of the individual will lead to increased competence in the three vital areas of productivity, relationships and quality

9.3.5 The benefits of TQM

TQM is a *philosophy* about quality that involves everyone in the organisation. It follows that the success of TQM depends on a genuine commitment to quality by every organisational member. Some benefits claimed for TQM include:

- improved customer satisfaction
- enhanced quality of goods and services
- reduced waste and inventory with consequential reduced costs
- improved productivity
- reduced product development time
- increased flexibility in meeting market demands
- reduced work-in-progress
- improved customer service and delivery times
- better utilisation of human resources.

9.3.6 Criticisms of TQM

TQM is not without its critics. Some objections include:

- that overly zealous advocates of TQM may focus attention on quality even though other priorities may be important, such as changes in the market – exemplified by the manager who said:

  > Before we invested in TQM, we churned out poorly made products that customers didn't want. We now churn out well-made products that customers don't want.

- that it creates a cumbersome bureaucracy of councils, committees and documentation relating to quality
- that it delegates the determination of quality to quality experts because TQM is a complicated entity beyond the comprehension of the average employee
- that some workers and unions regard TQM as management-by-stress and a way of de-unionising workplaces.

9.4　Specifications

9.4.1 Specifications and purchasing

Lysons[15] has suggested the following reasons for the importance of purchasing staff being knowledgeable about specifications.

- The primary purpose of purchasing is to contribute to the profitability of an undertaking by obtaining the best-quality products or services in terms of fitness for use at the least possible total cost.
- Purchasing staff are the intermediaries between the user and the supplier. They are therefore responsible for checking the completeness of product or service specifications. When negotiating with suppliers, purchasing staff must know what they are negotiating for.
- The satisfaction of user requirements depends on obtaining reliable suppliers.

- Purchasing staff should be expert in the application of value analysis and the provision at the design or specification stage of innovative suggestions aimed at achieving cost reduction without detriment to the required performance, reliability, quality and maintainability.

- Purchasing staff should be able to advise on whether or not any of the requirements stated in the specification are liable to cause commercial, environmental or legal problems.

9.4.2 Definitions

Specifications must be distinguished from standards and codes of practice. A *specification* has been defined as:

A statement of the attributes of a product or service.[16]

A statement of requirements.[17]

A statement of needs to be satisfied by the procurement of external resources.[18]

A *standard* is a specification intended for recurrent use.

Standards differ from specifications in that, while every standard is a specification, not every specification is a standard. The guiding principle of standardisation, considered later in this chapter, is the elimination of unnecessary variety.

Codes of practice are less specific than formal standards and provide guidance on the best accepted practice in relation to engineering and construction and for operations such as installation, maintenance and service provision.

9.4.3 The purpose of specifications

Both specifications and standards aim to:

- *indicate fitness for purpose or use* as indicated in Table 9.1 fitness for purpose or use was the definition of quality given by Joseph Juran, who also stated that quality is linked to product satisfaction and dissatisfaction, with satisfaction relating to superior performance or features and dissatisfaction to deficiencies or defects in a product or service

- *communicate* the requirements of a user or purchaser to the supplier

- *compare* what is actually supplied with the requirements in terms of purpose, quality and performance stated in the specification

- *provide evidence*, in the event of a dispute, of what the purchaser required and what the supplier agreed to provide.

9.4.4 Types of specification

As shown in Figure 9.2, specifications can broadly be divided into two types.

Several of the elements listed in Figure 9.2 may, of course, be combined in one specification. Thus, a specification for a component (a thing) may also state how it shall be made (a process) and how it shall be tested (a procedure). The specification may also state what the component is intended to do (function) and what a product or service should achieve under given conditions (performance).

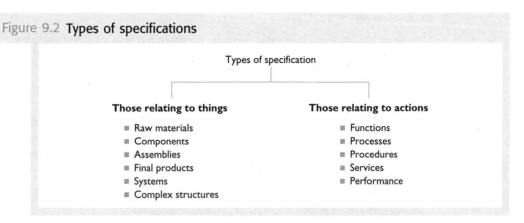

Figure 9.2 **Types of specifications**

9.4.5 Request for quotation (RFQ)

This is a specification on the basis of which a potential purchaser communicates his or her requirements to potential suppliers so that the latter have sufficient information to prepare quotations or tenders.

9.4.6 The contents of a specification

These will vary according to whether the specification is written from the standpoint of the user, designer, manufacturer or seller. The specification will also vary according to the material or item concerned. For a simple item, the specification may be a brief description, while in the case of a complicated assembly it will be a comprehensive document that perhaps runs to many pages. The following order of presentation for a specification relating to a product, process or service is adapted from BS 7373 (now BS 7373, 2:2001):

1 *identification* title, designation, number, authority
2 *issue number* publication history and state of issue, earlier related specifications
3 *contents list* guide to layout
4 *foreword* the reason for writing the specification
5 *introduction* description of the content in general and technical aspects of objectives
6 *scope* range of objectives/content
7 *definitions* terms used with meanings special to the text
8 *requirements/guidance/methods/elements* the main body of the specification
9 *index* cross-references
10 *references* to national, European or international standards or other internal company specifications.

The requirements specified may relate to the following:

■ conditions in which the item or material is to be installed, used, manufactured or stored

- characteristics, such as:
  - design, samples, drawings, models, preliminary tests or investigations
  - properties, such as strength, dimensions, weight, safety and so on, with tolerances where applicable
  - interchangeability – functional, dimensional
  - materials and their properties, including permissible variability and approved or excluded materials
  - requirements for a manufacturing process, such as heat treatment – this should be specified only when critical to design considerations
  - appearance, texture, finish, including colour, protection and so on
  - identification marks, operating symbols on controls, weight of items, safety indications and so on
  - method of marking
- performance:
  - performance under specified conditions
  - test methods and equipment for assessing performance, where, how and by whom they are to be carried out and reference to correlation with behaviour in operation
  - criteria for passing tests, including accuracy and interpretations of results
  - acceptance conditions
  - certification and/or reporting – that is, reports, test schedules or certificates required
- life
- reliability – under stipulated conditions and tests and control procedures required
- control of quality checking for compliance with specification:
  - method of checking compliance
  - production tests on raw materials, components, subassemblies and assemblies
  - assurance of compliance, such as by suppliers' certificates or independent manufacturer/supplier
  - instructions regarding reject material or items
  - instructions with regard to modification of process
  - applicability of quality control to subcontractors and others
- packing and protection
  - specifications of packaging, including any special conditions in transit
  - condition in which the item is to be supplied, such as protected, lubricant free and so on
  - period of storage
  - marking of packaging
- information from the supplier to the user, such as instructions and advice on installation, operation and maintenance.

9.4.7 Some principles of specification writing

Purdy[19] has identified four principles that should be observed by all specification writers. These and other principles are as follows.

■ *If something is not specified it is unlikely to be provided* The corollary is that all requirements should be stated in the specification before awarding the order. Suppliers will normally charge requirements subsequently added as 'extras'.

■ *Every requirement increases the price* All specifications should therefore be submitted to rigorous value analysis (considered later in this chapter).

■ *The shorter the specification, the less time it takes to prepare it* The expenditure in staff time devoted to the preparation of a specification can be high. This can be significantly lower when the length of a specification and the time taken in its preparation is reduced.

■ *The specification is equally binding on both the purchaser and the vendor* Omissions, incorrect information or imprecision in a specification can be cited by the vendor in any dispute with the purchaser. A rule of evidence is that words are construed against the party who wrote them. Where there is uncertainty about the meaning of a specification, the court will generally interpret it in the vendor's favour.

■ *Specifications, should, so far as possible, be presented in performance terms rather than as a detailed design* This is particularly applicable to items about which the purchaser has little expert knowledge. According to section 14(3) of the Sale of Goods Act 1979 as amended by the Supply and Sale of Goods Act 1994, where the seller sells goods in the course of a business and the buyer expressly, or by implication, makes known to the seller any particular purpose for which the goods are being bought, there is an implied 'term' that the goods supplied under the contract are of satisfactory quality. For the purpose of the Supply and Sales of Goods Act 1994 (SSGA), goods are of satisfactory quality if 'they meet the standard that a reasonable person would regard as satisfactory, taking account of any description of the goods, the price (if relevant) and all other relevant circumstances'.

■ *Specifications, should, whenever possible be 'open', not closed* Closed specifications are referred to in 9.5.3 below. Open specifications are written so that the stated requirements can be met by more than one supplier. By making the requirements sufficiently flexible to be met by several suppliers, competition is encouraged and prices reduced.

■ *Specifications must not conflict with national or international standards or health, safety or environmental laws and regulations* National and international specifications should be incorporated into individual specifications and identified by their numbers and titles.

9.5 Alternatives to individual specifications

9.5.1 Existing specifications

It should only be necessary to write a specification for non-standard requirements. For most standard industrial and consumer products it is usually sufficient to use:

■ manufacturers' standards, as stated in catalogues or other promotional literature
■ national or international standards.

All products or services will require materials, components or other elements for which existing standards will be available. An essential first step for designers or specification writers is to ascertain what relevant standards already exist. Searching for such standards is facilitated by consulting reference publications, especially the British Standards Catalogue (available in most large libraries), or databases. Especially useful are the services provided by Technical Indexes Ltd (Telephone: 01344 426 311), which offer comprehensive, reliable, full-text databases of manufacturers' technical catalogues, national and international standards and legislative material, delivered online via the Internet on an annual subscription basis. Technical Indexes' information services cover more than 90 per cent of the world's most commonly used standards, including:

- British Standards Online – a complete collection of over 35,000 British Standards
- worldwide standards on the Internet
- UK and US defence standards
- US Government Specifications Service.

9.5.2 Adapting existing specifications

This is often the most economical approach for construction projects or computer systems where architects or suppliers may be able to amend existing specifications to meet a new application.

9.5.3 Alternative methods of specifying

These include the use of brand or trade names and specifying by means of samples.

The use of a brand or trade names

England[20] lists the following circumstances in which descriptions by brand may be not only desirable but necessary, such as when:

- the manufacturing process is secret or covered by a patent
- the vendor's manufacturing process calls for a high degree of 'workmanship' or 'skill' that cannot be defined exactly in a specification
- only small quantities are bought so that the preparation of specifications by the buyer is impracticable
- testing by the buyer is impracticable
- the item is a component so effectively advertised as to create a preference or even a demand for its incorporation into the finished product on the part of the ultimate purchaser
- there is a strong preference for the branded item on the part of the design staff.

The main disadvantages of specifying branded items are as follows.

- The cost of a branded item may be higher than that of an unbranded substitute.
- The naming of a brand effectively results in what Haslam[21] refers to as a 'closed specification', which can take the form of naming a particular brand and the manufacturer or supplier not permitting the use of alternatives. Closed specifications

are most applicable when the need for duplication of an existing product is important or it is desirable to maintain a low spares range. Such specifications inhibit competition but also cut out fringe suppliers that may be unable to meet the quality requirements.

Specification by sample

The sample can be provided either by the buyer or seller and is a useful method of specification in relation to products such as printing or materials such as cloth. When orders are placed and products specified by reference to a sample previously submitted by a supplier, it is important that the sample on which the contract is based should be:

- identified
- labelled
- the signed and labelled samples retained by both purchaser and supplier.

Under sections 15 of the Supply of Goods and Services Act 1982 (SGSA) and section 15 of the SSGA there is an implied 'term' (later defined as a 'condition') that where goods are sold by sample:

- the bulk must correspond to the sample in quality
- the buyer must have a reasonable opportunity to compare the bulk with the sample
- the goods must be free from any defect making 'their quality unsatisfactory' (not unmerchantable), which a reasonable examination of the sample would not reveal.

Specification by a user or performance specification

Here, the purchaser informs the supplier of the use to which the purchased item is to be put. This method is particularly applicable to the purchase of items about which the buyer has little technical knowledge.

Under section 14(3) of the SSGA and sections 4 and 5 of the SGSA as amended by the SSGA, where the seller sells goods in the course of a business and the buyer, expressly or by implication, makes known to the seller any particular purpose for which the goods are being bought, there is an implied 'term' that the goods supplied under the contract are of satisfactory quality. For the purpose of the SSGA, goods are satisfactory if 'they meet the standard that a reasonable person would regard as satisfactory, taking account of any description of the goods, the price (if relevant) and all the other relevant circumstances'. Under section 2B of the SSGA, the quality of the goods includes their state and condition and the following (among others) are, in appropriate cases, aspects of their quality:

- fitness for all purposes for which goods of the kind in question are commonly supplied
- appearance and finish
- freedom from minor defects
- safety
- durability.

Under section 2C of the SSGA, the 'term' does not extend to any matter making the quality of goods unsatisfactory:

- that is specifically drawn to the buyer's attention before the contract is made
- where the buyer examines the goods before the contract is made as that examination ought to reveal such matters
- in the case of a contract of sale by sample, matters that would have been apparent on reasonable examination of the sample.

Section 4 of the SSGA provides that, when the seller can prove that the deviation from the specification is only slight, it would be unreasonable for the buyer to reject the goods. The buyer may not treat the breach of contract as a condition entitling him to reject the goods, but only as a warranty giving a right to damages arising from the breach.

Section 4 also makes a distinction between commercial buyers and consumers. If the buyer is a consumer, the right to reject the goods on the grounds that the quality of the goods is unsatisfactory is not affected.

Section 3(2) states that the section applies unless a contrary intention appears in, or is to be implied from, the contract.

As Woodroffe[22] observes:

> This time buyers must look to their own terms and conditions, for a well-drafted clause will enable a buyer to terminate a contract for any breach of sections 13–15 (SSGA) whether slight or not.

9.6 Standardisation

Standards are documents that stipulate or recommend minimum levels of performance and quality of goods and services and optional conditions for operations in a given environment. Standards may be distinguished according to their subject matter, purpose and range of applications.

9.6.1 Subject matter

This may relate to an area of economic activity, such as engineering, and items used in that field, such as fasteners. Each item may be further subdivided into suitable subjects for standards. Thus, 'fasteners' may lead to standards for screw threads, bolts and nuts, washers and so on.

9.6.2 Purpose

Standards may relate to one or more aspects of product quality. These include:

- *dimensions* thus encouraging interchangeability and variety reduction – for example, BS 308 is a British Standard that lays down technical drawing principles and conventions widely accepted in the UK and will be easily understood worldwide
- *performance requirements* for a given purpose, such as BS 1515, which covers all stressing and constructional features of fusion-welded pressure vessels necessary for a design to meet statutory requirements and those of manufacturers and users of safe performance

■ *environmental requirements* relating to such matters as pollution, waste disposal on land, noise and environmental nuisance – for example, environmental performance objectives and targets are covered by BS 7750 and ISO 14000.

In addition to the above, standards may also cover codes of practice, methods of testing and glossaries. Codes of practice, as stated earlier, give guidance on the best accepted practices in relation to engineering and construction techniques and for operations such as installation, maintenance and provision of services. Methods of testing are required for measuring the values of product characteristics and behaviour standards. Glossaries help to ensure unambiguous technical communication by providing standard definitions of the terms, conventions, units and symbols used in science and industry.

9.6.3 Range of application

This relates to the domain in which a particular standard is applicable. There are several kinds of standards.

■ *Individual standards* These are laid down by the individual user.

■ *Company standards* These are prepared and agreed by various functions to guide design, purchasing, manufacturing and marketing operations. Ashton[23] has drawn attention to the importance of keeping registers or databases of bought-out parts and company standards that can be referred to by codes listed in a codes register as a means of variety reduction and obviating variations in tolerances, finishes, performance and quality.

■ *Association or trade standards* These are prepared by a group of related interests in a given industry, trade or profession, such as the Society of Motor Manufacturers and Traders.

■ *National standards* British Standard specifications of particular importance are BS 4778 Quality vocabulary, BS 6143 Guide to the economics of quality, BS 7850 Total quality management and BS EN ISO 9000:2000 Quality management systems.

■ *International standards* The two principal organisations producing worldwide standards are the International Electrotechnical Commission (IEC) and the International Standards Organisation (ISO). The former, established in 1906, concentrates on standards relating to the electrical and electronic fields. The latter, founded in 1947, is concerned with non-electrical standards. Both organisations are located in Geneva. In Western Europe, progress is being made in the development of standards that will be acceptable as both European and international standards. This work is being done via the European Committee for Standardisation (CEN), formed by Western European standards organisations. The demarcation of European standardisation mirrors the international arrangement, with CEN covering non-electrical aspects and the European Committee for Electrotechnical Standardisation (CENELEC) and the European Telecommunications Standards Institute (ETSI) being responsible for the others.

Different standards and specifications can often be used in conjunction.

9.6.4 BS EN ISO 9000:2000

Although TQM preceded the ISO 9000 series as a method by which organisations could increase their reputation for quality and profitability, compliance with ISO standards and ISO certification is widely regarded as providing the framework and essential first step to TQM.

The British Standards Institution (BSI) was established in 1901 as the Engineering Standards Committee, but, after being granted a Royal Charter in 1929, changed to the present name in 1931.

The CEN (European Committee for Standardisation) and CENELEC (European Committee for Electrotechnical Standardisation) were created in the late 1960s – the former to 'promote technical harmonisation in Europe in conjunction with worldwide bodies and its partners in Europe'.

The ISO (International Standards Organisation) was founded in 1946 as the existence of non-harmonised standards for similar technologies can constitute technical barriers to international trade. ISO 9000, as the worldwide derivative of BSI's BS 5750 Quality Management System, launched in 1979, appeared in 1987. ISO standards, now adopted by over 140 countries, are revised every five years.

The current BS EN ISO 9000:2000 series, published in December 2000, provides the principles that are put into practice by the BSI system for the Registration of Firms' Assessed Capability. To be registered, an organisation is required to have a documented quality system that complies with the appropriate parts of BS EN ISO 9000 and a quality assessment schedule (QAS) that defines in precise terms the scope and special requirements relating to a specific group of products, processes or service. QASs are developed by the BSI in cooperation with a particular industry after consultation with purchasing and associated interests.

When an undertaking seeking registration has satisfactory documentation procedures, the BSI arranges for an assessment visit by a team of at least two experienced assessors, one of whom is normally from the BSI inspectorate. Afterwards, a report confirming any discrepancies raised and the outcome of the assessment is sent to the undertaking seeking registration. The initial assessment is followed by regular unannounced audit visits at the discretion of the BSI to ensure standards are maintained.

As shown by Figure 9.3, the main documents relating to the system are a vocabulary and separate standards.

Although the revised 9001:2000 and 9004:2000 are standalone standards, they constitute a 'consistent pair' aimed at facilitating a more user-friendly introduction of quality management systems into an organisation.

Figure 9.3 The main documents relating to ISO 9000:2000 standards

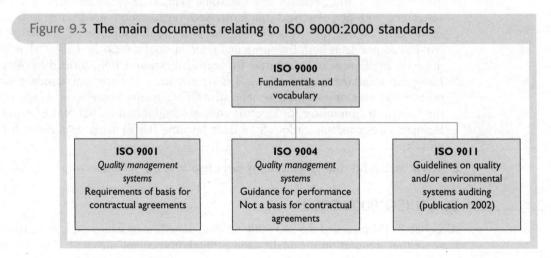

9.6.5 Purchasing and BS EN ISO 9000:2000

BS EN ISO 9000:2000 defines the standards for any requirements of a quality system under four main headings:

- management responsibility
- resource management
- product realisation
- measurement, analysis and improvement.

Purchasing is referred to under 'resource management' in clause 7.4. In this context, the word 'organisation' refers to the undertaking that is seeking conformity with the standard, that is 'us'. The term 'supplier' refers to 'our' suppliers. An 'interested party' is a person or group having an interest in the performance or success of an organisation.

Clause 7.4 contains provisions relating to the purchasing process (7.4.1), purchasing information (7.4.2) and verification of purchased produce (7.4.3). These sections should, however, be read in conjunction with BS EN ISO 9004:2000, which specified the activities that should be included in a quality system for purchasing. Subsection 7.4.2, for example, provides examples of ways in which an organisation can ensure that suppliers have the potential capability to provide required products 'effectively, efficiently and within schedule', such as:

- evaluation of relevant supplier experience
- performance of suppliers against competitors
- review of purchase product quality, price, delivery performance and response to problems
- audits of supplier management systems.

Cognisance should also be taken of the ISO 14000 series. This supercedes BS 7750, which was the world's first standard for environmental management systems.

9.6.6 Purchasing and standardisation

Purchasing staff should be aware of the major trade, national and international standards applicable to their industry and the items bought. They should also appreciate the advantages that standardisation offers to the buyer:

- clear specifications and the removal of any uncertainty as to what is required on the part of both buyer and supplier
- standardisation helps to achieve reliability and reduce costs
- saving of time and money by eliminating the need to prepare company specifications and reducing the need for explanatory letters, telephone calls and so on
- the saving of design time may also reduce the time for production of the finished product
- accurate comparison of quotations as all prospective suppliers are quoting for the same thing
- less dependence on specialist suppliers and greater scope for negotiation

- reduction in error and conflict, thus increasing supplier goodwill
- facilitation of international sourcing by reference to ISO standards
- saving in inventory and cost as a result of variety reduction (see Chapter 10) – by coordinating the efforts of purchasing, design and production, a company reduced 30 different paints to 15, 120 different cutting fluids to 10, 50 different tools steel to 6, and 12 different aluminium casting alloys to 3. Standardisation and coding of items also discovered 36 different terms in use for a simple washer
- reduced investment in spares for capital equipment
- reduced cost of material handling when standardisation is used
- elimination of the need to purchase costly brand names
- irregular purchases of non-standard equipment supplies are revealed.

9.6.7 Directories of ISO 9000-certified companies or organisations and standards

There is no complete database of ISO-certified organisations, but reference may be made to the following:

- ISO 9000 Web Directory
- ISO Register
- QSU Online ISO 9000 Registered Company Directory
- Quality Digest – International ISO Database
- The International Quality Systems Directory

Further information on standards can be obtained from Rhodes and Fallon.[24] Useful websites are:

- British Standards Institution at: www.bsi-global.com/
- British Standards Online at: http://bsonline.bsi-global.com
- Guide to British Standards Online at: www.swan.ac.uk/lis/help_and_training/pdf/bsonline.pdf
- BSI catalogue at: www.bsonline.bsi-global.com/server/index.jsp

9.6.8 Independent quality assurance and certification

Independent quality assurance and certification is of great benefit to the user, purchaser and manufacturer. The BSI, via its Kitemark, Safety Mark, Registered Firms and Registered Stockist Schemes, put into practice the principles of ISO 9000, setting out procedures by which a product's safety and a suppliers' quality management systems can be independently assessed.

About 30 third-party certification bodies are members of the Association of British Certification Bodies (ABCB). Some are set up by trade associations, such as the Manchester Chamber of Commerce Testing House for the Cotton Trade, Bradford Chamber of Commerce for the Wool Trade, the Shirley Institute, Manchester, and the London Textile Trading House. Certification bodies assessed by the National Accreditation Council for Certification Bodies (NACCB) are entitled to use the NACCB National Quality 'Tick'.

9.7 Variety reduction

Variety reduction can make substantial savings in inventory by standardising and rationalising the range of materials, parts and consumables kept in stock. Variety reduction can be proactive or reactive.

Proactive variety reduction can be achieved by using, so far as possible, standardised components and subassemblies to make end products that are dissimilar in appearance and performance so that a variety of final products use only a few basic components. Proactive approaches to variety reduction can also apply when considering capital purchases. By ensuring compatibility with existing machinery, the range of spares carried to insure against breakdowns can be substantially reduced.

Reactive variety reduction can be undertaken periodically by a special project team comprised of all interested parties who examine a range of stock items to determine:

- the intended use for each item of stock
- how many stock items serve the same purpose
- the extent to which items having the same purpose can be given a standard description
- what range of sizes is essential
- how frequently each item in the range is used
- what items can be eliminated
- to what extent sizes, dimensions, quality and other characteristics of an item can be standardised
- what items of stock are now obsolete and unlikely to be required in the future.

The advantages of variety reduction include:

- reduction of holding costs for stock
- release of money tied up in stock
- easier specifications when ordering
- narrower range of inventory
- a reduced supplier base.

9.8 Quality assurance and quality control

9.8.1 Quality assurance

Quality assurance is defined as:[25]

> All those planned and systematic activities implemented within the quality systems and demonstrated as needed to provide adequate confidence that an entity will fulfil requirements for quality.

Quality assurance is concerned with defect prevention. Therefore, it can involve a number of approaches, including:

- quality systems, including ISO 9000
- new design control, aimed at getting it right first time
- design of manufacturing processes aimed at eliminating defects at source

- incoming materials control – most organistion now require that their suppliers provide proof, such as ISO 9000 certification, that their processes are under statistical control
- supplier appraisal, to ensure that only suppliers able to meet quality requirements are approved – this is especially important with JIT purchasing.

9.8.2 Quality control

Quality control (QC) is defined as:[26]

> The operational techniques and activities that are used to fulfil requirements for quality. Quality control is concerned with defect detection and correction and relates to such activities as determining where, how and at what intervals inspection should take place, the collection and analysis of data relating to defects and determining what corrective action should be taken.

As defects are detected after they have been made, Schonberger[27] has referred to QC as 'the death certificate' approach.

9.9 Tests for quality control and reliability

It is impracticable in this book to attempt even an outline of quality assurance, control and liability techniques. So, in this section, brief mention is made of inspection, statistical quality control and six sigma, quality loss function, robust design, quality function deployment (QFD) and failure mode and effects analysis (FMEA).

9.9.1 Inspection

Although inspection is a non-value-adding activity, some form of inspection, either at source or on delivery, is often unavoidable. The four main inspection activities are shown in Figure 9.4.

Important aspects of inspection are as follows.

- *How much to inspect and how often* Only rarely is a 100 per cent inspection required, and the greater the frequency of inspections, the greater the cost. In general, operations

Figure 9.4 **The four main inspection activities**

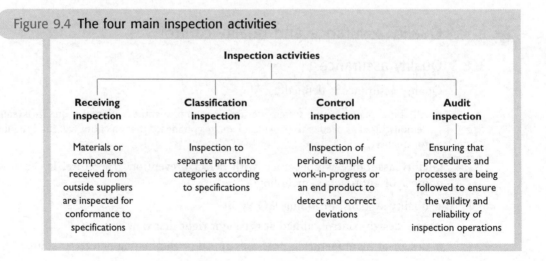

with a high human input necessitate more inspection than mechanical operations, which tend to be more reliable. The usual basis of inspection is an agreed sample, such as 5 per cent. The size of the sample will be determined by which statistical quality control method is to be used. Often the checking of dimensions or measurements can be done automatically by the use of go/no-go gauges.

■ *Where to inspect* Most operations have numerous possible inspection points. Generally, inspection should take place:

- when material is received from suppliers, although the tendency is for responsibility for quality to be placed with the supplier
- before dispatch, as repairing or replacing products after delivery is more costly than at the factory and there is also damage to customer goodwill
- before a costly operation
- before parts are joined irreversibly to other parts
- before a covering process, as painting or plating can often mask defects.

9.9.2 Statistical quality control

The basis of statistical quality control is sampling. A sample is a subset of a population or an entire set of objects or observations that have something in common. If a factory produces 1000 items of component X in one day, the population or 'universe' of component X for that day is 1000.

There are three main reasons for using sampling rather than 100 per cent inspection:

■ sampling saves time

■ sampling saves money

■ sampling provides a basis for control.

From the quality standpoint, sampling can take one of two forms.

■ *Acceptance sampling* tests the quality of a batch of products by taking a sample from each batch and testing to see whether the whole batch should be accepted or rejected. Acceptance sampling can be applied when bought-out items are received from suppliers or as a final inspection of goods produced before they are dispatched to customers.

■ *Process control* is a more proactive approach, aimed at ensuring that parts and components meet specifications during the production process, not after a batch has already been manufactured.

The concepts of the arithmetic mean and standard deviation (referred to in the next section) provide the basis for the book *Economic Control of Manufactured Products*, published in 1931 by Dr Walter Shewart of the Bell Telephone Company. This book is the foundation of modern statistical process control (SPC) and provides the basis for the philosophy of total quality management by means of sampling.

Shewart also developed the statistical process control chart to provide a visual indication of quality variations.

If, for example, the ideal length of a steel spindle is 6 cm and there is a tolerance of 0.005 cm, then components of 5.995 cm or 6.005 cm will be acceptable.

As sample batches of the spindle are taken, the average value of each batch is calculated and logged on the chart, as shown in Figure 9.5.

Figure 9.5 **Statistical process control chart**

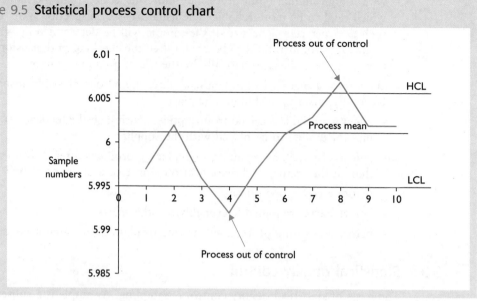

So long as the results are within the upper and lower limits, there is no need for action. However, if a value falls outside these limits – as with samples 4 and 8 – the reason(s) must be investigated and rectified. It is possible, for example, that the machine settings for these batches needed resetting or adjusting.

9.9.3 Six sigma

The concept of the arithmetic mean, standard deviation and normal curve are the basis of six sigma – an approach for improving customer satisfaction by reducing and eliminating product defects. Six sigma originated at Motorola in the early 1980s and aims to achieve virtually defect-free processes and products.

A normal distribution curve is shown in Figure 9.6.

The arithmetic mean (x) is obtained by dividing the sum of two or more quantities by the number of items. For example, the arithmetic mean of 5, 10 and 12 is 27/3 = 9.

The standard deviation measures the extent to which sample scores are spread around the mean or average. For example, suppose that the scores from a series of inspections are normally distributed with a mean of 80 and a standard deviation of 8. Then the scores that are within one standard deviation of the mean are between $80 - 8 = 72$ and $80 + 8 = 88$. One standard deviation from the mean in either direction accounts for somewhere around 68 per cent of all items in the distribution. Two standard deviations from the mean accounts for roughly 95 per cent and three standard deviations for 99 per cent of the distribution spread. The term 'sigma' is a Greek alphabet letter 'σ', used to describe variability. In six sigma, the common measurement is defects per million operations (DPMO). Six sigma – or six standard deviations from the mean – therefore indicates a target of 3.4 defects per million opportunities (or 99.99966 accuracy), which is as close as anyone is likely to get to perfection.

Achieving a six sigma level of quality output means reducing process variation by means of a technique called define, measure, analyse, improve and control (DMAIC),

Figure 9.6 **A normal distribution curve**

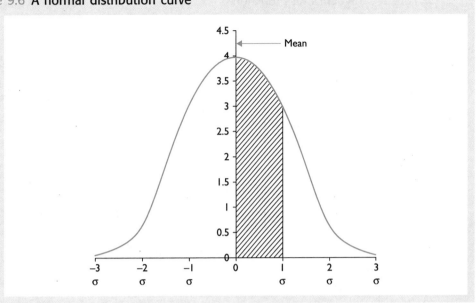

which uses a variety of statistical tools, including process maps, Pareto charts, control charts, cause and effect diagrams and process capability ratio, most of which are beyond the scope of this book. Suffice to say that, as a result of the application of DMAIC, organisations identify and eliminate special cause variations from their processes until six sigma quality output is achieved.

9.9.4 Quality loss function (QLF)

This, together with the concept of robust design referred to in 9.9.5, below, developed from work undertaken by Dr Genichi Taguchi while working for the Japanese telecommunications company NTT in the 1950s and 1960s.

Taguchi's approach is based on the economic implications of poor quality. He defines quality as:[28]

> The quality of a product is the minimum loss imparted by the product to society from the time the product is shipped.

The loss to society includes costs arising from the failure of the product to:

■ meet customers' expectations

■ achieve desired performance characteristics

■ meet safety and environmental standards.

QLF is based on the principle that 'quality should be measured by the deviation from a specific target value rather than by conformance to preset tolerance limits'. Thus, the greater the deviation from a given target, the greater will be customers' dissatisfaction and the larger the loss concept.

The QLF approach is shown in Figure 9.7. The aim is to keep the product as near to the target as possible.

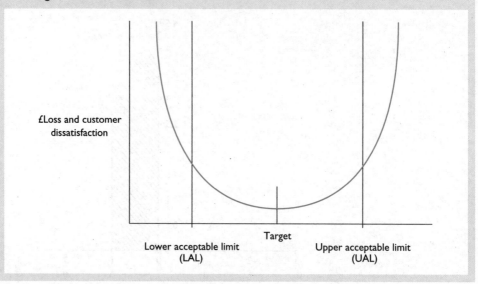

Figure 9.7 **Taguchi's loss function**

This loss function can be approximately calculated by using the formula:

$$L(x) = R(x - T)^2$$

Where:

L = the loss in monetary terms
x = any value of the quality characteristics
T = the target value
R = some constant

Example 9.1

Example of use of the loss function

Assume a quality characteristic has a specification of 0.500 ± 0.020. Further, assume that, on the basis of company records, it has been found that if the quality characteristic exceeds the target of 0.020 on either side, there is a probability that the product will fail during the warranty period and the cost of rectifying it will be £100.

Then:

$$£100 = R(0.020)^2$$

$$R = \frac{100}{(0.020)^2} = \frac{100}{0.0004} = 250,000$$

Therefore, the loss function is:

$$L(x) = £250,000(x - T)^2$$

Thus, if the deviation is only 0.005, the estimated loss will be:

$$L(0.005) = £250,000(0.005)^2 = £6.25$$

For a batch of 50 products, the cost would be 50 × 6.25 = £312.50

The loss function approach has been criticised on the grounds that the practicalities of determining the constant R with any degree of accuracy are formidable.

The Taguchi loss function can be applied to any non-conformance cost, such as complaint handling, inspection and testing, rework of defective parts, scrap and warranty repairs. All such costs arise from not doing the work right first time. By improving quality, such costs can be reduced. Thus, the cost of quality is a misnomer as quality can actually produce a profit.

9.9.5 Robust design

Some products are designed for use only within a narrow application range. Others will perform well in a much wider range of conditions. The latter have robust design. Think of a pair of bedroom slippers. These are clearly unsuitable for walking in mud or snow. Conversely, a pair of Wellington boots is exactly what is required. The Wellington boots are more robust than the slippers.

A product or service may be defined as 'robust' when it is insensitivie to the effects of source of variability, even though the sources themselves have not been eliminated. The more designers can build robustness into a product, the better it should last, resulting in a higher level of customer satisfaction.

Similarly, environmental factors can have a negative effect on production processes. Furnaces used in the production of food, ceramics and steel products may not heat uniformly. One approach to the problem might be to develop a superior oven. Another is to design a system that moves the product during operation to achieve uniform heating.

Taguchi's approach involves determining the target specifications of limits for the product or design process and reducing variability due to manufacturing and environmental factors. As shown in Figure 9.8, Taguchi distinguishes between controllable and non-controllable factors, or 'noise'.

'Noise' factors are primarily responsible for causing the performance of a product to deviate from its target value. Hence, by means of analytical methods or carefully planned experiments, parameter design seeks to identify settings of the control factors that make the product more robust – that is, less sensitive to variations in the noise factors. Taguchi states that many designers consider only system and tolerance factors. He maintains, however, that without parameter design it is almost impossible to produce a high-quality product.

Taguchi's concepts of QLF and design have been criticised mainly on the grounds that the constant R in the QLF equation is difficult to determine with any degree of accuracy and that the large number of possible parameters in robust design make it impossible to investigate all such combinations. Nevertheless, his methods are used by many world class organisations.

9.9.6 Quality function deployment (QFD)

QFD is a translation of the Japanese *Kanji* characters *Hin Shitsu Ki Ten Kai*, which can be broadly translated as meaning, 'how we do understand the quality that our customers expect and make it happen in a dynamic way?'

QFD has been defined as:

> a structured approach to defining customers' needs or requirements and translating them into specific plans to meet those needs.

Figure 9.8 **Taguchi's concept of controllable and non-controllable factors**

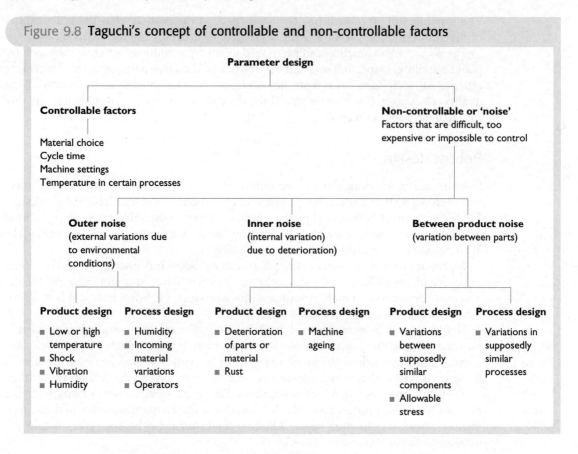

The term used to describe stated or unstated customer requirements is the 'voice of the customer'.

Information on customers' requirements is obtained in a multiplicity of ways, including market research, direct discussion, focus groups, customer specifications, observation, warranty data and field reports.

QFD ensures that customers' requirements are met by means of a tool called the 'house of quality' – an outline of which is shown in Figure 9.9. Using this tool, producers are able to reconcile customers' needs with design and manufacturing constraints.

The house of quality or product planning is, however, only the first of a four-stage process – the other three sequential phases being product design, product planning and process control. These four phases are shown in Figure 9.10.

The QFD process involves the following steps.

1 Details of customers' requirements, or 'attributes', are obtained from sources such as those referred to earlier and listed under 'Customers' requirements' in the house of quality.

2 The relative importance assigned to each attribute is expressed on a scale of 1–5 or in percentage terms and entered under 'Importance of each requirement' in the house of quality.

Figure 9.9 **House of quality**

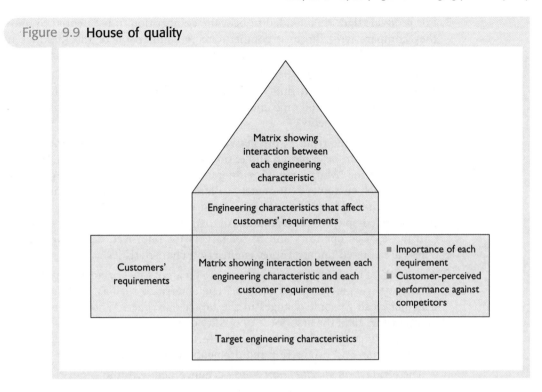

Figure 9.10 **The four phases in QFD**

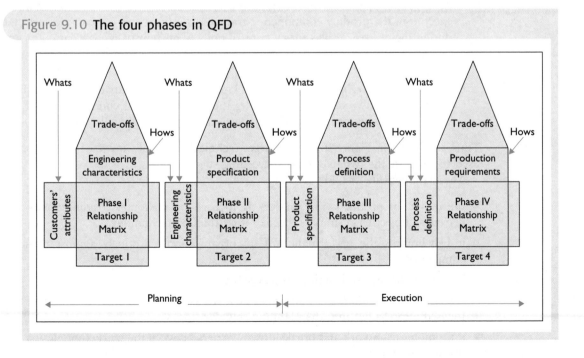

3 For products that are intended to beat the competition, it is essential to know how they compare with those of competitors. A comparison of the rankings of each attribute will be made under 'Customer-perceived performance against competitors'.

4 Customers' attributes are translated into key engineering characteristics. Thus, for a car, the customers' attribute of 'fast start' would be translated into a 'specified' acceleration from 0 to 60 mph and entered into 'Engineering characteristics that affect customers' requirements'.

5 The strength of the relationship between customers' requirements and the technical requirements can be explored and expressed as 'very strong', 'strong' or 'weak' and entered into the 'Matrix showing interaction between each engineering characteristic and each customer requirement'. Blank rows or columns indicate no relationship or technical requirements as no customer requirement exists. It is also now possible to compare the performance of the product against customers' requirements and those of competitors and to set targets for improved design or performance. These are entered under 'Target engineering characteristics'.

6 The 'roof' of the house matrix encourages creativity by considering potential trade-offs between engineering and customer characteristics, such as performance and cost. This may lead to some changes in the target outcomes. While some organisations go no further than the first house of quality concerned with customers' requirements, others continue the process through the further stages of product specification, process definition and production requirements shown in Figure 9.10.

■ The *production specification house* is concerned with the detailed characteristics of subsystems and components and the determination of target values for such aspects as fit, function and appearance.

■ The *process definition house* is where components characteristics are related to key process operations. This stage represents the transition from planning to execution. If a product component parameter is critical and is created or affected during the process, it becomes a control point. This tells us what to monitor and inspect and becomes the basis for a quality control plan for the achievement of customer satisfaction.

■ The *production requirements house* relates the control points to specific requirements for quality control and includes the specification of control methods and what sample sizes are required to achieve the appropriate quality level.

Thus, as shown in Figure 9.10, the target technical levels of 'hows' of one stage are used to generate the 'whats' of the succeeding stage.

The main benefits of QFD are that:

■ the design of products and services is focused on customers' requirements and driven by objective customers' needs rather than by technology

■ it benchmarks the performance of an organisation's products against those of competitors

■ it reduces the overall length of the design code

■ it substantially reduces the number of post-release design changes by ensuring that focused effort is put into the planning stage or stages

■ it promotes teamwork and breaks down barriers between the marketing, design and production functions.

9.9.7 Failure mode and effects analysis (FMEA)

What is FMEA?

FMEA, which originated in the USA aerospace industry, is an important reliability engineering technique that has the following main objectives:

- to identify all the ways in which failure can occur
- to estimate the effect and seriousness of the failure
- to recommend corrective design actions.

FMEA has been defined as:[29]

> A systematic approach that applies a tabular method to aid the thought process used by engineers to identify potential failure modes and their effects.

As a tool embedded within six sigma methodology, FMEA can help identify and eliminate concerns early in the development of a product or process. It is a systematic way to prospectively identify possible ways in which failure can occur.

Types of FMEA

It can take three forms.[30]

- *Systems FMEA* is used to analyse systems and subsystems in the early concept and design stages. System function is the design or purpose(s) of the system and is derived from customers' wants. It can also include safety requirements, government regulations and constraints.
- *Design FMEA* is used to analyse products before they are released to production.
- *Process FMEA* is used to analyse products before they are released to the customer.

The preparation of an FMEA

The Ford Motor Company, which was the first of the UK motor manufacturers to request suppliers to use FMEA in its advance quality planning, recommends a team approach led by the responsible system, product or manufacturing/assembly engineer, who is expected to involve representatives from all affected activities. Team members may be drawn from design, manufacturing, assembly, quality, reliability, service, purchasing, testing, supplier and other subject experts as appropriate. The team leader is also responsible for keeping the FMEA updated.

For proprietary designs, the preparation and updating of FMEAs is the responsibility of the suppliers.

With a design FMEA, for example, the team is initially concerned with identifying how a part may fail to meet its intended function and the seriousness of the effect of a potential failure, which is rated on a ten-point scale, as shown in Table 9.2.

Starting with the failure modes with the highest severity ratings, the design FMEA team then ascertains the possible causes of failure, based on two assumptions:

- that the part is manufactured/assembled within engineering specifications
- that the part design may include a deficiency that may cause an unacceptable variation in the manufacturing or assembling process.

Table 9.2 Severity rating table for design FMEA

Effect	Rating	Criteria
No effect	1	No effect
Very slight effect	2	Very slight effect on vehicle's performance. Customer not annoyed. Non-vital fault noticed sometimes
Slight effect	3	Slight effect on vehicle's performance. Customer slightly annoyed. Non-vital fault noticed most of the time.
Minor effect	4	Minor effect on vehicle's performance. Fault does not require repair. Customer will notice minor effect on vehicle's or system's performance. Non-vital fault always noted.
Moderate effect	5	Moderate effect on vehicle's performance. Customer experiences some dissatisfaction. Fault on non-vital part requires repair.
Significant effect	6	Vehicle's performance degraded, but operable and safe. Customer experiences discomfort. Non-vital part inoperable.
Major effect	7	Vehicle's performance severely affected, but drivable and safe. Customer dissatisfied. Subsystems inoperable.
Extreme effect	8	Vehicle inoperable but safe. Customer very dissatisfied. System inoperable.
Serious effect	9	Potentially hazardous effect. Able to stop vehicle without mishap – gradual failure. Compliance with government regulation in jeopardy.
Hazardous effect	10	Hazardous effect. Safety related – sudden failure. Non-compliance with government regulation.

Note: Severity rating corresponds to the seriousness of the effect(s) of a potential failure mode. Severity applies only to the effect of a failure mode.

Table 9.3 Probability of failure rating table

Probability of failure	Failure probability	Ranking
Very high: failure is almost inevitable	>1 in 2	10
	1 in 3	9
High: repeated failures	1 in 8	8
	1 in 20	7
Moderate: occasional failures	1 in 80	6
	1 in 400	5
	1 in 2000	4
Low: relatively few failures	1 in 15,000	3
	1 in 150,000	2
Remote: failure is unlikely	<1 in 1,500,000	1

The team then proceeds to ascertain:

- the probability of failures that could occur over the life of the part – see Table 9.3
- design evaluation techniques that can be used to detect the identified failure causes – see Table 9.4
- what design actions are recommended to reduce the severity, occurrence and detection ratings.

The completed design FMEA for a lighting switch subsystem is shown in Table 9.3. The technique is further described in BS 5750.

Table 9.4 Design evaluation – detecting causes of failure

Detection	Likelihood of detection by design control	Ranking
Absolute uncertainty	Design control *cannot* detect potential cause/ mechanical and subsequent failure mode	
Very remote	*Very remote* chance the design control will detect potential cause/mechanism and subsequent failure mode	
Remote	*Remote* chance the design control will detect potential cause/mechanism and subsequent failure mode	
Very low	*Very low* chance the design control will detect potential cause/mechanism and subsequent failure mode	
Low	*Low* chance the design control will detect potential cause/mechanism and subsequent failure mode	
Moderate	*Moderate* chance the design control will detect potential cause/mechanism and subsequent failure mode	
Moderately high	*Moderately high* chance the design control will detect potential cause/mechanism and subsequent failure mode	
High	*High* chance the design control will detect potential cause/mechanism and subsequent failure mode	
Very high	*Very high* chance the design control will detect potential cause/mechanism and subsequent failure mode	
Almost certain	Design control *will* detect potential cause/ mechanism and subsequent failure mode	

Advantages of the FMEA approach

These include:

- improved quality, reliability and safety of products and processes
- increased customer satisfaction
- early identification, rectification and elimination of potential causes of failure
- ranking of product or process deficiencies
- documentation and tracking of actions to reduce failure risk
- minimisation of late product or process changes and associated cost
- it is a catalyst for teamwork and the cross-functional exchange of ideas and knowledge.

Some disadvantages of the FMEA approach

A study undertaken by UMIST[31] concluded that engineers still view FMEA as a hard slog and more use should be made of computerised aids to reduce the effort of preparing and updating the FMEA. The main difficulties relate to time constraints, lack of understanding of the importance of FMEA and the cost and time required for training in FMEA approaches.

9.10 The cost of quality

9.10.1 Definitions

The cost of quality may be defined as the costs of conformance plus the costs of non-conformance or the cost of doing things wrong.

The cost of conformance (COC) is defined by BS 6143 as:

> The cost of operating the process as specified in a 100 per cent effective manner. This does not imply that it is efficient or even a necessary process but rather that the process when operated with the specified procedures cannot be achieved at a lower cost.

The cost of non-conformance (CONC) is defined as:

> The cost of inefficiency with the specified process, i.e. overresourcing or excess cost of people, materials and equipment arising from unsatisfactory inputs, errors made, rejected outputs and various other sources of waste. These are regarded as non-essential process costs.

BS 6143 points out that:

> Quality costs alone do not provide sufficient information for management to put them into perspective with other operating costs or to identify critical areas in need of attention.

To establish the significance of quality costs, it is necessary to use ratios showing the relationships between total quality costs and the costs of prevention, appraisal and failure. Typical ratios include:

$$\frac{\text{Prevention cost}}{\text{Total quality cost}} \qquad \frac{\text{Cost of supplier appraisal}}{\text{Prevention costs}}$$

The main costs of quality are set out in Table 9.5.

Table 9.5 **The costs of quality**

Cost of conformance

Prevention costs	*Appraisal costs*
Costs of any action taken to investigate, prevent or reduce defects and failures, including:	Cost of assessing the quality achieved:
■ quality engineering (or quality management, department or planning) ■ quality control/engineering, including design/specification review and reliability engineering ■ process control/engineering ■ design and development of quality measurement and control equipment ■ quality planning by other functions ■ calibration and maintenance of production equipment used to evaluate quality ■ maintenance and calibration of test and inspection equipment ■ supplier assurance, including supplier surveys, audits and ratings, identifying new sources of supply, design evaluation and testing of alternative products, purchase order review before placement ■ quality training ■ administration, audit and improvement.	■ laboratory acceptance testing ■ inspection tests, including goods inward ■ product quality audits ■ set-up for inspection and test ■ inspection and test material ■ product quality audit ■ review of test and inspection data ■ field (on-site) performance testing ■ internal testing and release ■ evaluation of field stock and spare parts ■ data processing inspection and test reports.

Costs of non-conformance

Internal failure	*External failure*
Costs arising within the manufacturing organisation before transfer of ownerships to the customer:	After transfer of ownership to the customer:
■ scrap ■ rework and repair ■ troubleshooting or defect/failure analysis ■ reinspect, retest ■ scrap and rework, fault of vendor, downtime ■ modification permits and concessions ■ downgrading – losses for quality reasons resulting from a lower selling price.	■ complaints ■ product or customer service, product liability ■ products rejected and returned, recall reject ■ returned materials for repair ■ warranty costs and costs associated with replacement.

9.11 Value management, engineering and analysis

The terms value management (VM), value engineering (VE) and value analysis (VA) are often regarded as synonymous. Each term may, however, be distinguished from the others.

9.11.1 Value management (VM)

VM is defined by BS EN 12973:2000 as:

> A style of management, particularly dedicated to mobilise people, develop skills and promote synergies and innovation with the aim of maximising the overall performance of an organisation.

As indicated by this definition, VM is a style of management aimed at instilling a culture of best value throughout an organisation. 'Best value' implies that a product or service will meet customers' needs and expectations at a competitive price. VM applies at both the corporate and operational levels of an organisation. At the corporate level it emphasises the importance of a value-orientated culture aimed at achieving value for customers and stakeholders. At the operational level it seeks to implement a value culture by the use of appropriate methods and tools.

The Society of American Value Engineers (SAVE), formed in 1959, became the prototype for similar institutions in other countries. In the UK, the Institute of Value Management was formed in 1966, while, in 1991, the European Committee for Standardisation (CEN) sponsored the Federation of National Associations to produce BS EN 12973:Value Management, published in 2000.

9.11.2 Value engineering (VE)

VE applies value analysis (VA) processes to cost reduction or value enhancement at the design stage and can be defined as:

> The application of value analysis techniques to new products, services, processes or systems commencing with the conceptual or design stage.

VE emphasises the importance of applying VA as early as possible in the design process and obtaining competitive advantage by means of designs that enhance customer satisfaction.

Research by Dataquest[32] has shown that the typical cost of a design change made during design of $1000 grows to $10,000 during testing, $100,000 during process planning, $1,000,000 during test production and $10,000,000 during final production.

The concept of VE is closely related to that of robust design (see 9.9.5 above). Clark[33] points out that many organisations combine VA and VE in one operation, which is referred to as concurrent design.

9.11.3 Value analysis

Value analysis (VA) was developed by the General Electric Company in the USA at the end of World War II. One of the pioneers of this approach to cost reduction was Lawrence D. Miles, whose book *Techniques of Value Analysis and Engineering* (McGraw-Hill, 1972) is still the classic on the subject.

The term 'value engineering' (VE) was adopted by the US Navy Bureau of Ships for a programme of cost reduction at the design stage, the aim of which was to achieve economies without affecting the needed performance, reliability, quality and maintainability. Miles has described value analysis as:

> A philosophy implemented by the use of a specific set of techniques, a body of knowledge, and a group of learned skills. It is an organised, creative approach which has for its purpose the efficient identification of unnecessary cost, i.e. cost which provides neither quality nor use, nor life, nor appearance, nor customer features.

VA results in the orderly utilisation of alternative materials, newer processes and the abilities of specialist suppliers. It focuses engineering, manufacturing and purchasing attention on one objective: equivalent performance at lower cost. Having this focus, it provides step-by-step procedures for accomplishing its objective efficiently and with assurance. An organised and creative approach, it uses a functional and economic design process that aims to increase the value of a VA subject.[34]

As will be shown later, the key words for an understanding of VA are 'function' and 'value'. The function of anything is that which it is designed to do, and should normally be capable of being expressed in two words – a verb and noun. Thus, the function of a pen is to 'make marks'. 'Value' is variously defined. The most important distinction is between use value – that is, that which enables an item to fulfil its stated function – and esteem value – factors that increase the desirability of an item. The function of a gold-plated pencil and a ballpoint pen, costing £70.00 and 50p respectively, is, in both cases, to 'make marks'. The difference of £69.50 between the price of the former over the latter represents esteem value.

9.11.4 Implementing VA

The necessary implementation of VA depends on choosing the right people and the right projects.

The right people

VA may be carried out by the following:

- a team of representatives from such departments as cost accounting, design, marketing, manufacturing, purchasing, quality control research and work study
- a specialist VA engineer, where the company's turnover warrants such an appointment, who will often have the responsibility of coordinating a VA team, so such a person should have:
  - experience of design and manufacturing related to the product(s)
  - understanding of a wide range of materials, their potentials and limitations
  - a clear concept of the meaning and importance of 'value'
  - creative imagination and a flair for innovation
  - knowledge of specialist manufacturers and the assistance that they can provide
  - the capacity to work with others and a knowledge of how to motivate, control and coordinate.

Just-in-time approaches emphasise the importance of consultation with suppliers and their co-option to VA teams.

The right project

In selecting possible projects, the VA team or engineer should consider the following:

- what project shows the greatest potential for savings – the greater the total cost, the larger the potential savings, so, for example, consider two hypothetical projects, A and B:

	A	B
Present cost each	10p	100p
Possible savings (10%)	1p	10p
Annual usage	100,000	1000
Projected annual savings	£1000	£100

Component A offers the greatest potential return for the application of VA

- what products have a high total cost in relation to the functions performed – that is, whether or not it is possible to substitute a cheaper alternative
- what suggestions for projects emanate from design, production staff and suppliers
- any there drawings or designs that have been unchanged in the last five years
- manufacturing equipment installed more than, say, five years ago that may now be obsolete
- any inspection and test requirements that have not been changed in the last five years
- single-source orders where the original order was placed more than, say, two years ago that may offer possibilities for savings.

Here are some typical areas warranting VA investigation.

- Product performance – what does it do?
- Product reliability – reducing or eliminating product failure or breakdown.
- Product maintenance – reducing costs of routine maintenance, such as cleaning, lubrication and so on and emergency repairs and replacement.
- Product adaptability – adding an extra function or expanding the original use.
- Product packaging – improving the saleability of or protection given to the product.
- Product safety – eliminating possible hazards, such as sharp edges, inflammability.
- Product styling – specifying lighter, stronger or more flexible materials or simplifying instructions.
- Product distribution – making it easier to distribute by, for example, reducing its weight or finding better transportation options.
- Product security – making the product less liable to theft or vandalism by using better locks, imprinting the customer's name on easily moveable equipment and so on.

9.11.5 Value analysis procedure

The job plan for a VA project involves the following six stages.

1 *Project selection* See the list above.
2 *Information stage*
   - Obtain all essential information relating to the item under consideration – cost of materials and components, machining and assembly times, methods and costs, quality requirements, inspection procedures and so on.
   - Define the functions of the product, especially in relation to the cost of providing them.
3 *Speculation or creative stage* Have a brainstorming session in which as many alternative ideas as possible are put forward for achieving the desired function, reducing costs or improving the product. Some questions that may promote suggestions at this stage include the following.
   - What *additional* or *alternative* uses can we suggest for the item?
   - How can the item be *adapted* – what other ideas does the item suggest?
   - Can the item be *modified*, especially with regard to changes in form, shape, material, colour, motion, sound, odour?

■ Can the item be *augmented* – made stronger, taller, longer, thicker or otherwise developed to provide an extra value and so on?

■ Can the item be *reduced* – made stronger, smaller, more condensed, lighter or unnecessary features omitted?

■ Can the item be *substituted* – would other materials, components, ingredients, processes, manufacturing methods, packaging and so on improve it?

■ Can we *rearrange* the item – change its layout or design, alter the sequence of operations, interchange components?

■ Can the item or aspects of the item be *reversed* – reversing its roles or functions or positions, turning it upside-down or front to back?

■ What aspects of the product can be *combined* – its functions, purposes, units, other parts and so on?

4 *Investigation stage* Select the best ideas produced at the speculation stage and evaluate their feasibility. When VA is organised on a team basis, each specialist will approach the project from his or her own standpoint and report back.

5 *Proposal stage* Recommendations will be presented to that level of management able to authorise the suggested changes. The proposals will state:

■ what changes or modifications are being suggested

■ statements relating to the cost of making the suggested changes, the projected savings, the period(s) over which the savings are likely to accrue.

6 *Implementation stage* When approved by the responsible executive, the agreed recommendations will be progressed through the normal production, purchasing or other procedures.

9.11.6 VA checklists

The following checklist, which every material, component or operation must pass, was prepared by the General Electric Company:

■ Does its use contribute value?

■ Is its cost proportionate to its usefulness?

■ Does it need all its features?

■ Is there anything better for the intended use?

■ Can a usable part be made by a lower-cost method?

■ Can a standard product be found that will be usable?

■ Is it made on the proper tooling, considering the quantities used?

■ Are the specified tolerances and finishes really necessary?

■ Do materials, reasonable labour, overheads and profit total its cost?

■ Can another dependable supplier provide it for less?

■ Is anyone buying it for less?

As stated earlier, whenever appropriate, suppliers should be invited to participate in a VA exercise. Miller[35] has prepared the checklist given in Figure 9.11. It can accompany requests for quotations or be used in supplier discussions relating to the design of a new product.

Figure 9.11 **Miller's checklist**

Question	Brief description of suggestion	Estimated savings of suggestion
1 What standard item do you have that can be satisfactorily substituted for this part? 2 What design changes do you suggest that will lower the cost of this item? 3 What part of this item can be more economically produced (considering tooling and so on) by casting, forging, extruding, machining or any other process? 4 What material can you suggest as a substitute? 5 What changes in tolerances would result in lower manufacturing costs? 6 What finish requirements can be eliminated or relaxed? 7 What test or qualification requirements appear unnecessary? 8 What suggestions do you have to save weight, simplify the part or reduce its cost? 9 What specifications, tests or quality requirements are too stringent?		

Will you attend a meeting to discuss your ideas if requested? Do you have a formal value analysis programme? If not, would you like help in setting one up?
Company:
Address:
Signature:
Title:
Date:

9.11.7 VA and functional analysis (FA)

As stated in 9.11.3, the function of anything is 'that which it is designed to do'. Value can be defined as:

$$\frac{\text{Performance capability}}{\text{Cost}} \quad \text{or} \quad \frac{\text{Function}}{\text{Cost}}$$

Functional analysis (FA) involves identifying the primary and secondary functions of an item and decomposing them into the sub-functions at an ever increasing level of detail. The application of FA particularly at the information and creative stages can indicate ways of reducing cost either by eliminating or modifying output functions. Conversely, a designer may seek to enhance value by adding new functions to an output. The latter can only be achieved when the target profit exceeds the cost of providing the additional functions. An extension of function analysis is cost function analysis, which identifies the cost of alternative ways of providing a given function.

9.11.8 Cost function analysis

This involves the following steps, which we shall illustrate by reference to a ballpoint pen, the existing components of which are shown in Figure 9.12.

Figure 9.12 **Using the components of a ballpoint pen as an example of cost function analysis**

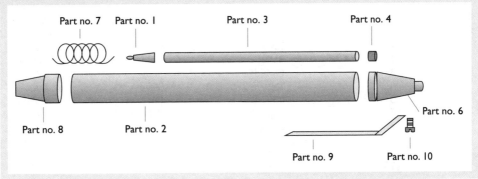

Step 1: Identify the primary and secondary functions of the item

Primary functions are those that the output must achieve. Thus, the primary function of a ballpoint pen is 'to make a mark'.

Secondary functions are support functions. These may be a necessary part of the function but do not themselves perform the primary function. Thus, to 'make a mark', secondary functions such as 'put colour' and 'hold pen' are required.

As stated earlier, the function should be capable of being expressed by two words – a verb and a noun – and, wherever possible, should have measureable parameters, such as 'prevent rust', 'reduce noise'.

Step 2: Arrange the functions in a tree model

Define the primary functions first and decompose them to lower-level functions. Thus, for the ballpoint pen, the resultant tree might be like that shown in Figure 9.13.

Step 3: Undertake a cost function analysis

A cost function analysis involves breaking down each function into components or general areas and allocating a target or estimated cost to each. A component or area may contribute more than one function. It is important to know how much each component

Figure 9.13 **Tree model of pen's functions**

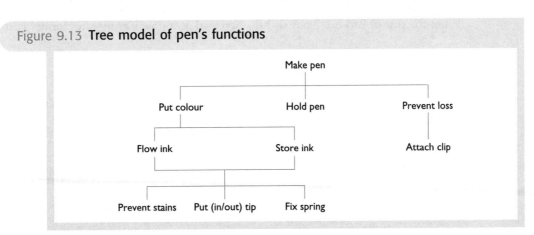

Table 9.6 **A cost function analysis of the parts of a ballpoint pen**

Part numbers	Names of parts	Functions		Cost (£)
		Transitive verb	Noun	
1	Tip	Flow	Ink	0.50
2	Barrel	Hold	Pen	0.70
3	Cartridge	Store	Ink	0.23
4	Top	Store	Ink	0.15
5	Ink	Put	Colour	0.10
6	Cap	Pull in/out	Tip	0.01
7	Spring	Pull in/out	Tip	0.09
8	Stopper	Fix	Spring	0.10
9	Clip	Prevent	Loss	0.10
10	Screw	Attach	Clip	0.02
				2.00

or area contributes to each function. Thus, the initial design for the ballpoint pen could include details of the parts and costs set out in a matrix, as shown in Table 9.6.

From such a matrix, it is possible to account for the total cost of each part by adding them together horizontally and the cost of each function by totalling them vertically. The total cost of each function is usually expressed as a percentage of the total cost of the activity. It is at this stage that the VA team will use its judgement to decide whether the cost of each function is high, reasonable or low – that is, whether or not it represents good value.

It should be noted that, of itself, cost function analysis does not provide savings or solutions. The purpose of such analysis is to:

■ provide the VA team with an in-depth understanding of the VA project by identifying the purpose of each element of cost
■ indicate what functions provide poor value or where, because of the high cost of a function relative to the total cost of the activity, there is a potential for reducing cost or increasing value.

Assume that, as a result of the cost function analysis, the ballpoint pen is redesigned, using the components shown in Figure 9.14. Also, assume that, by negotiating with suppliers and dealing with new suppliers, the price for Part no. 1 has been reduced, but the cost of Part no. 2 has slightly increased as it now incorporates former Part no. 6.

Figure 9.14 **The components of the ballpoint pen after redesigning**

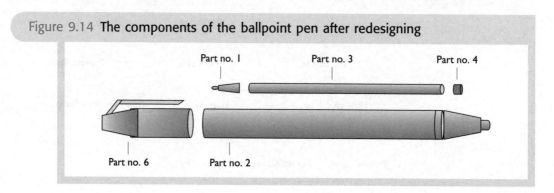

Table 9.7 Revised cost function analysis of the parts of the redesigned ballpoint pen

Part numbers	Names of parts	Functions		Cost (£)
		Transitive verb	Noun	
1	Tip	Flow	Ink	0.40
2	Barrel	Hold	Pen	0.80
3	Cartridge	Store	Ink	0.23
4	Top	Store	Ink	0.15
5	Ink	Put	Colour	0.10
6	Cap	Pull in/out	Tip	0.01
				1.69

The new cost function matrix is as shown in Table 9.7.

■ The above approach is particularly useful when the aim is to produce an item to a target cost. The aim in the above example might have been to produce a ballpoint pen at a target cost of below £1.75 (the component prices given in the example are for example only and bear no relation to reality).

■ In general, the more components required to make an item, the greater the complexity. The greater the complexity, the greater the cost. Product(s) should therefore be designed with as few components as possible.

■ Wherever possible, standard components should be used. Non-standard components increase costs and reduce flexibility. Standard components can be obtained from many suppliers, with short lead times at low cost and in smaller quantities.

9.11.9 Two simple examples of VA

Example 9.2

Example of VA

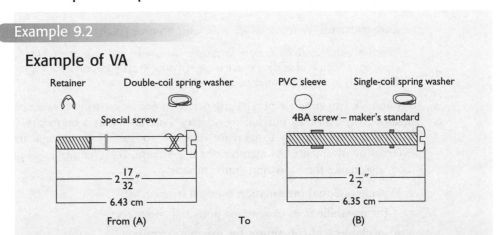

The function of the connecting screw shown in A is to secure parts and carry electrical current, the retainer holding the two items loosely together as a subassembly when the screw is released from a third point.

In B, a maker's standard screw is now in use, the retainer being replaced by a small PVC sleeve. A single-coil spring washer takes the place of the double-coil one. Total saving = 76 per cent.

Example 9.3

Another example of VA

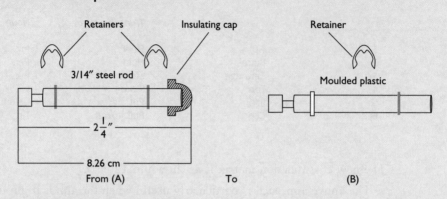

Retainers   Insulating cap   Retainer

3/14" steel rod   Moulded plastic

$2\frac{1}{4}''$

8.26 cm

From (A)   To   (B)

A push rod moving a contact operates against springs under digital pressure. It had been a machined steel rod with two retainers (for the springs) and an insulating cap because, on occasions, direct digital contact would be made (A).

It was decided to mould the rod in plastic, complete with a flange to replace one retainer. The insulating cap is no longer necessary because the rod itself is now an insulator. The cost of the new mould was recovered in less than four months and a total saving made of 60 per cent.

9.11.10 Value and purchasing

Two quotations from Miles,[36] himself a purchasing agent, indicate the close relationship between VE, VA, VM and purchasing.

> Close and extensive relationships must exist between purchasing and value analysis.

> Effective value analysis greatly improves the grade and degree of purchasing work and efficient execution of certain purchasing activities greatly improve the degree and amount of value analysis accomplishments.

VA and VE can enhance purchasing performance by creating a value culture that permeates every aspect of purchasing activity. Purchasing, as a boundary-spanning activity, has the opportunity to increase value as a result of its internal interactions and external involvements. As members of a VA team, representatives of purchasing can, inter alia, make the following contributions.

- Provide essential information on such matters as:
  - the capabilities of existing or potential suppliers
  - availability of substitutes for existing outputs
  - quality issues
  - prices and costs of suggested alternatives
  - delivery times
  - legal, economic, ethical and environmental issues
  - make-or-buy decisions.

■ Provide a purchasing perspective to contrast with the perspectives of design and production representatives on the value project team.

■ Establish buyer–supplier relationships. Purchasing can work closely with suppliers to reduce costs, improve quality and shorten lead times. It can also be a link between the value team and suppliers so that the latter can also be a source of innovation and creativity. Hartley[37] suggests that collaborative arrangements between purchasers and suppliers, such as partnerships, codevelopment, co-ownership and supplier associations can provide such benefits as:

  – access to the supplier's knowledge

  – greater understanding by the supplier of the customer's needs

  – greater trust

  – suppliers learning about VA

  – increased supplier motivation.

By active and aggressive participation in VA, purchasing professionals will not only enhance their individual reputations but also the status of purchasing throughout their organisation and, often, with suppliers.

Case study

Europa Airlines is an international airline with headquarters at London's Heathrow Airport, flying into 110 airports around the world. It operates short and long-haul flights, operating a range of 777, 747, 737 and Airbus aircraft. Some of the aircraft are over 5 years old and 45 have had major internal refits of aircraft seating and in-flight catering equipment, including ovens for cooking a variety of hot foods for passengers, cabin crew and flight crew. This case study will concentrate on a quality problem with the ovens.

The contract for the ovens was awarded, after a tendering and an e-auction process. The successful bidder was Ozland Flight Equipment (OFE), situated in Perth, Australia. At the prequalification stage, OFE demonstrated that it had quality accreditation and supplied Quantas, Air New Zealand and South African Airways with complete in-flight catering equipment. References were taken up and very positive feedback was received.

It is 9 months since the last of the 45 aircraft was refitted. The first aircraft was refitted 14 months ago. There has been a series of incidents in the past six weeks. This has affected 14 aircraft and, in all instances, the ovens have failed in flight. This equipment is not safety critical and would not lead to the mandatory grounding of an aircraft. There has been a flood of complaints received by the Catering Department of Europa Airlines and the Chief Executive Officer. Specifically, air crew have threatened a strike, first-class and business-class passengers are irate and other passengers have registered complaints. The airline has issued vouchers to a total value of £85,000 to passengers as a goodwill gesture.

You are the buyer now responsible for resolving the quality issue with OFE. Your Quality Manager has produced a report in which it is alleged that the oven wiring system is faulty, causing cut-outs. He has attributed the problem to the actual wiring, which is stamped 'OKRC KOREA'. The ovens were supplied and installed by OFE. Europa Airlines has no spare ovens and has removed 10 of the OFE ovens and rewired them, at a cost of

£3000 each, including wiring and labour. You have contacted OFE by e-mail and its response is not encouraging:

> Thank you for drawing this matter to our attention. We confirm that at the time of installation and acceptance the wiring was in working condition. If Europa Airlines rewires our ovens it will invalidate the product warranty. If you return the alleged faulty ovens to our Perth factory, we will conduct, at your cost, a full quality inspection. After that time, we will forward our report. At this stage we do not wish to predict an outcome. We can make available, on a conference call, our Manufacturing Manager, obviously by arrangement.

Task

It is vital that this matter is resolved at the earliest opportunity and you should prepare an ideal action plan to fully resolve the quality problem. Your plan should include consideration of the fact that your aircraft are continually in various parts of the world. What elements would you take into account? What would be your ideal solution?

Discussion questions

9.1 Take two similar products, such as two different makes of car intended for the same consumer group or two washing machines, and compare them to Garvin's eight dimensions of quality. On the basis of your comparison, recommend which of the two you consider gives the best value for money. What other factors apart from the eight stated might you have to consider when making your recommendation?

9.2 Consider the statement 'Without strong supplier–customer links both internally and externally TQM is doomed to failure'.
  (a) Can you think of four arguments to support this statement?
  (b) As Managing Director, what steps would you take to forge such links:
     (i) internally
     (ii) externally?

9.3 An important aspect of *kaizen* is the creation of a quality 'culture'. One definition of 'culture' is:

> The system of shared values, beliefs and habits within an organisation that interacts with the formal structure to produce behavioural norms.

  (a) How would you go about creating a 'quality culture'?
  (b) How might a quality culture sometimes clash with production and marketing cultures?

9.4 With what 'quality guru' do you associate the following:
  (a) quality loss function
  (b) 'End the practice of awarding business on the basis of price tag. Instead minimise the total cost'
  (c) 'The first principle is to recognise that quality is everybody's job'
  (d) *Poka-Yoke*
  (e) 'It is always cheaper to do the job right first time'
  (f) personal development of the individual will lead to increased competence in the three vital areas of productivity, relations and quality

(g) 'Quality is fitness for use'

(h) robust design

(i) 'Quality means conformity to requirements not elegance'.

9.5   Every requirement increases the price.
If something is not specified it is unlikely to be provided.

Why is it often difficult to reconcile these two principles, which should be observed by specification writers?

9.6 Specifications can be divided into two types: those relating to things and those relating to actions. Under which heading would you place each of the following?

(a) Services

(b) Raw materials

(c) Components

(d) Functions

(e) Assemblies

(f) Processes

(g) Procedures

(h) Final products

(i) Systems

(j) Complicated structures

9.7 BS 7373, 2:20001 suggests ten headings for a specification. How many can you recall?

9.8 Why should the purpose of a purchased item always be made known to the supplier?

9.9 Standards have roughly five areas of application. What are they?

9.10 What are the differences between standards prefixed:

(a) BS

(b) BS EN

(c) BS EN ISO?

9.11 Explain why the cost of detecting problems increases dramatically with the distance from the source of the problem.

9.12 Noriaki Kano identified three classes of consumer needs:

■ *dissatisfiers* those that the product or service is *expected* to provide

■ *satisfiers* the needs that customers say they want

■ *exciters/delighters* new or innovative features that customers would not expect but which they like.

(a) In relation to a car, give two examples of each of these consumer needs.

(b) Why is it important that designers are aware of these three categories of need?

9.13 Assume a product with tolerances of 0.500 ± 0.10. Further, assume that if the deviation from the target exceeds 0.10 on either side, the product will fail during the warranty period. From records, the cost of repairing the product under warranty is £100. Calculate the loss according to the Taguchi 'loss function' formula.

9.14 The number of defects found in 32 samples of an assembly taken on a daily basis over a month is given below. Plot the data on a control chart and work out the average value.

6, 1, 5, 5, 3, 4, 2, 2, 6, 4, 1, 2, 1, 3, 4, 1

4, 5, 6, 1, 12, 15, 3, 6, 3, 4, 3, 3, 5, 2, 4, 7

9.15 An alternative classification of 'effects' to those indicated in Table 9.2 in the text is:
- Category 1: catastrophic
- Category 2: critical
- Category 3: marginal
- Category 4: minor

Attempt definitions of each category and, imagining that they relate to a car, provide examples of each category.

9.16 The quality of the picture on a TV varies according to the room temperature. How would Taguchi describe the TV set?

9.17 What are the possible additional costs arising from the following?
(a) A rough casting is overspecified in terms of wall thickness.
(b) A component is specified with unnecessarily close tolerances.

9.18 For what reasons might a company seek BS or ISO registration?

9.19 Value analysis and 'creative thinking' are closely related. State, in each case, how you would counter the barriers to creative thinking quoted below.
(a) 'We always do it this way.'
(b) 'It won't work.'
(c) 'Why change it?'
(d) 'We tried that ten years ago.'
(e) 'We know more about this than anyone.'
(f) 'There is no better material.'
(g) 'We can't get it anywhere else.'
(h) 'The customers like it this way.'
(i) 'We'll try it next year.'
(j) 'We don't want to upset the staff/workers/suppliers/customers/...'
(k) 'It may work in theory but not in practice.'
(l) 'Lower costs mean lower quality.'

9.20 Take a simple everyday product, such as a pen, watch, lamp or similar, and carry out a value analysis exercise.

Past examination questions

The following questions are taken from the CIPS Professional Stage Examination: *Purchasing and Supply Chain Management II: Tactics and Operations.*

1 'Quality cannot be inspected into a product; it has to be built in from the outset.'
Explain, with reference to either manufactured goods or services, what you understand by this statement and explain how this view affects the role of purchasing.

(May 2001)

2 Analyse the contribution the purchasing manager can make to quality both at the design stage of a product and during the production stage. (November 2001)

3 Explain the importance of consistency and control in the production of goods and services and show how statistical process control (SPC) can assist in their achievement.

(May 2002)

4 'Inspection is a non-value-adding activity that can be avoided by giving quality greater attention at the design stage, and, subsequently, ensuring the careful selection and management of suppliers.'

Discuss this statement with particular reference to the role of the purchasing functions.
(November 2002)

5 Explain the importance of control, consistency and reduction of variability in the achievement of quality and outline some of the techniques that can be used in this context.
(May 2003)

References

1 Crosby, P. B., *Quality is Free*, Mentor Books, 1980, p. 15

2 Juran, J. M., *Quality Control Handbook*, 3rd edn, McGraw-Hill, 1974, section 2, p. 27

3 Garvin, D. A., 'What does product quality really mean?', *Sloan Management Review*, fall, 1984, pp. 25–38

4 Garvin, D. A., 'Competing in eight dimensions of quality', *Harvard Business Review*, Nov./Dec., No. 6, 1987, p. 101

5 Logothetis, N., *Managing Total Quality*, Prentice Hall, 1991, pp. 216–17

6 As 3 above

7 DTI, *Total Quality Management and Effective Leadership*, 1991, p. 8

8 Evans, J. R., *Applied Production and Operations Management*, 4th edn, 1993, p. 837

9 See Table 9.1

10 See Table 9.1

11 As 3 above, p. 10

12 Cannon, S., 'Supplying the service to the internal customer', *Purchasing and Supply Management*, April, 1995, pp. 32–5

13 Zaire, M., *Total Quality Management for Engineers*, Woodhead Publishing, 1991, p. 193

14 As 13 above, p. 216

15 Lysons, K., *How to Write Specifications*, CIPS, 2001

16 BSI, *British Standards Specification* (BS) 7373

17 Purdy, D. C., *A Guide to Writing Successful Engineering Specifications*, McGraw-Hill, 1991

18 The Office of Government Commerce, 'Specification writing', *CUP Guidance Note 30*, CUP, 1991

19 As 17 above

20 England, W. B., *Modern Procurement*, 5th edn, Richard D. Irwin, 1970, p. 306

21 Haslam, J. M., 'Writing engineering specifications', E. and F. N. Spon, 1988, p. 31

22 Woodroffe, G., 'So farewell then market overt', *Purchasing and Supply Management*, Feb., 1995, pp. 16–17

23 Ashton, T. C., 'National and International Standards', in Lock, D. (ed.) *Gower Handbook of Quality Management*, 2nd edn, 1994, pp. 144–5

24 Rhodes, J., and Fallon, E., *Information on Standards: A Guide to Sources*, British Library, London

25 BS EN ISO 8402 1995, section 3.5, pp. 25–6

26 BS EN ISO 8402 1995, section 3.4, p. 25

27 Schonberger, R. J., *Building a Chain of Customers*, Free Press, 1992

[28] Taguchi, G., *Introduction to Quality Engineering*, Asian Productivity Organisation, 1986, p. 1

[29] Ford Motor Co. Ltd, *Failure Mode and Effects Analysis Handbook*, 1992, p. 22

[30] As 29 above, pp. 24–5

[31] Dale, B. G., and Shaw, P., 'Failure mode and effects analysis: a study of the use in the motor industry', *University of Manchester, Institute of Science and Technology*, Occasional Paper 8904, 1990

[32] Quoted in Woodruffe, D., 'A smarter way to manufacture: how concurrent engineering can reinvigorate American industry', *British Week*, 30 April, 1990, p. 110

[33] Clark, L. J., 'Value analusis and value engineering at work', NAPM, *InfaEdge*, Vol. 3, No. 4, Dec., 1997

[34] BSI 'PD6663 Guidelines to BS EN 12973 Value Management', BSI, 2000, p. 26

[35] Miller, J., 'The evolution of value analysis', NAPM, *Insights*, 1 Dec., 1993, pp. 13–14. Original source of this checklist was George Fridholm Associates

[36] Miles, D., *Techniques of Value and Value Engineering*, 3rd edn, McGraw-Hill, 1989, p. 243

[37] Hartley, J. L., 'Collaborative value analysis: experiences from the automotive industry', *Journal of Supply Management*, Fall, 2000, pp. 27–36

Chapter 10

Matching supply with demand

Learning outcomes

With reference to purchasing and supply management, this chapter aims to provide an understanding of:

- inventory and inventory management
- the tools of inventory management
- dependent and independent demand
- 'push', 'pull' and hybrid demand systems
- inventory control.

Key ideas

- Inventory classifications.
- ABC analysis.
- Barcoding and RFID technology.
- Acquisition, holding and stockout costs.
- Safety stocks.
- Approaches to forecasting.
- Economic order quantities (EOQs) and periodic systems.
- Just-in-time (JIT) systems and their objectives.
- JIT II.
- MRP, MRP II, ERP, DRP and VMI systems.

10.1 Inventory, logistics and supply chain management

The Institute of Logistics and Transport[1] defines inventory as:

A term used to describe:

- all the goods and materials held by an organisation for sale or use
- a list of items held in stock.

An alternative definition is:[2]

> Materials in a supply chain or in a segment of a supply chain, expressed in quantities, locations and/or values (synonym stock).

As shown in Figure 3.2, inventory and its management are related both to materials management (MM) and physical distribution management (PDM). MM and PDM together constitute logistics management, or the process of managing both the movement and storage of goods and materials from their source to the point of ultimate consumption. As logistics is an aspect of the wider subject of supply chain management (SCM), it follows that inventory is a key business consideration in the attempt to achieve supply chain optimisation. As indicated in section 3.5, control of inventory is also an important element in demand management, which constitutes one of the eight supply chain processes identified by the International Centre for Competitive Excellence. In this chapter, inventory and demand management are considered primarily from the standpoints of materials management and production.

10.2 Reasons for keeping inventory

Notwithstanding such developments as just-in-time (JIT), discussed later in this chapter, computer-based production methods and the aims of lean production, a number of reasons may be deduced for all organisations keeping some inventory. These include wanting to:

■ reduce the risk of supplier failure or uncertainty – safety and buffer stocks are held to provide some protection against such contingencies as strikes, transport breakdowns due to floods or snow, crop failures, wars and similar factors

■ protect against lead time uncertainties, such as where supplier's replenishment and lead times are not known with certainty – in such cases an investment in safety stocks is necessary if customer service is to be maintained at acceptable levels

■ meet unexpected demands or demands for customisation of products as with agile production

■ smooth seasonal or cyclical demand

■ take advantage of lots or purchase quantities in excess of what is required for immediate consumption to take advantage of price and quantity discounts

■ hedge against anticipated shortage and price increases, especially in times of high inflation or as a deliberate policy of speculation

■ ensure rapid replenishment of items in constant demand, such as maintenance supplies and office stationery.

10.3 Inventory classifications

The term 'supplies' has been defined as:[3]

> All the materials, goods and services used in the enterprise regardless of whether they are purchased outside, transferred from another branch of the company or manufactured in-house.

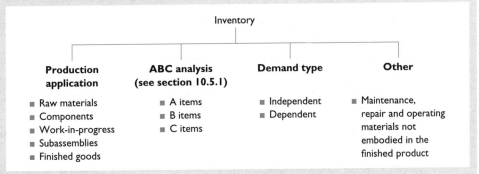

Figure 10.1 **Inventory classifications**

The classification of supplies for inventory purposes will vary according to the particular undertaking. In a manufacturing enterprise, for example, inventory might be classified as:

- raw materials – steel, timber, cloth and so on in an unprocessed state awaiting conversion into a product

- components and subassemblies – ball bearings, gearboxes, and so on that are to be incorporated into an end product

- consumables – all supplies in an undertaking classified as indirect and that do not form part of a saleable product and that may be subclassified into production, such as detergents, maintenance, such as lubricating oil, office, such as stationery, welfare, such as first-aid supplies and so on – all of which are often referred to as maintenance, repair and operating (MRO) items

- finished goods – products manufactured for resale that are ready for dispatch.

Following supply chain usage, inventory may also be classified into:

- primary inventory – raw materials, components and subassemblies, work-in-progress (WIP) and finished goods

- support inventories – MRO consumables of various categories.

A third classification is shown in Figure 10.1.

10.4 Scope and aims of inventory management

10.4.1 The scope of inventory management

Inventory management covers a wide variety of activities. These activities will vary from organisation to organisation. The scope of inventory management will also be influenced according to whether it is primarily concerned with MM or PDM or centralised or decentralised. There is clearly a significant difference in the complexity of managing inventory based at a single location and that where inventory is located at possibly hundreds of distribution centres. Globalisation is another factor that increases the complexity of inventory management. Irrespective of such considerations, however, inventory management is likely to be comprised of such activities as:

- demand management – ensuring that required operational and maintenance supplies are available in the right quantities and at the right time
- forecasting future demand requirements
- managing items with difficult supply and demand patterns related to seasonal demand, changes in end use applications or meeting demands for the customisation of products
- reviewing safety stock levels and controlling minimum and maximum amounts of inventory in terms of both quantity and value
- implementing lean inventory policies, such as JIT contracts to minimise investment in inventory
- liaising with purchasing to ensure that supplies are replenished in accordance with corporate and procurement policies
- developing cost-effective systems and procedures relating to the ordering, procurement and budgeting of supplies
- controlling the receipt, inspection (where necessary), recording, location and issue of supplies to users
- ensuring the safety and security of supplies and the avoidance of loss as a result of deterioration, theft, waste and obsolescence
- coordination of inventory to ensure that supplies can be rapidly located
- variety reduction and standardisation of inventory
- preparation and interpretation of reports on stock levels, stock usage and surplus stock
- liaison with auditors regarding all aspects of inventory
- appropriate disposal of scrap, surplus and obsolete items.

10.4.2 The aims of inventory management

The four main aims of inventory management are to:

- provide both internal and external customers with the required service levels in terms of quantity and order rate fill
- ascertain present and future requirements for all types of inventory to avoid overstocking while avoiding 'bottlenecks' in production
- keep costs to a minimum by variety reduction, economical lot sizes and analysis of costs incurred in obtaining and carrying inventories
- provide upstream and downstream inventory visibility in the supply chain.

10.5   Some tools of inventory management

ABC analysis, barcoding, radio frequency identification (RFID) and inventory software are four important tools of inventory management.

10.5.1 ABC analysis

A household will buy many different items in the course of a year. The weekly shopping will include a number of basic food items, such as bread, milk, vegetables and so on. These basic food items may account for the bulk of the annual expenditure in shops. Because these items are so important in the household budget, it is worth taking care to choose a shop that gives good value. Information about the prices charged elsewhere can be obtained from advertisements and visits to other supermarkets. In ABC analysis these items are known as Class A items. They merit close day-to-day control because of their budgetary importance.

Other items, such as replacement rubber washers for water taps, may be needed occasionally. A packet of washers costs between 30 and 50 pence. Spending hours comparing the prices of these at different suppliers does not make economic sense. The possible saving is at most a few pence and a year or more may elapse before another packet is needed. Items like these, that account for only a small proportion of spending, are known as Class C items.

Class B is the set of items that is intermediate between Class A and Class B. They should be regularly reviewed but are not as closely controlled as Class A items.

The Italian statistician Vilfredo Pareto (1848–1923) discovered a common statistical effect. About 20 per cent of the population own 80 per cent of the nation's wealth. About 20 per cent of employees cause 80 per cent of problems. About 20 per cent of items account for 80 per cent of a firm's expenditure. The terms 'Pareto analysis' and 'ABC analysis' are used interchangeably.

Table 10.1 summarises the main points of ABC analysis. In the table, the term 'usage' means the value in money terms of the stock items consumed.

Table 10.1 ABC analysis

	Percentage of items	Percentage value of annual usage	
Class A items	About 20%	About 80%	Close day-to-day control
Class B items	About 30%	About 15%	Regular review
Class C items	About 50%	About 5%	Infrequent review

The following example illustrates how items may be divided into classes A, B or C.

Example 10.1

ABC analysis

A purchasing department surveyed the ten most commonly used components last year.

Item number	101	102	103	104	105	106	107	108	109	110
Unit cost (pence)	5	11	15	8	7	16	20	4	9	12
Annual demand	48,000	2000	300	800	4800	1200	18,000	300	5000	500

Step 1

Calculate the annual usage in £s and the usage of each item as a percentage of the total cost.

Item number	Unit cost (pence)	Annual demand	Usage (£) $\dfrac{Demand \times Cost}{100}$	Usage as % of total $= \dfrac{Usage \times 100}{Total}$
101	5	48,000	2400	32.5%
102	11	2,000	220	3.0%
103	15	300	45	0.6%
104	8	800	64	0.9%
105	7	4,800	336	4.6%
106	16	1,200	192	2.6%
107	20	18,000	3600	48.8%
108	4	300	12	0.2%
109	9	5,000	450	6.1%
110	12	500	60	0.8%
Total usage			7379	

Step 2

Sort the items by usage as a percentage of the total. Calculate the cumulative percentage and classify the items (see Table 10.2).

Table 10.2 **Calculations for step 2**

Item number	Cumulative % of items	Unit cost (pence)	Annual demand	Usage (£)	% of total	Cumulative % of total	Classification
107	10	20	18,000	36,700	48.8	48.8	A
101	20	5	48,000	2400	32.5	81.3	A
109	30	9	5000	450	6.1	87.4	B
105	40	7	4800	336	4.6	92.0	B
102	50	11	2000	220	3.0	94.9	B
106	60	16	1200	192	2.6	97.5	B
104	70	8	800	64	0.9	98.4	C
110	80	12	500	60	0.8	99.2	C
103	90	15	300	45	0.6	99.8	C
108	100	4	300	12	0.2	100.0	C

> There are 10 items, so each item accounts for 10/100 = 10% of usage

Step 3

Report your findings (see Table 10.3).

Table 10.3 **Results of calculations for step 3**

Items	Item number	Percentage of items	Percentage usage	Action
A	107, 101	20	81.6	Close control
B	109, 105, 102, 106	40	16.2	Regular review
C	104, 110, 103, 108	40	2.5	Infrequent review

Step 4

Illustrate your report with a diagram if required. The diagram is a percentage ogive and is called a Pareto diagram. This is done by plotting the cumulative percentage usage against the cumulative percentage of items. The data needed has been extracted to create Table 10.4.

Table 10.4 **Data for Pareto diagram for step 4**

Item number	107	101	109	105	102	106	104	110	103	108
Cumulative % items	10%	20%	30%	40%	50%	60%	70%	80%	90%	100%
Cumulative % usage	48.8%	81.3%	87.4%	92.0%	94.9%	97.5%	98.4%	99.2%	99.8%	100%
Classification	A	A	B	B	B	B	C	C	C	C

In practice, there may be hundreds of items in inventory and use. Computer software can easily determine the percentage of annual usage for each item and sort the items into A, B or C categories.

10.5.2 Barcoding

Invented in the 1950s, barcodes accelerate the flow of products and information throughout business. The most familiar example of the use of barcodes is electronic point of sale (EPOS), which is when retail sales are recorded by scanning product barcodes at checkout tills. An EPOS system verifies, checks and charges transactions, provides instant sales reports, monitors and changes prices and sends intra- and inter-store messages and data.

Some production applications for barcoding include:

- counting raw materials and finished goods inventories
- automatic sorting of cartons and bins on conveyor belts and palletisers
- lot tracking
- production reporting
- automatic warehouse applications, including receiving, put away, picking and shipping
- identification of production bottlenecks
- package tracking
- access control
- tool cribs and spare parts issue.

Barcoding provides the following benefits:

- *faster data entry* barcode scanners can record data five to seven times as fast as a skilled typist
- *greater accuracy* keyboard data entry creates an average of one error in 300 keystrokes, but barcode entry has an error rate of about 1 in 3 million

- *reduced labour costs* as a result of time saved and increased productivity
- *elimination of costly over- or understocking* and the increased efficiency of JIT inventory systems
- *better decision making* barcode systems can easily capture information that would be difficult to collect in other ways, which helps managers to make fully informed decisions
- *faster access to information*
- *the ability to automate warehousing*
- *greater responsiveness to customers and suppliers.*

10.5.3 Radio frequency identification (RFID)

An RFID tag contains a silicon chip that carries an identification number and an antenna able to transmit the number to a reading device. This means improved inventory management and replenishment practices, which, in turn, results in a reduction of interrupted production or lost sales due to items being out of stock.

The reduction in the cost of chips to a point where they can be used to track high-volume, low-cost stores and individual items rather than an aggregate SKU (stock keeping unit) is revolutionary in its implications for inventory control and intelligence.

The following advantages and limitations of RFID technology are listed by GS1 UK.[4]

Advantages

- *line of sight* Tags can be read without being visible to the scanner. They can be read as long as they pass through the field emitted by the reader. This reduces manual handling and, therefore, cost.
- *Range* Tags can be read over a very long range – many hundreds of metres in the case of specialised tags. RFID devices used in mass logistics applications need a range of at least 1 metre and up to 4 or 5 metres.
- *Bulk read* Many tags can be read in a short space of time – a typical read rate is hundreds of tags per second.
- *Selectivity* Data can be inserted into the tags so that they are only read if the value requested from the reader is the same as the value embedded within the tag. This allows the reader to read only pallets or only outer cases.
- *Durability* Barcodes can be ripped, soiled and performance is impaired if they become wet. These are not issues that affect RFID tags.
- *Read/write* Data incorporated within the tags can be updated to accommodate simple changes in status – such as 'paid for' or 'not paid for' retail electronic article surveillance tags – or more complicated information, such as a car's warranty and service history.

Limitations

- *Cost* RFID tags will always be more expensive than barcodes. The cost is offset by the extra business benefits that RFID technology can provide. It is envisaged that the cost of tags will drop dramatically as production volumes are increased.
- *Moisture* Depending on the frequency used, radio waves may be absorbed by moisture in the product or the environment.

■ *Metal* Radio waves are distorted by metal. This means that tags might be unable to be read if there is metal within packaging or the environment (warehouse automation).

■ *Electrical interference* Electronic noise, such as fluorescent lights or electric motors, may produce interference with radio frequency communications.

■ *Accuracy* It can be difficult to identify and read specific tags separately from all the others that are within the range of the reader. For example, when attempting to read a tag identifying a pallet, the reader may also read the tags on all the cases on the pallet as well.

■ *Overcompensation* Additional data stored within the tag will provide functionality. However, this will increase both the cost of the tag and the time required to read it.

■ *Security* The ability to write information into tags is one of the main benefits of RFID technology. The mechanism required, however, needs to be secure to ensure that rogue parties are unable to write false information into the tag.

10.5.4 Software

Numerous software programs are available, providing complete inventory and stock management systems. Such software can provide such facilities as maintaining supplier and customer databases, create picking lists and receipts, provide instantaneous stock balances and automatic reordering, barcode reading, support grouping of inventory items, remove barriers between suppliers and customers, enhance profitability and implement such approaches as JIT, MRO, ERP, DRP and VMI, described later in this chapter.

10.6 The economics of inventory

The economics of inventory management and stock control are determined by an analysis of the costs incurred in obtaining and carrying inventories under the following headings.

10.6.1 Acquisition costs

Many of the costs incurred in placing an order are incurred irrespective of the order size, so, for example, the cost of an order will be the same irrespective of whether 1 or 1000 tonnes are ordered. Ordering costs include:

■ preliminary costs – preparing the requisition, vendor selection, negotiation

■ placement costs – order preparation, stationery, postage

■ post-placement costs – progressing, receipt of goods, materials, handling, inspection, certification and payment of invoices.

In practice, it is difficult to obtain more than an approximate idea of ordering costs as these vary according to:

■ the complexity of the order and the seniority of staff involved

■ whether order preparation is manual or computerised

■ whether or not repeat orders cost less than initial orders.

Sometimes the total cost of a purchasing department or function over a given period is divided by the number of orders placed in that time. This gives a completely false figure as the average cost per order reduces as the number of orders placed increases, which may be indicative of inefficiency rather than the converse.

10.6.2 Holding costs

There are two types of holding costs:

■ *cost proportional to the value of the inventory* such as:
  - financial costs, such as interest on capital tied up in inventory, which may be bank rate or, more realistically, the target return on capital required by the enterprise
  - cost of insurance
  - losses in value due to deterioration, obsolescence and pilfering.
■ *cost proportional to the physical characteristics of inventory* such as:
  - storage costs – storage space, stores' rates, light, heat and power
  - labour costs, relating to handling and inspection
  - clerical costs, relating to stores' records and documentation.

10.6.3 Cost of stockouts

The costs of stockouts – the costs of being out of inventory – include:

■ loss of production output
■ costs of idle time and of fixed overheads spread over a reduced level of output
■ costs of any action taken to deal with the stockout, such as buying from another stockist at an enhanced price, switching production, obtaining substitute materials
■ loss of customer goodwill due to the inability to supply or late delivery.

Often the costs of stockouts are hidden in overhead costs. Where the costs of individual stockouts are computed, these should be expressed in annual figures to ensure compatibility with acquisition and holding costs. Costs of stockouts are difficult to estimate or incorporate into inventory models.

10.7 Inventory performance measures

A number of key performance indicators (KPIs) have been devised to measure the extent to which an undertaking has the right quantity of inventory in the right place at the right time. Some of the most useful are the following.

■ *Lead times* the length of time taken to obtain or supply a requirement from the time a need is ascertained to the time the need is satisfied.
■ *Service levels* the actual service level attained in a given period, which can be ascertained from the formula:

$$\frac{\text{Number of times the item is provided on demand}}{\text{Number of times the item has been demanded}}$$

Service levels are closely related to safety stocks, as shown later.

- *Rate of stock turn* this indicates the number of times that a stock item has been sold and replaced in a given period and is calculated by the formula:

$$\frac{\text{Sales or issues}}{\text{Average inventory (at selling price)}}$$

What is considered a good stock turn varies by product and industry. Turnover of supermarket breakfast foods is 20–25 times that of pet foods. For car showrooms, a stock turn of six means that, on average, the stock of a particular car changes every two months.

- *Stockouts in a given period* this can be expressed as a percentage of the total stock population during a given period.

- *Stock cover* this is the opposite of stock turn and indicates the number of days the current stock of a stock keeping unit (SKU) will last if sales or usage continues at the anticipated rate. As an historic figure, it can be calculated by dividing the rate of stock turn into the yearly number of working days or 365 to give the average days' cover. For a simple SKU it can be calculated as:

$$\text{Days' stock coverage} = \frac{\text{Current quantity in stock}}{\text{Anticipated future daily rate of usage or sales}}$$

The ratio can be used to evaluate the effect of longer lead times or the danger of imminent stockouts.

10.8 Safety stocks and service levels

Safety stock is needed to cover shortages due to the agreed lead time being exceeded or the actual demand being greater than that anticipated.

Figure 10.2 shows that the service levels and safety stock are related. Thus, by increasing the investment on inventory, service levels can be increased.

Figure 10.2 **Service level to inventory trade-off curve**

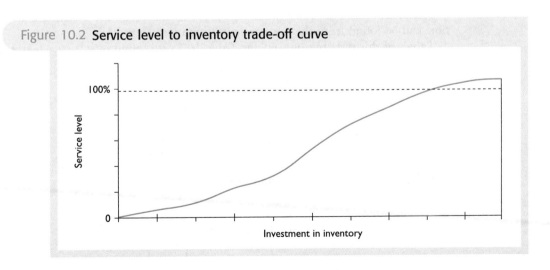

Figure 10.3 **The normal distribution curve**

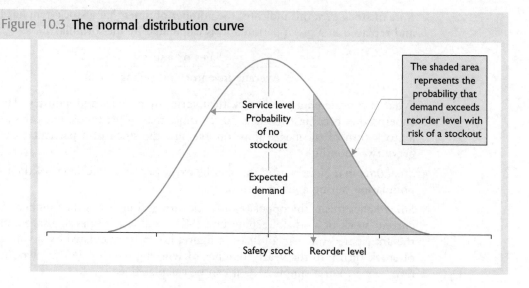

Service level
Probability
of no
stockout

Expected
demand

The shaded area
represents the
probability that
demand exceeds
reorder level with
risk of a stockout

Safety stock   Reorder level

For single items, an extra investment in inventory (higher levels of safety stock) will always increase customer service levels. Conversely, higher service levels imply larger quantities of safety stocks and an increased investment in inventory.

It is not possible to achieve 100 per cent service levels for the total inventory. High levels of safety stocks for all items would be uneconomical and the costs would be prohibitive.

JIT implies a low level of or zero inventory. This is achieved by removing uncertainty regarding supply. Safety stock is a cost-adding factor and so should, as far as possible, be eliminated.

If the uncertainty regarding supply cannot be eliminated, safety stocks are required.

In practice, the items that have high stockout costs can be identified by ABC analysis and, for such items, an acceptable risk of stockout should be determined.

Statistical theory provides methods for ensuring that the chances of a stockout do not exceed an acceptable risk level.

The probability that demand exceeds a particular distribution during a given lead time can be found from the normal distribution (see Figure 10.3).

Tables of this distribution, such as Table 10.5, are found in statistics textbooks.

- For each SKU, find the data on which the order was placed and the date of delivery. From stores' records, calculate the demand between these dates.

- Find the mean or arithmetic average demand during the lead time:

$$\text{Mean (x)} = \frac{\text{Sum of the demands}}{\text{Number of lead times}} = \frac{\Sigma x}{n}$$

- Calculate the standard deviation of demand from the formula:

$$\text{Standard deviation } (\sigma) = \sqrt{\frac{n}{n-1}\left(\frac{x^2}{n} - \left(\frac{x}{n}\right)^2\right)}$$

Table 10.5 **Probabilities table**

Reorder levels in standard deviations above the mean	Service level %	Probability of a stockout %
1.00	84.1	15.9
1.05	85.3	14.7
1.10	86.4	13.6
1.15	87.5	12.5
1.20	88.5	11.5
1.25	89.4	10.6
1.30	90.3	9.7
1.35	91.1	8.9
1.40	91.9	8.1
1.45	92.6	7.4
1.50	93.3	6.7
1.55	93.9	6.1
1.60	94.5	5.5
1.65	95.1	4.9
1.70	95.5	4.5
1.75	96.0	4.0
1.80	96.4	3.6
1.85	96.8	3.2
1.90	97.5	2.5
1.95	97.4	2.6
2.00	97.7	6.1
2.05	98.0	5.5
2.10	98.2	4.9
2.15	98.4	4.5
2.20	98.6	4.0
2.25	98.8	3.6
2.30	98.9	3.2
2.35	99.1	2.5
2.40	99.2	2.6
2.45	99.3	2.3
2.50	99.4	2.0
2.55	99.5	1.8
2.60	99.5	1.6
2.65	99.6	1.4
2.70	99.7	1.2
2.75	99.7	1.1
2.80	99.7	0.9
2.85	99.8	0.8
2.90	99.8	0.7
3.00	99.9	0.6

or by using the statistical functions on your calculator or spreadsheet. In simple terms, calculating the standard deviation involves the following steps:

1 Determine the mean (average (x)) of the set of numbers:

$$1, 2, 3, 4, 5 = \frac{15}{5} = x = 3$$

2 Determine the difference between each number and the mean:

$$(1) = -2, (2) = -1, (3) = 0, (4) = +1, (5) = +2$$

3 Square each difference:

$$-4 \quad -1 \quad 0 \quad +1 \quad +4 = 10$$

4 Calculate the square root of the average:

$$\text{Standard deviation } (\sigma) = 1.58$$

The reorder level required and stockout probability can then be found from Table 10.5.

Example 10.2

Calculating the required reorder level

The average (mean) demand is 10. A 99 per cent service level is required – that is, the probability of stockout is 1 per cent or less. Assume an average reorder level of 140.

Table 10.5 shows that, for a service level of 99.1 per cent, the reorder level should be 2.35 standard deviations above the mean.

Thus, the reorder level is $140 + 2.35 \times 10 = 163.5$ or 164

10.9 The right quantity

In manufacturing or assembly-type organisations, the most important factors that determine the right quantity are as follows.

- The demand for the final product into which the bought-out materials and components are incorporated.
- The inventory policy of the undertaking.
- Whether job, batch, assembly or process production methods are applicable.
- Whether demand for the item is independent or dependent (see section 10.10 below).
- The service level – that is, the incidence of availability required. The service level required for an item may be set at 100 per cent for items where a stockout would result in great expense due to production delays or, as with some hospital supplies, where lack of supplies may endanger life. For less crucial supplies, the service level might be fixed at a lower level, such as 95 per cent. The actual service level attained in a given period can be computed by the formula:

$$\frac{\text{Number of times the item is provided on demand in period}}{\text{Number of times an item has been demanded in period}}$$

- Market conditions, such as financial, political and other considerations that determine whether or not requirements shall be purchased on a 'hand-to-mouth' or 'forward' basis.
- Factors determining economic order quantities (see 10.13.2 below). In individual undertakings, the quantity of an item to be purchased over a period may be ordered or notified to purchasing in several ways, as shown in Table 10.6.

Table 10.6 **Purchasing and quantities**

Type of purchase	Indicators of quantities
Materials or components required for a specific order or application, such as steel sections not normally stocked	■ Material specifications or bill of material for the job or contract
Standard items kept in stock for regular production, whether job, batch or continuous flow	■ Materials budgets derived from production budgets based on sales/output target for a specified period ■ One-off material specifications or bills of materials showing quantities of each item needed to make one unit of finished product. These are then multiplied by the number of products to be manufactured ■ Material requisitions raised by storekeeping or stock control ■ Computerised reports provided at specified intervals – daily, weekly – relating to part usage, stocks on hand, on order and committed. With some programs, reordering can be carried out automatically.
Consumable materials used in production, plant, maintenance or office administration, such as oil, paint, stationery and packing materials	■ Requisitions from stores or stock control or computerised inventory reports as above. These may be ordered directly by users against previously negotiated contracts or purchasing consortia arrangements
Spares – these may be kept to maintain production machinery or bought-out components for resale to customers who have bought the product in which the component is incorporated	■ Requisitions from sales department ■ Computerised inventory reports as above

10.10 The nature of demand

When forecasting the future requirements for supplies, we have to distinguish between independent demand and dependent demand.

The main points of difference are set out in Table 10.7.

Table 10.7 **The main differences between independent and dependent demand**

Independent demand	Dependent demand
Independent demand items are finished goods or other end items	Dependent demand items are typically subassemblies or components used during the production of a finished or end product
Demand for independent items cannot be precisely forecast	Demand is derived from the number of units to be produced – for example, demand for 1000 cars will give rise to a derived demand for 5000 car wheels

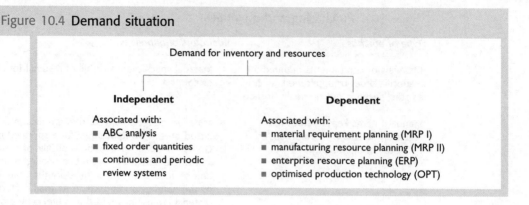

Figure 10.4 **Demand situation**

As shown in Figure 10.4, the distinction between dependent and independent demand is fundamental to inventory management.

10.11 Forecasting demand

10.11.1 What is forecasting?

Forecasting, which may be defined as the prediction of future outcomes, is the basis of all planning and decision making. We listen to the weather forecasts, for example, before planning a picnic. Similarly, the decision to enlarge a factory will be based on a forecast of increased demand for the product manufactured.

Forecasts, however, are rarely spot on, simply because they are always based on assumptions that may be wrong or affected by unforeseen events, such as war, economic and social factors and even the weather. All forecasts, therefore, are subject to uncertainty. This uncertainty will be enhanced as the time horizon of the forecast increases.

10.11.2 Forecasting issues

Forecasting involves asking six basic questions.

■ *What is the purpose of the forecast?* The answer to this question determines the accuracy required and expenditure on the resources necessary to obtain the required information.

■ *What is the time horizon?* All forecasts must have a time limit. Forecasts may be classified as being for the long, medium or short term.

  – Long-term forecasts – with time horizons exceeding two years – usually apply to strategic planning and carry the greatest uncertainty.

  – Medium-term forecasts – with time horizons of between three months and two years – apply to both strategic and tactical planning and carry less uncertainty than long-term forecasts.

  – Short-term forecasts – with time horizons of less than three months – apply to tactical planning and are likely to achieve a high level of accuracy.

The above times are, however, arbitrary and depend on circumstances. Thus, long, medium and short term may equally be one year, between three months and one year and three months respectively.

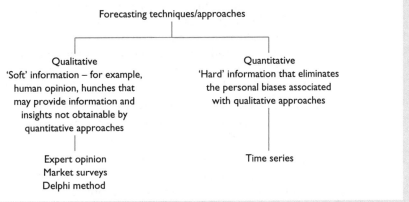

Figure 10.5 **Forecasting techniques**

- *What forecasting technique(s) is/are most appropriate?* See Figure 10.5.

- *On what data must the forecast be based and how shall it be analysed?* This depends on the purpose of the forecast, the accuracy required and the resources available for forecasting.

- *In what form shall the completed forecast be presented?* This will normally be in some form of report stating the purpose of the forecast, what assumptions have been made, the forecasting techniques used and the forecasts or conclusions reached.

- *How accurate is the forecast?* All forecasts should be monitored to ascertain the degree of accuracy achieved. Where actual events are substantially different from those predicted, the forecast, assumptions, techniques and validity of the data must be examined and, where necessary, the original forecast revised.

10.11.3 Forecasting techniques

As shown in Figure 10.5, forecasting techniques or approaches fall into two broad categories.

10.11.4 Qualitative approaches

- *Expert systems* Gathering judgements or opinions from people with special knowledge or experience. Such people may be executives, outside consultants or even sales or production personnel who have first-hand experience of what customers require or operating problems encountered. The value of their opinions, however, depends on the knowledge and experience of those giving them. Experts are sometimes wrong.

- *Test marketing* This is frequently used as a forecasting technique in connection with new products to ascertain the percentage of customers likely to adopt the product.

It may also be used to work out why sales are declining or what aspects of competing products appeal to buyers. It can also be used to see how a product will sell under actual conditions and the success of advertising and sales promotion campaigns. It has been estimated that only about a third of products tested in this way are finally put into production. An extension of test marketing is the market survey, which uses published data and survey techniques to find out what the total market is for all products serving a similar purpose, such as family cars, and the percentage of the market likely to be achieved by an individual manufacturer.

■ *Delphi method* Named after the ancient Greek religious site where the gods were believed to communicate answers to humans' questions about the future, this technique involves the following four steps.

1 Estimates or forecasts are solicited from knowledgeable people within a company or industry about the matter under consideration. The names of the people approached are not known to each other.

2 Statistical averages of the forecasts are computed. If there is a high level of agreement about the forecasts, the procedure ends there.

3 If, as often happens, there is considerable divergence between the forecasts, the group averages are presented to the individuals who made the original forecasts, asking them why their forecasts differ from the average or group consensus and asking for new estimates.

4 Steps 2 and 3 are repeated until agreement is reached.

The Delphi method is particularly useful where there is a lack of historical information on which to base a more objective forecast and predict changes in technology.

10.11.5 Quantitative approaches

A *time series* is a set of observations measured at successive times over successive periods. Time series forecasting methods make the assumption that past patterns in data can be used to forecast future data points. Time series demand consists of the following five components:

■ *average* the mean of the observations over time

■ *trend* a gradual increase or decrease in the average over time – a trend pattern exists when there is a long-term pattern of growth (upwards trend) or decline (downwards trend) in sales

■ *seasonal influence* a predictable short-term cycling behaviour due to the time of day, week, month or season, so, for example, sales of swimming costumes are greater in the summer than the winter

■ *cyclical movement* unpredictable long-term cyclical behaviour due to business or product/service lifecycles. Sales of dishwashers, refrigerators and similar household appliances reflect a fairly constant cyclical pattern

■ *random error* the remaining variation that cannot be explained by the other four components, such as when sales fluctuate in an erratic manner and reflect inconsistency.

The most frequently used methods of calculating time series are moving averages and exponentially weighted averages.

10.11.6 Moving averages

A *moving average* is an artificially constructed time series in which each annual (or monthly, daily and so on) figure is replaced by the average or mean of itself and values corresponding to a number of preceding and succeeding periods.

Example 10.3

Moving averages

The usage of a stock item for six successive periods was 90, 84, 100, 108, 116 and 127. If a five-period moving average is required, the first term will be:

$$\frac{90 + 84 + 100 + 108 + 116}{5} = 99.6$$

The average for the second term is:

$$\frac{84 + 100 + 108 + 116 + 127}{5} = 107$$

At each step, one term of the original series is dropped and another introduced. The averages, as calculated for each period, will then be plotted on a graph. There is no precise rule about the number of periods to use when calculating a moving average. The most suitable, obtained by trial and error, is that which best smooths out fluctuations. A useful guide is to assess the number of periods between consecutive peaks and troughs and use this.

10.11.7 Exponentially weighted average method (EWAM)

The moving average method has been largely discarded for inventory applications as it has a number of disadvantages:

- it requires a large number of separate calculations
- a true forecast cannot be made until the required number of time periods have elapsed
- all data are equally weighted, but, in practice, the older the demand data, the less relevant it becomes in forecasting future requirements
- the sensitivity of a moving average is inversely proportional to the number of data values included in the average.

These difficulties are overcome by using a series of weights with decreasing values that converge at infinity to produce a total sum of one. Such a series, known as an *exponential series*, takes the form:

$$a + a(1 - a) + a(1 - a)^2 + a(1 - a)^3 \ldots = 1$$

where a is a constant between 0 and 1.

In practice, the values of 0.1 and 0.2 are most frequently used. Where a small value such as 0.1 is chosen as the constant, the response, based on the average of a considerable number of past periods, will be slow and gradual. A high value – a = 0.5 – will result in 'nervous' estimates responding quickly to actual changes. With exponential smoothing, all that is necessary is to adjust the previous forecast by a fraction of the difference between the old forecast and the actual demand for the previous period – that is, the new average forecast is:

a (actual demand) + (1 – a) (previous average forecast)

Example 10.4

Exponentially weighted average

The actual demand for a stock item during the month of January was 300 against a forecast of 280. Assuming a weighting of 0.2, what will be the average demand forecast for February?

Solution

$$0.2(300) + (1 – 0.2)(280) = 60 + 224$$

Forecast for February = 284. By subtracting the average computed for the previous month from that calculated for the current month, we obtain the trend of demand.

10.11.8 The bullwhip effect

All forecasting depends on the reliability of the information on which the forecast is based. The so-called 'bullwhip effect' is the uncertainty caused by information flowing upstream and downstream in the supply chain. In particular, forecasts of demand become less reliable as they move up the supply chain from users or retailers to wholesalers, to manufacturers, to suppliers. Conversely, the forecast demand variability, though present, lessens as the point of forecast moves downstream.

The most common drivers of demand distortion are:

- unforecasted sales promotions, which have a ripple effect throughout the supply chain
- sales incentive plans when extended to, say, three months often result in sales distortion
- lack of customer confidence in the ability of suppliers to deliver orders on time, leading to overordering
- cancellation of orders, often resulting from previous overordering
- freight incentives, such as transportation discounts for volume orders, that may cause customers to accumulate orders and then order in bulk.

The results of the bullwhip effect are:

- excessive inventory quantities
- poor customer service
- cash flow problems
- stockouts
- high material costs, overtime expenses and transport costs.

Example 10.5

Impact of supply disruption due to the bullwhip effect

Customer demand forecast is 40 units

←			Information flow			→
Suppliers	Products	Manufacturers	Products	Distributors	Products	Retailers
Inventory 320 units	160 units	Inventory 160 units	80 units	Inventory 80 units	40 units	Inventory 0

← Cash flow →

The distributor anticipates a shortage and decides to keep a buffer stock of twice the demand forecast.

To accommodate anticipated demand fluctuations, manufacturers also increase their inventories by twice that required.

The suppliers, at the head of the supply chain, receive the harshest impact of the bullwhip effect. The result is a general lack of coordination throughout the supply chain.

In a worst-case scenario, working capital reduces, costs increase, customer service is unsatisfactory, lead times lengthen, production needs to be rescheduled and sales are lost.

The fundamental approach to resolving the bullwhip problem is to ensure transparency and information sharing throughout the supply chain. Many of the problems can be avoided by relying less on forecasting and more on direct demand data. Supply chain systems that provide open communication and reliable demand data avoid situations in which small demand fluctuations become high variability swings at the production stage.

10.12 'Push' and 'pull' inventories

'Push' and 'pull' inventories derive from push and pull strategies.

A *push strategy* is when products are manufactured in anticipation of demand and production is based on long-term forecasts and, therefore, uncertain. Push-based supply chains are associated with high inventory levels and high manufacturing and transportation costs, due to the need to respond quickly to demand changes.

A *pull strategy* is when products are manufactured to specific orders rather than forecasts. Thus, demand is certain and inventory is low or non-existent. Because information about customer demand is quickly transmitted to the various supply chain participants, the bullwhip effect is avoided.

Push–pull strategies are those in which some (usually the first stages) of the supply chain are operated on a push basis and the remaining stages on a pull basis. The interface between the push- and pull-based stages is known as the push–pull boundary and occurs at a place somewhere along the supply chain timeline. Postponement, which was mentioned earlier in section 4.6.3, aims to cater for customisation

Figure 10.6 **The push–pull concept**

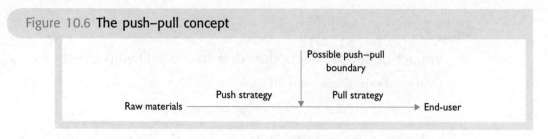

Figure 10.7 **Inventory control systems associated with different push and pull strategies**

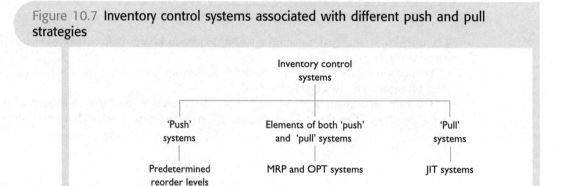

requirements by keeping products in a neutral or uncommitted state for as long as possible and this is a good example of a push–pull strategy. The concept of push–pull is shown in Figure 10.6.

The inventory control systems associated with each of the three above strategies are shown in Figure 10.7.

10.13 Independent demand

The nature of independent demand was discussed in 10.10 above. Independent demand is related to 'push' systems as (see Figures 10.4 and 10.7) both are concerned with fixed order quantities and periodic review systems.

10.13.1 Fixed order quantities

With fixed order quantities, inventory is replenished with a predetermined quantity of stock every time the inventory falls to a specific order level. The reorder level is the quantity to be used during the lead replenishment time plus a reserve. This level can be calculated by using the formula:

$$\text{Maximum usage} \times \text{Maximum lead time}$$

Thus, if the lead time is 25 to 30 days and the maximum usage in the lead time is 200 units, then the reorder level will be:

$$200 \times 30 = 6000 \text{ units.}$$

Reorder levels may be indicated by:

- simple manual methods, such as the two-bin system, which is that the stock of a particular item is kept in two bins and when the first bin is empty, a supply is reordered
- computerised systems, which trigger replacements when inventory has fallen to the specified reorder point – such systems usually use barcoding to record withdrawals from stock.

The fixed quantity is, however, usually based on an economic order quantity (EOQ).

10.13.2 Economic order quantity (EOQ)

The economic order quantity (EOQ) is the optimal ordering quantity for an item of stock that minimises cost.

To calculate the EOQ, a mathematical model of reality must be constructed. All mathematical models make assumptions that simplify reality. The model is only valid when the assumptions are true or nearly true, so, when an assumption is modified or deleted, a new model must be constructed.

The basic (or simple) EOQ model makes the following assumptions:

- demand is uniform – that is, certain, constant and continuous over time
- the lead time is constant and certain
- there is no limit on order size, due either to stores capacity or other constraints
- the cost of placing an order is independent of the size of the order – the delivery charge is also independent of the quantity ordered
- the cost of holding a unit of stock does not depend on the quantity in stock
- all prices are constant and certain – there are no bulk purchase discounts
- exactly the same quantity is ordered each time that a purchase is made.

The two basic types of inventory costs are:

- acquisition (see 10.6.1)
- holding (see 10.6.2).

There are several ways in which to calculate EOQs, but the basic formula is:

$$EOQ = \sqrt{\frac{2DS}{CI}}$$

where:

EOQ = economic order quantity
C = cost of the item
I = annual carrying cost interest rate
D = annual anticipated demand
S = order cost per order.

Example 10.6

Worked example of the basic EOQ formula

Assume the following figures:

- annual demand =1500 units
- unit cost per item = £10
- cost per order = £50
- carrying cost interest rate = 20 per cent.

Then:

$$EOQ = \sqrt{\frac{2 \times 1500 \times £50}{10 \times 0.20}} = \sqrt{\frac{150,000}{2}} = \sqrt{75,000} = 274$$

In practice, the EOQ would be increased to 300 items ordered 5 times yearly.

It should be recognised, however, that the EOQ may be misleading for the following reasons:

- annual demand is a forecast, so it is unlikely to be an exact figure
- order costs are assumed to be constant, but these may change due to use or the introduction of e-purchasing
- the interest rate is assumed to be constant, but, in practice, interest rates frequently change
- cost per item is likely to change in the course of a year, so we have to decide whether to use average cost, replacement cost, actual cost or anticipated future cost in the equation.

Many of the criticisms of EOQs derive from inaccurate data inputs, such as exaggerated carrying and order costs. Many ERP packages also have built-in programs that calculate EOQs automatically. Often, these built-in programs need modification to deal with changes in usages and products.

Sometimes EOQs are regarded as being in conflict with JIT approaches, but EOQs can be used to determine what items fit into the JIT model and what level of JIT is economically advantageous to the particular organisation.

While EOQs are not applicable to every inventory situation, they should be considered for repetitive purchasing situations and MRO items.

10.13.3 Periodic review system

As the name implies, in this system an item's inventory position is reviewed periodically rather than at a fixed order point. The periods or intervals at which stock levels are reviewed will depend on the importance of the stock item and the costs of holding that item. A variable quantity will be ordered at each review to bring the stock level back to maximum – hence, the system is sometimes called the 'topping-up' system.

Maximum stock can be determined by adding one review period to the lead time, multiplying the sum by the average rate of usage and adding any safety stock. This can be expressed as:

$$M = W (T + L) + S$$

where:

M = predetermined stock level
W = average rate of stock usage
T = review period
L = lead time
S = safety stock.

Safety stock may be calculated in a similar manner to that indicated for the fixed order point system.

Example 10.7

Periodic review system

Assume that:

- average rate of usage is 120 items per day
- review period is 4 weeks – say, 20 days
- lead time is 25 to 30 days
- safety stock is 900 items

$$M = 120 (20 + 30) + 900 = 6900 \text{ items}$$

If, at the first review period, the stock was 4000 items, an order would be placed for 2900 items – that is, 6900 maximum stock minus actual stock at the review date.

10.13.4 Advantages and disadvantages of fixed order point and periodic review systems

Fixed order point

Advantages:

- on average, levels of stock are lower than with the periodic review system
- EOQs are applicable
- enhanced responsiveness to demand fluctuations
- replenishment orders are automatically generated at the appropriate time by comparing actual stock levels with reorder levels
- appropriate for widely differing inventory categories.

Disadvantages:

- the reordering system may become overloaded if many items of inventory reach their reorder levels simultaneously
- random reordering pattern, due to items coming up for replenishment at different times.

Periodic review

Advantages:

- greater chance of elimination of obsolete items due to periodic review of stock
- the purchasing load may be spread more evenly, with possible economies in placing of orders
- large quantity discounts may be negotiated when a range of stock items is ordered from the same supplier at the same time
- production economies, due to more efficient production planning and lower set-up costs, may result from orders always being in the same sequence.

Disadvantages:

- on average, larger stocks are required than with fixed order point systems as reorder quantities must provide for the period between reviews as well as between lead times
- reorder quantities are not based on EOQs
- if the usage rate changes shortly after a review period, a stockout may occur before the next review date
- difficulties in determining appropriate review period, unless demands are reasonably consistent.

10.13.5 Choice of systems

- A fixed order point system is more appropriate if a stock item is used regularly and does not conform to the conditions for periodic review systems.
- A periodic review system is most likely to be appropriate if orders are placed with and delivered from suppliers at regular intervals, such as daily, monthly, or a number of different items are ordered from and delivered by the same supplier at the same time.

10.14 Dependent demand

Dependent demand is associated with pull systems and push–pull systems, discussed in section 10.12 above, and relates to just-in-time (JIT), materials and requirements planning (MRP), distribution requirements planning (DRP), enterprise resource planning (ERP) and vendor-managed inventory (VMI).

10.15 Just-in-time (JIT)

10.15.1 What is JIT?

The following comprehensive definition of JIT is provided by the American Production and Inventory Control Society:[5]

A philosophy of manufacturing based on planned elimination of all waste and continuous improvement of productivity. It encompasses the successful execution of all manufacturing activities required to produce a final product from design engineering to delivery and including all stages of conversion from raw material onward. The primary elements include having only the required inventory when needed; to improve quality to zero defects; to reduce lead time by reducing set-up times, queue lengths and lot sizes; to incrementally revise the operations themselves; and to accomplish these things at minimum cost.

In short, JIT production is:

Making what the customer needs, when it is needed and in the quantity needed using the minimum resources of people, material and machinery.

From the above definitions, it can be seen that JIT is more than delivering an item where and when required and at the right time. JIT is both a production scheduling and inventory control technique and an aspect of total quality management (TQM). As a production control technique, it is concerned with adding value and eliminating waste by ensuring that any resources needed for a production operation – whether raw material, finished product or anything in between – are produced and available precisely when needed. This emphasis on waste elimination means that JIT is an essential element in lean production, discussed in section 4.5.2. As a philosophy that aims at zero defects or never allowing defective units from the preceding process to flow into and disrupt a subsequent process, it is an aspect of TQM.

A useful distinction may be made between its two forms:

- *BIG-JIT* or lean production focusing on all sources of waste, as outlined in the first of the above definitions
- *Little-JIT* focusing more narrowly on scheduling goods, inventories and providing resources where needed.

It is with 'little-JIT' that the present section is primarily concerned.

10.15.2 The background of JIT

JIT is generally agreed to have been developed by Talichi Ohno, a vice-president of the Japanese Toyota motor company in the 1960s. It should be noted, however, that Henry Ford practised mass production with a JIT approach in 1921. By 1924, the production cycle of the Model T – from processing the core material to the final product – was only four days.

10.15.3 The objectives of JIT

These have been concisely summarised as:

- *zero defects* all products will more than meet the quality expectations of the customer
- *zero set-up time* no set-up time results in shorter production time, shorter production cycles and smaller inventories
- *zero inventories* inventories, including work-in-progress, finished goods and sub-assemblies, will be reduced to zero – this is the opposite of the traditional manufacturing philosophy of maintaining buffer stocks as a precaution against unreliable suppliers or fluctuating demand
- *zero handling* the elimination, so far as possible, of all non-value-adding activities
- *zero lead time* in some markets, this is impossible, but the aim is to increase flexibility by using small batches of components or assemblies

■ *lot size of one* this makes it possible to adapt quickly when demand is changing so if, for example, the lot size is 200 and demand is changing, either the supplier or customer ends up with a quantity of inventory that will either never or only very slowly reduce.

The requirements for successful JIT:

■ uniform master production schedules
■ 'pull' production systems
■ good customer–supplier relationships
■ short distance between customer and supplier
■ reliable delivery
■ consistent quality with zero defects
■ standardisation of components and methods
■ material flow system.

10.15.4 JIT and *kanban* systems

The *kanban* system is an essential aspect of JIT. In Japanese, the word *kanban* means 'ticket' or 'signal' and in JIT refers to an information system in which instructions relating to the type and quantity of items to be withdrawn from the preceding manufacturing process are conveyed by a card that is attached to a storage and transport container. The card identifies the part number and contained capacity. The two principal types of *kanban* are:

■ *production kanban, or P kanban* signals the need to produce more parts
■ *conveyance kanban, or C kanban* signals the need to deliver more parts to the next work centre.

The operation of a two-card *kanban* system within a work cell is shown in Figure 10.8. The rules for operating a two-card *kanban* system are therefore:

■ each container must have a *kanban* card
■ parts are only 'pulled' – that is, the user centre must go for them
■ no parts can be obtained without a conveyance *kanban*
■ all containers hold standard quantities and only standard quantities can be used
■ no extra production is permitted – production can only start with a production *kanban*.

It follows that the amount of work-in-progress inventory is equal to the number of *kanban* cards issued multiplied by the capacity of the container used. The *initial* number of *kanban* cards required is calculated by the formula:

$$\text{Number of K cards} = \frac{D\,(T_w + T_p)(1 + a)}{C}$$

Where:

D = average daily production rate, as indicated by the master production schedule
T_w = waiting time of *kanban* cards in decimal fractions of a day
T_p = the processing time per part in fractions of a day

Figure 10.8 A two-card *kanban* system – the flow within a cell

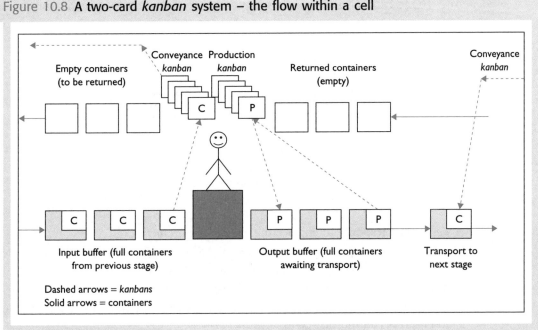

C = the capacity of a standard container
a = a policy variable determined by the efficiency of the work centre using the part

Thus, if:

$$D = 100 \text{ parts/day}, T_w = 0.25, T_p = 0.15, C = 10 \text{ and } a = 1$$

then the number of *kanban* cards will be:

$$\frac{100\,(0.25 + 0.15)(1 + 1)}{10} = 8$$

The dual card system described above is used by Toyota for car production. A more common approach is a one-card system, which signals requirements from the preceding work centre, as shown in Figure 10.9.

In Figure 10.9, a signal is sent back from the consuming work centre to the supplying work centre (or supplier). This is a signal:

■ to send some more (a transfer batch), via a buffer stock
■ to produce some more (a process batch), at the supplying work centre.

10.15.5 Benefits of JIT

The potential benefits of JIT to an organisation, and its purchasing function in particular, have been summarised by Schonberger and Ansari[6] as follows:

■ *part costs* low scrap costs, low inventory carrying costs
■ *quality* fast detection and correction of unsatisfactory quality and, ultimately, higher quality of purchased parts

Figure 10.9 **One-card system signalling requirements from previous work centre**

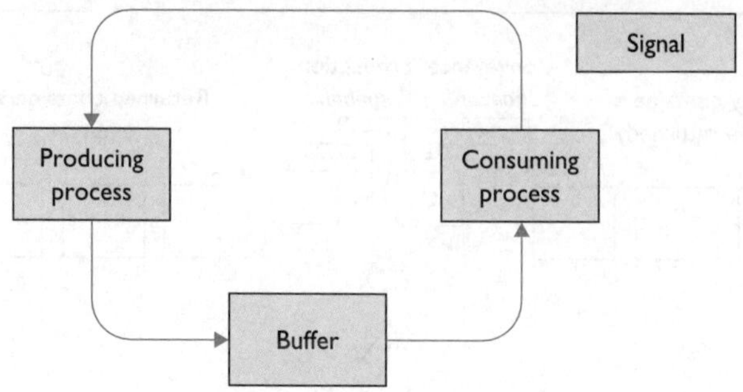

- *design* fast response to engineering change requirements
- *administrative efficiency* fewer suppliers, minimal expediting and order release work, simplified communications and receiving activities
- *productivity* reduced rework, reduced inspection, reduced parts-related delays
- *capital requirements* reduced inventories of purchased parts, raw materials, work-in-progress and finished goods.

10.15.6 Possible disadvantages of JIT

Some organisations have experienced problems with JIT for the following reasons:

- faulty forecasting of demand and inability of suppliers to move quickly to changes in demand
- JIT requires the provision of the necessary systems and methods of communication between purchasers and suppliers, ranging from vehicle telephones to EDI, so problems will arise if there is inadequate communication both internally – from production to purchasing – and externally – from purchasing to suppliers – and vice versa
- organisations with, ideally, no safety stocks are highly vulnerable to supply failures
- purely stockless buying is a fallacy – lack of low-cost C class items can halt a production line as easily as a failure in the delivery of high-priced A class items
- the advantages of buying in bulk at lower prices may outweigh the savings negotiated for JIT contracts as suppliers may increase their prices to cover costs of delivery, paperwork and storage required for JIT
- JIT is not generally suitable for bought-out items that have short lifecycles and are subject to rapid design changes
- JIT is more suitable for flow than batch production and may require a change from batch to flow methods, with consequent changes in the systems required to support the new methods
- even for manufacturers that mass-produce items, a substantial percentage of components are made by number, if not value, in batches, as well as a small number of high-value components, on dedicated flow lines

- apart from suppliers, JIT requires the total involvement of people from all disciplines and the breaking down of traditional barriers between functions within an organisation, which may involve a substantial investment in organisational development training
- Rhys et al.[7] have drawn attention to Japanese transport factors arising from some suppliers relocating at greater distances from purchasers (although these are normally still nearer to users than in Europe), road congestion and lighter vehicles – that is, for every one vehicle required in Europe, two or three are required in Japan, so JIT in Japan is now 'neither lean nor green'.

Further, Hayes and Pisano[8] suggest that the problems of implementing JIT derive from the fact that:

> most companies focus on the *mechanics* of JIT and TQM rather than on their *substance*, the skills and capabilities that enable a factory to excel and make it possible for improvement programmes to achieve their desired results. The consequence of this outlook is that managers have tended to view such programmes as solutions to specific problems rather than as stepping stones in an intended direction.

Hayes and Pisano also warn that, if an organisation lacks the skills, such as low set-up times and defect rates, that make JIT work, the adoption of the approach is likely to be costly. Adopting the system, will, however, provide strong incentives to develop such skills and induce an ethic of continuous improvement. Over time, a true JIT system may emerge.

10.15.7 JIT and purchasing

Apart from the general commitment to JIT mentioned above, two things essential to the successful implementation of JIT are that:

- all parts must arrive where they are needed, when they are needed and in the exact quantity needed
- all parts arriving must be usable.

Where these requirements are not achieved, JIT may easily become 'just-too-late'.
In achieving these requirements, purchasing has the responsibilities summarised below.

- *Liaison with the design function* The emphasis should be on *performance* rather than *design* specifications. Looser specifications enable suppliers to be more cost-effective by being more innovative with regard to the quality and function aspects of supplies. In JIT purchasing, value analysis is an integral part of the system and should include suppliers.
- *Liaison with suppliers* to ensure that they understand thoroughly the importance of consistently maintaining lead times and a high level of quality.
- *Investigation of the potential of suppliers* within reasonable proximity of the purchaser to increase certainty of delivery and reduction of lead time.
- *Establishing strong, long-term relationships with suppliers* in a mutual effort to reduce costs and share savings. This will be achieved by the purchaser's efforts to meet the supplier's expectations regarding:
  - continuity of custom
  - a fair price and profit margin

- agreed adjustments to price when necessary
- accurate forecasts of demand
- firm and reasonably stable specifications
- minimising order changes
- smoothly timed order releases
- involvement in design specifications
- prompt payment.

■ *Establishment of an effective supplier certification programme* which ensures that quality specifications are met before components leave the supplier so that receiving inspections are eliminated.

■ *Evaluation of supplier performance* and the solving of difficulties as an exercise in cooperation.

10.15.8 JIT II

This is a registered trademark of the Bose Corporation and is a customer–supplier partnerships concept practised by a number of companies and their suppliers. In a JIT II relationship, a supplier's representative – referred to as an 'in-plant representative' – functions as a member of the customer's purchasing department while being paid by the supplier. The representative issues purchaser orders to its own company on behalf of the customer. The representative is also involved in such activities as design, production planning and value analysis.

It is claimed that this arrangement provides benefits to both the customer and the supplier.

From the customer's perspective, benefits include that:

■ because the supplier's representatives are full-time employees of their customer's, they have ready access to information that can be used to reduce lead times and inventories and lead time reductions due to JIT II partnerships are generally greater than those achieved with conventional JIT

■ communications are improved because the representatives have a real-time awareness of the supplier's needs

■ transportation costs are lower as a result of organisations partnering transportation companies to deliver incoming items

■ the supplier is involved in concurrent design and value analysis so that it works with the customer from the inception of the design

■ material costs are reduced by large orders with consequent discounts and lower transportation costs

■ administrative costs are lower as there is a reduction in paperwork and the customer's purchasing staff are released for other duties.

From the supplier's perspective, benefits include that:

■ once a JIT II partnership has been agreed, an 'evergreen' contract is awarded, which has no end date and no requoting or tendering is required, and the resultant security enables the supplier to direct financial resources to managing the customer's account rather than seeking or renegotiating business.

JIT II is clearly not without risks and not always appropriate. There are obviously various factors to be considered:

- the volume of business must be sufficient to assign a representative exclusively to one customer and, unless this is achieved, the JIT II approach may not be effective, so it is only an option for a customer able to place a very substantial volume of business with one supplier

- a supplier may be reluctant to share costs or processes with a customer and, conversely, a customer may be reluctant to divulge information about new designs or processes to a supplier

- a customer may be reluctant to award a long-term contract because of the fear that the supplier's performance might deteriorate.

Pragman[9] states that the JIT II concept has expanded from merely purchasing materials to logistics, engineering and services. It does, however, demand a strategic alliance between partners based on trust.

10.16 Materials and requirements planning (MRP)

MRP, developed in the 1960s, is a technique that assists in the detailed planning of production and has the following characteristics:

- it is geared specifically to assembly operations
- it is a dependent demand technique
- it is a computer-based information system.

The aim is to make available either purchased or company manufacturing assemblies just before they are required by the next stage of production or for delivery. MRP enables orders to be tracked throughout the entire manufacturing process and assists purchasing and control departments to move the right supplies at the right time to manufacturing or distribution points.

10.16.1 MRP and JIT

MRP has many similarities to JIT. Some comparisons are shown in Table 10.8.

JIT and MRP should not, however, be thought of as opposing systems. In many organisations, the two systems are successfully combined. For example, it is important that a strong MRP II (see section 10.17) planning environment will facilitate JIT execution. Ideally the two systems are not alternative but complementary.

10.16.2 MRP terminology

MRP has its own terminology, as follows:

- a *bill of materials*, or BOM, contains information on all the materials, components and subassemblies required to produce each end item

- an *end item*, or master scheduled item, is the final product sold to the customer and the inventory for end items, from the accounting standpoint, will either be work-in-progress or finished goods

Table 10.8 **Comparison of MRP and JIT**

Operating system characteristics	MRP	JIT
System	'Push' system	'Pull' system
Focus	Bottlenecks	'Quality'
Rates of output	Variable production plan	Level schedule
Work authorisation	Master production schedule	*Kanban*
Inventory status	Inventory no problem, but the less the better	Reducing inventory to zero
Administrative personnel	Increased	Fewer
Forms of control	Management reports	Shop floor, visual
Capacity adjustment	Capital requirements planning (deferred)	Visual, immediate (demand surge)
Scheduling	MRP says 'which job next'	*Kanban* says 'make it now'

- a *parent* is an item manufactured from one or more component items
- a *component* is one item that goes through one or more operations to be transformed into a parent
- an *intermediate item* is one that has at least one parent and one component – classified as work-in-progress
- a *subassembly*, as it is 'put together', rather than other means of transformation, is a special case of intermediate item
- a *purchased item* is one that has no components because it comes from a supplier but has one or more parents, so, for accounting purposes, inventory or purchased items, is regarded as raw materials
- *part commodity* is the extent to which a component (part) has one or more parents – a concept related to standardisation – so a standard ball bearing may have numerous parents
- *usage quantity*, which is the number of units of a component required to make one unit of its parent
- a *bucket* is a time period to which MRP relates – for example, one week.

10.16.3 The essential elements of an MRP system

These are shown in Figure 10.10.

10.16.4 MRP inputs and outputs

The process starts at the top level with a master production schedule (MPS). The information in the MPS comes from a number of sources, including orders actually received and forecasts of demand, usually produced using the forecasting techniques described earlier. Two key MPS activities are the determination of planning horizons for the end product and the size of time buckets.

Figure 10.10 **Essential Elements of an MRP system**

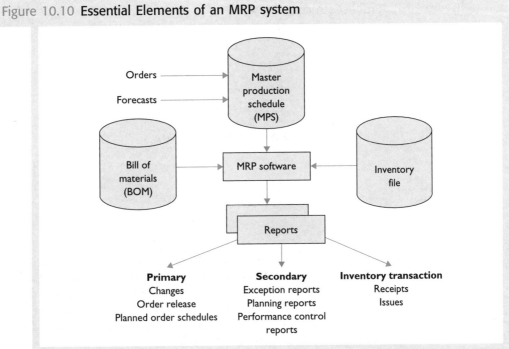

- *The master production schedule(s) (MPS)* uses the inputs from marketing and sales to forecast demand for quantities of the final product over a planned time horizon subdivided into periods known as time buckets (see Figure 10.11). These buckets are not necessarily of equal duration. Without the MPS(s), MRP cannot generate requirements for any item.
- *The bill of materials file (BOM)* also known as the product structure, this lists all the items that comprise each assembly and subassembly that make up the final product or end item. Each BOM is given a level code according to the following logic:
  - Level 0: the final product or end item not used as a component of any other product
  - Level 1: direct component of a level 0 item
  - Level 2: direct component of a level 1 item
  - Level n: direct component of a level $(n-1)$ item.

Figure 10.11 **Master production schedule**

Week	1	2	3	4	5	6	
Product X	30		14		10	8	Time buckets
Product Y		38	13	30	13	13	Time horizon

Figure 10.12 **Product structure for X**

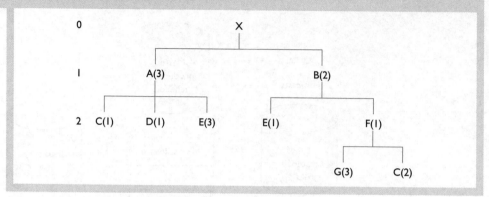

Assume the demand for product X is 30 units. Each unit of X requires three units of A and two of B. Each A requires one C, one D and three Es. Each B requires one E and one F. Each F requires three Gs and two Cs. Thus, the demand for A, B, C, D, E, F and G is completely dependent on the demand for X. From the above information, we can construct a BOM or product structure for the related inventory requirements, as in Figure 10.12.

■ *The inventory file* is the record of individual items of inventory and their status. The file is kept current by the online posting of inventory events, such as the receipt and issue of items of inventory or their return to store.

■ *The MRP package* uses the information provided by the MPS, BOM and inventory files to:

   – explode or cascade the end product into its various assemblies, subassemblies or components at various levels, so the number of units of each item needed to produce 30 units of product X would be:

     – Part A = 3 x no. of Xs   (3)(30)   = 90

     – Part B = 2 x no. of Xs   (2)(30)   = 60

     – Part C = 1 x no. of As + 2 x no. of Fs (1)(90) + (2)(60) = 210

     – Part D = 1 x no. of As   (1)(90)   = 90

     – Part E = 3 x no. of As + 1 x no. of Bs (3)(90) + (1)(60) = 330

     – Part F = 1 x no. of Bs   (1)(60)   = 60

     – Part G = 3 x no. of Fs   (3)(60)   = 180

   So, to produce 30 units of X, we shall need 90 units of A, 60 units of B, 210 units of C, 90 units of D, 330 units of E, 60 units of F and 180 units of G

   – offset for lead time – lead times for each item must be fed into the system, then, subtracting them from the date of the net requirement so as to position the planned order release date in advance of the timing of the net requirement it covers is called *offsetting the lead time*

– net out on-hand and on-order balances using the equation:

$$\underbrace{\text{Net requirements} = \text{Gross requirements}}_{\text{Total requirements}} - \underbrace{\text{Inventory on hand} + \text{Units on order}}_{\text{Available inventory}}$$

In an MRP system, net requirement quantities are always related to some date or period – that is, they are time phased (as shown by Figure 10.11). The primary outputs of the MRP system are:

■ order release instructions for the placement of planned – that is, future – production or purchasing orders

■ rescheduling instructions notifying the need to advance or postpone open orders to adjust inventory coverage to net requirements

■ expediting instructions that relate to overdue orders

■ cancellation or suspension instructions relating to open orders.

MRP systems also have the capacity to produce much secondary data, such as reports relating to exceptions or deviations from normal planning and performance.

10.16.5 Applications of MRP

While having elements in common to all inventory situations, MRP is most applicable where:

■ the demand for items is dependent

■ the demand is discontinuous – 'lumpy' and non-uniform

■ in job, batch and assembly or flow production, or where all three manufacturing methods are used.

10.17 Manufacturing resource planning (MRP II)

10.17.1 Definition

MRP II may be defined as:

> The extension of computerised MRP to link together such functions as production planning and control, engineering, purchasing, marketing, financial/cost accounting and human resource management into an integrated decision support system.

In MRP II, the production process is still driven by a master production schedule, but additional inputs are received from production control, purchasing and engineering. The computerised system also collects data to support financial or cost accounting, marketing and human resource management. An overview of MRP II is provided by Figure 10.13.

10.17.2 An overview of an MRP II system

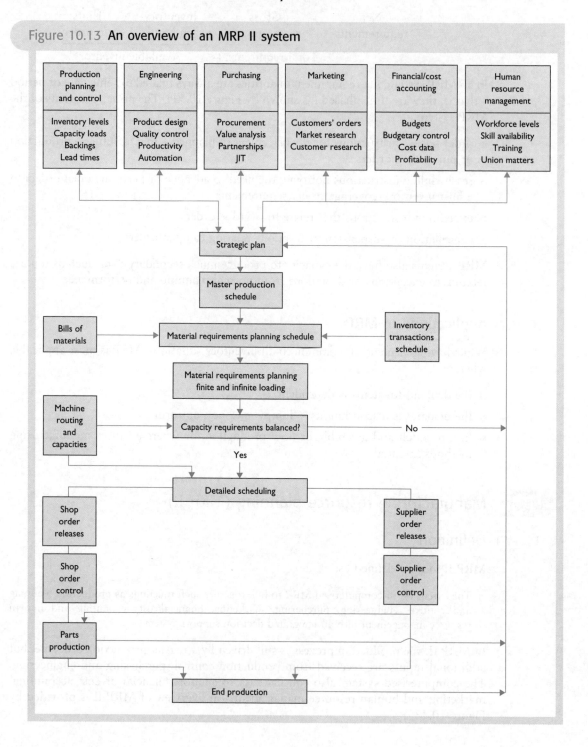

Figure 10.13 **An overview of an MRP II system**

10.17.3 The advantages of MRP II

- It coordinates the efforts of production, engineering, purchasing, marketing and human resources to achieving a common strategy or business plan.

- Managers are able to analyse the 'What if . . . ?' implications of their decisions, such as what if the sales forecasts of marketing cannot be met by the available production capacity? What would be the financial implications of outsourcing?

- Better utilisation of marketing, finance and human resources in addition to physical plant and equipment.

- Changes can be easily factored into the system as they arise, such as rush orders.

- Cost of resources used or considered for use can be converted into money values, thus facilitating budgeting and budgetary control.

- Coordination of production with purchasing, marketing and human resources in such ways as timing of supplies deliveries, using sales forecasts to determine master budgets and planning recruitment or run-down of personnel.

10.18 Enterprise resource planning (ERP)

10.18.1 What is ERP?

ERP is the latest and possibly the most significant development of MRP and MRP II. While MRP allowed manufacturers to track supplies, work-in-progress and the output of finished goods to meet sales orders, ERP is applicable to all organisations and allows managers from all functions or departments to have a consolidated view of what is or is not taking place throughout the enterprise. Most ERP systems are designed around a number of modules, each of which can be standalone or combined with others.

- *Finance* this module tracks financial information, such as accounts receivable and payable, payroll and other financial and management accounting information throughout the enterprise.

- *Logistics* this module is often broken down further into submodules covering inventory and warehouse management and transportation.

- *Manufacturing* this module tracks the flow of orders or products, including MRP and the progress and coordination of manufacturing.

- *Supplier management* this module tracks the purchasing process, from requisitioning to the payment of suppliers, and monitors delivery of supplies and supplier performance.

- *Human resources* this module covers many human resource management activities, including planning, training and job allocation.

ERP can be defined as:

> A business management system that, supported by multimodule application software integrates all the departments or functions of an enterprise.

Initially, ERP systems were enterprise-centric. The development of the Internet and e-business has, however, made the sharing of accurate real-time information across

Table 10.9 **Differences between ERP and ERP II**

Factor	ERP	ERP II
Role	Concerned with optimising within an enterprise	Concerned with optimising across the whole supply chain by collaborating with business partners
Domain	Focused on manufacturing and distribution	Crosses all sectors and segments of business, including service industries, government and asset-based industries, such as mining
Function	General applications	Designed to meet the needs of specific industries, thereby providing steep functionality for users
Process	Internally focused	Externally focused, especially on connecting trading partners, irrespective of location
Architecture	Monolithic and closed	Web-based and open to integrating and interoperating with other systems. Built around modules or components that allow users to choose the functionality they require
Data	Information on ERP systems is generated and consumed within the enterprise	Information available across the whole supply chain to authorised participants

the whole supply chain essential to business success. Gartner – the consultancy that coined the term ERP – now uses ERP II to refer to systems that facilitate collaborative commerce, or c-commerce, in which a key requirement is the sharing of information outside the enterprise. Some differences between ERP and ERP II are shown in Table 10.9.

10.18.2 The advantages of ERP

These can be summarised as:

- *faster inventory turnover* manufacturers and distributors may increase inventory turns tenfold and reduce inventory costs by 10 to 40 per cent
- *improved customer service* in many cases, an ERP system can increase fill rates to 80 or 90 per cent by providing the right product in the right place at the right time, thus increasing customer satisfaction
- *better inventory accuracy, fewer audits* an ERP system can increase inventory accuracy to more than 90 per cent while reducing the need for physical inventory audits
- *reduced set-up times* ERP can reduce set-up time by 25 to 80 per cent by grouping similar production jobs together, ensuring coordination of people, tools and machinery, together with the efficient use of equipment and minimising downtime by virtue of efficient maintenance

■ *higher-quality work* ERP software, with a strong manufacturing component, pro-actively pinpoints quality issues, providing the information required to increase production efficiency and reduce or eliminate rework

■ *timely revenue collection and improved cash flow* ERP gives manufacturers the power to proactively examine accounts receivable before problems occur instead of just reacting, which improves cash flow.

10.18.3 The disadvantages of ERP

■ *ERP implementation is difficult* this is because implementation involves a fundamental change from a functional to a process approach to business

■ *ERP systems are expensive* this is especially so when the customisation of standard modules to accommodate different business processes is involved – it has been estim-ated that some 50 per cent of ERP implementations fail to deliver the anticipated benefits and the cost is often prohibitive for small enterprises

■ *cost of training employees to use ERP systems can be high*

■ *there may be a number of unintended consequences* such as employee stress and a resistance to change and sharing information that was closely guarded by depart-ments or functions

■ *ERP systems tend to focus on operational decisions* and have relatively weak analytical capabilities (this topic is briefly dealt with below).

10.19 Supply chain management systems

While ERP systems can provide a great deal of planning capability, the various material, capacity and demand constraints are all considered separately in relative isolation from each other. Further, ERP systems have many tasks to fulfil. Analytical supply chain management systems, however, can consider all relevant factors simultaneously and perform real-time adjustments in the relevant constraints. Thus, while getting decisions or information from an overloaded ERP system can take hours, a separate SCM system may provide the required answers in minutes. SCM systems such as 1.2 Technologies and Manugistics usually span all the supply chain stages and have the analytical capabilities to produce planning solutions and strategic-level conditions. Analytical sys-tems do, however, rely on legacy systems or ERP systems to provide the information on which the analysis is based. Because of this, there is currently a rapid convergence of ERP and SCM software.

10.20 Distribution requirements planning (DRP)

10.20.1 What is DRP?

Distribution requirements planning (DRP) is an inventory control and scheduling technique that applies MRP principles to distribution inventories. It may also be regarded as a method of handling stock replenishment in a multi-echelon environment. An 'echelon' is defined by *Chamber's Dictionary* as 'A stepwise arrangement of troops,

Figure 10.14 **A supermarket multi-echelon distribution system**

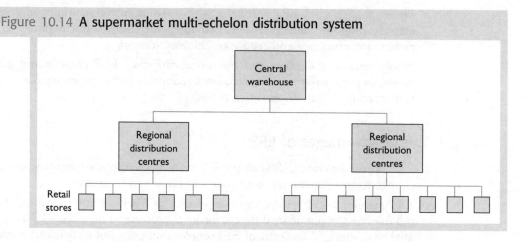

ships, planes, etc.'. Applied to distribution, the term 'multi-echelon' means that, instead of independent control of the same item at different distribution points using EOQ formulae, the dependent demand at a higher echelon (such as a central warehouse) is derived from the requirements of lower echelons (such as regional warehouses). DRP is useful for both manufacturing organisations, such as car manufacturers that sell their cars via several distribution points, such as regional and local distributors, and purely merchandising organisations, such as supermarkets (see Figure 10.14).

All levels in a DRP multiechelon structure are dependent, except for the level that serves the customer, which is the retailers in Figure 10.14.

10.20.2 DRP and MRP

DRP has been described as the mirror image of MRP. Some of the contrasts between the two approaches are set out in Table 10.10.

MRP and DRP approaches have, however, many common aspects:

- as planning systems, neither uses a fixed or periodic review approach
- both are computerised systems
- just as MRP has been expanded into MRP II, so DRP has been expanded into DRP II
- DRP utilises record formats and processing logic consistent with MRP.

Table 10.10 **Comparison of MRP and DRP**

MRP	DRP
■ The bill of materials applies time-phased logic to components and subassemblies to products in the MOM (management of materials) network	■ The bill of distribution (the network) uses time-phased order point logic to determine network replenishment requirements
■ An 'explosion' process from a master production schedule to the detailed scheduling of component replenishments	■ An 'implosion' process from the lowest levels of the network to the central distribution centre
■ Goods in course of manufacture	■ Finished goods

The last point is the most important of all as it provides the basis for integrating the database throughout the whole supply chain, from purchasing through to distribution. Thus, both MRP and DRP contribute to a logistics system, as shown in Figure 10.15.

Figure 10.15 Distribution requirements planning and logistics

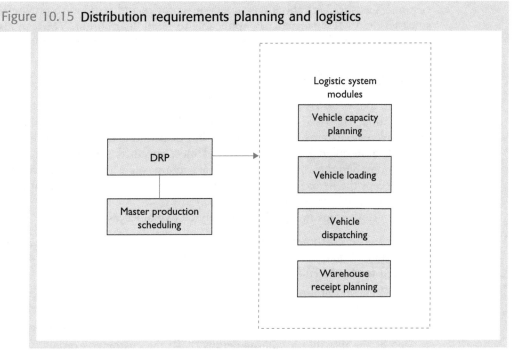

Source: adapted from Vollman, T. E., Berry, W. L., and Whybark, C. D., *Manufacturing Control Systems*, 2nd edn, Irwin, 1988, p. 788

Thus as Vollman et al.[10] observe:

> Distribution requirements planning serves a central role in coordinating the flow of goods inside the factory with the system modules that place the goods in the hands of the customers. It provides the basis for integrating the manufacturing planning and control (MRP) system from the firm to the field.

10.21 Vendor-managed inventory (VMI)

Vendor-managed inventory (VMI) is a JIT technique in which inventory replacement decisions are centralised with upstream manufacturers or distributors. Acronyms for VMI include:

- continuous replenishment programs (CRP)
- supplier-assisted inventory management (SAIM)
- supplier-assisted inventory replenishment (SAIR)
- efficient consumer response (ECR).

VMI may also be considered to be an extension of distribution requirements planning (DRP).

10.21.1 The aim of VMI

This is to enable manufacturers or distributors to eliminate the need for customers to reorder, reduce or exclude inventory and obviate stockouts. With VMI, customers no longer 'pull' inventory from suppliers. Rather, inventory is automatically 'pushed' to customers as suppliers check customers' inventories and respond to previously agreed stock levels. VMI is particularly applicable to retail distribution. VMI can also relieve the customer of much of the expense of ordering and stocking low-value MRO items.

10.21.2 Implementing VMI

A simple model of VMI is shown in Figure 10.16.

This model is based on the assumption that the customer has entered into a collaborative or partnership agreement with a distributor, under which the latter agrees to stock a specified range of items and meet specified service levels. In return, the customer undertakes to buy the specified items solely from the distributor and no longer keeps the items in stock. There must, therefore, be a high level of trust between the customer and the distributor.

The various steps in Figure 10.16 may be explained as follows.

- *Step 1* The customer sends information on items sold to the distributor. This information may be collected by barcoding and scanning technology and transmitted to the distributor by EDI or the Internet.

- *Step 2* The distributor processes the information and forwards an acknowledgement to the customer, giving details of the quantities and descriptions of the products to be delivered, delivery date and destination, and releases the goods.

- *Step 3* The distributor collects details of all the customer's orders, which are consolidated and sent daily to the manufacturers via EDI or the Internet.

- *Step 4* The manufacturer replenishes the distributor's stock.

- *Step 5* The distributor invoices the customer, who remits payment. Very large customers may transmit their requirements directly to the manufacturer, from whom they receive direct deliveries.

Figure 10.16 **A simple VMI model**

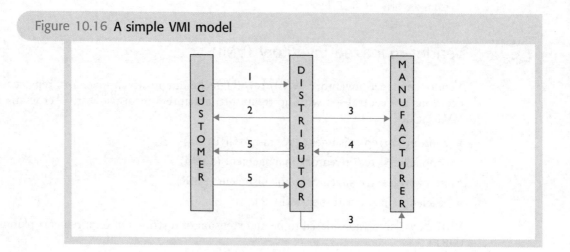

Normally, VMI implementation involves four stages.

1 *Preparation* In addition to initial negotiations between a customer and the supplier and setting up project teams with clearly defined roles and responsibilities, this stage involves collaborative planning, forecasting and replenishment (CPFR), the aim of which is to minimise inventories and focus on value-added process activities. By focusing on the flow of supply to consumers without the complication of inventory, the project's participants can often discover previously undetected hidden bottlenecks in the flow that can be eliminated.

2 *Pre-implementation* This is an extension of CPFR involving the determination of forecast quantities, safety stocks, lead time, service levels and key performance indicators and ownership issues.

3 *Implementation.*

4 *Refinement* Improvements that may be made in the light of experience, including the resolution of technical difficulties encountered subsequent to implementation.

10.21.3 Advantages of VMI

VMI is advantageous to both suppliers and customers. For suppliers, the advantages include:

■ *demand smoothing* VMI information improves forecasts of customers' requirements, thereby enabling manufacturers to plan production to meet customer demand

■ *long-term customer relationships* due to the high cost to the customer of switching to an alternative supplier

■ *enhanced operational flexibility* enabling production times and quantities to be adjusted to suit the supplier.

For customers, the advantages include:

■ *reduced administrative costs* due to the elimination of the need to monitor inventory levels, paper to computer entries and reduced reordering costs

■ *enhanced working capital* due to reduced inventory levels and obsolescence and enhanced stock turn with improved cash flow

■ *reduced lead times* with enhanced sales and a reduction of list sales due to stockouts.

10.21.4 Disadvantages of VMI

These also apply to both suppliers and customers. Disadvantages for suppliers include:

■ *transfers of customer costs to the supplier* these include those relating to administration and the cost of carrying increased inventory to meet customer demand

■ *reduced working capital* due to the enhanced inventory and administration costs stated above.

Disadvantages for customers include:

■ *increased risk*, resulting from dependence on the manufacturer or distributor

■ *disclosure of potentially sensitive information to the supplier* the possession of such information will put the supplier in a strong position when a contract is renegotiated

■ *customers may be better positioned than suppliers to make replenishment decisions*
Chopra and Meindl[11] point out that:

> One drawback to VMI arises because retailers often sell products from competing manufacturers that are substitutes in the customer's mind. For example, a customer may substitute detergent manufactured by Proctor & Gamble with detergent manufactured by Lever Brothers. If the retailer has a VMI agreement with both manufacturers, each will ignore the impact of substitution when making its inventory decisions. As a result, inventories at the retailer will be higher than optimal.

10.22 Purchasing and inventory

Inventories matter. The development of systems such as MRP, MRP II, ERP and VMI has meant that purchasing as a supply chain activity has possibly less involvement, especially with dependent demand items. In many organisations, an inventory management function will be responsible for many of the activities outlined in this chapter. It is important, however, that purchasing professionals should have a sound grasp of inventory management, for at least the following four reasons.

■ Inventory in many undertakings – for example, the construction industry – is an important asset. In some small companies, inventory may be the most important asset.

■ Inefficient inventory management will increase costs and reduce profitability. Too much working capital tied up in inventory can cause problems of cash flow, result in expensive borrowing and prevent desirable expenditure in other directions. There are also the ever-present risks of theft, deterioration and obsolescence. Conversely, holding inventory can, in a time of rising prices, be a source of windfall profits.

■ Holding inventory can enhance flexibility and provide competitive advantage, due to the ability to respond rapidly to customers' requirements, as with agile production. What inventory policy to pursue is therefore an important strategic decision.

■ Efficient and effective inventory management can only be achieved with the co-operation of efficient and effective suppliers. The selection of such suppliers and negotiation of all aspects of contracts relating to inventory are activities in which purchasing professionals should expect to play a leading role. The importance of sourcing is discussed in the next chapter.

Case study

James Johnson (JJ) is an organisation involved in manufacturing, distributing and providing after-sales service for lawnmowers and related powered garden products. It has a sales turnover of £210 million (compared with £150 million in 1999–2000), with the majority of its sales derived from the UK.

JJ remains a traditional organisation in terms of its attitudes towards working practices, management disciplines and functional approaches towards running the business.

Four months ago, JJ purchased a family business with a comparable product range – Knowles and Son (KS), located in Ipswich, with a £20 million turnover. JJ has achieved its growth by taking large amounts of business from 'trade' supermarkets. This has been a painful experience because all of them insist on two key trading conditions. They will agree to have products delivered in the winter months at a discount of 45 per cent. However, JJ must stock the products until the spring (when demand takes off) at JJ's cost. Payment is made 75 days after delivery.

JJ has a new Managing Director, who has invited his senior management team to a business briefing. You are the Purchasing and Supply Manager. The MD has told you all that profit this year is a disaster – 2.5 gross profit before tax. He said the money invested in the business would be better in the bank. He then launched an attack on yourself and the Production Manager for not getting inventory systems modernised, not getting suppliers engaged regarding the problem and failing to manage working capital. He has given you 48 hours to produce a high-level report that 'must be radical' in its approach. He then launched an attack on the Sales Director and told her to get a grip of customers, adding that the retailers made excessive profits without sharing the risks. The final attack was on engineering design, who had 'outdated products and ideas'.

Task

So, there you are, no doubt about what is required. It is obvious that things must change, and fast! You have accountability for purchasing and the supply chain (the latter including all inventory excluding work-in-progress, but including finished stock). What are the critical areas that you would study and offer comment on in your report?

Discussion questions

10.1 Calculate the rate of stock turn using the following information:

Turnover at *selling* price	= £125,000
Mark-up	= 25%
Opening stock at *selling* price	= £160,000
Closing stock at *selling* price	= £70,000

10.2 Calculate the rate of stock turn using the following information:

Turnover at cost price	= £100,000
Opening stock at cost price	= £48,000
Closing stock at cost price	= £56,000

10.3 How may the cost of ordering MRO items be reduced?

10.4 What information does an operations manager require to make effective use of dependent demand inventory models?

10.5 What are the implications for management of the following statements?
(a) The cost of carrying inventory has been estimated by leading logistics experts at between 1 and 75 per cent per year depending on the type of products and the business.
(b) The standard rule of thumb for inventory carrying costs is 25 per cent of the value of inventory on hand.

10.6 The total inventory cost of item 423 is estimated at 25 per cent. What percentage of the total inventory cost might be allocated to each of the following constituents?
(a) Cost of money, that is, interest on capital tied up in stock.
(b) Rates.

(c) Warehouse expenses.
(d) Physical handling.
(e) Clerical and stores control.
(f) Obsolescence.
(g) Deterioration and pilferage.

10.7 You have been asked to suggest four ways in which inventory costs might be reduced. What would you suggest?

10.8 A company categorises its inventory into three classes according to their usage value. Calculate the usage values of the following items and classify them along Pareto lines into A, B and C items.

Item no.	Annual quantity used	Unit value
1	75	£80.00
2	150,000	£0.90
3	500	£3.00
4	18,000	£0.20
5	3000	£0.30
6	20,000	£0.10
7	10,000	£0.04

10.9 The major disadvantages of barcoding are uniformity and cost. Discuss this statement.

10.10 As RFID systems make use of the electromagnetic system, they are relatively easy to jam using energy at the right frequency. What might be the implication for:
(a) customers at a supermarket checkout
(b) hospitals or military applications of RFID?

10.11 Carry out an ABC analysis on the basis of the following figures.

Item no.	Annual usage	Unit cost
1	2500	£0.20
2	1500	£5.00
3	1250	£0.16
4	6450	£20.00
5	8200	£15.00
6	5000	£45.00
7	1470	£100.00
8	200	£12.50
9	675	£200.00
10	20,000	£35.00
11	800	£15.00
12	84	£250.00
13	2900	£10.00
14	800	£80.00
15	9000	£0.50
16	300	£5.00
17	3250	£125.00
18	10,000	£35.00
19	5000	£25.00
20	2000	£65.00

10.12 Calculate the EOQ where:

Acquisiton cost	= £5
Holding cost	= 20% of stock value
Annual demand	= 1000 units
Price per item	= £20

For how long would the EOQ quantities last?

(EOQ = 50 units

Each order would last 2$^{1}/_{2}$ weeks)

10.13 Calculate the EOQ where:

Acquisiton cost	= £60
Holding cost	= £18 per item
Annual demand	= 240 units
Price per item	= £50

For how long would the EOQ quantities last?

(EOQ = 40 units

Each order would last 2 months as 240/40 = 1/6 of a year = 2 months)

10.14 Find the standard deviation for the following orders for product X received over a 12-week period.

0, 1, 0, 2, 1, 2, 4, 1, 2, 0, 3, 0

(Answer: 1.25)

10.15 Average order quantities are 150. The average demand is 20. Use the probability table 10.5 to determine what should be the reorder quantity to ensure a service level of 95 per cent – that is, a stockout probability of only 5 per cent.

(Answer: approx. 183 units or 185 rounded up)

10.16 What term would you use to describe the effect of information delays up and down the supply chain? What might be the consequences for inventory and profitability of such information delays?

10.17 A product is assembled from five components B, C, D, E and F. A BOM of X is as follows:

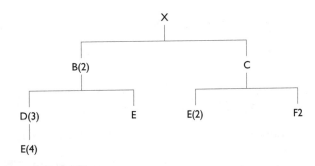

(a) Use the above information to compute the quantities of each component B, C, D, E and F to assemble one X.
(b) What quantities of each component will be required to manufacture 100 Xs?

10.18 **Attempt a BOM for:**

(a) a simple bicycle.

(b) a table lamp.

10.18.1 **Consider the following DRP display**

	Period						
	1	*2*	*3*	*4*	*5*	*6*	*7*
Gross requirements	30	30	30	30	30	30	30
Balance projected (in hand quantity) 44	14	64	34	84	54	24	74
Planned orders							

Safety stock = 20, Order quantity = 80, Lead time = 1

In what periods would the reorder points fall in the situation depicted above?

Past examination questions

All the following are taken from the CIPS Graduate Diploma papers in Purchasing and Supply Management II: Tactics and Operations.

1 Distinguish between dependent and independent demand items, outlining an inventory management system which would be suitable for each category of item.

(May 2001, also May 2003)

2 Many organisations find themselves in the apparently contradictory position of having high levels of financial investment in inventory, but at the same time frequently running out of stock of important components and materials.

(a) Explain how this situation could arise.

(b) Explain how you would deal with this problem and prevent it from recurring.

(November 2001)

3 (a) Explain the main principles of the Just-in-Time (JIT) approach to inventory management.

(b) Discuss the effect of the JIT approach upon purchasing operations.

References

[1] Institute of Logistics and Transport, *Glossary of Inventory and Materials Management Definitions*, 1998

[2] Institute of Logistics and Transport, *How to Manage Inventory Effectively*, Added Value Publication Ltd, 2003, p. 94

[3] Compton, H. K. and Jessop, D., *Dictionary of Purchasing and Supply Management*, Pitman, 1989, p. 135

[4] See GS1 UK's website at: www.e-centre.org.uk

[5] American Production and Inventory Control Society

[6] Schonberger, R. J., and Ansari, A., 'Just-in-time purchasing can improve quality', *Journal of Purchasing and Materials Management*, spring, 1984

[7] Rhys, D. G., McNash, K., and Nieuwenhuis, P., 'Japan hits the limits of Just-in-Time EIU', *Japanese Motor Business*, Dec., 1992, pp. 81–9

[8] Hayes, R. H., and Pisano, G. P., 'Beyond world class: the new manufacturing strategy', *Harvard Business Review*, Jan.–Feb., 1994, p. 75

[9] Pragman, C. H., 'JIT II: a purchasing concept for reducing lead times in time-based competition', *Business Horizons*, July–Aug., 1996, pp. 54–8

[10] Vollman, T. E., Berry, W. L., and Whybark, C. D., *Manufacturing Control Systems*, 2nd edn, Irwin, 1988, p. 788

[11] Chopra, S., and Meindl, P., *Supply Chain Management*, Prentice Hall, 2001, p. 247

Chapter 11

Sourcing and the management of suppliers

Learning outcomes

This chapter aims to provide an understanding of:

- tactical and strategic sourcing
- the sourcing process
- the location, appraisal and assessment of suppliers
- supplier performance and evaluation
- policy issues in sourcing
- sourcing decision making
- factors in deciding where to buy.

Key ideas

- Sourcing information.
- Analysis of market conditions.
- The main aspects of supplier appraisal.
- The purpose, scope and methods of evaluating supplier performance.
- The supplier base.
- Make-or-buy decisions.
- Outsourcing.
- Subcontracting.
- Partnering.
- Reciprocity.
- Intra-company trading, local suppliers and small or large suppliers.
- Purchasing consortia.
- Factors in deciding where to buy.
- Buying centres, teams and networks.
- Straight rebuy, modified rebuy and new buy purchasing situations.

11.1 What is sourcing?

Sourcing – the process of identifying, selecting and developing suppliers – is a key purchasing activity. Sourcing can be either at tactical and operational or strategic levels.

11.1.1 Tactical and operational sourcing

Tactical and operational sourcing is concerned with lower-level decisions relating to high-profit, low-risk, non-critical items. It is also concerned with short-term adaptive decisions as to how and from where specific supplier requirements are to be met. Thus, suggestions may be made to top management regarding temporary tactical deviations from strategic decisions. Although strategically it may have been decided to buy rather than to make a certain component, this decision may be tactically reversed in conditions of manufacturing for stock, work shortage or supplier failure.

11.1.2 Strategic sourcing

Strategic sourcing is concerned with top-level, longer-term decisions relating to high-profit, high supply risk strategic items and low-profit, high supply risk bottleneck products and services. It is also concerned with the formulation of long-term purchasing policies, the supplier base, partnership sourcing, reciprocal and intra-company trading, globalisation and countertrade, the purchase of capital equipment and ethical issues.

The status and importance purchasing now has requires a transition from thinking of it as a purely tactical activity to seeing it as a strategic activity. In transactional sourcing, purchasing is viewed as a function concerned with the placement of orders. In strategic sourcing, purchasing is viewed as a knowledge-based activity concerned with the total cost of ownership rather than the price paid per item with the optional mix of relationships to provide competitive advantage. Whether tactical or strategic sourcing applies in a particular situation depends on the nature of the purchase and the business environment in which purchasing takes place. A comparison, adapted from Dey,[1] is shown in Table 11.1.

Table 11.1 **Comparison of tactical and strategic sourcing business environments**

Tactical sourcing environment	Strategic sourcing environment
Clearly defined requirements and specifications	Development of a deep understanding of requirements – value analysis and engineering to identify operational value and trade-offs
Open bid process with little or no ability for suppliers to offer alternative designs or specifications – purchase price focus	Development of a deep understanding of the supply industry, product and service offerings and performance drivers of key suppliers

11.2 The sourcing process

Strategic sourcing is a complicated process involving a number of interrelated tasks. Not surprisingly, a number of models of the strategic process have been devised. A typical model is that of Novack and Simco,[2] who present the following 11-stage sourcing process.

- *Stage 1: Identify or re-evaluate needs*
  In some instances, needs must be re-evaluated because they have changed.
- *Stage 2: Define or evaluate users' requirements*
- *Stage 3: Decide to make or buy*
- *Stage 4: Identify type of purchase*
  The three types of purchases – from least amount of time and complexity to most amount of time and complexity – are:

  1 straight rebuy or routine purchase

  2 a modified rebuy, which requires a change to an existing supplier or input

  3 a new buy, which results from a new user need.

  These three types of purchases are discussed in section 11.30.
- *Stage 5: Conduct market analysis*
  A source of supply can operate in a purely competitive market (many suppliers), an oligopolistic market (a few large suppliers) or a monopolistic market (one supplier) – see section 12.3.
- *Stage 6: Identify possible suppliers*
  This may include suppliers that the purchaser has not previously used.
- *Stage 7: Prescreen possible suppliers*
  This process will reduce the number of suppliers to those that can meet the purchaser's demands.
- *Stage 8: Evaluate the remaining supply base*
  This activity is often accomplished by means of competitive bidding.
- *Stage 9: Choose supplier*
  The choice of supplier determines the relationships that will exist between the purchasing and supplier organisations and how the relationship will be structured and implemented. It will also determine how relationships with non-selected suppliers will be maintained.
- *Stage 10: Deliver product/perform service*
  The completion of this activity also begins the generation of performance data to be used for the next activity.
- *Stage 11: Post purchase/make performance evaluation*
  The supplier's performance must be evaluated to determine how well the purchaser's needs have been met. This will provide data for future sourcing.

11.3 Sourcing information

Sourcing information can be divided into the areas shown in Figure 11.1.

Figure 11.1 **Areas of sourcing information**

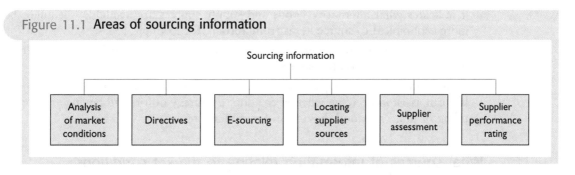

11.4 Analysis of market conditions

11.4.1 What is a market?

The term 'market' can mean:

■ a place where goods and services are bought and sold – for example, the European Union is a market created by agreement between the participating countries to reduce barriers to the internal movement of labour and capital

■ large groups of buyers and sellers of wide classes of goods, such as the consumer goods market, the equipment market and so on

■ demand and supply of a single class of community, such as the steel market, the cotton market

■ the general economic conditions relating to the supply of goods and services applying at a particular time – of special importance to purchasing is the distinction between a buyer's and a seller's market.

11.4.2 Why is the analysis of market conditions important to sourcing?

The horizon of purchasing awareness determines whether the contribution made by purchasing to an organisation is transactional or strategic.

Purchasing staff who never look beyond fulfilling the requirements of the current week are little more than expert expediters. Strategic purchasing involves using business intelligence to analyse the purchasing environment and make appropriate decisions and recommendations. Only on the basis of intelligence can strengths, weaknesses, opportunities and threats that impact supplies be evaluated. Business intelligence also provides information on how the organisation – and purchasing as an activity within the business – is performing relative to competitors. Analysis of market conditions as an aspect of business intelligence is useful for the following reasons:

■ it helps in forecasting the long-term demand for the product, of which bought-out materials, components and so on are part, so it has an interest in market research, too

■ it assists in forecasting the price trends of bought-out items and how material costs are likely to affect production costs and selling prices, so, for example, the need for cheaper prices may influence sourcing decisions

■ it indicates what alternative goods and supply sources are available – it might be more economical to source items from abroad, for example

■ it gives guidance on the security of supply sources, which is particularly important with sensitive commodities sourced abroad

■ information relating to pay trends, commodity prices, political factors and the like can assist in deciding whether to adopt a strategy of forward buying and stock-piling or hand-to-mouth buying and minimum stocks.

11.4.3 What sources of information relating to market conditions are available?

Information relating to market conditions may be obtained from the following sources:

■ *primary data* field research that can use one or more approaches, such as observation, analysis of internal records, such as sales trends and order book levels, visits to suppliers, questionnaires

■ *secondary data* statistics and reports issued by external information, many of which are on databases

■ *international sources* a useful survey of information sources is provided by GlobalEdge, created by the Center for International Business Education and Research for Michigan State University, which is a knowledge portal that connects business professionals worldwide to a wealth of information, insights and learning resources on global business activities, while a further useful site is Business Information on the Internet, provided by the Federation of International Trade Associations, and similar sources can be found by keying the phrase 'international sources of business data' into an Internet search engine

■ *UK government sources* full details of publications can be obtained from The Stationery Office, The most important sources including:
 – *Abstracts of Statistics*, published annually and monthly
 – *Economic Trends*
 – *Census of Production*
 – *Department of Employment Gazette*
 – *British Business*, published weekly by the Department of Trade and Industry
 – *Business Monitors* – the P series covers a wide sector of industrial activities
 – *Bank of England Reports*

■ *non-government sources* these include:
 – Economist Intelligence Unit
 – chambers of commerce
 – professional associations – of particular importance to procurement staff is *Supply Management*, the journal of the Chartered Institute of Purchasing and Supply (CIPS), and both the CIPS and the USA Institute of Supply Management have online databases – the CIPS databases relating to company information and data, universities and business schools, UK and European governmental and related sites, US government and associated sites, construction industry-specific resources, online newspapers, magazines and other links

- *the press in the UK* such as *The Economist, Financial Times* and the 'quality' daily and Sunday newspapers
- *economic forecasts* such as the Confederation of British Industries' (CBI) 'Economic Situation Report' and Oxford Economic Forecasting's range of publications, including *UK Economic Prospects, World Economic Prospects, UK Industrial Prospects* and *European Economic Prospects.*

11.5 Directives

A 'directive' is a general instruction. Typical directives relating to sourcing include those issued by the EU, central and local government offices and companies.

11.5.1 EU directives

Background

Most organisations that receive public funding are likely to be affected by European procurement legislation. Such organisations include central government departments, local authorities, NHS trusts and universities. The legislation covers most contracts for supplies (that is, goods), work and services. European directives take precedence over national law, irrespective of when the domestic law was enacted. The political aim is to create a single market for public procurement so that European companies may, in principle, have access to contracts without any kind of discrimination.

Breach of the EU public procurement rules may have significant legal consequences. Under the Remedies Directive and implementing regulations, for example, the High Courts of England and Wales, Northern Ireland and the Court of Session in Scotland have the power to review the award of a contract and apply a number of remedies, including:

- declaring the contract void
- varying the contract
- awarding damages to the injured party.

Details of current EU directives are available from regional EU information offices on the Internet. Directive 2004/18/EC requires the provisions of the Consolidated EU Public Procurement Directives to be transposed into national legislation by 31 January 2006. The directive simplifies and consolidates three pre-existing directives for public works, supplies and services into a single text. Provisions have been added to take account of modern procurement methods and developments in best practice. These include explicit provisions regarding framework agreements, central purchasing bodies, e-auctions and dynamic purchasing systems. A procedure called the Competitive Dialogue has also been introduced.

11.5.2 Central and local government purchasing directives and guidance

In the UK, current public procurement policy is based largely on the white papers 'Setting new standards: a strategy for government procurement', Cm 2840, 1995, and 'Modernising government', Cm 4310, March, 1999 (a 'white paper' is a statement of government policy or an explanation of proposed legislation).

The UK Office of Government Commerce (OGC) publishes guidelines on a range of procurement issues, such as strategic supplier management, e-procurement and contract innovation. A number of guidance notes issued when the Central Unit in Procurement (now superseded) formed part of the Treasury, covering topics such as post-tender negotiation and quality assurances, are still available. Guidelines on procurement and reports on the effectiveness of government initiatives aimed at improving central and local government procurement are also issued by the Audit Commission and the National Audit Office. Typical of the latter is the handbook *Getting Value for Money from Procurement* and the report 'Improving procurement progress' by the Office of Government Commerce in *Improving Department's Capability to Procure Cost-effectively* (2004).

In addition to EU directives, regulations and guidance for local authorities may be given in 'statutory instruments', which are laws written by a government minister exercising legislative powers delegated to him or her by an Act of Parliament. The 'National procurement strategy for local government in England and Wales', issued by the Office of the Deputy Prime Minister in October 2003, sets out how central and local government, working together with partners from the public, private and voluntary sectors, intend to improve local government procurement. The national strategy aims, by 2006, for all English and Welsh local authorities to be delivering 'significantly better and more cost-effective public services, through sustainable partnerships and a mixed economy of competitive suppliers from many sectors'. To do this, all councils need to:

- make the cultural changes needed
- provide leadership and build capacity
- engage in partnerships and collaboration
- do business electronically
- stimulate markets and thereby achieve local, economic and community benefits.

11.5.3 Company directives

Company directives may be issued by the top management of an organisation, instructing that, for reasons of strategy or in pursuance of agreements, particular supplies must be obtained from a specific source. An example would be directives relating to intra-company or reciprocal trading.

11.6 E-sourcing

E-procurement, along with e-marketplaces, e-catalogues and e-auctions, was discussed in Chapter 6. E-sourcing is defined by the CIPS[3] as:

> using the Internet to make decisions and form strategies regarding how and where services or products are obtained.

Although both e-procurement and e-sourcing are integral to the purchasing cycle, the two terms are usually distinguished. E-procurement is usually concerned with non-core goods and services. These can, however, cover far more than routine MRO items or office supplies. As Waller[4] has stated:

> For telecommunications companies network switches are indirect goods. For oil refineries, large condensers, costing millions of dollars are indirect goods. For companies that operate petrol stations, forecourts signs and fascias are indirect goods.

E-sourcing allows research, design and purchasing personnel to find parts, components and subassemblies for prototypes and subsequent production models. As ePedas[5] has explained:

> The difference between e-sourcing and e-procurement is that, in e-sourcing, decisions are made on the basis of functionality and characteristics, not purely on the basis of product and price. The e-sourced products form part of the finished products. Therefore e-sourcing is to determine which direct goods to buy.

The difference between e-procurement and e-sourcing is succinctly put in the following:

> e-procurement may be seen as the focus of local business administrators with one of the key goals being to devolve the buying process to local users, covering the requisition against contract, authorisation, order, receipt and payment.

> e-sourcing covers those parts of the buying process which are not wholly at the discretion of the specialist buyers, which includes knowledge (such as competence analysis, and spend analysis), specification; request for quotation/e-tender/e-auction and contract evaluation/ negotiation.

11.7 Locating suppliers

Suppliers can be located by checking a wide range of sources. This process has been made faster and easier by the World Wide Web. Microsoft[6] indicates a number of useful databases for sourcing suppliers, including:

■ a comprehensible searchable list of more than 1.7 million UK businesses, broken down into over 2500 distinct classifications, at the Ycll.com site from *Yellow Pages*: www.yell.com

■ some of the searchable databases intended to promote exports, such as the UK Trade and Investments database of suppliers: www.uktradeinvest.gov.uk

■ major overseas reference resources, such as the Thomas Global Register Europe at: www.tgreurope.com, which gives access to a searchable directory of over 210,000 industrial manufacturers, and a related website at: www.thomasnet.com, which covers 650,000 US and Canadian suppliers

■ the Purchasing Research Service at: www.touchbriefings.com, which provides sector-by-sector supplier listings and news items.

Specialised sites include:

■ the Applegate Directory at: www.applegate.co.uk, which covers suppliers in the electronics, engineering and plastics sectors

■ the Used Equipment Network at: www.buyused.com, which offers secondhand plant and machinery – from aircraft to X-ray machines – covering more than 75,000 items from more than 10,000 dealers.

Databases can provide up-to-date information and may be space-saving substitutes for large reference collections. Access to such databases may be free and unrestricted or subscriber only.

Thompson and Homer[7] point out that:

> In all cases the aim is the same, to provide a method whereby a company can search the various databases in order to satisfy their need for supplier information. For example, a company manufacturing forged components for vehicle steering systems might access such databases in order to identify and locate a company who has the capability to heat-treat their high molybdenum content forged components. In this example, the databases are being used to procure new suppliers (or sometimes, customers).

Thompson and Homer also highlight several problems that limit the value of these online searchable databases:

- the effort and time required to access several databases to find an answer to a query
- the quality of data content as reflected in differences in the method, terminology or units used to express quantitative data, which reduces the value of any Internet searches based on the data, resulting in the search excluding potentially useful companies simply because the format of units in which the data is held for a crucial field search to be inappropriate
- duplication of data, such as the same organisation being listed differently within the same database as, say, Small Parts Ltd and Small Engineering Ltd
- time out-of-date and incorrect data content – databases may contain information regarding organisations that have ceased trading or show wrong addresses, telephone numbers and so on
- the power and flexibility of available search methods – several online searchable databases investigated by the researchers revealed a considerable divergence in the search methods available to users, ranging from rudimentary – a mere list of suppliers – to more sophisticated methods allowing for an increasing identification of supplier capabilities

Other useful ways in which to locate suppliers include:

- *salespeople* the usefulness of salespeople is dependent on their knowledge of the product they are seeking to promote – they are often able to provide useful service information regarding suppliers, such as details of items other than those manufactured by their own undertaking.
- *exhibitions* these provide an opportunity to compare competing products, meet representatives of suppliers and attend presentations by exhibitors, and exhibition catalogues and other literature usually provide details of the main suppliers in a particular field, so should be retained for reference purposes
- *trade journals* these provide buyers not only with information regarding new products, substitute materials and so on, but also trade gossip, which keeps buyers informed about changes in the policies of suppliers and their personnel
- *trade associations* the Trade Association Forum[8] has a website aimed at assisting buyers, government departments, researchers and the public with access to information about UK trade associations and business sectors
- *informal exchange of information* between purchasing and other professionals.

11.8 Supplier appraisal assessments

11.8.1 When to appraise

Supplier appraisal may arise when a prospective vendor applies to be placed on the buyer's approved list or in the course of negotiation when the buyer wishes to assure him- or herself that a supplier can meet the requirements reliably.

Supplier appraisal can be a time-consuming and costly activity. It should therefore be selective. Lysons[9] states that there are situations in which appraisal is essential. These include:

- where potential suppliers do not hold BS EN ISO 9000:2000
- purchase of strategic high-profit, high-risk items
- purchase of non-standard items
- placing of construction and similar contracts
- expenditure on capital items, including plant, machinery and computer systems
- for purposes of supplier development – that is, what needs to done to bridge the gap between the present resources and competences of a supplier or potential supplier and the standard required by the purchaser
- when entering into JIT arrangements
- when contemplating joining a supplier association – a supplier association has been defined by Hines et al.[10] as 'a group of companies linked together on a regular basis to share knowledge and experience in an open and cooperative manner'
- when engaging in global sourcing
- when establishing e-procurement arrangements with long-term strategic suppliers
- when negotiating TQM and quality in relation to high-profit or high-risk items
- when negotiating outsourcing contracts
- before agreeing to a subcontract with a main supplier in relation to important companies
- when negotiating service-level agreements.

11.8.2 What should be appraised?

Supplier appraisal is situational. What to appraise is related to the requirements of the particular purchaser. All appraisals should, however, evaluate potential suppliers from eight perspectives:

- finance
- production capacity and facilities
- human resources
- quality
- performance
- environmental and ethical considerations
- IT
- organisational structure.

Such information may be obtained from questionnaires sent to prospective suppliers that have applied to be added to the purchaser's list of approved suppliers or prior to a supplier visit.

11.8.3 Finance

The UK Department of Trade and Industry[11] points out that financial appraisal should reduce, but will not eliminate, the risk of placing business with a company the financial viability of which is in doubt. It does, however, provide information enabling considered decisions to be made either when sourcing suppliers or when evaluating tenders. The checks recommended are:

■ the assessed turnover of the enterprise over three years
■ the profitability and the relationship between gross and net profits of the enterprise over three years
■ the value of capital assets, return on capital assets and return on capital employed
■ the scale of borrowings and the ratio of debts to assets
■ the possibility of takeover or merger affecting ability to supply
■ whether or not the firm is tied to a small number of major customers, so that if one or more withdrew their businesses it might cause the firm financial difficulties
■ whether or not the organisation has sufficient capacity to fulfil the order.

Such enquiries are advisable for small- and medium-sized enterprises (SMEs) in relation to one-off or annual contracts in excess of, say, £15,000. In the UK, an appraisal can be undertaken internally by accounting staff who can study the supplier's annual report and accounts for the past three or four years.

In the USA, 'FORM 10K' is an annual report submitted by US companies to the Securities and Exchange Commission, pursuant to Section 13 or 15(d) of the Securities Exchange Act of 1934. There is also the 'FORM 10Q', a quarterly report. The information contained in these documents exceeds, greatly, that typically found in UK companies' annual reports. There is vital company and market intelligence of value to procurement decisions. Examples of information contained are details of companies' major markets, products, business risks, outstanding legal writs and their nature, divisional financial results, investments and competition. These reports can be obtained free of charge from the companies themselves and many are available on the Internet.

Credit reports may also be obtained from bankers or credit references and credit reports provided by such agencies as Dun and Bradstreet. Important information provided by Dun and Bradstreet's supplier evaluation reports include:

■ *sales* gives a picture of the firm's financial size in terms of sales/revenue volume
■ *financial profile* evaluates how the enterprise is doing financially compared with its industry and, to understand the profitability and solvency of a supplier, five key financial ratios are calculated that provide industry benchmarks against a peer group of suppliers
■ *supplier risk score* an evaluation of the risk involved in dealing with a supplier that presents an at-a-glance 1–9 rating based on financial and public records and operational information, with 1 being the lowest and 9 the highest risk (this predictive score helps purchasing to understand the general financial status of a supplier and benchmark it against others).

Table 11.2 **Important balance sheet and income ratios when appraising potential suppliers**

Ratio source	Name of ratio	Calculation of ratio	Purpose of ratio
Balance sheet ratios measure the liquidity and solvency (ability to pay bills) and gearing (the extent to which the business is dependent on creditors' funding)	Liquidity ratios – current ratio	$\dfrac{\text{Total current assets}}{\text{Total current liabilities}}$	Can the business pay its current debts with a margin of safety for possible losses in current assets? A generally acceptable ratio is 2:1. The minimum acceptable ratio is 1:1
	Quick ratio (the 'acid' test)	$\dfrac{\text{Quick assets}}{\text{Current liabilities} - \text{Bank overdraft}}$	Answers question 'if all sales revenue should disappear, could the enterprise meet its current obligations with the readily convertible quick funds on hand?' Ratio of 1:1 is minimum acceptable
	Working capital	Total current assets – Total current liabilities	More of a measure of cash flow than a ratio. The result must be a positive number.
	Gearing ratio	$\dfrac{\text{Fixed interest capital}}{\text{Fixed interest} - \text{Equity capital}}$	Too high a gearing ratio is potentially unstable as it indicates undue dependence on external sources for long-term financing
Income statement Profit and loss account These ratios measure profitability	Gross profit margin ratio	$\dfrac{\text{Gross profit}}{\text{Net sales}}$	Gross profit = Net sales – Cost of goods sold. Measures the percentage of sales value left after deducting cost of manufacturing to pay the overhead costs of the enterprise. Can be compared to ratios of other businesses
	Net profit margin ratio	$\dfrac{\text{Net profit before tax}}{\text{Net sales}}$	Indicates percentage of sales revenue left after subtracting cost of goods sold and all expenses except tax

In addition, the Office of Government Commerce (OGC)[12] recommends that basic checks should be made on a UK company's title and its registered number at Companies House to see whether the company is dormant or trading and whether it is owned by another company or supported by a venture capital organisation.

Balance sheet and profit and loss ratio analysis (see Table 11.2) should also be used. The OGC indicates a number of warning signs, including:

- cash draining from the business
- falling profit margins
- increasing stocks and slower stock turnover
- high capital gearing
- changing auditors and bankers
- adverse press reports.

In the case of substantial contracts, the purchasing organisation should question whether or not the supplier is likely to become overly dependent on the buying company.

11.8.4 **Production capacity**

'Capacity' has been defined as:[13]

> The limiting capability of a productive unit to produce items within a stated time period normally expressed in terms of output units per unit of time.

Capacity is an elusive concept because it must be related to the extent that a facility is used – that is, it may be the policy to utilise production capacity five days weekly, one shift daily or produce a maximum of 2000 units monthly. Plant capacity can normally be increased by working overtime or adding new facilities.

In appraising supplier capacity, attention should be given to the following considerations:

- the maximum productive capacity in a normal working period
- the extent to which capacity is currently over- or undercommitted – for example, a full order book may raise doubts about the supplier's capacity to take on further work or else you have to wonder if a substantial amount of capacity is underutilised
- how existing capacity might be expanded to meet future increased demand
- the percentage of available capacity utilised by existing major customers
- what percentage of capacity would be utilised if the potential supplier were awarded the business of the purchaser – this can also be assessed in terms of annual turnover, but, in any case, care should be taken to avoid making the supplier overly dependent on one or two customers
- what systems are used for capacity planning.

11.8.5 **Innovation and design (where appropriate)**

Thought should be given to the company's:

- reputation for design and innovation
- design and research facilities, such as laboratories, drawing offices, specialist equipment
- R&D and design staff with regard to their qualifications and experience
- access to external sources of assistance, such as universities and research associations
- willingness to participate in collaborative projects
- ability to give examples, if any, of collaborative projects already undertaken and what they show.

11.8.6 **Production facilities**

An appraisal of production facilities depends on the purpose of it. Appraisal of machinery, for example, depends on what is to be produced. In general, attention should be given to answering the following kinds of questions.

- Has the supplier the full range of machinery needed to make the required product?
- How would any shortage of machinery be overcome?
- Are machines modern and well maintained? (Machine breakdowns will affect delivery.)

- Is the plant layout satisfactory?
- Is there evidence of good housekeeping?
- Has the supplier adopted such approaches as computer-aided design (CAD), computer-aided manufacture (CAM) or flexible manufacturing systems (FMS)?
- Are health and safety provisions satisfactory?

11.8.7 Human resources

No organisation is better than the people who work for it. Information should be obtained regarding the:

- number of people employed in manufacturing and administration
- use of human resources – whether economical, with everyone busy, or extravagant, with excess people doing little or nothing
- names, titles, qualifications and experience of managerial staff
- encouragement of teamwork and empowerment
- worker representation and recognised trade unions
- days lost due to industrial disputes in each of the past five years
- turnover of managerial and operative staff
- workers' attitudes to the organisation and concern for meeting customers' requirements.

11.8.8 Quality

For suppliers not included on the BSI's Register of Firms of Assessed Quality, appraisal may require satisfactory answers to such questions as the following.

- Has the supplier met the criteria for other BSI schemes, such as the Kitemark, Safety Mark and scheme for registered stockists?
- Has the supplier met the quality approval criteria of other organisations, such as the Ford Quality Awards, the Ministry of Defence, British Gas or others?
- To what extent does the supplier know about and implement the concept of total quality management?
- What procedures are in place for the inspection and testing of purchased materials?
- What relevant test and inspection process does the supplier use?
- What statistical controls are applied regarding quality?
- Does quality control cover an evaluation of quality?
- Can the supplier guarantee that the purchaser can safely eliminate the need for all incoming inspection? (This is especially important for JIT deliveries.)

11.8.9 Performance

Particularly when appraising suppliers of non-standard products such as construction projects or the installation of computer systems, questions should be asked regarding the following.

- What similar projects has the supplier already undertaken?
- What current projects are in hand?
- What are/were the distinctive features of such projects?
- What innovations might be introduced?
- What customers can the supplier cite as referees?

11.8.10 Environmental and ethical factors

ISO 14001 provides guidelines on environmental policies and, where applicable, suppliers should be expected to have an environmental policy and procedures for the implementation of such a policy. A large number of EU directives have also been issued relating to air, water, chemicals, packaging and waste.

Apart from those with reference to ISO 14001 and EU directives, suitable questions to ask include the following.

- Has responsibility for environmental management been allocated to a particular person?
- Are materials obtained, so far as possible, from sustainable sources – such as timber?
- What is the lifecycle cost of the suppliers' product?
- What facilities has the supplier for waste minimisation, disposal and recycling?
- What energy savings, if any, do the supplier's products provide?
- What arrangements are in place for the control of dangerous substances and nuisance?

Ethical questions may relate to the following.

- Has the supplier an ethical policy relating to the sale and purchase of items?
- Who is responsible for enforcement of such a policy?
- What guidelines and procedures are provided relating to the confidentiality of information provided by a customer?
- What guidelines apply to the receipt of gifts and hospitality?
- What principles apply with regard to conflicts of interest?

Further reference to ethical and environmental appraisal is made in sections 17.9 and 17.14.

11.8.11 Information technology (IT)

Research indicates that, at the time of writing, more than a third of buyers currently use the Internet to conduct transactions and such usage is likely to increase dramatically. Additionally, the Web also supports a variety of activities, such as identifying new sources of supply, finding product information, including products, prices and delivery, as well as tracking orders and receiving technical advice and after-sales service.

It is useful to ask mainly open-ended questions under this heading as the replies will indicate the extent to which the supplier is exploiting the possibilities of e-business. Here are some typical questions that might be asked.

- Does your organisation have a website?
- What information does the website provide?
- What business activities does your organisation process electronically?
- In what ways does your organisation
  - reduce or eliminate paper transactions
  - shorten order cycles
  - reduce inventory
  - provide real-time information on product availability and inventory
  - provide collaborative planning
  - integrate its supply chain?

11.8.12 Obtaining information for supplier appraisal

This may be done by means of a suitable questionnaire, supplemented where appropriate by a visit to the potential suppliers.

11.8.13 Appraisal questionnaires

The topics in sections 11.8.3 to 11.8.11 above can easily be adapted to use in a questionnaire. Some general principles relating to questionnaires should be remembered:

- keep the appraisal questionnaire as short as is reasonably possible
- ask only what is necessary and obtain only information that will be used
- divide the various sections of the questionnaire into 'fields', each relating to a particular area of investigation, as in sections 11.8.3 to 11.8.11 above
- consider whether or not it is likely that the respondent will know the answers to the questions and the trouble they are likely to have providing the information
- consider whether or not respondents will understand the wording of questions – are you using technical or cultural-specific words or abbreviations, for example
- ask only one question at a time – avoid the use of 'and' in the question
- start with factual and then go on to opinion-based questions
- ensure that the questionnaire is signed, dated and the title of the respondent is indicated.

11.8.14 Supplier visits

Supplier visits should always be undertaken by a cross-functional team that includes a senior member of purchasing and experts on quality and production engineering. Each member of the team is able to evaluate the supplier from a specialist viewpoint so this ensures shared responsibility for the decision to approve or reject a supplier. The purposes of a supplier visit include:

- the confirmation of information provided by the supplier in a preliminary questionnaire
- to discuss in depth the products and services offered by a potential supplier and ways in which the supplier can contribute to the requirements of the visiting organisation.

Prior to the visit, a checklist of matters to be investigated should be prepared. This ensures that no important questions are overlooked, provides a permanent record of the visit and reasons for the decisions reached can be recorded. On supplier visits, important sources of information are observation and informal conversations. Particular attention should be given to the following areas.

- *Personal attitudes* An observant visitor can sense the attitudes of the supplier's employees towards their work and this provides an indication of the likely quality of their output and service dependability. The state of morale will be evident from:
  - an atmosphere of harmony or dissatisfaction among the production workers
  - the degree of interest in customer service on the part of supervisory staff
  - the degree of energy displayed and the interest in getting things done
  - the use of manpower – whether economical, with everyone usually busy, or extravagant and costly, with excess people doing little or nothing.

- *Adequacy and care of production equipment* Close observation of the equipment in a plant will indicate whether it is:
  - modern or antiquated
  - accurately maintained or obviously worn
  - well cared for by operators or dirty and neglected
  - of proper size or type to produce the buyer's requirements
  - of sufficient capacity to produce the quantities desired.

  The presence or absence of ingenious self-developed mechanical devices for performing unusual operations will be indicative of the plant's manufacturing and engineering expertise.

- *Technological know-how of supervisory personnel* Conversations with foremen, shop superintendents and others will indicate their technical knowledge and ability to control and improve the operations of processes under their supervision.

- *Means of controlling quality* Observation of the inspection methods will indicate their adequacy to ensure the specified quality of the product. Attention should be given to:
  - whether or not the materials are chemically analysed and physically checked
  - frequency of inspection during the production cycle
  - employment of such techniques as statistical quality control
  - availability of statistical quality control.

- *Housekeeping* A plant that is orderly and clean in its general appearance indicates careful planning and control by management. Such a plant inspires confidence that its products will be made with the same care and pride as to their quality. The dangers of breakdown, fire or other disasters will also be minimised, with a consequent increased assurance of continuity of supply.

- *Competence of technical staff* Conversations with design, research or laboratory staff indicate their knowledge of the latest materials, tools and processes relating to their products and anticipated developments in their industry.

■ *Competence of management* All the above areas are, in essence, a reflection of management and, therefore, indicate its quality. Particularly in the case of a new supplier, an accurate appraisal of executive personnel is of paramount importance.

11.9 Supplier approval

Supplier approval is the recognition, following a process of appraisal, that a particular supplier is able to meet the standards and requirements of the particular buyer. The approval may be for a one-off transaction or mean that the supplier is put on a list of approved suppliers.

There are three important aspects of approved supplier lists:

■ the current emphasis is on having a small supplier base and so additions to an approved list must be carefully controlled

■ when an application to be placed on an approved list emanated from the supplier, this should have been considered fairly and, as far as possible with the minimum of bureaucracy

■ directives such as those of the EU have reservations about whether or not approved lists invalidate the EU principles of transparency, equality of treatment, proportionality and mutual recognition.

Approval should be decided by a cross-functional team that may give various levels of approval, such as A for unconditional, B for conditional subject to the potential supplier meeting prescribed conditions or C for unsuitable for approval.

Approved suppliers may also be graded into such categories as:[14]

1 *partnership* a one-to-one relationship with a supplier in which a corporate single-source agreement will be in place

2 *preferred* there is an agreed number of suppliers for one product or service with a corporate agreement

3 *approved suppliers* suppliers have been assessed as satisfactory suppliers for one or more products or services

4 *confirmed suppliers* those that have been specifically requested by a user, such as design or production, and accepted by purchasing – the acceptance process being:

   (a) no preferred, partnership or approved supplier is on the purchasing database for an identical requirement

   (b) there will be no continuing demand on the supplier

5 *one-off supplier* suppliers in this category are accepted on the following conditions:

   (a) no preferred, partnership or approved supplier is on the purchasing database for identical goods or services

   (b) purchasing card payment is not appropriate or possible

   (c) supplier will be closed after the transaction is complete.

In general, approval in the first instance should be for one year. Suppliers that consistently meet or exceed the prescribed standards over a period of, say, three years may be upgraded from 'approved' to 'preferred'. Conversely, suppliers that fail to meet performance standards should be removed from the database of approved suppliers.

11.10 Evaluating supplier performance

11.10.1 Why evaluate supplier performance?

There are various reasons for the evaluation of purchasing performance being important.

- Evaluation can significantly improve supplier performance. Emptoris[15] states that, properly done, supplier performance management can provide answers to questions such as the following.
  - Who are the highest-quality suppliers?
  - How can relationships with the best suppliers be enhanced?
  - How can supplier performance be incorporated into total cost analysis?
  - How can buyers ensure that suppliers live up to what was promised?
  - How can feedback be shared based on experience with a supplier?
  - How can underperforming suppliers' problems be tracked and fixed?
- Evaluation assists decision making regarding when a supplier is retained or removed from an approved list.
- Evaluation assists in deciding with which suppliers a specific order should be placed.
- Evaluation provides suppliers with an incentive for continuous improvement and prevents performance 'slippage'.
- Evaluation can assist in decisions regarding how to distribute the spend for an item among several suppliers to better manage risk.

11.10.2 What to evaluate?

Traditionally, the key performance indicators (KPIs) for the evaluation of supplier performance have been price, quality and delivery. While these are still basic to supplier evaluation, such developments as JIT, lean manufacturing, integrated supply chains and e-procurement have made the fuller evaluation of supplier relationships an important consideration. Such relationships, as Kozak and Cohen[16] point out, include such qualitative factors as intercompany communication and high levels of trust, which are not easy to assess other than subjectively. Apart from subjectivity qualitative evaluations are often subject to 'halo effects' – the tendency to bias in favour of a particular supplier due to irrelevant considerations, such as the friendly approach of its sales representatives. There is, however, an element of subjectivity in all evaluation systems.

The number of KPIs that may be used is almost limitless. A USA survey by Simpson et al.[17] reported 142 evaluation items, which they arranged under 19 categories of criteria, the first 10 of which are shown in Table 11.3.

The researchers conclude that, on the basis of these criteria, suppliers should concentrate on quality issues first – especially the ability to meet customers' order requirements – followed by continuous improvement and innovation efforts. Importantly, while not completely ignoring pricing issues, suppliers may want to place less emphasis on price when attempting to secure and retain customers.

Table 11.3 Supplier evaluation factors considered by relative frequency of mention and importance (Simpson, Siguaw, and White[17]) – first ten factors only

Evaluation criteria	Number of items by category	Percentage mentioning	Relative importance rating
Quality and process control	566	24.9	1
Continuous improvement	210	9.2	2
Facility environment	188	8.2	2
Customer relationship	187	8.2	2
Delivery	185	8.1	2
Inventory and warehousing	158	7.0	2
Ordering	132	5.8	2
Financial conditions	126	5.5	2
Certifications	81	3.6	3
Price	81	3.6	3

11.10.3 Quantitative approaches to supplier evaluation

The aim of quantitative ratings is to provide a sounder basis for evaluation than subjective ratings. The main problems of quantitative ratings relate to the following.

- The high cost of collecting the data on which ratings are based. Quality ratings, for example, require data relating to the costs of defect prevention, detection and correction, involving considerable subanalysis of what is involved under each heading. This problem has, however, been largely overcome by the development of appropriate software. Such programs collect and process quality and delivery performance data from all or specified suppliers (the latter are normally suppliers of critical or high-cost items identified on an A, B, C or Pareto basis). From the data, ratings and reports are provided monthly, quarterly or at other required intervals.

- Ratings may give the impression of scientific accuracy whereas, in fact, they are no more accurate than the assumptions on which they are based.

- Supplier performance is often affected by circumstances outside the control of the vendor.

Hollingsworth[18] lists seven common supplier rating methods, of which six are set out in Table 11.4. The other method – the matrix method – is seldom used.

11.10.4 Scorecards

Ratings are usually presented in the form of a scorecard that provides objective measurements of performance and indicates the supplier's conformance to requirements. Horton[19] points out that the term 'scorecard' is borrowed from the academic report card on which pupil performance is measured in terms of several subject grades and other performance indicators, such as homework, attendance, class participation and class behaviour. Scores for each performance indicator are then aggregated to give an overall grade that provides feedback that should act as an incentive to improvement.

Table 11.4 Common supplier performance rating methods (adapted from Hollingsworth[18])

Method	Description	Advantages	Disadvantages	Application
Subjective	Generally designed as questionnaires with a numerical rating scale (say 1–5), completed by a number of reviewers	■ Easy to develop and administer ■ Can be completed by an unlimited number of reviewers	■ After first survey, method loses its impact ■ No objective basis and ratings may be subject to 'halo' effect and short-term memory ■ If 5 evaluators can answer 10 questions for 50 suppliers on a quarterly basis, there will be 10,000 data entry points annually to enter into the database	■ Usually first attempt at a rating system ■ A simple approach for a small business with a small supplier base
Survey method	A purchased service in which a research organisation contacts a number of other customers and obtains their views on the performance of the supplier	■ Easy to implement ■ Research organisation provides regular updates	■ Expensive ■ Quality of data collected may be poor and depends on the source from which information is collected ■ Evaluation is based on the experience of other companies	■ Large corporations
Comparative method	Supplier is evaluated independently by evaluators on agreed factors, such as price, quality, delivery, etc. Individual ratings are then tabulated and a final rating awarded by the value team	■ Speed – can be used to quickly evaluate a supplier on a short-term basis ■ Easy to develop ■ May take the supplier's historical performance into consideration	■ Relative importance of various rating factors not considered ■ Not applicable to long-term evaluation of supplier performance ■ Dependent on subjective opinions of the evaluators ■ Easily 'rigged' by an evaluator to give desired outcome	■ Traditionally used to compare multiple suppliers prior to the award of a contract or select from an approved list ■ May be used in a manner similar to the subjective method

Method	Description			
Weighted point	A weighting factor is established for each of the areas that indicates the value of that area in relation to each of the other factors. A score is then assigned to each factor that indicates the supplier's performance. The score is multiplied by the weight and then averaged	■ Excellent tool for proposal evaluation ■ Allows evaluators to take all factors into account, yet provides the facility to emphasise the importance of one factor over another	■ Less useful for long-term evaluation as evaluators may lose interest ■ Data entry may become excessively time-consuming ■ Labour-intensive ■ The information has no objective basis and may be based on short-term memory	■ Used primarily as a tool for the long-term rating of suppliers
Percentage-based method	Percentage systems measure the percentage of quality defects or late deliveries – if a supplier has made 8 late deliveries out of 64, that supplier would be given a rating of $12\frac{1}{2}$ or 13, for example	■ Easy to accumulate data ■ Provides compliance targets and expectations, such as 'excellent' – 95–100 per cent; versus 'good' – 90–94 per cent and 'acceptable' – 85–89 per cent	■ Data may be accurate but misleading on the number of receipts or types of problems encountered by a particular supplier ■ Doesn't reflect the severity of quality problems ■ Doesn't accurately reflect level of on-time performance. If 1 delivery in 100 is late 3 days, or 60 days, a percentage-based system will still give a percentage of 1 per cent.	■ Initially the percentage method was applied to quality and later expanded to include delivery performance
Cost-based method	Evaluates supplier performance on total non-productive costs associated with each supplier's performance. Non-productive costs are estimated costs of non-compliance, such as cost of rejection – £200 returning suppliers – £75–£150 These are added to actual cost $$\text{Performance index} = \frac{\text{Purchase order price} + \text{Non-productive cost}}{\text{Purchase order price}}$$	■ Suppliers are held responsible for their actions ■ Promotes supplier improvement more rapidly than other methods ■ Provides suppliers with the level of detail they need to understand the issues and additional costs associated with their performance ■ Suppliers have greater motivation to improve their performance	■ Difficult to build internally ■ Difficulty of determining non-productive cost ranges	

Performance indicators such as product prices, delivery performance, customer satisfaction and percentage of defects and errors on delivered products are, as stated earlier, usually weighted to indicate their relative importance, such as:

Performance indicator	Weight × rating	Adjusted score
Price	20 × 4	80
Quality	40 × 3	120
Delivery	20 × 4	80
Customer satisfaction	20 × 3	60
		340

The weighted score is then averaged by dividing the number of performance indicators – that is, 340/4 = 85. The rating on a five-point scale may be:

1 = unsatisfactory

2 = marginal

3 = satisfactory

4 = very good

5 = outstanding

The level of performance achieved can then be compared with the level anticipated. Thus a level of 85 is unsatisfactory for quality if the standard prescribed is zero defects.

Supplier performance scorecards are, however, being increasingly superseded by integrated supplier performance management systems providing:

■ real-time visibility into performance across all products and suppliers

■ complicated supplier evaluations utilising data from all elements of the supply chain

■ actionable alerts whenever suppliers exceed defined KPI thresholds

■ immediate communication to suppliers regarding performance.

11.10.5 Service levels

Service levels are performance requirements that are usually divided in contracts for outsourcing and the provision of internal support services. Service-level agreements normally prescribe penalties for non-compliance with the prescribed levels.

Lysons[20] states that service levels should be:

■ *reasonable* as unnecessarily high service levels may entail higher charges and focus the attention of service providers on those aspects of service that they are being monitored on with possible reduced attention on those that are not

■ *prioritised by the customer* – that is, customers should identify the aspects of a required service that are important and prioritise them in order along an agreed scale, so computer software errors may be categorised as (1) 'critical'; (2) 'major'; (3) 'urgent'; (4) 'important' and (5) 'minor'. A three-point scale might be criteria that are (1) 'most important', (2) 'important', (3) 'less important'

■ *easily monitored* – this means avoiding the specification of levels that are subjective, intangible or incapable of quantification, such as 'the provider will furnish a high level of service', which is meaningless

■ *readily understood* by the staffs of both customers and providers.

Table 11.5 **Dimensions of service quality (Zeithaml, Parasuraman and Berry[21])**

Dimension	Definition	Example
Tangibles	Appearance of physical facilities, equipment, staff and communication material	Does the service provider have user-friendly sales material? Are staff members good at their jobs?
Reliability	Ability to perform the promised service dependably and accurately	Is the contracted service always delivered on time and to specification?
Responsiveness	Willingness to help customers and provide prompt service	Do service staff always try to assist customers, especially with exceptional problems and situations?
Assurance	Customer confidence in the service providers based on belief in their competence, courtesy, credibility and security	Customers return to the service provider whenever the need arises
Empathy	Customer confidence that the service provider will identify with the customers' service requirements and expectations in relation to ease of access, good two-way communication and understanding	Customers return to the service provider whenever the need arises

The performance criteria for service levels may be both general and specific.

General factors include those identified by Zeithaml et al.[21] that applied to an assessment tool SERVQUAL, the aim of which is to measure both customer expectations and satisfactions in specific service applications or providers. The five dimensions of service quality identified by the above writers are set out in Table 11.5.

Specific factors vary according to the nature of the service and individual customer.

11.10.6 The ten Cs of effective supplier evaluation

Many of the aspects of supplier appraisal are neatly summarised by Carter[22] as the 'seven Cs of supplier evaluation':

- *competency* of the supplier to undertake the tasks required
- *capacity* of the supplier to meet the purchaser's total needs
- *commitment* of the supplier to the customer in terms of quality, cost driving and service
- *control systems* in relation to inventory, costs, budgets, people and information
- *cash resources and financial stability* ensuring that the selected supplier is financially sound and is able to continue in business into the foreseeable future
- *cost* commensurate with quality and service
- *consistency* the ability of the supplier to deliver consistently and, where possible, improve levels of quality and service.

Figure 11.2 **Procurement targeting matrix**

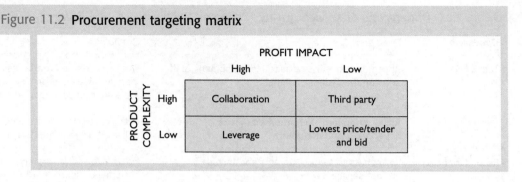

Three further 'Cs' not identified by Carter are:

- *culture* suppliers and purchasers should share similar values
- *clean* suppliers and products should satisfy legislative and other environmental requirements
- *communication* can the supplier communicate and receive information electronically?

Sadly, some suppliers are also confused, complicated, complacent, comedians and contradictory!

Carter goes on to state that, having established that the supplier has the appropriate attributes to be an effective supplier, the next step is to define some contingent system of weighting the seven Cs relative to each other and their impact on the business and offers the procurement targeting matrix shown in Figure 11.2 as a method of prioritising each 'C' according to the complexity of the product and the impact on profit. Thus, for a specification, such factors as cost, consistency and commitment might be given more weight than cash resources and financial stability.

11.11 Policy issues in sourcing

There are numerous aspects of sourcing policy and strategy, but eight of the main ones considered in this chapter are shown in Figure 11.3.

Figure 11.3 **Aspects of sourcing policy and strategy**

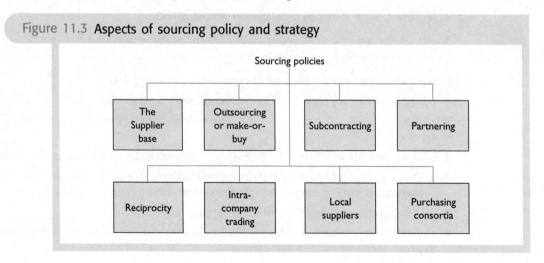

11.12 The supplier base

11.12.1 What is the supplier base?

The supplier base relates to the number, range, location and characteristics of the vendors that supply the purchaser.

Supplier bases may be described as broad, lean, narrow, single-sourced, local, national, international, diversified or specialised. They can relate to a 'family' of related products and suppliers or the totality of vendors with whom a purchaser does business.

Factors influencing the supply base of an enterprise include:

- the core competences of the enterprise
- make, buy, outsourcing and subcontracting decisions
- single, multiple and partnership decisions
- tiering
- international and global sourcing
- countertrade, intercompany trading and reciprocal trade
- risk aspects, especially in relation to ensuring continuity of supply
- miscellaneous factors, such as the social responsibilities of a large company to local industry or the support of small companies.

11.12.2 Supplier base optimisation

Supplier base optimisation or rationalisation is concerned with determining the approximate number of suppliers with whom the purchaser will do business. The need for such rationalisation derives from:

- the requirement to control cost and procurement processes as a large number of suppliers will entail higher administrative costs than a smaller number and e-procurement will usually lead to a rationalisation of supplier bases by integrating business processes and data with key suppliers and facilitating collaborative relationships
- the need to eliminate suppliers incapable of meeting the purchaser's performance requirements or from whom few purchases are made.

The aim of supplier base optimisation is therefore to leverage the buying power of an organisation with the smallest number of suppliers consistent with security of supplies and the need for high-quality goods and services at competitive prices.

Supplier base optimisation will therefore commence with an analysis of the existing supply base and the evaluation of suppliers according to criteria such as performance, cost, service and quality and the amount of business transacted during a specified period. Such an analysis may result in supplier base consolidation as a result of such approaches as:

- an approved or preferred supplier list
- selection of a single supplier with whom to develop partnership or other collaborative arrangements.

The advantages of supplier base rationalisation include:

- savings in administrative costs
- up to 80 per cent of supplies met by selected vendors
- the development of long-term partnerships and supplier associations
- improved standardisation
- elimination of or reduction in maverick purchases
- lower total production costs.

11.12.3 Possible risks of a reduced supplier base

These include:

- overdependency on a single supplier
- danger of supply disruption due to strikes, production breakdowns, floods or similar natural disasters, disruption of suppliers' suppliers
- loss of supplier's goodwill
- reduced competition
- failure to seek new or more competitive suppliers.

11.13 Outsourcing

11.13.1 What is outsourcing?

Verikatesan[23] observes that 'Today manufacturing focus means learning how *not* to make things – how *not* to make the parts that divert a company from cultivating its skills, parts that its suppliers can make more efficiently.'

Outsourcing, may be defined as:

> a management strategy by which major non-core functions are transferred to specialist, efficient, external providers.

Central to outsourcing are:

- make-or-buy decisions
- partnerships between purchasers and suppliers – as outsourcing relationships are often unequal, it is sometimes suggested that such arrangements should be termed 'cosourcing'.

11.13.2 What to outsource?

Outsourcing developed as a reaction to the overdiversification of the 1970s and early 1980s. This led many enterprises to review their core activities and concentrate on their core competences – what the organisations believe that they do best. What to outsource may be considered under the headings of manufacturing and services.

According to the British government's market testing programme (1993), the activities most easily outsourced are those that are:

- resource-intensive – especially those with high labour or capital costs
- relatively discrete
- require specialist competences

- characterised by fluctuating work patterns in loading and throughput
- subject to quickly changing markets, for which it is costly to recruit, train and retain staff
- subject to rapidly changing technology, requiring expensive investment.

11.14 Outsourcing manufacturing

11.14.1 Types of make-or-buy decisions

This is concerned with make-or-buy decisions. Probert[24] identifies three levels of make-or-buy decisions.

Strategic make-or-buy decisions

Strategic make-or-buy decisions (see Figure 11.4) determine the shape and capability of the organisation's manufacturing operation by influencing:

- what products to make
- what investment to make in machines and labour to make the products
- ability to develop new products and processes as the knowledge and skills gained by manufacturing in-house may be critical for future applications
- the selection of suppliers as they may need to be involved in design and production processes.

Conversely, inappropriate allocation of work to suppliers may damage an enterprise by developing a new competitor or damaging product quality or performance, profitabilities, risk and flexibility.

Strategic decisions also provide the framework for shorter-term tactical and component decisions.

Figure 11.4 Decision processes for make or buy

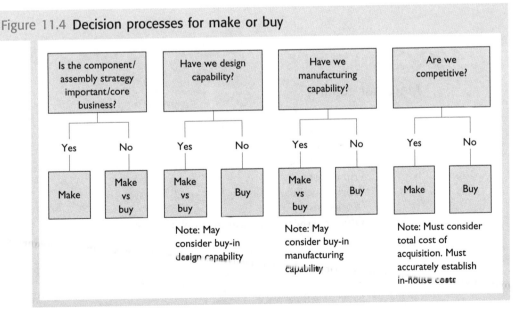

Source: by permission of the Society of British Aerospace Companies

Tactical make-or-buy decisions

These deal with the issue of a temporary imbalance of manufacturing capacity:

■ changes in demand may make it impossible to make everything in-house, even though this is the preferred option

■ conversely, a fall in demand may cause the enterprise to bring in-house work that was previously bought-out, if this can be done without damaging supplier relationships and without defaulting on a contract.

In such situations, managers require criteria for choosing between the available options. Such criteria may be quantitative, qualitative or both.

Component make-or-buy decisions

Component make-or-buy decisions are made, ideally, at the design stage and relate to whether a particular component of the product should be made in-house or bought-in.

11.14.2 Cost factors in make-or-buy decisions

Accurate make-or-buy decisions often require the application of marginal costing and break-even analysis.

Marginal costing

Marginal costing is defined as:[25]

> a (costing) principle whereby variable costs are charged to cost units and the fixed costs attributable to the relevant period are written off in full against the contribution for that period.

The term 'contribution' in the above definition is the difference between the selling (or purchase price) and the variable cost per unit.

The marginal cost approach is shown by Examples 11.1 and 11.2.

Example 11.1

Marginal costing

	£
Direct materials	60
Direct pay	30
Direct expenses	10
Prime cost	100
Works overhead (100 per cent on direct pay)	30
Works cost	130
Office overhead (20 per cent on works cost)	26
	156
Selling overheads £14 per item	14
Cost of sales	170
Net profit	30
Normal selling price	200

Assume that:

1 works overheads are 60 per cent fixed and 40 per cent variable

2 office overheads are constant

3 selling expenses are 50 per cent fixed and 50 per cent variable.

Then, the *marginal* cost will be:

	£	
Direct materials	60	
Direct pay	30	
Direct expenses	10	
	100	
Works overhead	12	(40 per cent of £30)
Selling overheads £14 per item	13	(50 per cent of £26)
	125	

Any price over £125 represents a *contribution* to fixed overheads. If fixed overheads totalled £75,000, a selling price of £200 would represent a contribution of £75 per item to fixed overheads and it would be necessary to sell 1000 items before the undertaking would *break even*. If, however, the selling price were reduced to £150, it would be necessary to sell 3000 units before reaching the *break-even point* as the contribution per item would be only £25.

In make-or-buy decisions, it is necessary to compare the vendor's price with the marginal cost of making, plus the loss of contributions of work displaced.

Example 11.2

Marginal costing

A company manufactures assembly JMA 423, the normal annual usage of which is 10,000 units. The current costs are:

	£
Materials	90
Labour	40
Variable overheads	10
Fixed overheads	20
	160

The component could be purchased for £156 but the capacity used for its production would then be idle. Only 30 per cent of the fixed costs is recoverable if the component is bought.

Assuming that there are no other relevant factors, should component JMA 423 be made or bought?

Solution

A superficial comparison suggests that the item should be bought rather than made. The correct comparison, however, is between the marginal cost of making and the buying price.

	Make	Buy	Difference
Variable costs (£90 + £40 + £10) = £140	£140	£156	£16
Variable costs × volume	£1,400,000	£1,560,000	
Fixed costs (30 per cent of £20 × 10,000 units)	£60,000	£60,000	
	£1,460,000	£1,620,000	£160,000

The above figures indicate that it is more profitable to make than buy. This is because the fixed costs of £60,000 would be likely to continue and, as the capacity would be unused, the fixed overheads would not be absorbed into production. Consequently, by buying instead of making, profits would be reduced by £160,000.

Opportunity cost

As shown by Example 11.3, this is the potential benefit that is forgone because one course of action has been chosen over another – that is, if the production facilities used in making had been applied to some alternative purpose.

Example 11.3

Opportunity cost

An undertaking manufacturers 100,000 of item X at a total cost of £120,000 and a marginal cost of £100,000. Item X could be bought-out for £1.50 each. The decision whether to make it in-house or buy-out depends on the cost of forgoing the opportunity to make something else. If the production capacity could be used to make an item with a contribution of £0.75 each, then the position would be:

Making	Buying but production capacity not used	Buying less opportunity cost
£100,000	£150,000	£150,000
		−£75,000
		£75,000

In this case, it would be more profitable to buy the item.

Break-even

The break-even point is:

The level of activity in units or value at which the total revenues equal total costs.

Estimated production quotas and actual usage may differ. See Example 11.4.

Learning curves

Learning curves are dealt with in 16.11. Suffice to say here, therefore, that when components are bought from a specialist manufacturer, there may be little opportunity for learning. When the items are new, however, the costs of both making and buying may have to be adjusted to take account of a learning factor. In comparing made in-house

> ### Example 11.4
>
> ## Break-even analysis
>
> Using the data in Example 11.2, at what volume will the company be indifferent between buying and making component JMA 423?
>
> ### Solution
>
> This is found by the formula:
>
> $$\frac{F}{(P - V)}$$
>
> where:
>
> F = fixed costs
> P = purchase price
> V = variable cost per unit
>
> In this case:
>
> $$\frac{£60,000}{(£156 - £140)} = \frac{£60,000}{16} = 3750 \text{ units}$$
>
> If only 3750 units are required, there will be no effect on profits from making or buying. If fewer than 3750 units are required, buying is the more profitable alternative. If more than 3750 units are required, making is the better alternative.

and bought-out prices, therefore, learning is a factor that must be considered, where applicable.

11.14.3 Other considerations in make-or-buy decisions

Apart from those mentioned above, a number of other quantitative and qualitative factors must be considered in deciding whether to make or buy.

Quantitative factors in favour of *making* include:

- chance to use up idle capacity and resources
- potential lead time reduction
- possibility of scrap utilisation
- greater purchasing power with larger orders of a particular material
- large overhead recovery base
- exchange rate risks
- cost of work is known in advance.

Quantitative factors in favour of *buying* include:

- quantities required too small for economic production
- avoidance of costs of specialist machinery or labour
- reduction in inventory.

Qualitative factors in favour of *making* include:

- ability to manage resources
- commercial and contractual advantages
- worries are eliminated regarding such matters as the stability and continuing viability of suppliers or possible repercussions of changes in supplier ownership
- maintaining secrecy.

Qualitative factors in favour of *buying* include:

- spread of financial risk between purchaser and vendor
- ability to control quality when purchased from outside
- availability of vendor's specialist expertise, machinery and/or patents
- buying, in effect, augments the manufacturing capacity of the purchaser.

11.14.4 Making the make-or-buy decision

From the above, it is clear that, irrespective of whether it relates to the strategic, tactical or component levels, many quantitative and qualitative factors have to be considered when arriving at a make-or-buy decision. The approach shown in Figure 11.4 earlier is a simple procedure for answering the question 'Shall we make or buy?'

11.15 Outsourcing services

11.15.1 Categorisation of services

Most outsourcing relates to services. The range of services that can be outsourced is almost limitless and those listed below represent just a few of the possibilities:

- car park management
- cleaning
- building repairs and maintenance
- catering
- security
- transport management
- waste disposal
- reception
- library
- medical/welfare
- travel administration
- pest control
- training centre management
- computers and IT
- research and development
- estate management
- staff recruitment
- internal audit
- legal services
- payroll
- quality assurance and control
- records management
- asset repair
- telemarketing
- translation services
- customs brokerage
- vehicle maintenance.

As service undertakings tend to be less capital-intensive than manufacturing companies, there is usually a large supplier base, especially for less specialised services, such as catering and building repairs. The drafting of service contracts and service-level agreements that may extend over several years does, however, tend to be complicated and involve considerable negotiation.

11.15.2 Outsourcing purchasing

Organisations may consider outsourcing purchasing in the following circumstances.

- Where purchasing is a peripheral rather than a core activity. The characteristics of peripheral work, as identified by Atkinson and Meager,[26] are that it has:
  - low or generalised skill requirements
  - internally focused responsibilities
  - well-defined or limited tasks
  - jobs that are easily separated from other work
  - no supply restrictions.

  These are also the characteristics of low-level operational purchasing. Beauchamp[27] also identified the following items as suitable for outsourcing consideration:
  - purchase orders, one-off and repeat needs
  - locally and nationally procured needs (international sourcing and procurement may be rather specialised for outsourcing)
  - low-value or low-value/large order acquisitions
  - brand name requirements
  - call-offs against internally approved agreements
  - set-up of commodity- or service-based contracts
  - obtaining goods for batch or volume manufacturing
  - stocking and providing for private- or public-sector needs
  - computerised purchasing or software-based manufacturing procurement
  - all administration and paperwork associated with purchasing needs
  - supply of stores staff at varying levels of skill
  - multidimensional and multidepartmental sourcing.
- Where the supply base is small and based on proven cooperation and there are no supply restrictions, the following may be outsourced:
  - well-defined or limited tasks
  - jobs that are easily separated from other work
  - jobs that have no supply restrictions.

  The above characteristics also apply to low-level operational purchasing.
- Where there is a small supplier base providing non-strategic, non-critical, low-cost/low-risk items. In such cases, purchasing may be outsourced to:
  - specialist purchasing and suppliers organisations
  - buying consortia.

  Such organisations provide the advantage of:
  - bulk purchasing, giving them a strong negotiating position over a wide range of products.

11.16 What not to outsource

Rothery and Robinson[28] state that none of the following should be outsourced without careful consideration:

- management of strategic planning
- management of finances
- management of management consultancy
- control of supplies
- quality and environmental management
- the supervision of the meeting of regulatory requirements such as product liability, misleading advertising, quality, environmental regulations, staff health and safety, public safety, product/service safety.

11.17 Drivers of outsourcing

Beulen et al.[29] suggest that there are five main drivers for outsourcing.

- *Quality* Actual capacity is temporarily insufficient to comply with demand. The quality motive can be subdivided into three aspects: increased quality demands, shortage of qualified personnel, outsourcing as a transition period.
- *Cost* Outsourcing is a possible solution to increasing costs and is compatible with a cost leadership strategy. By controlling and decreasing costs, a company can increase its competitive position.
- *Finance* A company has a limited investment budget. The funds must be used for investments in core business activities, which are long-term decisions.
- *Core business* A core business is a primary activity that enables an organisation to generate revenues. To concentrate on core business activities is a strategic decision. All subsequent activities are mainly supportive and should be outsourced.
- *Cooperation* Cooperation between companies can lead to conflict. In order to avoid such conflict, those activities that are produced by both organisations should be subject to total outsourcing.

A further factor is that of human resource management. The internal culture and attitude of employees may result in strong trade union and internal opposition to the introduction of necessary changes in work processes and restructuring. Such changes may also require the acquisition of new employee skills. Outsourcing may avoid conflicts and provide expertise and experience within a matter of days to fill gaps for which recruitment and training would take some time.

Monczka[30] observes that, historically, outsourcing decisions have been limited to decisions about a particular outsource instead of the more holistic approach of asking 'Looking at the entire supply chain, who would be doing what?'

11.18 Types of outsourcing

In relation to IT, Lacity and Hirscheim[31] provide a taxonomy of outsourcing options categorised as body shop, project management and total outsourcing.

- *Body shop outsourcing* is a situation where management uses outsourcing as a means of meeting short-term requirements, such as a shortage of in-house skills to meet a temporary demand.
- *Project management outsourcing* is employed for all or part of a particular project, such as developing a new IT project, training in new skills, management consultancy.
- *Total outsourcing* is where the outsourcing supplier is given full responsibility for a selected area, such as catering, security.

11.19 Benefits of outsourcing

The main benefit identified by organisations that have adopted outsourcing is the freeing of management time to concentrate on core business operations. Other benefits are shown in Figure 11.5. Additional reasons for outsourcing include to:

- gain access to world class capabilities
- improve organisational focus
- make capital funds available.

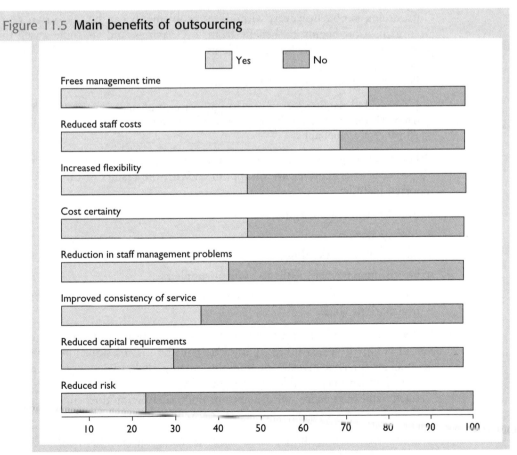

Figure 11.5 **Main benefits of outsourcing**

Source: taken from Carrington, L., 1994[32]

Figure 11.6 **Problems with outsourcing**

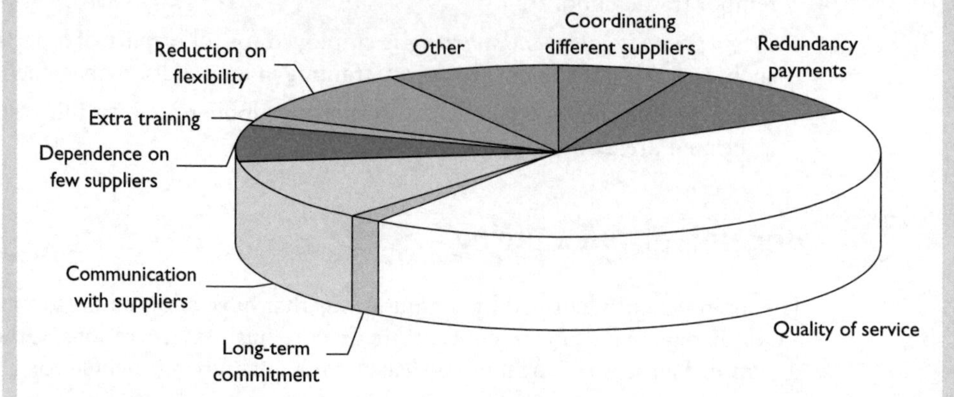

Source: taken from Carrington, L., 1994[33]

11.20 Problems of outsourcing

Outsourcing is not, however, without its problems. It can be up to two years before an organisation begins to benefit from any savings and in some cases the whole process is cost neutral. Some problems associated with outsourcing are shown in Figure 11.6.

Perkins[34] reports that an informal survey of his clients showed that:

> By the end of the first year, more than 50 per cent of the companies that have outsourced major IT functions are unhappy with their outsources . . . By the end of the second year 70 per cent are unhappy.

Other surveys relating to aspects of outsourcing have shown that between 30 and 50 per cent of executives are disappointed with the results of outsourcing. Problems reported include:

- overdependence on suppliers
- cost escalation
- lack of supplier flexibility
- lack of management skills to control suppliers
- unrealistic expectations of outsourcing providers due to over-promising at the negotiations stage.

Reilly and Tamkin[35] mention that a principal objection to outsourcing is the possible loss of competitive advantage, particularly in the loss of skills and expertise of staff, insufficient internal investment and the passing of knowledge and expertise to the supplier, which may be able to seize the initiative.

Lacity and Hirscheim[36] also point out that outsourcing does not seem to work well in the following areas:

- where a specific or unique knowledge of the business is required
- where all services are customised

■ where the employee culture is too fragmented or hostile for the organisation to come back together.

Problems reported in relation to outsourced suppliers include:

■ high staff turnover
■ poor project management skills
■ lack of commitment to the client or industry
■ shallow expertise
■ insufficient documentation
■ lack of control over larger suppliers
■ poor staff training
■ complacency over time
■ divergent interests of the customer and provider
■ cultural mismatches between customer and provider organisations.

11.21 Implementing outsourcing

The decision to outsource should be made after a consideration of the issues shown in Figure 11.7. Once it has been decided to outsource, the following steps need to be followed to implement that decision.

Figure 11.7 Seven steps to making a decision about strategic outsourcing

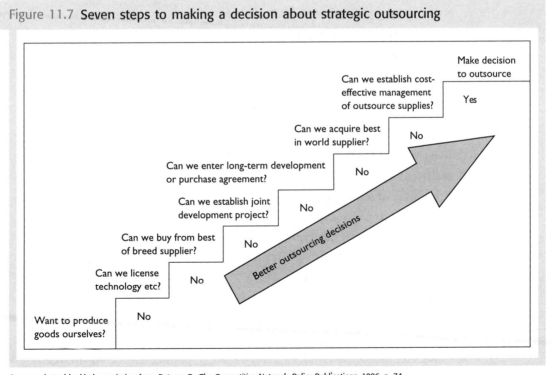

Source: adapted by kind permission from Batram, P., *The Competitive Network*, Policy Publications, 1996, p. 74

1 Consider the alternatives shown in Figure 11.7.

2 Set up a working party to consider:

- what to outsource
- why (strategic reasons)
- cost comparisons of internal and external provision
- anticipated benefits and problems
- possible effects on staff, capital, finance and competitiveness.

3 Prepare, as appropriate, a technical performance or technical specification. An example of a statement of source requirements (SSR) prepared by the Central Computer and Telecommunications Agency (CCTA)[37] for market testing in relation to IS/IT services is shown in Table 11.6. The SSR describes the job needing to be done, not the means for achieving it, and is not an invitation to tender. An SSR should be divided into three sections that:

- select the source (sections 1, 2 and 3)
- specify the requirements (sections 4, 5 and 6)
- provide rules for those responding to the SSR (section 7).

4 Consider possible suppliers.

5 Invite tenders against the specification.

6 Evaluate tenders against predetermined evaluation criteria.

7 Post-tender negotiation. Lacity and Hirscheim[38] provide the following advice relating to outsourcing contract negotiations:

- discard the vendor's standard contract
- do not sign incomplete contracts
- hire outsourcing experts
- measure everything in the baseline period
- develop service-level measures
- develop service-level reports
- specify escalation procedures
- include penalties for non-performance
- determine growth
- adjust charges to changes in business volume
- select your account manager
- include step in rights termination clause
- beware of 'change in character' clauses
- take care of your people.

8 Award contract.

9 Set up management control and monitoring processes.

Patton[39] recommends the following checklist of points to cover when negotiating outsourcing contracts. The checklist can be used to evaluate and compare the responses of potential outsourcing providers on the specified key issues, which are:

Table 11.6 **Model contents list for an SSR**

Section	Contents
1 Introduction	■ General information ■ Background to SSR ■ Purpose and composition of the SSR
2 Background	■ Description of business ■ Business requirements to be supported ■ Market testing objectives
3 Scope of SSR	■ Services included ■ Services excluded ■ Service options ■ Relationship with other providers
4 Service requirements	■ Service-specific requirements ■ Service levels ■ Performance measurement ■ Security and audit ■ Sustainability ■ Start-up and acceptance
5 Service management	■ Roles and responsibilities ■ Management review process ■ Change control
6 Constraints	■ Service constraints ■ Standards, methods and best practice ■ Contractual matters
7 Instructions to providers	■ Timetable for procurement ■ Format for proposals ■ Terms and conditions for submission of proposals ■ Evaluation approach ■ Further information

Supporting annexes	■ Business facts and figures
	■ Current IS/IT details:
	   – organisation
	   – costs and contractual commitments
	   – technical environment
	■ Mandatory requirements
	■ Desirable requirements

■ the total cost of providing outsourcing for the function
■ escalation requirements and response
■ asset valuation
■ hiring existing personnel
■ return of assets
■ change management

- escape clauses and exit strategies
- disposition of existing personnel
- reference checks from existing customers
- licence fees and transfers
- ability to extend or renegotiate the agreement
- transition planning and cost
- damage provisions
- dispute resolution process
- ownership of assets
- learning curve applications
- return of files, data and proprietary information
- non-competitive pay and benefit requirements
- insurance and/or bonding of the outsourcer.

Washington[40] suggests the following performance measures as being applicable to the outsourcing of IT functions. Such measures may, however, be adapted to other outsourcing areas.

- *Response time* an average or specific response time for the maintenance of critical equipment.
- *Availability* what is to be provided on a daily shift or application basis.
- *Downtime* equipment shall not be down or the supplier unavailable for more than a specified amount of time.
- *Turnaround time or schedule of performance* specify either a specific time for repairs to equipment or a particular performance time for services.
- *Performance reports* specify general performance criteria considered important to the outsourcing effort.
- *Penalties for non-performance* to emphasise the importance of meeting specific performance requirements.
- *Satisfactory performance statement* state the organisation's expectations of the vendor. These expectations need to be clearly specified.
- *Subcontractor approval rights* these should be built into the contract to aid in specifying what aspects of the work are to be handled only by the primary vendor.

Cost comparisons between those of the contractor and those of other providers should be undertaken at regular intervals. These comparisons can, for example, be made monthly on the basis of cost reports submitted by contractors. When compared with agreed target costs they can be the basis of incentive payments for improving on target costs or penalties for exceeding such standards or may provide a basis for negotiation.

11.22 Subcontracting

11.22.1 What is subcontracting?

Subcontracting may be distinguished from outsourcing in that the latter involves the total restructuring of an enterprise around core competences and outside relationships.

Whatever the degree of outsourcing, enterprises must retain certain core capabilities. Outsourcing is a strategic long-term decision. Subcontracting is a tactical, short-term approach.

> If you want the most beautiful lawn in the neighbourhood and you hire someone to take responsibility for every aspect of lawn care, including cutting the grass, weed control, watering and fertilising it's strategic sourcing. But hiring someone to only cut your lawn is subcontracting.[41]

11.22.2 Reasons for subcontracting

The buyer encounters problems that call for subcontracting in two main areas:

- where the buyer's organisation is the employer or client entrusting work to a main contractor who, in turn, subcontracts part of the work, which is the case with most construction contracts
- where the buyer's organisation is the main contractor and subcontracts work for such reasons as:
  - overloading of machinery or labour
  - to ensure completion of work on time
  - lack of specialist machinery or specialist know-how
  - to avoid acquiring long-term capacity when future demand is uncertain
  - subcontracting is cheaper than manufacturing internally.

11.22.3 Organisation for subcontracting

- When subcontracting is a regular and significant part of the activity of an undertaking, it may be desirable to set up a special subcontracting section within or external to the purchasing department.
- Arrangements must be made for adequate liaison between all departments connected with subcontracting – design, production control, construction and site staff, inspection, finance and so on.
- Friction over who should negotiate with the selected suppliers sometimes develops between purchasing and design or technical departments. This can be avoided by a proper demarcation of authority and responsibility, purchasing having a power of commercial veto, design a design veto and technical departments a technical veto.

11.22.4 Selection of subcontractors

It may be necessary to check whether or not external approval of the selected subcontractor is necessary, as in government contracts or where a specific subcontractor has been specified by the client. Certain construction contracts may provide that subcontractors must not be selected on the basis of Dutch auctions.

11.22.5 Liaison with subcontractors

Matters to be considered include the following:

- planning, to ensure that the subcontractor can complete by the required date – techniques such as program, evaluation and review techniques (PERT) are of assistance in this

■ ensuring that the subcontractor is supplied with the most recent copies of all necessary documentation, including drawings, standards and planning instructions

■ arranging with the subcontractor for the supply, by the main contractor, of materials, tooling, specialist equipment and so on and the basis on which this shall be charged

■ control of equipment and materials in the possession of subcontractors

■ arrangements for returns at stocktaking of free issued materials in the possession of the subcontractor

■ arrangements for visits to the premises of the subcontractor by progress and inspection staff employed by the main contractor

■ arrangements for transportation, especially where items produced by the subcontractor require special protection, such as components with a highly finished surface

■ payment for any ancillary work to be performed by the subcontractor, such as painting on of part numbers.

11.22.6 Legal factors

These will depend on the circumstances of the specific contract. All major contracts for subcontracting should be vetted by the legal department of the main contractor. Where the buyer's undertaking is the client entrusting work to a main contractor, it is useful to remember the following generic principles.

Unless the contract has been placed on the basis – express or implied – that the work will be wholly performed by the main contractor, the client will have no authority to prevent the subcontracting of part of the work (this will not apply to contracts for personal service). If, therefore, the client wishes to specify particular subcontractors or to limit the right of the main contractor to subcontract, these matters must be negotiated when the order is placed. With construction and defence contracts, tenderers are often required to state what parts of the work will be subcontracted. In particular, it is useful to include clauses stating that it is the duty of the main contractor to use best endeavours in the selection of subcontractors and that responsibility for the performance of these subcontractors shall lie with the main contractor exclusively.

11.23 Partnering

11.23.1 Partnering and outsourcing

Humbert and Passarelli[42] point out that, at its highest level, outsourcing can take the form of an alliance akin to a partnership or joint venture. Not all outsourcing agreements, however, are partnerships. Humbert and Passarelli state that 'the terms "partnering" or "strategic alliance" should not be used to describe an outsourcing agreement unless the contract is structured to reflect a true relationship of strategic alliance'. The characteristics of such an alliance include close working relationships built on trust, communication and mutual dependency 'where both parties have a vested interest in reducing costs and achieving a favourable business outcome'. Where these conditions obtain, the provider's 'reward' is based on results or attaining objectives rather than being compensated.

When comparing partnering and outsourcing, it is therefore important to distinguish between:

■ *different levels of outsourcing* at the lower levels it will be purely transactional – only at the higher, strategic levels is outsourcing likely to merge into partnering

■ *customer–supplier relationships and partnering* in the former, the emphasis is primarily on cost minimisation, while with the latter the emphasis is additionally on value enhancement and the achievement of joint venture objectives

■ *the contractual differences between outsourcing and partnering* with the former, the contract relates to clearly specified inputs and these are cost-based over a defined period of time, for which the supplier receives an agreed reward, whereas, as the CIPS[43] points out, because partnerships are based on trust, in theory no form of contractual documentation should be necessary, but it is still desirable that the parties should agree to a set of general guidelines to regulate the partnership, such as the 12 key areas identified by Partnering Sourcing Ltd:

 – general statement of principle
 – scope – what the partnership encompasses
 – costs
 – customer service levels
 – business forecasts
 – technological development strategies
 – continuous improvement policy
 – annual performance objectives
 – mutual assistance to resolve any problems that may arise
 – open book cost structures
 – minimising material costs
 – joint decisions on capital investment projects

(two important omissions from the above list are those relating to intellectual property rights and ownership of patents).

11.23.2 What is partnering?

Reference was made in 7.5 to the stepladder of external and internal relationships presented by Cox, from which the concept of partnership sourcing was omitted on two grounds:

■ the concept of partnering is generic and refers to a range of collaborative relationships

■ the term partnership sourcing refers to all forms of non-adversarial collaborative relationships.

The need for a broad approach to the concept of partnering is also recognised by Partnership Sourcing Ltd,[44] which defines partnering as:

> A commitment to both customers and suppliers, regardless of size, to a long-term relationship based on clear, mutually agreed objectives to strive for world class capability.

There may, however, be degrees of partnership. Lambert et al.,[45] for example, distinguish between:

- *type I partnerships* involving organisations that recognise each other as partners and, on a limited basis, coordinate activities and planning – such partnerships generally have a short-term focus and involve only a few areas within each organisation

- *type II partnerships* involving organisations that have progressed beyond coordination to integration of activities – such partnerships have a longer-term view of the partnership and involve multiple areas within both firms

- *type III partnerships* involving organisations sharing a significant level of operational and strategic integration – in particular, each partner can make changes to the other's systems without getting approval and such partnerships are of long-term duration with no end in sight, each party viewing the other as an extension of its own firm.

As Knemeyer et al.[46] state:

> the three types of partnership reflect increased strength, long-term orientation and level of involvement between parties . . . No particular type of partnership is better or worse than any other. The key is to try to obtain the type of relationship that is most appropriate given the business situation.

Partnering marks a shift from traditional pressures exerted by larger customers on small- and medium-sized suppliers in which the latter were regarded as subordinates. Partnering aims to transform short-term adversarial customer–supplier relationships focused on the use of purchasing power to secure lower prices and improved delivery into long-term cooperation based on mutual trust in which quality, innovation and shared values complement price competitiveness.

Some comparisons between traditional and partnering relationships are shown in Table 11.7.

11.23.3 The drivers of partnership sourcing

Some of the main drivers for partnerships have been summarised by Southey[47] as:

- drive for lowest acquisition cost
  - not only price, but all 'cost in use' elements, such as the benefits or exposure derived from actual product quality, delivery performance and the administration burden
- reduction in supplier base
  - need to reduce the supplier base to a number that can be managed effectively
- shortening of product lifecycles
  - need for faster response times
  - need for suppliers to be right first time
  - need for supplier involvement from day 1
- concentration on core business
  - where most value can be added
  - where distinctive competences exist
  - avoiding unnecessary capital expenditure

Table 11.7 **Comparison of traditional and partnering supplier relationships**

Traditional	Partnership
Emphasises competitiveness and self-interest on the part of both purchaser and supplier	Emphasises cooperation and a community of interest between purchaser and supplier
Emphasis on 'unit price' with lowest price usually the most important buyer consideration	Emphasis on total acquisition costs (TAC), including indirect and hidden costs, such as production hold-ups and loss of customer goodwill due to late delivery of materials and components. Lowest price is never the sole buyer consideration
Emphasis is on short-term business relationships	Emphasis on long-term business relationships with involvement of supplier at the earliest possible stage to discuss how the buyer's requirements can be met
Emphasis on quality checks, with inspection of incoming supplies	Emphasis on quality assurance based on total quality management and zero defects
Emphasis on multiple sourcing	Emphasis on single sourcing, although it is not, of necessity, confined to single sourcing. It will, however, reduce the supplier base
Emphasis on uncertainty regarding supplier performance and integrity	Emphasis on mutual trust between purchaser and supplier

- competitive pressures towards 'lean' supply
  - competition creating fewer, more technologically sophisticated suppliers that have to collaborate more closely with their customers
  - earlier involvement of predetermined suppliers for development of each individual component
  - pressure on inventory, forcing closer matching customer–supplier output levels and systems
  - need to optimise all linkages in the supply chain network (both internal and external)
- adoption of 'best practices', creating dependence
  - reduced system slack from TQM, JIT and EDI, creating greater dependence on suppliers
  - more dependency requiring forging of stronger supplier relationships
  - more dependency requiring closer integration of people, plans and systems, both internally and externally.

Southey states that customers enter into partnership sourcing arrangements because of their business-driven need to maximise competitive advantage. They see the benefits of partnering as being that it provides:

- a win–win scenario
- supply chain security

411

- close working relationships (arms around vs arm's length)
- a route to joint technological development
- ability to extend total continuous improvement (TCI) culture to critical suppliers
- improved profit contribution (or reduced profit exposure).

11.23.4 What types of relationships are suitable for partnering?

Partnership Sourcing Ltd[48] has identified seven types of relationships that may be suitable for partnership:

- *high spend* 'the vital few'
- *high risk* items and services that are vital irrespective of their monetary value
- *high hassle* vital supplies that are technically complicated to arrange and take a lot of time, effort and resources to manage
- *new services* new products or services that may involve possible partners
- *technically complicated* involving technically advanced or innovative supplies where the cost of switching would be prohibitive
- *fast-changing* areas where knowing future technology or trends or legislation is critical
- *restricted markets* markets that have few reliable or competent suppliers where closer links with existing or new suppliers might improve supply security.

11.23.5 Advantages of partnering

These are set out in Table 11.8 and Example 11.5.

Table 11.8 **Advantages of partnering**

To the purchaser	To the supplier
Purchasing advantage resulting from quality assurance, reduced supplier base, assured supplies due to long-term agreements, ability to plan long-term improvement, rather than negotiating for short-term advantage, delivery on time (JIT), improved quality	*Marketing advantage* resulting from stability due to long-term agreements, larger share of orders placed, ability to plan ahead and invest, ability to work with key customers on products and/or services, scope to increase sales without increasing procurement overheads
Lower costs resulting from cooperative cost-reduction programmes, such as EDI, supplier's participation in new designs, lower inventory due to better production availability, improved logistics, reduced handling, reduced number of outstanding orders	*Lower costs* resulting from cooperative cost-reduction programmes, participation in customer's design, lower inventory due to better customer planning, improved logistics, simplification or elimination of processes, payment on time
Strategic advantage resulting from access to supplier's technology, a supplier who invests, shared problem-solving and management	*Strategic advantage* resulting from access to customer's technology, a customer that recognises the need to invest, shared problem-solving and management

Benefits of partnering

A survey conducted by Partnership Sourcing Ltd in 1995 reported the following benefits (percentages are of those undertakings responding to the survey):

reduced cost	75.5 per cent
reduced inventory	72.9 per cent
increased quality	70.3 per cent
enhanced security of supply	69.4 per cent
reduced product development times	58.4 per cent

Partnership Sourcing Ltd[49] mentions the following important issues:

- ascertain your most important supplies by spend and criticality or customers by turnover and profit
- whether the potential partner is much bigger or much smaller than the enterprise initiating the partnership is relatively important – small undertakings are more responsive and flexible; larger ones may have better systems
- a potential partner may already have some experience of building partnership relationships and such a company is worth targeting
- that potential partners recognise that:
  - the business of the enterprise seeking to initiate the partnership is important to them
  - there is scope for improvement in the product or service received – in short, that partnering offers potential rewards.

11.23.6 Implementing partnership sourcing

1 *Identify purchased items potentially suitable for partnership sourcing* such as
   - high-spend items and suppliers – Pareto analysis may show that a small number of suppliers account for a high proportion of total spend
   - critical items where the cost of supplier failure would be high
   - complicated items involving technical and innovative supplies where the cost of switching sources would be prohibitive
   - 'new buy' items where supplier involvement in design and production methods is desirable from the outset.

2 *Sell the philosophy of partnership sourcing* to:
   - top management – demonstrating how partnership sourcing can improve quality, service and total costs throughout the organisation
   - other functions likely to be involved, such as accounting (will need to make prompt payments), design (will need to involve suppliers from the outset), production (will need to schedule supply requirements and changes)
   - stress the advantages in section 11.23.5 above.

3 *Define standards that potential suppliers will be required to meet* these will include:

- a commitment to TQM
- ISO 9000 certification or equivalent
- existing implementation of or willingness to implement appropriate techniques, such as JIT, EDI and so on
- in-house design capability
- ability to supply locally or worldwide as required
- consistent performance standards regarding quality and delivery
- willingness to innovate
- willingness to change, flexibility in management and workforce attitudes

Partnership Sourcing Ltd[50] state:

> Remember that people are key. It is people who build trust and make relationships work. Are the people right? Is the chemistry right?
>
> Partnership is two-way: if one of your customers was evaluating your business on the same criteria that you are using on suppliers, would you qualify? If not, perhaps you should think again about your minimum entry standards.

4 *Select one or a few suppliers as potential suppliers* do not attempt to launch too many partnerships at once as a byproduct of partnering is that a customer will be giving more attention to fewer suppliers, focusing available time where it will most benefit some issues.

5 *Sell the idea of partnering to the selected suppliers* stress the advantages in section 11.23.5 above.

6 *If a commitment to partnership sourcing is achieved, determine on the basis of joint consultation what both parties want from the partnership* and:

- decide common objectives, such as:
  - reduction in total costs
  - adoption of TQM
  - zero defects
  - on-time payment
  - JIT or on-time deliveries
  - joint research and development
  - implementation of EDI
  - reduction or elimination of stocks
- agree performance criteria for measuring progress towards objectives, such as:
  - failure in production or with end-users
  - service response time
  - on-time deliveries
  - stock value
  - lead time and stability
  - service levels

- agree administrative procedures:
  - set up a steering group to review progress and ensure development
  - set up problem-solving teams to tackle particular issues
  - arrange regular meetings at all levels with senior management steering the process
- formalise the partnership, which should be on the basis of:
  - a simple agreement
  - a simplified legal contract.

7 *Review and audit the pilot project* by:
  - reviewing against objectives
  - quantifying the gains to the business as a whole
  - reporting back to senior management on what has been achieved.

8 *Extend the existing partnership* by:
  - extending existing agreements
  - commiting to longer agreements
  - getting involved in joint strategic planning.

9 *Develop new partners for the future.*

11.23.7 Problems of partnership sourcing

- *Termination of relationships* The aim should be to part amicably, preferably over a period of time according to an agreed separation plan.
- *Business shares* The possibility of the customer being overdependent on the supplier. These issues need to be explored in joint consultation.
- *Confidentiality* Where prospective partners are also suppliers to competitors.
- *Complacency* Avoidance requires the regular review of competitiveness in regular meetings of a multifunctional buying team.
- *Attitudes* Traditionally adversarial buyers and salespeople will require retraining to adjust to the new philosophy and environment.
- *Contractual* Where, for reasons of falling sales, recession and so on, forecasts have to be modified.
- *Legislative* The CIPS[51] points out that it is less easy to establish partnership relationships in the public sector due to government and EU procurement directive rules. In general, partnership relationships in the public sector should not exceed three to five years, after which retendering should be required, although some partnering deals are 10 to 15 years in duration.

Other problems are that the sharing of information may create a competitor or potential competition and difficulties associated with sharing future profits and the possible foreclosure of other alliance opportunities.

Ramsay[52] rightly observes that:

As a sourcing strategy, partnerships may be generally applicable to only a small number of very large companies. For the rest, although it may be useful with a minority of purchases and a very small selection of suppliers, it is a high-risk strategy that one might argue ought to be approached with extreme caution. In Kraljic's terms [see 2.13.11] the act of moving the sourcing of a bought-out item from competitive pressure to a single-sourced partnership increases both supply risk and profit impact. Thus partnerships tend to push all affected purchases towards the strategic quadrant. Strategic purchases offer large rewards if managed successfully, but demand the allocation of large amounts of management attention and threaten heavy penalties if sourcing arrangements fail.

11.23.8 Why partnerships fail

Research by Ellram[53] covering 80 'pairs' of US buying firms and their chosen suppliers used 19 factors identified by previous studies as contributing to partnership failure. These factors, in the order of their ranking of importance by buyers, were:

1 poor communication
2 lack of top management support
3 lack of trust
4 lack of total quality commitment by supplier
5 poor up-front planning
6 lack of distinctive supplier value-added benefit
7 lack of strategic direction to the relationship
8 lack of shared goals
9 ineffective mechanism for cost revision
10 lack of benefit/risk sharing
11 agreement not supportive of a partnering philosophy
12 lack of partner firm's top management support
13 changes in the market
14 too many suppliers for customers to deal with effectively
15 corporate culture differences
16 top management differences
17 lack of central coordination of purchasing
18 low status of customer's purchasing function
19 distance barriers.

As shown in Table 11.9, five of the top seven factors were common to both buying and supplying organisations.

There were also strong differences. Suppliers ranked central coordination of the buyer's purchasing function as 12 compared with a ranking of 17 by buyers. Similarly, the low status of the customer's purchasing function, lack of strategic direction and lack of shared goals were ranked significantly higher by suppliers than buyers.

The above findings broadly agree with earlier research, although Ellram's sample regarded corporate culture and top management differences as relatively unimportant.

11.23.9 The termination of partnerships

The termination of supplier relationships is discussed in section 7.9.

Table 11.9 Top factors contributing to partnerships that have not worked out or have been resolved

Factor	Buyer ranking	Supplier ranking
Poor communication	1	1
Lack of top management support	2	10
Lack of trust	3	4
Lack of total quality commitment by supplier	4	18
Poor up-front planning	5	5
Lack of strategic direction for the relationship	7	3
Lack of shared goals	8	2

11.24 Reciprocity

11.24.1 What is reciprocity?

Reciprocity – often referred to as 'selling through the order book' – is a policy of giving preference to suppliers that are also customers of the buying organisation.

Reciprocity is influenced by two main factors:

- *the economic climate* pressures for reciprocity increase in times of recession when sales may attempt to put pressure on their suppliers to buy their products
- *the type of product* reciprocal dealing is greater when both supplier and buyer are producers of standard, highly competitive products – it does not arise where a purchaser has no alternative but to buy from a given supplier

11.24.2 Reciprocity policies

The responsibility of purchasing professionals is to make procurement decisions on such considerations as price, quality, delivery and service, so reciprocity may be expressly excluded by specific purchasing policy statements, such as:

> In no circumstances will the XYZ Co. Ltd use a buying decision as a means of inappropriately enhancing a sales opportunity. Reciprocal trading practices are prohibited.

A more liberal approach is that reciprocity may offer advantages to both parties as:

- supplier and buyer may benefit from the exchange of orders
- supplier and buyer may obtain a greater understanding of mutual problems, thus increasing goodwill
- more direct communication between suppliers and buyers may eliminate or reduce the need for intermediaries and the cost of marketing or procurement operations.

11.24.3 Purchasing and reciprocity

Normally decisions relating to reciprocity are taken by top management in the general interest of the whole organisation. The responsibility of professional purchasing is to point out the possible disadvantages of a reciprocal agreement to both marketing and purchasing.

- All purchasing factors, such as lifecycle costs, may not be considered.
- Costs may increase due to the reduced competitive position of the buyer without compensating benefits.
- Sales must increase substantially to provide an equivalent saving on purchases (see section 1.7.1).
- Selling through the order book uses purchasing to perform a market function. Credit may accrue to marketing while the performance of purchasing may be adversely affected.
- Marketing effort may slacken.
- Disputes may arise where the respective values of purchases and sales become substantially different.
- The opportunity to buy cheaper, better-quality alternatives may be denied to buyers if they are tied by a reciprocal agreement.
- Business may be taken from satisfactory suppliers.
- Difficulties may arise in finding alternative suppliers in an emergency.
- In practice, it is often difficult to terminate reciprocal relationships without friction.
- The morale of the buying staff may be adversely affected.

A second responsibility is to ensure that details of the agreement and, if possible, the reasons for the agreement are recorded in writing. In no circumstances should a reciprocal agreement be made with an oral contract. The objections of the purchasing professional should also be communicated and recorded.

11.25 Intra-company trading

Intra-company trading applies to large enterprises and conglomerates where the possibility arises of buying certain materials from a member of the group. This policy may be justified on the grounds that it ensures the utilisation and profitability of the supplying undertaking and the profitability of the group as whole. It may also be resorted to in times of recession to help supplying subsidiaries cover their fixed costs.

Policy statements should give general and specific guidance to the procurement function regarding the basis on which intra-company trading should be conducted. General guidance may be expressed in a policy statement such as the following:

> Company policy is to support internal suppliers to the fullest extent and to develop product and service quality to the same high standards as those available in the external market.

Specific guidance may direct buyers to:

- purchase specified items exclusively from group members regardless of price
- obtain quotations from group members that are evaluated against those from external suppliers with the order being placed with the most competitive source, whether internal or external.

Difficulties can arise where intra-company trading involves import or export considerations.

11.26 Local suppliers

What is 'local' must be determined bearing in mind such factors as ease of transport and communication. The advantages of using local rather than distant suppliers include the following:

- closer cooperation is facilitated between buyers and suppliers based on personal relationships
- social responsibility is shown by 'supporting local industries' and thus contributing to the prosperity of the area
- reduced transportation costs
- improved availability in emergency situations, such as the ease of road transport to collect urgently needed items, and the potential importance of localised confidence in the maintenance of lead times increases where a JIT system is adopted
- the development of subsidiary industries situated close to the main industry and catering for its needs is encouraged.

The main principle in deciding where to place orders must, however, be what is best for the buying undertaking.

11.27 Small or large suppliers

11.27.1 Advantages claimed for small suppliers

Advantages claimed for small suppliers include:

- closer attention to the buyer's requirements – many large suppliers, however, recognise that smaller accounts often grow
- relationships, especially at executive level, are more personal
- response to requests for special assistance from the buyer can be more rapid than with a large undertaking.

It is government policy to encourage the development of small firms and improve the access of such companies to public-sector business, not, however, by favouring small firms at the expense of competitiveness. The CIPS has issued 'A Guide to practice on use of small suppliers'[54] to use in such situations. This recommends, inter alia, that larger organisations should:

- facilitate access for small firms by publishing the names of the larger organisation's purchasing staff and details of its organisation structure
- confirm orders in sufficient time to allow small firms to meet completion dates
- provide assistance to small suppliers, especially by means of:
  - prompt payment, thereby easing liquidity problems
  - secondment of staff to deal with such problems as quality control, design and specification
  - supply of materials either as a free issue or at a price that the small firm would not have been able to negotiate

(if a large organisation merely wants to tender for price comparison purposes, the small company should be informed and, in certain circumstances, the cost of tendering should be paid)

■ limit overdependence of a small supplier on them by setting a ceiling to the percentage of sales taken, which, exceptional circumstances apart, should not be exceeded

■ by means of a written purchasing policy, state its policy towards small suppliers

■ be aware of and consider ameliorating the harmful impact that centralised purchasing *may* have on small local suppliers.

11.27.2 Advantages claimed for large suppliers

These include that they have:

■ greater reserve capacity to undertake extra work and cope with emergencies

■ special facilities and knowledge that can be made available to the buyer

■ greater likelihood of avoiding the trap of a supplier becoming too reliant on the buyer's business.

11.28 Purchasing consortia

11.28.1 Definition and scope

Purchasing consortia may be defined as:

> A collaborative arrangement under which two or more organisations combine their requirements for a specified range of goods and services to gain price, design, supply availability and assurance benefits resulting from greater volumes of purchases.

In public purchasing, for example, several separate authorities may establish a central purchasing organisation to provide three basic supply services to its constituent members, namely delivery from stores, direct purchasing of non-stock items for users in constituent authorities and the negotiation of call-off or 'standing offer' contracts. Such an organisation is usually self-financed by virtue of the mark-up on the items supplied from store and volume rebates received from suppliers that the consortium negotiates.

Purchasing consortia exist in a wide range of industries and cover for-profit and non-profit organisations, including universities and libraries.

The Yorkshire Purchasing Organisation

A typical example of such a consortium is the Yorkshire Purchasing Organisation (YPO), serving schools and local authorities mainly in Yorkshire, Greater Manchester and Merseyside.

Originally selling mainly to 12 constituent authorities, new autonomy, especially in education, means that the YPO is now selling to over 30,000 small customers whose orders have an average line value of under £10. Customers order by post or an EDI system devised by YPO using mail-order catalogues covering over 15,000 lines, ranging from alphabet pasta to xylophones. The consortium aims to meet a 97 per cent availability target.

11.28.2 Advantages of purchasing consortia

- The use of a consortium allows the constituent members to benefit from the economics of larger-scale purchasing than they could undertake individually.
- Members can utilise the relevant professional purchasing skills of the consortium staff who can develop wide-ranging product expertise.
- Saving of time in searching for and ordering standard items.
- Bulk purchasing enables the consortium to have strong buying leverage for a wide range of supplies.
- Costs are clearly identified.

11.28.3 Disadvantages of consortia

- A consortium cannot insist on the compliance of individual members, which may treat the consortium as only one of a number of suppliers. This may secure nominal price savings, but is unlikely to affect the administrative costs of appraising the consortium against alternative sources. It also weakens the strength of the consortium.
- When using a consortium, it may be more difficult to agree standard specifications than when dealing with one company.
- Significant areas of spend are not covered by what consortia can provide.
- Some forms of consortia may be prohibited under EU provisions. Thus, Article 85(1) of the EEC Treaty provides that:

  . . . all agreements, decisions and concerted practices (hereafter referred to as agreements) which have as their object or effect the prevention, restriction or distortion of competition within the common market are prohibited as incompatible with the common market . . . this applies, however, only if such agreements affect trade between Member States.

  In general, however, the Commission 'welcomes cooperation among small- and medium-sized enterprises where such cooperation enables them to work more efficiently and increase their productivity and competitiveness in a larger market'.[55]

11.29 Sourcing decisions

Sourcing decisions involve a consideration of:

- factors influencing organisational buying decisions
- buying centres or teams
- buying situations
- factors in deciding where to buy.

11.29.1 Factors in deciding where to buy

Webster and Wind[56] classify factors influencing industrial buying decisions into four main groups, as shown in Table 11.10.

Table 11.10 Factors in industrial buying decisions

Environmental	Organisational	Interpersonal	Individual
These are normally outside the buyer's control and include: ■ level of demand ■ economic outlook ■ interest rates ■ technological change ■ political factors ■ government regulations ■ competitive development	Buying decisions are affected by the organisation's system of reward, authority, status and communication, including organisational: ■ objectives ■ policies ■ procedures ■ structures	Involving the interaction of several people of different status, authority, empathy and persuasiveness who comprise the buying centre	Buying decisions are related to how individual participants in the buying process form their preferences for products and suppliers, involving the person's age, professional identification, personality and attitude towards the risks involved in their buying behaviour

11.29.2 Buying centres, teams and networks

A buying centre is essentially a cross-functional team, the characteristics of which were discussed in section 5.5. Essentially the buying centre is the buying decision-making unit of an organisation and is defined by Webster and Wind[57] as:

> all those individuals and groups who participate in the purchasing decision process and who share some common goals and the risks arising from the decision.

Normally a buying centre is a temporary, often informal, group that can change in composition according to the nature of the purchase decision.

Buying centres may also be more permanent groups responsible for the sourcing, selection, monitoring and evaluation of suppliers in relation to a specified range of items, such as food, drink, capital equipment and outsourced products and services. Such groups are often referred to as *procurement teams* and may also be responsible for framing purchasing policies and procedures. All teams should have a designated chairperson and clearly defined terms of reference and authority.

The composition of the buying centre or team can be analysed as follows.

- By individual participants or job holders, such as the managing director, chief purchasing officer, engineer or accountant.
- By organisational units, such as departments or even individual organisations, as when a group of hospitals decide to standardise equipment.
- The buying centre or team is comprised of all members of the organisation (varying from three to twelve) who play any of the following five roles in the purchasing decision process:
  - *users* who will use the product or service and often initiate the purchase and specify what is bought
  - *influencers* such as technical staff who may directly or indirectly influence the buying decision in such ways as defining specifications or providing information on which alternatives may be evaluated
  - *buyers* who have formal authority to select suppliers and arrange terms of purchase – they may also help to determine specifications, but their main role is to select vendors and negotiate within purchase constraints

- *deciders* who have either formal or informal authority to select the ultimate suppliers (in routine purchasing of standard items, the deciders are often the buyers, but in more complicated purchasing, the deciders are often other officers of the organisation)

- *gatekeepers* who control the flow of information to others, such as buyers, and may prevent salespeople from seeing users or deciders.

11.29.3 The buying network

The buying centre concept, developed in 1972, has proved remarkably durable and provided the basis for later models of organisational buying behaviour.[58] The Webster and Wind model, however, makes no reference to such aspects as the linkages between purchasing and corporate strategies and procurement decisions aimed at enhancing the competitive advantage of buying, such as the decision to source abroad.

Business practice has also changed since 1972 and process-driven management styles and philosophies such as partnering and the impact of IT have changed the way in which buyers and sellers interact.

Such considerations led Bristor and Ryan[59] to suggest that the concept of the buying centre as a group no longer captures the nature of buying behaviour and should be replaced by that of the buying network, which they define as:

> The set of individuals involved in a purchase process, over a specified time frame, and the set of one or more relations that link (or fail to link) each dyad [a dyad is a pair of units treated as one].

Networks have been discussed in section 4.3, but it is useful to mention here two dimensions of networks highlighted by Bristor and Ryan – structure and relationships. Structure relates to organisational aspects. Thus, the boundaries of a buying centre are those of the organisation. With buying networks, the issue arises as to whether or not it is appropriate to include buying network members from outside the organisation, such as customers or consultants. The nodes of buying centres can also represent roles rather than named individuals.

Relationship aspects of buying networks include communications and influence. IT not only makes information widely available to network members, but developments such as teleconferencing mean that they are no longer required to be in physical proximity.

11.30 The buying situation

Robinson et al.[60] identify three major types of organisational buying situations, which are described below.

11.30.1 Straight rebuy

Straight rebuy situations apply where:

- the item or commodity bought in is in continuous or recurrent demand
- suppliers are already known
- the item is dealt with routinely by current purchasing arrangements
- past experience has established a reliable supply pattern.

Subject to value and item constraints, straight rebuy requirements can be placed with approved suppliers by users using e-procurement without the intervention of the purchasing function. Buyers take a leading role in the initial contract, providing no technical differentiation is present.

11.30.2 Modified rebuy

Modified rebuy situations apply where:

- the demand for the item is continuous or recurrent, but at expanded or reduced levels
- minor changes have been made to the product's specification
- a significant change in specification is necessary due to some unforeseen event, such as a shortage of the material or the emergence of cheaper materials, or as the result of a value analysis exercise
- it is necessary to seek cost reductions, better service or quality
- for some reason a change in supplier is desirable
- a potential new supplier suggests possible economies resulting from the conversion of a straight rebuy into a modified rebuy.

Buyers, along with product design, take a leading role in modified rebuy situations, both as initiators of the change and the arbiters of the final purchase decision.

11.30.3 New task

New task situations apply where:

- the product or specification is new or unfamiliar
- the purchase is infrequently needed
- considerable expenditure on supplier sourcing and appraisal may be required as buyers may have little or no past experience on which to draw
- make-or-buy or outsourcing decisions may be required.

Buyers may not be involved in the early stages of new purchase decisions because it is generally accepted that the technical problems associated with new purchases must be solved before detailed commercial considerations of where to buy can be made.

Increasingly, however, important sourcing decisions are being made on a team or buying centre basis due to:

- the increased involvement of procurement in strategic as well as tactical and operational decision making
- the integration of purchasing into materials management and logistics functions
- the movement towards single and partnership sourcing
- the increasing complexity of purchasing, including global sourcing where many factors, including political, currency and similar considerations, enter into the purchasing decision
- the desirability of spreading responsibility for a high-risk purchasing decision
- the need to evaluate the risks and potential contribution to profitability of new materials, products technology and suppliers.

11.31 Factors in deciding where to buy

Assuming that the decision is made that a product should be bought out rather than made in, many factors determine where the order is placed and by whom the decision is made. Such considerations include:

11.31.1 General considerations

- How shall the item be categorised – capital investment, manufacturing material or parts, operating, supply or MRO item?
- Where does the item fit into our purchasing portfolio – leverage, strategic, non-critical or bottleneck (see section 2.13.11)?
- What are our current and projected levels of business for the item?
- Is the item a one-off or a continuing requirement?
- Is the item unique to us or in general use?
- Is the item a straight rebuy, modified rebuy or new task?
- If it is a straight or modified rebuy, from what source was it obtained?
- Is/was the present/previous supplier satisfactory from the standpoints of price, quality and delivery?
- With regard to the value of the order to be placed, is the cost of searching for an alternative supply source justified?
- Which internal customers may wish to be consulted on the sourcing of the item?
- Within what timescale is the item required?

11.31.2 Strategic considerations

- What supply source will offer the greatest competitive advantage from the stand-points of:
  - price
  - differentiation of product
  - security of supplies and reliability of delivery
  - quality
  - added value in terms of specialisation, production facilities, packaging, trans-portation, after-sales services and so on?
- Is the source one with whom we would like to:
  - single source
  - share a proportion of our requirements for the required item
  - build up a long-term partnership relationship
  - discuss the possibilities of supplier development
  - outsource
  - subcontract?

- Does the supply source offer any possibilities for:
  - joint product development
  - reciprocity or countertrade
- what would be our relationship profile with that supply source – market exchange, captive buyer, captive supplier or strategic partnership (see section 7.6)?
- What relationships has the supplier with our competitors?
- Is it desirable that at least part of our requirements should be sourced locally for political, social responsibility or logistical reasons?
- What risk factors attach to the purchase? Is the product high profit impact/high supply risk, low profit impact/high supply risk, high profit impact/low supply risk, low profit impact/low supply risk?

11.31.3 Product factors

- Can the product or components and assemblies be outsourced?
- What critical factors influence the choice of suppliers? Chisnall[61] reports a research finding that seven critical factors were found to influence buyers in the British valve and pump industry in the choice of their suppliers of raw materials: delivery reliability, technical advice, test facilities, replacement guarantee, prompt quotation, ease of contact and willingness to supply range. These attributes helped to reduce the risk element to purchase decisions.
- What special tooling is required? Is such tooling the property of the existing supplier or the vendor?
- To what extent are learning curves applicable to the product? Are these allowed for in the present and future prices?
- Is the product 'special' or 'standardised'?
- In what lot sizes is the product manufactured?
- What is the estimated product lifecycle cost?

11.31.4 Supplier factors

Such factors are those normally covered by supplier appraisal and vendor-rating exercises.

11.31.5 Personal factors

Personal factors relate to psychological and behavioural aspects of those involved in making organisational buying decisions. All purchasing professionals should constantly keep in mind the exhortation of the Greek Philosopher Diogenes: 'Know thyself'.

Knowledge of our strengths, weaknesses, prejudices, motivations and values will often prevent us from making purchasing or other decisions on irrational grounds or as a member of a team being pressurised by 'group-think' influences. Among the many personal factors that may influence decisions relating to where to buy and who to buy from are:

- cultural factors – the way in which we have been taught to do business
- the information available to us
- professionalism, including ethical values and training
- experience of suppliers and their products
- ability to apply lateral thinking to purchasing problems.

Purchasing professionals should also develop the capacity to understand the preferences of users for a particular product and the motivations of suppliers.

Case study

The Wright Group designs and manufactures a wide range of equipment for civil and military aircraft. Three years ago, it won two large contracts for supplying landing gear on two overseas civil aircraft developments. There was a requirement for machining castings and forgings. The surge in demand required 1000 hours of machinery each month to be subcontracted. This meant that more than twice that capacity was kept in-house. The subcontracted work was tendered by the procurement department and was awarded to a local, small company – Standish Manufacturing. When it won the work, it invested in special purpose machining equipment, having negotiated a bank loan. The Wright Group now takes more than 60 per cent of Standish Manufacturing's output, by value.

The Wright Group's own machine shop is now short of work because a military support contract has ended. The Production Director, Chuck Briggs, has asked the Buying Manager to cancel the arrangements with Standish Manufacturing. It was an 'arrangement' because the Buying Manager took advantage of Standish Manufacturing's lack of contract expertise and agreed a form of words that items would be 'called off as and when required'. A weekly production schedule has been issued and that has become the method of advising the requirements.

Last week, the Buying Manager called in Joe Sopwith, the Managing Director of Standish Manufacturing, and told him that no more subcontracting would take place. Sopwith was horrified and said that the decision would bankrupt the business. He added that local labour would be made redundant and that the decision was illegal and unethical. He further added that not only had he invested in machinery, he had also invested over £60,000 in special tooling. To make matters worse, he had just declined a large subcontracting job from a competitor of the Wright Group. The Buying Manager was very sympathetic but added he had no choice but to stop subcontracting.

In the last few days, things have got worse. Standish has now stopped machining components and refuses to answer telephone calls from anyone at the Wright Group. The Managing Director has told his Buying Manager to ensure that the matter is resolved 'immediately', otherwise the Wright Group will be paying £40,000 a week in liquidated damages to a Swedish company.

Tasks

1 What actions will you now take?

2 Analyse the history of this deal and suggest how it could have been done differently.

Discussion questions

11.1 It is important, however, that purchasing staff at tactical and operational levels are also aware of their roles in providing value-adding support services to sourcing and thereby contributing to the competitive advantage of their enterprise.

As a logistics manager responsible for purchasing processes, how would you seek to ensure that tactical and operational purchasing staff are aware of their roles and responsibilities as described above?

11.2 Situation analysis is concerned with taking stock of where an organisation or activity within an organisation has been recently, where it is now and where it is likely to end up using present policies, plans and procedures. As the executive in charge of the purchasing of production materials and components, you are asked to effect procurement economies without prejudicing the final product quality. How might an analysis of market conditions help you to make constructive recommendations?

11.3 You purchase a 'sensitive commodity', such as zinc, copper or rubber. From what sources can you obtain information relevant to market conditions that might help you to decide whether or not to stockpile the commodity?

11.4 Discuss the advantages and disadvantages of using the Internet as a means of locating possible suppliers.

11.5 You have been asked to prepare a report on the anticipated market conditions in the next 12 months. How and from what sources ought you to obtain the required information?

11.6 How would you answer a manager who refuses to approve your visit to a trade exhibition on the grounds that such exhibitions are 'only an excuse for a day out'?

11.7 Draft a questionnaire designed to enable you to make a preliminary assessment of a supplier who asks to be considered for inclusion on your approved supplier list.

11.8 When evaluating the production capacity of a potential supplier, it is useful to distinguish between:
   (a) design capacity – the maximum output that can possibly be achieved
   (b) effective capacity – the maximum possible outputs given a product mix, scheduling difficulties, machine maintenance, quality factors and so on
   (c) actual output – the rate of output actually achieved, which is often less than effective capacity, due to breakdowns, material shortages and so on.

   Two useful measures are *efficiency*, or the ratio of actual output to effective capacity, and *utilisation*, or the ratio of actual output to design capacity.
      Compare, in purchasing terms, the efficiency and utilisation of a potential supplier given the following figures:
   ■ design capacity 500 items weekly
   ■ effective capacity 400 units weekly
   ■ actual output 360 units weekly.

11.9 Your management recognises that plant visits are one way in which purchasing personnel can learn about the capabilities of potential suppliers. However, such visits must be controlled. Prepare a set of brief guidelines informing purchasing staff of the procedure for obtaining authorisation to make such visits and how such visits should be conducted.

11.10 The cost of measuring the performance of suppliers can be high.
  (a) What arguments would you use to justify the expenditure of measuring performance?
  (b) What steps might you take to minimise such expenditure?

11.11 Suggest one way in which you might evaluate the performance of a supplier against each of the 'ten Cs' listed in section 11.10.6 of this chapter.

11.12 Although supply bases may be drastically reduced, many companies have found that, over time, they tend to grow again.
  (a) Is this true of your experience?
  (b) Why may such renewed growth take place?
  (c) What steps might you take to ensure that your supply base remains reasonably constant?

11.13 On the basis of the following figures, you have been asked whether a certain component should be made in or bought out. You decide to base your decision on a marginal cost approach – that is:

Total cost = Fixed cost + Volume × Variable cost

	Make	Buy
Annual fixed costs	£300,000	None
Variable cost/unit	£120	£160
Annual volume (units)	24,000	24,000

What is your recommendation?

Would your recommendation be different if the annual volume in terms of units were 12,000?

11.14 In section 11.20 of this chapter, a number of problems associated with outsourcing were reported, such as high staff turnover, poor project management skills and so on. How, prior to entering into an outsourcing contract, would you attempt to minimise the likelihood of such problems arising?

11.15 On what grounds would you advise your management against outsourcing purchasing?

11.16 Due to overloading in your machine shop, you have been asked to find a sub-contractor able to produce spindles to close limits from stock mild steel round bars. You arrange for the steel bars to be delivered directly to the subcontractor by the steel producer. What controls might you devise over the use and security of the bars by the subcontractor?

11.17 Why may it be important for first-tier suppliers to be located nearer to the assembler than second-tier suppliers?

11.18 Partnering involves the exchange of information that may previously have been available to only a few senior managers in their own companies. Open book accounting, where the partners have access to each other's accounts, is a perfect example of where complete trust is needed. While no agreement can replace complete trust, some organisations find it useful to prepare guidelines on the use of confidential information. What matters might you include in such guidelines?

11.19 What problems might arise in a reciprocal trading agreement when, due to a change in demand, the quantity and value of goods bought by A from B falls substantially below the quantity and value of goods bought by B from A?

11.20 The main manufacturing base of your company is located in a relatively small town. Over the years, a number of smaller undertakings have developed that rely mainly on your company for their business and survival. In some cases, for social responsibility reasons, you are paying local suppliers more than you would pay non-local suppliers. Because of enhanced competition, you do not consider that this practice can continue. What steps might you take to improve the competitiveness of the local suppliers?

11.21 A construction company has drawing offices in both Glasgow and London. Staff from Glasgow often visit London for technical consultations with customers and colleagues and vice versa. Such visits may extend over two or three days and entail substantial hotel costs. Your directors have decided to establish a team to source and negotiate with hotel groups in both centres with a view to offering special rates for accommodation and meals in return for exclusive business. Draft the terms of reference for the team.

11.22 Consider the following definition:[62]

Company politics is the byplay that occurs when people want to advance themselves or their ideas regardless of whether or not these ideas would help the company.

How may company politics influence sourcing decisions?

Past examination questions

The following are taken from the CIPS Professional Stage Examination in Purchasing and Supply Chain Management II: Tactics and Operations

1 Recent research by Brunel University shows that 33 per cent of companies in the UK cancelled their outsource contracts within 5 years and 50 per cent found themselves in dispute with the outsourced contractor.
   (a) Discuss the reasons for this apparent failure.
   (b) Suggest how the outsourcing exercise should be conducted to maximise the possibilities of successful outcome.

(May 2002)

2 As the purchasing manager for a manufacturer of domestic appliances you are to source the door seal for a new model of microwave oven. The component has caused problems in the past but the design problems have now been overcome. The market has become increasingly competitive and any problems with the new model could be disastrous. Preliminary sourcing indicates that Permaseal Ltd has a substantially lower price than other potential suppliers, including your current supplier Thermalbond Ltd. However, the last time you did business with Permaseal was six years previously and at the time you experienced some quality and delivery problems.

Explain in detail how you would undertake this sourcing exercise in order to ensure that you select the best possible supplier for the long term.

(November 2001)

3 Deltic PLC produces a wide range of industrial products. One of the product ranges is a specialised plastic moulding produced for a customer who is very demanding on quality requirements. Unfortunately none of the current suppliers is performing consistently to a satisfactory quality standard. As you have some spare capacity available internally it may be viable to manufacture it in-house. As the procurement manager, discuss the factors you would consider.

(November 2003)

References

1 Dey, P. K., *Supply Chain Management on Construction through Partnership*, AACE International Transactions, 2002, pp. 1–7

2 Novack, R. A., and Simco, S. W., *Journal of Business Logistics*, Vol. 12, Issue 1, 1991

3 CIPS, 'Reference file: *e-sourcing*',

4 Waller, A., quoted by Lascelles, D., in his *Managing the E-supply Chain*, Business Intelligence, 2001, p. 19

5 ePedas at: www.epedas.com.my/who.html

6 As 2 above

7 Thompson, D. M., and Homer, G. R., 'Internet-searchable supplier database in the supply chain', Proceedings of the 10th Annual Conference, 2001, pp. 815–25

8 Trade Association Forum: www.taforum.org

9 Lysons, C. K., 'Supplier appraisal', CIPS How to Series, CIPS, 2002

10 Hines, P., Lamming, R., Jones, D., Cousens, P., and Rich, N., *Value Stream Management*, Prentice Hall, 2000, p. 326

11 DTI, 'Sourcing and supplier appraisal', Document 5

12 OGC, *Supplier Financial Appraisal Guidance*, Oct., 2001

13 Buffa, E. S., and Kakesh, K. S., *Modern Production Operations Management*, 5th edn, John Wiley, 1987, p. 548

14 These categories are used in the supplier management policy document of the University of Nottingham

15 Emptoris Supplier Performance Module at: www.emptoris.com/solutions/supplier_performance_management_module.asp

16 Kozak, R. A., and Cohen, D. H., 'Distributor–supplier partnering relationships: a case in trust', *Journal of Business Research*, Vol. 30, 1997, pp. 33–8

17 Simpson, P. M., Siguaw, J. A., and White, S. C., 'Measuring the performance of suppliers: an analysis of evaluation processes', *Journal of Supply Management*, Feb., 2002

18 Hollingsworth, B., 'Rating system options', NAPM *InfoEdge*, Vol. 4, No. 3, Nov. 1998

19 Horton, S., 'Creating and using supplier scorecards', *Contract Management*, Sept., 2004

20 Lysons, C. K., 'How to prepare service level agreements', CIPS, 2001

21 Zeithaml, V. A., Parasuraman, A., and Berry, L. L., *Delivering Quality Service: Balancing Customers' Perspectives and Expectations*, Free Press, 1990

22 Carter, R.., 'The seven Cs of effective supplier evaluation', *Purchasing and Supply Chain Management*, April, 1995, pp. 44–5

23 Verikatesan, R., 'Strategic sourcing: to make or not to make', *Harvard Business Review*, Nov.–Dec., 1992, pp. 98–107

24 Probert, D. R., 'Make or buy: your route to improved manufacturing performance', DTI, 1995

25 ICMA, 'Management accounting', Official Terminology, ICMA, 1996

26 Atkinson, J., and Meager, N., 'New forms of work organisation', IMS Report 121, 1986

27 Beauchamp, M., 'Outsourcing everything else? Why not purchasing?', *Purchasing and Supply Management*, July, 1994, pp. 16–19

28 Rothery, B., and Robinson, I., *The Truth about Outsourcing*, Gower, 1995, p. 66

29 Beulen, E. J. J., Ribbers, P. M. A., and Roos, J., *Outsourcing van IT-clienstverlening:een-make or buy beslissing*, Kluwer, 1994. Quoted by Fill, C., and Visser, E., *The Outsourcing Dilemma: Management Decision 2000*, Vol. 38.1, MCB University Press, pp. 43–50

30 Quoted in Duffy, R. J., 'The outsourcing decision', *Inside Supply Management*, April, 2000, p. 38

31 Lacity, M. C., and Hirscheim, R., *Information Systems Outsourcing*, John Linley, 1995

32 Carrington, L., 'Outside chances', *Personnel Today*, 8 Feb., 1994, p. 34

33 As 32 above

34 Perkins, B., *Computer World*, 22 Nov., 2003

35 Reilly, P., and Tamkin, P., *Outsourcing: A Flexibility Option for the Future*, Institute of Employment Studies, 1996, pp. 32–3

36 As 31 above

37 CCTA, 'Producing a SSR', July, 1993. The same model is reproduced in *Producing a Statement of Service Requirements*, BUY IT Guidelines, 1993

38 As 31 above

39 Patton, M. G., 'Outsourcing: a strategy whose time has come', Proceedings of the NAPM 3rd Annual Conference, May, 1998

40 Washington, W. N., 'Subcontracting as a solution, not a problem, in outsourcing', *Application Review Quarterly*, winter, 1999, pp. 79–86

41 The source of this quotation cannot be traced

42 Humbert, X. P., and Passarelli, C. P. M., 'Outsourcing: avoiding the hazards and pitfalls', Paper presented at the NAPM International Conference, 4–7 May, 1997

43 CIPS, 'Partnership Sourcing'

44 Partnership Sourcing Ltd, *Making Partnerships Happen*, p. 4

45 Lambert, D. M., Emmelhaing, M. A., and Gardner, J. T., 'Developing and implementing supply chain partnerships', *International Journal of Logistics Management*, Vol. 7, No. 2, 1996, pp. 1–17

46 Knemeyer, A. M., Corsi, T. M., and Murphy, P. R., 'Logistics outsourcing relationships: customer perspectives', *Journal of Business Logistics*, Vol. 24, No. 1, 2003, pp. 77–101

47 Southey, P., 'Pitfalls to partnering in the UK', PSERG Second International Conference, April, 2003, in Burnett, K. (ed.), 'Readings in partnership sourcing', CIPS (undated)

48 PSL, *Creating Service Partnerships*, Partnership Sourcing Ltd, 1993, p. 7

49 As 48 above

50 As 48 above

51 As 43 above, pp. 5–6

52 Ramsay, J., 'The case against purchasing partnerships', *International Journal of Purchasing and Materials Management*, fall, 1996, pp. 13–24

53 Ellram, Lisa M., 'Partnering pitfalls and success factors', *International Journal of Purchasing and Materials Management*, spring, 1995, pp. 36–44

54 CIPS, 'Guide to practice on use of small suppliers', CIPS, undated

55 *E.C. Journal* 84–28.8, 1968

56 Webster, F. E., and Wind, Y. J., *Organisational Buying Behaviour*, Prentice Hall, 1972, pp. 33–7

57 As 56 above

58 A useful summary of research in the 25 years prior to 1996 is provided by Johnston, W. J., and Lewin, J. E., 'Organisational buying behaviour: towards an integrative framework', *Journal of Business Research*, Vol. 35, No. 1, 1996

59 Bristor, J. M., and Ryan, M. S., 'The buying centre is dead, long live the buying centre', *Advances in Consumable Research*, Vol. 4, 1987, pp. 255–8

60 Robinson, P. J., Farris, C. W., and Wind, Y. J., *Industrial Buying and Creative Marketing*, Allyn & Bacon, 1967, p. 14

61 Chisnall, P. M., *Strategic Industrial Marketing*, 2nd edn, Prentice Hall, 1989, pp. 82–3

62 Hegarty, E., *How to Succeed in Company Politics*, McGraw-Hill, 1976

Chapter 12

Buying at the right price

Learning outcomes

With reference, where applicable, to purchasing and supply chain management, this chapter aims to provide an understanding of:

- price
- competition
- pricing agreements
- price analysis
- price variation
- price adjustments
- price and value.

Key ideas

- Perfect, imperfect competition and monopoly.
- Competition legislation.
- Cost-based and market-driven pricing models.
- Firm price agreements.
- Cost price agreements.
- Variations in firm and cost price agreements.
- Price analysis for the purposes of comparison and negotiation.
- Price index numbers.
- Price adjustment formulae.
- Procedure for price adjustment.
- Techniques for obtaining best value for money spent.

12.1 Price

Price can be defined as:

the value of a commodity or service measured in terms of the standard monetary unit.

Figure 12.1 **Supply, demand and the equilibrium price**

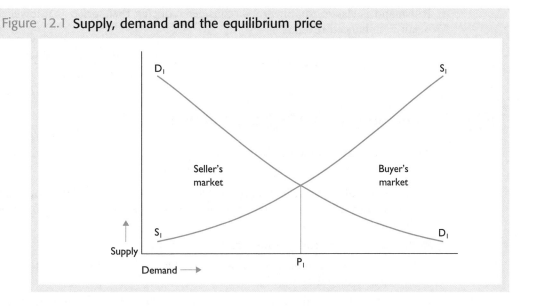

When comparing two quotations, price enables us to appraise the relative value offered by each supplier.

Economic theory shows that demand and supply are balanced by the influence of price, the *equilibrium price* indicating the point at which demand and supply are equal. The equilibrium price can be represented diagrammatically, as in Figure 12.1 in which D_1–D_1 is the demand curve, indicating quantities demanded at various prices, and S_1–S_1, is the supply curve, indicating quantities demanded at various prices, and P_1 is the equilibrium price, where demand and supply will be balanced.

A seller's market exists when demand exceeds supply, so prices generally rise. Conversely, a buyer's market exists when supply exceeds demand, so then prices generally fall. Some of the determinants of supplier and buyer power as identified by Porter are shown in Figure 2.6.

At a particular moment in time, the market price may differ from the equilibrium price because the effect of temporary influences may not have had the chance to work themselves out. When these factors have stabilised, however, a normal – that is, equilibrium – price will apply. In the above analysis, the shape of the demand and supply curves will be influenced by 'elasticity', or the degree of responsiveness of demand or supply to changes in price. Where a slight change in price will cause a substantial change in demand, then demand is said to be *elastic*. Demand is *inelastic* where a substantial change in price makes little difference to the amount demanded.

$$\text{Price elasticity of demand} = \frac{\%\ \text{change in quantity demand}}{\%\ \text{change in price}}$$

Demand is likely to be less elastic where the following conditions obtain:

- there are few or no substitutes or competitors
- there is 'buyer inertia' – that is, buyers are slow to change their buying habits and search for alternative sources or lower prices
- buyers do not notice or fail to challenge the higher price.

If demand is elastic, suppliers will consider reducing their price as a lower price will result in enhanced revenue:

$$\text{Price elasticity of supply} = \frac{\%\ \text{change in quantity supplied}}{\%\ \text{change in price}}$$

12.2 Conditions for perfect competition

The above theory is based on the concept of 'perfect' competition. For perfect competition to exist, the following five conditions must apply:

- the item dealt in must be homogeneous so that buyers are indifferent regarding the sellers from whom they make their purchases – there is an absence of trade or proprietary names, for example
- the item must be easily transportable
- there must be many buyers and sellers so that the former cannot artificially restrict demand or the latter supply
- there should be an absence of preferential treatment of or discrimination against any buyer or seller
- easy communication must exist between buyers and sellers so that they are immediately aware of what is happening anywhere in the market.

Under perfect competition, there is only one price at which the entire quantity available can be sold.

12.3 Imperfect competition and monopoly

While perfect competition applies in the commodity markets, as outlined later in Chapter 13, most buyers operate under conditions of *imperfect* competition. Under imperfect competition there is no single selling price for an item.

Imperfect competition may take several forms, according to the number of suppliers and the ease with which additional suppliers may enter the market. The commonest forms of imperfect competition are shown in Table 12.1.

It would be impractical to deal with the effects of each of these conditions on demand, supply and price here and, in any case, a full treatment is contained in any standard textbook of economics. However, there are a few points to note. Buyers should remember that even a monopolistic supplier is not all-powerful. It can control the price or quantity sold but not both and is thus subject to the 'sovereignty' of the consumer. If suppliers overexploit their monopoly power, buyers will be provoked into searching

Table 12.1 **Forms of imperfect competition**

Type	Numbers of suppliers	Entry of suppliers into the market
Monopoly	One	No entry
Oligopoly	Few	Limited entry
Monopolistic competition	Many	Competition between suppliers

for alternative products. Monopolies and restrictive trading may also give rise to intervention by central government.

12.4 Competition legislation

12.4.1 Anti-competition agencies

Almost every nation has legislation designed to regulate competition and restrict the exploitation of monopoly power. The International Competition Network is an organisation of national and multinational competition agencies entrusted with the enforcement of anti-competition legislation.

12.4.2 UK anti-competition agencies

In the UK, the Secretary of State for Trade and Industry (DTI) sets the overall policy for competition, but is only involved in public interest decisions under the Enterprise Act 2002. The four main UK competition bodies are the following.

- *Office of Fair Trading (OFT)* an independent body with statutory powers under the Competition and Enterprise Acts of 1998 and 2002 respectively. The DTI is committed to work together with the OFT and share information. The OFT addresses anti-competition practices by means of a mix of enforcement and communication. It is to the OFT that complaints relating to competition should, in the first instance, be made.
- *Competition Commission* conducts in-depth inquiries into markets, mergers and the regulation of major industries at the request of the DTI and OFT.
- *Competition Appeal Tribunal (CAT)* hears and decides appeals and other applications or claims involving competition.
- *European Commission (Directorate General for Competition)* has powers to deal with restrictive agreements and anti-competition practices when trade between EU members is affected.

12.4.3 The Competition Act 1998 and the Enterprise Act 2002

The Competition Act 1998 prohibited both anti-competition agreements and the abuse of a dominant position.

An 'agreement' is an undertaking or contract between companies or associated companies, whether in writing or otherwise. Examples of such agreements include:

- agreeing to fix purchasing or selling prices or other trading conditions
- agreeing to limit or control production, markets or technical developments of investment
- agreeing to share markets or supply sources
- agreeing to apply different trading conditions to equivalent transactions, thereby placing some parties at a competitive advantage.

An agreement is, however, considered to be unlikely to have an appreciable effect where the combined market share of the parties involved does not exceed 25 per cent. This said, agreements to fix prices, impose minimum resale prices or share markets may be regarded as having an appreciable effect even when the parties' combined market share is below 25 per cent.

Whether or not a company is in a 'dominant position' will be decided by the OFT according to its market share. In general, a company is unlikely to be regarded as dominant if it has a market share of less than 40 per cent, although a lower market share may be considered dominant if the market structure enables it to act independently of its competitors.

Ways in which a dominant company may abuse its position include:

- imposing unfair purchasing or selling prices
- limiting production, markets or technical development to the prejudice of customers
- applying different trading conditions to equivalent transactions and thereby placing certain parties at a competitive advantage
- attaching unrelated supplementary conditions to a contract.

12.5 Pricing agreements

An important aspect of purchasing is the negotiation of the price to be paid to the supplier. Negotiation is the subject of Chapter 15, but it is useful to look at the factors that suppliers and purchasing will consider in arriving at pricing agreements.

12.6 Supplier considerations in pricing agreements

These will relate both to general considerations and pricing models.

12.6.1 General considerations

- Their position in the market, ranging from a monopoly position, in which there is no product differentiation and the *seller* (subject to government control) sets the price, to pure competition, in which the *market* sets the price.
- The nature of demand for the product – that is, is it elastic, as will be the case where there are substitutes, or inelastic, where demand is not affected by the price?
- What the market or a particular purchaser will pay – that is, charging what the market will bear.
- Prices charged by competitors in general. Higher prices can only be charged where it can be shown that the higher price is justified by product differentiation or other added value.
- The supplier's need for the business.
- The potential long-term value of the purchaser to the supplier in terms of continuity of orders, promptness of payment and so on.
- Is the product standard or a special?
- The order volume – long production runs make lower prices possible.
- The stage of the product in its lifecycle. In general, the earlier a product is in its lifecycle, the higher will be the price.

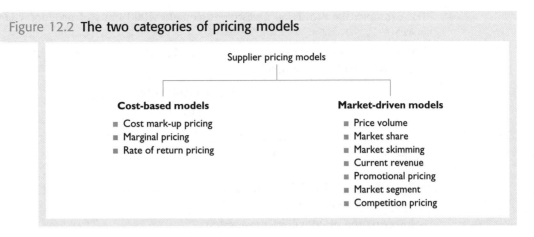

Figure 12.2 **The two categories of pricing models**

12.6.2 Pricing models

Suppliers aim to cover their costs and achieve a margin of profit that will provide for future growth, meet long-term borrowings, update plant and equipment, build up reserves and reward shareholders. The pricing models aimed at meeting these objectives generally fall into two categories, as shown in Figure 12.2.

Cost-based models

- *Cost mark-up pricing model (also known as cost-plus pricing)* The supplier adds a mark-up percentage to the estimated costs. Estimated costs may be product cost (direct material + direct labour + production overheads) or total cost (product cost + general, administrative and marketing overheads). For example, a supplier's estimated total costs is £100, desired mark-up is 20 per cent so the selling price is £120.

- *Marginal pricing model* The supplier fixes a price (based on product or total costs) that will yield a predetermined percentage of the quoted price. Selling price is computed using the formula:

$$\frac{\text{Total (or product) cost price} \times \text{Cleared margin}}{\text{Cost price} - \text{Desired margin}}$$

∴ e.g. Estimated total costs = £100, desired margin = 20%

Then:

$$\therefore \frac{£100 \times 20}{£100 - 20} = £25 + £100$$

∴ Selling price = £125

- *Rate of return pricing model (also known as target return pricing)* The supplier places the profit on the desired return on the investment rather than the estimated cost per product. The selling price is computed using the formula:

$$\frac{\text{Unit cost of product} + \text{Desired margin} \times \text{Total investment}}{\text{Number of units from investment}}$$

For example, the estimated investment to make 4000 units of product = £600,000 = £150.

This will be more than the *product* cost of £100 as general administrative and marketing costs will also be involved:

$$\therefore £100 \times \frac{(0.20 \times £600,000)}{4000} = £30$$

$$\therefore \text{Selling price is } £100 + £30 = £130$$

Market-driven models

■ *Price volume model* This involves break-even analysis (see section 11.14.2) and is based on two assumptions:
 – lowering the price will increase sales
 – the greater volume will spread the cost of fixed overheads over more units, thereby enabling the supplier to offer quantity discounts.

A knowledge of cost-volume-profit analysis is indispensable when conducting price negotiations.

■ *Market share model* This approach is based on the premise that profitability, in the long run, depends on the market share or penetration achieved by the supplier. To win customers or discourage or eliminate competition, suppliers initially set low prices and may even incur losses. As market share increases, the cost per unit falls and long-term profits are achieved.

■ *Market skimming* is a pricing approach in which the supplier sets a high introductory price to attract buyers who have a strong desire for the product and the financial resources to buy it and then gradually reduces the price to attract the next and subsequent market layers.

■ *Current revenue pricing model* This approach aims to cover operating costs rather than achieve profits. A company may accept an order to supply at or below cost because, without the order, the lack of work will necessitate shutting down part of its production, incurring large lay-off costs, training costs if the skilled workforce does not return after the lay-off and high start-up costs after a lengthy shutdown. The aims, therefore, are primarily to cover fixed costs and retain skilled labour until market conditions improve. Buyers taking advantage of such a situation should ensure that, to achieve a profit, the suppliers do not attempt to cut costs at the expense of quality.

■ *Promotional pricing models* In this approach, a short-term discount is offered to promote sales. Book clubs, mobile phone manufacturers and car distributors are examples of suppliers offering their products at reduced cost to enhance sales.

■ *Market segment pricing model (also known as status pricing)* Different prices are set for different market segments based on the value each segment receives from the product or service. Suppliers may, for example, offer lower prices to overseas markets. With market segment pricing, the supplier's unit cost remains the same, even though different prices obtain.

■ *Competition pricing model (also known as dynamic pricing)* An example of this approach is found in the reverse auction process described in section 6.9. The supplier's pricing strategy is based on obtaining orders by quoting the highest possible price, but which is still lower than the prices tendered by competitors.

12.7 Purchasing considerations in pricing agreements

Purchasers will consider:

- the risk attached to the purchase and the method of pricing
- the purchaser's position in the market as, where the supplier is in a monopoly position, the purchaser must exploit the fact that, except for products with an inelastic demand, the monopolist can control either the price or the quantity demand but not both
- whether the purchase is a leverage, strategic, non-critical or bottleneck product
- whether the purchase is a rebuy, modified rebuy or new buy item
- the number of suppliers in the market and the possibility of alternative products
- prices paid by competitors – this information may be difficult to obtain
- whether or not learning curve factors are applicable to the product
- the relationship between price and value in terms of competitive advantage
- the period for which the price is to be agreed
- what is a reasonable price based on a price analysis
- what quantities are likely to be involved and over what period
- what may be considered a fair price from both the purchaser's and supplier's viewpoints.

All the above factors influence the selling or purchase price of a product. In practice, price agreements are essentially of two types: firm and cost type. As shown in Figure 12.3, firm and cost agreements are at opposite ends of a continuum, with a number of intermediate pricing arrangements aimed at reducing the risks to the purchaser.

Figure 12.3 Risks of different pricing arrangements to the purchaser

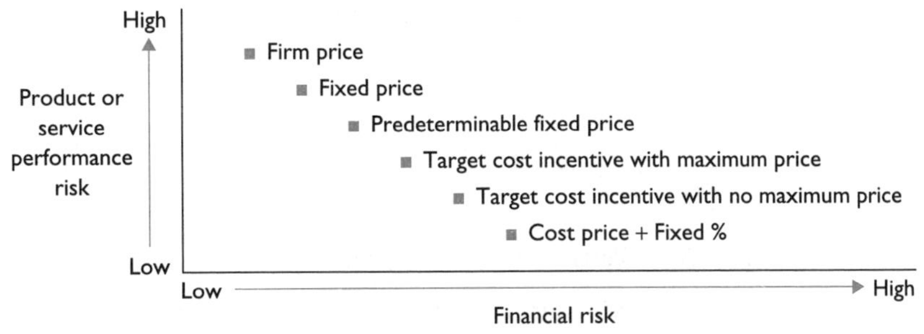

Source: adapted from Behan, P., *Purchasing in Government*, Longman, 1994, p. 57

12.8 Firm price agreements

Fixed price agreements are contracts that are negotiated with fixed payment schedules, payment based on milestones or payment based on fixed fees for a service. These agreements are generally used when reasonably definite specifications are available and when fair and reasonable prices can be estimated and established.

Although, as shown later, variations may be negotiated, firm price agreements are not subject to any provision for variation. Such agreements are advantageous to purchasers for the following reasons:

- all risks are borne by the supplier and the purchaser knows from the start what is to be paid
- suppliers have the maximum incentive to produce efficiently and complete the work on time as all cost savings *below* the price are kept by the supplier, while all costs incurred *above* the price are met by the supplier
- a minimum of administration is involved, such as auditing of costs.

12.9 Cost price agreements

Cost price agreements – in which a fixed percentage is added to the production or construction cost – are more disadvantageous to the purchaser, for the following reasons:

- all financial risks accrue to the buyer
- such agreements are difficult to administer as the suppliers' cost schedules have to be checked by financial and management accountants and possibly other specialist staff, such as engineers, architects, quantity surveyors and so on.

12.10 Variations in firm and cost price agreements

In practice, factors such as the escalation in material costs, as a result of inflation or pay rises during the period of a contract, the need to provide incentives or the difficulty of measuring the work to be done make it desirable to reduce the risks to both purchaser and supplier by incorporating variations into both firm and cost type contracts, as shown in Examples 12.1 and 12.2. Some possible variations to firm and cost type agreements are shown in Table 12.2.

Example 12.1

Target cost with maximum price

Target price = £11, including £1 profit. Ceiling price = £12 with no profit. Cost savings shared in the ratio 80/20 between supplier and purchaser.

Cost (£)	Profit (£)	Price (£)
11.00	–	11.00
10.00	1.00	10.80
9.00	2.00	10.60
8.00	3.00	10.40

Example 12.2

Target cost without maximum price

Target cost per item = £10.00, with a profit of £1.00. Increases or decreases above or below this target cost are shared equally between supplier and purchaser.

Cost (£)	Profit (£)	Price (£)
10.00 (target)	1.00	11.00
11.00	1.00	11.50
9.50	1.50	10.75

Table 12.2 **Variations on firm and cost price agreements**

Type of agreement	Characteristics	Application
Firm agreements Fixed price	Once determined, price remains fixed until completion of the contract, apart from changes in the scope of the contract	Standard items from stock or for short-term production
Firm fixed price with economic price adjustment	Provides for upward or downward revision of the fixed price on the occurrence of specified contingencies. The adjustments may be: ■ based on the fixed or contract price ■ based on actual increases/decreases in labour or material costs ■ based on specially mentioned indexes relating to labour or material	When the stability of market or labour conditions during the period of the contract are uncertain Contingencies that might occur can be identified and covered separately in the contract
Fixed price incentive contracts	Provide for an adjustment of profit and a final price based on a formula relating final negotiated total cost to a total target cost. The final price is subject to a maximum negotiated at the outset	Where a firm fixed price contract is unsuitable Where it is desirable to give the contractor a positive incentive to control cost To provide incentives to the contractor for technical performance or delivery on time
Fixed price contracts with prospective price redetermination	A firm fixed price applies for an initial, specified period, after which price will be renegotiated or amended at stated times during the contract	Where it is possible to agree on a fair and reasonable fixed price for an initial period, but not for subsequent periods of contract performance Where a learning element is involved, as in prices subject to learning curves
Firm fixed price, level of effort term contracts	Require the contractor to provide a specified level of effort over an agreed period on work that can only be specified in general terms in return for a fixed amount	Appropriate for research and development contracts where a firm and reasonable fixed price cannot be negotiated due to cost uncertainties For research and development contracts Where payment is for effort expended rather than results achieved

Table 12.2 (cont'd)

Type of agreement	Characteristics	Application
Cost type agreements		
Target costs with maximum price	This is the same as the fixed price incentive contract described above. The maximum price is fixed, including an agreed profit, and any reductions are shared on an agreed percentage basis between purchaser and supplier	Where target cost can be fixed with reasonable certainty but exact costs cannot be determined when the contract is placed
Target costs without maximum price	No maximum price is fixed. Excess or reduced costs over target price are shared between supplier and purchaser in agreed proportions	Contracts extending over any period of time, during which the supplier may require to be compensated for costs incurred over target or rewarded for cost savings

12.11 Price analysis

Price analysis can be regarded in the following two ways.

12.11.1 Price analysis as comparison

First, it may be considered as:[1]

> the process of examining and evaluating a proposed price without evaluating its separate elements of cost and profit.

In this case, a quoted price is compared with competing prices. Graw[2] has listed seven bases on which such comparisons can be made.

■ *Comparison with competing offers on the immediate purchase* This is simply ensuring that the quoted price is the lowest among those received.

■ *Comparison with established catalogue prices* The price analysis must take care to ensure that those specified are actual prices, as catalogue prices may be discounted. The price listed must also apply to a product sufficiently similar to the required item to prove a basis for comparison.

■ *Comparison with established market prices* Prices for a particular item may fluctuate over short intervals.

■ *Comparison with prices set by law or regulation* Prices for some utility services, such as water or electricity supply, are regulated by government-appointed commissions. Commission-approved rates are published and available to purchasers.

■ *Comparison with producer price and other market indexes* The use of index numbers (discussed later in this chapter) makes prices from different points in time comparable with respect to a specific point in time. Thus, the UK Retail Price Index measures changes in the value of money over different periods of time.

■ *Comparison with in-house estimates* This is the comparison of the quotes received from external suppliers with the calculation of what would be a fair price prepared by a competent external estimator.

■ *Comparison with values determined by value and visual analysis* As described in section 9.11.3, value analysis is the task of determining why seemingly similar products should be priced differently. Visual analysis involves the visual inspection of an item or representations of the item in drawings to develop a rough estimate of value.

12.11.2 Price analysis as price breakdown

This involves the breaking down of a quoted price into its constituent elements for the purpose of determining the reasonableness, or otherwise, of the proposed charge.

The reasonableness of the proposed charge is an analysis of the quoted price to ensure that it covers the costs of an efficient procedure and allows a fair profit commensurate with the risks involved in undertaking the work. An analysis of price can be based on:

■ cost experience of the buyer's company, such as when subcontracting items previously manufactured

■ cost estimates prepared by the estimating or costing staff of the buyer's company

■ cost information provided by the vendor.

Price analysis can also be undertaken as a joint exercise by the purchaser in association with the supplier.

12.11.3 Advantages of price analysis

Price analysis has the following advantages:

■ it provides buyers with an indication of what they ought to pay

■ it highlights possible mistakes in quoting on the part of the supplier – that is, where the price is exceptionally high or low

■ management accounting provides a number of approaches that can be applied to price analysis, including lifecycle costing, target costing, absorption costing, activity-based costing and standard costing – these approaches are discussed in Chapter 16, while marginal costing and its application to make-or-buy decisions was discussed in section 11.14.2.

Most suppliers have flexibility in their pricing and it is not uncommon for a negotiation allowance to be built into the quoted purchase price. Suppliers will not make this allowance visible in cost breakdowns, but initial prices are often submitted to 'test the temperature'. There is an obvious risk with this practice as there is no guarantee that the purchaser will attempt to negotiate.

12.11.4 Examples of price analysis applications

■ *Challenge assumptions in the pricing proposal* For example, on a major project, the supplier may assume that the mobilisation period will require the full-time involvement of a project manager and will have been costed on this basis. The project may only require 50 per cent of the manager's time and, if specific accountabilities are identified, that may not be a problem.

■ *Challenge the nature of 'equipment' costs* For example, it is not unusual on some construction contracts for the contractor to include IT costs and software in the costs. Exploration of this may show that there is 'double counting', in that these costs are in overheads and separated elsewhere as well. The buyer may wish to explore who owns the equipment at the end of the contract if the buyer were to find these costs.

■ *Determine what cash flow assumptions have been made* It is not unusual for the supplier to build in the cost of capital on the assumption that the buyer will be late with payment. If the buyer is asked to make up-front payments and is willing to do so, a discount should be obtained and, of course, a bank guarantee obtained to secure the money.

■ *Press for disclosure of the cost drivers of the price proposal* For example, on engineering purchases, material will probably be the key cost driver – often over 50 per cent of the selling price. The buyer may be able to help the supplier purchase more effectively if there is access to a bill of materials (BOM).

■ *Labour costs are always worthy of challenge* Labour costs come from many directions, such as within service costs, such as cleaning, IT maintenance, consultancy, legal services, auditing and security. The cost of labour may range from, say, £8.00 per hour to £3000 per day. The origins of the labour cost will include pay, pension, National Insurance, training, clothing and other items. The buyer must ensure that overheads are not recovered within the labour costs and also in overheads.

■ *Challenge the estimated number of hours or days estimated* A good example is IT implementation contracts. The buyer should obtain a work programme resourced on a daily basis, by number and grade/status of staff. The supplier will, on occasions, be quite happy to provide excess resources, simply to recover their costs.

■ *Evaluate whether or not the grade of labour being proposed is necessary* Consultancy and legal services provide examples of senior partners being proposed when most of the work can be done by lesser grades. Where possible, the purchase enquiry should request details of work content and have this related to the skills required to undertake specific duties.

■ *Challenge contingency inclusions* On some projects, this may be 5–15 per cent of the tendered price. It is not unreasonable for a supplier to plan for contingency, after all there are unknowns on most projects. One solution is to take the contingency out of the price and create a 'contingency fund'. The circumstances under which the supplier may access the fund should be defined and agreed. This introduces a control mechanism and there may be a division of the fund at the end of the project when a surplus remains.

■ *Scrutinise the level of overheads being applied to base costs, such as labour and materials* This area is subject to the influence of accountants and they may need to get involved in negotiations. There is no accepted way of recovering overheads, hence a scrutiny is necessary. In some cases, overheads may be recovered as a percentage on labour, in others as a percentage on materials or in some other way dictated by accountants.

■ *Probe the profit margin being proposed by the supplier* One approach is to link profit returns to the contractual risks. For example, a lower profit level may be expected on a routine provision of a service than, say, for a contract in the nuclear engineering field where safety considerations are paramount. The buyer's attitude should be to accept profit as a genuine business objective. A profitable supplier has capital to invest in new solutions and capital equipment.

■ *Scrutinise the deal for concessions that may not cost the supplier a great amount* For example, the supplier may have specialist marketing expertise that can be made available to support the buyer's marketing. In the retail sector, suppliers have a promotional budget that can be used for radio, press or television marketing. This activity is particularly prevalent at Christmas and other special seasons.

■ *Consider aggregation of demand to negotiate discounts and/or rebates* The former may be available for a single purchase, if the buyer asks! In the electrical wholesaler sector, discounts in excess of 50 per cent may be available on selected lines.

■ *Examine the impact of learning on costs when repetitive tasks are involved* This is referred to as the learning curve, which establishes a relationship between the quantity manufactured and the reduced labour time required to produce them.

12.12 Price variation and adjustment

12.12.1 Price variation

Prices may vary from one supplier to another and at different times owing to the following factors.

■ *Quantity considerations* Quantity discounts are often given as an incentive to the buyer to give the vendor a larger share of the available business. The vendor may also pass on to the buyer a proportion of savings accruing from large quantities, such as reductions in production, selling, transport and administration costs.

■ *Payment considerations* Cash discounts are given as an incentive to prompt payment, enabling the vendor to reduce borrowing and the risk of bad debts. Buyers do not always appreciate the true value of cash discounts. Note that it would be necessary for the bank rate to exceed 36.1 per cent before it would pay an undertaking to forgo a cash discount of 2.5 per cent monthly account. Cash discounts also offer scope for negotiation. A cash discount of 3.5 per cent for 7 days is preferable to 2.5 per cent monthly.

■ *Time considerations* Vendors may sometimes offer discounts to encourage buying in slack trading periods or for buying out of season.

■ *Quality considerations* These reflect the cost of producing from more expensive materials, to higher standards of accuracy or from a brand name.

■ *Distribution considerations* Trade discounts are given to compensate suppliers or buyers for undertaking distributive functions. Manufacturers of original equipment give trade discounts as their market is widened both by the initial sale and the subsequent business in spares.

■ *Transport considerations* The meaning of such terms (Incoterms) as CIF (cost, insurance, freight), FOB (free on board) and DDP (delivered duty paid) should be known and understood.

■ *Annual rebate based on the volume of business in a financial year.*

■ *Trade-in allowances.*

12.13 Price index numbers

A price index number is a measure designed to show average changes in the price of an item or group of items over a period of time.

12.13.1 Simple and weighted index numbers

Simple index numbers calculate price changes over time for a simple item, such as coal or oil imports or population changes. They are calculated by using the formula:

$$\text{Price or relative index} = \frac{P_1}{P_0} \times 100$$

where P_0 is the price in a base year and P_1 the year to be compared.

12.13.2 Weighted index numbers

Where more than one item is involved, as in the index of retail prices (IRP) – usually referred to as the 'cost of living index' – the calculation of an index is more complicated. In the cost of living index, for example, which involves the prices of some 650 items in 14 categories and the collection of about 150,000 separate price quotations, there are the following kinds of differences:

- some prices will fall and others will rise
- prices will vary for different weights and quantities of the same item
- some items are of greater importance to the cost of living than others
- households spend their money in different ways.

Example 12.3

Price index calculation

The average price of an item for the years shown is as follows.

	2000	2001	2002	2003	2004
Price(£)	85	90	95	102	105

Assume for P_0 that the base year is 2000 so the price is £85. The calculation will be as follows.

Year	Price	Base price	Price relative calculation	Price relative	Index number
2000	85	85	85/85	1 × 100	100
2001	90	85	90/85	1.06 × 100	106

Weighted index numbers attempt to make prices directly comparable. The weights used reflect the relative importance of a particular item.

The two most popular weighted indexes are those of Laspeyres and Paasche. The *Laspeyres index* uses base year quantities and weights and indicates how much the cost of buying base-year quantities at current-year prices is compared with base-year costs. Different years can be compared with each other. The Laspeyres formula is:

$$\frac{\Sigma p_1 q_0}{\Sigma p_0 q_0}$$

where p_0 and p_1 are the base-year and current-year prices and q_0 the base-year quantity.

The *Paasche index* uses current-year quantities and weights and indicates how much current-year costs are related to the cost of buying current-year quantities at base-year prices. The different years can be compared only with the base-year and not with each other. The Paasche formula is:

$$\frac{\Sigma p_1 q_1}{\Sigma p_0 q_1}$$

The IRP may be defined as:

> An average measure of change in the prices of goods and services bought for the purpose of consumption by the vast majority of households in the UK.

The IRP is based on the Laspeyres formula.

Example 12.4

Cost of living index calculation

Assume a family's budget is influenced by four main items, A, B, C and D, the weightings (w) of which are 3, 1, 2 and 4 respectively. The price per unit is shown for the years 2003 (p_0) and 2004 (p_1)

Commodity	Weighting	Price/unit 2003	Price/unit 2004
A	3	0.50	0.58
B	1	1.60	1.40
C	2	1.28	1.36
D	4	2.50	2.60

Using 2003 as base, the weighted price relative to index will be:

$$\frac{\Sigma \frac{p_1}{p_0} w}{\Sigma w} \times 100 = \left(\left(\frac{0.58}{0.50} \right) \times 3 + \left(\frac{1.40}{1.60} \right) \times 1 + \left(\frac{1.36}{1.28} \right) \times 2 + \left(\frac{2.60}{2.50} \right) \times 4 \right) \times 100$$

$$= 1.064 \times 100 = 106.4$$

The cost of living is higher in 2004 by 6.4 per cent.

12.13.3 The use of index numbers

Index numbers can be used to:

- estimate current average product prices or costs using the prices or costs of similar items or groups of items at a previous base date
- facilitate the analysis of a time series of prices and costs by eliminating the effects of inflation or deflation
- estimate or negotiate future prices or costs, allowing for changes in the value of a currency
- identify and define price or cost changes as a basis for contract cost or price adjustments (see the example of BEAMA in the next section)
- index numbers can also be utilised to compare the performance of a supplier or two or more suppliers with reference to a given factor such as quality or delivery from one year to another.

Example 12.5

Using index numbers to compare suppliers' performance

A buyer divides the purchase of Part 723 between two suppliers, X and Y, and wishes to compare their performance with regard to quality and delivery for the two years 2003 and 2004.

Solution: Taking 2003 as the base year

Quality rating Part 723

Year	Vendor	Intake	Rejects	Rejects	Index
2003	X	2000	54	2.7	100
2003	Y	1000	23	2.3	100
2004	X	2500	72	2.9	107.4
2004	Y	1500	30	2.0	87

Index X – 2.9/2.7 = 107.4; Index Y – 2.0/2.3 × 100 = 87

Delivery rating Part 723

Year	Vendor	Deliveries	Total days late	Average days late	Index
2003	X	5	35	7	100
2003	Y	4	22	5.5	100
2004	X	8	48	6	85.7
2004	Y	6	38	6.3	114.5

Index X = 6/7 × 100 = 85.7; Index Y = 6.3/5.5 × 100 = 114.5

In 2004, the performance of X has shown a 14.3 per cent improvement compared with the previous year, while that of Y has deteriorated by 14.5 per cent.

The overall rating of Part 723 gives an indication of the supplier's overall performance. Each factor considered is weighted in accordance with its relative importance. Assuming that quality and delivery are weighted 60 per cent and 40 per cent respectively, the overall weighting would be:

Factor	Supplier	
	X	Y
Quality	107.4	87
Delivery	85.7	114.5

$$\text{Overall index X} = \frac{107.4\,(60) + 85.7\,(40)}{100} = 98.7$$

$$\text{Overall index Y} = \frac{87\,(60) + 114.5\,(40)}{100} = 98$$

There is little difference in the overall performance of X and Y, the latter being only marginally superior.

12.14 Price adjustment formulae

12.14.1 The BEAMA formula

Examples of methods of price variation have been given in section 12.10 above. Contract price adjustment (CPA) formulae have been developed for certain industries. The CPA formula originally developed by the British Electrotechnical and Allied Manufacturers Association (BEAMA), was the prototype for similar formulae used by other trade associations, local and central government departments and others.

The fundamental principle of the BEAMA formula is to calculate the variation of labour and material costs in relation to the incidence of expenditure and manufacture throughout the contract period. In the case of electrical machinery, the procedure is as follows.

1 The contract price is divided: 47.5 per cent labour, 47.5 per cent materials and 5 per cent fixed portion.

2 Materials costs are varied using indices provided by the Office for National Statistics at two points in time – the tender date and the average of the indices between the two-fifths and four-fifths points of the contract period.

3 Labour costs are varied by using a labour index published by the BEAMA and based on a Department of Employment figure of average earnings modified to include statutory payments made by the employer. Adjustments in labour costs are made by considering the labour index at the date of tender and the average of labour indices published for the last two-thirds of the contract period.

4 If the cost to the contractor of performing his or her obligations under the contract is increased or reduced due to a rise or fall in labour costs or materials, the amount of such increase or reduction is added to or deducted from the contract price as the case may be. No account is taken of any cost incurred by the contractor that is due to his or her error or negligence.

5 Variations in the cost of materials and labour are calculated in accordance with the following formula:

$$P_1 = P_0\left(0.05 + 0.475\left(\frac{M_1}{M_0}\right) + 0.475\left(\frac{L_1}{L_0}\right)\right)$$

where:

$P_1 =$ final contract price

$P_0 =$ contract price at date of tender

$M_1 =$ average of producer price index figures for materials and fuel purchased for basic electrical equipment as provided by the Office for National Statistics, commencing with the index last provided before the two-fifths point of the contract period and ending with the index last provided before the four-fifths point of the contract period

$M_0 =$ producer price index figure of materials and fuel purchased for basic electrical equipment last provided by the Office for National Statistics before the date of tender

$L_1 =$ average of the BEAMA labour cost index figures for electrical engineering published for the last two-thirds of the contract period

$L_0 =$ BEAMA labour cost index figure for electrical engineering published for the month in which the tender date falls.

Example 12.6

BEAMA price adjustment calculation

Basis of claim for contract price adjustment

Customer: A. N. EXAMPLE   *Customer's Order No......*

A	Contract price	£20,000
B	Tender of cost basis date	20 January 2003
C	Date of order	14 February 2003
D	Date when ready for dispatch/taking over*	12 August 2004
E	Contract period between C and D days	545
F	Date at one-third of contract period	15 August 2003
G	Date at two-fifths of contract period	20 September 2003
H	Date at four-fifths of contract period	25 April 2004
I	Labour cost index at tender or cost basis date	583.1
J	Average of BEAMA labour cost indices for period F to D	614.9
K	BEAMA figures of materials for 'basic electrical equipment/ mechanical engineering' last published before tender or cost basis date	90.9
L	Average BEAMA index figures of materials commencing with the index last published before date at G and ending with the index last published at H	94.5
M	Labour adjustment $47.5 \times \dfrac{J - I}{I} = \dfrac{31.8}{583.1} \times 47.5 =$	2.5905%
N	Material adjustment $47.5 \times \dfrac{L - K}{K} = \dfrac{3.6}{90.9} \times 47.5 =$	1.8812%
P	Total percentage adjustment for labour and materials	4.4717%
	Assumed contract price £20000 × 4.4717% adjustment =	£894.34

12.14.2 Procedure for price adjustment

The procedure adopted for dealing with price increases should include the following:

- adjustments should, wherever possible, be authorised by a single responsible official
- adjustments should be notified to all interested departments, such as design, estimating and so on, or people, such as the project manager
- adjustments should be confirmed in writing
- where standard costing is in operation, a procedure for monitoring price adjustments and variances against standard material uses will be necessary
- where adjustments are calculated in accordance with an agreed formula, the base date of both the original contract and the circumstances giving rise to an adjustment should be clearly identified
- suppliers should be asked to provide data to justify a price increase – an increase of 10 per cent on labour costs only justifies 1 per cent on the total price, for example.

Where the vendor and the buyer cannot reconcile the request for a price adjustment, the latter may consider such strategies as:

- alternative suppliers
- alternative materials
- make-or-buy
- value analysis
- longer-term contracts requiring longer notification of adjustments
- where the supplier is in a monopoly position, the buyer may, as a last resort, take the matter to the Restrictive Practice Court.

12.15 Price and value

Both Oscar Wilde and John Ruskin recognised that price and value are not the same thing. Oscar Wilde[3] defined a cynic as 'A man who knows the price of everything and the value of nothing.' John Ruskin[4] is alleged to have declared:

> There is hardly anything in the world that some men can't make a little worse and sell a little cheaper, and the people who consider price only are this man's lawful prey.

The DTI[5] has defined value for money as:

> taking into account the optimum combination of whole life cost and quality necessary to meet the customer's requirement.

A number of purchasing techniques may be used to obtain the best value for money, including:

- value analysis, especially the elimination of non-essential features
- consolidation of demand – that is, aggregating several orders to negotiate reduced prices or increased discounts
- negotiating contracts and prices centrally
- proactive sourcing – ensuring competition by challenging the repeated use of regular suppliers

- buying complete subassemblies rather than constituent components
- investigating the refurbishment or upgrading of existing or second-hand items, rather than buying new
- encouraging standardisation, thus reducing the cost of spares and maintenance
- adoption of a whole-life methodology rather than an initial price approach
- negotiation with existing or potential suppliers aimed at ensuring additional features or concessions
- application of learning curve analysis to negotiation
- post-tender negotiation
- elimination or reduction of inventory, thereby avoiding unnecessary storage and holding costs
- applications of e-procurement
- global purchasing
- evaluating non-productive cost drivers, such as travel expenses, training, energy, consulting services and similar items
- challenging design or other specifications from a cost function perspective – often the cost of purchased outputs is increased as a result of overspecification.

Case study

The East Shires Utility (ESU) company owns a number of companies engaged in the storage and distribution of water, including complicated pumping stations. There is a 5 year engineering asset renewal and refurbishment programme, for which a budget of £450 million exists. Until six months ago, the Engineering Projects Division (EPD) handled the procurement process from start to finish. The situation changed when ESU appointed a new Managing Director. Within two weeks, he issued a mandatory instruction: 'All purchases will, in future, be handled by procurement.' The Director of EPD did not welcome this change and made it very clear to ESU's Procurement Director that he did not agree with the instruction. Relationships are very strained between EPD and procurement.

There is a need to place a contract for the refurbishment of the Westhead Pumping Station. This is a medium-sized pumping station. The work will require labour, site management, the presence of construction plant and equipment, materials (such as electric motors, switchboards and turbine parts), scaffolding, painting, installation, testing, commissioning and provision of drawings. EPD and procurement have agreed to use the Westhead project as a model for all similar future projects.

EU procurement procedures were followed (the negotiated procedure) and three companies were selected to tender. Even before the process began, EPD made it known that it wanted the contract to be awarded to Tinnion Ltd, which has done pumping station work for ESU in the past. Internal records show that Tinnion has been a very effective contractor. EPD argued that experience of ESU plant is a vital factor and persuaded procurement to make 'experience of similar plant' a tender evaluation criteria, weighted at 20 per cent.

Yukon Construction was also shortlisted. It is owned by a French water utility, but is a registered UK business. It has satisfied all prequalification criteria and has relevant technical expertise.

The third shortlisted company is Normand Ltd – a large engineering project company. It has never done any work for ESU and has made it clear to procurement staff that Normand has been prevented from winning contracts by EPD, which has, in effect, run a closed shop in the past.

Tenders have been received and all three potential suppliers have satisfied all technical requirements, so the price negotiations will decide who wins the contract.

The invitation to tender document requested a price breakdown in a specified form and the information that has been submitted is shown in the table below.

Price element	Normand £	Yukon £	Tinnion £
Site management	40,000	–	156,000
Labour	75,000	–	92,224
Construction plant and equipment	42,000	–	35,890
Materials	27,500	–	*(see below)
Subcontracted work	110,000	–	22,000
Subtotal	294,500	–	306,114
Overheads	29,450	–	61,222
Subtotal	323,950	–	367,336
Profit	32,395	–	45,917
Grand total	£356,345	£280,000	£413,253

* Materials at cost +5% handling fee +6.5% profit (estimated at £38,000)

The analysis and subsequent actions on a pricing decision are to be carried out by Evan Evans, a senior buyer with ESU. He first of all contacted Yukon to ask why it had not provided a price breakdown. It replied that it had not been a mandatory requirement in the invitation to tender document, which is correct. Its stance was that it would stand by its price and its policy was against breaking down costs or prices. Evans noted that 'under no circumstances will Yukon supply a price breakdown'.

Evans next contacted the Director of EPD to ask for the budget figure for the work to be carried out at Westhead Pumping Station. The reply was £450,000. This assumed that the work would be completed within 24 weeks of the contract being awarded. All tenderers have agreed to that date. Evans asked how the £450,000 figure had been determined. The answer was experience and the Director quickly pointed out some of the cost elements. Evans noted:

- crane hire
- helicopter
- design
- transport of equipment to site
- scaffolding
- painting
- site management
- site establishment
- inspection
- on-site machining

- divers
- materials.

The discussion ended with the EPD Director saying that procurement could not possibly evaluate these costs and it should be left to technical staff!

Tasks

1 If you were Evans, what actions would you now take with the tenderers?
2 What lessons are there to be learned for procurement?
3 What type of pricing agreement would you put in place?

Discussion questions

12.1 Which of the following statements are true?
Market prices:
(a) communicate information
(b) determine supply
(c) measure scarcity
(d) provide incentives.

12.2 Price elasticity of demand measures the responsiveness of demand to a given change in price.
(a) Give three examples of household commodities for which demand is (i) elastic and three of those for which demand is (ii) inelastic.
(b) Now give three examples of the items purchased by a manufacturing organisation for which demand is (i) elastic and three for which it is (ii) inelastic.

12.3 Complete the following table by indicating whether demand will be elastic or inelastic and why.

Characteristics	Elastic items	Inelastic items
Whether item is cheap or expensive		
Whether demand can or cannot be postponed		
Whether a rise in price will result in a large or smaller fall in demand		
Whether item is a luxury or necessity		
Whether or not there are substitutes		
Will the demand curve be steep or flat?		

12.4 The most dramatic change brought about by the Internet revolution is that it is establishing something like the textbook condition of perfect competition across a wide range of activities.

What arguments would you use (a) to support or (b) to refute this statement?

12.5 A monopoly has been defined as a firm that is the only producer of a good or service for which there are no close substitutes. Before privatisation, the UK gas, electricity, coal, steel, railways and postal services were all state monopolies.
Discuss the advantages and disadvantages of public utilities being state monopolies. What might be the consequences of nationalising the motor car industry?

12.6 Covisint is an electronic marketplace set up by six major automotive manufacturers – Ford, General Motors, Daimler, Renault, Nissan and Peugeot-Citroën – to serve their procurement needs and those of their providers.
- (a) What benefits did the members expect to derive from the establishment of Covisint?
- (b) On what grounds might Covisint have been considered to violate competition and anti-trust legislation?
- (c) On what grounds did the US Federal Trade Commission and the European Commission give regulatory approval for Covisint?

12.7 Draft some policy statements suitable for inclusion in a purchasing manual:
- (a) stressing the importance of encouraging competition when sourcing
- (b) providing for an exception in the case of small local suppliers.

12.8 What types of pricing agreement would you recommend for the following situations?
- (a) A pharmaceutical company wishes to commission the testing of a newly developed drug by a teaching hospital that will prepare a detailed report at the end of a fixed trial period.
- (b) An engineering company wishes to place an order for the supply of a new component that will entail a lengthier learning period on the part of the supplier.
- (c) A contract for the erection of a new school where there is some uncertainty regarding the depth of the foundations that will be required.
- (d) A contract for a bridge over a river.
- (e) A contract extending over two years for the supply of a standard product to be delivered on a just-in-time basis.
- (f) Where it is essential that a delivery date should not be exceeded and, if possible, should be improved upon.

12.9 Determine, from the following date, the new selling price for a set of 10,000 components as at 1 December 2004.
Base price 1 December 2003 = £768,450
Costs of labour, materials and fuel:

Year	Labour	Materials	Fuel
2003	102.2	128.6	68.5
2004	107.2	133.4	91.0

Weightings: labour 40 per cent, materials 40 per cent, fuel 20 per cent.
(Answer: Index no. = 110.00. New price £845,295.)

12.10 The cost of salad vegetables in consecutive years is given in the following table.

Vegetable	Cost in year 1 (p)	Weighting	Cost in year 2 (p)
Tomato	45	0.4	54
Lettuce	27	0.3	28
Spring onion	15	0.1	20
Peppers	89	0.1	160
Sweetcorn	25	0.1	20

Calculate the index for the cost of salad vegetables in year 2 based on their cost in year 1 and interpret the index.

(Answer: Index no. = 128.2. This indicates that the cost of a salad has risen by 28.2 per cent over the period.)

12.11 Using the following figures, calculate the labour adjustment, material adjustment and the total price adjustment using the BEAMA formula.

Basis of claim for contract price adjustment

A	Contract price	£20,000
B	Tender of cost basis date	20 January 2002
C	Date of order	14 February 2002
D	Date when ready for despatch/taking over*	12 August 2003
E	Contract period between C and D days	545
F	Date at one-third of contract period	15 August 2002
G	Date at two-fifths of contract period	20 September 2002
H	Date at four-fifths of contract period	25 April 2003
I	Labour cost index at tender or cost basis date	464.9
J	Average of BEAMA labour cost indices for period F to D	499.0
K	BEAMA figures of materials for 'basic electrical equipment/mechanical engineering last published before tender or cost basis date	91.0
L	Average BEAMA index figures of materials commencing with the index last published before date at G and ending with the index last published at H	92.2

(Answer: Labour adjustment = 3.4841 per cent
Material adjustment = 0.6264 per cent
Total adjustment = 4.1105 per cent.)

Assumed contract price £20,000 × 4.1105 per cent Adjustment = £822.10

Past examination questions

The following are taken, with permission, from the CIPS Professional Stage Examinations.

1 Explain the concept of price/cost analysis and show how it can be used in the preparation stage of negotiation.

Purchasing and Supply Management II. Tactics and Operations, November 2001

2 Compare and contrast the features of incentive clauses and contract price adjustment clauses to supplier relationships and explain their usage.

Commercial Relationships, May 2002

3 Explain how prices of transport or logistics services would be affected if there was only one logistics or transport provider. List the supply and demand conditions that would be needed to enable a more equitable pricing of transport or logistics services.

Institute of Logistics and Transport. Level 4 Professional Diploma in Logistics and Transport, Mock examination for November 2003

References

[1] Graw, L. H., *Cost/Price Analysis: Tools to Improve Profit Margins*, Van Nostrand Reinhold, 1994

[2] Graw, L. H., 'Is price analysis a lost art', NAPM, International Purchasing Conference, May, 1998

[3] Wilde, Oscar, *Lady Windermere's Fan*, Act 3

[4] Ruskin, John (no date) – this statement is attributed to Ruskin, but found in none of his writings

[5] DTI, *Statement of General Procurement Principles*, HMSO, 2000

Part 3

Strategy, tactics and operations 2: buying situations

Chapter 13

Contrasting approaches to supply

Learning outcomes

This chapter aims to provide an understanding of the purchase of:

- capital equipment
- production materials, including raw materials, semi-finished goods and processed materials and component parts and assemblies
- commodities, including 'sensitive' commodities
- gas and electricity
- component parts and assemblies
- consumables
- construction supplies
- services.

Key ideas

- Categories of capital equipment.
- Characteristics of capital equipment and factors to be considered in its acquisition, financing and evaluation.
- Methods of buying raw materials, including forward buying and futures dealing.
- Commodity dealing.
- Gas and electricity supply chains.
- Energy markets, pricing, switching suppliers using online energy marketplaces.
- Categories and characteristics of consumables.
- Bills of quantities.
- Differences in the purchasing of goods and services.
- Service level agreements.

Introduction

The considerations that apply to purchasing products, and services, can be contrasted according to the nature of the product, the types of production and the principal uses to which a purchased item will be put. We can also distinguish between purchasing consumer, industrial and resale items and services.

- *Consumer products* used in this context, are goods purchased by individuals and households for personal consumption.
- *Industrial products* are purchased by organisations for use in the manufacture of other products to make profits or achieve other objectives.
- *Resale products* are those purchased by organisations in order to resell them at a profit.
- *Services.*

This chapter is concerned with industrial products, consumables or maintenance and repair and operating (CMRO) supplies and services. Consumer products and retailing and wholesale purchasing will not be covered as they are beyond the scope of this book.

13.1 Industrial products

These may be subdivided into:

- Capital equipment items.
- Production materials.

13.2 Capital investment items

13.2.1 Definitions

Capital equipment has been defined by Aljian[1] as:

> One of the subclasses of the fixed asset category and includes industrial and office machinery and tools, transportation equipment, furniture and fixtures and others. As such, these items are properly chargeable to a capital account rather than to expense.

Alternative terms include 'capital goods', 'capital assets' and 'capital expenditure', which can be defined as follows:

- *capital goods*

> Capital in the form of fixed assets used to produce goods, such as plant, equipment, rolling stock.[2]

- *capital assets*

> Assets used to generate revenues on cost savings by providing production, distribution or service capabilities for more than one year.[3]

- *capital expenditure*

> An expenditure on acquisition of tangible productive assets which yield continuous service beyond the accounting period in which they are purchased.[4]

Of the above definitions, that for capital expenditure is the most useful as it emphasises the three most important characteristics of capital equipment, namely:

- *tangibility* capital equipment can be physically touched or handled
- *productivity* capital equipment is used to produce goods or services
- *durability* capital equipment has a life longer than one year.

13.2.2 Categories of capital equipment

From the marketing standpoint, Marrian[5] has distinguished six types of industrial equipment.

- *Buildings* permanent constructions on a site to house or enclose equipment and personnel employed in industrial, institutional or commercial activities.
- *Installation equipment (capital equipment, plant)* essential plant, machinery or other major equipment used directly in producing the goods and services.
- *Accessory equipment* durable major equipment used to facilitate the production of goods and services or enhance the operations of organisations. Installation and accessory equipment often coincide, but there is a distinction. Aircraft purchased by an airline, for example, would be installation equipment; aircraft purchased by a manufacturing organisation to facilitate the movement of executive personnel would be accessory equipment.
- *Operating equipment* semi-durable minor equipment that is movable and used in, but not generally essential to, the production of goods and services, such as special footwear, goggles, brushes and brooms.
- *Tools and instruments* semi-durable or durable portable minor equipment and instruments required for producing, measuring, calculating and so on, associated with the production of goods and services, such as word processors, all tools, surgical instruments, timing devices, cash registers and other such items.
- *Furnishings and fittings* all goods and materials employed to fit buildings for their organisational purposes, such as carpets, floor coverings, draperies, furniture, shelving, counters, benches and so on, but not that equipment used specifically in production.

Some capital equipment can be placed in more than one classification. Thus, a computer system might be either installation or accessory equipment according to its primary application. The classifications are also useful headings for a 'register of capital equipment', in which all acquisitions, replacements and disposals are recorded. An alternative categorisation is given in section 13.5 below.

13.3 Capital expenditure

From the *accountancy* standpoint, expenditure on capital equipment results in the acquisition of fixed rather then current assets. One useful definition of capital expenditure other than those already quoted is:

> all expenditure that is expected to produce benefit to the firm over a period longer than the accounting period in which the expenditure was incurred.

13.3.1 Characteristics of capital expenditure

Expenditure on capital equipment differs from that on materials and components in many ways, including the following:

■ the cost per item is usually greater

■ the items bought are used up gradually to facilitate production rather than as a part of the end product

■ capital expenditure is financed long-term capital or appropriations of profit rather than from working capital or charges against profit

■ tax considerations, such as capital allowances and investment grants, have an important bearing on whether or not to purchase capital equipment and the timing of such purchases

■ government financial assistance towards the cost of capital equipment may be available, such as where a manufacturing organisation is located in a development area

■ the purchase of capital equipment is often postponable, at least in the short term

■ the decision to buy capital equipment often results in consequential decisions relating to sales, output and labour – in the latter case, consultations with the appropriate unions may be necessary.

It is probable that the terms and conditions of purchase will have to be tailored to meet the circumstances arising from the acquisition of capital equipment.

All of these things mean that the purchase of capital equipment is usually more complicated than that of materials and components, a large proportion of which can be handled using repeat procedures.

13.4 Factors to be considered when buying capital equipment

Apart from the mode of purchase, finance and the return on the investment made, the following factors should be considered when buying capital equipment.

■ *Purpose* What is the prime purpose of the equipment?

■ *Flexibility* How versatile is the equipment? Can it be used for purposes other than those for which it is primarily being acquired?

■ *Spares* Cost and ease of availability.

■ *Standardisation* Is the equipment standardised with any already installed, thus reducing the cost of holding spares?

■ *Compatibility and existing equipment.*

■ *Life* This usually refers to the period before the equipment will have to be written off due to depreciation or obsolescence. It is, however, not necessarily linked to the total lifespan of the item if it is intended that the asset will be disposed of before it is obsolete or unusable.

■ *Reliability* Breakdowns mean greater costs, loss of goodwill due to delayed deliveries and possibly a high investment in spares.

■ *Durability* Is the equipment sufficiently robust for its intended use?

- *Product quality* Defective output proportionately increases the cost per unit of output.
- *Cost of operation* Costs of fuel, power and maintenance. Will special labour or additional labour costs be incurred? Is discussion with the trade unions advisable?
- *Cost of installation* Does the price include the cost of installation, commissioning and training of operators?
- *Cost of maintenance* Can the equipment be maintained by your own staff or will special agreements with the vendor be necessary? What estimates of maintenance costs can be provided before purchase? How reliable are these?
- *Miscellaneous* These include appearance, space requirements, quietness of operation, safety and aspects of ergonomics affecting the performance of the operator.

13.4.1 Lifecycle costing

Lifecycle costing – Terotechnology – is an important aspect of capital expenditure. Lifecycle costing is further considered in Chapter 16.

13.5 Controlling the acquisition of capital equipment

Acquisitions of capital equipment may be transformational or incremental. With *transformational acquisitions*, the new equipment may result in a fundamental change in the working of the whole organisation, as would be the case with the installation of a new computer system or the adoption of computer-integrated production. With *incremental acquisitions*, the new or replacement machinery will not fundamentally change the working of the organisation and the effects will generally be confined to the user, function or department. It follows, therefore, that the acquisition of certain items of capital equipment require considerably more deliberation regarding cost, suitability, lifespan and the consequences of acquisition than others. In order to determine the amount of deliberation that should be accorded to a request for permission to acquire capital items, it is useful to assign such requests to a particular category.

- *Category A* strategic new equipment – that is, equipment not already in use that, if acquired, would replace or fundamentally change working methods throughout the company.
- *Category B* operational new equipment – that is, equipment the use or application of which will be confined to a particular function, department, project or operation.
- *Category C* replacement equipment – that is, equipment that replaces existing equipment that is obsolete or has depreciated to a point where repair or renovation would be uneconomical. The replacement of an obsolete machine will entail the acquisition of operational new equipment and is therefore Category B expenditure.
- *Category D* vehicles and transportation – that is, new or replacement motorcars and lorries.
- *Category E* administrative equipment – that is, office machinery, fixtures and fittings required to facilitate the provision of administrative support or office services.
- *Category F* miscellaneous – that is, equipment not exceeding a prescribed value that cannot be assigned to any of categories A to E.

The amount of expenditure and therefore the level of management that will have to give approval of the expenditure will vary for each category.

■ *Levels A and B* will usually require approval by the board or chief executive. Both the board and the chief executive will normally take specialist advice before making a decision.

■ *Levels C, D and E* will, within prescribed limits and subject to budget approval, usually be at the discretion of senior managers.

■ *Level D* will usually be on the basis that vehicles shall be disposed of and replaced at the end of a prescribed 'life', such as three years or on the attainment of a given mileage.

Such policies, when published in the form of a capital equipment guide circulated to all senior managers, provide clear guidelines on the procedures for obtaining approval of capital expenditure and such related matters as the disposal of redundant items.

13.6 New or used equipment

Various aspects of new and used equipment and their respective advantages and disadvantages are examined in Tables 13.1 and 13.2.

England[6] has suggested using the criteria set out in Table 13.3 when deciding whether to buy new or used equipment.

Used equipment may be either rebuilt or reconditioned. With the former, the equipment will usually have been stripped down and built up again from the base. Worn and broken parts will have been replaced and worn surfaces reground and realigned to meet the original tolerances. The rebuilt machine will also have been thoroughly tested and will carry a limited warranty. Such machines will typically cost between 50 and 70 per cent of the cost of a new counterpart.

Table 13.1 **Factors to consider when buying new and used equipment**

New equipment	Used equipment
■ Likely to incorporate the most up-to-date technology	■ Less likely to provide state of the art technology
■ Will provide maximum capital allowances	■ Capital allowances will be based on lower acquisition cost
■ Will probably provide lower maintenance costs, fewer problems and better warranties	■ Maintenance problems will only reveal themselves when the equipment is operating
■ Procurement will be more straightforward, requiring fewer tests and investigations	■ Manufacturers' warranties may not be available
■ Availability of spares may be better	■ Much used equipment is sold as seen. To avoid expensive mistakes, all potential purchases should be vetted by an expert
	■ Difficulties in obtaining spares may be encountered

Table 13.2 **Advantages and disadvantages of used equipment**

Used equipment – advantages	Used equipment – disadvantages
■ Acquisition costs often significantly lower than for new equipment and may therefore offer a better return on investment and price–performance ratio	■ Equipment may be old, with a high risk of early obsolescence
■ Equipment may be thoroughly run in and the teething troubles associated with new equipment eliminated	■ Low cost of equipment may be offset by lower productivity, resulting in increased production costs
■ Used equipment may be available immediately, thus obviating the time required for the acquisition of new equipment	■ warranties may not be given even when available
■ Maintenance records should be available for inspection	■ Warranties are generally short and maintenance costs relatively high
	■ Maintenance records require careful investigation. Who did the maintenance? Have any parts been replaced? Why were they replaced and when?

Table 13.3 **Criteria to use to decide whether to buy new or used equipment**

New equipment should be bought	Purchase of used equipment should be considered
■ When relative efficiency is great enough to be important	■ When price is important, either because the differential between new and used is vital or the buyer's funds are low
■ When the guarantee is better	■ For use with pilot or experimental plant
■ When better essential service is provided	■ For use with a special or temporary order over which the total cost can be amortised
■ When better credit terms are stated	■ When the machine will be idle for a substantial amount of time
■ When longer life is anticipated	■ For use by learners or apprentices
■ When less maintenance is required	■ For maintenance (not production) departments
■ When government finance is available	■ For better delivery time when time is essential
■ When it is desirable to strengthen vendor relationships	■ When a used machine can be easily modernised or is the latest model
■ When repair parts on used equipment may not be available	■ When labour costs are unduly high

Reconditioned machines will not have been as thoroughly overhauled as rebuilt machines. They will, nevertheless, have been cleaned and had all broken or worn parts replaced and been repainted to look like new. However, the guarantee or warranty may be less inclusive than for rebuilt equipment. Reconditioned items generally sell at between 40 and 50 per cent of the cost of new items.

13.6.1 Precautions to take when buying used equipment

Although protection is given by the Sale of Goods, Trades Description and Misrepresentation Acts, the purchaser of used equipment should work on the principle of caveat emptor – let the buyer beware. Some questions that a prospective buyer of used equipment should ask include the following.

- Is a history of the equipment available?
- Is there any indication of age, such as a serial number?
- How well has the equipment been maintained?
- Are spares readily available? Will they continue to be?
- How does the price asked for used equipment compare with the cost of buying new?
- Is the vendor well established? Has the vendor got a sound reputation?
- What special contractual terms and conditions, if any, apply to the purchase?
- Do any guarantees or warranties supersede the protection given under the Sale of Goods Act?
- What trials, test or approval period will the vendor allow?
- Will the vendor permit an inspection by an independent assessor?
- What will be the cost, where appropriate, of dismantling, transporting and re-erecting/installing equipment?

13.7 Financing the acquisition of capital equipment

The acquisition of new or capital equipment may be financed by:

- straight purchase
- hire purchase
- leasing.

13.7.1 Straight purchase

Table 13.4 **Advantages and disadvantages of straight purchase of equipment**

Advantages	Disadvantages
■ The total cost, particularly in comparison to rental, is low	■ Investment in fixed capital resources will reduce liquidity
■ Equipment may have a residual or second-hand value	■ Obsolescence or market changes may drastically reduce residual or second-hand market expectations
■ User has total control over the equipment (there may, however, be maintenance and software constraints)	■ Long-term commitment to maintenance and software may be necessary to protect the capital equipment investment
■ Capital allowances (normally 25 per cent annually on the reducing balance) may be set against tax	■ Equipment may rapidly become obsolete and the costs of upgrading by means of sale, trade-in or leasing may be expensive

The effect of a straight purchase is to increase fixed (equipment) and reduce current (cash) assets. The capital cost of acquisition and the revenue cost of maintenance may adversely affect the working capital of an enterprise and so must, in the long term, be expected to create a positive return on the investment.

Some assistance towards the purchase of capital equipment may be available from central or local government sources, particularly if the company is located or prepared to locate in an 'assisted area'. Enquiries regarding help under the Enterprise Grant Scheme should be made to the regional office of the UK Department of Trade and Industry.

Full information on capital allowances is given on the UK Inland Revenue's website at: www.inlandrevenue.gov.uk/manuals/camanual/

13.7.2 Hire purchase

Table 13.5 Advantages and disadvantages of hire purchase for equipment

Advantages	Disadvantages
■ Provides a compromise between straight purchase and leasing. Hire purchase agreements are easily negotiated and available	■ Financing arrangements impose more restrictions than when equipment is purchased outright
■ Subject to such factors as interest rates and the user's rate of return, hire purchase may be more financially effective than outright purchase or leasing	■ Interest rates and the user's rate of return may make hire purchase a less financially effective method than outright purchase or leasing
■ The most up-to-date technology may be hired and used to increase the company's productivity and efficiency	■ There will, in general, be no opportunity to upgrade
■ After all the payments have been made, the user becomes the owner of the equipment, either automatically or on payment of an option to purchase fee	■ The disadvantages of outright purchase stated in Table 13.4
■ For tax purposes, the user is, from the start, regarded as the owner of the equipment and can claim capital allowance and VAT on the equipment	

13.7.3 Leasing

Leasing is a contract between the leasing company – the *lessor* – and the customer, the *lessee*.

■ The leasing company buys and owns the asset that the lessee requires.

■ The customer hires the asset from the leasing company and pays rental over a predetermined period for the use of the asset.

As shown in Figure 13.1 there are two types of leases: finance leases and operating leases.

Leasing has advantages and disadvantages, as listed in Table 13.6.

Figure 13.1 **Types of lease**

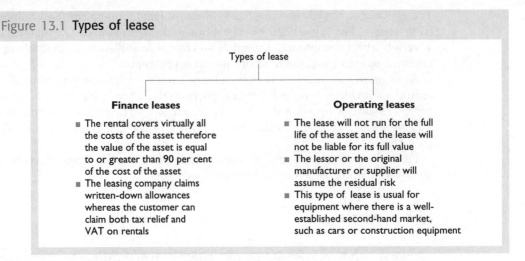

Table 13.6 **Advantages and disadvantages of leasing equipment**

Advantages	Disadvantages
■ Costs are known in advance and cannot be amended without agreement once the lease has been signed	■ Fixed obligation to pay rental may create an embarrassment in depressed conditions
■ Reduced need to tie up capital in fixed assets. Use of an asset can be obtained without capital outlay	■ Does not provide the prestige or flexibility of ownership
■ Leasing is concerned only with rentals and not with grants, allowances, depreciation or other calculations	■ Large organisations may be able to obtain capital or equal terms with lessors and, because of a steady flow of taxable profit, be able to obtain the use of capital allowances for themselves
■ Leasing provides a hedge against the risk of obsolescence	■ The flexibility to dispose of obsolete equipment before the end of the lease may be reduced

Other advantages of leasing include easier replacement decisions. Ownership of an asset sometimes has the psychological effect of locking the owner into the use of an asset that should be replaced by a more efficient item of equipment. Leasing is also a hedge against inflation. The use of the asset is obtained immediately. The payments are met out of future earnings and are made in real money terms with the real costs falling over the years.

13.7.4 Leasing or buying

In practice, the decision to lease or buy is complicated, depending on operating, legal and financial considerations.

■ *Operating factors* relate to the advantages of a trial period before purchase, the immediate availability of cost-saving equipment, the period for which the assets are required and the hedges provided against obsolescence and inflation.

■ *Legal factors* are important as the leasing agreements are one-sided in that most risks are transferred to the lessee. The lessee should therefore carefully examine the terms and conditions of the contract, especially with regard to such aspects as limitations on the use of the equipment and responsibilities for its insurance, maintenance and so on. Where possible, improved terms should be negotiated.

■ *Financial factors* are usually crucial in deciding whether to lease or buy. These include:
  – the *opportunity cost* of capital – that is, what the purchase price of the equipment would earn if used for other purposes or invested elsewhere
  – the *discounted cost* of meeting the periodical rental payments over the period of the lease – note that 'flat' interest rates, calculated on the initial amount owing rather than on the average amount owed, can be misleading.

Example 13.1

How to work out whether it is best to lease or buy

(Taken from *The Lease–buy Decision*, BIM)

Cash price of asset £1000	Leased cost – 20 payments of £75 per quarter over 5 years £1500	Excess cost of leasing over purchase £500 or 50 per cent	Annual flat rate of interest $50\%/5 = 10\%$

The true rate, however, is just over 20.4 per cent per annum, as can be seen from the following table.

Quarterly periods	Balance brought forward £	Repayment in advance £	Interest 20.4064% compound £	Balance carried forward £
1	1000.00	−75.00	43.95	968.95
2	968.95	−75.00	42.48	936.43
3	936.43	−75.00	40.94	902.37
4	902.37	−75.00	39.32	866.69
5	866.69	−75.00	37.62	829.31
6	829.31	−75.00	35.85	790.16
7	790.16	−75.00	33.98	749.14
8	749.14	−75.00	32.04	706.18
9	706.18	−75.00	29.99	661.17
10	661.17	−75.00	27.85	614.02
11	614.02	−75.00	25.62	564.64
12	564.64	−75.00	23.27	512.91
13	512.91	−75.00	20.81	458.72
14	458.72	−75.00	18.23	401.95
15	401.95	−75.00	15.54	342.49
16	342.49	−75.00	12.71	280.20
17	280.20	−75.00	9.75	214.95
18	214.95	−75.00	6.65	146.60
19	146.60	−75.00	3.40	75.00
20	75.00	−75.00	0.00	0.00
		−£1500.00	£500.00	

▶

Ignoring tax, the lessee will be indifferent, on cost grounds, about whether to lease or buy if the opportunity cost of capital is about 20.4 per cent. If the cost of capital exceeds 20.4 per cent, however, then leasing will be cheaper in net present value (NPV) terms. If it is less, then leasing will be the most expensive proposition.

Excluding such factors as the time value of money, capital allowances and maintenance and other ownership costs, the simple lease versus buy break-even point can be calculated by using the formula:

$$N = \frac{P}{L}$$

Where:

P = purchase cost of equipment
L = monthly leasing payment
N = the number of months needed to break even

Thus, if the equipment costs £5000 and the leasing payment is £200 monthly, the simple break-even point is 25 months. This indicates that, other considerations apart, owning is preferable to leasing if the equipment is going to be used for more than 25 months.

13.8 Selecting suppliers of capital equipment

Because the acquisition of capital equipment is a high-risk, high-cost issue, the decision about which of several possible suppliers to accept is normally undertaken by a buying centre.

In general, the greater the technical nature and complexity of an item, the greater will be the influence of the technical staff as both users and deciders. This will apply to both the acquisition of new or used equipment and purchase or lease decisions and, although there tend to be differences between the criteria for purchasing and leasing, the most important considerations in both cases are technical and cost factors.

13.8.1 Technical factors relating to capital equipment

A simple matrix for the comparison and evaluation of quotations or tenders received from, say, three potential suppliers on the basis of technical factors is shown in Table 13.7.

To ensure compatibility, points may be awarded to each factor or, where this is not feasible, to each group of factors. The points given may be weighted according to the importance of the factor, as shown in Table 13.8.

The example given in Table 13.8 points up the major pitfall of the points system of evaluation. The equipment supplied by B scores higher than that of A. The equipment supplied by A, however, is regarded as most having the greater suitability for the user's purpose. The value of checklists such as that in section 13.4 is that they ensure all relevant factors receive consideration, but the final criteria must be fitness for use.

Table 13.7 **Capital equipment: technical factors evaluation sheet**

Factor	Supplier			Points	Aggregate	Recommendations
	A	B	C			
General suitability for purpose						
Ease of installation						
Convenience of operation						
Ease of maintenance						
Power demand (kVA) ■ Normal running ■ Peak running						
Energy consumption ■ Power (kWh) ■ Fuel						
Other utility consumption ■ Steam ■ Water ■ Compressed air						
Equipment warranties						
Estimated life						
Life of items not subject to equipment warranties: estimates of normal operational wear						
Environmental considerations ■ Noise ■ Pollution ■ Effluent treatment						
Appraisal of ■ Electrical equipment ■ Instrumental and control equipment						
Standardisation with existing equipment						
Spare parts to be carried						
Interchangeability of spare parts						
Initial spares or tools to be supplied						
Services to be provided (if any) by supplier regarding: ■ installation ■ commissioning ■ operator training						
Supplier's after-sales service and spare parts availability						
Other relevant factors ■ Delivery time ■ Insurance ■ General reputation or previous experience of supplier						
Totals						

kVA – kilovolt ampere; kWh – kilowatt hour

Table 13.8 **Weighting factors according to their importance for capital equipment**

Factor	Assigned number of points	Points achieved	
		A	B
Overall suitability for purpose	500	400	300
General quality of technical design	400	300	400
Estimated life	400	300	400
Economy of performance and reliability	300	200	300
Economy of maintenance and after-sales service	300	250	200
Environment factors	300	200	300
General reputation of supplier	200	200	300
Estimated trade-in value at end of life or on disposal	200	200	300
Totals	**2600**	**2050**	**2500**

13.8.2 Cost factors

References to the important financial factors relating to the acquisition of capital equipment are made in sections 13.7 and 13.9. Some additional cost aspects that apply to the acquisition of capital items are set out in Table 13.9.

Table 13.9 **Factors to be considered in quotations for capital equipment**

Factor	Supplier			Notes
	A	B	C	
	£	£	£	
Ex-works cost of equipment				
Delivery and handling costs				
Cost of insurance				
Additional costs for essential spares				
Installation costs for essential spares				
Installation costs payable to supplier				
Cost of extra work specified by purchaser				
Customs or other duties/tariffs for imported equipment				
Price escalation charges computed by using accepted formulae				
Terms of payment				
Warranty/guarantee payments				
Servicing, if any by supplier				
Less discounts				
trade-ins				
other deductions				
Less capital allowances				
Final cost				

13.9 Evaluating capital investments

Although this is the province of the management accountant, buyers should have an awareness of the methods of appraising expenditure on capital items. Three highly simplified examples of these approaches – payback, average rate of return and two applications of discounted cash flow – are briefly considered below.

13.9.1 Payback

This is the time required for cash returns to equal the initial cash expenditure.

Example 13.2

The payback approach

An enterprise buys two machines, each costing £20,000. The net cash flows – after operating costs and expenses but not allowing for depreciation – are expected to be as shown below.

Year	Cash flow machine A (£)	Cash flow machine B (£)
1	5000	4500
2	5000	4500
3	5000	4500
4	5000	4500
5	5000	4500
6	–	4500
7	–	4500
	£25,000	£31,500

$$\text{Payback} = \frac{£20,000}{5000} = 4 \text{ years or } \frac{£20,000}{4500} = 4.4 \text{ years}$$

Example 13.2 shows the principle and fallacy of the payback approach. Machine A has the better payback figure as the initial cost is recovered in less time than for machine B. Machine B has an inferior payback, but the return extends over two further years.

The payback method, because of its simplicity, is probably the most popular method of investment appraisal. With this approach, the emphasis is on risk rather than profitability – that is, the risk with machine B is somewhat greater because it has a longer payback period.

13.9.2 Average rate of return (prior to tax)

This method aims to assess the average annual net profit after depreciation and other cash outlays as a percentage of the original cost. Three simple calculations are required:

1 *The annual rate of depreciation* This is calculated by the 'straight line' method, namely:

$$\frac{\text{Cost} - \text{Residual value}}{\text{Estimated value}}$$

Assuming that machines A and B each had an estimated residual value of £1000, their annual depreciation rates would be:

$$\text{Machine A} = \frac{£20,000 - £1000}{5} = £3800$$

$$\text{Machine B} = \frac{£20,000 - £1000}{7} = £2714$$

2 *Deduct depreciation from the average annual profit*

$$\text{Machine A} = £5000 - £3800 = £1200$$
$$\text{Machine B} = £4500 - £2714 = £1786$$

3 *Express net annual profit after depreciation as a percentage of the initial cost*

$$\text{Machine A} = \frac{£1200 \times 100}{£20,000} = 6 \text{ per cent}$$

$$\text{Machine B} = \frac{£1786 \times 100}{£20,000} = 8.93 \text{ per cent}$$

An alternative formula is that of return on capital employed (ROCE):

$$\frac{\text{Average annual profit after depreciation}}{\text{Original capital invested}} \times 100 \text{ per cent}$$

This method shows that the investment in machine B is the most profitable and allows comparison with the returns anticipated from alternative investments.

13.9.3 Discounting

Discounting is the opposite process to compounding. *Compounding* shows the extent to which a sum of money invested now will grow over a period of years at a given rate of compound interest. Thus, £100 invested now at 10 per cent compound interest will be worth £110 in one year's time and £121 at the end of two years.

Discounting shows the value at the present time of a sum of money payable or receivable at some future time. This present value can be obtained by dividing the amount now held by that to which it would have grown at a given rate of compound interest. So:

$$\frac{£100}{£110} = 0.9091 \text{ or } \frac{£100}{£121} = 0.8264 \text{ or } \frac{1}{(1 + r)^n}$$

where r is the rate of interest and n the number of years we are discounting.

These present values are *discount factors* and state that £100 at the end of one year at 10 per cent is worth £0.9091 or £0.8264 at the end of two years. In practice, the discount factors would be obtained from present value tables, which give the following for £1 at 10 per cent and 12 per cent respectively:

Years	10%	12%
1	£0.9091	£0.8923
2	£0.8264	£0.7972
3	£0.7513	£0.7118
4	£0.6830	£0.6355
5	£0.6209	£0.5674
6	£0.5645	£0.5066
7	£0.5132	£0.4523

Net present value and yield methods illustrate two of a number of approaches based on discounted cash flow.

13.9.4 Net present value (NPV)

In this method, the minimum required return on the capital investment is determined. The present value of anticipated future cash flows is that discounted at this rate. If the sum if these discounted cash flows exceeds the initial expenditure, then the investment will be given a higher return than forecast. Using the figures given above and a minimum required rate of 10 per cent, the discounted cash flows for machines A and B would be:

Machine A

Year	Cash return	10% factor	Net present value
1	£5000	£0.909	£4545
2	£5000	£0.826	£4130
3	£5000	£0.751	£3755
4	£5000	£0.683	£3415
5	£5000	£0.621	£3105
6	–	–	–
7	–	–	–
	£25,000	–	£18,950

Machine B

Year	Cash return	10% factor	Net present value
1	£4500	£0.909	£4090
2	£4500	£0.826	£3717
3	£4500	£0.751	£3880
4	£4500	£0.683	£3073
5	£4500	£0.621	£2795
6	£4500	£0.565	£2542
7	£4500	£0.513	£2309
	£31,500		£22,406

Machine A has a total return that is less than the initial expenditure of £20,000 – that is, less than the 10 per cent required. In contrast, machine B will exceed the given figure. This approach is very useful in evaluating which of two alternative investment propositions to adopt.

13.10 The buyer and capital investment purchases

Research findings indicate that:

- capital equipment is more likely to be bought centrally than products of relatively continuous consumption, such as materials and component parts
- purchasing decisions relating to capital items will be made by a buying centre, with the ultimate user, such as the production manager in the case of machinery, playing a dominant role
- the greater the technical nature and complexity of an item, the greater the influence of technical staff in the buying decision.

A respected professional buyer can, however, do more than contribute a list of possible vendors to buying centre decisions. Other contributions may include:

- emphasis on lifecycle considerations relating to capital purchases
- countering prejudice of users in favour of one make of capital equipment, which may exclude consideration of more innovative or competitive equipment available from other manufacturers
- provision of commercial, contractual and negotiating expertise
- identification of alternatives to purchasing new machines, such as the availability of second-hand items, leasing or subcontracting
- identification of central or regional government grants towards the purchase of capital equipment
- investigation of the cost of sourcing capital equipment abroad (see Chapter 14)
- assisting with the disposal of the displaced asset.

13.11 Production materials

Risley[7] has classified materials and parts for use in manufacture under the following three headings.

- *Raw materials* primarily from agriculture and the various extractive industries – minerals, ores, timber, petroleum and scrap – as well as dairy products, fruits and vegetables sold to a processor.
- *Semi-finished goods and processed materials* to which some work has been applied or value added. Such items are finished only in part or may have been formed into shapes and specifications to make them readily usable by the buyer. These products lose their identity when incorporated into other products. Examples include: metal sections, rods, sheets, tubing, wires, castings, chemicals, cloth, leather, sugar and paper.

■ *Component parts and assemblies* completely finished products of one manufacturer that can be used as part of a more complicated product by another manufacturer. These do not lose their original identity when incorporated into other products. Examples include: bearings, controls, gauges, gears, wheels, transistors, radio and TV tubes, car engines and windscreens.

13.12 Raw materials

13.12.1 Characteristics of raw materials

Raw materials are:

■ often 'sensitive' commodities
■ frequently dealt with in recognised commodity markets
■ safeguarded in many organisations by backward integration strategies.

13.12.2 Sensitive commodities

Sensitive commodities are raw materials – copper, cotton, lead, zinc, hides and rubber – the prices of which fluctuate daily. Here the buyer will aim to time purchases to fulfil requirements at the most competitive prices.

The main economic and political factors that influence market conditions are:

■ interest rates, such as the minimum lending rate
■ currency fluctuations, such as the strength of sterling
■ inflation, such as the effect of increased material and labour costs
■ government policies, such as import controls or stockpiling
■ 'glut' or shortage supply factors, such as crop failure
■ relationships between the exporting and importing country, such as oil as a political weapon.

13.12.3 Information regarding market conditions

The main sources of information regarding present and future market conditions for a commodity such as copper are as follows:

■ *government sources* in the UK, the Department of Trade and Industry
■ *documentary sources* these may be 'general', such as the *Financial Times*, or specialised, such as *World Metal Statistics*, published by the World Bureau of Metal Statistics, or the *Metal Bulletin*
■ *federations* the British Non-ferrous Metals Federation or International Wrought Copper Council, for example
■ *exchanges* these include independent research undertaken by brokers and dealers into metal resources and the short- and long-term prospects for the commodity and daily prices of commodities dealt with by the exchange
■ *analysts* these include economists and statisticians employed by undertakings to advise on corporate planning and purchasing policies and external units, such as the Commodities Research Unit

- *databases* these can provide up-to-date information and may be space-saving substitutes for large institutions
- *chambers of commerce* the London Chamber of Commerce, for instance.

The task of the buyer is to evaluate information and recommendations from the above sources and put forward appropriate policies that fall broadly into two classes: hand-to-mouth and forward buying.

13.12.4 Hand-to-mouth buying

This is buying according to need rather than in the quantities that are most economical. Circumstances in which this policy might be adopted are where prices are falling or where a change in design is imminent and it is desirable to avoid large stocks.

13.12.5 Forward buying

This applies to all purchases made for the purpose of increasing stocks beyond the minimum quantities required to meet normal production needs based on average delivery times.

Forward buying may be undertaken:

- to obtain the benefit of economic order quantities (EOQs)
- when savings made by buying in anticipation of a price increase will be greater than the interest lost on increased stocks or the cost of storage
- to prevent suspension of production, due to occurrences such as strikes, by stockpiling to avoid shortages
- to secure materials for future requirements when the opportunity arises, for example, some steel sections are only rolled at infrequent intervals.

Forward buying can apply to any material or equipment. A particular aspect of forward buying applicable to commodities is dealing in 'futures'.

13.13 Futures dealing

Futures dealing is an example of dealing in derivatives. *Derivatives* are financial contracts that have no intrinsic value but instead derive their value from something else. They hedge the risk of owning things that are subject to unexpected price fluctuations, such as foreign currencies and sensitive commodities. There are two main types of derivatives: futures and contracts for future delivery at a specified price and options that give one party the opportunity to buy from or sell to the other at a prearranged price.

A commodity such as copper may be bought direct from the producer or a commodity market. The latter provides the advantages of futures dealing. The London markets are divided into two main areas: metals and soft commodities. The six major primary non-ferrous metals dealt with on the London Metal Exchange (LME) are:

- primary high-grade aluminium
- 'A' grade copper
- high-grade zinc
- primary nickel
- standard lead
- tin.

The LME also offers contracts for secondary aluminium and silver. The soft commodities markets dealing in cocoa, sugar, vegetable oils, wool and rubber are the concern of the Futures and Options Exchange. The International Petroleum Exchange covers crude oil, gas, gasoline, naphtha and heavy fuel oil.

13.13.1 Functions of exchanges

Four functions of exchanges are to:

- enable customers, merchants and dealers to obtain supplies readily and at a competitive market price – on the LME, for example, contracts traded are for delivery on any market day within the period of three months ahead, except for silver, which can be dealt in up to seven months ahead
- smooth out price fluctuations due to changes in demand and supply
- provide insurance against price fluctuations by means of the procedure known as 'hedging' (see Example 13.3 below)
- provide appropriately located storage facilities to enable participants to make or take physical delivery of approved brands of commodities.

13.13.2 Differences between forward and futures dealing

- Futures are always traded on a recognised exchange.
- Futures contracts have standardised terms (see section 13.13.4 below).
- Futures exchanges use clearing houses to ensure that futures contracts are fulfilled. The London Clearing House (LCH), for example, is a professional, international clearing house owned by the six UK clearing banks. The responsibility for completing the execution of trade across the LME ring is transferred from the brokers to the LCH by what is called *novation*. The clearing house is, thus, the buyer and seller of last resort.
- Futures trading requires margins and daily settlements. A *margin* is a cash deposit paid by a trader to a broker who, in effect, lends money to enable the futures contract to be purchased. Traders hope to sell their futures contracts for more than their purchase price, enabling them to repay the broker's loan, have their margins returned and take their profits. No broker may margin a contract for less than the exchange minimum. Each trading day, every futures contract is assessed for liquidity. If the margin drops below a certain level, the trader must deposit an additional, or 'maintenance, margin'. Futures positions are easily closed as the trader has the option of taking physical delivery.

13.13.3 The purpose of and conditions for futures dealing

The purpose of futures dealing is to reduce uncertainty arising from price fluctuations due to supply and demand changes. This benefits both producers and consumers as the producer can sell forward at a sure price and the consumer can buy forward and fix material costs in accordance with a predetermined price. Manufacturers of copper wire, for example, might be able to obtain an order based on the current price of copper. If they think the price of copper may rise before they can obtain their raw materials, they can immediately cover their copper requirements by buying on the LME at the current price for delivery three months ahead, thus avoiding any risk of an increase in price.

For futures dealing to be undertaken, five conditions must apply:

- the commodity must be capable of being stored without deterioration for a reasonable period
- the commodity must be capable of being graded for the purpose of providing a basis for description in the contract
- the commodity must be capable of being traded in its raw or semi-raw state
- producers and consumers must approve the concept of futures dealing in the commodity
- there must be a free market in the commodity, with many buyers and sellers, making it impossible for a few traders to control the market and, thus, prevent perfect competition.

13.13.4 Some terms used in futures contracts

- *Arbitage* the (usually) simultaneous purchase of futures in one market against the sale of futures in a different market to profit from a difference in price.
- *Backwardation* the backwardation situation exists when forward prices are less than current 'spot' ones.
- *Contango* a contango situation exists when forward prices are greater than current 'spot' ones.
- *Force majeure* the clause that absolves the seller or buyer from the contract due to events beyond their control, such as unavoidable export delays in producing countries due to strikes at the supplier's plant. Note that there is now no force majeure clause in a London Metal Exchange contract. Customers affected by a force majeure declared by a producer or refiner can always turn to the LME as a source of supply. Equally, suppliers can deliver their metal to the LME if their customers declare force majeure.
- *Futures* contracts for the purpose of selling commodities for delivery some time in the future on an organised exchange and subject to all the terms and conditions included in the rules of that exchange.
- *Hedging* the use of futures contracts to insure against losses due to the effect of price fluctuations on the value of stocks of a commodities either held or to be acquired. Essentially, this is done by establishing a position in the futures market opposite one's position in the physical commodity. The operations of hedging can be described by means of a simplified example, given in Example 13.3.

Example 13.3

Hedging

1 On 1 June, X (manufacturer) buys stocks of copper to the value of £1000, which X hopes to make into cable wire and sell on 1 August for £2000, of which £750 represents manufacturing costs and £250 profit.

2 The price of copper falls by 1 August to £750 so X sells at £1750 – that is, X makes no profit.

3 To insure against the situation in (2), X, on 1 June, sells futures contracts in copper for £1000.

4 In August, if the price remains stable X will buy at this price, thus making a profit of £250 on the futures contract, which will offset any loss in manufacturing. If the price rises to £1250, X will lose on the futures contract, but this will be offset by gains on manufacturing. While trading refers to actual physical copper trading, a futures transaction is really dealing in price differences and the contract would be discharged by paying over or receiving the balance due.

- *Options* a buyer who expects the price of a commodity to rise may pay option money to a dealer for the right to buy it at a stated future date – a *call option* – or sell at a future date – a *put option*.
- *Spot price* the price for immediate cash payment.
- *Spot month* the first deliverable month for which a quotation is available in the futures market.
- *Options contracts* relate to the sale or purchasing of commodities that will occur at a specified price on a specified future date, but only if the prospective buyer or seller wishes to exercise the option to buy or sell at the predetermined *strike* or *exercise price*. Options, as we saw above, can be either 'call' or 'put'. Buyers of call options are exposed to limited risk as the most they can lose is the amount of the premium or the sum of money paid when the option is purchased. They have, however, an unlimited profit potential. Conversely, writers of put options have unlimited risk but limited profit potential. Mathematically, however, the odds favour the put option writer.

13.13.5 Commodities at the right price

Buying commodities is the province of specialists who have access to current and relevant information. Such specialists use two approaches to determine the right price, namely *fundamental analysis* and *technical analysis*.

- *Fundamental analysis* relies heavily on an assessment, both statistically and in other ways, of supply and demand. Statistics in particular, indicate whether the trend of prices is up or down. In addition to trends, fundamentalists take into account production, consumption and stocks. Thus, an imbalance in production and consumption will affect prices. Prices will rise or fall according to whether less or more of a commodity is being produced than is consumed. Stock figures, according to the mood of the market, may be counted either way. In a *bull*, or rising, *market*, stocks tend to be held by producers or merchants, thus forcing consumers to bid higher for available stocks of the commodity. In a falling, or *bear market*, consumers hive off their stocks and buy less of the commodity than they are using, while producers reduce prices to a level at which they can turn unsold stock into cash. Additionally, fundamental analysis pays attention to news items that affect sensitive commodities, such as wars, weather, natural disasters, political developments, environmental legislation, labour unrest and macroeconomic statistics from major economies.

■ *Technical analysis* claims to be quicker and more comprehensive than fundamental analysis as the market is efficient and the current market price clears the market or brings it into equilibrium. If this is so, it is unnecessary to do more than look at the record of prices to read the future of prices. Technical analysis, therefore, makes great use of chart formations, such as can be obtained from plotting prices on two different timescales, such as daily price movements and the one year rolling average – that is, every day, the latest day's price is added to the list of prices, the oldest year ago price is dropped and a new average for the past year is calculated. Chartists have developed a language of their own for interpreting their charts, such as 'base formation', 'break out', 'overprofit', 'oversold' and so on, to name a few. The results of charting are offered to commodity market makers, often at a considerable charge. The basic concept is that of using the past to predict the future. Chartists, however, are no more able to forecast the effects of news than those who rely on fundamental analysis. In practice, a combination of the two approaches is often used. It has been rightly observed that 'the whole point of having an idea of the "right price" is to spot when the market price is wrong'. Companies have been forced into liquidation by making long-term forecasts on the assumption that today's price is right when, in fact, it is wrong and vice versa.

13.14 Methods of commodity dealing

Dealing in commodities or derivatives is a highly complicated activity, involving the possibilities of heavy gains or losses. In 1995, Barings Bank 'went bust' when one of its employees, Nick Leeson, gambled that the Nikkei 225 index of 225 leading Japanese company shares would not move materially from its normal trading range. That assumption was shattered by the Kobe earthquake on 17 January 1995. Leeson, who attempted to conceal his gamble, lost the bank $14 billion. Warren Buffett[8] said:

> We view them [derivatives] as time bombs both for the parties that deal in them and the economic system . . . In our view derivatives are financial weapons of mass destruction, carrying dangers that, while now latent, are potentially lethal.

An organisation buying large quantities of a commodity will therefore employ a specialist buyer who has made a specialist study of that commodity and its markets. Often, commodity buying will be a separate department distinct from other purchasing operations. Where quantities or the undertaking are smaller, a broker may be retained to procure commodity requirements – in effect, subcontracting this aspect of purchasing.

Other approaches are designed to enable non-specialists to undertake commodity buying with a minimum of risk. These include the following.

13.14.1 Time budgeting or averaging

This is an application of hand-to-mouth buying in which supplies of the commodity are bought as required and no stocks are held. As supplies are always bought at the ruling price, losses are divided, but, of course, the prospect of windfall gains are obviated. This policy cannot be applied if it is necessary to carry inventory.

13.14.2 Budgeting or cost averaging

This approach is based on spending a fixed amount of money in each period – say, monthly. The quantity purchased therefore increases when the price falls and reduces when the price rises.

Example 13.4

The budgeting or cost averaging approach

Assume the monthly requirement for commodity X is 100 tonnes, the average price of which, from experience, is estimated at £100. We therefore budget to spend £100 × 100 = £10,000 monthly. The price fluctuates as shown below.

Date	Cost per tonne	Amount spent	Tonnes purchased
January	£98	£10,000	102.04
February	£97	£10,000	103.09
March	£95	£10,000	105.26
April	£96	£10,000	104.16
May	£95	£10,000	105.26
June	£93	£10,000	107.52
July	£92	£10,000	108.69
August	£95	£10,000	105.26
September	£97	£10,000	103.00
October	£100	£10,000	100.00
November	£102	£10,000	98.03
December	£104	£10,000	96.15
		£120,000	1238.46

$$\text{Average cost per tonne, total cycle} = \frac{£120,000}{1238.46} = £96.89$$

Purchases over the total cycle exceed requirements by 38.46 tonnes. There is thus an average saving of £3.11 per tonne.

13.14.3 Volume timing of purchases

This approach is based on forward buying when prices are falling and hand-to-mouth buying when prices are rising. Its success depends on accurate forecasting of market trends.

Example 13.5

The volume timing approach

Assume that the price of a commodity with a constant monthly requirement of 100 tonnes is between £100 and £120 per tonne. The buyer is authorised to purchase up to 3 months' supply.

In January, market intelligence is that the current price of £100 is likely to rise over the next three months to £120. An order is therefore placed for 300 tonnes at £100 per tonne.

In early March, intelligence is that, over the next 3 months – April to June – the price of £120 will rise further to £135. A further 300 tonnes are ordered at £120 per tonne. In early June, it is forecast that prices will fall. For each of the months July, August, September and October, therefore, only one month's supply is bought, at £130, £125, £120 and £110 respectively. In September, the forecast is of a further rise to £125. Therefore, a forward order for 3 months' supply is placed at £110 per tonne.

The savings from forward buying on the upswing and hand-to-mouth buying on the downswing are shown in the table.

Date	Quantity purchased (tonnes)	Price paid per tonne £	Market price per tonne £	Actual cost £	Market cost £
January	100	100	100	10,000	10,000
February	100	100	110	10,000	11,000
March	100	100	120	10,000	12,000
April	100	120	125	12,000	12,500
May	100	120	130	12,000	13,000
June	100	120	135	12,000	13,500
July	100	130	130	13,000	13,000
August	100	125	125	12,500	12,500
September	100	120	120	12,000	12,000
October	100	110	110	11,000	11,000
November	100	110	120	11,000	12,000
December	100	110	125	11,000	12,500
	1200			136,500	145,000

$$\text{Average price paid per tonne over year} = \frac{£136,500}{1200} = £113.75$$

$$\text{Average market price per tonne} = \frac{£145,000}{1200} = £120.83$$

$$\text{Saving over total period} = \frac{\text{Average market price} - \text{Average price paid}}{\text{Average market price}}$$

$$= \frac{£120.83 - £113.75}{120.83} \times 100 = \frac{7.08}{120.83} \times 100$$

$$= 5.86\%$$

13.15 Purchasing non-domestic gas and electricity

The deregulation of energy supply started in the UK with the implementation of the Gas Act 1986. Then the Electricity Act 1989 brought chances and opportunities, risks and complexities for those responsible for purchasing non-domestic energy supplies. To exploit these opportunities and minimise the risks, purchasers of gas and electricity require a knowledge of energy regulation, the relevant supply chains and energy markets, pricing, the process of switching suppliers, the use of online retail energy marketplaces and energy consultants and management.

13.16 Energy regulation

The Office of Gas and Electricity Markets (Ofgem) is the regulator of Britain's gas and electricity. Ofgem was established in 1999 by the merger of the Office of Gas Supply (Ofgas) and Office of Electricity Regulation (Offer), set up under the Gas Act 1986 and the Electricity Act 1989 respectively. Under the Utilities Act 2000, Ofgem ceased to be an independent regulator and now reports to the Gas and Electricity Markets authority (GEMA) and the Gas and Electricity Consumers Council. The Utilities Act also put Ofgem under the direct control of the Secretary of State for Trade and Industry.

Ofgem also has enforcement powers under the Competition Act 1998 and the power to enforce consumer protection law under the Enterprise Act 2002. It can also name and shame companies that it believes are acting against the interests of gas and electricity consumers. Up until March 2004, Ofgem had imposed or proposed penalties totalling £3.6 million on five companies.

Any organisation seeking to supply gas and electricity to customers has to be licensed by Ofgem, which is one of its powers under the Gas and Electricity Acts. One area it does not licence is the offshore gas industry, which is regulated by the Department of Trade and Industry (DTI).

13.17 Energy supply chains

The UK supply chains for gas and electricity are shown in Figures 13.2 and 13.3.

Most UK gas is produced in the North and Irish seas. Declining reserves, however, mean that it is also necessary to import natural gas from other countries – principally Norway, the Netherlands and Algeria – and liquefied natural gas (LNG) from the Middle East, Africa and the Caribbean. Offshore gas is collected at certain shore locations. Shippers buy this gas and transport it to customers using Transco's distribution system. In 2004, there were over 60 suppliers licensed by Ofgem to sell gas to customers. Many suppliers are also shippers. In 2003, Ofgem published proposals for the separation of Transco price controls into eight regional areas.

Generators produce electricity using coal, oil, natural gas, nuclear energy or 'renewables', such as wind and hydroelectric methods. The bulk of electricity is transmitted, often over long distances, from generating stations to distributing companies and a small number of large industrial companies. There are four UK electricity transmission systems: one for England (National Grid Transco), two in Scotland (Scottish Power and Scottish Southern Energy) and one in Northern Ireland (Northern Ireland Electricity).

Figure 13.2 The gas supply chain

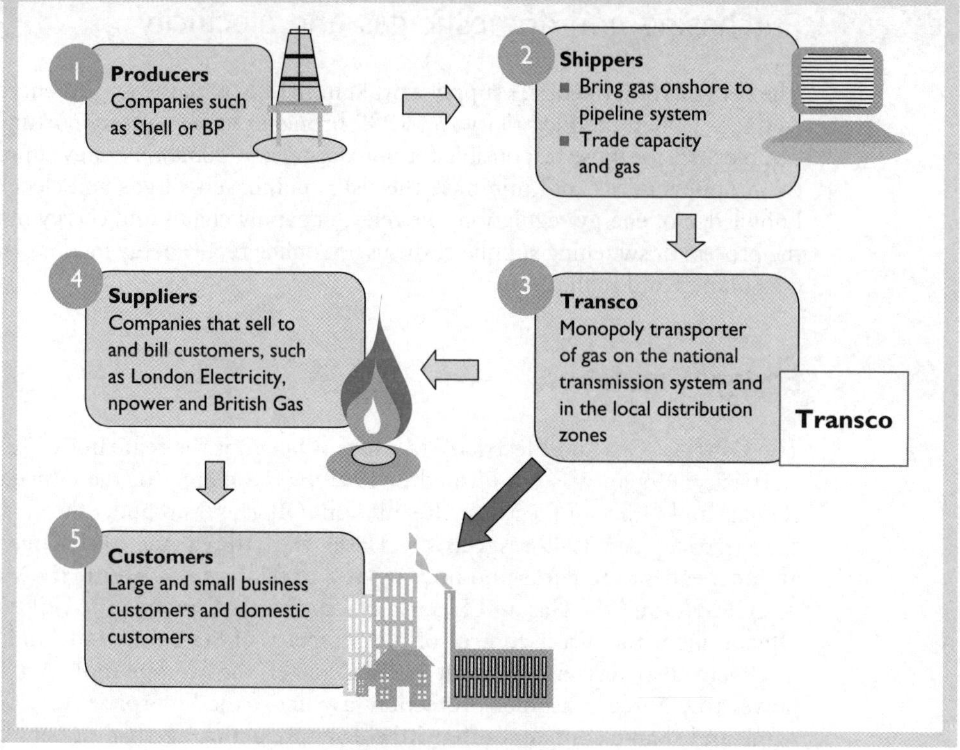

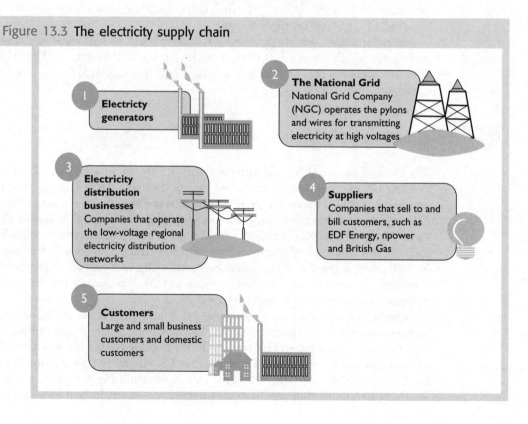

Figure 13.3 The electricity supply chain

The transfer of electricity from the transmitters to suppliers is called distribution. In England and Wales, there are 9 distribution companies operating in 12 distribution areas. In Scotland, distribution is operated by the two vertically integrated energy companies Scottish Power and Scottish Southern Electricity.

Suppliers of electricity, like those for gas, are licensed by Ofgem. At the time of writing there are over 30 suppliers of electricity. A full list of licensed gas and electricity suppliers can be seen on Ofgem's website at: www.energywatch.org.uk

Because of mergers, a number of suppliers – such as British Gas – have become multinational utilities, offering gas, electricity and other services, such as telecommunications.

13.18 Markets

Markets for gas and electricity are both wholesale and retail.

13.18.1 Wholesale markets

Wholesale markets are those in which electricity and gas are traded between parties before being sold to suppliers that, in turn, sell to consumers. In the present context, the parties to the wholesale market are gas producers, electricity generators, transmitters, distributors and suppliers.

The distributors or transmitters are monopolies regulated by price controls based on the RPI – X formula. Using this formula, the prices that transmitters or distributors can charge is limited to the increase in the Retail Price Index less a proportion to drive up transmitter or distribution efficiency. Thus, if the RPI is 3 per cent and X is 2 per cent prices cannot be increased by more than 1 per cent annually.

In 1999, Ofgem announced new (wholesale) trading arrangements for gas (NGTA) and electricity (NETA), which have been implemented. These arrangements are designed to produce prices that respond to competitive pressure and balance the supply for a utility. The aims are to be achieved by online trading on power exchanges – a balancing mechanism operated by the National Grid, a settlement process and associated derivatives markets. Like other exchanges, those for energy enable suppliers to place contracts with producers and generators either for several years ahead or on a daily basis for gas and at half-hour intervals for electricity. They can also reduce price volatility by means of the classic approaches of futures, hedging and options.

The process of balancing is best illustrated by reference to electricity supply. Approximately 24 hours before its physical delivery, suppliers begin to fine-tune their positions to cover any shortfall between their actual positions and that covered by their contracts on the forwards and futures market. Any shortages will be covered by short-term spot trading. Suppliers must declare their positions up to 35 hours before delivery. This is known as *gate closure*. From gate closure to the time of physical delivery, the operator (the National Grid) works to ensure that 'the lights stay on'. This is possible because the UK transmission systems are fully interconnected and the operator can use the bids made on the power exchanges to balance demand and supply.

13.18.2 Retail markets

Retail markets are those in which suppliers sell gas or electricity to consumers.

13.19 Pricing

13.19.1 Gas pricing

Gas was traditionally invoiced in therms, but now, like electricity, is charged in kilowatt hours (kWh). There are approximately 29.3 kilowatt hours to a therm.

The price paid for gas is comprised of:

■ the supply price – that is, the price of the gas itself

■ the price paid for transportation via Transco's distribution system.

Customers pay a total price to the supplier.

The price of gas can vary due to such factors as:

■ the season – the price of gas is more in winter than summer

■ the annual volume of gas used

■ the location of the customer

■ the duration of the contract

■ whether the contract for the supply of gas is firm or interruptible – a firm supply is guaranteed unless there is an emergency whereas, due to weather or market conditions, interruptible customers may be required to interrupt their use of natural gas either by switching to an alternative fuel source or to curtail their use, but, in return, they enjoy lower rates than firm commercial customers.

13.19.2 Electricity pricing

A typical invoice for electricity will be broken down into the following elements.

■ *Total kilowatts used* This is known as the *energy charge*. The energy charge, along with the profit, are the only negotiable elements. The most important aspect of the energy charge is the time at which the energy is used.

■ *Transmission charge* This is the amount paid to the National Grid (NG) in England and differs according to capacity and location. Such charges, for example, tend to be low in the North and high in the South of England. Suppliers pay three forms of transmission charges:

– demand charges, based on demand during the three annual peak demand periods (triads), which differ depending on zones

– energy consumption charges, based on the energy consumed between 1600 and 1900 hours throughout the year

– charges for non-energy ancillary services, covering reserve generation and standby services to facilitate balancing.

■ *Distribution charges* These also vary according to the customer's regional location and the capacity held for the customer.

■ *Meter charges* These are discussed later.

■ *Fossil fuel levy (FFL)* A charge to reduce consumption of electricity produced by using fossil fuels, such as coal and oil, and increase usage of electricity produced by renewable energy sources, such as wind power and geothermal energy.

- *Climate change levy (CCL)* At the Kyoto Summit in 1997, the UK agreed to reduce greenhouse gas emissions by 12.5 per cent of 1990 levels by 2010. The levy is collected by the energy supplier on behalf of Customs and Excise. Energy-intensive industries that enter into a legal commitment to achieve usage reductions over a ten-year term are eligible for discounts of up to 80 per cent.

Ofgem[9] has commented that, while customers have achieved price reductions following falls in wholesale gas and electricity prices, they have been less successful in attempts to secure improvements in service quality in areas such as supplier communication channels, accuracy of billing, frequency of meter readings and rapid resolution of problems. This is partly because customers have little information on which they can base informed decisions about supplier performance.

13.20 Negotiating energy contracts

Buyers of gas and electricity should review their existing contracts and suppliers at least annually. If the decision is made to 'test the market', consideration should be given to timing, usage, negotiation position, the process of switching and the use of e-retail marketplaces.

13.20.1 Timing

This is important because customers must give notice to their existing suppliers (up to three months) and, for all negotiations, customers, should, if possible, avoid approaching suppliers in the six weeks prior to the three busy starting months of April, July and August. Customers should therefore commence tender preparation at least 12 weeks before the expiration of their existing contracts.

13.20.2 Usage

Customers should be able to furnish suppliers with details of their annual usage of gas and electricity and patterns of usage – whether or not it is seasonal, has daily peak periods and so on. This information may be obtained from the customer's current supplier.

13.20.3 Negotiating position

In general, larger users are in a stronger position to negotiate non-standard (bespoke) contracts than smaller ones. What 'large' and 'small' users are can be roughly determined by the type of meter used to measure their usage of gas and electricity.

Larger users of gas have daily meters. Larger users of electricity have half-hourly meters. Smaller users generally have standard contracts with prices set at standard rates. To protect their costs and profits, smaller users should try to negotiate two- or three-year fixed-price contracts. Larger users may be able to negotiate bespoke contracts. Only larger users of gas, for example, can apply for interruptible rates and non-standard pricing options. Larger users of electricity may be able to negotiate seasonal quarterly or monthly contracts, thereby reducing the risk of price volatility.

13.20.4 The process of switching suppliers

Smaller gas customers requiring firm – that is, non-interruptible – contracts only need to furnish potential suppliers with details of their:

- metering point administration number (MPAN) – this is stated on all invoices
- address, telephone number and postcode
- existing supplier
- approximate annual usage and any potential future changes.

For larger suppliers, additional information required may relate to:

- whether the contract required is for firm or interruptible supply
- the type of offer required – standard or bespoke
- the length of contract required
- any other relevant information
- closing date for the receipt of offers.

Essentially, the same information should be furnished by small and large electricity customers, except that it is useful to state:

- the capacity and voltage, as agreed with the regional distribution company, which can be given as low (LV), high (HV) or extra high (EHV) voltage
- electricity usage for each month of the previous year split into day and evening usage.

For most electricity contracts, a quotation should be requested based on a fixed monthly charge, a monthly charge, based on capacity, and unit charges, based on day and night usage. Prices should normally stay fixed for the duration of the contract.

When soliciting offers, consideration may also be given to joint gas and electricity contracts that might attract supplier discounts. It may, however, be cheaper to buy from different suppliers.

Purchasers of energy, large or small, should consider a joint approach to suppliers by a consortium. This might consist of organisations in close geographical proximity or individual tenants of a multistorey office block, for example.

13.20.5 The use of online retail energy marketplaces

The Internet is increasingly the channel for securing energy supply deals efficiently and economically. By utilising the Internet, the time taken to prepare and negotiate an energy contract can be reduced from weeks to days and substantial savings on contract prices can be achieved.

Energy-specific purchasing systems are provided by a number of exchanges, including Utilyx (the largest Web-based auction system), buyENERGYonline and EnergyQuote. The most important approaches to energy buying on retail e-marketplaces are requests for proposals (RFPs) and requests for quotations (RFQs), bulletin boards and reverse auctions.

- RFPs and RFQs automate the paper-based process and save buyers some time. Additionally, energy buyers gain access to more suppliers than they might discover on their own.

Figure 13.4 **Typical transparent price discovery path**

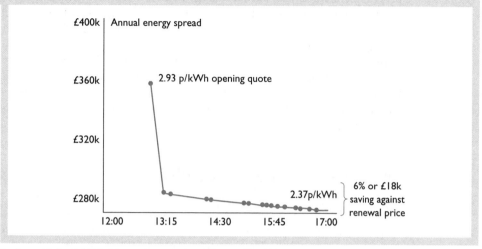

Requirement 1 site 12.5 Gwh (Gigawatt hours – a gigawatt is one million kilowatt hours)
Competition: 7 suppliers – 15 quotes

- Bulletin boards are where an Internet marketer posts the prices offered by affiliated suppliers on its website. Customers seeking an alternative supplier visit the Internet marketer's site and discover the available prices. The bulletin board prices are fixed and stable and the supplier specifies the terms and conditions of the contract.

- Reverse auctions are the most widely used method in the UK. Multiple suppliers bid for an energy buyer's requirement on a 'going, going, gone' basis so that prices keep falling until the energy need has been fully met or the buyer accepts a bid and closes the auction. Suppliers have the ability to see competing bids and react accordingly. With real-time, transparent reverse auctions, suppliers usually undercut each other in the final moments of an auction, as shown in Figure 13.4.

Figure 13.4 shows how a reverse auction can result in thousands of pounds in savings for a customer using £300,000-worth of electricity.

Marks & Spencer and the John Lewis Partnership are competitors, but joined forces to save money by purchasing energy online in a reverse auction on the e-market Utilyx.

The two companies ran three separate reverse auctions – one for each user to obtain independent bids and one with their loads aggregated. The auction covered 347 Marks & Spencer and 154 John Lewis stores.

Eight suppliers submitted a total of 40 bids in a two-week auction. When the final bid was recorded, the offer for the aggregated loads delivered a 1 per cent saving compared with the auction where individual bids had been requested. Overall, Marks & Spencer beat its previous contract by 15 per cent.

13.21 Energy consultants and management

Because of the complexity of energy management, companies may outsource both their energy buying and energy management. Consultants such as EnergyQuote undertake both to negotiate the best deals on behalf of clients and provide services beyond the procurement stage, too, such as energy audits, monitoring and bill checking. A register of approved energy consultants is kept by the Energy Institute, established in 2003. When consultants are used they should be remunerated with fixed fees, not shared savings agreements.

Buyers of gas and electricity can obtain much help from associations of purchasers that share information and expertise in exchange for a fee. Such associations include the Energy Information Centre, the government's Energy Efficiency Best Practice Programme and, for big companies, the Major Energy Users Council. Details of these organisations are available on the Internet.

13.22 Component parts and assemblies

A *component* is a structure that has parts and connections. The parts are also components and the *connections* are to other components. A number of connected components is an *assembly*. Components and assemblies may be either standard, such as a ball bearing, or specific, such as a casting or gearbox made to a particular customer's design. Standard components are, generally, readily available and have the advantages listed in section 9.6.6.

Specific components:

- offer opportunities for liaison between design and purchasing regarding material costs, suppliers and alternatives
- may be jointly developed by purchaser and supplier
- may involve detailed negotiation over such aspects as tooling costs, learning curves and so on
- should always be subject to value analysis
- raise make-or-buy issues
- can often be combined into subassemblies.

13.23 Consumables

13.23.1 Categories of consumables

These are categorised by Risley[10] into operating and maintenance, supply and overhaul items. Often the two categories are jointly referred to as maintenance, repair and operating (MRO) items.

- *Operating supplies* are defined by Risley as 'consumable items used in the operations of the business enterprise', such as stationery, office supplies, machine oil, fasteners, insecticides, fuel, small tools and packaging materials.
- *Maintenance, supply and overhaul items* are defined as 'items which are needed repeatedly or recurrently to maintain the operating efficiency of the business', such as electrical supplies, caretaking requirements, lubricants, paint, plumbing accessories and a wide range of repair parts or spares for plant and equipment.

13.23.2 Characteristics of consumables

Consumables and MRO items are, generally:

- low-cost, low-risk items – with the exception of 'critical' items, such as some spares
- Pareto category items
- revenue items, usually relating to one financial period in contrast to capital items relating to many financial periods
- 'called off' by the actual consumers against orders negotiated with approved suppliers by the purchasing function
- independent demand items suitable for fixed order and periodic stock control systems
- purchased by one of the simplified procedures for small orders
- linked to maintenance policies in the case of MRO items.

13.23.3 Maintenance and replacement policies

Breakdowns and repairs can never be totally avoided, but regular, systematic and thorough maintenance will reduce their number and consequential costs, such as lost production, idle time and hold-ups for other production items. Pareto analysis can provide a useful guide as to where maintenance attention should be placed – that is:

- *Class A* or critical items, which are essential parts of the machine or system, failure of which would result in total breakdown with high repair and other consequential costs
- *Class B* or major components, but where failure would not result in stoppage of the total system
- *Class C* or minor components, the failure of which would not, in the short term, affect the overall process or system.

There are five approaches to planned maintenance that are aimed at keeping equipment or facilities in good operating condition:

- *inspection* by visual means on a regular, planned basis
- *breakdown (or corrective) maintenance* actually waiting for the item to break down and then repairing it
- *preventive maintenance* combining inspection, repair and regular servicing, based on a detailed plan
- *planned replacement* setting fixed times or dates when components or machines will be replaced, irrespective of their condition
- *breakdown replacement* a positive policy, particularly appropriate for small items where maintenance costs would be disproportionately high or items that rapidly become obsolete.

13.23.4 Purchasing and consumables

Apart from negotiating the actual purchase of consumables and MRO items, the purchasing function can:

- liaise with maintenance staff to ensure that information regarding the cost, availability and delivery times is available, especially for 'critical' items
- advocate a policy of standardisation to avoid holding a variety of 'critical' spares

- suggest alternatives, such as outsourcing of catering and cleaning, which can obviate the need to hold stocks of food and cleaning materials
- minimise administrative and storage costs by the application of small order procedures and direct requisitioning by users against 'call-off' contracts, subject to approved safeguards
- analyse proposed maintenance contracts offered by suppliers and advise whether or not these should be accepted.

13.24 Construction supplies and bills of quantities

13.24.1 Construction supplies

These differ in a number of respects from supplies purchased for manufacturing and service organisations.

- Construction supplies are purchased for use on a site that may be distant from the office that placed the orders or even in another country altogether.
- Many construction supplies have a high bulk relative to their value, such as bricks, steel. Because of the high cost of transport, it is desirable that construction supplies are procured as near as possible to the site where they will be used.
- With many construction schemes, the purchasing department will probably be asked to negotiate agreements for electricity, gas and water supplies and, occasionally, for sewage or effluent disposal.
- Specification of construction supplies will often be on the basis of:
  - instructions given by the client to an architect or civil engineer
  - architect's specifications.
  These specifications are often stated in the bill of quantities.
- In the interests of security, it is important that purchased supplies are delivered to site as close as possible to the time that they will be used.
- Because of the remoteness of the site from the contractor's office, procedures for recording of supplies received and issued will have to be agreed between the contractor's purchasing department and site engineer.
- Some construction supplies may be 'free issue' supplies or 'customer furnished equipment' (CFE) – that is, items provided by the client for use in connection with a construction project that is being undertaken on the client's behalf.
- Subcontracting is an important aspect of purchasing for construction projects. Examples would be contracts for foundations, drainage, air-conditioning, lift installation, ventilation, structural steelwork and so on.
- Some construction supplies involve intra-company purchasing. Thus, a construction company may also own stone, sand and gravel quarries that supply other companies within the group.
- Supplies may be transferred from one site or construction contract to another. It is therefore important to know what supplies are available at each site.
- Some discretion must be allowed to the site engineer to arrange for the supply of materials and services, such as hiring plant for particular parts of the project. All such orders should be notified to the contractor's purchasing department to ensure that orders are placed and amounts due to suppliers are duly paid.

13.24.2 Bills of quantities

Bills of quantities are documents prepared by quantity surveyors from drawings and specifications prepared by architects or engineers, setting out as priceable items the detailed requirements of the work and the quantities involved.

Bills of quantities are usually formidable documents running to many pages and incorporating schedules of conditions of the contract in addition to the specifications of labour and materials required for the particular construction project. A typical bill of quantities will have the following six sections.

■ *Section 1: Preliminary items and general conditions* This sets out the terms and conditions of the contract and responsibilities of the contractor, architect and other parties involved in the contract, altogether with provision for the settlement of disputes arising from the contract.

■ *Section 2: Trade preambles* This sets out the general requirements relating to such aspects of a construction contract as:
 – excavation and earthwork
 – concrete work
 – brickwork and blockwork
 – roofing
 – woodwork
 – structural steelwork
 – metalwork
 – plumbing installation
 – foul drainage above ground
 – holes/chases/covers/supports for services
 – electrical and heating installations
 – floor, wall and ceiling finishes
 – glazing
 – painting and decorating.

■ *Section 3: Demolition and spot items* Foundation work
■ *Section 4: General alteration and refurbishment work*
■ *Section 5: Provisional sums and contingencies*
■ *Section 6: Grand summary*

These sections set out the quantities of work to be done

Typical extracts from Sections 2 and 4 relating to plumbing installations are shown in Figures 13.5 and 13.6.

The main aims of bills of quantities are to:

■ enable tenderers to show against each item on the unpriced bill of quantities a price per unit covering labour, materials, overheads and profit and, when totalled in the 'grand summary', the items will provide the tender price for the contract
■ enable the quantity surveyor, on receipt of the successful tender, to ensure that the contractor has made no serious errors that could cause complications at a later date
■ avoid the inclusion by the tenderer of a large amount for contingencies
■ assist in verifying the valuation of variations due to changes in design requested or agreed by the client after the contract has been placed.

Figure 13.5 **Extract from a bill of quantities**

Clause	SECTION 2 Plumbing installation Trade Preambles
R1	**General** Before pricing the specification, contractors tendering are requested to visit the site, peruse the drawings and make themselves fully conversant with the nature of the works for which they are tendering. **HOT AND COLD WATER** **GENERAL INFORMATION/REQUIREMENTS**
R2	**The installation** – Drawing references: See architect's layout – Cold water: Mains fed – Hot water – direct system(s): Unvented direct water storage cylinder Heat source(s): Immersion heaters Control: Thermostat on immersion heater – Other requirements: Remove existing pipework Allow for general builder's work
R3	ELECTRICAL WORK in connection with the installation is not included, and will be carried out by the electrical contractor. Provide all information necessary for the completion of such work.
R4	SERVICE CONNECTIONS are covered elsewhere by a provisional sum.
R5	FUEL FOR TESTING: Costs incurred in the provision of fuel for testing and commissioning the installation are to be included in clause B40 section 1. **GENERAL TECHNICAL REQUIREMENTS**
R6	PIPELINE SIZES: Calculate sizes to suit the probable simultaneous demand for the building and to ensure: – a water velocity of not more than 1.3 m/s for hot water and 2.0 m/s for cold water – suitable discharge rates at draw-off points – a filling time for the cold water storage cistern of not more than 1 hour.
R7	INSTALLATION GENERALLY: – Install, test and commission the hot and cold water systems so that they comply with BS 6700, water supply bye-laws, and the requirements of this section to provide a system free from leaks and the audible effects of expansion, vibration and water hammer. – All installation work to be carried out by qualified operatives. – Store all equipment, components and accessories in original packaging in dry conditions. – Protect plastic pipework from prolonged exposure to sunlight. Wherever practicable retain protective wrappings until practical completion. – Securely fix equipment, components and accessories in specified/approved locations, parallel or perpendicular to the structure of the building unless specified otherwise, using fixing brackets/mountings etc. recommended for the purpose by the equipment manufacturer. – In locations where moisture is present or may occur, use corrosion-resistant fittings/fixtures and avoid contact between dissimilar metals by use of suitable washers, gaskets, etc. – All equipment, pipework, components, valves, etc., forming the installation to be fully accessible for maintenance, repair or replacement unless specified or shown otherwise.

Figure 13.6 **Extract from a bill of quantities**

	SECTION 4			
			Plumbing Installations	
Item	PLUMBING INSTALLATION		£	p
	GENERAL			
A	Bring to site and remove from site on completion all plant required for the work in this section	} Item		
B	Maintain on site all plant required for the work in this section	... Item		
	Installation as shown in the following sections to be carried out to the architect's drawings and specifications			
C	Soil and waste pipes	... Item		
D	Hot and cold water supply including all fittings and rising mains	... Item		
E	Dry riser installation	... Item		
F	Sanitary fittings	... Item		
G	Allow for carrying out all builder's work in connection with the plumbing installations as described including cutting and forming chases, cutting and forming holes, forming ducts through walls and floors, timber support battens, all dire stopping to walls and floors and everything necessary to complete the whole of the works to the reasonable satisfaction of the architect	Item		
H	Allow for testing and commissioning to plumbing installations including obtaining any certificates to be handed to the architect	Item		
J	Hand to the architect at practical completion of the works copies of the manufacturer's operation and maintenance instructions together with two sets of 'as fitted' drawings.	Item		
	PLUMBING INSTALLATIONS CARRIED TO SUMMARY FOLIO NO. 4/63			
			£	

13.24.3 Purchasing and construction contracts

Purchasing will be involved at both the tendering and implementation stages of construction contracts. At the tendering stage, the purchasing function will provide estimators with prices for materials and subcontracted work on which the tender can be based. As tendering is highly competitive, the prices obtained by purchasing can determine whether a tender is expensive or otherwise. Of particular importance will be:

- ensuring that transport costs for materials are kept low by purchasing building items from sources as near as possible to the point of use
- negotiating with subcontractors
- obtaining the best quality commensurate with the life of the item where tenderer/contractor has discretion over what is bought
- effecting suitable delivery arrangements to ensure that supplies are delivered to site as near to when they are going to be used in the project as possible.

13.25 Purchasing services

13.25.1 Purchasing and services

In any large organisation, expenditure on services is a major component of the total spend. Fearon and Bales[11] in a study of 116 large USA organisations reported that:

- over half of the purchase dollars (54 per cent) were spent on services
- only 27 per cent of the expenditure on services in their sample organisation was handled by purchasing staff
- of the total spend, the largest categories were utilities (9 per cent), insurance (82 per cent), sales/promotions (7.2 per cent), health benefit plans (6.1 per cent) and travel – air tickets (58 per cent), and in none of these areas was the purchasing department handling more than half the total expenditure
- two explanations for the low involvement of purchasing departments in the procurement of services are:
  - the users of services considered that they had greater expertise in the particular area of service buying than purchasing department staff
  - the purchase of services involves a closer personal relationship with suppliers than does the purchase of goods, yet Fearon and Bales suggest that 'if a logical purchasing process as normally used by purchasing professionals was employed substantial savings might be possible regardless of by whom the actual buying is done' and they also concluded that 'the opportunity to increase profits through more effective purchasing probably is greater in the buying of services than in the purchase of goods'.

13.25.2 Differences in the purchasing of goods and services

Services can be defined as:[12]

> All those economic activities that are intangible and imply an interaction to be realised between service provider and consumer.

Characteristics of services are:

- *intangibility* the result of a service transaction is not a transfer of ownership as with physical goods – a service is a process or act
- *simultaneity* the actualisation of a service implies the presence of a supplier as well as a customer – both of whom play an active part in the realisation of services.

Intangibility and simultaneity imply two further service characteristics:

- intangibility implies *perishability* – unlike tangible goods, services cannot be stored and used or resold at a future date
- simultaneity implies *heterogeneity* – or the large risk of a service being performed differently depending on such factors as the provider of the service, the particular customer, the physical setting or even the hour of the day.

These differences between services and goods are shown in Table 13.10.

Table 13.10 Comparison of services and goods

Services	Goods
■ An activity or process	■ A physical object
■ Intangible	■ Tangible
■ Service is produced and consumed simultaneously	■ Separation of production and consumption
■ Customers participate in production	■ Customer may or may not participate in production
■ Heterogenous	■ Homogenous
■ Perishable – cannot be stored for future use	■ Can be stored for future use or sale

From a purchasing perspective, there are other differences.

■ Boshoff[13] suggests that, because of their intangibility, services are riskier to purchase than physical products. This enhanced risk is due to:

– service buyers only knowing what they have bought after the buying decision

– the high level of human involvement and interaction, which makes the standardisation of a service not only difficult but, over time, almost impossible

– customers differing in the amount of information they seek before purchasing a service and satisfaction depending on factors such as prior experience and recommendations.

Boshoff suggests that service guarantees reduce the anxiety and uncertainty of potential service buyers.

■ Specifications for goods are generally more specific than service statements of work.

■ Cost analysis and negotiation are more difficult with services than for goods.

■ Services are likely to become a significant proportion of total spend as many non-core service competences are outsourced.

13.25.3 Segmentation of services

Services can be segmented or categorised in several ways.

■ The Kraljic matrix (see section 2.13.11) is equally applicable to services as it is to goods.

■ Hadfield[14] provides a matrix that categorises services according to their cost and strategic impact on a particular organisation. As applied to a bank, an example of this matrix is shown in Figure 13.7.

In Figure 13.7 the lower and upper quadrants respectively reflect lower and higher cost services. The left quadrants show services of the commodity type, of less importance to the bank's operations. The right quadrants hold services that are either essential or of strategic importance to the particular bank. Thus, security is of critical importance, dry cleaning is not.

■ Lallatin[15] suggests simple groupings of five major types of service – personal, professional, support, personnel and construction – each of which has special characteristics from a purchasing standpoint. Typical examples of each type are shown in Figure 13.8.

Some services in Figure 13.8 can be categorised under more than one heading. Finance, for example, can be either 'support' or 'professional'.

Figure 13.7 **Hadfield's matrix of services arranged according to their cost and strategic impact for a bank**

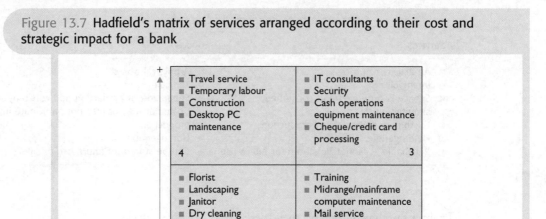

Figure 13.8 **Lallatin's typology of services**

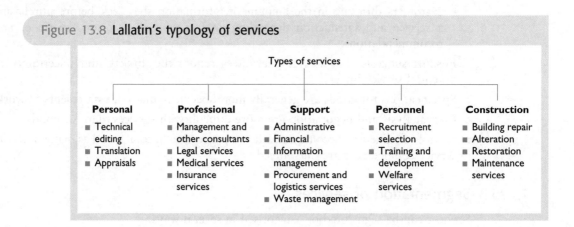

Segmenting services as described above is essential for the analysis of what to spend and their importance.

From the standpoint of *spend*, such analysis shows:

■ *volume aggregation* – that is, the process of collecting and categorising purchasing spend to determine what services are being purchased throughout the entire organisation, who buys and from which suppliers

■ the percentage of spend relating to each category of service

■ areas of excessive service spending where control is required.

From the standpoint of importance, such analysis shows:

■ where a particular service falls on a Kraljic matrix or a cost/strategy matrix

■ whether a service should be provided internally or outsourced.

13.25.4 Processing the purchasing of services

This normally involves six steps.

- *Step 1: Determine the appropriate process for procuring the service*

  This involves consideration of:

  - the nature and strategic importance of the service, with reference to the Kraljic matrix – Duffy and Flynn[16] advise:

    > In general automate or routinise non-critical and leverage buys; identify a champion for each strategic service and form a team to eliminate bottlenecks

  - where purchasing of services such as insurance, advertising, transport or energy is done by non-purchasing personnel, provide training in specialist purchasing techniques.

- *Step 2: Prepare a statement of work*

  A statement of work is defined as:[17]

  > A statement outlining the specific services a contractor is expected to perform, generally indicating the type, level and quality of service as well as the time schedule required.

  Much of the information relating to the content and principles of specification writing given in section 9.4.3 applies equally to statements of work. Statements of work should clearly indicate:

  - the services required

  - where, when and to whom the services are to be provided

  - under what conditions

  - standards or levels of performance required

  - period of initial provision and renewal intervals

  - roles, if any, to be undertaken by the purchaser of the service(s), such as assistance with coordination, equipment, staff or research.

  As with specifications, special attention should be given to language, such as the use of mandatory words 'shall', 'will' and 'must' and avoidance of ambiguous words or words with multiple meanings, such as 'adequate', 'necessary', 'as required'.

- *Step 3: List the statement of work as the basis of a request for proposals (RFP) or quotations (RFQ)*

  - Request that potential suppliers suggest their solution(s) for a given requirement.

  - Provide scope for supplier innovation and suggestions.

  - Such documents are useful for locating solutions or sources of supply.

- *Step 4: Obtain quotations or tenders from potential suppliers*

  Invitations may be advertised generally, thus giving all potential suppliers an equal opportunity to make proposals or quotations. Alternatively, RFPs or RFQs may be restricted to three or four selected suppliers. Reverse auctions are increasingly used as a means of obtaining the lowest price and allowing bidders to see those submitted by competitors. Reverse auctions need the requirements for a service to be clearly specified.

- *Step 5: Evaluate quotations or tenders*

  Evaluation should be by a cross-functional team. Individual evaluators should rank the offers received. The team should then discuss the individual rankings. The final decision should be on the basis of a consensus rather than a majority vote and should be recorded.

- *Step 6: Notification and issue of contract*

  Notify the successful and unsuccessful suppliers and issue the contract. Pohlig[18] states that it is critical – to make the contract enforceable – that the statement of work is either incorporated into the contract or included as an appendix.

13.25.5 Service level agreements (SLAs)

These are defined by Hiles[19] as:

> An agreement between the provider of a service and its user which quantifies the minimum quality of service which meets business needs.

Normally an SLA is not a separate agreement covering service levels additional to the main contract terms and conditions. It is generally a part of the outsourcing agreement and should be regarded as a schedule (or part of a schedule) to the agreement.

The main advantages of SLAs are that:

- the customers for and providers of specific services are clearly identified
- attention is focused on what a particular service or services actually do, as distinct from what it is believed to do
- customers are more aware of what services they receive and what additional services and levels of service a provider can offer
- the real needs and levels of service required by the customer are identified and whether or not these can be modified, which could possibly reduce the cost
- services and service levels adding value can be distinguished from those that do not
- customers have a heightened awareness of what a service or level of service costs and can then evaluate the service or level on a cost–benefit basis
- monitoring of services and service levels is facilitated
- customer reporting of failure to meet service levels enables providers to eliminate the causes and effect improvements
- understanding and trust is fostered between customers and providers.

Lysons[20] lists the principal reasons for SLAs failing as being the following:

- lack of commitment by customers and service providers
- an inadequate support structure, such as failure to implement the SLA concept by means of a project team, appointing an SLA manager and holding regular service level review meetings
- additions to workloads – SLAs require an additional reporting system and, internally, transfer pricing, for example – so attention should be given to compensating for such extra work by relieving staff concerned of some existing duties
- they are too detailed

- they are not detailed enough
- inadequate staff training relating to the purpose, advantages and implementation of SLAs.

13.25.6 Reducing the cost of services

The Institute of Supply Management[21] has identified seven strategies that buying organisations can use to reduce the cost of purchased services. Some of these strategies have already been referred to in section 13.20 relating to the purchasing of gas and electricity.

- Take advantage of volume aggregation to negotiate quantity discounts.
- Commit to supplier development, thereby creating trust and cooperation, which can lead buyers and suppliers to work together to cut costs.
- Develop integrated sourcing strategies so that purchasing professionals can work with users of services to:
  - delay and control maverick spending
  - ensure adherence to agreed purchasing policies and procedures
  - ensure that advantage is taken of contracts negotiated with suppliers for the provision of services at reasonable rates
  - enforce financial controls, such as the verification of services, deliveries, prices and expense limits to prevent overcharging and cost overruns.
  - take advantage of discounts for prompt or early payment.
- Assign responsibility for service purchases to the right people who possess appropriate expertise, such as insurance and travel services.
- Consider consortium buying. This is especially beneficial to small organisations that have only a small requirement for a particular service.
- Outsource service purchases, such as advertising, insurance and so on, to a third party.
- Use reverse auctions.

Case study

The Universal Mining Company (UMC) is engaged in many countries, undergoing deep mining of precious metals. There is a decentralised engineering and procurement function located in each country of operation. One of the countries is in Southern Africa. A need has been identified for the design, preparation of detailed drawings, manufacture, supply, delivery to site, installation and commissioning of a vacuum ice pilot plant with a capacity of 350 tons per day. This will be a pilot plant, offering the design potential to increase the capacity to 700 tonnes per day.

The engineering function has been in discussions with UBV, a German company, for in excess of eight months. A decision has been made to invite a single tender from UBV. Procurement issued the tender, were engaged in its evaluation and, with the necessary approach, placed a contract four weeks ago. The agreed completion date is 14 months from the date of the contract. The internal audit department (a centralised unit) selected the

UBV contract for audit and requested the relevant documents. The audit was conducted by Irene Philips.

Some key extracts from her report are as follows.

1 Only lump sum prices were obtained in the tender (see the details in the table).

Item	Description of work	Total price
1	Design and detailed drawings	Included
2	Manufacture and supply plant	£5,000,000
3	CIF and port charges (estimated)	£195,000
4	In-country delivery	£87,500
5	Site establishment charges	Included
6	Installation charges	Included
7	Commissioning charges	Included
8	Initial spares	£1,250,000
9	Special insurance charges	£100,000
		£6,632,500

Auditor's extract from the report: 'I regret to conclude that this is an unsatisfactory situation. There is inadequate detail and there is no guarantee that the tendered figure will be the final invoiced figure.'

2 Payment terms have been agreed at 30 per cent, with the contract (and this has already been paid but without a bank guarantee); 15 per cent of contract value 8 weeks after contract placement; 25 per cent of contract value prior to shipment, 10 per cent of contract value when plant on site, 15 per cent when installation completed: 5 per cent when the commissioning and the engineer's acceptance have been completed.

This is unacceptable practice in that payments should be made against milestones and retrospectively. There should be a retention for at least six months of 10 per cent of contract value.

3 The supplier's technical commentary includes the following (accepted and mentioned in our contract):

■ as this is a pilot plant, we are unable to offer a plant guarantee, but will use our reasonable endeavours to deal with plant failures

■ the initial list of spares is provided in good faith, but in the event that other parts are required, we will advise on the lead time

■ all parts supplied by our subcontractors shall be repaired or replaced at their option

■ we reserve the right to collect data and operating experience and use it in future plant design – the resultant output will be our intellectual property.

No negotiations have taken place, no risk assessment has been undertaken and the impact of the above on our standard contract terms has not been assessed.

4 It is evident that many meetings have been held with UBV. All minutes of meetings on file were written and issued by UBV. One meeting's minutes included the following notes:

■ the tendered price was accepted and no technical problems were identified

■ UBV confirmed that the planned capacity of 350 tonnes per day would be an objective, but not a contractual obligation

- UBV confirmed that the extent of subcontracting is a commercial confidentiality and could not be released – this also applies to the names of subcontractors (notes should be written and issued by UMC and the points above should have been challenged).

5 The first invoice carries the following comment on foreign currency: 'The above quoted exchange rate is indicative only as per today's rates and will be adjusted according to actual rates obtained on date of completion of transaction.' This is unacceptable financial practice and leaves currency risk entirely with UMC.

The report concludes, 'This is a disasterous contract, for which the relevant internal specialists should be disciplined. Despite a contract having been issued, urgent negotiations should be conducted with UBV to deal with the identified issues.'

Tasks

1 Based on the information provided, if you were representing procurement in any negotiations with UBV, how would you deal with the above issues?

2 Using only the points in this case study, produce a checklist that could be used for future capital asset procurements.

3 How would you deal with the future relationship with UBV?

Discussion questions

13.1 How many of the 'factors' to be considered in buying capital equipment listed in section 13.4.1 do you take into account when purchasing:
   (a) a new or second-hand car
   (b) a new washing machine?

13.2 Explain the statement that it is necessary to classify capital equipment for the purposes of identification and control.

13.3 (a) Give an example of each of the following categories (i–iv) of capital equipment:
      (i)   strategic new equipment
      (ii) replacement equipment
      (iii) vehicles and transportation
      (iv) administrative equipment, such as PCs.
   (b) How may acquisition policies and procedures differ in each case?
   (c) At what management level may decisions be taken for each category?

13.4 Draft a capital expenditure request form that can be used by senior managers seeking board approval for the acquisition of expensive capital equipment.

13.5 XYZ is considering whether to lease or buy a machine. The machine will cost £2000 and have a life of 3 years, at the end of which it will have no residual value. A loan for the purchase of the machine can be obtained for an annual interest rate of 7 per cent, payable at the end of each of the three years. The machine can also be leased from an equipment hire company in return for an annual payment of £762.50, payable at the end of each year.

Ignoring taxation factors, which option will be the lowest-cost solution? What factors might you consider when making a decision?

13.6 Calculate the ROCE from the following figures.

Cost of machine	£160,000
Expected life	5 years
Estimated scrap value	£20,000
Estimated profits before depreciation	
Year 1	£40,000
Year 2	£80,000
Year 3	£60,000
Year 4	£30,000
Year 5	£10,000

Answer: 10 per cent

Note: Average profit before depreciation £220,000/5 = £44,000
Total depreciation = £160,000 − £20,000 = £140,000
Average depreciation = £140,000/5 = £28,000
Average annual profit after depreciation = £44,000 − £28,000 = £16,000

$$\therefore \text{ROCE} = \frac{£16,000}{£160,000} \times 100\% = 10 \text{ per cent}$$

13.7 A machine costs £100,000 and would generate net cash receipts each year as follows:

Year 1	£30,000
Year 2	£60,000
Year 3	£20,000
Year 4	£10,000
Year 5	£4000

Assuming it has a life of five years and no scrap value at the end of that time, calculate the payback period.

[Answer: 2.5 years]
Note: at the end of Year 1, we have recouped £30,000
At the end of Year 2, we have recouped £90,000
We require an additional £10,000, therefore, as this is half of the £20,000
For year 8 the payback period will be 2.5 years

13.8 What lessons can be learned from the February 1995 collapse of Barings Bank due to losses in the derivatives market?

13.9 Under what circumstances would you stockpile a sensitive commodity?

13.10 In relation to futures markets, ascertain the meaning of the following terms:
(a) going long
(b) going short
(c) spot market price index.

13.11 What are the main factors likely to affect the price of petrol?

13.12 As a purchasing officer, what action may you take if you expect a substantial (i) rise or (ii) fall in the price of steel?

13.13 Enquire whether or not your organisation has:
  (i) data on its usage of gas and electricity
  (ii) data on the pattern of usage
  (iii) switched suppliers
  (iv) considered an energy audit.

13.14 (a) As a purchasing officer, are there any services in your organisation that you consider you could buy more effectively than the staff currently responsible for their procurement?
  (b) How would you go about buying:
    (i) private health insurance
    (ii) advertising?

Past examination questions

1 (a) Explain why the markets for commodities tend to be less stable than the markets for manufactured goods.
  (b) Outline some of the ways in which buyers of commodities can attempt to bring a degree of stability into their purchasing.

CIPS Purchasing and Supply Chain Management II: Tactics and Operations, May 2001

2 The difference between service contracts and product contracts is becoming increasingly irrelevant.

Discuss this statement with particular reference to some of the specific issues faced in the drafting and management of service contracts.

CIPS Commercial Relationships, May 2003

3 Identify and explain the particular problems associated with the acquisition of services, to the extent that these problems impact upon relationships.

CIPS Commercial Relationships, November 2001

4 Identify and discuss the ways in which e-commerce and information technology in general have affected the management and operations of the purchasing functions and how they may continue to do so in the future.

CIPS Purchasing and Supply Chain Management II: Tactics and Operations, May 2003

5 Lease and hire agreements offer a number of advantages for the purchasing professional operating in a volatile, fast-changing market. Explain these advantages and the issues that might require consideration in using such agreements.

CIPS Commercial Relationships, November 2003

6 Consortia purchasing seems at first glance to be a desirable option in developing supply chain policy. Evaluate the strengths and weaknesses of consortia purchasing arrangements.

CIPS Commercial Relationships, May 2003

References

[1] Aljian, G. W., *Purchasing Handbook*, National Association of Purchasing Management, 1958, section 16.1

[2] Van Nostrand, *Dictionary of Business and Finance*, Van Nostrand, 1980

[3] Barfield, J. T., Raibon, C. A., and Kinney, M. R., *Cost Accounting*, West Publishing, 1994, p. 709

[4] Definition provided by the Inland Revenue

[5] Marrian, J., 'Marketing characteristics of industrial goods and buyers', in Wilson, A. (ed.) *The Marketing of Industrial Products*, Hutchinson, 1965, pp. 10–23

[6] England, W. B., *Modern Procurement Management*, Irwin, 1970, p. 743

[7] Risley, G., *Modern Industrial Marketing*, McGraw-Hill, 1972, pp. 24–5

[8] Buffett, W., 'Apocalypse is nigh: Buffett tells Berkshire Faithful', *Money Telegraph*, 4 April 2005

[9] Ofgem, 'Review of competition in the non-domestic gas and electricity markets', July, 2003, p. 59

[10] As 7 above

[11] Fearon, M. E., and Bales, W. A., *Purchasing of Non-traditional Goods and Services*, Center for Advanced Purchasing Studies, USA, focus study executive summary, 1995

[12] Desmet, S., Van Looy, B., and Van Dierdonck, A., 'The nature of services' in Van Looy, B., Van Dierdonck, A., and Gemmel, P. (eds), *Service Management*, FT Management, 1998, p. 5

[13] Boshoff C., 'Intention to buy a service: the influence of service guarantees: general information and price information advertising', *South African Journal of Business Management*, Vol. 34(1), 2003, pp. 39–43

[14] Hadfield, J. E., 'Purchasing services on the Internet', *Inside Supply Management*, May, 2002, p. 20

[15] Lallatin, C. S., 'How can I categorise my service purchases', *Purchasing Today*, Nov., 1997

[16] Duffy, R. J., and Flynn, A. E., 'Services purchases: not your typical grind', *Inside Supply Management*, Vol. 14, No. 9, p. 28

[17] ISM, 'Glossary of Purchasing and Supply Terms'

[18] Pohlig, H. M., 'Legal issues of contracting for services', *Inside Supply Management*, September, 2002, pp. 22–5

[19] Hiles, A., 'Service level agreements', *Payroll Manager's Review*, No. 7, July, 1989, pp. 70–1

[20] Lysons, C. K., 'How to prepare service level agreements', CIPS, 2001, p. 18

[21] ISM, 'Reducing the costs of purchased services', 2004

Chapter 14

Buying from overseas

Learning outcomes

This chapter aims to provide an understanding of:

- the terminology of international and global sourcing
- motives for buying overseas
- difficulties in buying overseas
- Incoterms
- distribution costs
- methods of payment in overseas trade
- countertrade
- factors in successful overseas buying.

Key ideas

- Benefits of overseas buying.
- Information sources relating to buying overseas.
- Cultural, political, ethical, quality, exchange risk and legal factors in overseas buying.
- The format and meaning of Incoterms.
- Factors in freight costs.
- Freight agents.
- Open accounts, bills for collection and letters of credit.
- Purchasing and countertrade.
- The true cost of overseas buying.

14.1   Terminology

Birou and Fawcett[1] distinguish between international sourcing, multinational sourcing, foreign sourcing and strategic global sourcing. They define the first three terms as:

> buying outside the firm's country of manufacture in such a way that does not coordinate requirements among worldwide business units of a single firm.

Strategic global sourcing is defined as:

> the coordination and integration of procurement requirements across worldwide business units, looking at common items, processes, technologies and suppliers.

Trent and Monczka[2] also differentiate between international and global sourcing. International purchasing is:

> a commercial transaction between a buyer and a seller located in different countries.

Global sourcing involves:

> positively integrating and coordinating common items and materials, processes, designs, technologies and suppliers across worldwide purchasing, engineering and operating locations.

Among other important findings, Trent and Monczka conclude that firms engaging in global sourcing are likely to have competitors and be larger than those engaging in international purchasing and that 'one can easily conclude that international purchasing is best described as a functional activity while global sourcing represents a strategic direction and organisational process'.

These views are supported by Rexta and Miyamoto[3] who suggest that, in general, smaller firms are restricted in their capacity to search for and secure overseas suppliers by their lack of managerial knowledge and capital resources so that 'any supplier found among a small pool of qualified overseas suppliers is a potential candidate so long as it can meet their procurement requirements'. Moreover, the small quantities they are purchasing makes the business of smaller firms less attractive to first-class overseas suppliers. In contrast, 'a depth of resource capacity allows large firms to aggressively pursue the full potential of international sourcing by capitalising on the world's best suppliers'.

Regarded from a strategic perspective, global sourcing is more complicated than international purchasing. There are, however, aspects where the two approaches converge and international purchasing is strategic as well as tactical. Smaller firms also engage in the development and early involvement of their overseas suppliers. Because of such convergence, Trent and Monczka use the generic term 'worldwide sourcing' to describe international purchasing and global sourcing. The phrase 'buying from overseas' used in this chapter, while also generic, is probably more closely equated with 'international purchasing'.

14.2   Motives for buying from overseas

The primary reason for buying overseas is to obtain some form of competitive advantage. Reasons for international sourcing include changes in the business environment and factors relating to the needs or competitiveness of the enterprise.

■ *Changes in the business environment* Carter and Narasimhan[4] identify the following such changes:

- intense international competition
- pressure to reduce costs
- the need for manufacturing flexibility
- the need for shorter product development cycles
- stringent quality standards
- ever-changing technology.

■ *Factors relating to the needs or competitiveness of the particular enterprise* Such factors include:

- domestic non-availability of, for example, commodities such as rubber, cotton or copper
- insufficient domestic capacity to meet the demand
- insurance reasons, such as buying abroad to maintain continuity of supplies when domestic sources are threatened by shortages or strikes
- competitiveness of overseas sources, including lower prices, improved delivery and better quality
- reciprocal trading and countertrade resulting from policy reasons or government pressures due to balance of payments considerations
- access to worldwide technology
- to obtain penetration of a growth market – Toyota, for example, sources from the Pacific Rim not only to achieve lower costs but also to enter markets with restrictive quotas by increasing the local content component of the cars.

Typical of the findings of a number of research studies into why companies buy overseas are those of Birou and Fawcett.[5] They found that two of the most prevalent reasons for firms sourcing internationally were the lower prices available from foreign sources (for 74 per cent of firms surveyed) and availability of foreign products not obtainable domestically (for 49 per cent of respondents). Ranked on a seven-point Likert scale, with seven indicating the greatest benefit, the advantages reported by Birou and Fawcett's respondents are shown in Table 14.1.

Table 14.1 **Benefits of international sourcing (Birou and Fawcett, 1993)**

Rank	Benefits from international sourcing	Rating
1	Access to lower-priced goods	5.56
2	Enhanced competitive position	5.29
3	Access to higher-quality goods	4.89
4	Access to worldwide technology	4.49
5	Better delivery performance	3.48
6	Better customer service	3.38
7	Increased number of suppliers	2.76
8	Helps meet countertrade obligations	2.60

All ratings are on a seven-point Likert scale, with seven for greatest benefit

14.3 Information regarding buying from overseas

Before firms can commit themselves to purchasing abroad, they must obtain information on potential suppliers. Min and Galle[6] in a survey of ISM's (USA) purchasing managers found the most used information sources to be:

- professional contacts – 48 per cent
- trade journals – 43.7 per cent
- directories such as *Kompass*, *Thompson*, *Jaegar* and *Waldman* – 31.1 per cent
- trading companies – 30.4 per cent
- import brokers – 24.4 per cent. A company new to importing may be wise to use the services of an importer until some expertise in buying overseas has been established.

Other sources of information include:

- visits to the proposed overseas supplier (it is only by such visits that the buyer will be able to see at first hand the potential supplier's factory and the conditions under which the goods are made, but a multidisciplinary approach should be used, which, taking into consideration travel, subsistence and hotel costs, can make it an expensive exercise, but then, if the items to be bought are important enough, the cost of visiting is more than justified)
- references furnished by the proposed overseas supplier
- commercial attachés and other government departments of foreign nations
- the Department of Trade and Industry
- *The Official Journal of the European Communities*
- shipping and forwarding agents
- the banks
- the World Bank
- chambers of commerce, especially the London Chamber of Commerce
- specialist enquiry agents, such as Dun and Bradstreet, offer a product-finding service and run credit checks on prospective suppliers
- trade fairs and exhibitions
- professional and trade organisations, including the CIPS and other national professional purchasing organisations
- Customs and Excise departments
- the Internet, although there is always the possibility that you will be swamped with information if you are not highly selective.

14.4 Difficulties when buying from overseas

Many buyers are reluctant to buy from overseas because of difficulties not encountered or of less significance when buying from home suppliers. The principal challenge to international sourcing mentioned by the Birou and Fawcett survey referred to above are shown in Table 14.2.

Table 14.2 **Challenges to international sourcing (Birou and Fawcett, 1993)**

Rank	Challenges to international sourcing	Rating
1	JIT sourcing requirements	5.14
2	Finding qualified foreign sources	4.92
3	Logistics support for longer supply links	4.91
4	Culture and language differences	4.61
5	Duty and customs regulations	4.41
6	Fluctuations in currency exchange rates	4.39
7	Knowledge of foreign business practices	4.42
8	Nationalistic attitudes and behaviour	3.86
9	Understanding the political environment	3.82

All ratings are on a seven-point Likert scale, with seven for major challenge

Apart from finding qualified foreign suppliers, as discussed in section 14.3 and Customs and Excise regulation referred to in section 14.6, all the items listed in Table 14.2 fall under two headings: risk factors – 1, 3 and 6 – and cultural factors – 4, 7, 8 and 9.

Thus, longer supply lines and the risk of delays resulting from transportation difficulties make JIT arrangements with overseas suppliers difficult, if not impossible. To safeguard against such risks, it may be necessary to hold large buffer stocks, with consequential high inventory costs. Such costs should be considered when evaluating the prices quoted by overseas suppliers. A further brief consideration below of possible cultural, political and ethical, communication, quality, foreign exchange and legal difficulties that may be encountered when buying abroad is followed by a consideration of terminology and the true cost of buying from overseas suppliers.

14.4.1 Cultural factors

Culture is the system of shared beliefs, values, behaviours and artefacts that the members of a particular society use to cope with their world and with one another. Culture differs with nationality and an understanding of such differences is essential when buying from or negotiating with overseas suppliers.

> An American exporter went to negotiate with a Saudi Arabian official. He sat in a chair and crossed his legs, with the sole of his shoe exposed to his Saudi host; an insult had been delivered. He passed documents with his left hand, which Muslims consider unclean. Finally, he refused coffee, suggesting criticisms of his host's hospitality. The price for these unintentional cultural gaffes was the loss of a substantial contract to a competitor better versed in Arab ways.

Cultural aspects that are important in international purchasing include the following.

- *The pace of negotiation* It may be more leisurely than in the West, where the focus is on gaining agreement for a set of specific proposals during a finite period of time

- *Relationships* In Eastern countries, relationships are more important than contracts.

- *Language* In some countries – Japan, China and Korea, for example – communication is often by non-verbal signals and verbal communication is secondary in importance, while in Western countries the converse applies. The language of business may be English, but English words may not be understood in the same way.

- *Time orientation* Delivering on time may be regarded as less important than in Western countries.

- *Information sharing and decision making* In Japan, information sharing is emphasised at all levels of responsibility. Japanese managers prefer group decisions that spread responsibility and emphasise teamwork to a single person making all the decisions.

- *Values* In some countries, the giving and receiving of bribes may be expected. The maxim 'when in Rome, do as the Romans do' thus raises ethical problems of cultural relativism and cultural imperialism. *Cultural relativism* is based on the principle that what is ethical depends on the values of the particular country and that no one set of values is better than another. *Cultural imperialism* is based on the idea that values espoused by us must prevail over those of the country or supplier with whom we seek to do business. Purchasing professionals buying overseas can benefit from studying the analysis of national cultures made by Hofstede,[7] Hampden-Turner and Trompenaars[8] and Lesem and Neubauer.[9]

14.4.2 Political and ethical factors

Political events can destabilise trading conditions. Several agencies – the Political Risk Services, Risk Intelligence and the Economic Intelligence Unit – exist to evaluate country risk. *The Economist*'s index of risk includes measures for bad neighbours, Islamic fundamentalism, authoritarianism, war/armed insurrection, ethnic tension, urbanisation pace and generals in power.

Ethical issues include those of buying from overseas suppliers that operate sweatshops, employing child labour and offering barely subsistence-level pay. Many companies insert clauses into their contracts specifying that suppliers must only employ children who are at least 14 years old, offer the local minimum or prevailing industry levels of pay and respect the right of employees to unionise.

14.4.3 Difficulties in supplier communication

These are due to differences in time zones and working days. The further east you go from the UK, the greater the time difference. In Christian countries, weekends are typically Saturday and Sunday. In Muslim countries, the weekend is Friday and Saturday. The effective working week may therefore be only four days. Physical communication difficulties of the past, however, have been largely overcome by the Internet, e-mail, fax machines and mobile communications.

14.4.4 Quality

Overseas buying will not be competitive if the quality of the items purchased is erratic. The rectification of substandard items is more difficult when buying overseas due to distance and transportation costs. It is therefore important to pay extra attention to:

- specification writing (see section 9.4.7)
- supplier appraisal (see section 11.8)
- quality assurance and quality control (see section 9.8)
- international standardisation (see section 9.6)
- the submission and approval of samples before giving the go-ahead to bulk production
- independent certification of suppliers
- on-site inspection (where appropriate), either by means of personal visits or third-party agents
- preshipment inspection by a third party, such as crown agents, Lloyd's of London and Société Générale de Surveillance (SGS).

14.4.5 Foreign exchange risk

This is the risk that a purchaser of an overseas product will be required to pay more (or less) than expected as a result of fluctuations in the exchange rates between the purchaser's currency and that of the supplier's currency in which payment may be made.

Assume that a UK company buys an item of capital equipment costing $100,000 at a 'spot' price of $2 to the pound, payable in six months' time. If, at the time of payment, the pound has strengthened against the dollar, so that the exchange rate is $2.5 to the pound, the number of pounds required will be lower – in fact, £44,445. Conversely, if the pound has weakened against the dollar so that the exchange rate is $1.75 to the pound, the number of pounds required to buy $100,000 will be greater – in fact, £57,142. The risk of a rise in price due to an adverse exchange rate is termed *transaction exposure*.

Companies buying overseas can minimise foreign exchange risk in several ways, including the following.

- *Arranging to buy in the currency of the buyer* This effectively transfers the risk of fluctuations in exchange rates to the supplier. This may not, however, be the best policy. Scott[10] suggests that, when negotiating international deals, purchasers should:
  - research exchange rates for one or two years previously to benchmark the range of fluctuations in the respective currencies
  - price goods in the currency of the supplier if it is anticipated that the purchaser's currency will strengthen further
  - price goods in the currency of the purchaser if it is anticipated that the purchaser's currency will weaken
  - when agreeing to price adjustment clauses, ensure that currency fluctuations are kept separate from cost increases.

- *Reduce the uncertainty by hedging with forward contracts* for a period of no longer than six months. If a purchaser knows that a supplier must be paid a fixed amount in foreign currency in, say, six months, the purchaser can arrange a six-month forward contract with the bank under which the bank will provide a fixed amount of the foreign currency at the end of that time.

■ *Buy currency options* Such contracts give the purchaser the right (but not the obligation) to buy or sell foreign currency at a specified price within a specified time period. Under forward contracts, options allow the purchaser to benefit from favourable fluctuations in exchange rates.

■ *Buy the overseas currency at the spot price on the day on which the overseas purchase is made* This uses up capital, but interest may be earned on the currency held and the exchange rate is known from the outset.

■ *Negotiate currency adjustment clauses* These may include clauses specifying that:

   – payments may be in a currency other than that of the purchaser or supplier, such as sterling, dollars, Swiss francs

   – 'this contract is subject to an exchange rate of X plus or minus Y per cent. If the exchange rate exceeds these parameters then the contract price shall be renegotiated'

   – 'the contract shall be subject to an exchange rate fluctuation equal to the average of the exchange rate at the time of signing the contract and that at the date of the delivery'.

Developments such as that of the single European currency may help to simplify currency prices and exchange rates in an international context.

14.4.6 Legal difficulties

It is necessary to determine, inter alia, the following:

■ what law shall govern the transaction – that is, whether it is to be that of the importing or exporting nation, but, in general, this will be the law of the country in which the contract is made

■ arrangements for arbitration

■ terms and conditions applicable to cancellation, deliveries and delays and the passing of property

■ protection of the buyer against infringements of patents

■ protection of the buyer against product liability

■ redress of complaints – that is, the return to the supplier of goods rejected or damaged in transit – and, as the recovery of damages is awarded to the buyer by the courts or arbitration, it is useful to ascertain what assets, if any, the supplier has in the buyer's country so these can be restrained by the courts in payment of damages due

■ delays in delivery due to the weather, cargo transfer, dock strikes and customs action

■ transportation, including the terms of delivery

■ import duties and insurance (see the next section on Incoterms)

■ documentation, such as bills of lading, certificates of origin and customs entry forms that are unnecessary for home trade

■ price rises due to increased costs incurred by the supplier and the basis on which these shall be computed or allowed

■ specifications, especially where there are differences in units of measurement.

The United Nations' Convention on Contracts for the International Sale of Goods (CISG) and the Principles of European Contract Law (PECL) are attempts to simplify international trade by harmonising the contract law of individual states. There are 62 'contracting states', including Canada, China, France, Germany, the Russian Federation and the USA (but not the UK), that are signatories to the CISG, the purpose of which is to make it easier and more economical to buy and sell raw materials, commodities and manufactured goods in international markets. In 1999, the UK's Department of Trade and Industry issued a position paper stating that the CISG should be brought into UK law when time is available in the legislative programme, but in 2004, nothing further had been done. Where both the buyers and the sellers have signed it, the CISG will be applicable, unless a statement that 'the United Nations Convention for the International Sale of Goods will not apply' is included in the contract.

The Principles of European Contract Law (PECL), two parts of which have so far been published, were drawn up by an independent body of legal experts from each member state of the EU under a project supported by the European Commission. It is envisaged that the general principles of the law of contracts provided in the PECL will be integrated into what may eventually become a European Civil Code.

The International Chamber of Commerce (ICC) Court of Arbitration is a final recourse for companies situated in member countries. ICC arbitrations are conducted under 'Rules that became operative in January 1998. In all matters not expressly covered by the Rules, the Court and the Arbitral Tribunal act in the spirit of the Rules and endeavour to ensure that their awards are legally enforceable'.

International trade is also facilitated by Incoterms.

14.5 Incoterms

14.5.1 What are Incoterms?

Incoterms refer to the set of international rules for the interpretation of the chief terms used in foreign trade contracts first published by the International Chamber of Trade in 1936 (now International Chamber of Commerce) and amended in 1953, 1967, 1976, 1980, 1990 and 2000.

The reason Incoterms are periodically revised is to ensure that they represent current practice. In the 1990 version, for example, the clause dealing with the seller's obligation to provide proof of delivery allowed paper documentation to be replaced by e-mail for that purpose for the first time.

Although the use of Incoterms is optional, they can reduce difficulties encountered by importers and exporters.

14.5.2 Format of Incoterms

Each Incoterm is referred to by a three-letter abbreviation. The International Chamber of Commerce (ICC) recommends that 'Incoterms 2000' be referred to specifically whenever the terms are used together with a location. For example, the term FOB (free on board) should always be accompanied by a reference to the exact place to which delivery is to be made. An example of the correct use of an Incoterm is:

FOB Liverpool Incoterms 2000

Incoterms are grouped into four categories, each denoted by the first letter of the three-letter abbreviation:

■ under the *'E' term (EXW)*, the seller only makes the goods available to the buyer at the seller's own premises – there is only one Incoterm in this category

■ under the *'F' term (FCA, FAS and FOB)*, the seller is to deliver the goods to a carrier appointed by the buyer

■ under the *'C' term (CFR, CIF, CPT and CIP)*, the seller has to contract for carriage, but without assuming the risk of loss of or damage to the goods or additional costs due to events occurring after shipment or dispatch

■ under the *'D' term (DAF, DES, DEQ, DDU and DDP)*, the seller has to bear all costs and risks needed to bring the goods to the place of destination.

The most used Incoterms are probably FOB, CIF and CFR. Incoterms suitable for any mode of transport, including inter- or multimodal, are EXW, FCA, CPT, CIP, DES and DEQ. Those shown as (S) are used for sea and inland waterways.

14.5.3 An explanation of Incoterms

An explanation of the transport obligations, costs and risks attached to each Incoterm is provided by Table 14.3.

14.5.4 The advantages of Incoterms

■ Incoterms, as stated, are suitable for any mode of transport, although six of the terms are intended only for sea and inland waterway transport.

■ If, when drawing up a contract, buyers and sellers specifically refer to one of the ICC Incoterms, they can be sure of defining their respective responsibilities – especially for passing of title, risks and costs – simply and safely, eliminating any possibility of misunderstanding and subsequent dispute. Thus, while Incoterms do not enter into a contract of sale automatically in the same way that local, national or international conventions do, they may be incorporated into the contract in five ways:

– the custom of the trade

– standard forms

– statutory rules, such as Sale of Goods Acts

– implied terms

– express intention.

■ Incoterms are subject to regular revision so that they reflect transportation and communication changes. FOB Airport and FCA for Shipments by Aircraft, for example, were introduced in 1976 and 1990 respectively. The 1990 revision related FCA, CPT and CID to container vessels.

Table 14.3 Incoterms

Group	Incoterm	Meaning	Carriage	Risks	Costs
E Departure	EXW	Ex-works (named place) Goods are made available at the seller's premises for collection by the buyer	Arranged by buyer. Seller does not clear the goods for export nor load them on to any collecting vehicle	Transfer from the seller to the buyer when the goods are at the buyer's disposal Seller's risks at a minimum	Transfer from seller to buyer when the goods are at the buyer's disposal
F Main carriage not paid by seller but seller must hand over the goods to the buyer's nominated carrier. Free of risk and expense to the buyer	FCA	Free carrier (named place) Unless otherwise agreed, seller arranges export clearance and pays for the precarriage in the country of origin	Carriage to be arranged by buyer or seller on buyer's behalf. If seller's premises chosen, seller is responsible for loading. At any other place, seller not responsible for loading	Transfer from seller to buyer when goods have been delivered to carrier at the named place	Transfer from seller to buyer when goods have been delivered to the carrier at the named place
	FAS	Free alongside ship (named port of shipment) Delivery is deemed to have taken place when goods are placed alongside the ship or inland waterway vessel at named port of shipment. Seller clears goods for export (S)	To be arranged by buyer	Transfer from seller to buyer when the goods have been placed alongside the ship	Transfer from seller to buyer when the goods have been placed alongside the ship
	FOB	Free on board (named port of shipment) Delivery has taken place when the goods pass the ship's rail at named port of shipment. Seller clears goods for export (S)	To be arranged by buyer	Transfer from seller to buyer when the goods pass the ship's rail	Transfer from seller to buyer when the goods pass the ship's rail

Table 14.3 *continued*

Group	Incoterm	Meaning	Carriage	Risks	Costs
C Main carriage paid by seller but without assuming the risk of the main carriage. Seller must, however, bear certain costs even after critical point for the division of risk of loss or danger to the goods has been reached	CFR	Cost and freight (named port of destination) Seller clears goods for export, delivers to nominated carrier and pays costs and freight to bring them to the named port of destination. Risk and additional costs pass to buyer after time of delivery (S)	Carriage to be arranged by seller	Transfer from the seller to the buyer after the goods pass the ship's rail	Transfer from seller to buyer at port of destination, buyer paying such costs as are not for the seller's account under the contract of carriage
	CIF	Cost, insurance and freight (named port of destination) As CFR above, with the additional obligation that the seller is required to obtain and pay for minimum cover marine insurance for goods during carriage (S)	Carriage and insurance to be arranged by the seller	Transfer from the seller to the buyer after the goods pass ship's rail	Transfer from seller to buyer at port of destination, buyer paying such costs as are not for the seller's account under the contract of carriage
	CPT	Carriage paid to (named port of destination) Seller clears goods for export, delivers to buyer's nominated carrier and pays the cost of carriage to named destination. Buyer bears all risks after delivery. If subsequent carriers are used, the risk passes on delivery of goods to the first carrier	Carriage to be arranged by the seller	Transfer from the seller to the buyer when the goods have been delivered to the carrier	Transfer from seller to buyer at place of destination, buyer paying such costs as are not for the seller's account under the contract of carriage

CIP	Carriage and insurance paid (named port of destination) Seller clears goods for export and delivers to the nominated carrier, paying the costs to bring the goods to the named destination. Seller also obtains and pays for insurance against the buyer's risk of loss or damage to the cargo during carriage on minimum cover. Risk passes when goods delivered to the first carrier	Carriage and insurance to be arranged by the seller	Transfer from the seller to the buyer when goods have been delivered to the carrier	Transfer from seller to buyer at port of destination, buyer paying such costs as are not for the seller's account under the contract of carriage
D Arrival Seller's cost/risk is maximised as goods must be made available on arrival at a stated destination				
DAF	Delivered at frontier (named place) Seller delivers when goods are at the disposal of buyer on the arriving means of transport, cleared for export but not import at the named point of frontier. Contract of sale to state if risk and costs of unloading from arriving means of transport to be borne by seller	Carriage to be arranged by seller	Transfer from seller to buyer after goods have been delivered at frontier	Transfer from seller to buyer when goods have been delivered to the frontier
DES	Delivered ex ship (named port of destination) Seller delivers when goods are placed at disposal of buyer on board ship not cleared for import. Seller bears all costs and risks to port of destination prior to unloading (S)	Carriage to be arranged by seller	Transfer from seller to buyer when goods are placed at the disposal of the buyer on board ship	Transfer from seller to buyer when goods are placed at the disposal of the buyer on board ship

Table 14.3 continued

Group	Incoterm	Meaning	Carriage	Risks	Costs
	DEQ	Delivered ex quay (named port of destination) Delivery takes place when goods, not cleared, are placed at the disposal of the buyer on the quay at the named port of destination. Seller incurs all costs and risks on boarding goods to the port of destination, including cost of unloading. Buyer clears goods for import and pays all customs-related formalities and duties. Contract of sale to specify any further seller obligations on import (S)	Carriage to be arranged by seller	Transfer from seller to buyer after goods placed at the disposal of the buyer on the quay	Transfer from seller to buyer after goods are placed at the disposal of the buyer on the quay
	DDU	Delivered duty unpaid (named place of destination) Seller delivers goods to buyer not cleared for import and not unloaded from any arriving means of transport at named place of destination. Seller bears costs and risks of bringing goods to this point, but not customs formalities or payment of duties. Contract of sale to specify if seller's responsibility extended to customs formalities	Carriage to be arranged by seller	Transfer from seller to buyer when goods are placed at the disposal of the buyer	Transfer from seller to buyer when the goods are placed at the disposal of the buyer
	DDP	Delivered duty paid (named port of destination) Seller's maximum obligation, involving delivery of goods to buyer, all costs and risks in bringing goods to that point cleared for import and paying duties, but not unloaded from arriving means of transport at place of destination. Contract of sale to state if seller is excused from any costs payable in connection with import. Not to be used if seller is unable to obtain import licence	Carriage to be arranged by seller	Transfer from seller to buyer when the goods are placed at the disposal of the buyer	Transfer from seller to buyer when the goods are placed at the disposal of the buyer

14.6 Customs and Excise

All goods, new or used, imported into the EU from outside the EU are subject to customs duty (import duty or import tax) and value added tax (VAT) according to their value and import tax classification. All goods imported into the UK from outside the EU must be declared to HM Customs and Excise and, in most cases, this includes goods bought via the Internet. The importer is legally liable for import duty and VAT.

Import duty rates are set annually by the EU and published by each EU country in a 'Customs Tariff'. The *HM Customs and Excise Integrated Tariff of the UK* (known as *the tariff*) is published by the Stationery Office in three large loose-leaf binders. The tariff, based on the Common Customs Tariff (CCT) of the EU, provides general information on tariffs affecting the import, export and transport of goods, valuation of goods for import duty purposes, VAT and excise duties (excise duties are payable on certain goods such as wines, spirits and tobacco and are payable in addition to import duty).

The rate of import duty varies according to the type of goods imported and the country of origin. Normally, import duty is based on a percentage of the value of the goods, plus the transport and insurance costs to the country of destination and may also include such costs as tools, dies, moulds, design work, royalties and licence fees. VAT, which varies across EU member states, is then added. The process is exemplified by the following illustration:

	£	£
Value of goods, say	100.00	
Shipping and insurance costs to the UK, say	15.00	
Total value for import duty	115.00	
Import duty payable at, say, 5 per cent	5.75	5.75
	120.75	
VAT on £120.75 at 17.5 per cent	21.13	21.13
	141.88	26.88

From the above example, it can be seen that, in most cases, VAT will be the largest tax to pay on importation. The total tax payable is £26.88 on the original price of these goods.

In addition, a customs clearance fee will be charged by the courier, carrier, freight forwarder or import agent (including the Royal Mail or Parcel Force) for clearing the product through customs. There can be further charges for storage if the goods are held up in customs or due to late payment.

Further details of customs charges can be obtained from the websites of HM Customs and Excise and the UK Department of Trade and Industry. Rates of import duty on a particular product can be found at the EU TARIC (Integrated Tariff of the European Communities) database on the Internet.

14.7 Total distribution costs

14.7.1 Definition

The total cost of distribution may be defined as:

The sum total of all the costs incurred in the distribution of the goods.

Clearly costs will differ from organisation to organisation and a company may have specific 'total' distribution costs that may include such items as a private goods vehicle fleet (either owned or leased) or IT costs for hardware and software to manage the total supply chain operation. In general, however, the total cost of distribution will include such items as transportation charges, inventory carrying costs, service factors, packaging, insurance and miscellaneous costs.

14.7.2 Elements of freight costs

Fixed and variable costs

All costs may be divided into either fixed or variable. In relation to the five main modes of transport, these may be summarised as in Table 14.4.

Table 14.4 Fixed and variable costs of differing modes of transport

Mode of transport	Suitable for	Fixed cost	Variable cost
Road	Medium/light loads	Low	Medium
Rail	Heavy bulk loads	High	Low
Air	High-value goods where rapid delivery is important	Low	High
Water	Heavy bulk loads, including oil and timber	Medium	Low
Pipelines	Petrol, chemicals	High	Low

Critical transport elements

On a five-point scale, with one for best and five for worst, the critical operating characteristics may be rated as shown in Table 14.5.

Table 14.5 Operating characteristics of five modes of transport

Operating characteristics	Mode of transport				
	Road	Rail	Air	Water	Pipeline
Speed	2	3	1	4	5
Availability	1	2	3	4	5
Dependability	2	3	5	4	1
Capability	3	2	5	4	1
Flexibility	1	3	5	2	5
Environmental	5	3	4	1	1
Composite	14	16	23	19	18

Rates

Rates paid to hire carriers can be classified as follows.

- *Volume rates* Volume is reflected in the rate structure, which may take account of such factors as the size of shipments – that is, consistently high-volume shipments being given lower rates than those for smaller shipments. Such special rates are considered to be deviations from the usual rates that apply to lower-volume shipments.

- *Distance-related rates* Such rates may be:
  - *uniform rates* – that is, one transport rate for all origin–destination distances
  - *proportional rates*, in which the rate varies with the distance
  - *tapering rates*, in which rates increase with distance, but by a decreasing amount
  - *blanket rates*, which are single rates covering a specified area for specified products, such as coal or grain – often adjusted so that they are competitive.
- *Demand-related rates* These rates are often set at levels that are claimed to be what the traffic will bear and so the level is determined by the competition for a particular freight service.

Other factors that may influence rates include:

- the product – its bulk, volume, fragility
- the freight provider – there are conference and independent rates for ocean shipping
- incentive rates – shippers may be offered reduced rates if an agreed minimum tonnage is moved within a specified time period or increased rates may be offered to carriers for an assurance that goods will reach their destination ahead of normal times.

Inventory carrying costs

With global sourcing, deliveries will usually be in the form of large consignments, which means that storage space is needed so holding costs can be increased. This element is rarely considered in the total cost model for global procurement.

Service factors

Transportation costs are strongly influenced by the level of service that a supply chain aims to provide. If, for example, a supplier aims to dispatch goods on the same day an order is received, it will have many small outbound loads, resulting in high transport costs. Conversely, by aggregating orders over a period, it will be able to make larger deliveries at lower transport costs by exploiting economies of scale.

A second factor in transportation costs is the *transportation network*. The achievement of low-cost responsiveness depends, to a large extent, on a well-designed transportation network that provides the infrastructure for efficient vehicle scheduling and routing.

Networks can be direct or indirect. With a *direct delivery*, the routing of each consignment is from supplier to customer. Direct delivery, usually by road, is justified when each consignment is large enough for consignments to constitute a full load to each customer. Consignments can be consolidated to enable one vehicle to make 'drops' to a number of customers, such as when a supplier makes deliveries within an area of high customer density.

Indirect delivery is where, instead of making deliveries directly, suppliers make use of distribution centres. Such distribution centres facilitate cross-docking, which is the merging of goods flows from several sources at a distribution centre before final delivery but without any inventory being held at the distribution centre. Cross-docking, as shown in Figure 14.1, is appropriate when volumes are predictable and it enables economies of scale to be achieved by both suppliers and customers.

An effective distribution plan will determine the optimal network to ensure that customers are provided with the right quantity of goods in the right places at the right times for the lowest total distribution costs.

Figure 14.1 **Indirect delivery and distribution centre**

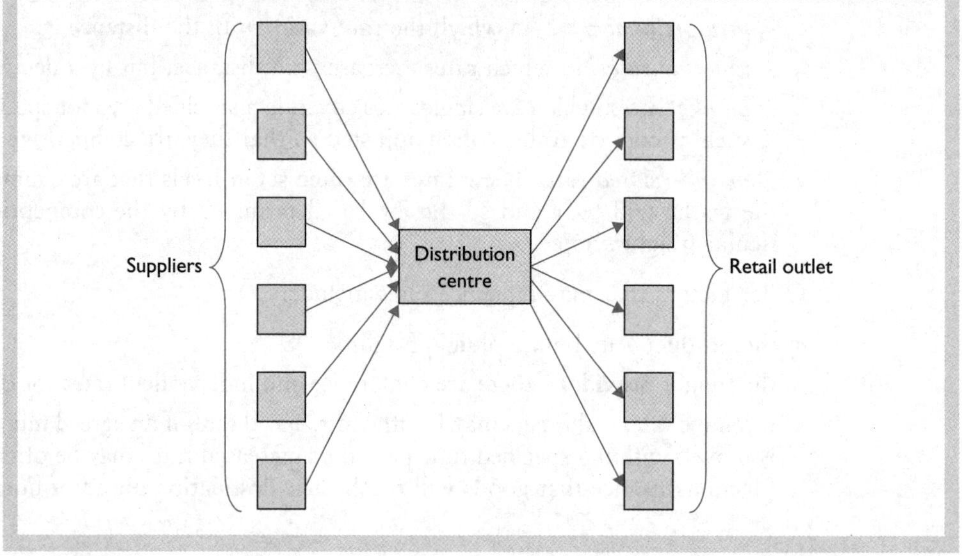

Packaging

Packaging influences both the efficiency and effectiveness of logistics implementation. Industrial packaging focuses on such aspects as:

■ handling, such as palletisation and stock picking

■ protection and security, such as containerisation

■ communication, such as the package content identification, tracking of goods in transit and instore, as well as handling instructions relating to such aspects as fragility, hazards and environmental issues.

An important innovation in tracking is that, using the Internet, the tracking and tracing of consignments by all the parties involved has been improved enormously.

Insurance

Suppliers of goods will wish to insure the goods during the period when they are at their risk. Although such risks end with the passing of the title, insurance may also be taken out against contingencies such as stoppage of goods in transit, insolvency of the buyer and refusal of the buyer to accept goods on arrival at their destination. Incoterms, referred to in section 14.5 earlier in this chapter, help to achieve clarity concerning the passing of the title of goods in transit. The cost of freight insurance is a specialised field and will obviously vary according to the risks attached to a specific consignment.

Pilfering

High-value and consumer goods especially face an enhanced risk of theft or pilfering. In general, the use of door-to-door intermodal containers significantly reduces the exposure to such risks, although container highjacking targeted at high-value consumer and electrical goods, usually as a result of dishonest 'insider' carrier information, has become increasingly common.

Miscellaneous costs

Additional costs may be incurred for documentation for customs clearance, proof of delivery, delivery outside working hours, cash on delivery, abnormally shaped cargo, hazardous cargo and similar items.

14.8 Minimising freight costs

There are numerous ways in which freight costs may be minimised, including:

- siting manufacturing and assembly processes nearer to customers and suppliers
- cross-docking
- aggregating loads to prevent part-empty running when delivering
- avoiding, if possible, empty vehicles on return journeys
- using smaller vehicles, particularly for transportation in urban areas
- arranging delivery times at off-peak periods to avoid idle or waiting times (demurrage)
- negotiating lower rates, either directly or via freight forwarders
- undertaking a cost analysis of total costs to ascertain where possible economies may be made
- requiring reductions in the cost per unit of distance as the distance increases on the grounds that fixed costs will be spread over a larger distance base
- requiring reductions in the cost per unit of weight as the size of the shipment increases on the grounds that fixed costs can be spread over a larger weight base
- analysing the relative importance of such factors as speed, availability, dependability, security and so on to a particular customer and as a value-adding element for the product and producer in order to enable possible trade-offs to be identified – speed and cost, cost of carrying inventory and cost of stockouts and cost of alternative modes of transport, for example.

14.9 Freight agents

Large companies will often have staff specialising in import and freight procedures. Others will rely on the services of import or freight agents.

14.9.1 What is a freight agent or forwarder?

A freight agent or forwarder is a person or company, who, for a fee, undertakes to have goods carried and delivered to a destination. The services of freight agents are normally engaged when the carriage of goods involves successive carriers or the use of successive means of transport.

Traditionally, freight agents make contracts of carriage for their principals. Under the principles of the law of agency, a freight agent is under an obligation to the principal to conclude the contract on the agreed terms. Although in civil law freight agents are distinguished from carriers, the latter sometimes also act as freight agents.

14.9.2 The services of freight agents

In 1970, a report by the National Economic Development Office[11] defined the traditional functions of forwarders as involving:

■ the preparation and handling of documentation, the main types of which are:
- bills of lading
- airway bills or equivalent
- customs papers
- certificates of origin
- exchange control forms
- insurance certificates
- shipping notes
- calling forward notes
- collection orders
- port rate forms

and help in preparing invoices

■ planning and costing the route to give the desired combination of speed, economy and reliability, trading times against cost

■ booking and coordinating transport and freight space, domestic, international and foreign

■ arranging any ancillary services, such as warehousing, packing

■ consolidating and paying charges payable to transport, such as operators, port authorities, customs and so on

■ presenting goods for customs clearance, both for imports into the UK and abroad via overseas offices, and correspondence and so on for UK exports

■ advising on special requirements, trade and financial, of foreign countries and providing necessary documents

■ providing exporters with the necessary information to prepare quotations, particularly CIF or delivered to importers' premises

■ advising importers of details and any changes in UK import procedures.

Other services offered by forwarders may include:

■ consolidation or groupage – that is, the grouping of consignments from several consignors in a single load

■ road haulage, such as the operation of a cargo collection and delivery service to and from sea or airports

■ containers – some forwarders may operate container services or lease containers

■ provision of warehousing, packing, insurance, financial and market research services

■ coordination of the deliveries of multiple consignments.

14.9.3 Freight agents' fees

Freight agents or forwarders are paid a negotiated fee by the shipper or importer depending on the service or documents required. Fees are related to Incoterms in that they depend on the responsibilities undertaken by the different parties. They will be lower, for example, if the responsibilities end FOB at the departure port and increase as responsibilities extend DDP to the destination terminal.

14.9.4 Freight agents and the future

Willmott[12] points out that the development of logistics and supply chain management requires:

> the services of 'logistics practitioners' who can mesh themselves into the overall pattern, not just as suppliers of freight forwarding services but as links that might encompass several business functions.

Such functions are listed by Willmott as being:

- customerisation, or tailoring for individual markets or customers
- sourcing and delivery of raw materials
- allocation of materials and packaging
- manufacturing and capacity planning
- inventory determination and allocation to warehouses
- international movement by sea, road, rail and air
- domestic trunking and primary and multidrop distribution
- order fulfilment, including picking, packing and dispatch/delivery to customers
- e-commerce support of supply chain visibility
- reverse logistics, perhaps involving call centre management and collections for repair or servicing and so on.

Possible developments include:

- establishing 'one stop' entities by merging logistics and forwarding services, providing increased capabilities as suppliers of materials and components, enabling manufacturers to outsource non-core logistic and transport activities
- the secondment of the freight forwarder's staff to major customers to provide on-site freight expertise
- whole supply chains setting up in competition with each other rather than individual companies in that chain doing so, with the consequence that a freight forwarder may become a link in more than one chain.

14.10 Methods of payment

Overseas suppliers (exporters) may be unwilling to release goods until they have received payment. Conversely, buyers may be unwilling to pay before the goods have been delivered. SITPRO[13] (Simplifying International Trade) has produced the payments risk ladder shown in Figure 14.2, setting out some methods of payment and the risks of each to exporters and importers respectively.

Each of the four methods of payment shown in Figure 14.2 is briefly described below. SITPRO also advises that importers and exporters should consider their options

Figure 14.2 **The payments risk ladder for exporters and importers**

Exporter	Least secure →	Less secure →	More secure →	Most secure →
	Open account	Bills for collection	Documentary credits	Advance payment
Importer	← Most secure	← More secure	← Less secure	← Least secure

carefully and hedge the risks with appropriate insurance and credit checks on overseas suppliers or customers.

14.10.1 Open account

This is similar to most home transactions. Goods are shipped and documents remitted to the buyer with an invoice for payment on previously agreed terms, such as 'net 30 days'.

14.10.2 Bills for collection

Under this system, the shipping documents – including the *bill of lading* (which is a receipt signed by a ship's master specifying the goods shipped on board and constituting a negotiable bill of title to such goods) are sent to the buyer's bank rather than direct to the buyer. These will be handed to the importer only when payment has been made (documents against payment) or against a promise to pay (documents against acceptance) and, until the documents are received, the title to the goods remains with the exporter. Documents against acceptance are usually accompanied by a *draft* or *bill of exchange* drawn on the buyer. Bills of exchange are the oldest method of payment for goods bought overseas. A bill of exchange (B/E) is defined as:[14]

> An unconditional order in writing, addressed by one person to another, signed by the person giving it, requiring the person to whom it is addressed to pay on demand, or at a fixed or determinable future date, a sum certain in money to or to the order of a specified person or to the bearer.

A cheque is a specialised form of B/E drawn on a bank to pay a specified sum to X on demand.

When a buyer (drawee) agrees to pay on a certain date – say, '30 days from acceptance' – the draft is said to have been accepted. It is against this acceptance that the goods are released to the buyer.

The *bills for collection* process is governed by the 'Uniform rules for collections' (Document 522, published by the International Chamber of Commerce). Over 90 per cent of the world's banks adhere to Document 522.

14.10.3 Letters of credit

With bills for collection, the bank acts only as an intermediary and enters into no payment undertaking. It is therefore a cheaper arrangement than a *letter of credit*

(LOC), which is a legal instrument constituting a cash guarantee, obligating the bank to make a payment to a named beneficiary, such as an exporter, within a specified time against the presentation of documents such as the bill of lading, certificate of quality, insurance and origin, packing list and a commercial invoice. The risk of non-payment by the buyer is therefore transferred to the issuing bank. Letters of credit are governed by the ICC rules 'Uniform customs and practice for documentary credits' (Document UCP 500).

An LOC is opened by an importer (applicant) to ensure that the documentation requested proves that the seller has fulfilled the requirements of the underlying sales contract by making such requirements conditions of the LOC.

From the exporter's perspective, apart from cash in advance, an LOC is the most secure method of payment in international trade. The conditional nature of an LOC means that payment will not be made to the exporter unless all the credit terms have been precisely met.

LOCs may be conditional, standby or transactional:

- a *conditional LOC* may require some burden of proof by the owner that the contractor has not failed to perform before the bank will pay
- a *standby LOC* is normally used for open accounts (see section 14.10.1) and deals only with payment of documented sums within a specified period
- a *transactional LOC* applies to one specific transaction.

Most LOCs are irrevocable, which means that both parties must agree to any changes in terms.

While LOCs are a very secure method of payment, the security comes at a price. The security must therefore be weighed against the cost of higher bank charges.

14.10.4 Payment in advance

As shown in Figure 14.2, this is the least secure and most secure method of payment from the standpoint of buyers and sellers respectively. Often this method takes the form of a payment up front of, say, 50 per cent of the selling price, with the remainder payable on agreed credit terms.

14.10.5 What method of payment to use?

SITPRO[15] lists the following factors to bear in mind when deciding which method to choose:

- company policy
- cash flow considerations
- relationship with the overseas supplier
- the market conditions under which the overseas supplier operates
- the buyer's gut feeling.

The effectiveness and expeditiousness of all the processes involved in the exchange of documents and payments has been greatly facilitated by the various electronic means at our disposal.

14.11 Countertrade

14.11.1 What is countertrade?

Yasvas and Freed[16] define countertrade (CT) as:

> a generic term for parallel business transactions, linking sellers and buyers in reciprocal commitments that usually lie outside the realm of typical money-mediated trade.

Essentially, CT is a form of international reciprocal trading in which an order is placed by a purchaser with a supplier in another country (or vice versa) on condition that goods of an equal or specified value are sold or bought in the opposite direction.

Countertrade often, but not necessarily, takes place in less well-developed, more centrally planned economies. The rising price of oil, higher interest rates and foreign debt have meant that many countries are unable to generate sufficient hard-core earnings by means of their exports to service their debts, but desperately need imports. As a result of economic, financial and political forces, countertrade has become an established feature of modern markets. Estimates vary but approximately 25 per cent of all world trade is accounted for by countertrade.

14.11.2 Forms of countertrade

Carter and Gagne[17] identify five distinct types of countertrade.

- *Barter or swaps* a one-off, direct, simultaneous exchange of goods or services between trading partners without a cash transaction, such as an exchange of New Zealand lamb for Iranian crude oil. The term 'swap' is used when goods are exchanged to save transportation costs.

  Kreuze[18] instances the shipping of Russian oil to Greece rather than Cuba and the sending of Mexican oil to Cuba instead of Greece, thereby saving considerable transportation costs for both nations.

- *Counterpurchase* occurs when a company in country X sells to a foreign country Y on the understanding that a set percentage of the sale's proceeds will be spent on importing goods produced in country Y. Both trading partners agree to fulfil their obligations within a fixed time period and pay for the major part of their respective purchases in cash.

  In 1977, Volkswagen sold 10,000 cars to the then East Germany and agreed to purchase goods from a list compiled by the East Germans up to the value of the cars over the ensuing two years.

- *Buy-back or compensation* occurs when the exporter agrees to accept, as full or partial payment, products manufactured by the original exported product.

  Occidental Petroleum negotiated a deal with the former USSR under which they agreed to build several plants in the Soviet Union and receive partial payment in ammonia over a 20-year period.

The main differences between buy-back and counterpurchase are that, in buy-backs:

- the goods and services taken back are tied to the original goods exported, while this is not the case with counterpurchase

- buy-back deals usually stretch over a longer period of time than counterpurchase ones.

The Xerox Corporation sold plant and technology for the production of low-value photocopying machines to the People's Republic of China and contractually agreed to repurchase a large proportion of the machines produced in the Chinese plant.

■ *Switch trading* refers to the transfer of unused or unusable credit balances in one country to overcome an imbalance of money by a trading partner in another country. Country X sells goods of a certain value to country Y. Country Y credits country X with the value of the goods, which X can use to buy goods from Y. Country X, however, does not wish to buy goods from Y. X therefore sells the credits to a third-party trading house at a discount. The trading house then locates a country or company wishing to buy goods from Y. In return for a small profit, the trading house sells the credits to the country or company wishing to buy from Y.

■ *Offset* this is similar to counterpurchase, except that the supplier can fulfil the undertaking to import goods or services of a certain percentage value by dealing with any company in the country to which the original goods were supplied.

14.11.3 The advantages and disadvantages of countertrade

These have been identified by Forker,[19] as shown in Table 14.6.

Table 14.6 Advantages and disadvantages of countertrade

Advantages	Disadvantages
Acceptance of goods or services as payment can: ■ avoid exchange controls ■ promote trade with countries with inconvertible currencies ■ reduce risks associated with unstable currency values Overcoming the above financial obstacles enables countertrading enterprises to: ■ enter new or formerly closed markets ■ expand business and sales volume ■ reduce the impact of foreign protectionism on overseas business Countertrade has enabled participants to: ■ make fuller use of plant capacity ■ have longer production runs ■ reduce unit expenses due to greater sales volume ■ find valuable outlets for declining products	Countertrade negotiations tend to be longer and more complicated than conventional sales negotiations and must, sometimes, be conducted with powerful government procurement agencies Additional expenses, such as brokerage fees and other transaction costs, reduce the profitability of countertrade deals There may be difficulties with the quality, availability and disposal of goods taken as countertrade Countertrade may give rise to pricing problems associated with the assignment of values to products/commodities received in exchange Offset customers can, later, become competitors Commodity prices can vary widely during the lengthy periods of countertrade negotiation and delivery

14.11.4 Risks of countertrade

As shown in Table 14.6, CT has its disadvantages. Some risks include:

- exchanged goods may find their way back to the original market at discount prices
- CT can entail long and complicated negotiations with less than successful outcomes
- goods received can be lacking in quality, backed unattractively and difficult to sell or service
- CT can be used to offload products that cannot be sold elsewhere
- products received may be unrelated to normal product lines and not fit easily into normal distribution channels
- a company that has acquired the countertrading partner's know-how may become a competitor.

14.11.5 Purchasing's contribution to countertrade

Forker[20] points out that purchasing's traditional role in countertrade has been to find either a use or sales outlet for the compensatory items that must be bought. Purchasing can also play a major part in countertrade by:

- identifying low-cost sources of supply that may be exploited on a countertrade basis
- providing negotiating expertise when discussing countertrade arrangements with prospective overseas suppliers
- ensuring that payment-in-kind products are properly inspected before the CT agreement is signed, thus guarding against the receipt of poor-quality items
- advising that raw materials are taken in compensation as raw materials are often graded, making comparison easier, and have greater flexibility in terms of use
- developing long-term CT partnerships
- recognising that, properly used, CT can be:
  - a major source of low-cost, quality materials
  - a means of preserving hard currency
  - a means of upgrading manufacturing capabilities.

14.12 The true cost of overseas buying

As indicated in earlier sections of this chapter, while the benefits of buying overseas can be substantial, there are also significant financial costs and risks. It is therefore important that such costs and risks should be evaluated before deciding to source abroad. Tables such as 14.7 facilitate comparisons between the true costs of buying from abroad and from home-based suppliers. They also provide a list of some possible items for negotiation.

Many of the costs shown in Table 14.7 will also attract VAT. Costs will vary according to different weights, sizes and quantities, too. The effects of such variances are easily computed with the aid of a spreadsheet.

Table 14.7 Comparisons of costs of overseas and UK suppliers

Expense category	Costs: areas of expenditure	Overseas supplier	Home supplier
Basic price	Supplier's quoted price per item Packaging Sea/air freight Marine insurance Supplier's final price CIF/destination		
Handling/transportation charges	Handling charges (port of entry) Storage Port costs Internal transport to buyer Freight forwarding fees Insurance		
Customs and associated charges	Customs duties Customs clearance fees		
International financing	Costs of documentation Currency conversion rates Exchange rate fluctuations Bank fees		
Inventory costs	Holding costs of higher inventory Levels at x per cent per annum		
Sourcing costs	Costs of visit to overseas supplier Estimated communication costs Costs of inspection by overseas agent Special fees, such as translation, legal		
Total actual or estimated costs			

14.13 Buying capital equipment abroad

14.13.1 Reasons for buying abroad

Capital equipment can be sourced abroad for numerous reasons – lower prices, compatibility with existing equipment, the need for technology only available from overseas suppliers and to equip factories in or adjacent to the country in which the equipment is manufactured to name but a few.

14.13.2 Technical requirements of equipment bought abroad

Essentially these are the ones listed in section 13.4, although special attention will be given to lifecycle costs and the availability of spares – especially the speed at which they can be provided by air transport or other methods. Other important factors are international standardisation and, with some complex equipment, the provision of assistance with installation and post-purchase maintenance advice and services.

14.13.3 Cultural, contractual and currency factors

The cultural, political and ethical and foreign exchange factors referred to in sections 14.4.1, 14.4.2 and 14.4.5 apply equally to the purchase of capital equipment.

Legal factors will also need special consideration, especially what legal system is applicable, and the provision for the international settlement of disputes by means of such agencies as the International Chamber of Commerce (ICC). Special clauses may need to be included in the contract, such as an undertaking by the supplier of the equipment to maintain stocks of spare parts for a prescribed minimum number of years.

Currency considerations to take into account are as those referred to in section 14.4.5. In some cases countertrade may be applicable, especially buy-back arrangements, whereby the country exporting capital equipment undertakes to buy back some of the products made in the buyer's country.

14.13.4 Import factors

These include the most suitable forms of transport and the way in which freight and import agents can provide assistance. All buyers of capital equipment from overseas should have a thorough understanding of Incoterms especially FOB, CIF and CFR.

Finally it is essential to make an evaluation, as shown in section 14.12, of the comparative costs of buying capital equipment from overseas and home sources, when these alternatives are available.

14.14 Factors in successful overseas buying

The Birou and Fawcett research referred to earlier in this chapter identified the factors listed in Table 14.8.

Other important considerations include ascertaining the total cost of ownership for all significant purchases, using overseas suppliers that practice TQM, providing overseas suppliers with accurate demand forecasts, a boundary-spanning philosophy for supply chain participants, as opposed to a narrow vision of business processes, and

Table 14.8 Factors influencing success in international sourcing (Birou and Fawcett, 1993)

Rank	Factor	Rating
1	Top management support	5.68
2	Developing communication skills	5.67
3	Establishing long-term relationships	5.65
4	Developing global sourcing skills	5.62
5	Understanding global opportunities	5.13
6	Knowledge of foreign business practices	5.09
7	Foreign supplier certification and qualifications	5.02
8	Planning for global sourcing	5.02
9	Obtaining expert assistance	4.79
10	Knowledge of exchange rates	4.53
11	Use of third-party logistics services	4.12

Note: all ratings are on a seven-point Likert scale, with seven for major challenge

sensitivity to the interests and cultures of overseas suppliers. Most purchasing professionals can benefit from training in buying overseas, but hands-on experience is usually the best teacher of all.

Case study

The Vermont Engineering Company (VEC) manufactures high-quality, specialised equipment for railway signalling systems. There are two manufacturing sites in the UK – one in Hull, the other in Birmingham. Over the past two years, VEC has lost major orders because of cost. The feedback from two major customers – one in Germany and one in Australia – has been that VEC's prices are at least 18 per cent higher than those of their competitors.

A 'Cost Reduction Team' (CRT) was set up, with representatives from sales, design, purchasing, finance, manufacturing and marketing. As Procurement Manager, you were an active member. In the past, there has not been any international sourcing, other than some electronic motors from France. It was agreed that you would consider sourcing subassemblies, machined components and wiring harnesses from overseas.

A friend of the Managing Director – Eugene Smooth, an import agent – was commissioned to look for sources of supply. He has now issued his report and presented the outline findings shown in the table.

	Subassembly 'A'	Machined component 'B'	Wiring harness 'C'
Current cost	£46.33	£8.53	£121.80
Comparative cost	£21.10	£3.15	£33.97
Country of origin	India	China	Vietnam
Incoterm	DDP	CIF	EXW

When Eugene Smooth made his presentation, he faced hostile questioning from the Quality Manager. It was obvious, he said, that quality would suffer and he could not support the idea of purchasing from these alternative sources. The Sales Director thought it was a good idea, but asked why Procurement had not handled the exercise. When Finance questioned the quoted figures, Eugene explained that the prices were based on 'current exchange rates'.

The Managing Director listened to the discussion with patience and then appointed you as Procurement Manager to conduct an exercise, to be completed within 8 weeks, with the objective of moving 40 per cent of all purchases overseas by month 9 of the current year. He suggested that Procurement and Quality personnel visit the three countries and sources identified by Eugene Smooth.

Tasks

You are now reflecting on your next steps and need to answer the following questions.

1. How will you obtain quotations and from which companies?
2. Which six contractual clauses will be really important?
3. How will you deal with major risks?
4. How will you expedite deliveries?

Discussion questions

14.1 Why, from the standpoint of supply chain management, is the distinction between international purchasing and global sourcing important?

14.2 'Economics' refers to the principle of comparative costs – that is, under given technological conditions, the increased product or output obtainable from specialisation and exchange, rather than from a policy of self-sufficiency, is maximised when each country or region specialises in the production of goods or services in which its relative advantage is largest (the comparative cost of production is least).
   Why may the purchasers of goods not always be able to apply this principle?

14.3 What sources of information relating to overseas suppliers would you use when looking for:
   (a) commodities
   (b) components or assemblies
   (c) capital equipment?

14.4 What are the implications for overseas sourcing of longer supply chains?

14.5 Why is it important for buyers to have an awareness of ethical factors when buying abroad? What might be the consequences of buying from an overseas supplier using child labour?

14.6 Draw a diagram showing how a letter of credit transaction works.

14.7 Draft a contract clause containing provisions for safeguarding the purchaser against increased costs arising from fluctuating exchange rates.

14.8 'The most used Incoterms are probably FOB, CIF and CFR.'
   Why?

14.9 Identify four items that you might buy from overseas that are suitable for sending by sea but not by air and vice versa.

14.10 One USA company incurred a million dollar loss on car touch-up paint that formed part of a countertrade transaction in which the paint was to be sold overseas. The loss was attributable to the fact that, in the country to which the paint was sent, the colour was uncommon and the right equipment to apply the paint was not available.
   What lessons can be learned from this example about the risks of countertrade?

Past examination questions

1 The purchase of capital items, despite being some of the most important acquisitions made by organisations, are frequently conducted very badly. The purchasing professional often is brought in during the later stages to correct the mistakes already made. This situation is generally worse when the capital acquisition is being made from overseas.
   Discuss how these problems arise and explain how capital acquisitions from overseas should be made in order to ensure that such problems are minimised.
   CIPS, *Purchasing and Supply Chain Management II:*
   Tactics and Operations, May 2001

2 Define global sourcing and evaluate its importance from the buyer's perspective.

CIPS, *International Purchasing*, November 2002

3 (a) Explain how developments in technology and transport have made buying overseas an increasingly attractive option.

(b) Although the overseas buying option has become easier, there are still risks to be managed. Identify these risks and suggest ways in which the buyer may manage them.

CIPS, *Purchasing and Supply Chain Management II: Tactics and Operations*, May 2003

4 Explain the concept of countertrade, illustrating your answer with appropriate examples.

CIPS, *International Purchasing*, May 2002

5 Evaluate the importance of national and international standards when establishing supply contracts from overseas.

CIPS, *International Purchasing*, May 2002

6 (a) Identify the factors that have contributed to the increased trend towards international sourcing for both goods and capital equipment.

(b) Discuss the specific issues the buyer should take into account when considering the purchasing of capital equipment from an overseas buyer.

CIPS, *Tactics and Operations*, May 2004

References

1 Birou, L. H., and Fawcett, S. E., 'International purchasing benefits and requirements and challenges', *International Journal of Purchasing and Supply*, Jan., 1993, pp. 22–5

2 Trent, R. J., and Monczka, R. M., 'International purchasing and global sourcing: what are the differences?', *Journal of Supply Chain Management*, Nov., 2003

3 Rexta, N., and Miyamoto, T., 'International sourcing: an Australian perspective', ISM, *Resource Article*, Winter, 2000

4 Carter, J. R., and Narasimhan, R., 'Purchasing in the international marketplace', *Journal of Purchasing and Supply Management*, Sept., 1990, pp. 2–11

5 As 1 above

6 Min, H., and Galle, W., 'International negotiation strategies of multinational US purchasing professionals', *International Journal of Purchasing and Materials Management*, Vol. 29, No. 3, 1993, pp. 40–50

7 Hofstede, G., *Cultures and Organisations*, McGraw-Hill, 1991

8 Hampden-Turner, C., and Trompenaars, F., *The Seven Cultures of Capitalism*, Piatkus, 1994

9 Lesem, R., and Neubauer, F., *European Management Systems*, McGraw-Hill, 1994

10 Scott, S., 'Strong dollar, weak contract', *Purchasing Today*, July, 1997, pp. 8–9

11 National Economic Development Office, 'The freight forwarder', HMSO, 1970, pp. 1–3

12 Willmott, K., 'Understanding the freight business', in as 3 above, pp. 203–4

13 SITPRO (Simplifying International Trade) at: www.sitpro.org.uk/trade/paymentmethods.htm

14 Bills of Exchange Act 1882, section 3(1)

15 As 13 above – SITPRO is the UK's Trade Facilitation Agency, supported by the DTI

16 Yasvas, B. F., and Freed, R., 'An economic rationale for countertrade', *The International Trade Journal*, Vol. XV, No. 2, summer, 2001, pp. 127–56

17 Carter, J. R., and Gagne, J., 'The dos and don'ts of countertrade', *Sloan Management Review*, spring, 1988, pp. 31–7

18 Kreuze, J. G., 'International countertrade', *Internal Auditor*, Vol. 5, No. 2, April, 1997, pp. 42–7

19 Forker, L. B., 'Purchasing's views on countertrade', *International Journal of Purchasing and Materials Management*, spring, 1992, pp. 10–19

20 Forker, L., 'Countertrade's impact on the supply function', *International Journal of Purchasing and Materials Management*, fall, 1996

Part 4

Strategy, tactics and operations 3: negotiation, support tools and performance

Negotiation

This chapter aims to provide an understanding of:

- the nature of negotiation
- the content of negotiation
- the negotiation process
- negotiation and relationships.

- The distinction between adversarial or distributive and collaborative or integrative negotiations.
- Substance and relationship negotiating roles.
- Time as a factor in negotiations.
- Planning as a key negotiation element.
- The stages of the negotiation process.
- Negotiating behaviour.
- Negotiation post-mortems.
- Positional and principled negotiation.
- Ethical aspects of negotiation.

Introduction

Negotiation has been described as:[1]

> perhaps the finest opportunity for the buyer to improve his (or her) company's profits and obtain recognition.

Definitions

There are numerous definitions of negotiation. Three typical examples are quoted and commented on below.

The process whereby two or more parties decide what each will give and take in an exchange between them[2]

This definition of negotiation highlights:

- its interpersonal nature
- the interdependence of the parties
- its allocation of resources.

A formal negotiation is:

An occasion where one or more representatives of two or more parties interact in an explicit attempt to reach a jointly acceptable position on one or more divisive issues about which they would like to agree[3]

This definition highlights that negotiation:

- is *formal* negotiation is restricted to occasions when two or more parties need to reach agreement
- involves *representatives of the parties* – the purchaser and a supplier, for example
- is *explicit* – that is, the process genuinely and deliberately attempts to reach an agreement
- involves *divisive issues* about which the parties would like to agree

Third, negotiation is:

Any form of verbal communication in which the participants seek to exploit their relative competitive advantages and needs to achieve explicit or implicit objectives within the overall purpose of seeking to resolve problems that are barriers to agreement.[4]

This definition stresses three elements of negotiation:

- it involves communication – that is, the exchange of information
- it takes place in a context in which the participants use their comparative competitive advantages and the perceived needs of the other party to influence the outcome of the negotiation process
- each participant has implicit as well as explicit objectives that determine the negotiating strategies – a supplier will explicitly wish to obtain the best price, for example, but, implicitly, will be seeking a contribution to fixed overheads and endeavouring to keep the plant and workforce employed.

15.1 Approaches to negotiation

Approaches to negotiation may be classified as adversarial or collaborative:

- *adversarial negotiation* – also termed *distributive* or *win–lose negotiation* – is an approach in which the focus is on 'positions' staked out by the participants and the assumption is that every time one party wins, the other loses, so, as a result, the other party is regarded as an adversary

- *collaborative negotiation* – also called *integrative* or *win–win negotiation* – is an approach in which the assumption is that, by means of creative problem-solving, one or both parties can gain without the other having to lose and, as the other party is regarded as a collaborator rather than an adversary, the participants may be more willing to share concerns, ideas and expectations than would otherwise be the case.

The characteristics of adversarial and collaborative negotiation are summarised in Table 15.1.

Table 15.1 Adversarial and collaborative negotiation contrasted

Adversarial negotiation	Collaborative negotiation
■ The emphasis is on competing to attain goals at the adversary's expense	■ The emphasis is on ascertaining goals held in common with the other party
■ Strategy is based on secrecy, retention of information and low level of trust in the perceived adversary	■ Strategy is based on openness, sharing of information and high level of trust in the perceived partner
■ The desired outcomes of the negotiation are often misrepresented so that the adversary does not know what the opponent really requires the outcome of the negotiation to be. There is little concern for or empathy with the other party	■ The desired outcomes of the negotiation are made known so that there are no hidden agendas and issues are clearly understood. Each party is concerned for and has empathy with the other
■ Strategies are unpredictable, based on various negotiating ploys designed to outmanoeuvre or 'throw' the other	■ Strategies are predictable. While flexible, such strategies are aimed at reaching an agreement acceptable to the other party
■ Parties use threats, bluffs and ultimatums with the aim of keeping the adversary on the defensive	■ Parties refrain from threats and so on, which are seen as counterproductive to the rational solution of perceived problems
■ There is an inflexible adherence to a fixed position that may be defended by both rational and irrational arguments. Essentially, the approach is destructive	■ The need for flexibility in the positions taken is assumed. The emphasis is on the use of imaginative, creative, logical ideas and approaches to a constructive resolution of differences
■ The approach is essentially hostile and aggressive – 'us against them'. This antagonism may be enhanced in team negotiations where members of the team may seek to outdo their colleagues in displaying macho attitudes	■ The approach is essentially friendly and non-aggressive – 'we are in this together'. This involves downplaying hostility and giving credit to constructive contributions made by either party to the negotiations
■ The unhealthy extreme of an adversarial approach is reached when it is assumed that movement towards one's own goal is facilitated by blocking measures that prevent the other party from attaining the goal	■ The healthy extreme of the partnership approach is reached when it is assumed that whatever is good for the other party to the negotiation is necessarily good for both
■ The key attitude is that of 'We win, you lose'	■ The key attitude is 'How can the respective goals of each party be achieved so that both win?'
■ If an impasse occurs, the negotiation may be broken off	■ If an impasse occurs, this is regarded as a further problem to be solved, possibly by the intervention of higher management or an internal or external mediator or arbitrator

15.1.1 An evaluation of adversarial and collaborative strategies

Adversarial strategies may, on occasion, be appropriate in the following situations:

■ where there is no ongoing relationship or the potential for one exists or it is desired – the deal is a one-off

■ a quick, simple solution to a disagreement is required.

Collaborative strategies, while more time-consuming and difficult to achieve, have the following advantages:

■ they are more stable and lead to long-term relationships and creative solutions to mutual problems

■ they may also be the only way to obtain agreements when both parties to a negotiation have high aspirations and resist making concessions on these issues.

15.1.2 Transforming adversarial attitudes

Fisher and Ury[5] suggest five tactics designed to transform an adversarial into a collaborative approach. These approaches are discussed in section 15.10 on negotiation ethics.

15.2 The content of negotiation

In any negotiation, two types of goals should receive consideration. These may be referred to as *substance goals* and *relationship goals*.

15.2.1 Substance goals

Substance goals are concerned with the content issues of the negotiation. The possible content issues are legion and depend on the requirements relating to a situation. Most negotiations will be about high-value/usage items – that is, the 15–20 per cent that constitute the major portion of inventory investment. Negotiation also relates to non-standard items, although a large user will seek, if possible, to negotiate preferential terms for standard supplies. Most negotiation topics affect price, either directly or indirectly. There are numerous ways in which content issues can be grouped, including overseas buying and buying for construction projects. Groupings may also relate to products, such as IT or commodities. Three typical groupings – shown in Figures 15.1, 15.2 and 15.3 respectively – relate to price, contractual and delivery issues in negotiation. The issues listed are in no way exhaustive and the lists often overlap.

15.2.2 Relationship goals

Relationship goals are concerned with outcomes relating to how well those involved in the negotiations are able to work together once the process is completed and how well their respective organisations or 'constituencies' may work together. Some areas for relationship goals include:

■ partnership sourcing

■ preferred supplier status

■ supplier involvement in design, development and value analysis

■ sharing of technology.

Figure 15.1 The price content of negotiation – some issues

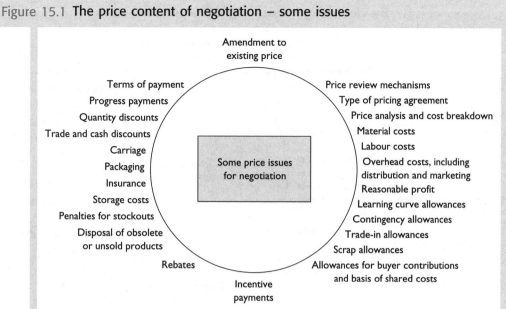

Figure 15.2 The contractual content of negotiation – some issues

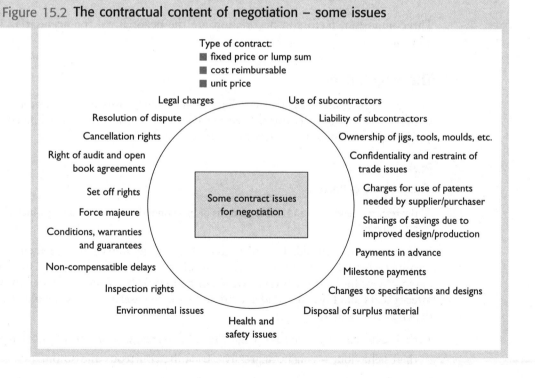

Figure 15.3 **The delivery content of negotiation – some issues**

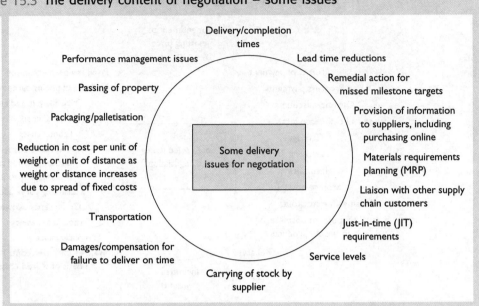

15.3 Factors in negotiation

Three important factors in negotiation are the negotiators, the negotiating situation and time.

15.3.1 The negotiators

In negotiations, purchasers and suppliers are individuals usually acting as representatives of their respective organisations. Their behaviour in negotiations will be influenced partly by their personalities and partly by their roles as representatives.

Personality

This may be defined as:[6]

> the relatively enduring and stable patterns of behaving, thinking and feeling which characterise an individual.

It should be recognised, however, that there is no universal agreement about the meaning of personality because behavioural scientists define the term from different perspectives. In the present context, it can be loosely considered to mean 'how people affect others and how they understand and view themselves'. How people affect others depends primarily on:

- their external appearance – height, facial features, colour and physical aspects
- their behaviour – vulgar, aggressive, friendly, courteous and so on.

Studies have shown that personality variables, such as authoritarianism, anxiety, dogmatism, risk avoidance, self-esteem and suspiciousness, affect the degree of cooperation or competitiveness present in a negotiating situation. The implementation of negotiating strategies may be affected by personality factors and, equally, the mix of personality characteristics of the participants may determine the outcome of negotiations.

Transactional analysis, developed by Eric Berne in the 1950s, has considerable relevance to the understanding of negotiating behaviour. A 'transaction' is the unit of social interaction: 'If two or more people encounter each other . . . sooner or later one of them will speak, or give some other indication of acknowledging the presence of others.' This is called the *transactional stimulus*. Another person will then say or do something that is in some way related to the stimulus and that is called the *transactional response*. Transactions tend to proceed in chains, so that each response is in turn a stimulus. Transactional analysis is based on the concept that people respond to each other in terms of three ego states – namely Parent, Adult and Child – or frames of mind, which lead to certain types of behaviour. It is impractical to fully describe transactional analysis in this book. Readers should refer to Eric Berne's book *Games People Play*[7] or the later account by T. Harris, *I'm OK – You're OK*.[8]

Negotiators as representatives

In negotiations, it is important for participants to know the extent of their authority to commit the organisations that they are representing as such authority prescribes their options and responsibility for the outcome of the negotiations.

The degree of authority may range from that of an emissary commissioned to present, without variation, a position determined by his or her superiors to that of a free agent.

There is evidence that the fewer constraints imposed on a negotiator, the greater will be the scope for his or her personal characteristics, such as knowledge, experience and personality to influence the negotiation process. Five sets of conditions prevent negotiators from responding spontaneously to their opposite number:

- when they have little latitude in determining either their positions or posture
- when they are held responsible for their performance
- when a negotiator has sole responsibility for the outcome of negotiations
- when negotiators are responsible to a constituency that is present in the negotiations
- when they are appointed rather than elected.

In the above situations, the behaviour of negotiators will be constrained by their obligations. The more complicated and open-ended the negotiations, the greater should be the status of the negotiators.

15.3.2 The negotiating situation

This relates to the strengths and weakness of the participants in the negotiation. The factors identified by Porter as affecting the relative strengths of supplier and buyer groups are outlined in Chapter 2 (see Figure 2.6). Some additional factors influencing the relative strengths of buyers and suppliers are listed below.

- *The buyer's negotiating position* The buyer will be in a strong position where:
  - demand is not urgent and can be postponed
  - suppliers are anxious to obtain the business
  - there are many potential suppliers

- the buyer is in a monopolistic or semi-monopolistic position – that is, the only or one of few firms requiring a particular item
- demand can be met by alternatives or substitutes
- 'make' as well as 'buy' alternatives are available
- the buyer has a reputation for fair dealing and prompt payment
- the buyer is well briefed regarding the supplier's order book, financial situation, manufacturing processes and other relevant intelligence.

■ *The supplier's negotiating position* The supplier will be in a strong position where:
  - demand is urgent
  - suppliers are indifferent about accepting the business
  - the supplier is in a monopolistic or semi-monopolistic position
  - buyers wish to deal with the suppliers due to their reputation for quality, reliability and so on
  - the supplier owns the necessary jigs, tools or specialised machinery
  - the supplier is well briefed regarding the buyer's negotiating position.

In any negotiating situation, it is important to consider the sources of power of each party. Sources of power include the ability to apply:

■ *sanctions* withdrawal of other contracts placed with the supplier, for example

■ *force* such as physically withholding access to tooling or the site where work is to be done

■ *moral authority* claiming that the supplier's position is untenable, for instance

■ *relationships* for example, use of previous good personal relationships or past favours to impact the particular situation

■ *dependence* the extent to which each party is dependent on the other, especially in the short term, say

■ *expertise* such as the extent to which one party relies on the other's knowledge, skills and resources.

The basic power equation is that:

$$P = \text{Resources (used)} \times \text{Importance (to purchaser/supplier)} \times \text{Scarcity (goods or services).}$$

15.3.3 Time

Senior management, design, production and stores staff should understand that 'necessity never made a good buyer'. They should therefore notify buyers of their requirements well in advance to ensure that the purchasing function has adequate procurement and lead time to obviate having to negotiate under the constraint of urgency.

Negotiations may have a past, present and future context. The past is important to negotiations as:

■ past experience governs expectations and perceptions, as it is the expectation of the most likely reaction from the other side on a particular issue that determines whether or not the bargaining situation is perceived as predominantly integrative or distributive

■ a second way in which the past influences negotiations is that previous encounters usually produce precedents, conventions, custom and practice, which become identified with a particular relationship and influence the behaviour of the negotiating parties, so, where there is no previous history of negotiation, as in new buy situations, the past can have no direct influence.

15.3.4 Influential factors

McCall and Norrington[9] have modelled the relationship between the behavioural predispositions of the negotiators and other factors influencing negotiation outcomes. This model is shown in Figure 15.4.

Figure 15.4 **Factors influencing negotiations and their outcomes**

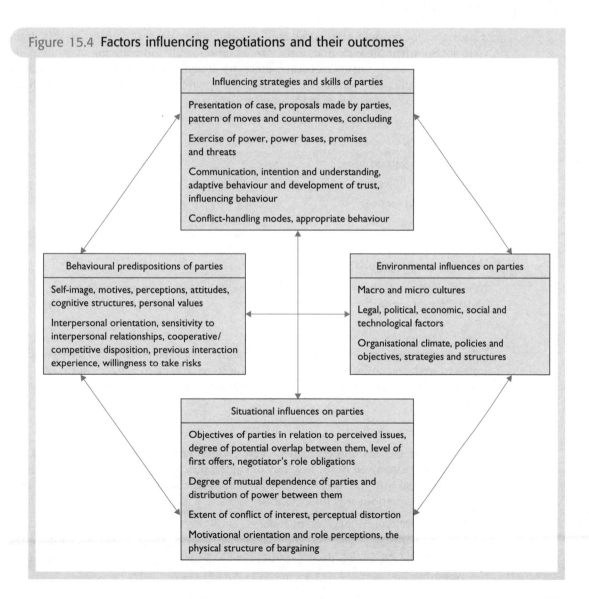

Influencing strategies and skills of parties

Presentation of case, proposals made by parties, pattern of moves and countermoves, concluding

Exercise of power, power bases, promises and threats

Communication, intention and understanding, adaptive behaviour and development of trust, influencing behaviour

Conflict-handling modes, appropriate behaviour

Behavioural predispositions of parties

Self-image, motives, perceptions, attitudes, cognitive structures, personal values

Interpersonal orientation, sensitivity to interpersonal relationships, cooperative/competitive disposition, previous interaction experience, willingness to take risks

Environmental influences on parties

Macro and micro cultures

Legal, political, economic, social and technological factors

Organisational climate, policies and objectives, strategies and structures

Situational influences on parties

Objectives of parties in relation to perceived issues, degree of potential overlap between them, level of first offers, negotiator's role obligations

Degree of mutual dependence of parties and distribution of power between them

Extent of conflict of interest, perceptual distortion

Motivational orientation and role perceptions, the physical structure of bargaining

15.4 The negotiation process

Some negotiations concern a single issue and are relatively straightforward. A simple example is that of a product priced at, say, £9.70 each, when the buyer's objective is to purchase it at a price of, say, £8.30. All other aspects of the transaction may be agreed and it is the buyer's task to negotiate the lower price.

As shown by Figures 15.1, 15.2 and 15.3 other negotiations can be far more complicated and give rise to a multiplicity of issues relating to price, contracts and delivery. Whether simple or complicated, however, the negotiation process will involve three phases: prenegotiation, the actual negotiation and post negotiation.

15.5 Prenegotiation

'Cases are won in chambers' is the guiding principle in prenegotiation – that is, legal victories are often the outcome of the preceding research and planning of strategy on the part of counsel. Buyers can learn much by studying the strategies and tactics of legal, diplomatic and industrial relations and applying them to the purchasing field. The matters to be considered at the prenegotiation stage include:

- who is to negotiate
- the venue
- intelligence gathering
- negotiation objectives
- strategy and tactics
- dummy runs.

15.5.1 Who is to negotiate?

Negotiations can be between individual representatives or teams representing the buying and selling organisations respectively.

The *individual approach*

When negotiations are to be between two individuals, both should normally have sufficient status to settle unconditionally without having to refer back to a higher authority. The majority of rebuy and modified rebuy negotiations are conducted on an interpersonal basis.

The *team approach*

For important negotiations, especially where complicated technical, legal, financial and other issues are involved or for new buy or capital purchases, a team approach is usual as an individual buyer is rarely qualified to act as sole negotiator in such situations.

In team negotiations it is important to:

- *allocate roles* typical 'players' include:
  - the *spokesperson*, who actually presents the case and acts as captain of the team in terms of deciding how to respond to the situations arising in the course of the negotiation

- the *recorder*, who takes notes of the negotiation
- the *experts*, such as management accountants, engineers or other technical design or production staff, legal advisers, who provide back-up for the spokesperson – it is not essential for every member of the team to speak during negotiations in order to make a useful contribution to the negotiation

- *avoid disagreement* there should be no outward disagreement between team members while negotiations are in progress, so any differences should be resolved in private sessions, but the desirability of devising a code of signals, enabling team members to communicate imperceptibly during negotiations, should be considered to avoid having to wait to make a decision.

There are drawbacks to team negotiation. These include:

- *the tendency for groupthink* that is, for team members to hold illusions of group invulnerability, stereotyped perceptions of perceived opponents and unquestioning belief in group morality
- *the emphasis on win–win* is, unless modified by the spokesperson, greater in team negotiations as team members may wish to demonstrate their 'toughness', inflexibility and ability to demolish rather than consider the merits of proposals made by the other side, so the importance of the role of spokesperson on each side in setting the 'tone' of the negotiations cannot be overemphasised.

15.5.2 The venue

Buyers should normally expect the vendor to come to them, unless there are good reasons to do otherwise, such as the buyer is seeking concessions or it is desirable to inspect the vendor's facilities. There are advantages in negotiating on home ground. Not only are the surroundings familiar, but access to files and expert advice is facilitated. The buyer is also under no obligation, which can be felt if you have accepted the hospitality of the the vendor.

15.5.3 Gathering intelligence

This normally involves:

- ascertaining the strengths and weaknesses of the respective negotiating positions
- assembling relevant data relating to costs, production, sales and so on
- preparing data that is to be presented at the negotiation in the form of graphs, charts, tables and so on so that is can be quickly assimilated.

Three important negotiation tools are:

- cost and price analysis (see section 12.11)
- situational analysis (see section 15.9)
- value analysis (see section 9.11.3).

15.5.4 Determining objectives

Buyers should be clear about what they expect the negotiations to achieve. They should also empathise with the likely objectives of other parties to the negotiation. Pena-Mora

Figure 15.5 **Varying interests of participants in negotiations relating to design and construction projects (adapted from Pena-Mora and Tamaki[10])**

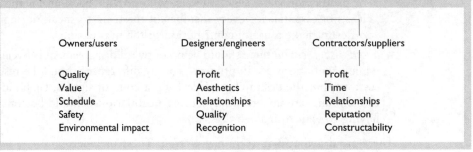

and Tamaki,[10] in a study of collaborative negotiations for large-scale infrastructure projects, draw attention to the different interests of owners/users, designers/engineers and contractors/suppliers. These differing interests are shown in Figure 15.5.

Players in a negotiation process will have both cooperative and competitive characteristics. Sensitivity to the goals of other players by all participants will set the tone of negotiations and contribute to win–win outcomes. A model of bargaining applicable to negotiations relating to purchasing issues is shown in Figure 15.6.

Figure 15.6 **A model of bargaining in a purchasing context**

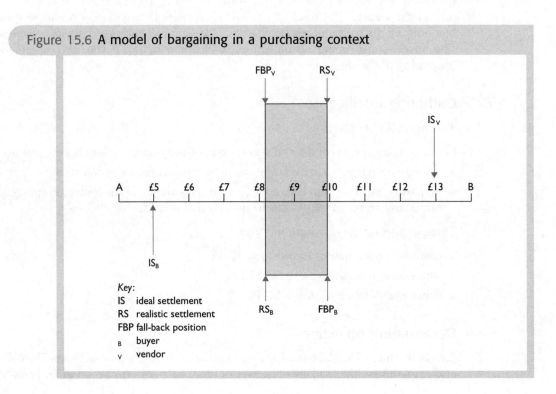

Thus, assuming that the negotiation relates to a pricing issue:

- axis A–B represents the range of positions that the negotiators could take
- IS_B represents the buyer's ideal settlement – the most favourable price that can, realistically, be achieved in negotiation – that is, £5
- IS_V represents the vendor's ideal settlement which is £13.

(*Note*: In most cases, IS will represent the starting position of each of the negotiators, subject, of course, to the fact that, if there is to be negotiation, the initial demands must not be too far apart to preclude bargaining.)

- RS_B is the buyer's realistic settlement – here, about £8 – or that point of settlement fully justified by bargaining power that would be reached with reasonable skill in negotiation and no adverse, unforeseen circumstances
- RS_V is the vendor's realistic settlement – around £10
- FBP_B is the buyer's fall-back position – around £10 – or the price beyond which they will not go. After this point, they break off negotiations or seek alternative means of meeting their requirements
- FBP_V is the vendor's fall-back position – around £8
- the shaded portion represents the area of settlement and this model is based on the convention that each side will normally be prepared to move from their original positions, so the negotiated price will be between £8 and £10, depending on the skills of the negotiators and assuming that the bargaining positions are approximately equal.

Before commencing negotiations, the buyer should have a clear mandate from his or her superiors to settle at any point not exceeding an agreed fall-back position. It is important to stress the importance of determining in advance what is a *good* agreement. Too often, negotiators consider that their goal is to arrive at *an* agreement or even *any* agreement. They should therefore determine what is their own and what is likely to be the other side's BATNA. A BATNA is the 'best alternative to a negotiated agreement' – a concept introduced by Fisher and Ury.[11]

While BATNAs and fall-back or reserve positions are similar in many respects, they are not the same. For example, if you are trying to outsource your catering function, the BATNA may be to continue to provide this facility in-house.

15.5.5 Strategy and tactics

Strategy is the overall plan that aims to achieve, as nearly as possible, the objectives of the negotiation as seen from the perspective of each participant. A *tactic* is a position, manoeuvre or attitude to be taken or adopted at an appropriate point in the negotiation process. Among the tactics to be decided are the following.

- The order in which the issues to be negotiated shall be dealt with.
- Whether to speak first or allow the other side to open the negotiations. Galinsky[12] states that 'substantial psychological research suggests that, more often than not, negotiators who make first offers come out ahead' and suggests that 'making a first offer is related to one's confidence and sense of control at the bargaining table'. The same writer, however, suggests that making the first offer may not be advantageous when the other side has much more information about the item to

be negotiated or the relevant market or industry than they do. This situation can be remedied by information gathering prior to the negotiation so that a more level playing field is achieved.

- Whether to build in recesses for discussion. Recesses may cause a negotiation to lose its momentum. Conversely, recesses provide opportunities for reflection on the negotiation so far, for devising new or alternative proposals and sometimes for 'cooling down' and face-saving.

- What concessions to make should the need arise? Some writers suggest that negotiators should only make concessions in return for trade-offs – that is, they should seek to get something in return for everything they give up.

- The timing of concessions.

- What issues can be linked, such as price and quality.

- What the other party's likely reaction will be to each tactic you're thinking of using.

- What tactics the opponent is likely to adopt and how these can be countered.

15.5.6 The dummy run

Before an important negotiation, it is advisable to subject all arguments, tactics and overall strategies to critical scrutiny.

15.6 The actual negotiation

15.6.1 Stages

Even with a philosophy of collaborative negotiation, the activities of the participants will change at each stage of the negotiation process. These activities alternate between competition and cooperation. It is useful for a negotiator to recognise this pattern of interaction and the stage that has been reached in a particular negotiation. The stages that occur during negotiation are indicated in Figure 15.7.

15.6.2 Techniques

Specialist books of negotiation usually list a number of techniques available to negotiators. It is not possible to detail these in this book, although a more detailed description of Fisher and Ury's approach is given in section 15.10. Some general findings include the following.

- In framing an agenda, ensure that the more difficult issues appear later, thus enabling some agreement to be reached early in the negotiation on less controversial matters, smoothing the way to agreement on less straightforward points.

- Questions are a means of both eliciting information and keeping pressure on an opponent and can also be used to control the pattern and progress of the negotiation.

- Concessions are a means of securing movement when negotiations are deadlocked. Research findings show that losers tend to make the first concession and that each concession tends to raise the aspirational level of the opponent, so buyers should avoid a 'pattern of concession' in which, due to inadequate preparation, they are forced to concede more and more. The convention is that concessions should be reciprocated.

Figure 15.7 The stages in the negotiating process

Stage 1	Introductions, agreement of an agenda and rules of procedure
Stage 2	Ascertaining the 'negotiating range' This means the issues that the negotiation will attempt to resolve With *adversarial* negotiations, this may be a lengthy stage as the participants often overstate their opening positions With *collaborative* negotiations, 'openness saves time'
Stage 3	Agreement of common goals that must be achieved if the negotiation is to reach a successful outcome This will usually require some movement on both sides from the original negotiating range, but the movement will be less or unnecessary in partnership negotiations
Stage 4	Identification of and, when possible, removal of barriers that prevent attainment of agreed common goals At this stage there will be: ■ problem solving ■ consideration of solutions put forward by each ■ determination of what concessions can be made It may also be useful to: ■ review what has been agreed ■ allow a recess for each side to reconsider its position and make proposals or concessions that may enable further progress to be made If no progress can be made, it may be decided to: ■ refer the issues back to higher management ■ change the negotiators ■ abandon the negotiations with the least possible damage to relationships
Stage 5	Agreement and closure Drafting of a statement setting out as clearly as possible the agreement(s) reached and circulating it to all parties for comment and signature

While flexibility is essential, there is no compulsion to make a counter-concession and the aim should be to concede less than has been obtained. The outcome tends to be more favourable when the concessions made are small rather than large. An experienced negotiator will often 'throw a sprat to catch a mackerel'.

■ Negotiation is between people, so it is essential to be able to weigh up the personalities of one's opponents and the drives that motivate them, such as achievement, fear and similar factors.

15.6.3 Deadlocked negotiations

Negotiations sometimes come to an impasse when both sides see no prospect of further movement or concessions. Techniques for resolving such deadlock include those suggested by Fisher and Ury's concept of principled negotiation (see section 15.10 below).

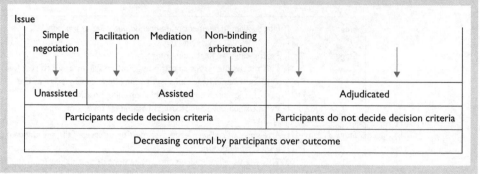

Figure 15.8 **The dispute resolution continuum (adapted from Susskind and Cruikshank[13])**

Other approaches to such situations include:

- taking a break for each party to refocus
- lightening the atmosphere by the use of humour
- breaking down an issue into sub-issues
- agreeing to 'agree in principle' – if the parties agree in principle, they also agree on objectives
- considering the consequences of non-agreement for the parties concerned
- obtaining third-party assistance as they can listen objectively to arguments, clarify issues and, where required, adjudicate.

The degree of third-party involvement can vary. Susskind and Cruikshank[13] provide a useful model of this, expressing their involvement as lying on along a continuum and depending on whether the final decision is made by the parties to the negotiation or an adjudicator. This model is shown in Figure 15.8.

Not every situation can be negotiated. For example, the decision of a contractor to refuse to work in situations that might put them in breach of Health and Safety Regulations or expose their employees to physical danger, such as from violent protests or terrorists, has to be accepted.

15.6.4 Negotiating behaviour

All negotiations involve interpersonal skills. The negotiating styles that are applicable vary according to the specific situation. Training in negotiation should, therefore, include training in behaviour analysis, which should lead to an understanding of the responses likely to be evoked by particular behaviour. For example, shouting usually causes the other person to shout back, while humour may diffuse a tense situation.

Lee and Lawrence[14] have identified seven categories of behaviour, all of which may be encountered in negotiations (see Table 15.2).

15.6.5 Effects of behaviour on other parties

The main fact that the negotiator can learn from the generalisations given in Table 15.2 is that our outward behaviour must be arranged to have the desired effect on those

Table 15.2 Types of behaviour and likely responses to them

Types of behaviour	Likely response
Proposing behaviour Such as suggesting actions – 'Shall we look at subcontracting?'	Usually elicits either development behaviour in the form of support or reasoned negative behaviour in the form of difficulty solving
Development behaviour Such as building on or supporting proposals made by others. 'Having decided to subcontract, who shall we approach?'	Usually leads to further development behaviour or, perhaps, a question in return, asking for further explanation
Reasoned negative behaviour Such as disagreeing with others in a reasoned way, stating difficulties with their ideas. 'Price is likely to be a difficulty because their material costs don't attract our quantity discounts'	Tends to evoke similar negative behaviour in response, leading to a downward spiral in terms of communications and emotions. This spiral can be avoided by stating difficulties and identifying differences as reasonably as possible, perhaps by asking further questions
Emotional negative behaviour Such as attacking others, being critical, defending against attacks in the same way. 'Rubbish'	In general, attack begets either attack or defence. It can make resumption of constructive negotiation difficult
Clarifying behaviour Such as checking whether or not people understand, summarising previous discussion. 'As I see it, this is what we agreed'	Tends to lead to supportive development behaviour, although there can be disagreement
Seeking information behaviour Such as seeking facts, opinions, ideas. 'How much discount if we doubled the quantity?' 'What if . . .'	This almost always results in information being given. The certainty of response makes this a powerful shaping behaviour
Giving information behaviour Such as giving facts, opinions, ideas. 'We need to reach a decision today'	This is usually a response to other behaviour, especially seeking information. It is uncertain in its effect, as it depends largely on the content of the statement

with whom we are negotiating. The desired effect depends on the negotiator's goals. Thus, development behaviour is more likely than emotional disagreement to persuade the other party to accept our viewpoint. Providing and giving information is indispensable to influencing a group. Sometimes it is better to begin a negotiation by asking questions than giving information about the subject matter.

15.6.6 Ploys

A *ploy* is a manoeuvre in a negotiation aimed at achieving a particular result. Most of the ploys mentioned below are appropriate to adversarial rather than partnership negotiating. Such ploys are of doubtful utility, partly because they are easily recognised and countered by experienced negotiators and partly because they are detrimental to long-term relationships. Some ploys identified by Rowntree[15] include:

- the 'time's getting on' ploy – suggesting that a quick settlement is essential
- the 'yes, but . . .' ploy – acceptance of one part of the opponent's proposal, but in terms that may be unacceptable
- the 'believe it or not' ploy – straight bluff, such as 'I've already had three lower prices', which should be called with, in this case, 'Why don't you accept one of them?'
- the 'or else' ploy – a straight threat – 'I'll take the business elsewhere' – that should never to be used unless it is meant
- the 'hand on the door' ploy – another straight threat, saying to the other party 'That is my final offer, if not accepted immediately, I shall leave', and, again, should never be used unless it is meant
- the 'divide and rule' ploy – endeavouring to get agreement on issues one by one rather than deferring final agreement on one of the issues at stake until all the others have been settled
- the 'think of your reputation' ploy – suggesting loss of an opponent's credibility unless your proposals are agreed
- the 'trust me' ploy – in effect saying, 'Accept my proposals now and I'll try to get you a better deal later'
- the 'beyond my remit' ploy – suggesting that a settlement cannot be reached until you have had advice from others not represented at the negotiation.

Part of a negotiator's skill is being able to appraise people and situations quickly. Everything seen and heard should also be taken with a grain of salt. Learn to discern the hidden meanings in the other person's words. Evaluate statements against what you know. Be patient and play for time. Often a little stubbornness can yield high returns.

15.7 Post negotiation

This involves:

- drafting a statement detailing as clearly as possible the agreements reached and circulating it to all parties for comment and signature
- selling the agreement to the constituents of both parties – that is, what has been agreed, why it is the best possible agreement and what benefits will accrue
- implementing the agreements, such as planning contracts, setting up joint implementation teams and so on
- establishing procedures for monitoring the implementation of the agreements and dealing with any problems that may arise.

15.8 What is effective negotiation?

15.8.1 Characteristics

An effective negotiation may be said to have taken place when:

- substance issues are satisfactorily resolved – that is, an agreement has been reached that is satisfactory to all parties
- working relationships are preserved or even enhanced.

Fisher and Ury[16] have identified the following three criteria for an effective negotiation:

- the negotiation has produced a *wise agreement* – one that is satisfactory for both sides
- the negotiation is *efficient* – no more time-consuming or costly than necessary
- the negotiation is *harmonious* – fosters rather than inhibits good interpersonal relationships.

15.8.2 Negotiation post-mortems

Many organisations hold post negotiation meetings for the purpose of discussing:

- *negotiating strategies and tactics* the extent to which they were satisfactory and how they might be improved
- *negotiating costs* the number and duration of negotiating sessions and how these might be reduced
- *negotiating methods* tools such as e-mail and video conferencing enable more rapid and frequent communication exchange, both of which are key components in the negotiation process, while reverse auctions provide an online marketplace for supply managers to invite potential suppliers to visit to bid on defined goods and services, which can reduce the whole negotiation process to little more than half an hour's duration, though, while useful for low-cost, high-volume commodities, they are less applicable to high-cost or high-quantity items and are not conductive to long-term relationships, for which meeting the buyer's requirements involves more than just quoting a price.

15.9 Negotiation and relationships

15.9.1 Situational and institutional approaches

Ertel[17] states that only rarely do companies think about their negotiating activities as a whole:

> Rather they take a situational view, seeing each negotiation as a separate event, with its own goals, its own tactics and its own measures of success. That approach can produce good results in particular instances, but it can be counterproductive when viewed from a higher, more strategic plane. Hammering out advantageous terms in a procurement contract may torpedo an important long-term relationship with a supplier.

15.9.2 Changing from a situational to an institutional approach

Ertel, therefore, advocates treating negotiation as an institutional capability rather than a series of discrete events. He identifies four changes instituted by companies that had moved away from a situational view of negotiation to a corporate approach concerned with long-term relationships.

- *Creation of a company-wide negotiation infrastructure* This implies that the outcome of a negotiation does not rely solely on the skill of an individual negotiator. Such negotiators can be supported by databases providing better information to negotiators, drawing lessons from past negotiations, guidance in strategy selection, examples of creative bargaining approaches and evaluation of outcomes. Such an infrastructure not only improves negotiating results but also breaks down the assumption that every negotiation is 'unique and immune to coordination and control'.

- *Broadening the measures used to evaluate the performance of negotiators beyond matters of cost and price*

   To be judged successful, negotiators have to show, for example, that they explicitly discussed several creative alternatives, used objective criteria to choose among the alternatives and that the final deal fulfils not only the company's interests but the other parties' as well.

Such an approach forces negotiators to think more broadly and creatively about negotiations, both when strategies are initially established and as the bargaining develops.

- *Recognition of the distinction between deals and relationships* Too frequently, negotiators confuse the deal with the broader relationship. To improve a strained relationship, they may offer a price concession. To gain a price concession, they may threaten to terminate the relationship. Such approaches, however, are counterproductive in that they create an adversarial climate in which both parties withhold information to protect their bargaining positions, thereby creating enhanced suspicion, which may adversely affect both the present deal and long-term relationships. If there is a previously established climate of trust, in which the terms of a deal can be discussed without prejudice to long-term relationships, this facilitates the free exchange of information and enhanced creative and collaborative problem-solving, leading to more valuable deals and stronger trading relationships.

- *Understanding of when to walk away from a deal* Successful and unsuccessful negotiations are usually evaluated respectively in terms of deals completed or uncompleted. Completion of deals, however, usually involves concessions on the part of one or both parties that may be in the interests of neither. When, however, a deal is struck that is unattractive to the purchaser, supplier or both, the possibility arises that less time and effort will be invested in working together and relationships will be strained. Companies should therefore encourage their negotiators to see their role not as producing *agreements* that may be mutually unsatisfactory, but, rather, as making good *choices*. Prior to meeting, the negotiators of each side should have established their respective BATNAs or the objective hurdles that any negotiated agreement has to clear. Neither should accept an agreement that is not at least as good as their BATNA. To do so is likely to have an adverse effect on relationships. Before concluding a deal, purchasers should consider whether or not a prospective supplier can possibly meet quality, delivery and other requirements, such as the price. If not, they should reject the deal and seek other supply sources. Negotiators should be made aware of the fact that, rather than arrive at a deal on the basis of concessions that would take the agreement below their BATNA, it is better to walk away. Ertel points out that not only do executives have to send the right messages internally, they also need to be aware of how external communications may affect negotiations and quotes the following example:

   In an interview published in a widely read magazine the CEO of a large computer company stated that when he was a sales representative he never lost a customer. . . . Imagine how the statement was interpreted by the company's sales force. The CEO was in effect telling the sales representatives that they could never say no and signalling customers that they held all the leverage. The negotiators' BATNAs were instantly rendered inconsequential with one public statement.

15.10 Negotiation ethics

Negotiation ethics is an aspect of the wider subject of purchasing ethics, considered in Chapter 17, and relationships, covered above. This topic is considered here because ethical perspectives largely determine whether or not a particular negotiation is adversarial or integrative.

Fisher and Ury[18] distinguish between positional and principled negotiation.

15.10.1 Positional negotiation

Positional negotiation views negotiation as an adversarial or conflict situation in which the other party is the enemy. It is based on four assumptions:

- we have the correct and only answer to a particular problem
- there is a 'fixed price'
- opposite positions equal opposite interests
- it is not our responsibility to solve the problems of the other party.

Positions and interests are closely related. Often negotiators will not move from a fixed position because of psychological pressures or needs. A leader of a negotiating team may refuse to consider alternatives for fear of losing face or being seen by team members as backing down.

Positional negotiation has at least two drawbacks:

- it is win–lose – it has only two ways to go, which are forwards to victory or backwards to defeat
- from an ethical standpoint, positional negotiation leads to such questionable tactics as:
  - misrepresentation of a position
  - bluffing (see section 17.10.3)
  - lying or deception
  - only providing selected information or being economical with the truth
  - threatening
  - manipulating.

15.10.2 Principled negotiation

Principled negotiation is fundamentally different from positional negotiation. The very term 'principled' has an ethical connotation. Fisher and Ury criticise positional negotiating on four grounds:

- *arguing about positions produces unwise agreements* compromising, for example, involves both parties giving up something, so neither is completely satisfied with the outcome
- *arguing about positions is unwise* time is wasted in trying to reconcile extreme positions
- *ongoing relationships are endangered* anger and resentment result when one side sees itself as being forced to bend to the rigid will of the other
- *positional bargaining is worse when there are many partners* it is harder to change group or constituency positions than those of individuals.

Fisher and Ury also see principled bargaining as an alternative to 'hard' or 'soft' bargaining. Soft bargainers may make concessions to cultivate or maintain relationships. Hard bargainers demand concessions as a condition of the relationship.

15.10.3 The Fisher and Ury principles

Apart from 'Don't bargain about positions', Fisher and Ury lay down four elements that parties must follow to obtain an ideal settlement.

Separate the people from the problem

This involves viewing the problem as the central issue to be resolved rather than regarding the other person as an adversary. Failure to do so can lead to antagonism between the parties. Fisher and Ury put forward 18 propositions under the 4 headings of perception, emotion, communication and prevention, of which the following are typical.

- *Perception*
  - Put yourself in the other party's shoes.
  - Don't blame the other party for your problem.
  - Discuss each other's perceptions.
  - Look for opportunities to act inconsistently with their perceptions.
- *Emotion*
  - First, recognise and understand emotions – theirs and yours.
  - Allow the other side to let off steam.
  - Don't react to emotional outbursts.
- *Communication*
  - Listen actively and acknowledge what is being said.
  - Speak about how you feel, not how you feel about them.
- *Prevention*
  - Where possible, build prenegotiation relationships that will enable parties to absorb the knocks incurred in the actual negotiation.

Focus on interests, not positions

Positions are symbolic representations of a participant's underlying interests. Each side has multiple needs. To find out about interests, ask 'Why?' and 'Why not?' questions.

Invent options for mutual gain

Again, Fisher and Ury classify their approaches under five headings – diagnosis, prescription, broadening options, searching for mutual gain and facilitating the other party's decisions.

- *Diagnosis*
  This includes avoiding:
  - premature judgements
  - searching for a single answer
  - assuming a 'fixed price'.

■ *Prescription*
  - Separating inventing from deciding.
  - Engaging in brainstorming, including brainstorming with the other party.

■ *Broadening options*
  - Look through the eyes of different experts.
  - Invent agreements of different strengths, such as substantive versus procedural, permanent versus provisional and so on.

■ *Searching for mutual gain*
  - Identify shared interests.
  - Dovetail differing interests.

■ *Facilitating the other party's decision*
  - Help the other party to sell a decision to his/her constituency.
  - Look for precedents.
  - Provide a range of options.

Insist on using objective criteria

This requires:

■ fair standards, such as objective criteria, including market value, professional or moral standards, legal criteria, custom and practice

■ fair procedures for resolving conflicting interests

■ reasoning and openness to reasoning

■ never yielding to pressure, only to principle.

15.10.4 Criticisms of principled negotiation

A number of criticisms have been made of principled negotiation, some of which Fisher and Ury recognise. Thus, where the other party has some negotiating advantage, they suggest that the answer is to improve your BATNA. The only reason we negotiate is to produce something better than the results we could obtain without negotiating. BATNAs offer protection against accepting terms that are too unfavourable and rejecting terms that it would be beneficial to accept.

Where the other party will not play or uses dirty tricks, the answer is to insist on principled negotiation in a way that is most acceptable to the competitor. Thus, principled negotiators might ask about the other party's concerns to show that they understand such concerns and ask the competitor to recognise all concerns.

Where the other party refuses to respond, two techniques to try are those of 'negotiation jujitsu', in which, instead of directly resisting the force of the other party, it is channelled into exploring interests, inventing options and searching for independent standards, and using outside intervention or mediation.

McCarthy[19] offers two main criticisms of the Fisher and Ury approach. The first is that it does not provide an adequate analysis of the role of power. The concept of negotiation jujitsu, for example, does not actually turn power back on the other party, but encourages both to ignore dirty tricks and minor power plays. McCarthy holds that the balance of power between the two parties is the key element in determining the limits of a mutually acceptable settlement and concludes 'in the area of collective bargaining at least I know of no set of maxims or principles that will enable any of us to escape from the limits set by a given power situation'.

McCarthy's second point is that Fisher and Ury assume rather than argue that the factors that make for effective negotiation in widely differing situations from domestic quarrels to international disputes are the same. There may be situations in which positional is preferable to principled negotiation.

15.10.5 Can negotiation be ethical?

Arguments that negotiation cannot be completely ethical include:

- it is commonly believed that success in negotiation is enhanced by the successful use of deceitful tactics, such as bluffing and outright misrepresentation
- negotiators have the responsibility of obtaining the best results for those they represent
- what is ethical is affected by cultural factors, such as bribery and deception that may be acceptable in some global negotiations, that 'When in Rome, do as the Romans do'
- self-interest is the most powerful of all motivations – few negotiations can be wholly altruistic
- ethical negotiation is an idealistic concept that does not work in practice
- sharing information may put a negotiator at a disadvantage.

Crampton and Dees[20] list a number of reasons for it being possible to gain from deceptive tactics:

- information asymmetry is great – the greater the information disparity between the two parties, the greater the opportunity one has for profitable deception
- verification of such details as long-term maintenance costs and performance is difficult
- the intention to deceive is difficult to establish – it is hard to distinguish it from a mistake or an oversight
- the parties have insufficient resources to adequately safeguard against deception
- interaction between the parties is infrequent – deception is more likely in one-off relationships
- ex-post redress is too costly – the deceived party may, however, prefer to make an effort, even when the costs exceed the expected compensation
- reputable information is unavailable, unreliable or very costly to communicate
- the circumstances are unusual in a way that limits inferences about future behaviour and deceptions are unlikely to damage future negotiations because they occur in distinctly different circumstances
- one party has little to lose (or much to gain) from deception – a negotiator may not be concerned about the prospect of being caught, providing that it does not occur before the deal has been closed.

Crampton and Dees state that they cannot recommend a single strategy that will work effectively to promote honesty in all negotiations, but they make the following suggestions.

- *Assess the situation* This involves considering the incentives for deception. What incentives are there for suppressing or misrepresenting information? What is known about the principles of the other side? What is the competence and character of the other side?

■ *Build mutual trust* In most cases, the incentive for deception in negotiation is defensive. It arises from the fear that the other party will unfairly exploit any weakness. This also involves building mutual benevolence, creating opportunities for displaying trust and demonstrating trustworthiness.

■ *Place the negotiation in a long-term context Caveat emptor* is reasonable advice for negotiators. Select negotiating partners wisely, verify when you can, request bonds and warranties, get important claims in writing and, where applicable, such as in IT and outsourcing negotiations, it may be advisable to hire a skilled intermediary.

Ethical negotiation can only take place in a climate of trust. Ascertaining whether or not such a climate exists requires negotiators to answer two questions – 'Can the other party trust us?' and 'Can we trust them?' Each party can answer the first question with some certainty, although they should be aware of self-deception. Not until both sides have established a working relationship can a certain answer be given to the second question. In the interim, both sides should show diligence in obtaining information to provide assurance that the other party will negotiate ethically.

Case study

Angela Cheetham is the buyer for HPS, a large building services organisation. Angela's scope for expenditure includes consultancy agreements. The Managing Director has invited four specialist consultancy companies to provide him with a tender to provide organisational change services. They have all responded and he has selected Thomasen Services as his 'preferred' consultancy provider. He has now given Angela the task of negotiating what he calls the important points. While Thomasen is his preferred supplier he has said that he would be quite prepared to deal with Fox and Standwell (FS). There is no problem agreeing the consultancy brief and that is not an issue. In the table below are the focus issues that need to be resolved.

Issue	Details
Costs	Thomasen has quoted £350,000 lump sum in fees, plus travel and hotels (neither has been defined), whereas FS has quoted £450,000 as an all-inclusive fee (lump sum). Both prices exclude VAT
Insurance	Thomasen has limited its liability to 50 per cent of the fees, while FS has £5m of professional indemnity insurance
Start date	Thomasen wants an eight-week lead time, but FS could begin in two weeks' time. The Managing Director wants the work started 'more or less immediately'
Key personnel	Thomasen has not named the consultants who would undertake the work, but FS has named the lead consultant and the five other consultants in support roles.

Tasks

Assuming you are Angela, prepare:

1 an agenda for negotiation with each of the potential service providers
2 an outline of the style you would adopt to deal with the situation.

Discussion questions

15.1 In a negotiation, each party knows that the other has some power to influence the outcome. What powers have:
   (a) trade unions and employees in a pay negotiation
   (b) two superpowers in a negotiation over weapons limitation
   (c) a monopoly supplier and a customer in a price negotiation?

15.2 Using the approach shown in Figures 15.1, 15.2 and 15.3, list at least 15 issues that might be the subject of negotiation when:
   (a) buying capital equipment
   (b) sourcing overseas.

15.3 Why might an adversarial strategy *not* be appropriate when a quick, simple solution to a disagreement is required?

15.4 Why are most negotiations likely to take place in relation to high-value items – that is, the 15–20 per cent that constitute the major portion of inventory management? Is it possible to agree any substantial expenditure or project, such as a construction project, without considerable negotiation?

15.5 Many writers confuse consultation with negotiation. What is the difference between the two concepts?

15.6 It has been said that our personalities are revealed by how we react to given situations. Try to think of six ways in which a person who fails to get his or her own way in a negotiating situation may react. Divide such reactions into those that are productive and those that are counterproductive to the negotiation.

15.7 Why is it important that you should know the limits of your authority to commit your organisation in negotiations? Why is it equally important for you to know the extent of the authority possessed by your opposite number?

15.8 As a buyer, you find yourself in a strong buying position due to a combination of the factors mentioned in section 15.3.2. Why is it essential that you use such power sensitively and responsibly?

15.9 How may time affect your negotiating position with regard to price, quality, negotiating style and future supplier relationship?

15.10 Explain, with examples, the working of the basic power equation in section 15.3.2.

15.11 In the industrial relations context, it is usual for employees and trade unions to have joint negotiating procedures. Such agreements can contain clauses on such matters as:
   (a) the stages in the agreement – that is, the levels at which the procedure will operate, time limits and provision for adjustments
   (b) what matters can be dealt with in the negotiating procedure
   (c) what happens if there is a failure to agree.

   What are the possible benefits of an organisation having a negotiating procedure for bargaining in relation to the placing of long-term supply or project contracts?

15.12 As part of the preparation for negotiation, is it useful to draft ground rules that, if approved by the other party, can provide the framework for a negotiation. What aspects of negotiating would you include within such ground rules?

15.13 Suggest five ways in which to resolve an apparent deadlock in a negotiation.

15.14 Discuss the following statements:
(a) 'Once you consent to some concession, you can never cancel it and put things back the way they were'
(b) 'We cannot negotiate with those who say "What's mine is mine, what's yours is negotiable"' (John F. Kennedy)
(c) 'Flattery is the infantry of negotiation' (Lord Chander)
(d) 'Always define your terms' (Eric Partridge).

Past examination questions

1 Discuss the stages in the negotiation process and how buyers can ensure that they are negotiating effectively at each stage of a negotiation.
CIPS. *Purchasing and Supply Chain Management II:*
Tactics and Operations, May 2001

2 Negotiation is like a major sporting event. The game is usually won or lost in the planning and preparation stages. P. Evans, *Supply Management*, October 2000

Explain what is meant by this statement, showing what these stages would consist of and how they could be incorporated into the negotiation itself.
CIPS. *Purchasing and Supply Chain Management II:*
Tactics and Operations, November 2001

3 Explain why some organisations use adversarial relationships and evaluate where the use of such relationships might be appropriate.
CIPS. *Commercial Relationships*, May 2003

4 (a) Explain how knowledge of negotiating styles can assist in the preparation for a negotiation.
(b) Describe three tools of analysis that can be used to assist the purchasing manager in the preparation stage of negotiation.
CIPS. *Tactics and Operations*, November 2003

5 (a) Discuss the advantages and disadvantages of the different styles of negotiation that can be adopted.
(b) Explain how you would measure the effectiveness of an important negotiation.
CIPS. *Tactics and Operations*, May 2004

References

[1] Aljian, G. W., *Purchasing Handbook*, 4th edn, McGraw-Hill, 1982, section 11, p. 11.5

[2] Rubin, J. Z., and Brown, B. R., *The Social Psychology of Bargaining and Negotiation*, Academic Press, 1975

[3] Gottschal, R. A. W., 'The background to the negotiating process' in Torrington, D., *Code of Personnel Management*, Gower, 1979

4 Lysons, C. K., Modified version of definition in *Purchasing*, 3rd edn, Pitman, 1993

5 Fisher, R., and Ury, W., *Getting to Yes*, Penguin, 1983

6 Cooper, C. L., and Makin, P., *Psychology for Managers*, British Psychological Society in association with Macmillan, 1988, p. 58

7 Berne, Eric, *Games People Play*, Penguin, 1968

8 Harris, T. A., *I'm OK – You're OK*, Pan Macmillan, 1986

9 McCall, J. M., and Norrington, M. B., *Marketing by Agreement: A Cross-cultural Approach to Business Negotiations*, Wiley, 1986

10 Pena-Mora, F., and Tamaki, T., 'Effect of delivery systems on collaborative negotiations for large-scale infrastructure projects', *Journal of Management in Engineering*, April, 2001, pp. 105–21

11 As 5 above

12 Galinsky, A. D., *Negotiation Strategy: Should You Make the First Offer?* Harvard Business School, 2004

13 Susskind, L., and Cruikshank, J., *Breaking the Impasse*, Basic Books, 1987

14 Lee, R., and Lawrence, P., *Organisational Behaviour: Politics at Work*, Hutchinson, 1988, p. 182

15 Rowntree, D., *The Manager's Book of Checklists*, Gower, 1989, pp. 207–8

16 As 5 above

17 Ertel, Danny, 'Turning negotiation into a corporate capability', *Harvard Business Review*, May–June, 1999, pp. 55–70

18 As 5 above

19 McCarthy, W., 'The role of power and principle in getting to yes', in Breslin, J. W., and Rubin, J. Z., *Negotiation Theory and Practice*, Cambridge University Press, 1991, pp. 115–22

20 Crampton, P. C., and Dees, J. G., 'Promoting honesty in negotiation', *Journal of Business Ethics*, March, 2002, pp. 1–28

Chapter 16

Support tools

Learning outcomes

This chapter aims to provide an understanding of:

- tendering or competitive bidding
- costing techniques and their application to purchasing
- budgets and budgetary control
- learning curves
- scheduling
- project managements
- operational research.

Key ideas

- Types of tenders and tendering procedure.
- Post tender negotiation (PTN).
- Lifecycle costing.
- Target costing.
- Absorption costing.
- Activity-based costing and management.
- Standard costing.
- Purchasing budgets.
- The learning curve theorem.
- Types of projects.
- Gantt charts.
- Network analysis.
- CPM and PERT.
- Operational research and suppliers.

16.1 Tendering

16.1.1 Definitions

A *tender* or *bid* is a formal offer to supply goods or services for an agreed price. From a purchasing perspective tendering (or competitive bidding) is:

> A purchasing procedure whereby potential suppliers are invited to make a firm and unequivocal offer of the price and terms on which they will supply specified goods or services, which, on acceptance, shall be the basis of a subsequent contract.

Normally tenders are based on a specification of requirements prepared by the purchaser. An alternative is to invite potential providers to submit solutions and prices to a problem stated by the purchaser. Tendering is based on the principles of competition, fairness and accessibility, transparency and openness and probity. The process of obtaining tenders should also aim at obtaining the best value and not necessarily the lowest price.

16.1.2 Types of tender

- *Open tenders* Prospective suppliers are invited to compete for a contract advertised in the press or on the Internet – the lowest tender generally being accepted, although the advertisers usually state that they are not bound to accept the lowest or any tender.
- *Restricted open tenders* Prospective suppliers are invited to compete for a contract, the advertising of which is restricted to appropriate technical journals or local newspapers.
- *Selective tenders* Tenders are invited from suppliers on an approved list that have been previously vetted regarding their competence and financial standing.
- *Serial tenders* Prospective suppliers are requested on either an open or a selective basis to tender for an initial scheme on the basis that, subject to satisfactory performance and unforeseen financial contingencies, a programme of work will be given to the successful contractor, the rates and prices for the first job being the basis for the rest of the programme. Advantages claimed for this system include:
  - contractors are given an incentive to maintain a high performance level
  - savings in cost and time by eliminating one-contract negotiations for each stage of a programme
  - teams of employees and plant can be moved to successive jobs without disruption
  - supplier security of contract should enable purchasers to negotiate keener prices.
- *Negotiated tenders* A tender is negotiated with only one supplier so that competition is eliminated. This type of contract is unusual. In the case of a local authority, it would require the waiving of standing orders.

16.1.3 The application of tendering

Although tendering is used by private-sector undertakings, particularly for construction and service contracts, it is in the public sector that tendering is most used to ensure conformity to such principles of public accountability as openness or transparency, avoidance of a conflict of interests and recognition that 'a public office is a public trust'. Guidance regarding public tendering is found in the following sources.

■ UK Law, Section 135(3) of the Local Government Act 1972, for example, states:

> Standing orders made by a local authority with respect to the supply of goods or materials for the execution of works shall include provision for securing competition for such contracts and for regulating the manner but may exempt from any such provisions contracts for a price below that specified in standing orders and may authorise the authority to exempt any contract from such provision when the authority is satisfied that the exemption is justified by special circumstances.

Part 1 of the Local Government Act 1999 (which repeats Part III of the Local Government Planning and Land Act 1980; Part 1 Section 3.2 Schedule 6 of the Local Government Act 1988 and Sections 8–11 Schedule 1 of the Local Government Act 1992) imposes a duty on 'best value authorities' to make arrangements to secure continuous improvement in the way that their functions are exercised having regard to 'economy, efficiency and effectiveness'. In addition to local authorities, 'best value authorities' include police, fire, waste disposal, transport, National Parks and Broads authorities.

■ Most European law on public-sector purchasing is contained in UK regulations or statutory instruments. The UK Public Contracts (Works, Service and Supply (amendment) Regulations 2000 (SI2000 No. 2009)), for example, sets out:

– the thresholds for contracts, above which, under EU directives, must be applied to the tendering and award of contracts

– rules relating to the advertising by public bodies by which their requirements must be advertised in the *Official Journal of the European Union* (OJEU).

European directives on public-sector purchasing recognise three forms of tendering procedure:

– *open tenders* all suppliers that respond to the contract notice are invited to tender

– *restricted tenders* only those suppliers that have been invited by the contracting authority may submit tenders, but restricted procedures will only apply where:

– the contract value does not justify the procedural costs of an open tender

– the product required is highly specific in its nature

– *negotiated tenders* allow the terms of the contract to be negotiated with one or more suppliers without prior publication of a tender notice, but the negotiated procedure is only available in certain defined circumstances, such as:

– where, because bids were irregular or unacceptable, no suitable supplier has been found by open or restricted tender procedures

– where such procedures have resulted in no tender being received

– where the required product is manufactured purely for research and development or experimental purposes

– where, for technical or artistic reasons or the existence of exclusive rights, there is only one supplier.

16.1.4 Tendering procedures

General procedures

In public purchasing, procedures are usually codified within standing orders that usually prescribe a cash limit above which tenders must be invited, the forms of contract to be used and to whom and under what circumstances responsibility for the evaluation of tenders may be delegated, such as to senior officers. In general, the procedure for open tenders involves:

1 the issue of a public advertisement inviting tenders
2 the issue of tender documentation to those responding to the advertisement, which will normally include:
   - a letter of invitation and instructions to tenderers
   - a pricing document and/or form of tender
   - specification and/or schedule of rates
   - contract conditions or conditions of purchase
   - any relevant supporting invitation
   - pre-addressed tender return label

   the documentation will include a date by which tenders must be submitted and any received after the specified deadline will be excluded from the evaluation process
3 on the date arranged for the opening of tenders, appointed officers from the procurement department and an external department, such as the treasurer's department, will attend
4 tenders will be initialled, listed and entered on an analysis sheet or spreadsheet showing details of prices, rates, carriage charges, delivery, settlement terms and other information necessary for their evaluation
5 tenders will be evaluated on an agreed basis, such as lowest bid or most economically advantageous tender (MEAT), but the public body is under no obligation to accept the lowest or any of the tenders received
6 the successful tenderer will be notified
7 unsuccessful tenderers will also be notified, although they will not automatically be given reasons for their tender not being accepted – this information should be made available if it is requested.

Reverse auctions and e-tendering

The process of tendering is greatly expedited by the use of reverse auctions and e-tendering.

- in reverse auctions (see sections 6.9 and 13.20.5), all prospective suppliers submit competitive bids based either on lowest price or most economically advantageous criteria
- e-procurement is the conduct of the complete tendering process – from the advertising of the requirement to the placing of the contract, including the exchange of all relevant documentation – all of it by electronic means of communication.

Bryden and Luther[1] list the following benefits to be realised by both the tender authorities and the contractors if they use a completely online process. For tender authorities, these include:

- savings in document preparation and reproduction costs
- a larger group of bidders
- improved communication of changes
- consistent bid format
- savings in the processing of bids received
- elimination of bidding errors, as incomplete bids will be rejected automatically.

For the contractors (tenderers), these include:

- savings in reviewing possible bid opportunities
- the ability to review an expanded list of opportunities
- round the clock access to documents
- savings in travel costs, as bids are submitted from the office
- no risk of travel delays disrupting a last-minute submission
- bids may be efficiently resubmitted before the submission deadline
- automatic rejection of incomplete bids, allowing for resubmission.

The UK's Ministry of Defence[2] has identified the following key principles as ones that should be considered when conducting e-tendering:

- security
- confidentiality
- integrity
- authentication
- equity/transparency
- liability
- trust
- business benefits
- portability of data
- flexible process
- future-proofing
- audit trail
- affordability
- compatibility/interoperability
- firewalls
- scalability
- reliability/availability.

16.1.5 The disadvantages of tendering

- Contractors may quote a price that is too low, leading to subsequent disputes if goods or services supplied are unsatisfactory.

- Tendering is unsuitable for certain contracts. With plant contracts, for example, consultation with one or more of the more favourable tenderers is often essential to clear up technical points. These often result in the tenderer making suggestions that will result in cheaper running and maintenance costs. The extent to which technical changes can be allowed without affecting the validity of open competition is a matter of difficulty.

- The tendering procedure is too slow for emergencies – this is usually recognised by standing orders.

- Where tenders are accepted on the principle of the lowest price, credit may not be given to suppliers for past performance.

- The tendering procedure, particularly with open tendering, may be expensive from the standpoint of clerical, stationery and postage costs. This can be largely reduced by e-tendering.

- Tendering is expensive for contractors. For this reason, selective tendering is usually preferable. Again, e-tendering reduces such expenses.

16.2 Debriefing

The practice of debriefing unsuccessful tenderers adopted by most public-sector purchasers might usefully be adopted by the private sector as it supports the procurement principle of promoting open and effective competition.

16.2.1 The benefits of debriefing

Debriefing, however, can be costly. It is often done verbally rather than by written communication. The UK Treasury[3] recommends that government departments should balance the resource costs against the likely benefits. The benefits accruing to a purchasing organisation as a result of adopting a policy of responding to requests from unsuccessful tenderers for debriefing information include:

- establishing a reputation as a fair, honest, open and ethical client

- providing unsuccessful tenderers with some benefits from the time and money spent on preparing their tenders – this is likely to be of most value to smaller and newer suppliers, but will help all tenderers to be more competitive in the future.

16.2.2 Debriefing topics

The UK Office of Government Commerce[4] lists the following:

- *Cost* The actual prices or rates offered in tenders are confidential and should never be disclosed. It is permissible, however, to disclose a prospective supplier's ranking in the tender list. The UK Office of Government Commerce observes that:

  > if the tenderer was the lowest bidder in cost terms but not selected on VFM this need not be disclosed: it is unlikely to lead to constructive debate. The tenderer could, however, be told that although the price was competitive, other factors were more significant in the award decision.

- *Schedules* Exceptionally long production and/or construction schedules.

- *Design* Deficiencies, higher operating costs.

- *Organisation/administration weaknesses.*
- *Experience* Where the experience of the tenderer is deemed to be inadequate for the demands of the contract.
- *Personnel* Where the numbers, experience and quality of personnel, including management, are deemed inadequate.
- *Facilities/equipment* Outdated equipment or facilities.
- *Subcontracting* Too much reliance on subcontractors and inadequate control arrangements.
- *Cost and schedule control inadequacies.*
- *Industrial relations* Where the tenderer has an unsatisfactory record and no plans for improvement.
- *Quality management* Where control procedures relating to materials, methods, systems and people are deemed unsatisfactory.
- *Contract terms* Where these differ fundamentally from those of the client.
- *After-sales service* Inadequate arrangements for servicing and the supply of spares.

16.2.3 Conducting a debriefing

The UK Inland Revenue[5] recommends that debriefing:

- should not disclose information about other tenderers that could breach commercial confidentiality
- should not become an argument about rights or wrongs or an attempt to justify the reasons for awarding the contract to a particular tenderer
- should be confined to the unsuccessful bid and the weaknesses that led to its rejection – cost, delivery dates, inadequate experience, failure to meet quality standards and so on, as appropriate
- should indicate the perceived strengths of the unsuccessful tender
- should conclude by asking for the supplier's view on the debriefing process.

Results of debriefing interviews should be recorded for reference should there be any further audit in the case of follow-up by the unsuccessful bidder or some other party.

16.3 Post-tender negotiation (PTN)

The disadvantages of traditional tendering procedures have indicated the importance of post-tender negotiation. PTN is defined by the CIPS[6] as:

> Negotiation after the receipt of formal tenders and before the letting of contract(s) with the supplier(s)/contractor(s) submitting the lowest acceptable tender(s) with a view to obtaining an improvement in price, delivery of content in circumstances which do not put other tenderers at a disadvantage or affect their confidence or trust in the competitive tendering system.

'Post-tender negotiation', issued by the former Central Unit on Procurement,[7] points out that, if it is not considered unethical for a supplier to tender at the highest level that it is considered the purchaser will pay, the converse is that it is not unethical for buyers to challenge the prices tendered.

The former Central Unit on Procurement (CUP)[7] has stated that post-tender negotiation can apply to almost any order or contract, although care should be taken to ensure that the cost of negotiation does not outweigh any resultant savings. In particular, post-tender negotiation is recommended for:

- all orders potentially worth £10,000 or over
- where the final bid evaluation does not present overwhelming evidence for one tenderer
- where there is doubt regarding quality or performance or where clarification of terms and conditions is required
- all supply agreements made for a period of 12 months or longer.

It is important that the same general questions and propositions are put to short-listed tenderers, although, as stated above, this does not preclude asking questions for clarification. A record should be kept of the negotiation process for audit purposes. This should include:

- date and time of communications, such as meetings, phone calls, correspondence
- people present or contacted
- matters discussed
- outcomes.

The former CUP also identifies eight common areas for direct price negotiation:

- where a single-tender action has been authorised
- where it is known or suspected that price-fixing or cartel arrangements are operating
- where tender prices appear grossly inflated compared to known or reliably estimated market prices or the price(s) paid for similar or identical items
- where, despite competitive tendering, a particular supplier is consistently successful in obtaining the contract
- where the enquiry is based on a functional or development specification rather than a detailed specification
- where the purchaser needs to justify selections by testing the market
- where the quantity to be ordered justifies splitting requirements between more than one supplier
- to evaluate whether or not market conditions are in the buyer's favour or otherwise.

The CIPS[6] has also identified a 'position statement' on PTN in which it suggests that:

> One way of obtaining Best and Final Offers (BAFO) is to send to suppliers, on an anonymous basis, a list of all the costs/prices obtained, inviting their BAFO. It is important that suppliers are advised at the ITT stage that this process is scheduled to take place and that suppliers make their own decision as to whether they wish to participate. A similar method is the reverse auction, whereby suppliers are requested to submit offers which progressively reduce in price until either a) they are accepted by buyers, or b) until those other suppliers decline to reduce their prices any further.

This practice is, of course, only feasible when there is time to conduct PTN without delaying the contract's completion date.

16.4   Application of costing techniques

No purchasing professional can afford to be unaware of the various cost accounting approaches to make-or-buy decisions, negotiation, price appraisal and purchasing performance, to mention just four such applications. Relevant approaches include lifecycle costing, target costing, absorption costing, activity-based costing (ABC) and standard costing. Marginal cost as applied to make-or-buy decisions is considered in section 11.14.2.

16.5   Lifecycle costing

The concept of lifecycle analysis with its stages of development, growth, maturity, decline, and withdrawal was introduced in section 2.13.2. As stated in section 13.4.1 lifecycle costing is an important factor when making decisions relating to capital expenditure.

16.5.1 Definition

Lifecycle costing has been defined by the Chartered Institute of Management Accountants (CIMA)[8] as:

> The practice of obtaining over their lifetime the best use of the physical assets at the lowest cost to the entity (Terotechnology). This is achieved through a combination of management, financial, engineering and other disciplines.

The term *Terotechnology*, coined in 1970, is derived from the Greek verb *tereo* and means literally 'the art and science of caring for things'. Lifecycle costs are therefore those associated with acquiring, using, caring for and disposing of physical assets, including feasibility studies, research, development, design, production, maintenance, replacement and disposal, as well as the associated support, training and operating costs incurred over the period in which the asset is owned.

16.5.2 The importance of lifecycle costing

Unless lifecycle implications are taken into consideration, there is a danger that initial cost on delivery will be used as the sole criterion when selecting a physical asset. This simplistic approach can, however, have detrimental implications for the total lifecycle cost of the item.

Lifecycle costing is of particular importance for products liable to rapid technological or style changes. From the standpoint of producers, rapid technological change may mean that revenue from sales may be insufficient to make the original investment in design and development worthwhile. From the buyer's viewpoint, the asset may, to a greater or lesser extent, be obsolete before the amount invested in its purchase has been recouped.

Purchasing executives concerned with the acquisition of capital items are therefore advised to:

■ ensure that specifications include reference to factors that have a bearing on the cost of ownership of an asset, such as maintenance and the availability of spares

- create a communication bridge with the supplier regarding developments in the particular field
- treat initial costs as only one of many factors that will contribute to their total lifecycle costs
- ensure all factors that may have implications for the total lifecycle costs are given due consideration before recommending the purchase of a particular asset.

16.5.3 Application of lifecycle costing

Apart from the purchase of capital equipment, lifecycle costing can be applied to:

- *acquisition control* estimating the future costs of large-scale acquisitions
- *optioneering* comparing the returns on a number of expenditure options
- *pricing* ensuring that, in addition to direct and general overhead costs (not including depreciation), an interest charge is included that reflects the overall cost of capital required to satisfy all capital providers so that the annual equivalent cost of fixed assets will recover both depreciation and a profit margin that satisfies all providers
- *project analysis* measurement of the cost of a project against its targets
- *product design* provision of data that will enable designers to modify or improve designs that will improve consumer satisfaction and give a product greater cost advantage over those of competitors
- *replacement decisions* as the cost of using and repairing physical assets increases with age, lifecycle costing can indicate when it is more beneficial to dispose of an asset and purchase a replacement than it is to meet increasing maintenance costs
- *supplier support* provision by suppliers of comparative lifecycle estimates for their products.

16.5.4 Lifecycle costing methodology

The lifecycle costing methodology involves the following four basic steps.

1 Identify all relevant costs. As shown in Figure 16.1, these are initially broken down into acquisition and operation, maintenance and disposal costs, then broken down further under each heading.

2 Calculate the costs over the anticipated life of the asset of all the elements identified above. Such costs may be:
   - known rates, such as operator pay, maintenance charges
   - estimated rates based on historical figures or other empirical data
   - guesstimates based on informed opinion.

3 Use discounting to adjust future costs to apply to the present – that is, the time when the purchase decision is made. This reduces all options to a common base, thereby ensuring fair comparison. Discounting was discussed in section 13.9.3.

4 Draw conclusions from the cost figures obtained by the above procedure.

Figure 16.1 **Lifecycle costing breakdown structure**

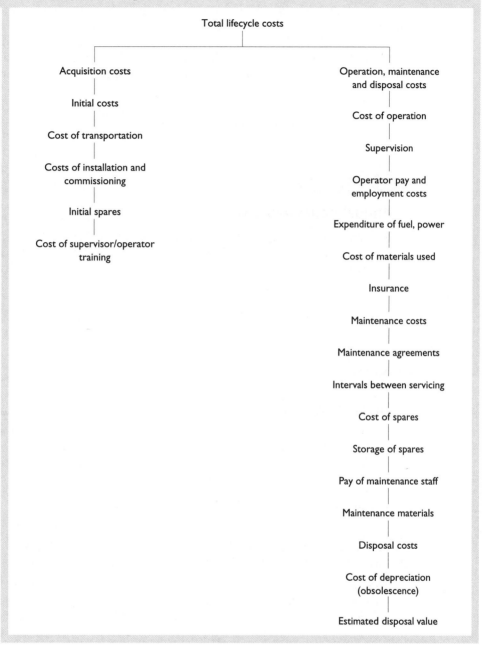

In its simplest form, lifecycle costs (LCC) are:

> Initial cost
> + Operating/maintenance costs over life of item
> + Energy costs
> + Disposal costs or salvage value

16.5.5 Annual equivalent costs

This involves expressing the initial purchase and subsequent running costs of an asset in terms of annual equivalent costs for the purpose of comparing the lifecycles of assets with different lives. The calculation involves dividing the capital cost – that is, the purchase and installation costs – by the relevant cumulative present value factor (obtained from cumulative present value tables) for the specified life and rate of interest.

The formula is:

$$\text{Annual equivalent cost} = \frac{\text{Capital cost}}{\text{Cumulative present value factor}}$$

Example 16.1

Annual equivalent cost

A company buys a machine for a capital cost of £10,000, plus £1000 for installation. The machine has an anticipated life of 5 years and cumulative present value factor of 3.933, representing 8 per cent for 5 years. The annual equivalent cost is therefore:

$$\frac{£11,000}{3.993} = £2755$$

Example 16.2

Lifecycle costing

A department has a requirement for 50 photocopiers, capable of producing 40,000 copies per month from each copier.

There are two copiers that fully meet the department's technical specification together with the quality requirements. The anticipated life of the copier is five years.

The metered cost per copy offered by the suppliers includes maintenance charges and all consumables. The two proposals are as follows:

	Copier A	Copier B
Unit price for an order of 50	£10,745	£8625
Metered cost per copy, fixed in cash terms for 5 years	0.9p	1.9p

To ascertain the most cost-effective acquisition in lifecycle cost terms, an LCC analysis is carried out. A discount rate of 6 per cent in real terms (that is, after adjusting for inflation) is used in the analysis, which gives the following discounting factors:

Year 0	1
Year 1	0.943
Year 2	0.890
Year 3	0.840
Year 4	0.792

The following example sets out the steps involved in this procedure. All costs are expressed at year '0' prices. Staff costs and consumables will almost certainly rise in line with inflation, but any costs that will remain the same in cash terms over the five years will need to be adjusted to year '0' prices using a forecast of inflation that your finance division will be able to give you. In this example, inflation is assumed to be 4 per cent per year. It is also assumed that the machines are deployed at separate locations around the building, not as part of a continuous flow print room. In the case of the latter, it would be necessary to allow for some standby facility to maintain the required level of output.

Step 1

Produce a cost breakdown structure (see Figure 16.2).

Figure 16.2 **Cost breakdown**

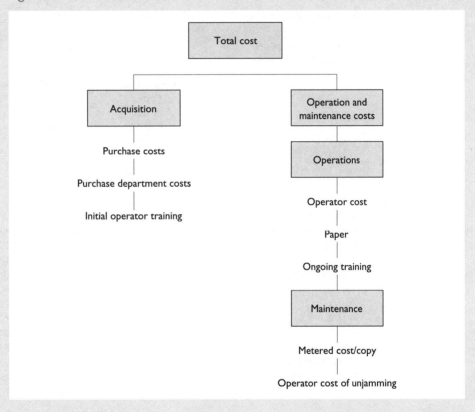

Step 2

Produce a cost estimate.

Acquisition	Copier A	Copier B
Purchase costs	£537.25k	£431.25k
Purchase department costs (2 people/weeks)	£2.5k	£2.5k
(Operator training time required per copier)	(3 hrs)	(2 hrs)
(2 operators per copier) at £10 per hour × 50 copiers	£3k	£2k
Total acquisition cost	**£542.75k**	**£435.75k**

Operation (5 years)			Copier A	Copier B
Operator cost			£k	£k
Year 0			600.0	600.0
Year 1			565.8	565.8
Year 2			534.0	534.0
Year 3			504.0	504.0
Year 4			475.2	475.2
(£5 per 1000)			£k	£k
Year 0			120.0	120.0
Year 1			113.2	113.2
Year 2			106.8	106.8
Year 3			100.8	100.8
Ongoing training			95.0	95.0
			1.5	1.5
Total operation cost			**£3216.3**	**£3216.3**

Maintenance (5 years)			Copier A	Copier B
Metered cost per copy			0.9p	1.0p

	Adjusted at 4% per year		Then discounted at 6%	
	Copier A	Copier B	Copier A	Copier B
	£k	£k	£k	£k
Year 0	216.0	240.0	216.0	240.0
Year 1	207.7	230.8	196.7	217.4
Year 2	199.7	221.9	177.7	197.2
Year 3	192.0	213.3	161.3	179.2
Year 4	184.6	205.1	146.2	162.5

Operator/supervisor cost of unjamming
Mean number of copies between jams
(source: previous experience)

	Copier A	Copier B
Mean number of copies between jams	5000	3000
Average downtime	0.5 hr	1 hr
5 year cost at £10/hour	£k	£k
Year 0	24	80
Year 1	22.6	75.4
Year 2	21.4	71.2
Year 3	20.2	67.2
Year 4	19.0	63.4
Total maintenance cost	**£1004.1**	**£1353.7**
Total 5 year LCC	**£4.831m**	**£5.080m**

Step 3

Analysis

The example shows that the acquisition cost is far exceeded by the maintenance costs. The cost of operation although large is incurred by the decision to buy the copier and is not affected by the choice. Therefore, it was unnecessary to discount these costs as they apply equally to both options.

The maintenance costs show the major cost drivers over which the procurer has some control. Not only are the metered costs important, but also the time expended by the operator in unjamming the machine.

Before the decision can be fully assessed, the options should be evaluated in performance terms. The prime criterion for copiers of equal performance is availability for use. This can be calculated as follows:

$$\text{Availability} = \frac{\text{Uptime}}{\text{Total time}}$$

With the following data:

	Copier A	Copier B
Total possible availability	176 hrs	176 hrs
Downtime for replacement of consumables/ month/copier (company brochures)	3 hrs	4 hrs
Downtime for operator unjamming/ month/copier (user experience)	4 hrs	13.3 hrs
Downtime for maintenance engineers/month/copier	5.4 hrs	10.8 hrs
Average downtime/month/copier	12.4 hrs	28.1 hrs
$\dfrac{\text{Uptime}}{\text{Total time}}$	$\dfrac{(176 - 12.4)}{176}$	$\dfrac{(176 - 28.1)}{176}$
Availability	93%	84%

Step 4

Draw conclusions.

Copier A, although over £100,000 more expensive to buy, is some £349,000 cheaper to own when considered in LCC terms over 5 years (that is the difference between the operation and maintenance costs of copiers A and B). Additionally, Copier A, as it is a better-quality machine with greater reliability than Copier B is, on average, 9 per cent more available than its competitor or, viewed alternatively, Copier B would be unavailable for twice as long as Copier A. Therefore, the additional investment in purchasing it will be more than recouped during the life of the copiers.

Source: HM Treasury, *Life Cycle Costing*, BCUP Guidance Note 35, HMSO, pp. 7–8. Reproduced by kind permission of HM Treasury and HMSO

16.6 Target costing

16.6.1 Definition

Target costing is defined by CIMA[9] as:

> A product cost estimate derived from a competitive market price. Used to reduce costs through continuous improvement and replacement of technologies and processes.

16.6.2 Target cost procedures

Target cost, as defined above, is simply the target price minus the target profit.
Target costing has the following characteristics:

- it is proactive and forward-looking rather than reactive and historical, as is the case with standard costs

Figure 16.3 **Initial target cost statement**

Component X

Estimated lifecycle		5 years
Estimated annual sales		40,000
Estimated total sales over lifecycle		200,000
Initial target sales price per unit		£342 (50% on target costs)

	Target costs	
	Per unit	*Total lifecycle*
Design and development	£12.50	£2,500,000
Production	£125.50	£25,100,000
Packaging	£10.00	£2,000,000
Marketing	£35.00	£7,000,000
Transportation	£25.00	£5,000,000
After-sales service	£10.00	£2,000,000
	£218.00	£43,600,000

- it is dynamic as target costs are revised not only in the design and development stages but throughout the lifecycle of a product or service – the emphasis on continuous improvement implies that target costs over this period are expected to decrease
- it is market-driven in the sense that targets are fixed according to the costs of competitors
- it is linked closely to the concept of *functional analysis*.

A *function* is that which a product or service is designed to do, and functional analysis 'contributes to cost management by eliminating or modifying functions of the product or service'.[10] Functional analysis is undertaken by a team comprised of representatives of design, engineering, production, purchasing, marketing and management functions. The team's aim is to determine how costs can be managed to meet the desired target. Functional analysis can, on occasion, lead the designer to add new functions if the target profit is greater than the target cost generated by the additional functions.

An initial target cost statement prepared by the supplier would resemble the one shown in Figure 16.3.

Each cost element will be considered by the team to ascertain how target costs can be modified or the competitiveness of the product can be enhanced by means of:

- improved design specifications
- improved production techniques
- alternative materials
- eliminating or combining functions
- control of packaging, marketing and transportation costs
- a reduction in after-sales service required due to improved reliability.

16.6.3 Target costing and purchasing

Target costing is primarily associated with the search for competitiveness by product manufacturers and service providers. It is, however, an approach that can be utilised by purchasing, particularly in relation to negotiation, in such ways as the following:

- providing suppliers with a target price that the purchaser is prepared to pay
- identifying, in association with a supplier, the means by which the target price may be achieved, including a fair profit
- incorporating improvements into the product or price at agreed intervals or when a contract is due for renewal
- providing suppliers with an estimate of the lifecycle of parent products in which bought-out components or assemblies will be incorporated – it is then possible to estimate the total demand that a supplier may expect to receive over a defined period of time and this can be used to negotiate quantity discounts, price reviews and learning allowances.

16.6.4 Target and *kaizen* costing

Kaizen costing is a Japanese approach to cost reduction and management. The principal difference between target and *kaizen* costing is that target costing applies to the design stage while *kaizen* costing applies to the manufacturing stage of the product lifecycle. Target costing focuses on the product and seeks to achieve cost reductions by means of product design. Thus, target costing at Toyota is a rigorous engineering process that uses value engineering to reduce the cost of products. *Kaizen* costing focuses on production processes and cost reduction is achieved by improving manufacturing efficiency. The aim of *kaizen* costing is to reduce the cost of components and production processes by a specific amount.

16.7 Absorption costing

16.7.1 Definition

Approaches such as lifecycle and target costing are concerned with price comparison and price control and reduction rather than day-to-day costing methods. Probably the simplest and best understood method of ascertaining costs is absorption costing, defined by the CIMA[11] as:

> A principle whereby fixed as well as variable costs are allotted to cost units and total overheads are absorbed according to activity level.
> The term may be applied where (a) production costs only or (b) costs of all functions are allotted.

16.7.2 The elements of cost

Cost is the amount of expenditure incurred on a given thing. Costs can be classified in several ways, according to the purpose for which they are required. The most usual classifications are into:

- *direct costs* direct pay, materials and expenses that can be allocated to specific cost units or centres
- *indirect costs* expenses such as indirect pay, materials and expenses that cannot be allocated but which can be apportioned to or absorbed by cost units or centres.

Costs can also be classified as:

- *fixed* a cost that tends to be unaffected by variations in volume of output
- *variable* a cost that tends to vary directly with variations in volume of output
- *semi-variable* a cost that is partly fixed and partly variable.

16.7.3 Price composition

The price quoted will be built up as follows:

Direct costs	Materials, labour and expenses	Prime cost
Indirect costs	Works or factory expenses (Production overheads)	Work costs
	Office and administrative expenses (Establishment overheads)	Cost of production (Gross cost)
	Selling and distribution expenses (Selling overheads)	Cost of sales (Selling cost)
Net profit		= Selling price

By means of price analysis, the buyer, with the assistance of design, production and financial colleagues, will be able to arrive at a reasonably close estimate of the prime cost of a bought-out item. There will, however, be less precision in arriving at estimates of indirect costs and profit. The preparation of such an estimate is an essential preliminary to negotiation. When presented to a vendor, the estimate puts the prospective supplier in the position of having to explain why the buyer's estimate is wrong or providing cost data to support the quotation.

The questions that the buyer might raise in analysing the prices quoted by vendors will be peculiar to the particular item or job, but below are some examples of the kinds of questions that are applicable to each of the elements that constitute selling prices to indicate the approach that should be taken.

16.7.4 Material costs

Material costs are arrived at by the following sum:

$$\text{Quantity of material} \times \text{Purchase price of material}$$

- What material is used – that is, would an alternative material reduce costs?
- What standardisation is possible?
- Is it possible for the buyer to purchase materials on behalf of the vendor at a cheaper cost?
- What weight of material has been allowed for?
- What scrap allowances are included?
- Has scrap any resale value?

16.7.5 Labour costs

These can be calculated by multiplying time by the rate of pay.

- What time allocations have been made?
- Has any allowance been included for idle time?

- What element of overtime is included?
- Has any allowance for 'learning' been included? (See section 16.11)
- What production methods will be used?

16.7.6 Indirect costs

All material, labour and expense costs that cannot be identified as direct costs are termed indirect costs and are usually separated into:

- *production overheads* indirect production *materials*, such as lubricating oil and spare parts for machinery, indirect *labour*, such as supervisory and maintenance pay, and indirect *expenses*, such as factory rates and insurance
- *administration overheads* management, secretarial and office services and related expenditure, for example
- *selling overheads* costs incurred in securing orders, such as salespeople's salaries, commissions and travelling expenses, while overheads may be:
  - *allocated* that is, charged against an identifiable cost centre or unit – a *cost centre* being a location, function or item of equipment for which costs may be ascertained and related to cost units for control purposes, such as the drawing office or the purchasing department
  - *apportioned* spread over several cost centres on an agreed basis – rates and lighting may be apportioned on the basis of floor area or space occupied respectively, for example
  - *absorbed* charged to cost units by means of rates separately calculated for each cost centre – in most cases the rates are predetermined.

16.7.7 Production overhead costs

Production overhead costs are usually absorbed in one of six ways, shown by the following example:

Total overhead for period	£24,000
Total units produced in period	180
Total direct labour hours for period	3200
Total direct pay	£6400
Total direct material used	£12,000
Total machine hours	£4800

From the above, the following overhead absorption rates (OAR) can be calculated:

- Cost unit OAR $= \dfrac{£24,000}{180} = £133.33$ overhead per unit produced

- Direct labour OAR $= \dfrac{£24,000}{3200} = £7.50$ per labour hour

- Direct pay OAR $= \dfrac{£24,000}{£6400} = 375\%$ or £3.75 per £ of pay

- Direct material OAR $= \dfrac{£24,000}{£12,000} = £2$ or 200% of materials

- Material hours OAR $= \dfrac{£24,000}{£4800} = £5$ per machine hour

- Prime cost OAR $= \dfrac{£24,000}{(£6400 + £12,000)} = 130\%$ or £1.30 per £ of prime use

16.7.8 Non-production costs

These are typically absorbed on an arbitrary basis, such as:

$$\text{Administration overhead} = \frac{\text{Administration costs}}{\text{Production cost}}$$

$$\text{Selling overheads} = \frac{\text{Selling + Marketing costs}}{\text{Sales value or production cost}}$$

Price analysis in relation to overheads should therefore involve asking the following kinds of questions.

- What is the basis on which indirect costs are allocated, apportioned or absorbed?
- To what extent can the fixed overhead element per unit be reduced by increased quantities?
- What is the vendor's break-even point per item or contract?
- What is the proportion of selling and administrative overhead as a proportion of production cost?

Attention should also be given to marginal and activity costing approaches, as described in sections 11.14.2 and 16.8.

16.7.9 Profit

The vendors are entitled to a fair profit as this is the reason for their acceptance of the order. Profit expectation may also provide an incentive to do the work efficiently. The following seven points should be considered when analysing a vendor's anticipated profits:

- *competitive price* the buyer who offers the lowest price should be allowed what profit can be made, providing this is not excessive
- *initial orders* a large profit may need to be allowed on initial orders to persuade the vendor to undertake the risks of a new line or production
- *size of order* a bigger profit may be justified on a small order
- *amount of value added to a product* vendors that produce all the components incorporated in a product generally make larger profits than assemblers of purchased parts
- *management expertise required* with products requiring a high degree of designer production expertise, large profits may be required to keep vendors interested in the buyer's business, while subcontracted items usually require less skill and therefore the profit should be smaller
- *risks assumed by vendor* the greater the risk the greater the allowable profit
- *efficiency of vendor* a vendor that has demonstrated reliability with regard to quality and delivery should not be lost because the process does not allow that vendor adequate profit.

16.8 Activity-based costing (ABC) and management

16.8.1 Definition

Activity-based costing is:[12]

> A cost attribution to cost units on the basis of benefit received from indirect activities, e.g. ordering, setting up, assuring quality.

16.8.2 Activity management and activity-based costing

Activity-based costing (ABC) is an aspect of activity-based management (ABM). ABM has been defined as:[13]

> A discipline that focuses on the management of activities as a route to improving the value received by the customer and the profit achieved by providing this value.

ABM is based on the principle that 'activities consume costs'. Whereas traditional cost systems focus on the 'worker', ABM systems focus on the work. The field of ABM covers the following activities:

- activity analysis
- activity-based budgeting
- activity-based costing
- benchmarking
- business process re-engineering
- cost driver analysis
- continuous improvement
- operational control
- performance evaluation.

16.8.3 The distinction between absorption-based and ABC costing

Within traditional absorption costing, overhead costs are assigned to products, services, labour or other cost objects using one of the approaches indicated in section 16.7 above. Overhead costs are allocated in proportion to production volume. With ABC, an overhead is allocated to cost objects according to the activities and resources consumed.

16.8.4 Terminology

The following key terms are used in relation to ABC.

An *activity*, in this context, is a repetitive action performed in fulfilment of business functions, such as designing, purchasing, production set-up, assembly, quality control, packaging and shipping.

Activities can be classified as shown in Figure 16.4. Time, for example, can be classified as production or service inspection, transfer time and idle time such as storage or waiting for materials. Only production or service time add value. The other categories of time should be reduced to a minimum or eliminated.

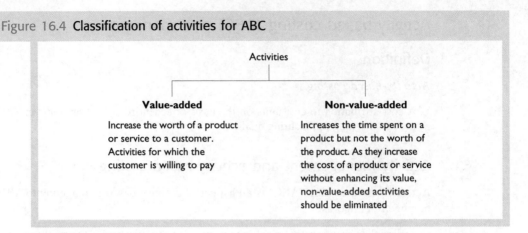

Figure 16.4 **Classification of activities for ABC**

A *resource* is a cost or costs that support activities. The purchasing activity, for example, incurs costs in the form of salaries and benefits, office space, computer time, travelling, training and so on. Thus, as Lapsley et al.[14] state:

> Activities consume resources
> and
> Products (or services) consume activities

A *cost object* can be almost anything that incurs costs, such as products, services, units, batches, jobs, customers, sales territories and so on.

A *cost driver* is a factor that has a direct cause–effect relationship to a cost. Activities creating cost drivers may be either:

- resource drivers or
- activity drivers.

Resource drivers assign costs to activities, thereby forming activity costs pools, each containing their appropriate shares of resource costs. A number of cost pools can be assigned to an activity cost centre.

For each activity or resource one or more cost drivers must be identified – these are activity drivers. Cost drivers set activity levels. The cost driver for creating a purchase order, for example, may include the number of orders processed or the number of suppliers.

In general, the appropriate cost driver – that is, activity or resource driver – is the one that represents the primary output of the activity. Usually, a cost driver that captures the *number* of activity transactions is preferable to drivers based on the time duration or monetary amount of the activity transaction because it is readily available, easy to understand and apply and motivates people to act in ways likely to achieve organisational goals.

As Cooper and Kaplan[15] point out:

> A company that wants to reduce the number of unique parts that it processes in order to simplify activities such as vendor selection, purchasing, inspection, maintenance of the bill of materials, storage and accounting may decide to apply the costs of these activities using 'number of part numbers' as the cost driver. Then by evaluating and rewarding product designers according to their ability to design low-cost products, they will be motivated to design products with fewer part numbers.

An *activity cost centre* is a segment of the production or service process for which management wants to separately ascertain the costs of the activities performed, such as purchasing, production, marketing. Activity centres should be created where a significant amount of overhead cost is incurred and several key activities are undertaken.

Direct costs inputs, as with traditional costing, consist of direct labour and direct material and, sometimes, direct technology.

16.8.5 A simple example of ABC

Activity-based costing involves the following steps.

1 Total overhead costs for a given period are computed either prospectively from budgets or retrospectively from departmental and general ledger records.

2 A project team is formed by top management to plan and implement the ABC system. The team – normally led by the management accountant – may be comprised of representatives of the design, production, purchasing/logistics, marketing and financial accounting functions.

3 The estimated or actual total overheads will be divided into service and production categories. Functional managers will then be interviewed and asked questions, such as the following.

■ What activities does your function undertake?

■ What activities are undertaken by each member of staff in the function?

■ What are the outputs of each activity?

■ What equipment and supplies are used for each activity?

■ What overtime is worked?

■ Why does idle time occur?

This activity analysis describes what is done by the enterprise and each function within the enterprise – that is, how resources, including time and effort, are spent and what inputs and outputs are involved.

4 The team will then assign resource costs to activity cost centres and cost pools using first-stage resource drivers, as shown in Figure 16.5 (for simplicity, only three resources – salaries, office costs and computers – are shown here).

5 Second-stage activity drivers, such as the number of purchase orders, items stored, deliveries made, will be chosen. These will normally be outputs and are used to assign the cost pools to cost products, as shown in Figure 16.5.

6 A bill of activities will be prepared for each product, as shown in Table 16.1. This enables the unit cost of each product to be ascertained using ABC.

16.8.6 The application of ABC

Burch[16] states that ABC is especially appropriate in companies where:

■ competition is high

■ product mix is diverse in terms of batch sizes, physical sizes, degree of complexity and raw material characteristics

■ product lifecycles are short – of three years or less

Figure 16.5 **Allocation of service resources to cost pools**

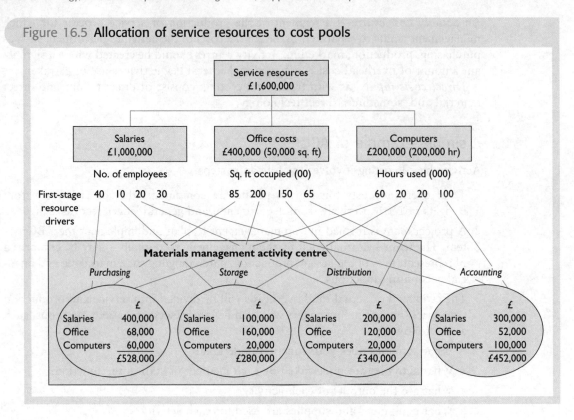

- collection and manipulation of data are performed by an integrated computer-based information system (ICBIS).

16.8.7 Activity-based costing and purchasing

Barker[17] states that purchasing is 'a key activity for using ABC' and points out that 'much of the literature uses the purchasing and supply function to illustrate how to apply ABC'. Barker identifies a number of ways in which ABC can be implemented within purchasing, including:

- the attribution of purchasing function costs to products
- the provision of information that can be utilised in relation to make-or-buy and sourcing decisions, such as Ness and Cucuzza's[18] observations that the introduction of ABC at Chrysler showed the actual costs of some low-volume parts were as much as 30 times greater than the stated costs, which made it clear that the company would be better off outsourcing these parts and making more high-volume parts
- analysis of the total acquisition cost of purchased items 'may give buyers the information to prove what they have long suspected: paying more often costs less'.

ABC can also:

- highlight procurement activities that do not add value to products, such as inspection and storage, and which activities should be cut

Table 16.1 Bill of activities for products X and Y for the 52 weeks ending 31 March

	Pool driver rate	Product X = 20,000 units			Product Y = 12,000 units		
		Second stage Driver quantity	Activity cost Activity cost	Unit cost	Activity driver Quantity	Activity cost Activity cost	Unit cost
Purchasing	£264 per order	800	£211,200	£10.56	1200	£316,800	£26.40
Storage	£200 per item stored	600	£120,000	£6.00	800	£160,000	£13.33
Distribution	£10,625 per delivery	200	£212,500	£10.63	120	£127,500	£10.63
Accounting	£200 per a/c	904	£180,800	£9.04	1356	£271,200	£22.60
Factory administration	£1000 per factory hour	1100	£1,100,000	£55.00	1500	£1,500,000	£125.00
Set-ups	£2000 per set-up	100	£200,000	£10.00	200	£400,000	£33.34
			£2,024,500			£2,775,500	
Activity costs per unit				£101.23			£231.30
Direct materials cost per unit £65				£65.00			£127.50
Direct labour cost per unit £25				£25.00			£46.20
Total costs per unit				£191.23			£405.00

With traditional absorption costing, the overhead rate per unit produced would be £4,800,000/32,000 = £150 per unit. The costs would therefore be:

	Product X	Product Y
Direct materials	£65.00	£127.50
Direct labour	£25.00	£46.20
Overheads	£150.00	£323.70
	£240.00	£497.40

- identify ways in which savings in procurement costs can contribute to the competitive advantage of the enterprise, such as a reduction in the number of suppliers and transactions, elimination of unnecessary purchasing documentation, improved design with fewer and standardised parts
- control of the overall procurement function by regarding it as an activity centre in which all purchasing activity-related cost pools are aggregated, which may provide data on drivers and rates that allow comparisons to be made across functions and with potential external suppliers
- have the potential to make a significant contribution to TQM as costs are a key factor in any decision.

16.9 Standard costing

16.9.1 Definition

Standard costing is defined by the CIMA[19] as:

> A control technique which compares costs and revenues with actual results to obtain variances which are used to stimulate improved performance.

Standard costing is therefore a technique of comparisons – the actual with the standard. This approach is used mainly in companies engaged in repetitive production and assumes the use of materials or components the design, quality and specifications of which are standardised. The standard cost of materials is made up of the following elements.

16.9.2 Quantity

Normally this is derived from technical and engineering specifications, frequently as indicated in the bill of materials. Standard quantities normally include an allowance for normal losses due to factors such as scrap, breakages, evaporation and the like.

16.9.3 Price

Prices used are the forecast expected prices – normally the latest prices for the item from approved sources in the quantities estimated for the relevant budget period. Another approach – which takes into account that an item may have to be bought from several suppliers – is to base prices on the average expected to be paid over the period under consideration.

16.9.4 Variances

The difference between the standard and actual cost is termed a *variance*. The most important material variances are those relating to price and usage, which are calculated by using the following formulae:

- *direct materials price variance* the difference between the standard price and actual purchase price for the actual quantity of material, which can be calculated at the time of purchase or the time of usage – generally the former is preferable – using the formula:

$$\text{(Actual purchase quantity} \times \text{Actual price)} - \\ \text{(Actual purchase quantity} \times \text{Standard price)}$$

■ *direct materials usage variance* the difference between the standard quantity specified for the actual production and the actual quantity used, at standard purchase price, calculated by using the formula:

$$\text{(Actual quantity used for actual production} \times \text{Standard price)} - \\ \text{(Standard quantity for actual production} \times \text{Standard price)}$$

■ *direct materials total variance* the sum of the usage and price variances, calculated as follows:

$$\text{(Standard direct materials cost of the actual production volume)} - \\ \text{(Actual cost of direct materials)}$$

Example 16.3

Worked examples of price variance formulae

Assume the *standard* quantities and prices of the direct materials used for product X are 75 kg at £3.75 per kg. The *actual* usage and price were 74 kg at £3.85 per kg.
The direct materials price variance is:

$$(74 \text{ kg} \times £3.85) - (74 \text{ kg} \times £3.75) = £284.90 - £277.50 \\ = £7.40$$

making an adverse variance of £7.40
The direct materials usage variance is:

$$(74 \text{ kg} \times £3.75) - (75 \text{ kg} \times £3.75) = £277.50 - £281.25 \\ = £3.75$$

making a favourable variance of £3.75
The direct materials total variance will therefore be:

$$\text{(Adverse direct materials total price variance)} - \\ \text{(Favourable direct material usage variance)} \\ = £7.40 - £3.75 = £3.65 \text{ (adverse)}$$

It is also possible to calculate the *direct materials yield* and *mixed variances* for production processes involving the mixing of various materials. Information on these variances and their calculations can be found in any cost accounting text.

16.9.5 Causes of material price variances

Such variances can occur because:

■ actual prices are higher or lower than budgeted

■ quantity discounts may be lost or gained by buying smaller or larger quantities than expected

■ prices paid may be affected by buying higher or lower qualities than anticipated
■ buying substitute materials from stockists due to the non-availability of the planned material.

16.9.6 Causes of material usage variance

These variances can be due to:

■ the actual production yield from the material being greater or not as great as planned
■ the amount of scrap or shortage being more or less than expected.

Standard costing is an application of the management principle of exceptions. Where a variance exceeds a prescribed level, it will be analysed with a view to identifying controllable and uncontrollable factors. Particularly with regard to prices, standard costs provide a widely used measure of purchasing effectiveness.

16.10 Budgets and budgetary control

16.10.1 Definitions

The CIMA[20] provides the following:

> Budget: A plan quantified in monetary terms, prepared and approved prior to a defined period of time, usually showing planned income to be generated and/or expenditure to be incurred during that period and the capital to be employed to attain a given objective.

> Budgetary control: The establishment of budgets relating the responsibilities of executives to the requirements of a policy, and the continuous comparison of actual with budgeted results, either to secure by individual action the objective of that policy or to provide a basis for its revision.

16.10.2 Purchasing budgets

These are derived from sales and production budgets and will be divided into:

■ A *materials budget* based on:
  – whole units of products to be completed in the budget period converted into individual direct material requirements expressed in terms of physical quantities and monetary expenditure
  – the company's end inventory policy based on the availability of materials and components – an example of a materials/components budget is given in Table 16.2.
■ A *purchasing department's operating budget* covering projected expenditure for the budget period on salaries, training, computer time, travelling, entertainment, office space occupied, stationery and so on.

Although budgetary control and standard costs are interrelated, the former can be operated in enterprises where the latter is difficult to apply. The value of budgeting is, however, enhanced when it is used with standard costing.

Table 16.2 **A materials/components budget**

Material/components for budget period 2004–2005								
Material (units)	A	B	C	D	E	F	G	
Stock in hand 1 April 2004	20,000	25,000	16,000	3500	9800	7500	28,600	
Required stock 31 March 2005	18,000	27,000	15,000	4000	9000	8000	25,000	
Standard price per unit	£0.06	£0.35	£1.20	£3.25	£0.90	£2.00	£1.20	

Procurement budget for the period 1 April 2004 – 31 March 2005								
Material (units)	A	B	C	D	E	F	G	Total
Required stock 31 March 2005	18,000	27,000	15,000	4000	9000	8000	25,000	
Budgeted usage during period	125,000	150,000	18,000	24,000	18,000	22,000	137,000	
Totals	143,000	177,000	33,000	28,000	27,000	30,000	162,000	
Stock in hand 1 April 2004	20,000	25,000	16,000	3500	9800	7500	28,600	
Items to be purchased	123,000	152,000	17,000	24,500	17,200	22,500	133,900	
Standard price per unit	£0.06	£0.35	£1.20	£3.25	£0.90	£2.00	£1.20	
Value of budgeted purchases (£)	73,800	53,200	20,400	79,625	15,480	45,000	160,680	448,185

16.11 Learning curves

16.11.1 Definition

A learning curve (sometimes termed a 'skill acquisition or experience curve') is:

> a graphical representation of the rate at which skills or knowledge is acquired over a period of time.

16.11.2 The basis of the learning curve

'Skill to do comes by doing.' A task is performed more quickly with each subsequent repetition until a point is reached where no further improvement is possible and performance levels out. In industry, cost reductions arising from 'learning' are due to the following factors:

- less time required for the operative to weigh up the job
- improved speed and proficiency in performing the actual operations
- reduction in scrap and rectification
- improved operational sequences
- improved tooling as a result of production experience
- the application of value engineering and analysis
- larger lot sizes with reduced setting-up costs.

Learning curves are therefore developed on the basis of the following assumptions:[21]

- the direct labour required to product the (n + 1)th unit will always be less than the direct labour required for the nth unit

- direct labour requirements will decrease at a steeper rate as cumulative production increases
- the reduction in time will follow an exponential curve.

16.11.3 The learning curve theorem

The learning curve theorem is that each time the number of production units is doubled, the cumulative average labour hours per unit figure declines by a specific and constant percentage of the previous cumulative average.

If the learning rate is 80 per cent and the number of items made doubles, the average time per unit is reduced to 80 per cent of its previous value. This is illustrated in Table 16.3. To make one unit required one day but to make two units required 1.6 days. Thus, the average time taken per unit has fallen to 0.8 days – 80 per cent of its original value. As you can see from Table 16.3, this does not mean that the second item took 0.8 days.

If the number of units produced is doubled from two to four and then doubled again to eight, the average time per unit should fall to:

$$80\% \times 80\% = 64\%$$

of the average time per unit when only two were produced, and then to:

$$64\% \text{ of } 0.8 = 0.512 = 0.51$$

of the initial average time per unit. As you can see from the table, this does not mean that the eighth unit took 0.51 days to produce.

Table 16.3   Reduction in the average time taken to produce 1 unit

Units produced	1	2	3	4	5	6	7	8	9	10	11	12
Time of last unit produced	1.00	0.60	0.51	0.45	0.42	0.39	0.37	0.35	0.34	0.33	0.32	0.31
Total time so far	1.00	1.60	2.11	2.56	2.98	3.37	3.74	4.10	4.44	4.77	5.08	5.39
Cumulative average time	1.00	0.80	0.70	0.64	0.60	0.56	0.53	0.51	0.49	0.48	0.46	0.45

It can be shown mathematically that the equation for the learning curve is:

$$y = ax^b$$

where:

y is the cumulative average time per unit
x is the number of units produced so far
a is the time taken to produce the first item

$$b = \frac{\log(\text{learning rate})}{\log(2)}$$

It should be noted that learning curves vary according to:

- the complexity of the operation – the learning rate for simple products is less pronounced than for more complicated items because the opportunity to improve work is greater with the latter

- the opportunity to reduce labour hours in machine-paced operations is limited because the output rate is controlled by the machine

- learning will be affected by the introduction of automation or improved equipment, so, because of this variability in learning rates, it is necessary when several operations are involved in manufacturing a part, to prepare an aggregate learning curve by multiplying the percentage of the total task for a given operation by the learning rate for that operation – the learning rate for all the operations involved will then be aggregated.

Example 16.4

The learning curve theorem applied to a process with several operations

The manufacture of a product involves four operations.

Operation	Improvement rate	Percentage of task
1	90%	30%
2	92%	20%
3	85%	20%
4	80%	30%

The aggregate learning curve slope will be:

$$(0.90 \times 0.30) + (0.92 \times 0.20) + (0.85 \times 0.20) + (0.80 \times 0.30)$$
$$= 0.28 + 0.18 + 0.17 + 0.24$$
$$= 0.87$$

16.11.4 Drawing the learning curve

The cumulative average hours per unit could be plotted on graph paper, when they would appear as shown in Figure 16.6.

Figure 16.6 Learning curve

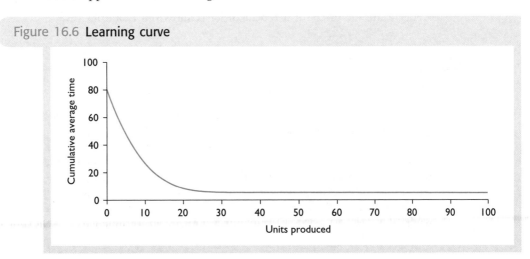

Figure 16.7 **An 85 per cent learning curve on log-log scale**

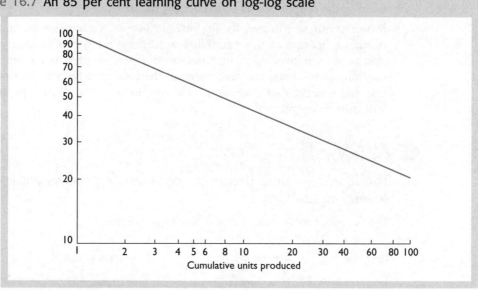

In practice, log-log paper is used (see Figure 16.7) because it has the following advantages:

- all lines will be approximately straight
- the cumulative total can be plotted within the confines of the paper
- for forecasting, a ruler can be laid on the actual line and the results read off.

16.11.5 The application of learning curves

The greatest potential for savings resulting from learning curve analysis lies in high-cost items, those with a high direct labour content and those at the beginning of the curve.

Price determination

The learning curve approach indicates the areas in which to concentrate on a price analysis in order to obtain the greatest savings. The method of using learning curves to renegotiate the price for a repeat order is shown in Example 16.5.

Example 16.5

Using learning curve analysis to gain cost savings

Let us say that 200 items were purchased at £100 each. A repeat order for an additional 200 items is under negotiation.

Analyse the supplier's costs based on the following information: £2000 was spent on tools, half of which was written off on the first order. Raw material costs per item were £40 for the first order, but will now be £45. The supplier has given a 10 per cent pay rise to his workforce. Direct labour costs amounted to £50 for the first order.

The supplier made no profit on the first order and considers that he is entitled to a profit of at least 10 per cent. Assuming a 90 per cent learning curve, what should the new price be?

Solution

	£
Original price per item	100
Deduct tooling cost	10
	90
Deduct cost not subject to learning – raw materials	40
Balance subject to learning	50
Add pay rise of 10 per cent	5
	55
90 per cent of £55	49.50
Add half cost of tooling	10.00
Add material costs	45.00
	104.50
Add 10 per cent profit	10.45
Price per item for repeat order	114.95

Make-or-buy decisions

When comparing the costs of making and buying, the effect of learning on each production run should be determined and taken into consideration as well as the planned quantity.

Delivery times

Knowledge of the learning curve principle can enable a supplier to offer improved delivery times. The principle is illustrated by Example 16.6.

Example 16.6

Using learning curve analysis to promote delivery times

A contract is placed for 100 units of a component. By allocating 7200 labour hours, the manufacturer expects to produce 10 units in the first month. Assuming that an 80 per cent learning curve applies, how long should it take to complete the order?

Solution

The contract should take just over five months – not ten months as might be expected from a constant output of ten units, which would be the case if no learning took place.

Month	Capacity (labour hours)	Cumulative average values (80% learning curve, from tables)	Units produced	Cumulative total
1	7200	1.00	10	10
2	7200	0.80	16	26
3	7200	0.70	21	47
4	7200	0.64	25	72
5	7200	0.59	26	98

16.11.5 When not to use learning curves

Learning curves are not useful in the following cases:

- when learning is not constant – that is, where a straight line cannot be fitted to the data reasonably accurately
- where the direct labour content of the job is small
- where the cost or volume does not justify the expensive periodic time studies or job costing required to obtain the data from which the learning curve is constructed
- when production is largely automated so that human input is relatively small.

16.12 Project management

16.12.1 Definitions

In the present context, a project may be defined as:[22]

> an activity (or usually, a number of related activities) carried out according to a plan in order to achieve a definite objective within a certain period of time and that will close when the objective has been achieved.

Project management is:[23]

> The function of evaluating, planning and controlling a project so that it is finished on time, to specification and within budget.

16.12.2 Types of project

Lock[24] classifies projects under four headings:

- *civil engineering, construction, petrochemical, mining and quarrying projects* these are normally undertaken at a site, exposed to the elements and remote from the contractor's office
- *manufacturing projects* aimed at the production of a piece of equipment or machinery, ship, aircraft, land vehicle or some item of specially designed hardware
- *management projects* operations involving the management and coordination of activities to produce an end result that is not identifiable principally as an item of hardware or construction, such as the relocation of offices or installation of a new computer system
- *research projects* aimed at extending the boundaries of current scientific knowledge that are high risk because the outcomes are uncertain.

16.12.3 Purchasing and project management

Although not always designated as such, a project manager will have responsibility for the overall direction and control of a particular project and the staff involved. Such staff may be organised on:

- a *matrix* basis
- a *functional* or *team* basis.

Matrix structures and their advantages and disadvantages are described in section 4.1.2. Teamwork is discussed in sections 5.4–5.10.

With either form of organisation, however, purchasing may contribute to ensuring that the project is 'finished on time, to specification and within budget' in such ways as the following:

- liaising at each stage with appropriate members of the project's organisation, such as the project manager, architects, designers, consultants, quantity surveyors, site engineers, concerning the specification, procurement and scheduling of materials, equipment and services required for the contract
- agreeing where, and by whom, purchasing will be undertaken, although Lock[25] points out that:

    The purchasing agent could be an independent organisation from the contractor's purchasing department, or even the client's own purchasing department. There can also be various combinations of these arrangements. In international projects the client's purchasing department might issue purchase orders to local suppliers, with the contractor's head office dealing with other suppliers worldwide (possibly operating through purchasing agents overseas where their location and local experience provides for greater efficiency)

- advising on the most economic approaches to procurement, such as whether purchasing or leasing capital equipment is the best option
- assistance with the preparation of tender specifications and negotiation with subcontractors for, typically, brickwork, civil engineering, drainage, electrical installations, heating and ventilation, painting and decorating, pipework, plumbing and structural steelwork
- evaluating tenders and post-tender negotiation
- placing orders and subcontracts, ensuring that the terms and conditions are appropriate to the particular contract
- expediting orders placed to ensure that deliveries meet the schedule and requirements
- inspecting materials received and maintenance of quality records
- dealing with requests from suppliers and subcontractors for price variances
- controlling 'free issue' supplies – that is, items provided by the customer or client for use in connection with the project, so, for example, a glass manufacturer might provide the glass for use in a contract for its new office building
- certifying payment of invoices for goods and services provided by external suppliers and subcontractors.

16.13 Scheduling

Of the above contributions, one of the most important is that of ensuring that materials and equipment are on site as needed to obviate delays in meeting the scheduled times for the completion of each part of the project.

Two useful scheduling tools are Gantt charts and networks.

16.13.1 Gantt charts

Devised by Henry L. Gantt in 1917, Gantt charts depict the occurrence of the activities comprising a project across time. An example of a Gantt, or bar, chart is shown in Figure 16.8.

Figure 16.8 **Gantt chart**

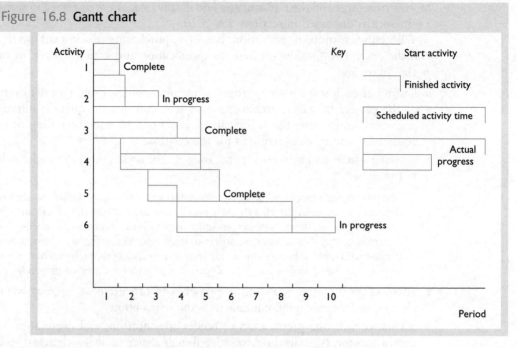

Gantt activity progress charts perform several functions:

- they show at a glance how project activities are progressing, so, in Figure 16.8, for example, activities 2 and 6 are behind schedule, activities 1 and 4 are on time and activities 3 and 5 are ahead of schedule
- they can facilitate the coordination of activities and labour as activities represented by overlapping bars can be performed concurrently to the degree that they overlap, while activities shown by non-overlapping bars must be performed in the sequence indicated, so activity 4 in Figure 16.8 cannot be started until the completion of activity 1, but can be performed concurrently with activities 3 and 5
- they are most useful in scheduling a series of unrelated activities, but where many activities must be correlated, network analysis (see next) is more appropriate.

16.13.2 Network analysis

BS 4335 defines network analysis as:

A group of techniques for presenting information to assist the planning and controlling of projects. The information . . . includes the sequence and logical interrelationships of all project activities.

There are two common types of networks:

- critical path analysis (CPA) and
- program evaluation and review techniques (PERT)

16.13.3 Critical path analysis

Like Gantt charts, CPA is used to plan the tasks that must be completed on time if the whole project is to meet a promised delivery or completion date. CPA also identifies tasks that can be delayed to enable resources to be diverted to more urgent requirements. A further benefit of CPA is that it indicates the minimum time in which a project can be completed.

16.13.4 CPA and sequencing

CPA is similar to Gantt charts in that it is based on the concept that some activities cannot start until others have been completed. Thus, with building, walls cannot be constructed until the foundations have been prepared and roofing cannot take place until the walls have been built. The foundations and walls are thus critical and on the critical path.

Other activities, such as making window frames, are not dependent on the completion of other tasks and can be done either before or after a certain *milestone* in the project has been reached. These are non-dependent, or *parallel*, tasks.

16.13.5 CPM/PERT terminology

Some basic terms are shown in Table 16.4.

Table 16.4 Key terms used in network analysis

Term	Explanation
Activity	A task or job requiring resources, such as digging foundations. An *activity* is represented by an arrow
An event	A point in time at which an activity or a number of activities start or finish. An *event* is represented by a circle, or *node*, in which the number of the event appears
Path	A sequence of events that leads from the starting node to the finishing node. Thus, the sequence 1, 2, 3, 4, 5, 6 is a *path*. The length (of time) of any path can be determined by adding the estimated times for the activities on that path. The longest path governs the completion time and so is referred to as the *critical path*
Duration	The estimated time in hours or days needed to perform the activity
Earliest start (ES)	The earliest time (measured from the start of the project) when an activity can begin. An activity cannot begin until all the necessary preceding activities have been completed
Earliest finish (EF)	The sum of its earliest start time and duration
Latest finish (LF)	The latest time (measured from the start of the project) when an activity may be completed without delaying any activity that immediately follows it and thereby delaying the completion of the project
Latest start (LS)	The latest finish time minus its duration
Slack	The amount of leeway allowed in either starting or finishing an activity. *Slack* can be calculated as either LS – ES or LF – EF

Figure 16.9 **A node, representing an activity with its key schedule details completed**

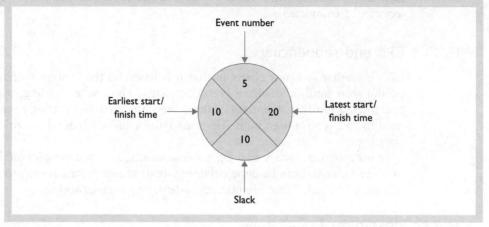

All the above can be shown in one node as depicted in Figure 16.9.

16.13.6 Network conventions

A precedence diagram indicates the sequence in which activities must be completed. Thus, in the A–C diagram in Figure 16.10, activity A must be completed before activity B can begin and activity B before C.

Figure 16.10 **A precedence diagram**

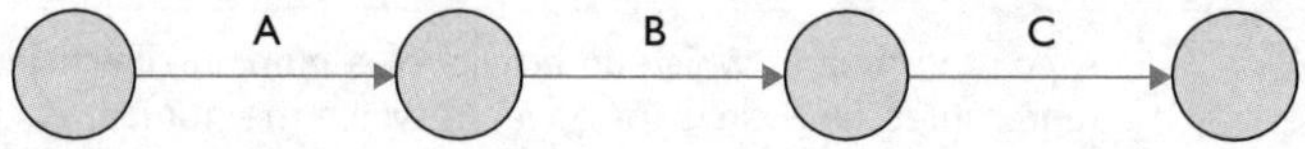

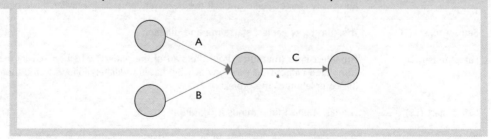

If two activities – A and B – have to be completed before activity C can begin, the diagram would be as shown in Figure 16.11.

Figure 16.11 **Non-dependent activities that need to be completed before the next**

A and B can, however, be performed simultaneously and independently of each other.

If a number of activities enter a node, it means that each activity must be completed before the activity beginning at that node can commence (see Figure 16.12).

Figure 16.12 Several activities need to be completed before the next two can start

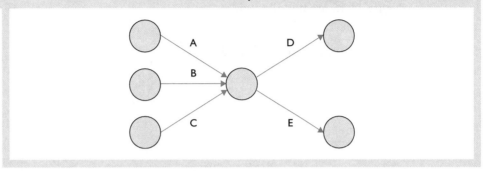

Thus, activities A, B and C must be completed before either activity D or E can start.

Two activities may not, however, share the *same* tail and head event as this would imply that the two activities have the same duration, which may not be the case. A diagram such as Figure 16.13, therefore, is not allowed.

Figure 16.13 Two activities cannot share same head and tail events

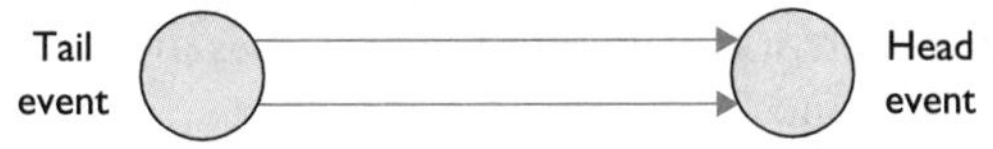

Tail event → Head event

The above can be avoided by using a so-called *dummy node*. The dummy node or activity is used to preserve the separate identities of each activity. An example of a dummy node is shown in Figure 16.14.

Figure 16.14 A dummy node

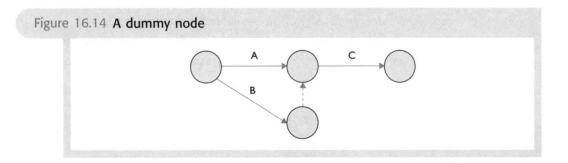

Dummy nodes are indicated by dotted lines. In the activities shown in Figure 16.14, A and B must be completed before C can be started. Dummy activities have a time activity of zero.

For reference purposes, nodes are numbered from left to right. Each activity must have a preceding 'tail' event and a subsequent 'head' event. Many activities may have the same tail event or same head event (but not both). Activities that do not have a tail are not allowed. Such activities are known as *danglers*. Further, a series of activities that lead back to the same event are termed *loops*. Loops such as that shown in Figure 16.15 are not allowed.

Figure 16.15 **Loops are not allowed**

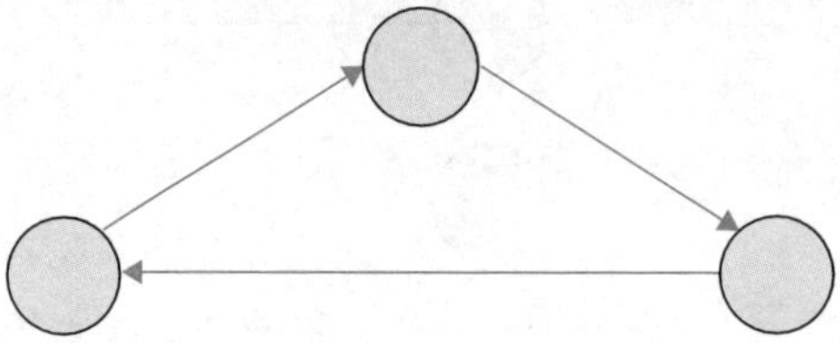

16.13.7 CPM/PERT project scheduling procedure

This involves the following steps:

1 identify and list the activities that comprise the project
2 identify the immediate predecessor activity for each activity in the project
3 estimate the duration (time from start to finish) for each activity
4 draw a network depicting the activities and their immediate predecessors identified in steps 1 and 2
5 using the network and the estimated activity times, calculate the earliest start and earliest finish times for each activity by making a forward pass through the network – the earliest finish time for the last activity in the project identifies the total time required to complete the project
6 using the project completion time arrived at in step 5, make a backwards pass through the network to identify the latest start and latest finish times for each activity
7 use the difference between the latest start time and the earliest start time for each activity to identify the slack time available for that activity
8 find the activity or activities with zero slack – these are the critical path activities
9 use the information from steps 5 and 6 to develop the activity schedule for the project.

16.13.8 Network analysis and cost

Time is not the only consideration associated with project management. The cost is of equal importance.

What is known as PERT/Cost is a technique used to plan, schedule and control project costs and ensure adherence to a specified budget. Essentially, it involves identifying all the costs associated with a project and then developing a schedule of when the costs are expected to occur. As with other budgets, actual costs are compared with what was

Example 16.7

Network analysis

Steps 1, 2 and 3

A project is comprised of the following activities and their estimated duration times. You are asked to draw the critical path network and ascertain the duration of the critical path and slack times for all the activities.

Activity	Immediate predecessor	Estimated duration (days)
A	–	4
B	A	2
C	B	2
D	C	4
E	C	10
F	D, E	10
G	F	2

Step 4 Draw the network

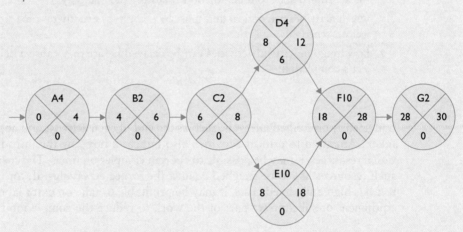

Step 5

Determine the earliest start and earliest finish times and insert them in the nodes as above:

$$\text{Time required to complete the project} = 30 \text{ weeks}$$

Steps 6 and 7

Determine the latest starts and latest finish times by working backwards from the completion date. The latest finish time for an activity entering a particular node is equal to the smallest of the latest start times for all activities entering the node.

$$\text{Slack time} = \text{Latest start (LS)} - \text{Earliest start (ES)}$$
$$\text{or}$$
$$= \text{Latest finish (LF)} - \text{Earliest finish (EF)}$$

▶

Activity	Latest start	Earliest start	Slack
A	0	0	0
B	4	4	0
C	6	6	0
D	12	18	6
E	8	8	0
F	18	18	0
G	28	28	0

Insert slack times into nodes.

Step 8

Activities with zero nodes are A + B + C + E + F + G. This forms the critical path.

Step 9

We are now able to state:

- the total time to complete the project, which is 30 weeks
- the scheduled start and completion times for each activity
- which activities are critical and must be completed exactly on time to keep the project on schedule
- how long non-critical activities can be delayed before they cause a delay to the project's completion.

budgeted at prescribed intervals, such as the end of each activity, and appropriate action taken. Attention to critical activities also indicates how, by the introduction of additional resources, it may be possible to shorten completion times. The cost of introducing such resources has to be weighed against the projected savings. If, for example, a project has high daily fixed costs, it may be profitable to take on extra labour, buy or hire equipment or subcontract part of the work to reduce the completion time.

16.13.9 CPM and PERT

CPM and PERT use much of the same terminology and techniques. Both aim to show the logical sequence of activities in a project. CPM, however, was developed mainly for use in industrial projects where activity times could be estimated with reasonable accuracy. In contrast, PERT was devised in the late 1950s in connection with the Polaris missile project where the times could not be forecast because the associated activities had not been previously encountered. Unlike CPM, which provides only one time estimate for each activity, PERT provides three – namely:

- *normal (n)* the most realistic assessment of the time required, without allowing for unforeseen contingencies
- *pessimistic (p)* the longest times that will be required, allowing for all foreseeable contingencies

- *optimistic (o)* the shortest duration within which the activity can be accomplished if all circumstances work out favourably.

These three times are used to calculate expected time on the basis of the following weighted average:

$$\text{Expected time} = \frac{(o + 4n + p)}{6}$$

In practice, the estimate would normally be based on the most likely time.

The differences between CPM and PERT have, however, now largely disappeared and the two terms tend to be used interchangeably as a generic term to embrace the whole network planning and control process.

Computerised scheduling

A large project involves many activities, so manual calculations for CPM and PERT would be both tedious and require considerable checking. Computer-generated CPM graphs and schedules, however, can show the relationships between project tasks, identify contingencies and conflicts, anticipate resource needs, permit the updating of networks and allow project managers to easily project the impacts of alternative schedules. Many software packages are currently available for project scheduling and control using network analysis techniques.

Resource constraints

So far, CPM has only been discussed in relation to the time aspect of project management. In practice, managers may wish, or be required, to reduce the duration of a project for several reasons, such as to receive incentive payments for early completion or release resources committed to the project for use on other contracts. This shortening of completion times, which can normally be achieved only by adding resources such as labour, overtime or subcontracting, is referred to as *crashing*. Crashing can therefore be defined as the process of reducing the time it takes to complete an activity by adding resources. The aim is to ascertain which activities should be crashed and at what cost. To describe crashing and other CPM/PERT techniques is outside the scope of this book.

16.13.10 Network analysis and purchasing

- Generally, network analysis is applicable to large, complicated, long-running projects, such as construction contracts, and subcontracted work.

- Network analysis provides purchasing with an overview of the complete project and the significance of the contribution of purchasing to its successful completion.

- Network analysis is a team activity to which purchasing contributes essential information, such as the availability of materials and the duration of lead times.

- The network enables purchasing to compare actual with promised deliveries and take early expediting action on 'slippage' to prevent delays in delivery having a cumulative effect on the whole project.

- Purchased items can be scheduled for delivery in the right sequence and to the right location, for instance, materials for construction projects can be delivered direct to site immediately before use, thus reducing the possibility of loss from theft or deterioration.

- In subcontracted work, progress payments can be linked to the completion of specified events.

- Networks can be used to control expenditure with long-running contracts. Computer printouts can show:

  - actual costs incurred at a given date

  - estimated costs for the rest of the project

  - statements of future expenditure, such as purchase orders still outstanding

16.14 Operational research (OR)

16.14.1 Definition

Operational research (OR) is defined by the UK Operational Research Society as:

> The application of the methods of science to complex problems arising in the direction and management of large systems of men, machine, materials and money in industry, business, government and defence. The distinctive approach is to develop a scientific model of the system incorporating measurement of factors, such as chance and risk, with which to predict and compare the outcomes of alternative decisions, strategies or controls. The purpose is to help management determine its policy and action scientifically.

In this context, 'research' has the narrower meaning of the application of new mathematical models, methods and techniques to the solution of business or other problems.

The above definition emphasises that:

- OR is concerned with problems of organisation and the allocation of resources, which are labour, machines, materials and money, to achieve a specified objective

- a model or system can be built

- OR is a service to management

- alternative decisions can be evaluated against some measure of effectiveness.

16.14.2 OR procedures

The application of quantitative techniques to management practice is known as operational research. The major phases of an OR project have been identified as being:

- stating the problem for which a solution is required

- constructing a mathematical model as an analogue (a symbolic model or simulation) of the real system – generally taking the form:

$$E = f(x_1 y_1)$$

where E represents the effectiveness of the system, and x and y the controllable variables and non-controllable variables in the system respectively

- deriving an optimum solution from the model either *analytically* – that is, by the manipulation of the mathematical model – or *numerically* – which is when a large number of iterations of possible values of the variables are created and the equation solved repetitively
- testing the model and the solution
- establishing controls over the solution – that is, indicating changes in the values of the uncontrollable variables or the relationships between variables that would render the solution invalid
- implementation – translating the tested solution into a set of operating procedures capable of being understood and applied by those who will be responsible for their use.

16.14.3 OR and supplies

Some reference to applications of OR techniques have been made earlier in this book, namely:

- elementary inventory control (sections 10.4 and 10.5)
- network analysis (section 16.13.2 above)
- materials requirements planning (section 10.17)
- replacement theory and capital expenditure evaluation (section 13.9).

Many supplies problems can be solved by the application of techniques from such OR fields as linear programming, queuing theory and probability theory. The application of OR to supplies work has been assisted by computerisation, which can deal easily with a large number of variables, such as many different items of stores in inventory control. In fact, with the increasing use of computers and availability of specialist software, many OR studies can now be performed by purchasing staff without the need for specialist assistance. In addition to the approaches referred to above, some other applications of OR are given in Table 16.5.

16.14.4 Limitations of OR

Decision making is the process or activity of selecting a future course of action from a number of possible alternatives. Decisions can be grouped into different categories, such as strategic, operational and administrative, and into those that are programmable and non-programmable. Programmable decisions can be worked out by computer as all the variables are quantifiable and the decision rules or constraints clearly defined. Non-programmable decisions cannot be quantified and require the exercise of human judgement. It is important therefore to recognise that OR is limited in its effectiveness, working best in situations where the analysis and comparison of relationships between controllable and uncontrollable variables can be expressed in terms of a mathematical model.

There are times when the subjective judgement of the decision-maker must act contrary to the OR recommendation. OR, for example, can indicate the EOQs and most economic inventory levels for raw materials and components, but these recommendations may be disregarded by the purchasing function if it is known that a threatened strike will seriously disrupt production unless sufficient supplies can be obtained to ensure continuity of output, at least in the short term.

Table 16.5 **Applications of OR**

Aspect of OR	Typical supplies applications
■ *Linear programming (LP)* A mathematical technique for determining the optimum allocation of resources, such as capital, raw materials or labour, or plan to obtain a desired objective, such as minimum cost of operations or maximum profit when there are alternative uses of the resource in question. LP can also help to analyse alternative objectives, such as the economics of alternative resources	■ Analysis of quotations from several suppliers that, because of limited resources, can accept only certain combinations of the business offered. Linear programming can indicate the combination of quotations that will minimise purchasing expenditure ■ Determining the relative advantages of a low price and a high probability of late delivery against a higher price with a better chance of achieving ideal delivery time
■ *Queuing theory* Mathematical analysis and solution of problems in which items requiring or providing service stand idle and when optimising either the arrival rate or service rate or both is required	■ Sequencing and scheduling arrivals of parts or components to achieve minimum costs ■ The most economical staffing of stores to provide the minimum waiting time.
■ *Games theory* A mathematical technique or decision-making tool in competitive situations in which the outcome depends not only on the actions of a manager but also on those of competitors. The aim of the game is to devise a strategy that maximises returns and minimises losses	■ *Negotiation* Decisions are based on the assumption that the rival is shrewd and will always play to minimise the opponent's gain
■ *Decision trees* A decision tree is a type of flow chart or visual aid that summarises the various alternatives and options available in a complicated decision process. Decision trees consist of three parts: – the initial decision point – the branches representing various outcomes – the paths, which may consist of several branches representing the various probabilities and events of a particular outcome. The whole tree represents the decision problem. The object of decision trees is not to find optimum solutions, but instead represent visually a wide range of alternatives that can apply to specific policies and procedures	■ Virtually any supplies problems that can be reduced to: – a set of mutually exclusive decisions – for each decision, a set of possible outcomes, together with an assessment of the likelihood of each outcome occurring – revenues or costs for each outcome
■ *Forecasting* The process of estimating future quantities required, normally by using past experience as a basis. OR methods of forecasting include: – exponential smoothing – moving averages – trend analysis – multiple regression analysis – curve fitting	■ Any supplies problem involving the prediction of future requirements, such as stock levels, purchasing expenditure, stores space, purchase of sensitive commodities in various market conditions
■ *Probability theory* An aspect of forecasting based on mathematical techniques for establishing the likelihood of particular events taking place. The probability of an event ranges from 0 to 1 (0 = event will certainly not occur; 1 = event is certain)	■ The application of statistical techniques, such as sampling, as a means of controlling quality ■ Determining the life expectancy of materials and components ■ Predicting the probability of stockouts at given levels of inventory

Case study

The Vanguard Group manufactures a high-quality range of caravans. Seven months ago, it recruited a new Engineering Design Manager who initiated a design review of the whole range of caravans. This has led to significant changes to the bills of materials for each product within the range.

At a recent trade show at the Birmingham International Exhibition Centre, the new range was shown to trade buyers. The demand has been exceptional and the current year's sales are already showing an increase of 24 per cent. This has led to the five-year business plan being revised. Year on year, sales are predicted to carry on rising by a least 15 per cent.

The Managing Director called a senior management meeting, which included you as Procurement Manager. The meeting dealt with the increase in production and its impact on existing skills and manufacturing facilities and the discussion focused on procurement issues. The Engineering Design Manager voiced the view that, given the increase in quantities, the purchase prices should 'come tumbling down'. He mentioned the learning curve as being very relevant and proposed that your department immediately undertake an investigation into how the purchase prices could be dramatically reduced. In that he was supported by the Managing Director.

The Manufacturing Director then said that some existing manufacturing lines would have to be outsourced because he could not create the necessary facilities in the available time. The Vanguard Group has never previously outsourced anything.

You have promised that, within a week, you will have a list of all the items to be outsourced. It is likely to include ten lines, each with considerable subassembly work being needed, prior to assembly.

The Managing Director has asked you to prepare a project plan to deal with the outsourcing actions. These parallel actions will be a major challenge for you and your department.

Tasks

1 What techniques are available to you to deal with the pricing issue?

2 What actions would you include in the project plan to ensure that you deliver the outsourcing strategy, on time?

Discussion questions

16.1 Turner[26] records that when Neil Armstrong was being interviewed about the Moon landing, he was asked to state the most frightening moment. Was it as the Moon lander came down and he thought it might crash or was it as he stepped off the ladder or was it when they came to blast off from the Moon and he thought that the rockets might not be powerful enough? No, he said, the most frightening moment was being on the launch pad at Cape Canaveral and under him were 2000 components, every single one of which had been bought on minimum price tender! One of them did indeed fail in 1986.

(a) List the possible dangers of accepting the lowest tender.

(b) If you must accept the lowest tender, how might you seek to ensure that quality or performance does not fall below specified standards?

16.2 When debriefing unsuccessful suppliers, what procedures:

(a) would you suggest to ensure that the debriefing session does not become confrontational or dissolve into recriminations

(b) how would you respond to requests from an unsuccessful bidder:

   (i) asking for information relating to the tenders of competitors?

   (ii) referring disparagingly to competing suppliers?

   (iii) asking for copies of the minutes of the meeting at which the decision was made not to accept their tender?

16.3 Opposition to post-tender negotiation is usually based on ethical considerations. What arguments would you use to reassure an objector that PTN is honest, open, fair and beneficial to both potential purchasers and suppliers?

16.4 The following figures show the monthly percentages of all deliveries that have been received on time over a period of 12 months.

90   92   94   93   93   94   95   94   92   93   94   93

(a) Compare a three months' moving average forecast with an exponential smoothing forecast using a = 0.2.

(b) Which of the two averages provides the better forecast?

(c) What is the forecast for the next month?

16.5 Your company, a manufacturer of cleaning machinery, has undertaken a market research exercise that has ascertained the selling price of a new vacuum cleaner must not exceed £350. It has also discovered that, to be an effective competitor, it needs to achieve a profit of £75 per machine sold. A preliminary estimate is that, providing these targets are met, the estimated sales over the first three years should be 250,000 units. A preliminary estimate of costs is as follows:

	£
Development costs	20
Production costs	120
Materials and components	80
Marketing costs	20
Logistics costs	40
Service costs	10
	290

Clearly the initial estimate is above the target cost price of £275. What action would you take to ensure that the target cost is achieved?

16.6 The XYZ Co. Ltd incurred the following overhead costs.

	£
Depreciation of factory buildings	2000
Repairs and maintenance of buildings	1200
Factory administrative costs (treat as production overheads)	3000
Depreciation of machinery	1600
Insurance of machinery	400
Heating	780
Lighting	200
Canteen	1800

Information relevant to the factory production and service departments is:

	Production A	Production B	Service C	Service D
Floor space (square metres)	2400	3200	1600	800
Volume (cubic metres)	6000	12000	4800	3200
Number of employees	60	60	30	30
Machinery at book value	£60,000	£40,000	£20,000	£40,000

How do you suggest the overhead costs should be apportioned for departments A, B, C and D?

16.7 An application of activity-based costing is the measurement of supplier performance. Non-conformance to the purchaser's requirements means that the purchaser has to perform otherwise non-value-adding activities.

The management accountant of the XYZ Co. Ltd has assigned labour hours to non-value activities. Thus, material received too early may entail stores disruption and costs estimated at 2 labour hours while material received too late incurs costs of 8 labour hours. Each labour hour is currently costed at £50 so that the cost of a delivery can be obtained by multiplying the labour hours by the total cost per labour hour.

The scores in pounds for each delivery by each supplier are kept in a database and evaluated at six-monthly intervals. This score is used to compute a vendor performance index (VPI) calculated by:

$$VPI = \frac{\text{Cost of purchased items} + \text{Cost of non-value-added activities}}{\text{Cost of purchased supplies}}$$

A score of 1.2 or under is deemed satisfactory. Anything higher may be a factor in deciding to discontinue using the supplier. The score for Supplier A is as shown below. Assuming purchases for the period of £34,542, work out the VPI and decide whether the score is satisfactory or otherwise.

Non-value-added activity	Labour hours	Cost at £50 per labour hour
Inspection rejection	0.3	
Paperwork rejection	0.3	
Rework at buyer's premises	5.0	
Materials received too early	2.0	
Materials received too late	8.0	
Excess of materials	2.0	
Shortage of materials	4.0	

16.8 The standard material costs for part number 423 are 50 kg at £5 per kg. During January 2002, 150 units were produced. The actual material costs for part number 423 for January 2002 are direct material purchases 7000 kg at a cost of £36,400:
- opening stock of material 1300 kg
- closing stock of material 850 kg

Calculate the price, usage and total material variances.

16.9 Match the terms on the left with the concepts and definitions on the right

(a) Activity-based costing	(1) Something that increases the worth of a product or service
(b) Lifecycle stages	(2) Expected selling price less desired profit
(c) Value-added activity	(3) The process of attaching costs based on activities
(d) Target cost	(4) Idle time, transfer time, storage time
(e) Non-value-added activities	(5) A principle whereby fixed as well as variable costs are allotted to cost units and total overheads are absorbed according to activity level
(f) Variance	(6) Development, introduction, growth, maturity, decline
(g) Absorption costing	(7) Difference between standard and actual prices and quantities
(h) Cost driver	(8) Something that causes or influences costs

16.10 A manufacturing company has just completed the first two units of a new product subject to an 80 per cent learning curve at a labour cost of £20,000. It has received an enquiry for a further two units, but the purchaser intimates that a reduced price should be applicable as the learning element involved in the initial two products should be considered.

Assuming that variable overheads amount to 20 per cent of direct labour cost, what should be the estimated labour and variable overheads for the two new units?

Past examination questions

1 It has been suggested that the competitive tendering method could achieve the lowest total acquisition cost.
   (a) Critically appraise this statement.
   (b) Identify situations in which the competitive tendering method is appropriate.
   (c) Identify situations in which the competitive tendering method is *not* appropriate.

   CIPS, *Purchasing and Supply Chain Management II: Tactics and Operations*, November 2000

2 A project to reorganise and move a credit operation to a new office location is represented by the following tasks:

	Immediate predecessors	Expected duration (weeks)
A Select office site	–	3
B Develop financial plan	–	5
C Determine personnel requirements	B	3
D Design office layout	A, C	4
E Construct office interior	D	8
F Select personnel to move	C	2
G Hire new employees	F	4
H Move records, personnel, etc.	F	2
I Make financial arrangements	B	5
J Train new personnel	H, E, G	3

(a) Draw a network to represent the project.

(b) Calculate earliest start, latest finish and total slack for each activity and determine the earliest finish for the project and its critical path.

(c) One week into the project you are informed that activity F will go late by 4 weeks and activity G will go late by 3 weeks. What will be the effect on the project completion date?

(d) What would be the order of priority of crashing to reduce the overall project duration?

CIPS, *Operations Management*, May 2000

3 Explain the concept of price/cost analysis and show how it can be used in the preparation stage of negotiation.

CIPS, *Purchasing and Supply Chain Management II:
Tactics and Operations*, November 2003

4 (a) To what extent do you believe that the competitive bidding method of supplier selection is compatible with the concept of total acquisition cost in the selection of suppliers?

(b) Under what circumstances would you use the competitive bidding method?

CIPS, *Purchasing and Supply Chain Management II:
Tactics and Operations*, May 2002

5 Evaluate the procedures and the techniques relevant to the selection, management and development of suppliers where the procurement emphasis has moved from price alone to total acquisition cost.

CIPS, *Tactics and Operations*, May 2004

Solutions to selected exercises

16.4 (a)

Month	Y^1	3-month moving average forecast	(Error)^2	A = 2 forecast	(Error)^2
1	90				
2	92			90.00	4.00
3	94			90.40	12.06
4	93	92.00	1.00	91.12	3.53
5	93	93.00	0.00	91.50	2.25
6	94	93.33	0.45	91.80	4.84
7	95	93.33	2.79	92.24	7.62
8	94	94.00	0.00	92.79	1.46
9	92	94.33	0.43	93.03	1.06
10	93	93.67	0.45	92.83	0.03
11	94	93.00	1.00	92.86	1.30
12	93	93.00	0.00	93.09	0.01
			11.12		39.06

$$\text{Mean square error for 3 months} = \frac{11.12}{9} = 1.24$$

$$\text{Mean square error } (a = 0.2) = \frac{39.06}{11} = 3.65$$

Use 3 months' moving average.

(b) $(93 + 94 + 95) = \dfrac{282}{3} = 94$

16.5 The equivalent annual cost for Machine X is:

$$\frac{\text{Purchase + Installations cost}}{\text{Cumulative PV factor at 8\%}}$$

$$= \frac{£3200}{3312} = £966 \text{ per annum}$$

The EAC for Machine Y is:

$$\frac{\text{Purchase + Installations cost}}{\text{Cumulative PV factor at 8\%}}$$

$$= \frac{£4100}{3992} = £1027 \text{ per annum}$$

To the above figures must be added the annual running costs:

Machine X: £966 + £800 = £1766

Machine Y: £1027 + £760 = £1787

Taking into account the life of each machine, it would seem that Machine Y is actually the cheaper option.

16.6

Cost	Basis of apportionment	Total	A	B	C	D
Depreciation of factory buildings	Floor area	2000	600	800	400	200
Repairs and maintenance	Floor area	1200	360	480	240	120
Factory administration	No. of employees	3000	1000	1000	500	500
Depreciation of machinery	Book value	1600	600	400	200	400
Insurance of machinery	Book value	400	150	100	50	100
Rates	Volume	780	180	360	144	96
Lighting	Floor area	200	60	80	40	20
Canteen	No. of employees	1800	600	600	300	300
		£10980	3550	3820	1874	1736

16.7

Non-value-added activity	Labour hours	Cost at £50 per labour hour (£)
Inspection rejection	0.3	15
Paperwork rejection	0.3	15
Rework at buyer's premises	5.0	250
Materials received too early	2.0	100
Materials received too late	8.0	400
Excess materials	2.0	100
Shortage of materials	4.0	200
		1080

$$\text{VPI} = \frac{(£34542 + £1080)}{£34542} = \frac{35622}{34542} = 1.03$$

Based on a satisfactory score of 1.092, the achieved score is unsatisfactory.

16.8 (a) Material price variance

$$\text{Standard} \quad 7000 \text{ kg at £5} \quad = £35,000$$
$$\text{Actual} \quad 7000 \text{ kg at £5.20} = £36,400$$

Therefore £36,400 − £35,000 = adverse material price variance of £1400

(b) Materials usage variance

$$\text{Standard for 150 units at 50 kg per unit} = 7500 \text{ kg}$$
$$7500 \times £5 \qquad\qquad = £37,500$$

Actual usage

Opening stock	1300 kg	
Add purchase	7000 kg	
	8300	
Less closing stock	850	
	7450 kg at £5	£37,250
		£250

Material usage variance = favourable

(c) Total material variance = £1400 + 250 = £1650 *adverse*

16.10 Cumulative average labour cost for units 1 and 2 was:

$$\frac{£1000}{2} = £500 \text{ per unit}$$

Cumulative average labour cost for first four units will be:

$$\left(\frac{20,000}{4}\right)\left(\frac{80}{100}\right) = £4000 \text{ per unit}$$

Labour cost for the two new units will be computed as follows:

$$\text{Labour cost for 4 units at £4000 per unit} = £16,000$$
$$\text{Less labour for 2 units at £5000 per unit} = £10,000$$
$$\text{Cost for new order of 2 units} \qquad = £6000$$

The estimated cost of the two additional units will be as follows:

$$\text{Direct labour cost for 2 units} \qquad = £6000$$
$$\text{Variable overheads (20\% of £6000)} \qquad = £1200$$
$$£7200$$

References

[1] Bryden, P., and Luther, R., 'E-tendering – from electronic notices to electronic bidding: how close is the complete online process?', *Atlantic Construction Journal*, August, 2004

[2] Ministry of Defence, 'Defence e-business' at: www.contracts.mod.uk/dc/public/ebusiness/etendering.htm

[3] UK Central Unit on Procurement, *CUP Guidance Note 45, Debriefing*

[4] As 3 above, pp. 2–3

5 Inland Revenue, 'Award of contract debriefing of suppliers', PUM 2840

6 CIPS, 'Practice position statement: tendering and post tendering negotiation', CIPS

7 Central Unit on Procurement, CUP Guidelines Note 1, 'Post-tender negotiation', HM Treasury

8 Chartered Institute of Management Accountants, 'Management accounting official terminology', CIMA, revised 1991, p. 44

9 As 8 above, p. 49

10 Yoshikawa, Y., Innes, J., and Falconer, M., 'Cost management through functional analysis' in Brinker, B. (ed.), *Emerging Practices in Cost Management*, Warren Gornam Lamont, 1990, p. 243

11 As 8 above, p. 26

12 As 8 above, p. 90

13 Raffish, N., and Turney, P. B. B. (eds), 'Glossary of activity-based management', *Journal of Cost Management*, fall, 1991, pp. 53–63

14 Lapsley, J., Llewellyn, S., and Falconer, H., *Cost Management in the Public Sector*, Longman, 1994, p. 90

15 Cooper, R., and Kaplan, R. S., 'How cost accounting systematically distorts product costs', in William, J. B. (ed.), *Accounting and Management Field Study Perspectives*, Harvard Business School, 1987, Paragraph D–15

16 Burch, J., *Cost and Management Accounting*, West Publishing, 1994, p. 458

17 Barker, J., 'How to achieve more effective purchasing through activity-based costing', paper presented to Second PSERG Conference, University of Bath, 1993

18 Ness, J. A., and Cucuzza, T. G., 'Tapping the full potential of ABC', *Harvard Business Review*, July/Aug., 1995, pp. 130–8

19 As 8 above, p. 38

20 As 8 above, p. 58

21 Karjewski, L. J., and Ritzman, I. P., *Operations Management*, Addison Wesley, 1990, p. 208

22 French, D., and Saward, H., *Dictionary of Management*, Pan, 1975, p. 333

23 Lock, D., *Project Management*, Gower, 1994

24 As 23 above, pp. 3–4

25 As 23 above, p. 401

26 Turner, J. R., *The Handbook of Project-based Management*, 2nd edn, McGraw-Hill, 1999, p. 234

Chapter 17

Purchasing research, performance and ethics

This chapter aims to provide an understanding of:

■ purchasing research
■ purchasing performance evaluation
■ purchasing ethics
■ purchasing and fraud
■ environmental aspects of purchasing.

■ Areas, organisation and methods of purchasing research.
■ Quantitative and qualitative approaches to purchasing performance, evaluation and measurement.
■ Purchasing audits and benchmarking.
■ Principles of personal and global ethics.
■ Ethical issues relating to suppliers.
■ Ethical codes, training and decisions.
■ The nature and indications of fraud and fraud prevention.
■ Environmental legislation.
■ Environmental purchasing policies and management.
■ Screening suppliers for good environmental performance.

17.1 Purchasing research

17.1.1 Definition

Purchasing research has been defined by Fearon[1] as:

> The systematic gathering, recording and analysing of data about problems relating to the purchasing of goods and services.

The importance of purchasing research has been enhanced by the following:

■ rapid changes in technology and economic circumstances are increasing the complexity of purchasing

■ much purchasing is undertaken in conditions of uncertainty so that strategic decisions have to be made involving individuals, organisations and events outside the direct control of the purchasing company

■ electronic data processing provides the facility to store and process vast quantities of data that, when processed, can improve decision making

■ the increased outsourcing of non-critical functions

■ the new focus on partnering and evaluation of the benefits

■ e-procurement facilitating real-time ordering and payment by line employees

■ purchasing as a function is increasingly required to quantify its contribution to profitability and its strategic function in the supply chain.

17.1.2 Areas of research

In selecting topics for research, it should be remembered that the greater the expenditure on an area, the greater is the potential for significant cost savings. Among the most important areas of research are the following:

■ *materials and commodities*
  - trends in the requirements of the company for specific materials
  - price analysis
  - substitute materials or items
  - specifications and standardisation
  - value analysis
  - usage analysis
  - use of learning curves

■ *purchasing policies and procedures*
  - whether or not any policies are in need of revision
  - if it be more economical to make in rather than buy out or vice versa
  - whether or not any opportunities exist for the consolidation of purchasing requirements
  - purchasing contributions to competitive advantage
  - forms design, distribution and elimination
  - the application of activity-based costing to the purchasing function
  - how the information made available by EDP can be used more effectively
  - whether or not the purchasing organisation for materials can be improved by regrouping the purchasing, stores and other related subsystems, such as by means of materials or logistics management approaches
  - to what extent operational research methods can be applied to purchasing
  - internal and external customer satisfaction with the purchasing function

- *suppliers*
  - supplier appraisal
  - supplier performance
  - the possibilities for supplier development
  - contracting simultaneously with two suppliers to design and build
  - supplier reviews – how often suppliers are changed and how new suppliers are found
  - supply chain – analysis of at least one level back
  - purchasing consortium
  - price monitoring after contracting
  - outsourcing the procurement process
  - global sourcing
- *staff*
  - staff responsibilities
  - staff turnover, absenteeism, morale
  - what overtime, if any, is worked
  - staff succession
  - staff training and development
  - staff remuneration, facilities and incentives
- *miscellaneous*
  - purchasing applications of IT
  - expert systems and artificial intelligence
  - transportation of bought-out items
  - securing supplies in conditions of uncertainty
  - disposal of scrap and obsolete stores equipment
  - terms and conditions of purchase
  - the measurement of purchasing performance
  - purchasing ethics.

17.1.3 Organisation for research

Some research is undertaken by all purchasing departments, even though this may be only rudimentary, such as consulting directories or the Internet to locate possible suppliers of an item not previously bought. Some willingness to initiate research is essential to the development of the status of purchasing. Unless such an initiative is taken by purchasing, the research role will be assumed by other functions, such as design, marketing and production. Purchasing research may be formal or informal.

- *Small business units* These may be unable to allocate resources such as personnel and finance to establish a formal purchasing research section. Staff should nevertheless be encouraged to keep up to date by meeting representatives, attending trade exhibitions, attending appropriate short courses, having access to and opportunities for studying journals and other relevant literature, as well as networking with other purchasing staff at meetings of professional bodies, such as the CIPS.

■ *Research sections* Systematic research requires time and freedom from other distractions. These conditions can be best provided by establishing a special purchasing research section as a centralised staff activity to provide assistance to line members of the purchasing function. Experience has shown that companies with formal purchasing research arrangements:

– engage in more research projects
– do so in greater depth
– make a significant contribution to profitability.

■ *Other approaches* When a specialised research section is not feasible, formalised purchasing research may be undertaken by the following groups.

– *Project teams* concerned with a specific problem or range of problems – probably including staff from outside the purchasing function, such as design, production, finance and marketing, as in a value research or engineering project.

– *Supplier associations.*

– *Membership of a research consortium.*

– *Use of specialised outside research facilities*, such as the Commodities Research Unit of the International Monetary Fund.

– *Collaboration with universities* This may be 'contract' or 'collaborative' research. In contract research, the agenda for a project is set by the industrial partner with a university providing a research service at a commercial price on the same basis as any other supplier, while collaborative research's goals are jointly defined by both company or companies and the university. 'Clubs' or 'networks' are often set up by an individual university or consortium of universities to focus on a particular research topic. Companies wishing to become members usually pay an agreed annual subscription. Thus, the Centre for Research in Strategic Purchasing and Supply at Bath University claims to work, at any one time, with over 100 companies, often organised into 'project clubs'.

– *Support of individuals working for higher degrees* in purchasing and supply chain management.

– *Use of consultants* to investigate a specific matter. Some large consultancies also undertake independent research that is made available to the relevant industries at a cost. An example is the *Purcon Index* – a specialised survey of the salaries and total remuneration packages of purchasing and supplies staff throughout Britain. This index is updated annually in March and September. Similar research is undertaken by Market Focus Research Ltd.

– *Professional institutes* The Institute of Logistics and Transport maintains a logistics research network – a special interest group of academics with some interested practitioner members. The network produces the *International Journal of Logistics Research and Applications*. The CIPS supports chairs in purchasing at several UK universities. In the USA, the Center for Advanced Purchasing Studies was established in 1986 as a national affiliation agreement between the NAPM and Arizona State University.

17.1.4 Research methodology

As with all other research, the first step in a purchasing or supply chain investigation is to adopt a plan or model of the research, from inception to completion. Sarantakos[2] states that the general assumption made by researchers who employ a research model in their work rests on the belief that:

- research can be perceived as evolving in a series of steps that are closely interrelated and the success of each depends on the successful completion of the preceding step
- the steps must be executed in a given order
- planning and execution of the research is more successful if a research model is employed – a typical one being that shown in Figure 17.1.

Figure 17.1 **A purchasing research model**

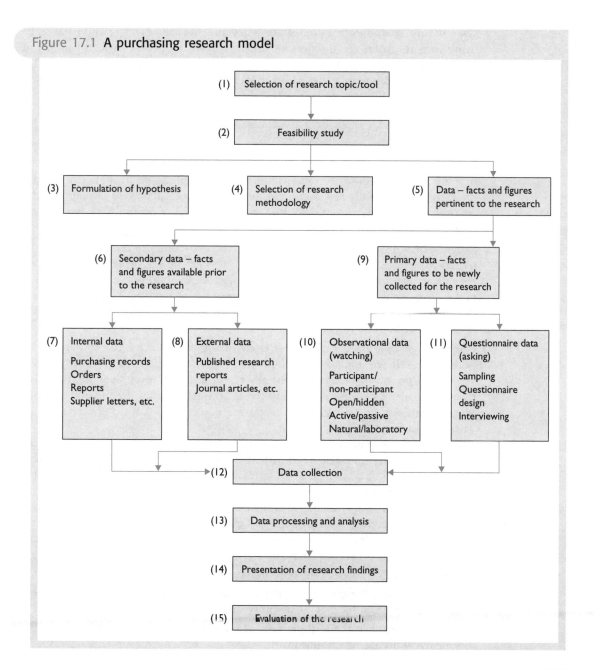

633